AN UNCOMMON MAN

THE TRIUMPH OF

HERBERT HOOVER

Richard Norton Smith

★

SIMON AND SCHUSTER
New York

Copyright © 1984 by Richard Norton Smith
All rights reserved
including the right of reproduction
in whole or in part in any form
Published by Simon and Schuster
A Division of Simon & Schuster, Inc.
Simon & Schuster Building
Rockefeller Center
1230 Avenue of the Americas
New York, New York 10020
SIMON AND SCHUSTER and colophon are registered trademarks of
Simon & Schuster, Inc.
Designed by Pat Dunbar
Manufactured in the United States of America

1   3   5   7   9   10   8   6   4   2

Library of Congress Cataloging in Publication Data
Smith, Richard Norton, date.
An uncommon man.

Includes index.
1. Hoover, Herbert, 1874–1964.   2. Presidents—
United States—Biography.   3. United States—Politics
and government—20th century.   I. Title.
E802.S68   1984   973.91'6'0924   [B]   83-27175
ISBN 0-671-46034-X

FOR FRANK AND RUTH SMITH—
who understood

One must wait until the evening,
to see how splendid the day has been.
—Sophocles

CONTENTS

★

10 CONTENTS

ACKNOWLEDGMENTS

★

"There is little importance to men's lives except the accomplishments they leave to posterity," Herbert Hoover once wrote. "When all is said and done, accomplishment is all that counts." Even by that narrow measurement, Hoover's own legacy has been clouded by his indelible association with America's Great Depression. Only with the opening of his presidential and other archives in 1966 has a parade of scholars been able to assemble a fresh view of this *wunderkind* turned scapegoat. In the course of their work, they have vastly broadened our grasp of what he did and tried to do to combat the worst crisis since Lincoln faced a disintegrating Union. Even now, Dr. George Nash is engaged in a multivolume biography that promises a definitive assessment of a flawed giant. Meanwhile, the Hoover Institution has published a far-ranging academic study of its founder's life after he left the White House, exhaustively researched by Gary Dean Best.

Yet Hoover rarely permitted access to his emotions. His distaste for personal revelation has left him shrouded in myth and vulnerable to every persuasion of historical partisanship. Revisionists of varied stripe, from Old Right to New Left, flock to West Branch, Iowa, to sift his papers or practice a latter-day phrenology on history's couch.

Therein lies a problem—and a motivation. Uncomfortable with personal drama, in their professional specialization the Hoover academics have thus far devoted surprisingly few pages to the private man behind the public character, or his desperate struggle for reacceptance after 1933. The inner resentment and outer resolve, the bitterness leavened with humor and shot through with the ideological fervor of an Old Testament prophet—even the historic relationship or rivalries with the likes of Franklin Roosevelt, Win-

11

ston Churchill, Harry Truman, Dwight Eisenhower and others—have been largely abandoned to the footnoters and monograph writers. As a result, few know Hoover much better than on the gunmetal gray day he left the presidency.

From the beginning, my own emphasis has been on portraiture, the dark as well as the light side of Hoover's complex nature, and a long passage through the political wilderness that only death could fully resolve. Unlike his hero Woodrow Wilson, Hoover lived long enough to influence history's judgment. He benefited as well from an entire generation of friends and admirers too young to recall the agonies of 1932, or attracted out of their own distaste for the Roosevelt revolution. Their memories, preserved in more than three hundred interviews comprising the Hoover Oral History Project (HOHP), provided an invaluable source for what follows. So did thousands of pages of personal correspondence, diaries (including the first use of a diary kept by the president's military aide, Campbell Hodges), memoranda and other privileged glimpses into the man's life and times.

Originally, this volume was intended nearly exclusively as a study of Hoover's post–White House career. The focus remains fixed on the three decades of desert-crossing that began in March 1933. But I have found it impossible to isolate those years from earlier ones. To understand Hoover's tragedy, one must explore his triumph. One must trace his motives to their roots, seeing the man whole, in the turbulent context of the mid-twentieth century. This would be impossible were it not for the wholehearted cooperation of those who work at the Herbert Hoover Presidential Library in West Branch. I am deeply indebted to Thomas Thalken, the library's director, as well as Dr. Robert Wood, Dwight Miller, Dale Mayer, Shirley Sondergard, Mildred Mather and J. Patrick Wildenberg for guiding me through the historical treasure trove preserved in its collections. The same holds true for Donald Johnson and the other officers of the Herbert Hoover Library Association. One of the pleasures of my stay in West Branch was the opportunity to know George Nash, who shared his insights and sharpened my own interpretations.

I appreciate as well the assistance of Columbia University's Oral History Collection, the Franklin D. Roosevelt Library at Hyde Park, New York, the Library of Congress in Washington, and Justice Department officials who processed my Freedom of Information Act request for FBI files. Steve Neal made available to me correspondence between the former president and Senate Minority Leader Charles McNary, as well as a thick file pertaining to Hoover's 1940 political activities, and a wealth of Hoover photographs. Two sons of presidents, Allan Hoover and John Coolidge, answered questions by mail. Senator Mark Hatfield and Edward L. Bernays, an early pioneer in public relations, shared their own recollections of Hoover. By permitting me to quote from her father's remarkable diary, with its intimate portrait of the ex-president as viewed through the unique perspective of his lifelong friend Edgar Rickard, Marguerite Rickard Hoyt contributed much to this volume. George Cheffy steered me to a revealing memoir by Atlee Pomerene, who served on Hoover's Reconstruction Finance Corporation and came to know the president as few others. Kay Luther did an expert job typing the manuscript. Alice Mayhew proved once more to be a sensitive editor, and my agent, Rafe Sagalyn, was helpful as always in refining my initial vision. When energy flagged, I was fortunate to be able to turn to friends like Steve Chapman, Bob Rapp, Jim Strock, Sally Ironfield and Ed Cheffy. Laura J. Connolly demonstrated again her formidable gift for friendly encouragement.

Finally, I owe a debt of gratitude beyond payment to the two persons whose names grace the dedication page. Their own dedication has never wavered; I am lucky indeed to have been a beneficiary of such unselfishness.

—Richard Norton Smith
October 2, 1983

OLD MAN IN A HURRY

★

I don't have too much time to finish what I'm doing.   —Herbert Hoover[1]

★

As an old man who had tasted popular acclaim and virulent hatred, supreme authority and the political wilderness, Herbert Hoover liked to wax philosophical. When visitors to his "comfortable monastery" in New York's Waldorf Towers asked how he managed to survive the ostracism that lasted a dozen years after he turned the presidency over to Franklin Roosevelt in 1933, Hoover's eyes twinkled. "I outlived the bastards," he explained. More reflectively, he looked back on those who had succeeded in attaching his name, once revered throughout the world, to the most deadening depression on record, and claimed to have converted nearly all those he hadn't buried.[2]

"If you live long enough," he went on, "the wheel turns, the pendulum swings."[3]

For abundant evidence, he needed to look no further than the record of his own hyperactive existence. It had begun in a whitewashed cottage of two rooms, perched at the corner of Main and Downey streets, in the idyllic hamlet of West Branch, Iowa, population 265. It came to a peaceful close, ninety years and two months later, in a $32,000-a-year suite of rooms high above Park Avenue. Along the way, it traced the emergence of a modern superpower and the slow strangulation of the old values Hoover never abandoned. America was barely out of her own infancy on August 10, 1874, when Huldah Hoover gave birth to her second son and her husband Jesse announced to his neighbors that "we have another General Grant at our house." In common with his pious Quaker wife, Jesse Hoover would prove something of a prophet: like Grant, Herbert Hoover would rise from obscurity to the status of international hero, cap his career with the White House, and see his reputation tarnished by events and men too large or corrupt to yield before mere idols. In the end, his presidency would be little more than an aberrant footnote to a fabulous adventure.[4]

There were 44 million Americans in August 1874; Hoover's passing in 1964 was marked by nearly 200 million of his countrymen. His father's family traced a receding frontier over five generations before Jesse wed Huldah, whose ancestors journeyed south from Canada in a lumbering prairie schooner. Bert was not yet twenty when Frederick Jackson Turner revealed the close of America's frontier and pronounced a benediction on the fierce individualism and acquisitive ethic that thrived in a raw, tentative republic. By the end of Hoover's life, the frontier was defined by men who donned bulky suits and traveled high above the air he breathed; his last public appearance came in May 1963, at a dinner honoring astronaut Gordon Cooper.

Washington, D.C., was an unwashed irrelevancy in 1874, tinged with graft (Grant's Treasury Secretary resigned that year, to avoid congressional censure, and his private secretary was implicated in the Whiskey Ring scandal, which bilked the government out of millions), and content to allocate $300 million a year to sustain the public welfare. It was far more concerned with eradicating the Sioux and Apache than aiding factory workers and farmers against an economic panic Grant called "a blessing in disguise." By the time Herbert Hoover moved into Suite 31-A of the Waldorf, Washington was entrenched in the nation's economic life, its coffers swollen by the income tax first levied when Huldah's son was a forty-year-old self-made millionaire, its annual outlays fast approaching the astronomical sum of $50 billion.

As a student at Stanford University, Hoover had led an antifraternity element against campus swells, criticized Grover Cleveland's hands-off attitude toward the depression of the 1890s ("We cannot squander ourselves into prosperity" was Cleveland's defense of traditional laissez-faire, a phrase Hoover repeated verbatim when congressmen pressed forty years later for direct relief payments to the jobless), and refused to let the president's predecessor, Benjamin Harrison, into a campus baseball game until the great man duly purchased a twenty-five-cent ticket. During his own unhappy term in the White House, Hoover came to represent the forces of high-collared indifference. He was assailed bitterly for failing to halt what became known as the Great Depression, and those who booed him lustily at the 1931 World Series gave vocal expression to the contempt felt by millions who had once regarded their president as a superman and now made him the butt of a hundred jokes.

His ninety years were crowded with controversy and irony. In Europe and Asia he saved more people from starvation than Hitler and Stalin together could murder—yet he drove to his final campaign appearance in 1932 through crowds of angry New Yorkers shouting, "We want bread." He crossed the Mississippi for the first time at the age of twenty-three—and returned a quarter century later to direct a massive relief effort that made his name more than ever synonymous with humanitarian generosity and prompted Will Rogers to remark, when the flood waters receded and Hoover returned to the Commerce Department in Washington, "Bert's just resting between disasters."

He sat with Woodrow Wilson at Versailles as that eloquent prophet of a new world order ("too great a man to employ European methods") saw his dreams incinerated in the furnace of age-old jealousies—and he lived to compose a moving memoir on Wilson's ordeal and warn his countrymen in stentorian tones of the untrustworthiness of an Old World polluted with racial and political hatreds. Thirty-one-A was just eleven floors below the official residence of America's Ambassador to the United Nations, talkative successor to Wilson's doomed league. Hoover celebrated his eighty-eighth birthday by returning to the scene of his boyhood, to dedicate his presidential library and float a proposal to replace the UN—and the obstreperous Russians who paralyzed its best intentions—with a new Council of Free Nations.

"An unabashed individualist," Hoover derided the Century of the Common Man. "The great human advances have not been brought about by mediocre men and women," he wrote in 1949. "They were brought about by distinctly uncommon people with vital sparks of leadership. . . . It is a curious fact that when you get sick you want an uncommon doctor; if your car breaks down you want an uncommonly good mechanic; when we get into war we want dreadfully an uncommon admiral and an uncommon general."

To a friend, he expressed the philosophy that made him the talisman of rugged individualism and the living embodiment of the Horatio Alger myth. "Look how I have risen," he said. "You have dreams. You have to rise to your dreams."[5]

Yet as Secretary of Commerce, Hoover gloried in the elimination of waste and the gray majesty of standardized production. "When I go to ride in an automobile," he told a skeptical Sherwood Anderson in 1927, "it does not matter to me that there are a million other automobiles on the road just like mine. I am going somewhere and I want to get there in what comfort I can and at the lowest cost." After the second world war, when some Americans prophesied a new depression as savage as the one that crippled his own presidency, he called for greater reliance on labor-saving devices and industrial ingenuity. Progress remained for Hoover a benign, all but inevitable force in American life, subject only to the greed or stupidity of a bloated government that failed to understand the creative impulses set loose through what he called his "inheritance of freedom."

He did not take seriously the prospect that Americans content to produce identical bricks and boxsprings might also discard human individuality. It was as if society could appreciate equally Ralph Waldo Emerson and Henry Ford's assembly lines, or crossbreed a Mercury space capsule with one of the gangling camels Hoover rode before the turn of the century in search of Australian gold. An evangelist of efficiency, he nonetheless rued the regimentation of the potato, "once the happiest of vegetables," by his freewheeling successors. He wore a dollar watch on his wrist and mourned the fact that his doctors denied him Beluga caviar at eighty-nine. He found God in a trout stream before a church pew, mailed out Christmas greetings attacking "godless Communism" and insisted on wearing a business suit and tie, even while casting a line upstream, or cleaning the bonefish he outwitted each winter in Florida.[6]

Work was his refuge; even while floating off Key West, he took along a couple of secretaries to help transcribe one or another of the volumes he worked upon daily. He kept four desks in 31-A, one for each book he wrote simultaneously to add to the two dozen already bearing his name. His celebrated neighbors included the Duke and Duchess of Windsor, Cole Porter, and Elsa Maxwell, but Hoover lived according to a different ethic from that of the partygoers and socialites. Slackers were sinners, he believed, and the doggedness and gumption of a curious intellect propelled him through a series of thick tomes, each written with the stubby yellow pencils he used as an aid to terseness (dictating machines, like smooth-flowing ballpoint pens, were ruled out as "invitations to verbosity"). The Ordeal of Woodrow Wilson was one. The American Epic was another, four volumes chockablock with statistics and nutritional minutiae to tell the story of his own crusade against hunger in a world accustomed to reliance on bullets and bombs rather than grain sacks.

Only his closest friends knew how intensely Hoover toiled on his final literary project, a three-volume study (the Magnum Opus to his five secretaries) of U.S.–Soviet relations after Franklin Roosevelt first recognized Lenin's successors in 1933. As a concession to age, he rose each morning at seven instead of six, to plant himself at a desk littered with manuscripts and his signature pipes. Scribbling away for up to ten hours, pausing only to check a fact, strike a kitchen match against the rough stone kept nearby for the purpose—presented with suitable fanfare after Waldorf employees wearied of putting strips of sandpaper on every flat surface Hoover was accustomed to using to light his ubiquitous pipes—and sample the special tobacco he had blended at the nearby University Club, the former president rejoiced in December 1963 when doctors promised him time to complete the project he called "Freedom Betrayed" if only he would curtail his schedule for a year.[7]

He was not always so cooperative. Only a few months earlier, after an attack of internal bleeding laid him low, Hoover had called his son, Herbert, Junior, to his Waldorf bedside. He knew he was worried, he said, then dismissed such fears as impractical. "I am going to pull through. I still have a great deal of work to do." For young Hoover, who had already alerted the Kennedy White House to prepare for his father's funeral, the next morning brought startling confirmation of the old man's resolve. At 7:30 A.M. the patient sat up in bed, called for his pipe and announced, "We're back in business."[8]

He never lost his appetite for the strenuous life. In his eighty-fifth year, Hoover traveled 14,000 miles and delivered twenty speeches. He had long since shed the wooden manner and mumbling style that made earlier platform appearances as painful for the audience as the speaker. He gleefully held up an invitation to address the New York Chamber of Commerce, after noting he first spoke to its members on returning from Belgium, and "in the 32 years afterward they never invited me again." In that same year, Hoover accepted twenty-three awards from groups as diverse as the Jewish Theological Seminary and the U.S. Lawn Tennis Association, laid three cornerstones, dedicated four Boys Clubs for his beloved "pavement boys" (with $10 million to put into Harlem, he maintained, he could do more than any band of policemen to eliminate juvenile delinquency), gave his name to four schools, raised more than a million dollars for the Hoover Institution at Stanford, and answered more than 21,000 letters. (He was puzzled, he said, by the strangely inactive behavior of his Waldorf neighbor Douglas MacArthur. After all, Hoover reasoned, Mac was "a younger man"—born in 1880 instead of 1874.[9]

Some thought him lonely, with only his books, his memories and a Siamese named Mr. Cat to provide company. He wanted a dog, he told

friends, as his late wife Lou always loved dogs, but what could you do with
a dog on the thirty-first floor of the Waldorf? Lou's portrait hung over the
mantel in his combination living room–office (the only other painting was
of Benjamin Franklin), and the suite was filled with the cobalt-colored
porcelains the Hoovers had collected since they first took up residence in
China in 1899. It had been said of the resourceful Lou at the time of the
Boxer Rebellion that no other woman in the small Western colony then
under siege could do such miraculous things with horsemeat. In the years
since her death in 1944, her husband had given away most of her collection
of semiprecious stones, just as he would present colleagues with costly Austrian watches in the last weeks of his life, on the theory that when a man
got to be ninety, he should give presents on his birthday instead of receiving
them.[10]

But the blue and whites from the K'ang-hsi and Ming dynasties remained,
a handsome memorial to the wife he rarely mentioned, and never called by
her first name. One of them, bearing the odious image of a malevolent
dragon, was named "Charlie"—Hoover's characteristically wry way of getting even with Charlie Michaelson, the Democratic genius of public relations who had, nearly alone, managed to demolish Hoover's miracle-worker
image and poison the nation's mood against a president elected in 1928 and
defeated four years later—both times by record margins.[11]

But the wheel turns, the pendulum swings. For proof, Hoover had only
to stroll along Third Avenue, where construction workers too young to have
felt the sting of 1933 greeted him warmly, or to the garage of the Waldorf,
where a self-professed Al Smith Democrat acknowledged the error of his
ways and was rewarded with a tip of the presidential hat and a barely
audible, "God bless you." Even the more shadowy elements of New York's
population seemed to take a protective interest in the old man, whose
exercise was limited to strolling around the hotel where he lived. "Mr.
Hoover," proclaimed a solicitous burglar one evening, "you should not be
walking around in the dark this time of night. Now go home."[12]

Once there, Hoover could cast his glance around walls generously lined
with a sampling of his 85 honorary degrees—still a record—and 468 awards
and citations. "I do not get a swelled head over the 96th gold medal," he
wrote in December 1960, "but they are good for aged persons." He might
have taken more pride in a framed certificate of graduation from the Friends'
Academy in Newburg, Oregon, dated 1887, commemorating a declamation
from "Bertie Hoover" entitled "Keeping his word. . . ." Near the entrance
to the suite sat a tommy-knocker, an iron gremlin alleged to cast a protective
spell over the miners Hoover once supervised in the Urals. A Finnish sword

called to mind his campaign to feed the Finns following their invasion by the Soviet Union in 1939; his name had since been added to the language. "To Hoover" in Finnish meant to help.[13]

The proprietor of 31-A liked sometimes to display a handsome scroll, presented to him in 1923 by a grateful Soviet Union, in recognition for his apolitical crusade to save fifteen million Russians from starvation in the desperate aftermath of World War I. "They've forgotten all that now," he said with a shake of his head, "but I have proof, right here." With typical stubbornness, he refused to hand the scroll back when Moscow rewrote history, although he did return the first edition of *Izvestia* from its place in his Stanford collections on war and revolution.[14]

Next to the souvenirs, the predominant physical feature of 31-A was the mail, bales of it stacked in chairs and piled on desks. Hoover liked to read aloud from favorite children's letters to guests who called him Chief. He took pains in answering those seeking advice on a career to replace the word "politician" with "public servant." He had never slept well, and it wasn't unusual for him to switch on a lamp at 3 A.M. and scrawl out a thick sheaf of correspondence for his secretaries to type up first thing in the morning. Visitors were astounded to find the old man answering individually the birthday or Christmas greetings that poured in from the King of the Belgians and the staff of Boise, Idaho's, J. C. Penney store. Anyone thoughtful enough to spend twenty-five cents on a card for him, he explained, was owed a response in kind.[15]

Perhaps his most cherished correspondent was also the most unlikely. "Yours has been a friendship which has reached deeper into my life than you know," he told Harry Truman in 1962. "I gave up a successful profession in 1914 to enter public service. I served through the First World War and after for a total of about 18 years. When the attack on Pearl Harbor came, I at once supported the President and offered to serve in any useful capacity. Because of my various experiences . . . I thought my services might again be useful, however there was no response. My activities in the Second World War were limited to frequent requests from Congressional committees. When you came to the White House," Hoover continued, "within a month you opened the door to me to the only profession I know, public service, and you undid some disgraceful action that had been taken in prior years."[16]

It was all there in two paragraphs: the gratitude mingled with bitterness over past slights, the awkward syntax and muffled emotions of an orphaned boy from Quaker West Branch, with all the limitations of the self-made man, and a surprising vein of humor as rich as any exploited during Hoover's globe-trotting days as a doctor of sick mines. After sitting through the dedicatory speeches when Truman opened his Independence library in 1957, Hoover left the 91-degree heat for some refreshments at the Truman home on nearby Delaware Avenue. A fluttery admirer approached the historical centerpiece of the program, to ask what it was that ex-presidents did with their days.

"Madame," Hoover answered, "we spend our time taking pills and dedicating libraries."

His own schedule, punishing as it was, suggested otherwise. It was interrupted only by some pungent rattrap cheese and crackers, plus one and a half of his patented Gibson cocktails (wherein an onion replaced the traditional martini olive) during the hour he called "the pause between the errors and trials of the day and the hopes of the night." Then came dinner—Hoover couldn't abide eating alone—and the nightly game of canasta with guests. As ever a tinkerer, he changed the rules to make for more cutthroat competition, even if the stakes never exceeded fifty-eight cents. He shushed diversionary chatter around the card table, as he turned off his hearing aid when confronted by tedious visitors. He took canasta, like his own place in the history books he now sought to influence, seriously. He didn't play bridge anymore; being pressed into round-the-clock games by an anguished Warren Harding in the last days of that tormented president's life had cured him permanently of any fondness for the game.[17]

With his books, his travels, and what he called his "unending public chores," Hoover lived the routine of an old man in a hurry. For the regulars who frequented 31-A, he was a towering figure, belatedly cleansed of the mud hurled by two generations of Democratic orators. To others, he was the prototype reactionary, Daddy Warbucks with a chip on his shoulder.

"You will discover," Hoover wrote Richard Nixon in January 1961, "that elder statesmen are little regarded by the opposition party until they get over 80 years of age, and are harmless." This was a misreading of history, one of the ways his historic feud with FDR warped Hoover's interpretation of events. In fact, he had always gotten along better with Democratic chief executives than with the leaders of his own party. Wilson and Truman showed that. So did Coolidge and Eisenhower. The new President, young John F. Kennedy, admired Hoover more than his campaign speeches could allow. He invited the old man to become honorary chairman of the Peace Corps, donated $10,000 to the Boys Clubs, and listened carefully as Hoover warned him against cutting his administration to fit Roosevelt's pattern. "This country cannot stand another New Deal" was the way he put it to one friend.[18]

The Kennedy administration sought Hoover's advice. More surprisingly, it often heeded what it heard. Robert McNamara delighted the occupant of 31-A by adopting a number of cost-cutting measures first proposed by Hoover's old commission on government reorganization; perhaps five billion dollars were shaved off the Pentagon's budget as a result. George McGovern, the earnest young administrator of Kennedy's Food for Peace program, wrote to tap Hoover's wealth of experience in feeding the hungry and was told that not even Red China should be excluded from a share of America's agricultural bounty. When JFK manfully accepted personal responsibility for the disastrous invasion of Castro's Cuba at the Bay of Pigs, Hoover sounded downright hawkish in his support.[19]

"You know I'm a Quaker and I loathe war," he snapped, "but, by heavens, if I were President of the United States, I would order the necessary forces into the Bay of Pigs, and I would decimate that Cuban army while they're there. . . . I'd end the thing forthright." (Ironically, it was a man of war, General MacArthur, who advised caution on the Kennedy White House. The President, said Mac, should emulate a bamboo plant, and "bend with the wind").[20]

Eight weeks after the abortive campaign to liberate Cuba, Hoover traveled to Philadelphia. The subject of freedom was much on his mind, as well as in the pages he was composing for future publication. On the steps of Independence Hall, where the founding fathers had welded a patchwork puzzle of squabbling colonies into the first enduring republic since the time of Plato, he delivered an impassioned valedictory. He seemed anxious that day to warn the young of dangers to freedom, from within as well as beyond the borders of their nation. His own childhood, he said, had been marked by the absence of many conveniences taken for granted by modern Americans. Iowans in the Gilded Age knew nothing of electric lights or telephones, automobiles or paved roads, airplanes or atomic bombs that might rain death from a deceptively benevolent sky.

But they had enjoyed something greater than all material goods, if only because it set the stage for all material progress and lifted America to the forefront of nations. Personal liberty, said Hoover, provided a powerful incentive to individual success. The entrepreneurial temperament of West Branch more than made up in opportunity for an impoverished childhood and an early life made rootless by the death of his parents. America had taken their place, given him schooling and a launching pad for achievement, handed him a passport and an insight into a world that offered at best a pale replica of Turner's frontier. "In no other land," he liked to exclaim, "could a boy from a country village, without inheritance or influential

friends, look forward with unbounded hope." He had seen the rise of tyranny and the death of liberty in other lands, he said outside Independence
Hall. Each time he returned, it had been for Hoover "a reaffirmation of the
glory of America. Each time my soul was washed by relief from the grinding
poverty of many nations, by the greater kindliness and frankness which
come from acceptance of equality and wide open opportunity to all who
want a chance."

But he was worried about the land of his birth, concerned whether it was
becoming a nation of sheep and selfish special interests. In seeking economic
security, might not latter-day descendants of Jefferson and Franklin permanently close the door to opportunity? If modern legislatures eager to curry
popular favor were willing to restrict individual activity, might they not
inadvertently stifle the creative impulse that the frontier had generated?
"Freedom is the open window," Hoover was fond of saying, "through which
pours the sunlight of the human spirit, of human dignity. With the preservation of these moral and spiritual qualities, and with God's grace, will
come further greatness for our country."

To the end, his own ambitions remained as limitless as the treeless terrain
of his native Cedar County, Iowa. On the eve of his ninetieth birthday, a
frail, toothless man sat in his wheelchair, clutching a blue robe and savoring
the World Series on one of the new color television sets American consumers were being introduced to that year. Reluctant to have his picture taken,
Hoover relented when it was pointed out that the only other president to
reach such a milestone, John Adams, would doubtlessly have leapt at such
an innovative disruption to his palsied old age. Suddenly, Hoover turned to
the wife of a younger friend. What did she want most out of life, he wanted
to know? Truthfully, she replied, she was content with her lot, satisfied with
her home, happy with her husband. For her, the status quo was a worthy
aspiration.[21]

Herbert Hoover drew back in horror. "How can you say a thing like
that?" he demanded. "I want more. I want to write a better book. I want to
have more friends. I *just want more!*"[22]

Like the country he loved with a passion that had itself become unfashionable, Hoover wanted it all. He wanted individual Americans to live their
lives without restriction or burdensome taxes. He wanted science and technology unleashed, to guarantee that tomorrow would be better than today.
He wanted government contained within the channels of individual conscience and Christian charity. He wanted America to enjoy the same respect
and affection he had stoked by feeding hungry Belgium. He wanted Americans to share his engineer's taste for a society perfected gradually. He wanted

them to take the long view, to be as detached from noisy contentiousness, as suspicious of the political glad-hander, as disinterested in personal gain.

Even in the closing scenes of a long and emotional drama, Hoover remained a hungry actor anxious to prove himself. His oddly American combination of nostalgia for what had been and optimism about a better, bolder future was an article of faith. He didn't accept that the wheel might not turn for nations as for individuals, or that the pendulum had swung irrevocably away from the middle course he spent his life pursuing, the rational ideal of voluntary cooperation as an alternative to both paternal government and the law of the jungle. The pointed fingers and poison pens had long since moved on to other targets, and his own life had taken on the trappings of Greek tragedy, albeit with a happy epilogue of rediscovery and restoration in the years since 1945. But the ordeal of Herbert Hoover did not end with Franklin Roosevelt's death, nor even with his own. It still haunts America's image of herself, still reproaches the dream that we think of as uniquely ours and that the technology Hoover himself celebrated has all but obliterated.

One can trace the Passion of Herbert Hoover back to its roots, in an individualism that was truly rugged and a predecessor whose term of office was as sterile as his own was stormy. He was the last of the old-fashioned presidents, and the first of the modern ones, and his ordeal is bracketed neatly by a man from rural Vermont and another from a Hudson Valley estate. Both were legends, crushing the more prosaic Iowan like a pair of historical millstones. Calvin Coolidge and Franklin Roosevelt spoke for their times, evoking something fundamental within the people they led in opposite directions. In January 1933, a crossroads on the calendar, they shared the headlines and relegated Hoover, the man who was still president, to a prison cell of shadows. He would spend the next thirty-one years trying to escape.

CHAPTER ONE

A DEATH IN NORTHAMPTON

★

I no longer fit in with these times . . . new ideas call for new men to develop them. —Calvin Coolidge, December 1932

I am so tired that every bone in my body aches. —Herbert Hoover

★

January 5, 1933, dawned a clear, crisp Thursday in Washington, D.C. At the White House, the nation's thirty-first president waged a forlorn campaign to remain relevant. Two months after his overwhelming defeat at the hands of Franklin Roosevelt, Herbert Hoover clung to power in the study once occupied by another hero, Abraham Lincoln. Maintaining a heavy schedule, Hoover could barely conceal a gloomy demeanor appropriate to one who presided over little more than the rubble of his own reputation.

The day's single triumph suggested how low his stock had plunged. That morning, a Washington courtroom heard the confession of one John Hamill, a native of Liverpool and author of *The Strange Career of Mr. Hoover, Or, Under Two Flags*, the latest in a smarmy clown's parade of pseudo-biographies, with titles like "Tough Luck—Hoover Again," and "Herbert Hoover, An American Tragedy." With help from J. Edgar Hoover (who owed his 1925 appointment to direct the new Federal Bureau of Investigation at least in part to a recommendation from the then Secretary of Commerce), the president and his confidential assistant, Larry Richey, had unearthed shadowy ties between Hamill and a Tammany cop named James J. O'Brien. O'Brien hoped to sell fifteen million copies of a work alleging Hoover to be a British citizen ("Sir Herbert"), a profiteer from wartime suffering, a contributor to the deaths of 126,000 American doughboys, a conspirator in the execution of British war nurse Edith Cavell on spy charges, and a shameless exploiter of Chinese and South African laborers during his meteoric career as the world's premier mining engineer early in the century.[1]

Hamill publicly repudiated the book bearing his name. It was published, he said, by William Faro, alias Samuel Roth, a convicted pornographer best known for earlier works like "Venus in Furs" and "Self-Abusement." Left unclear was the book's place in a million-dollar assault on the president mounted by the Democratic National Committee under John J. Raskob and others anxious for a rematch with Hoover's 1928 rival, Al Smith. Ironically, Raskob and his chosen agent, a brilliantly vituperative publicist named Charlie Michaelson, had succeeded too well by half; Smith was shouldered aside in favor of Roosevelt, who went on to crush Hoover beneath the accumulated layers of economic hardship and political disillusionment. The president was not merely rejected in November 1932. He was virtually excommunicated to the warm and spicy countryside around his Palo Alto, California, home. The years ahead promised a series of battles to regain at least the respect of the nation now eager to forget him. Hamill's retraction was a melancholy beginning.

No courtroom confession, however, could erase persistent doubts about the chief executive. No legal verdict could, by itself, silence those who held Hoover personally responsible for Army troops who fired into the tattered ranks of protesting veterans in July 1932, believed him guilty of diverting public funds to build a weekend retreat in Virginia's Shenandoah Mountains, or implicated him in the kidnap-murder of Charles Lindbergh's baby. The fiercely devoted Lou Hoover said it was not surprising the voters had turned on the man she called Daddy. She would too, she said, if she believed half of what they had been told.[2]

Her husband struck a bloody but unbowed stance. "I cannot take the time from my job to answer such stuff," he replied to those who urged a counteroffensive. "No man can catch up with a lie. If the American people wish to believe such things . . . about me, it just cannot be helped."

It wasn't supposed to have been like this at all. The Lincoln study, originally intended to serve as the pivot of a broad national advance, had become instead the static center of a desperate defense. In its own way, the room symbolized the failed hopes and desperate aura surrounding Herbert

Hoover's presidency. Seventy years in the past, its floorboards had resounded to the restless pacing of the great Civil War president whom Hoover idolized. Here, he had signed the Emancipation Proclamation, an event commemorated by an inscription over the fireplace and a vivid portrait of Lincoln and his divided Cabinet. Characteristically, Hoover had studied the picture's history in detail, explaining to small children the discrepancy between William Seward's white trousers in the White House version, and the black pair on display in an otherwise identical scene at the Capitol. Hoover was good with children; advisers wished he could extend his talent at communicating with ten-year-olds to their parents.

The president found strength in Lincoln's study, and a suitably heroic if misunderstood model in the leader martyred on Good Friday 1865. Along with his cosmopolitan wife, who spoke five languages, read sociology and economics for pleasure, and employed a secretary and two assistants to help her channel anonymous contributions to victims of the depression, he had rounded up four chairs from the Lincoln era, banished the electric horse kept by his unathletic predecessor, Calvin Coolidge, and hung up a steel engraving of the Great Emancipator which had accompanied him and Lou on all their overseas journeys.[3]

The president himself sat behind a desk once used by Woodrow Wilson, whom he had served as America's wartime Food Administrator ("Food Will Win The War") and whom Hoover admired both for his reforming instincts and his belief in a world order responsive to moral imperatives. From this spot, hallowed in history and memory, Hoover could gaze out the window at the grassy Ellipse and Arlington's low hills beyond, where Confederate bonfires once burned and Robert E. Lee's family manse stood sentinel over thousands of white crosses. It was with Lincoln's ghost looking over his shoulder that he broadcast an appeal and a warning to a troubled nation in February 1931: "The moment that responsibilities of any community, particularly in economic and social questions, are shifted from any part of the nation to Washington," he admonished those demanding exactly that, "then that community has subjected itself to a remove bureaucracy. . . . It has lost a large part of its voice in the control of its own destiny."

But constitutional purity seemed less urgent than survival to the residents of tin and cardboard shanty towns called Hoovervilles, or in streets where shivering residents stuffed old newspapers in their coats to keep out the cold —and labeled them Hoover Blankets. In boxcars called Hoover Pullmans by more than a million Americans riding away from their roots; in New York City, where architects worked for $20 a week and the new Empire State Building didn't have a single tenant above the Model Brassiere Company on the forty-first floor; in Chicago, where hungry men fought each other over pails of garbage set outside elegant restaurants; in Newport, where jobless breadwinners raced for the rights to a greased pig; in Kentucky's snow-dusted hollows, where miners dug coal for thirty cents a ton; in the drought-plagued landscape of the president's homestate of Iowa, where farmers dumped milk along the roadsides and talked of the Boston Tea Party; in Pennsylvania sawmills whose work force took home a nickel an hour; in Texas cotton fields left empty because the going price of thirty-five cents per hundred pounds didn't lure pickers; in a stricken, belligerent land where the Federal Council of Churches labeled capitalism a failure, and a hundred thousand persons applied in the fall of 1931 for six thousand jobs in Soviet Russia, the man labeled President Reject by *Time* magazine was the most hated in America.

> "Mellon pulled the whistle," people sang,
> "Hoover rang the bell,
> Wall Street gave the signal,
> And the country went to hell."

With each passing day, Hoover's "war on a thousand fronts" was being reduced to self-parody. Given his own disdain for the dramatics of popular leadership, it was not surprising. "Nothing could be more abhorrent to me in the wide world than to go into politics in any shape or form," he had written in 1916, after turning down "the one chance which has been my life ambition," the Stanford presidency. Belgium was starving, and a Quaker conscience dictated that the hungry be fed, even if his own appetite for advancement went unmet. When the war ended, Hoover wrote, he looked forward to resuming his mining career, and repairing his fortunes, "with a sufficient amount of experience in public affairs to know that it is an evil connection if one values contentment or even constructive results."[4]

Since then, he had overcome his reluctance to hold public office, but Hoover never discovered the joys of political gamesmanship, nor developed the skin as thick as an elephant's hide with which most politicians deflect criticism. As a member of Coolidge's official family, he had complained about the severity of attacks on administration farm policies in *Wallace's Farmer,* a bellwether midwestern journal whose masthead contained the family name of Coolidge's own Secretary of Agriculture. The president was less concerned. "You mean that one in the magazine with the green cover?" he asked nonchalantly after Hoover mentioned a censorious article in *American Mercury.* "I started to read it, but it was against me, so I didn't finish it."

Hoover read everything printed about his own administration. He sub-scribed to a clipping service to sample firsthand the disillusionment felt by millions of Americans who had elected him as a more dynamic version of the Yankee president whose prosperity barely outlasted his term of office. As a young man, Hoover had helped revolutionize the techniques of mining. Those auditing a series of lectures he delivered at Columbia University in 1908 were not prepared for his endorsement of labor unions as "normal and proper antidotes for unlimited capitalistic organizations. . . . The time when the employer could ride roughshod over his labor is disappearing with the doctrine of laissez-faire upon which it was founded." Hoover and his cadre of bright, idealistic young men who formed the Commission for Relief in Belgium (CRB) had outraged every convention of diplomatic etiquette, disregarding national borders and rejecting wartime jingoism to keep eleven million Europeans from starvation—at an overhead of less than one half of one percent. "We do not kick a man in the stomach after we have licked him," Hoover informed those he angered by feeding the defeated Germans. And when President Wilson asked him to oversee a postwar industrial com-mission, Hoover fought hard for collective bargaining, the minimum wage, an end to child labor, and guaranteed equality of pay for working women.

Back in 1920, resigned to Harding and Coolidge as his party's standard-bearers, Hoover buried his disappointment and rationalized his own defeat at the hands of professional vote-counters. "Our only chance," he told his friend Lewis Strauss at the time, "is to let the Old Guard swallow us and then work to make the Republican Party wiser and better in the years ahead." His own sympathies lay in the activist tradition of Theodore Roo-sevelt, whose 1912 Bull Moose campaign had been enriched by a thousand-dollar Hoover contribution. In his inauguration address, Hoover redeemed the promise of 1920, heralding a New Day in the life of his country and party. Hardly had he sworn the oath of office—itself an act of disobedience to the hard-shell Quakerism of his youth—than the new executive was waist-deep in an ambitious agenda of overdue reforms.

He wanted child care made a top priority, along with conservation, bank-ing regulation, executive reorganization, Indian rights and the first steps toward old-age pensions and unemployment insurance. Anxious to tap the best minds and inspire grass-roots enthusiasm, Hoover called sixty-two con-ferences under White House auspices, to take apart the nation's shortcom-ings and lay the groundwork for their solution. Once he had sent shivers up the spines of his critics by announcing that an engineer could create a more handsome waterfall than any to be found in nature's realm. In the White House, he soon found both his reforming and his engineering instincts blocked by the untidy, irrational element called human nature. Before the depression curdled his hope for voluntary cooperation as the surest route to security as well as freedom, Hoover was swamped by Prohibition and the unbridled lawlessness it fostered among a thirsty, rebellious people.

Himself a connoisseur, who boasted of the finest port in California until Lou Hoover emptied out his wine cellar ("I don't have to live with the American people," he said, "but I do have to live with Lou"), the president's rigid adherence to constitutional mandate ruled out even the suggestion of repealing the social experiment he called noble in motive but came to view as a blood-drenched failure. Fred Clark, head of the Crusaders, more than a million young men who stood behind the dry decade but wished to placate growing public opposition, went to the Lincoln study and proposed a way out. He would send Hoover a telegram asking for the president's position on a pending bill to legalize the sale of beer, to which Hoover could respond with tepid support, refusing to commit himself until he had seen the actual language it contained but promising not to oppose legal beer if it was the sentiment of Congress. The president listened to all this, jingling coins in his pocket and looking out the window for a long while. "Well, Mr. Clark," he finally replied, "I can't agree to your proposal. If I have to resort to such tactics, I do not want to be in public life."[5]

Such stiff-necked refusal to play the games on which popular government depended was not the only reform instituted in the Hoover White House. Hardly had Coolidge moved out than his successor placed the presidential yacht in mothballs, shut down the White House stables—Hoover detested horses, what he called a "cockeyed" creation from an impractical deity— and executed the threadbare "White House spokesman" behind whom Coolidge had taken refuge in dealings with the press. He installed the first Oval Office telephone, hired four secretaries in place of Coolidge's one, and divided their responsibilities among the press, Congress, and, in Larry Richey's case, his own most confidential errands. He disliked Coolidge's daily receptions for the public and chafed under the impromptu greetings for visiting beauty queens and Hollywood idols ("Who is Rudy Vallee?" he huffed) which other presidents relished. To save time, for Hoover the most precious of commodities, he replaced the noontime handshaking ritual with a mass picture session on the South Lawn. He remodeled the executive offices during his first month in residence—only to see them ravaged by a Christmas Eve fire in 1930.

Efficiency was his hallmark. Back in his days as Food Administrator, he once called his namesake son into the study of their S Street home and with suitable ceremony inquired if the boy had any objection to dropping his middle initial. Personally, he was required to sign his name hundreds of times each day, he explained. Without the encumbrance of a capital C, he could save at least a few minutes for meatier duties. Washington's less standardized sorts didn't know what to make of a chief executive who played medicine ball each morning because it provided him with three times as much exercise as tennis, and six times as much as golf, who wolfed down five courses of a state dinner in eleven minutes and gave signals to eliminate a course if the meal ran over an hour, and whose mania for competence played havoc with political protocol.[6]

Colonel Edmund Starling of the Secret Service, who abandoned his plan to join Coolidge in retirement at Hoover's request, found himself protecting the new president from red-faced lawmakers, as well as an alarming covey of cranks and would-be assassins. When proud residents of Bangor, Maine, sent the White House a fresh salmon, they did not reckon with Hoover's spit and polish. Before a beaming congressman could be photographed with its presumably delighted recipient, the scaly gift was dispatched to the kitchen. Colonel Starling was forced to sew its head back on. Maine, he noted afterward, "did not go Democratic for three years."

Ill-suited as he was at political logrolling, Hoover was still less adept at the modern arts of mass leadership. He built his speeches as an engineer builds a bridge. Less charitable observers compared the endless revising—the president liked to sit at his desk, shears in hand, cutting and pasting paragraphs of a message to Congress—to digging a canal. "I can't imagine that the American people aren't willing to listen for an hour to the subjects that are vital to their lives," he reproached advisers urging him to shorten his addresses and enliven his statistic-laden arguments. Persuasive in private, Hoover frittered away opportunities for public guidance, speaking in a dishwatery monotone, burying his head in a text, conveying the pained expression of a condemned man instead of a confident leader.[7]

So preoccupied was he with the urgent economic conferences that filled his days that the president overlooked the educational and inspirational functions of his office. It was not a showman's job, he insisted: "You can't make a Teddy Roosevelt out of me." When someone suggested he boost his sagging reelection campaign in the fall of 1932 by going aloft with Charles Lindbergh and Coolidge, the notion was rejected out of hand, even though Franklin Roosevelt had roused the nation with his precedent-shattering flight to Chicago earlier that summer, to accept his own party's presidential nomination.[8]

Together with Walter Hope, his Assistant Secretary of the Treasury, Hoover once happened upon a sandlot ball game not far from the White

House. He stopped to watch the kids at play for half an hour, cheered them on, and chatted with them informally when the game was over. Then he returned to his office and more work.

"Mr. President," Hope said to his chief, "I wish you'd come out here tomorrow if it's a nice day and let me have some photographers get a picture of you watching this game."[9]

Hoover would do nothing of the kind, for the same reason he banned pictures of his daily medicine-ball game. Unthinkingly, he did allow himself to be pictured feeding his dog on the White House lawn, setting off a barrage of accusations. A Batesville, Arkansas, man complained of a *Time* magazine story in which the president fed milk to an alley cat. "Is this at the expense of the American people," demanded the letter-writer, "or does the President furnish his own milk?"

Americans who scratched their heads over Hoover's failure to visit a single soup kitchen or breadline were not privy to his horror of suffering. "Don't you ever let me see one of these again!" he had commanded a Belgian relief worker who insisted on showing him a Brussels field kitchen. To the end of his life, the memory of starving Belgium could bring tears to his eyes. His own methods of greeting the public more often displayed an aptitude for disaster. Before the Washington State football team played in the 1932 Rose Bowl, it was invited to the Rose Garden. His mind elsewhere, Hoover casually inquired if the boys had had a good season. They'd beaten Stanford fifty to nothing, someone answered, and everyone chuckled indulgently.[10]

At White House musicales arranged by his wife, the president sat with his eyes closed, seemingly oblivious to the artistry of Rosa Ponselle, Jascha Heifetz and other luminaries of the concert hall invited to entertain state guests. Every evening, surrounded by people to whom he was barely civil, Hoover dined in formal dress. "You have to hammer and hammer at him," Lou commented. "He said he is too busy to think about it." Yet when an aide suggested that perhaps her husband would prefer to be by himself one weekend, she instantly vetoed the idea. "He always wants to have people around him," she explained. He would undoubtedly turn around and come straight back to the White House if he reached Camp Rapidan and found it empty of weekend guests.[11]

The public barely knew him. To most Americans, he was a rubber face perched atop a stiff size 17 collar, blandly reassuring them that nothing fundamentally wrong afflicted their economic system. They saw nothing of his private anguish, or of the dozens of personal bequests he made to individuals in need—after first having them checked out by trusted associates.

Hoover's personal fortune, developed in a breathless decade of globe-trotting to sniff out gold and copper, zinc or lead, was reduced to less than $1,000,000 by 1932. He sank at least $25,000 of what remained into a camp on the Rapidan River, 109 miles from Washington, where he found temporary release in a trout stream, read newspapers dropped each morning by a Marine Corps plane, and laid plans for a World Disarmament Conference while sitting on a log with British Prime Minister Ramsay MacDonald.[12]

At his camp, he was content to don rubber boots and wade into a mountain brook, discard the formal gear of the capital for white flannels and a Panama hat, pitch horseshoes and mix up jigsaw puzzles to confuse his guests and bring a chuckle in the midst of his troubles. In the evening, he told droll stories before the fireplace in Town Hall, a central meeting place and dining room, not far from the Hoovers' own lodge, another house designated "the Prime Minister's" for MacDonald's occupancy during his visit, and a group of smaller cabins set aside for individual guests and identified by a sign reading, "The Slums."

A lifelong conservationist, who added two million acres to the national forest system and tightened controls over oil drilling on public lands, Hoover refused to burn firewood at his camp. When trout pools were called for, the president and his guests moved boulders to create them. "I have discovered," he said, "that even the work of the government can be improved by leisurely discussions out under the trees." Yet for all the fresh air and woodsy ambience of the Rapidan camp, Hoover could not wholly flee the national crisis. Striding back and forth, fretting over a proposed moratorium on European war debts, he devoted much of his time along the Rapidan to front-porch conferences with congressmen and economic advisers. One weekend in 1932, he spent twelve hours on a long-distance hookup, personally directing a rush order of $35 million so that a major Chicago bank could open on Monday morning.

When a boy from nearby Dark Hollow wandered into the camp with an opossum he'd shot, Hoover discovered that the children of the area had no school. He and Lou promptly donated funds to build one and with the help of Robert Hutchins, then dean of Yale's Law School, they found a young woman to conduct classes in the two-room cabin with loft that the state of Virginia had been unwilling or unable to construct on its own. The Hoovers also enjoyed inspecting the state's new Skyline Drive, ordered by the president as part of his public works program. Lou was especially fond of the area, whether racing along in the open Ford V-8 that outdistanced Secret Service agents or making light of the copperheads cleaned out of the camp by a detachment of Marines and razorback hogs. On Sundays, few bothered to attend services in Luray, twelve miles away. Lou's husband excused his absence from church by explaining that there were two things no man should be forced to do before the public eye—fish and pray.[13]

The same mask concealed a complex, paradoxical personality, and a preoccupation with private virtue that smothered any chance for dynamic or intuitive leadership. Hoover's boyhood, with all its hardships and emotional deprivation, had bred into him both insecurity and rigid self-reliance. His subsequent successes, dazzling as they were, taught him a narrow formula of the public good. They instilled as well a stubbornness and suspicion that imputed evil motives to those who would block his program or take issue with his methods. The very quality of disinterested, rational management that had propelled Hoover so far, so fast, was precisely the wrong tack in governing a people requiring inspiration as well as legislation. When Hoover denied any resemblance to T.R., he told the truth in a way that heralded the tragedy of his administration. Uncomfortable with the superficiality of most political relationships, the president withdrew to the things he understood best—only to discover the limitations of managerial government in a time of national emergency.

Few penetrated the shell of crisp efficiency in which Hoover guarded himself from outsiders. Those who did were treated to a master raconteur with a waspish wit. Appalled by the gimcracks Americans love to shower on their presidents, Hoover remarked that some enterprising showman ought to start a museum for ugly things; he'd gladly make several contributions. One of Lou's secretaries quit her job to get married and informed the president that had it not been for him, she might never have met her intended. Taken aback, Hoover gave a feeble imitation of the boyish grin preserved in hundreds of pictures snapped during less arduous days. "I have been held responsible for everything under the sun," he told her. "It is a pleasure to know that I am responsible, even to so small a degree, for your future happiness."[14]

For the rest of his long life, he would savor Coolidge stories, none more than the tale about the evening he sat across from the dour New Englander in the State Dining Room and a vexed chief executive glanced repeatedly at some distraction in the hallway. "Mr. Hoover," he ventured near the end of their meal, "don't you think the light has been a little too shiny on Mr. John Quincy Adams' head?" Without pausing for a reply, Coolidge summoned a servant and a stepladder, rubbed a rag in some fireplace ashes, and proceeded to black out the sixth president's bald, ample cranium. Only later, when Hoover himself occupied the presidential chair, did it fall to him to apologize to his own Secretary of the Navy, Charles Francis Adams.

Adams, it seemed, failed to see the humor in the disfigurement of his ancestor. One way or another, it appeared that Hoover was fated to suffer from his predecessor's conduct, even while making excuses for it.[15]

It was cruelly ironic that he should find himself succeeding Coolidge, only to attend the deathbed of the old order, feeling its pulse weaken along with the flickering vital signs of an economy *in extremis*. His predecessor had galvanized a strike-weary nation in 1919, declaring that the police of Boston had no right to strike against the public safety anywhere, anytime. Thirteen years later, Americans hooted at their president when he dispersed the Bonus Army and proclaimed his willingness to mete out similar treatment to any other mob. Few complained in 1927 when Coolidge dispatched U.S. Marines to help suppress the Nicaraguan Rebellion of Augusto Sandino— or cheered Hoover for withdrawing the troops during the last week of Coolidge's life. Almost overnight, the Great Engineer became "Super Babbitt" to a hostile press corps. Reporters derided the president as a victim of his own self-pity, hiding behind a protective wedge of second-rate retainers. Theodore Joslin, Hoover's personal secretary after 1931, was classified as the only known rat ever to clamber aboard a sinking ship.

Hoover responded by lashing out, at friend and foe alike. "The only trouble with capitalism," he remarked to friendly columnist Mark Sullivan, "is capitalists; they're too damned greedy." When 2,300 banks collapsed in 1931 alone, it confirmed his judgment that the entire system he hoped to bring within the protective embrace of the Federal Reserve was "rotten." He reserved still harsher words for officeholders of both parties who insisted on business as usual.[16]

Hoover was "in a state," Joslin reported to one capital journalist in the summer of 1931, invited in to hear the president blow off steam at a crucial juncture in global efforts to combat the Depression and reduce war reparations. His hair rumpled, his face red, Hoover overflowed with rhetorical anger. "Is it my fault that these selfish men over the whole world have refused to see the folly of their policies until it was too late?" he demanded. "Is it my fault that Jim Watson, although he is supposed to be the Republican leader of the Senate, prefers to play his own politics against me? Is it my fault that France, our ally, has stood blindly in the way of settlement and co-operation?" Americans were passing through the most difficult days in their history, concluded the president. At least during the war, Wilson could rely on "militant co-operation." "That," said Hoover, "we cannot get now."[17]

It was "damned inconsiderate" to force him out of an economic conference in the Lincoln study to help Alexandria's Masons dedicate a memorial to George Washington, he stormed. The country was burning—and loquacious congressmen wanted him to cut ribbons. He complained, but he also went. He would observe the amenities, just as his imagination would not overstep the bounds of constitutional precedent. His response to the emergency was cerebral, not emotional. Lacking the gift of ruthlessness, he persisted in thinking ruthless men vulnerable to his own rationality. At each of his meals, throughout sixteen-hour days and often late into the night, Hoover kept on talking, jawboning industry to maintain wage levels, cajoling legislators to support tax increases and oppose direct relief payments, plugging an endless series of fiscal dikes. He worked as hard on Sundays as on the other six days of the week, pouring himself into veto messages that would, he felt certain, "rattle their bones" on Capitol Hill. Yet nothing halted the steep decline of the nation's economy.[18]

"I saw more than a dozen people today," an exhausted president confided to his Kansas ally, editor Roy Roberts, "and only one of them contributed so much as the glimmer of an idea." "I have heard that so often," he told another well-wisher professing to see bright omens of economic recovery, "and have always been disappointed." He deleted any trace of humor from his already ponderous speeches; a president could not afford to be funny in the midst of such suffering. When the Portuguese minister celebrated thirty years of diplomatic service in Washington by recalling Theodore Roosevelt as the most fun-loving president in memory, Hoover replied with a hint of acid, "I doubt if he would get much fun out of it in a period like the present."[19]

A man less hardened to adversity might not have endured. Even though Hoover's frame had been toughened by decades of harsh existence, weeding fields as a boy, wading through hip-deep snow to make contact with Americans in Manchuria after the Boxer Rebellion, the Depression left its mark. His face became a bas-relief of the sorrows overwhelming millions of Americans. His hands shook as he lit one of the fistful of Juan Alones cigars he smoked each day. His hair grew white and his frame shed twenty-five pounds. Whatever else the American people might call him, they could no longer agree with H. L. Mencken that he was merely a "fat Coolidge." His doctor told him to get a haircut: it would make him look younger, said Joel Boone. But there was no time for haircuts in the Hoover White House. The hero of Belgium, prophet of a New Day and New Era, was gone now, replaced by a grim-faced man in a blue double-breasted suit who doodled at his desk and stared at the floor as visitors tried to engage his attention. Some of Hoover's friends doubted he would survive a year out of office.[20]

His innovations in office turned out to be the bitter harvest of mass privation. As the initial recession turned ugly late in 1930, and joblessness soared to record levels, Hoover conducted a cautious flirtation with novelty. He expanded government's role far beyond the hands-off stance taken in earlier depressions, if not far enough to satisfy his critics. He spent more money on public works than all his predecessors combined, added 37,000 miles of highway, and threw a double-decked span of steel and cable across San Francisco's Golden Gate. He created Federal Land Banks to halt farm foreclosures, and Home Loan Discount Banks to afford homeowners similar protection. He launched the National Credit Association, with half a billion dollars in capital, and sent it out into the field to salvage tottering banks. But 522 financial institutions withered in the NCA's first month, and the program died aborning.

Cutting federal salaries by 15 percent, donating his own to charity, the president grew progressively bolder in his remedies. He persuaded the Interstate Commerce Commission to reduce rates charged rail lines carrying water and forage to farmers desperate for both. He set up an Emergency Relief Organization and pressured state and local authorities to cooperate with efforts at grass-roots assistance. "A voluntary deed," he maintained, "is infinitely more precious to our national ideas and spirit than a thousandfold poured from the Treasury." Hoover's Agriculture Department gave seed loans to the farm belt, and diverted Lake Michigan to relieve a growing dust bowl, where crops and hope alike refused to take root.

Continuing his foxhole conversion to government intervention, Hoover thought back to his own wartime experiences. He unveiled the Reconstruction Finance Corporation, fitted out with $3 billion dollars to ransom financial institutions in the throes of deflation and a depositors' panic. He violated the gospel of balanced budgets, called a moratorium on payment of European war debts, and acquiesced in the public demand for direct relief payments—only to see a few states exhaust most of the $300 million relief fund within two weeks of its creation. On Janaury 5, 1933, a House committee listened to feverish demands from Illinois officials for a fresh infusion of $72 million. The president should send the money immediately, declared the mayor of Chicago, or else send troops to maintain order.

At the White House, Hoover sat beneath an old magnolia tree, its spidery branches sheltering such men as Chief Justice Harlan Stone, Interior Secretary Ray Lyman Wilbur, Dr. Boone and other members of his Medicine Ball Cabinet. To these intimates, he apologized for failing to persuade his successor to stay true to the gold standard, and mused out loud about a different kind of government emerging from the present travail as Joseph had prophesied to Pharaoh an end to Egypt's ruinous cycle of bust and boom.

The demise of the dominant role of private charity in countering hardship was at hand, Hoover announced. At other times, he muttered about crimes worse than murder, and in his imagination, lined up Wall Street brokers and crooked bankers alike before the firing squad of public opinion.[21]

Once applauded as an administrative maestro, now reduced to a pawn, the president sat behind his desk an unwilling spokesman for discredited truths. Holding office in such a time, he said ruefully, was akin to being a repairman behind a dike. "No sooner is one leak plugged up than it is necessary to dash over and stop another that has broken out. There is no end to it." Like a leading man being struck by collapsing scenery while stagehands look on, his own position was rapidly crumbling to the floor. Not even the imminent prospect of his departure from power could prevent a handful of congressmen from joining a Pennsylvania colleague in voting for a twenty-four-count bill of impeachment against Hoover. The same House of Representatives was working its way methodically toward rejection of the president's cherished government reorganization plan, while the Senate adopted an even more sweeping blueprint for change, carefully reserving to Franklin Roosevelt the authority to abolish agencies at will and impound funds already appropriated by Congress.

On the Senate floor, Alabama's Hugo Black spent January 5 arguing for his bill to mandate a thirty-hour workweek, thereby creating 6.5 million jobs and defusing a general strike threat from the American Federation of Labor. His colleagues were turning thumbs down on one of their own, an Ohio Democrat named Atlee Pomerene, to serve on the board of Hoover's Reconstruction Finance Corporation, and House Speaker John Nance Garner was crowing over his victory in compelling disclosure of all RFC loans, a step sure to enrage a public out of sympathy with banks, insurance companies, and a president derided by radio priest Charles Coughlin as "the Holy Ghost of the rich, the protective angel of Wall Street."

Hoover could only throw up his hands. "Whatever the subject," he told Ted Joslin, "there are not thirty senators we can depend on. It's a rout." In the twilight of his own presidency, sandwiched between the prosaic stand-pattism of Coolidge and the as-yet unfathomable liberalism of Roosevelt, Hoover might well reflect on the twists of timing and fate. His calendar for January 5 included luncheon with Secretary of State Henry Stimson. Given Stimson's announced desire to meet the following week with FDR at the latter's country estate at Hyde Park, it was certain to be an acrimonious affair.

The president could not guess that by the time his lunch broke up, it would be Coolidge rather than Roosevelt who held his attention. His relationship with both men said a great deal about Hoover, the reputed miracle worker turned political misfit.

★   ★

Calvin Coolidge was a creature of habit. His was a life of accidental pageantry, wherein faithfulness to small things paid rich dividends. The red-haired Vermonter, with a nasal twang in his voice and a surprising streak of sentiment in his character, could thank both habit and exquisite timing for propelling him from the City Council of Northampton, Massachusetts, to the White House. Succeeding Warren Harding in August 1923, Coolidge promptly replaced his predecessor's boozy card parties with sober six-o'clock suppers. Habit ruled his life and set the well-regulated tone of his administration. It forbade thirteen at his table and Cabinet conferences after four in the afternoon. ("I don't work at night," the new president had announced. "If a man can't finish his job in the daytime, he's not smart.") It made him don huge suspenders before stepping out each morning to window-shop along the capital's F Street—and flee his South Dakota summer retreat on a special train at first sight of a snake.

Habit demanded eleven hours out of every twenty-four for sleep. Indeed, it said much about Coolidge's administration when his nominee for Attorney General was voted down by the Senate as Vice President Charles Dawes napped in his hotel room.

Above all else, habit dictated thrift. Coolidge was as frugal with innovation as with the Vermont cheese he grumpily sliced for Colonel Starling. He halted the twenty-one-gun salutes customarily fired as the presidential yacht drew up alongside George Washington's Mount Vernon. They made Prudence Prim, his white collie, howl. "Besides," Coolidge explained, "it costs money to fire so many guns. So I have the band play the Star Spangled Banner." When he set foot in Key West after a visit to Cuba, a curious mayor was eager to hear about the presidential excursion into diplomacy. Coolidge wanted to know if the city manager had any free passes to the local moving picture show; as mayor of Northampton, twenty years earlier, he had enjoyed just such a privilege.[22]

An admiring public thought him taciturn. They didn't know the Coolidge who held three press conferences in a week and could be garrulous as a filibustering senator in private. Biting characterization came naturally to "the little fellow," as White House retainers called him. They witnessed firsthand a peevish man with an entourage of doormen and butlers on whom he loved to play practical jokes, who rebuked bluebloods from self-satisfied Boston ("That's just ol' man Stearns," he explained after hearing his chief financial backer, a Tremont Street storeowner, pace outside his door. "He wants to come in and have some of our supper, but I'm not going to let him. He's eaten enough of my food already"), and forced long-suffering Secret Service men to bait the presidential fishhook and retrieve trout taken by an itinerant sportsman testing the waters within two miles of Coolidge's summer White House. "They are my fish," Coolidge insisted, with the same matter-of-fact petulance he displayed in ordering the White House automobile cleared, in terminating official receptions at 10:45 P.M., and in supervising provisions for the executive mansion from the nearest Piggly Wiggly store.

His wife, Grace, as tolerant as the nation was bemused, humored her eccentric husband into abandoning white kid gloves at the fish pond. Grace deflated the deification of 1600 Pennsylvania Avenue. "What's the matter, Poppa," she asked as he blew a whistle to summon a pet raccoon, "don't your teeth fit tonight?"

"The greatest man ever to come out of Plymouth, Vermont," H. L. Mencken called the thirtieth president, who provided Americans with five and a half years of cautious governing, made spectacular only by the feverish growth of an economy reborn in the wake of war. Coolidge Prosperity, people called it, and the ordinarily somber-faced Yankee let pride flicker about his features. Why not? Between 1925 and 1929, the New York Stock Exchange rose by 250 percent. Before the decade was over, Americans had retired nearly half the $26 billion debt bequeathed by the victory sealed at Versailles. Sympathetic to commerce in all its forms—he once likened a factory to a temple—Coolidge did not wholly embrace the Darwinist idea that worldly goods provided a better yardstick of individual worth than spiritual values. Instead, he made business into a religion, telling the New York Chamber of Commerce in 1925 that theirs was a calling that rested on "a higher law" of "truth and faith and justice."

Delighted with the torrent of wealth, the 800,000 new homes being built annually to meet postwar demand, the new highways snaking out into the American countryside, the bustling steel plants and booming auto sales, Coolidge found it easy to dismiss the warnings of his Secretary of Commerce, Herbert Hoover, that credit was too easy, and the stock market dangerously inflated. Instead, the president issued a bullish proclamation early in 1928: $4 billion worth of broker loans struck him as a sign of robust economic health.

"Did that man say *that*?" asked an incredulous Hoover.[23]

As creative in his approach to government as Coolidge was pinched, Hoover proved a nettlesome inheritance for his nominal superior. "What's our wonder boy done now?" Coolidge drawled as his dynamic colleague dipped a finger into every Washington pie. At Commerce, Hoover hatched countless schemes to fix airplane routes and regulate the infant medium of radio, dam the Colorado River, and erect tent cities for a hundred thousand victims of the Mississippi River floods of 1927. Peripatetic and single-minded, the secretary was not the sort to let obstacles block his path or divert him from his myriad goals. As Woodrow Wilson's domestic food czar, a position created for the man called the Great Humanitarian for his brilliant efforts to feed ten million Europeans in the path of warring armies, Hoover was riding with an associate in a Washington taxi one day when it collided with another vehicle on the capital's slick streets. The two taxi passengers promptly got out and walked to work, neither of them breaking the train of official conversation.[24]

A city whose conventional wisdom was conventional indeed, Washington had trouble interpreting this self-made millionaire who rejected a $500,000 offer from the Guggenheims to take the helm at Commerce, an orphan who founded the American Child Health Association, a shameless patriot who had already spent a third of his life abroad. On top of it all, Hoover was also a philosopher of sorts, preaching a new brand of grass-roots idealism even as he pointed out the limitless possibilities in standardized tires and bottle caps.

"We have long since abandoned the laissez-faire of the 18th Century," he wrote in *American Individualism*, a 1922 volume that moved the *New York Times* to compare its author to James Madison as a practitioner-prophet of the governing process, "in part because we have learned that it is the hindmost who throws the bricks at our social edifice, in part because we have learned that the foremost are not always the best. . . . We have learned that the impulse to production can only be maintained at a high pitch if there is a division of the product."[25]

Hoover's individualism insisted on service to the community. It hinted broadly at society's franchise on free enterprise. Relying on legal structures to guarantee equality of opportunity, the author of *American Individualism* did not confuse the law and real life. The notion that all men were created equal in brains, character or ambition, wrote Hoover, "was part of the claptrap of the French Revolution." Worse yet, he warned, was the emotionalism and greed of masses of individuals. "The crowd only feels," he concluded, "it has no mind of its own which can plan. The crowd is credulous, it destroys, it consumes, it hates, and it dreams—but it never builds." From such soil sprang demagoguery and false leadership.

To prevent the crowd from taking command, Hoover's prescription was for "a better, brighter, broader individualism," with the sluiceways of change always kept open, and the path of social and economic advance maintained by a government committed to social mobility. To him, life was a race, on a track maintained by a democratic government determined to provide the runners with an equal chance at the start. Others thought this naive. Hoover's race, they insisted, was really a steeplechase, and government little more than a monitor of spills and collector of broken bodies.[26]

If Hoover cast the human race in abstract terms, his burst of activity nonetheless stood out boldly in the somnolent atmosphere of postwar Washington. Coolidge held the steering wheel, providing direction without engine power. Hoover was in the engine room. The secretary envisioned a complete reorganization of the executive branch of government. He urged construction of power plants along the Saint Lawrence River. He cooked up a plan to enable migrant farmers to buy land in the cotton South, promoted foreign exports of U.S. farm products, and persuaded local fish and game clubs to join the federal government in producing half a billion baby fry to stock the nation's streams. Hoover reported the problem with a whimsy infrequently glimpsed in public.

"America is a well watered country," he told the Izaak Walton League, of which he had become president, "and the inhabitants know all the fishing holes. The Americans also produce millions of automobiles. These co-ordinate forces of inalienable right, the automobile and the call of the fishing hole, propel the man and boy to a search of all the water within a radius of 150 miles at weekends alone. He extends it to a radius of 500 miles on his summer holidays. These radii of operations . . . greatly overlap. Not surprisingly," he concluded, "the time between bites has become longer and longer, and the fish have become wiser and wiser."[27]

A world traveler, familiar with Mandalay rain forests and the Australian outland, an indefatigable worker, who found relaxation on Sunday afternoons by going to Rock Creek Park and damming the waters while family and friends dug into a picnic basket, Hoover was by all odds the biggest man in Washington. Warren Harding called him "the smartest 'geek' I know." His prominence and vigor made certain the disapproval of Harding's cranky, suspicious successor. Coolidge enjoyed dampening rumors that Hoover might replace Frank Kellogg, the timid, hypersensitive Secretary of State derided by official Washington as Nervous Nellie. His brows arched in horror at the price tag attached to Hoover's good intentions. His ego suffered in the penumbra of Hoover's dazzling reputation.

"That man has offered me unsolicited advice for six years," Coolidge stormed near the end of his term. "All of it bad."

Elected overwhelmingly in 1924, applauded since for his tax cuts and cracker-barrel aphorisms, swathed in myth by a people who found him aromatic as a russet apple, Coolidge could easily have extended his White House lease in 1928. But on August 3, 1927, the fourth anniversary of his lamplit inaugural in a Vermont farmhouse, the president stunned Americans with the cryptic disclosure that he did not choose to seek another term.

Grace said he smelled a depression coming. Her interpretation was bolstered by a prophecy her husband made to Colonel Starling shortly before leaving office.

"Well," he told his friend, "they're going to elect that superman Hoover, and he's going to have some trouble. He's going to have to spend money. But he won't spend enough. Then the Democrats will come in and spend money like water. But they don't know anything about money. Then they will want me to come back and save some money for them. But I won't do it."

Only a handful knew of the anguish Coolidge kept within, sitting misty-eyed at his desk while glancing out at George Washington's obelisk and remembering his dead son, Calvin, Junior. The boy had died from blood poisoning in the summer of 1925 after contracting a blister on the White House tennis court. "When he went," his father said, "the power and the glory of the Presidency went with him." Others watched the grueling pace of official life take its toll on Mrs. Coolidge, who called down the full force of her husband's wrath after returning late from a hike in the Black Hills with a handsome Secret Service man in the summer of 1927. Shortly thereafter, the president reassigned the agent permanently and let it be known that he and Grace would be returning to Northampton, and their thirty-six-dollar-a-month duplex come March 1929.[28]

He sat back and enjoyed the spectacle as ambitious suitors, Hoover among them, called in hopes of clarifying the ambiguous declaration of noncandidacy, or enlisting Coolidge's own potent support for their campaigns. For his part, Hoover came away convinced that the president was his ally in a fight against Old Guard senators, an elitist oligarchy despised by the Vermont democrat even more than upstart pretenders to his throne. Those around the Oval Office were less certain. They saw Coolidge, on the very day his party anointed Hoover as its new champion, demand a bottle of Green River whiskey and retreat to his room. They noticed his peremptory demand for Hoover's resignation from the Cabinet and his refusal to name the outgoing secretary's personal favorite to succeed him. Following Hoover's landslide win that fall over Al Smith, relations between the once and future presidents did not thaw noticeably. Hoover went off on a precedent-shattering goodwill tour of Latin America, avoiding Coolidge's baleful stare and inspiring "the little fellow" to revenge. "We'll leave it for the Great Engineer," Coolidge cracked to intimates as he filed away the knottiest dilemmas on his desk until after March 4.[29]

"You have to stand every day three or four hours of visitors," he warned Hoover shortly before handing over power. "Nine-tenths of them want something they ought not to have. If you keep dead still, they will run down in three or four minutes. If you even cough or smile they will start up all over again."[30]

It was curious advice for a man of Hoover's energy. Having imparted it, Coolidge was content to pack his things and bid farewell to a city and a political establishment that had often mocked and rarely understood him. Habit did not desert him. It always rained on his moving days, he remarked on Inauguration morning; Hoover would have to ride down Pennsylvania Avenue in a downpour. When the new chief executive got back to the White House, an address he had coveted for at least eight years, he would find one last example of Coolidgean denial.

The night before, the outgoing president had said goodbye to Colonel Starling, then pointed to a table groaning under the weight of the jams and preserves he liked to devour at all hours of the day. "I'm not going to leave them here," he told Starling. "I'm going to eat them in Northampton."

When Herbert and Lou Hoover arrived at the White House, drenched and chilled, they found the cupboard bare.

★   ★

For Coolidge, the habits of a thrifty lifetime, plus the acquaintance of rich friends, ensured against any personal rainy days. Unlike Hoover, who donated his presidential salary to charity, Coolidge saved most of his. His nest egg was enlarged in July 1929 by the acquisition of eight thousand shares of J. P. Morgan securities at eight dollars below market value. Others talked the ex-president into writing his memoirs at a dollar a word and composing a daily newspaper column for $3,000 a week.

The editors of The Nation compared Coolidge's two-hundred-word bromides to advertisements for Wanamaker's Department Store. Unfazed, the sage of Northampton promised to write a book entitled "The Importance of the Obvious." After all, he concluded, if Americans would only do the few simple things they knew were their obligation, "most of our big problems would take care of themselves."

Before he abandoned the journalistic grind in June 1931, Coolidge mingled tributes to springtime in the north country and sympathy for victims of a Santo Domingo hurricane with some tart criticism of his successor's farm policies. But about the biggest problem confronting his own economically ravaged land—the Depression born in the fall of 1929 and grown since to engulf half the nation's wealth and a quarter of her jobs—Coolidge could offer little more than exhortations to self-reliance.

"All that is needed," he told those who doubted private charity alone could satisfy a growing army of the destitute, "is for us to give what we think America is worth to us." The Depression might even have a silver lining, he concluded, if it turned Americans to planting gardens. Friends pressed in vain for more aggressive steps to halt the worsening spiral of bank closings and plant layoffs. He rejected any suggestion to offer journalistic advice to his successor. "I refuse to be Deputy President," he snapped. He told Al Smith that the whole situation was too confusing to understand. "The big men of the country have got to get together, and do something about it," he informed his barber. "It isn't going to end itself."

The big men could not prevent the Northampton Savings Bank from shutting its doors in 1932. Coolidge heard the news, then silently placed a check for $5,000 on the desk of Ralph Hemenway, his financially distressed partner in the law practice they shared. He gave another friend a handsome cedar chest with five $20 gold pieces inside. Publicly, he struck a note of optimism. The government still functioned, he wrote in his final newspaper column. The people stood firm in the face of adversity, "whatever excesses they tolerated in the time of prosperity."

It came as close to an apology as anyone ever heard from Coolidge, a thin-lipped confession of error without penance. His typewriter fell silent, with Coolidge telling friends he'd run out of things to say. Others thought him defensive about earning so much for saying so little, while seventeen thousand New Yorkers a month were being evicted from their homes, and a distraught woman marched into the Animal Rescue League in Washington, D.C., and begged to have her baby put out of its misery.

Even without the Depression to haunt his days and assail his pride, Coolidge discovered that being an ex-president carried demands to match the rewards. Free to spend summers at the old homestead in Plymouth, a hundred miles and a world away from Northampton, he rehabilitated his father's farmhouse, installed electricity and indoor plumbing, and added on a library to house some of his four thousand books. At Plymouth he could savor the purple hills and sugar lots of his boyhood, forget his hay fever and escape a clamoring public for the more welcome sounds of the bobolink and partridge.

With comfort came an intense craving for privacy. There was not a line of work, Coolidge complained a few months after leaving office, that he might take up without engendering public censure. His own celebrity ruled out travel through an admiring nation; he could not set foot in Europe without "detracting from the influence of Washington." The euphemism for Hoover was obvious. So was his own dissatisfaction with the public's curiosity. Motor cars by the thousands invaded the quiet side street in Northampton where he and Grace tried to resume their previous lives. Tourists made him give up window-shopping and his customary morning stroll. Now, he was forced to ride to the spartan suite of offices he rented on the second floor of the red brick Masonic block on Main Street, and the flat-topped desk of oak on which he ground out his epigrammatical sermonettes. In the evening, admirers stared into his living room and reporters clambered into the former president's bathroom as he showered.

In the spring of 1930, Coolidge took his newfound wealth and taste for seclusion to The Beeches, a handsome shingled residence of fourteen rooms clinging to the heights above the Connecticut River. He paid $40,000 for the estate, nestled at the end of a quiet cul-de-sac and protected from the inquisitive by nine acres of clipped lawn and scrubby wood. To newsmen he explained his purchase as an altruistic act: now, he said, his "doggies" would have room to play. He settled into his new routine, emerging from behind his iron gates each morning in a car once belonging to the White House.

Downtown, he rode an old-fashioned cage elevator to the rooms marked "Coolidge and Hemenway, Partners in Law," kicked off his shoes, lit up a powerful black cigar, and pondered his mail and papers. There was little else to fill his time. Often, he stood at a window, staring out at the crippled storefronts of commercial Northampton, and a bereaved people he no longer commanded or understood. He cut himself off from partisan politics, refusing any role in choosing a new Republican chairman for Massachusetts, pleading health to stay away from Hoover's renomination ceremony in August 1932.

"I suppose no one knows how I hate making speeches," he muttered before agreeing to make one for the embattled president on October 11. When it was over, an admirer gushed her desire to have Coolidge, not Hoover, carry the GOP banner against Franklin Roosevelt. "It would be the end of this terrible depression," she told him.

"It would be the beginning of mine," he replied.

Coolidge did manage a legalistic appeal for the president's cause, which ran in the *Saturday Evening Post* ("a warming remembrance from a true friend," Hoover called it), and an election eve broadcast from his library at The Beeches. In both he struck a cautionary note, calling voters home to a safe harbor of values enshrined in the very laissez-faire rejected by Hoover. Yet all his warnings against experimentation could not save Herbert Hoover from overwhelming defeat. Bewildered by the strident voices abroad in his land, surprised by the size of Roosevelt's mandate, the former president began speaking of himself as a museum piece. No longer did the American people share his priorities of tax and debt reduction, or a stable tariff, he noted. "Socialistic" remedies seemed certain to be applied to those caught up in their own suffering.[31]

But he was not bitter, or apocalyptic. He struck a sympathetic note for the president-elect, whose unwieldy coalition of the dissatisfied might prove as centrifugal as Warren Harding's had a decade before. Early in January 1933, he confessed to sympathy for anyone holding office just then. He declined an invitation to attend his Amherst class reunion; an accompanying police squad would disrupt the occasion. "It's my past life that makes all the trouble," he went on. "If only I could get rid of my past life. But that always stays with one."[32]

He climbed out of bed at seven o'clock on the morning of January 5, breakfasted with Grace and rode downtown. By ten he had finished what little business cluttered his desk, and was back at The Beeches, fiddling with a jigsaw puzzle and reminiscing about the previous autumn's partridge hunt at Plymouth. Prowling around like a caged animal, Coolidge went to the kitchen to fetch a glass of water, descended into the cellar for a word with the handyman, and climbed wordlessly to the second floor to shave. Habit still consoled him: lunch was an hour away, his customary nap more distant in the recesses of a short winter afternoon.

In his dressing room, he removed his coat and faced himself in the mirror. Noiselessly and with massive certainty, death reached out to embrace Calvin Coolidge. Returning from a shopping excursion on Main Street a few minutes later, Grace found him sprawled on the floor, the victim of an exhausted heart unable to beat any longer. Gently, she stretched him out on his bed, where the soft light of a single bulb caressed his sharp Yankee features into contentment. Outside, neighborhood children were joined by journalists and photographers. The world beyond Northampton took note of the news. Andrew Mellon, coarchitect of Coolidge Prosperity, more recently exiled by Hoover to the Court of St. James's, called the death of his friend an irreparable loss to the nation. The president-elect, conferring with Democratic congressional leaders in New York over ways to raise taxes and honor a campaign pledge of a balanced budget, interrupted the talks long enough to pronounce himself "shocked beyond measure" and designate his wife, Eleanor, and son James to represent him at the funeral.

Across the Atlantic, the *Times* of London eulogized rugged individualism. "The old American belief," it judged, "so cherished by New Englanders like

Mr. Coolidge, that the honest man should depend on himself and earn the bread he eats is now challenged by millions of decent citizens who must . . . eat by charity because there is no work for them. This lonely, inarticulate, simple, shrewd man," concluded the *Times*, "was not of today."

Walter Lippmann, who had written with faintly disguised contempt of Coolidge's "genius for the commonplace," proclaimed himself amazed that the dead man's popularity should have survived the end of his era. Dorothy Parker, who used the Depression as a platform from which to extol the glories of an age without individuals, was suitably irreverent. Informed of Coolidge's death, she had a question:

"How could they tell?"

Notwithstanding the wisecracks and head-scratching by sophisticates, no one could ignore the fresh grief deepening the pall over a nation accustomed to three years of black headlines. Perhaps it was the quality defined as "pure New England" by Lippmann's rivals at the *New York Times*, a fierce, often funny individuality cackling before the impersonal forces of modern life, or simply the longing of a profligate people in the twilight of their speculation for what Coolidge himself called "a solemn ass" in the White House; whatever the source of their bond, Americans were feeling poorer on the afternoon of January 5, and not just materially.

Tears, however, were out of season. Having left office just seven months before Black Tuesday cast a permanent shadow over "the wonder boy," Coolidge drew his last breath eight weeks before Franklin Roosevelt and his new order could sweep away the moorings of all that was familiar and comfortable. For the prone figure on his Northampton fourposter, the ordeal was over. For his successor and victim, less blessed with good timing, less endowed with the qualities of personal legend, it was just now beginning.

★　　★

It was a few minutes before two o'clock when chief usher Ike Hoover knocked on the door of the Lincoln study bearing a bulletin from Northampton. For most Americans, news of Coolidge's death evoked emotions distilled by memory or tainted by more intimate glimpses of suffering. For Secretary of State Stimson, eager to conclude a prolonged, contentious lunch with his chief, Ike Hoover's bulletin was at least a useful shock. Stimson itched to return to his office and a meeting with Japanese diplomats certain to be chastised for their government's latest aggression in Manchuria.

It wasn't merely unfinished business that made him uneasy. White House conferences with the perpetually gloomy Hoover reminded the fastidious diplomat of a bath in ink. On January 5, the two men sparred as expected over Roosevelt's invitation to Stimson for a face-to-face encounter. The subject was highly sensitive. Both had served in Wilson's official family, Hoover as the nation's food czar, young FDR as Assistant Secretary of the Navy. Eleanor Roosevelt was one of millions of American housewives who "hooverized" during the war, declaring porkless Tuesdays, limiting sugar to two pounds per person per month, and developing a taste for cornbread and milk puddings.

When the earnest Mrs. Roosevelt attributed her success in food conservation to the helpful presence of ten servants, she provoked hilarity among Washington cynics and a choice barb or two from her husband. He was proud indeed, wrote FDR, to be married to "the Originator, Discoverer and Inventor of the New Household Economy for Millionaires! Please have a photo taken showing the family," he continued, tongue firmly planted in cheek, "the ten cooperating servants, the scraps saved from the table and the hand book. I will have it published in the Sunday Times."

Despite the contretemps over her hooverizing, Eleanor, like her husband, remained on good terms with Bert and Lou Hoover. The two men met over the dinner table in the S Street home of their mutual friend Franklin K. Lane. At the start of 1920, Hoover received from his own friend, Ambassador Hugh Gibson, a copy of a Roosevelt letter containing the wish that Hoover might be elected president that year ("There could not be a better one"). Louis Brandeis, Jane Addams, Harvard's faculty and the *New Republic* echoed FDR's sentiments, but Hoover's lack of political finesse was painfully evident, and ultimately Harding and Coolidge were pitted against Ohio's James Cox—and, for Vice President, Roosevelt himself.

Following the attack of polio which clouded his once bright prospects, Roosevelt busied himself with Wall Street speculation, dabbling—and losing heavily—in Maine lobsters and transatlantic dirigibles. He also became chairman of the American Construction Council, where Secretary Hoover advised him to let regulation of building standards appear to originate within the industry itself. This was only logical, wrote Hoover, since "the vast sentiment of the business community against Government interference tends to destroy even a voluntary effort if it is thought to be carried out at Government inspiration."[33]

Still regarding Roosevelt as his friend, Hoover was appalled to read a confidential letter mailed by FDR on behalf of Al Smith's 1928 campaign. Himself a candidate for Smith's Albany office, Roosevelt attacked "materialistic and self-seeking advisers" around Hoover and suggested that Smith had far more genuine interest in suffering humanity. Roosevelt also attempted to downplay Hoover's relationship with Woodrow Wilson. "To me," FDR wrote, "the contemptuous casting aside of all of President Wilson's wonderful dreams of a better world, and the substitution of crass materialism and a dollar-and-cents viewpoint of everything has been a world tragedy." If Hoover were not personally at fault, Roosevelt implied, he stood in the shadow of Harding and Coolidge, surrounded by apostles of greed and isolation.[34]

Hoover did not have access to another Roosevelt letter, which combined political promotion and personal prophecy. "I have known Mr. Hoover personally for many years," Roosevelt explained to a wavering voter in September 1928, "and would be the last one to decry his abilities as an administrator of a department, but that very quality which enables him to take some particular brand of activity and by concentration of effort, carry whatever the project may be to a triumphant conclusion, is a very serious handicap to a man in the Presidential office, where what is needed is a wide previous experience in government problems generally and a versatility of mind that can take up one subject after another during the day and find itself equally at home in all of them."[35]

Hoover found bitter humor in his rival's own "versatility." Over and over during a harsh campaign against Roosevelt in 1932, he pointed to inconsistencies in his opponent's words. Roosevelt, he said near the end of a cross-country trail littered with tomatoes hurled at his train, was nothing less than "a chameleon on plaid." He demanded that the Democratic candidate spell out frankly how he would balance the budget, lower tariffs, create jobs, and restore stability to the international economic system. In November he got his answer: resounding defeat by a man he already was beginning to hate.

Two weeks after the election, Hoover and Roosevelt met at the White House. They discussed the war debt situation, fast becoming a crisis with the impending expiration of Hoover's moratorium, and Britain's signaled desire to renegotiate outstanding loans. Before the session broke up, the two men spent seventeen minutes alone. A patronizing Hoover judged his successor, with his note cards and genial vagueness, "amiable, pleasant, anxious to be of service, very badly informed and of comparatively little vision."[36]

In the weeks that followed, frustrated in his efforts to commit Roosevelt to a plan of joint action, Hoover's attitude turned venomous. By the time Henry Stimson approached him with the invitation to go to Hyde Park, the president was describing his recent electoral rival as "a gibbering idiot," who could barely grasp the economic intricacies at hand, whose only predictable action would be to take the United States off the gold standard—something Hoover had fought desperately to avoid—and whose personal untrustworthiness made Stimson's boss rule out any further dealings with FDR except in the presence of friendly witnesses.[37]

For his part, Roosevelt brushed aside the president's plan for a committee of three prominent Democrats to conciliate their differences and construct a common front at a time of mounting economic dangers. Without illusions as to its results ("You won't get anything," he reminded Stimson), Hoover finally gave his consent for the Secretary of State to see Roosevelt on January 9. It was at this point that Ike Hoover's knock brought an abrupt end to the discussion. Stimson left for the State Department; the president went immediately to his Oval Office, to dictate in the indistinct mumble that confounded stenographers and embarrassed his wife, an official proclamation of the nation's sympathy.[38]

It wasn't easy for Hoover, with his Quakerish preference for plain words and diamond-hard logic, to express his feelings. So shy that he blushed when asked the color of his eyes, given to denunciations of what he called "the pneumatic drill of constant personal contact," Hoover was reticent over matters of the heart, a reticence undoubtedly mingled with his memories of an arm's-length relationship. His wife was much closer to the gregarious Grace Coolidge. They addressed each other as "Bleeding Heart" and "Lily of the Valley" and had shared a common sorrow in young Calvin's death and the subsequent hospitalization of Herbert, Junior, for tuberculosis. Gently probing her friend's wishes concerning funeral arrangements for Coolidge, Lou learned that there was to be no public lying-in-state in Washington or Boston, no military presence, and a minimum of pomp. By nightfall, Lou had canceled the heart of the White House social season.[39]

Meanwhile, her husband scribbled away, struggling with his emotions, assuring Mrs. Coolidge of his sympathy over the loss of "my dear friend and distinguished predecessor. . . . To lose the comrade of so many high enterprises in the public service and the understanding private friend gives us a peculiar capacity to share your grief," he went on. "We may all take comfort in the universal recognition of his character and career and in the affection felt for him by all the people."[40]

The president dispatched his own military and naval aides to Northampton to assist the widow. He lowered the nation's flags and made ready for a somber journey through the midwinter landscape. A brooding silence fell over the White House, as Lou substituted for a party gown the black tweeds and conservative hat of a traveler, bound for frigid New England and a final act of homage.

★　★

It always rained on his moving days. As if to confirm Calvin Coolidge's maxim, a cold torrent drummed against the room of The Beeches, where a nervous party of mourners looked at their watches and fretted over a casket yet to be delivered from a Worcester funeral home. Close to midnight, a truck appeared at the gates. Coolidge luck held fast. In Washington, it was 1:30 A.M. when Hoover convened a meeting on board the special train bound for Northampton. Never before had there been greater need for unity of action, the president said by way of prelude to the Stimson-Roosevelt talks scheduled to take place within seventy-two hours. The economic pestilence was endangering national survival. Bank failures were up sharply since the election, half the outstanding mortgages in America were in default, and joblessness had increased by half a million during the previous thirty days. Public psychology must be cushioned—a favorite Hoover word —in the perilous weeks of transition that lay before them.[41]

For thirty-eight months, he had stuck to his resolve that no man filling his office in such times could afford to aggravate the crisis with pessimistic reports, however honest. Now, according to Chief Justice Charles Evans Hughes, it was a "pretty bad picture" painted by the president. Six million of his countrymen were receiving some sort of relief assistance on the morning of January 7. Two or three times that number were without jobs; seven or eight times as many lived in poverty. According to the Federal Reserve, a quarter-billion dollars of gold left U.S. shores during the final week of Calvin Coolidge's life. More than anything else, it was this financial hemorrhage that preyed on Hoover's mind as his train climbed the Eastern seaboard through a curtain of darkness.[42]

★   ★

Northampton's businesses were open, despite the death of the city's most prominent citizen. Coolidge would have opposed any interruption in trading, explained the mayor. Outside the plain Congregational church whose congregation had once thrilled to the eloquent brimstone of Jonathan Edwards, the rain plastered flags to their masts and turned stained-glass windows into murky mirrors of the external gloom.

Three years earlier, leaving the obsequies of another former president, William Howard Taft, Hoover had barely managed to suppress his longing for a cigar. "When they have my funeral," he revealed on the way back down Pennsylvania Avenue, "I want arrangements made so that everyone will have permission to smoke."[43]

This morning, there wasn't a stogie in sight as the president and Mrs. Hoover made their way through pressing crowds outside the church. As they appeared inside, a few minutes after ten o'clock, the congregation rose in respect. Hoover stood with his head bowed, oblivious to the attentions of congressmen and Northampton's gentry. Looking neither right nor left, he lifted his eyes and fixed them on the dull silver casket, fifteen feet from his place in the front row of pews. Ten minutes later, the widow arrived on the arm of her son—"a good representative of American Puritan stock" she seemed to Henry Stimson—and managed a pale smile for the president and First Lady.[44]

The church organ played the Largo from Handel's *Xerxes*. A quartet sang "Lead, Kindly Light." The Reverend Albert Penner, youthful and towering in the pulpit, read from the Forty-sixth Psalm and a prayer of his own composition. "Amid all the change and decay which all around we see, Thou never changest." Hoover sat immobile, eyes lined with work and shaded by grief riveted on his predecessor's bier. His face, ruddy from a recent fishing trip in the South, looked out of place in a Massachusetts winter. He said nothing. Only the rustling sound of pages in the Pilgrim Hymnal, and the subdued weeping of Vice President Curtis interrupted the young pastor's lulling voice. There were no trumpets, and no eulogy. As the sign of the cross was given, the president abruptly raised a hand, as if to second the gesture. He looked at Lou, then returned his attention to the casket, flanked by a fragrant honor guard of irises and roses.

Dvořák's New World Symphony filled the small church, its familiar "Going Home" movement bouncing off the brick walls as Grace prepared to leave, followed by the Hoovers and other eminent guests. Secret Service agents clambered onto the running boards of the presidential auto as it pulled out of line for the five-minute trip to The Beeches. Inside the Coolidge home, Hoover renewed his wish to accompany his predecessor north in a final tribute. Grace insisted that road conditions from Ludlow to Plymouth would be too hazardous to permit such a gesture, however thoughtful. She told her visitors she would have chosen no other passing for Calvin, then expressed condolences of her own for the president. It was, she told him, a hard twist of fate, to have performed the terrible work of the last four years only to have unappreciative voters turn him out of office. Hoover's eyes were red as he left the house.[45]

Less than thirty minutes later, Calvin Coolidge, his widow and son were on their way home, past knots of bareheaded farmers and factory workers at Brattleboro and Proctorsville. Glistening birches and the soft, wet humps of Vermont's Green Mountains lined the road north. A requiem of hail greeted the cortege as it arrived late that afternoon at the Notch, and reporters and townspeople alike stood a respectful distance from the hillside lot where five generations of Coolidges rested, and a freshly dug grave now received a casket covered with Japanese Leothe leaves, a floral tribute from Herbert and Lou Hoover. Reverend Penner stepped forward to read the lines by Robert Richardson that Grace had requested:

"Warm summer sun, shine kindly here,
Warm southern wind, blow softly here;
Green sod above, lie light, lie light,
Good night, dear heart, good night, good night."

It snowed that night in Plymouth. When morning came, the new mound was itself buried, under the frozen benediction of a Yankee God. No one knew better than Coolidge's successor, now back in Washington, that a life had ended in Northampton—and a way of life had been buried at Plymouth. In a few weeks he would be retracing the route to Union Station, departing from a city he had entered in triumph nearly sixteen years earlier. Another train would take him—where? For now, such speculation would have to wait its turn. A nation doubting its own future laid first claim to his attention.

But in Coolidge's wake, and with the understated grief of Northampton behind him, perhaps Hoover traveled back in time, to another mound, in the rich, black earth of Cedar County, Iowa. Perhaps he dwelt, if only for a moment, on the remembered plight of an eleven-year-old boy, without parents or prospects, who rode an emigrant train of the Union Pacific bound for Oregon and an uncertain welcome in the home of a strict Quaker uncle. In his pocket the orphaned boy carried two prayer cards. "Leave me not," read one, "neither foresake me, Oh God of my salvation." From the church of Jonathan Edwards, it was fifty-eight years and 1,500 miles to a clapboard cathedral on the banks of an Iowa stream. Measured in the perspective of a man's values, however, distances have a way of vanishing. Surely, Hoover's West Branch was emotionally nearer to Northampton or Plymouth Notch than the nation's capital, or the Hudson Valley hamlet about to take over as the unofficial seat of a government in waiting.

West Branch, Iowa, a Quaker settlement of poke bonnets and abolitionist politics. Hoover remembered breakfasts of milk and mush, an aunt who held winter sledding to be a godless activity and parents who were dead by his tenth birthday.

Enrolled as the youngest freshman in the new Stanford University (fifth from the left), Bert never managed an A—but he cut a swath as a manager, a rival of campus swells, and a budding geologist. He graduated in May 1895, with $40 in his pocket, and the prospect of Miss Lou Henry's hand in marriage.

Growing a mustache to make himself look older, Hoover was soon off to the hellish outland of western Australia, "three yards inside civilization." Within a few years, he was the world's most renowned mining engineer, and a self-made millionaire.

Hoover's crusade to feed starving Belgium made him a household word. Woodrow Wilson (seen touring Louvain) made him domestic food czar, and soon, Americans whipped to patriotic frenzy were "hooverizing" on meat, wheat and sugar.

As Secretary of Commerce, Hoover undertook regulation of the new radio industry. Here he is participating in the first public demonstration of television.

On the day Hoover was nominated to succeed him, Calvin Coolidge took to his bedroom with a bottle of Green River whiskey. Pleased with the prosperity that bore his name, Coolidge was content to leave future problems to the man he called "the wonder boy."

"People expect more of you than they have of any other President" warned a friend in the days before Hoover's 1929 inauguration. In his first months in office, he gave them what they wanted—a whirlwind of reform proposals that reminded Washington journalists of Woodrow Wilson or Theodore Roosevelt at their most energetic. The First Lady shared her husband's drive, refurbishing the White House and causing a national storm by inviting the wife of a black congressman to tea.

But with the collapse of the nation's economy late in 1929, Hoover's White House became the frontline stand of a doomed defense. "Why is it, that when a man is on this job as I am day and night," he demanded, "doing the best he can, that certain men . . . seek to oppose everything he does, just to oppose him?" Franklin Roosevelt, once a friend who had urged Hoover to seek the Democratic presidential nomination, more recently a foe whose call for an end to "foolish tradition" struck a responsive note in a desperate electorate, replaced the exhausted, embittered president in March 1933.

Hoover went to Union Station the object of death threats and popular contempt. On the same day both men began a new rivalry, Hoover accusing FDR of tapping his phone and opening his mail, of striking his name from Hoover Dam, and of making him synonymous with a generation of soup kitchens and hard times. The Wilderness Years had begun.

"The greatest men's club in the world," the Bohemian Grove *(above)* provided an opportunity for bad, sometimes bawdy jokes, good liquor, and the healing balm that existed in few other places. Here, Hoover could indulge a whimsey hidden from all but his closest companions. "I'm the only person of distinction," he later acknowledged, "who's ever had a depression named after him."

When not writing books, making speeches, or plotting electoral revenge, Hoover delighted most in the homely art of rod and reel. "All men are equal before fish," he proclaimed, and his joy in the wordless company of old retainers like Larry Richey *(left)* was as evident as his disdain for Calvin Coolidge.

After 1937, home for Hoover was New York's Waldorf Towers. Here, amidst celebrated neighbors like the Windsors, Cole Porter and Elsa Maxwell, he kept four desks (one for each book he was simultaneously writing), passed up French cuisine for baked beans, played furious canasta, and maintained a salon of anti–New Dealers and anti-interventionists.

Bunny Miller, who was with Lou the day she died in January 1944, became even more indispensable in running Hoover's office, with its five secretaries and more than 20,000 pieces of mail to be answered annually.

The former president's controversial 1938 European journey included an unplanned meeting with Adolf Hitler. The two men sparred verbally over the merits of democracy versus dictatorship, with Hitler arguing cogently—until the word Jew was mentioned. The German fuehrer, judged his visitor, had certain "trigger spots" that sent him into furious rages.

Hoover's hopes for vindication at the polls in 1936 were dashed by Kansas Governor Alfred M. Landon, whose feeble chances against FDR seemed to rest on repudiation of the last Republican administration. Later they became reconciled in common opposition to U.S. entry into the Second World War.

No such agreement united Hoover and his party's 1940 nominee, Wendell Willkie. Less than ten weeks before Willkie's miraculous victory in Philadelphia, he called the ex-president "the ablest man in the country." Hoover hoped for a miracle of his own when the convention met to choose between Willkie, Tom Dewey, Bob Taft—and Herbert Hoover.

In later years, Hoover came to regard Willkie as a political turncoat, a dreamer whose call for "One World" overlooked global realities and dismissed Hoover's own carefully worded peace plans.

"Have I sounded too much like an Old Testament prophet?" Hoover asked friends during World War II. Shut out of its execution (FDR told Bernard Baruch, "I'm not Jesus Christ. I'm not raising him from the dead."), the former president returned to active public service at Harry Truman's invitation. In the spring of 1946, the 72-year-old Hoover embarked on a famine-fighting tour of 38 nations.

Working around the clock, wrapped in blankets against the cold, and grumbling at the extravagance of state dinners, Hoover begged and borrowed enough food to save tens of millions from starvation. In Rome, he and Hugh Gibson visited Pope Pius XII, who promised the church's support while renewing an old friendship that predated World War I.

In Poland, he was surrounded by the children he related to so well. In Argentina, he said he would eat dirt in order to wangle foodstuffs from dictator Juan Perón. In India, he told an arrogant maharajah who warned him of Indian hostility should America fail to do its "duty" that Americans "don't give a good goddamn whether your people hate them for all time."

He returned to a hero's welcome—and a friendship with Harry Truman that grew steadily more intimate.

Dwight Eisenhower might have seemed too liberal for Hoover's fundamentalist tastes—but the first Republican president in twenty years carried on a warm courtship of his prickly predecessor, dispatching him to Belgium in 1958 and inviting him to fish in the streams of Colorado.

Hoover preferred Douglas MacArthur, whom he had made Army Chief of Staff and whom he backed publicly while privately disapproving MacArthur's violent dispersal of the Bonus Army in 1932. Using his own contacts with the Truman White House, Hoover helped arrange the joint session of Congress that heard MacArthur deliver his famed "Old Soldiers Never Die" speech—and even wrote several paragraphs that the eloquent general polished into his own prose.

In their last years, Hoover and MacArthur were neighbors at the Waldorf, the former president wondering why his younger friend seemed so inactive. His own activities included a vast correspondence, numerous speeches, travel and, best of all, time for his beloved Boys' Clubs. Here an old man in a hurry takes time out to receive yet another award from those he called his "pavement boys."

A VICTIM OF VIRTUE

★

1 8 7 4 – 1 9 3 2

CHAPTER TWO

THE PRICE OF SUCCESS

★

Ah, woe is me!
I hoped to see my country rise to heights
Of happiness and freedom yet unreached
By other nations, but the climbing wave
Pauses, lets go its hold, and slides again
Back to the common level, with a hoarse
Death-rattle in its throat. I am too old
To hope for better days.
　　　　　—"Michael Angelo," Henry Wadsworth Longfellow

I am sure I'd have made a better all-around man if I hadn't lost so much time
just making a living.
　　　　　　　　　　　　　　　　　　　—Herbert Hoover

★

On the western side of the ragged line separating a mature society from its rambunctious country cousin, Hoover and the Quaker gentry of Iowa stood in confident contrast to Longfellow's opulent spinster of Boston. The Quakers of West Branch pursued divinity without dogma and prosperity without guilt. They invoked the Lord's name in a meetinghouse as plain and uncompromising as their speech. Without stained glass or sacrament, they sat in silence, awaiting direction from the Inner Light first discerned in 1647 by their English prophet, George Fox.

Fox and his followers held that "every man was enlightened by the divine

59

light of Christ." Instead of a hierarchy to provide guidance, "Friends of Truth" by official nomenclature, Quakers in the vernacular, regularly asked themselves a list of demanding Queries, a self-examination of virtues ranging from human brotherhood to moderation of speech and honor in one's worldly dealings.

"Debts to be punctually paid," decreed the Quaker elders of Balby, England, in 1656, "that nothing may the Children of Light owe to any man but love to one another." Herbert Hoover said the same thing with different words. "If any man by his vices was on his way to pauperism," he explained, "he stopped being a Quaker." But Quakers were admonished to do more than pay their bills and love one another. Their faith was not confined to an hour of Sunday morning soul-searching. Overlapping the sacred and secular, it blended the laws of man and God. There was but one divorce on record in the little village Hoover's grandparents helped found in 1854 as a refuge from slavery in North Carolina. West Branch became a way station on the Underground Railroad that ferreted slaves to Canada and freedom, and a supporter of Negro suffrage even before the Civil War. Hoover's mother was equally vocal on behalf of a woman's right to vote.

Poke bonnets and abolitionist politics predominated along the banks of the Wapsinonac Creek, where Jesse Hoover built a cottage for his wife Huldah with lumber imported from neighboring Wisconsin. Huldah's own family was noted for its piety and its allegiance to the colorless clothing and absence of formalism that ironically became as much a symbol of exclusiveness as any rosary or skullcap. It was Huldah who saw to it that her son read his Bible in daily installments and charted every expenditure in a miniature account book. She took in sewing from neighbors so that her own offspring could sample for themselves the traditional Quaker emphasis on education. She conducted prayer meetings for local children, nursed the sick, and quickly gained the admiration of those moved by her spontaneous eloquence in meeting.

But Huldah was no establishmentarian. When a younger group of the faithful called for singing and psalms in the service, she joined their ranks. Such divisions were to be expected in a group that mirrored America's own contradictory urges for reform and self-glorification, generosity and grasping ambition.

For all its moral underpinnings, its condemnation of alcohol and cigars, its pacifism and literal acceptance of Scripture, the Quakerism of West Branch had a highly practical element to its otherworldliness. Hoover's devout Aunt Rebecca might denounce the melodeon and screens that kept horseflies out of the meetinghouse, and fret over the prospect that the Lord's tabernacle might one day be converted to immoral purposes as a theater (a prophecy that bore fruit in the 1920s), but her nephew was reared in an atmosphere not far removed from the money-conscious mainstream of an adolescent nation.

Like the Americans who attacked their clannishness and impulse to martyrdom (Jefferson had called them Protestant Jesuits), the Friends were a self-anointed chosen people, doing battle for the faith while making a comfortable living. Thrift was central to their loose credo. So were tolerance and the assumption of individual responsibility for the lot of one's home and country. Not for nothing had William Penn informed a woman accused of witchcraft in his Quaker colony of Pennsylvania that, as for riding a broomstick, "that is thy right if thou chooses to execute it." Most of Penn's followers, who knew firsthand the savage intolerance of which other chosen people, like New England's Puritans, were capable, circled their wagons and behaved like a family entrusted with heaven's favor.

"Persons who walk disorderly are to be spoken to in private," ruled the first Quaker elders, "then before two or three witnesses; then, if necessary, the matter is to be reported to the Church." With their ideals divorced from the impersonal clutches of public authority, the people of West Branch did for themselves. Theirs was a prosaic democracy, drawing no class distinctions, and looking down only on those who assumed for themselves superior airs.

Upholding the dignity of labor, they believed that every man was entitled to the bounty of his work, but that the possession of property carried with it an obligation of service to one's neighbors. Idleness degraded talents handed down by God. Intellectual laziness was a mockery of mankind's unique inheritance—the ability to reason and fathom right from wrong. God provided a common Fatherhood, to which they must respond with a common, if emotionally restrained, brotherhood.

"Put on old clothes and stop Herbert Hoover on the street and ask him for a dime," wrote one admirer years later. "You will be unlikely to get it. You will be likely, on the contrary, to find yourself giving him something: namely, your name and address. You will then be likely, further, to get a visit from an agency which will strive to induce you to go to work. Only if there is no work to be got for you, or only if you are physically or mentally unable to take it, will you find that Hoover has given the agency a fund to be freely spent upon cases such as yours."

Hoover phrased this impersonal compassion in words of his own in a 1924 radio address. Americans, he said, wanted to get ahead. They demanded more security, finer education, greater justice in society and stronger moral fiber, "for everybody who will work, and for nobody else." The residents of West Branch could not have put it better. On First Day and Fifth Day, they occupied hard benches in an unheated place of worship. Outside, the icy perfume of a winter morning gave way to the dim brilliance of a retreating sun as the Friends sat for hours, their stillness interrupted only by the sounds of infants not already confined to the "crying room" or the abrupt inspiration of a member moved to speak. Male and female worshippers were separated by a long, low partition. Up front, there was no pulpit, and no ordained minister, only a "facing bench" occupied by elders and lay pastors, men or women sufficiently inspired by the Inner Light as to convince the most skeptical brethren that theirs was a unique insight.

Quakers told the story of one elderly member of their denomination being driven home past a group of once-woolly animals. "Oh look," said the driver, "there is a flock of sheep that have been sheared."

"I see a flock of sheep," replied the Elder, "that have been sheared on this side." [1]

Jesse Hoover was of this hardheaded, softhearted school. The wooden partition in the meetinghouse provided more than a symbolic barrier from his fervent wife. Huldah conducted revival meetings and parked her children outside the polls on election day while she waged rhetorical war on whiskey-loving sin. She enrolled Bert in the Band of Hope, a prohibitionist circle of Quaker children, by the time he was ten. His early reading, Hoover recalled, was limited to the Bible, school texts, "certain novels showing the huge danger of Demon Rum" and a copy of the *Youth's Companion,* surreptitiously stashed behind his father's blacksmith shop lest its corruptive influence invade Huldah's godly home. [2]

Jesse Hoover was not irreligious; he attended services regularly and prayed with everyone else for the Inner Light to illumine his life. But his wise-cracking, leg-pulling ways (Bert he called his "little stick-in-the-mud") did not endear him to the rulers of West Branch. On at least one occasion they were forced to reprimand him, and he seems to have been a reluctant convert to his wife's evangelical search for grace. Jesse valued success in this life as well as spiritual preparation for the next one. A natural-born tinkerer and promoter, he did well in his blacksmith shop, selling his neighbors the newfangled barbed wire and a cattle-powered water pump invented by his father, Eli.

Farmers in Iowa as elsewhere might be suffering from the Depression precipitated by Jay Fiske and Jay Gould on distant Wall Street, but with seven million or so agricultural yeomen relying on horsepower for their livelihood, the purveyor of Sulky Plows and iron shoes could evade hard times. By 1878, Jesse Hoover was able to move his wife, two sons and a daughter into a larger home, not far from the smithy he sold in favor of a farm implements store on Main Street. Elected by the townspeople to serve on the town council, teasing his wife when he wasn't tallying his newfound prosperity on a cash register, Jesse Hoover seemed a model of the Quaker burgher: successful, self-contained, public-spirited.

His achievements, modest as they were, placed him squarely in the tradition of a fertile age. By 1900 the nation boasted five times as much rail track as in 1865. Young Bert Hoover could hear the piercing whistle of the Burlington engines as they rumbled across the trestle where he liked to catch sunfish with a willow pole and trap rabbits with a crackerbox, in mischievous defiance of Quaker morality. Men of equally inventive but more advanced cast were reshaping Iowa, expelling darkness for light, replacing scarcity and sweat with plenty and comfort. Hoover was born in the year Thomas Edison invented the duplex telegraph. His childhood unfolded amid explosive changes: Sousa marches, a ten-story skyscraper peering over Chicago's horizon, awakening labor, and the muscular exuberance of Walt Whitman's highly individualized poetry. Hoover was not yet an adolescent when the air brake and Pullman car revolutionized train travel, hastening the final chapters of an exploratory tale begun at Jamestown in 1607, and hardly old enough to vote when the Spanish-American War introduced imperialism into the popular language, suggesting the possibilities of a frontier more expansive than any Frederick Jackson Turner could imagine.

Even amid the country smells of woodsmoke and new-mown hay, it was a time of feverish ingenuity. Between 1860 and 1890, Americans took out 440,000 patents, twelve times the number applied for in the first seventy-five years of nationhood. Typewriters and talking machines took up residence in city homes and offices. They were complemented on the farm by reapers and mowers, tractors and threshers. Machines replaced human muscle in planting and plowing, husking and shelling, separating cream and distributing manure. A bushel of wheat that required more than three hours of labor to produce in 1830 could be on its way to market in less than ten minutes by the end of the century. America was still a rustic nation in Hoover's boyhood. The plank sidewalks and boxy architecture of West Branch testified to that. More than 80 percent of the population clung to farms and small villages that dotted the landscape, cherishing their GAR chapters, cotillions and Republican politics. But farming, like government, was becoming a science, and Jesse Hoover's barbed wire and water pumps stood on the threshold of a rural revolution.

Jesse's wife spoke for the other half of Victorian America, the moralist and reformer offended by unbridled capitalism, which Theodore Roosevelt in his *Autobiography* would label "a riot of individual materialism under which complete freedom for the individual . . . turned out in practice to mean perfect freedom for the strong to wrong the weak." Eighteen seventy-four witnessed the first restriction on working women and children, Massachusetts's 10 Hour Act to safeguard factory laborers from burning out before they reached voting age. Prompted by the growing Grange movement, Iowa followed the example of neighboring Illinois, and passed laws to regulate rail traffic and protect farmers from extortionate prices to move their cattle or grain.

Bigness was capturing the American economy. John D. Rockefeller organized the Standard Oil Trust in 1879. Similar visionaries watered railroad stock and purchased state legislatures. Even the GOP, according to Iowa's Senator James W. Grimes in the heyday of Grant's rule, was "going to the dogs . . . the most corrupt and debauched political party that has ever existed." Bert Hoover was churning butter and weaving homespun when Congress adopted the Sherman Antitrust Act in 1890. He was a freshly minted Stanford graduate five years later when the same Supreme Court that invalidated a 2 percent tax on incomes over $4,000 demolished the trustbusters by ruling a sugar conglomerate controlling 98 percent of the trade was not in violation of the law since technically it was not engaged in interstate commerce. Eighteen ninety-six was the year of William Jennings Bryan, the farmers' savior hailed by admirers as a "Gigantic troubadour, speaking like a siege gun, smashing Plymouth Rock with his boulders from the west."

By 1905, when Hoover was beginning his spectacular rise to preeminence in the mining field, Oliver Wendell Holmes was reminding his fellow justices on the Supreme Court that Herbert Spencer's ode to laissez-faire was not written into the U.S. Constitution. Another son of Quaker parents named Frederick W. Taylor was revolutionizing business with his standardized system of scientific management. Taylor became what Daniel Boorstin has called "the Apostle of the American Gospel of Efficiency." He insisted that civilized and uncivilized countries were distinguished by the productivity of their citizens. Taylor lived the productive life. He wore slip-on shoes in the age of high buttons, invented his own tennis racket and golf putter, avoided tobacco and tea and maintained that even shoveling could be turned into a science if treated with the principles of scientific management.

"In the past," wrote Taylor in 1911, "the man has been first; in the future the system must be first." Dependent on the stopwatch and industrial departments organized by function, "Taylorization" became the watchword of the new Harvard Business School, which first opened its doors in 1908. It set the tone for an age in which public accountants, business economists, marketing specialists and consulting engineers first stepped forward to fine-tune an economy that would expand with increasing velocity until one of their own, Herbert Hoover, was in the White House.

Then as later, Hoover said little about his boyhood, "a Montessori school in stark reality." His parents were ghostly images, fleeting apparitions of piety and entrepreneurship. In a three-volume autobiography, he could spare only eight pages for West Branch, and his tributes to simple joys were seasoned with regret. He conjured up breakfasts of milk and mush, consumed under "stiff moral pressure," popcorn balls at Christmas, sliding down Cook's Hill on frosty winter nights—an activity his Aunt Hannah thought godless—and picking potato bugs, at a hundred per penny, to buy fireworks for the Fourth of July celebrations that enlivened even sober Quaker households. "If that wage still prevails," Hoover noted in his memoirs, "it ought now to be adjusted to the commodity dollar and is entitled to a hearing by the Labor Board. It may be that the use of arsenic on bugs has created technological unemployment in the firecracker industry. If so," he asserted, with an obvious swipe at the New Deal's agricultural policies, "the recent remedy would be to dig up the potatos while they are young."[3]

In addition to an economic system that "absolutely denied collective bargaining to small boys," Hoover remembered sitting for hours in the meetinghouse, unable even to wiggle his toes while his elders awaited inspiration. "Its recreational aspects," he noted, "were . . . somewhat limited." To friends he sounded a modestly contradictory, almost apologetic note. "I was a Quaker," he liked to say, "but I didn't work very hard at it." More poignantly, he confessed that he was twelve years old before realizing he might do a thing solely for the joy it gave without worrying that an angry Lord would strike him down for faithlessness.[4]

It was not a happy way to spend a childhood, and it was made immeasurably worse by Jesse Hoover's death in 1880, at the age of thirty-four. Village elders reproached his widow for marking the grave with a headstone too prominent for prevailing tastes. Her own faith deepened into mysticism, and she left Bert with his Uncle Laban Miles, once a U.S. Indian agent to the Osage Nation, while she attended Quaker meetings in Kansas and Iowa, and preached in nearby Springdale. The next summer the boy stayed with another uncle, who lived in a sod house and who allowed his young guest to ride up front as a team of oxen helped break ground for future development. Then, in February of 1884, Huldah Hoover was caught in a winter storm en route home from a prayer meeting in Muscatine. Her cold turned into pneumonia, complicated by typhoid fever, and on February 24 she died.

"As gentle as are the memories of those times," her son wrote with oblique feeling half a century later, "I am not recommending a return to the good old days. Sickness was greater, and death came sooner."[5]

Still another uncle, Allan Hoover, played host to Bert on his farm near West Branch, after Huldah's death left three children to be parceled out among relatives. The youth wasted no time in displaying his father's mechanical gifts. With his cousin, he rigged a heifer to a battered old mowing machine. More successfully, he turned a decrepit clothes wringer into a crude imitation of the sorghum mills that provided Iowans with sweet molasses for their tables. For the rest of his life, Hoover would try to stamp his mark wherever he went, mastering events in defiance of his early vulnerability.

When he was eleven, an orphaned boy of muted intellect and no singular talents, his prospects took an uncertain turn. A message came to Allan Hoover's farm from Huldah's physician brother in Oregon, recently deprived of his own son. "Send the boy to us," it said. A few days later, Bert climbed on board a Union Pacific train, enriched by two dimes and a hamper stuffed with homemade delicacies. Ahead of him lay a seven-day journey through a still primitive continent, and a future whose rigors and rewards were beyond anything imaginable in the cool ardor of West Branch's meetinghouse.[6]

★　　★

> The needs of widows and the fatherless to be supplied. Such as can work, and do not, are to be admonished. If they refuse to work, neither let them eat.
> —Disciplines of the Friends, 1656

The Rocky Mountains were not really made of rock at all, Bert Hoover reported to Miss Mollie Brown, a maiden teacher whose offer to adopt the boy had been spurned by his guardians. As far as he could tell from the window of his train, they were composed of very ordinary dust and dirt. This early geological discovery did not exhaust the catalogue of disappointments in the new home for which he was bound. "Play every chance you get," Hoover advised children who wrote him in his old age, "including fishing." His Uncle John Minthorn, educator and businessman, moralist and money changer, was not the sort to encourage play.

Among his fellow Quakers, Minthorn was regarded as an eccentric, theologically suspect and financially aggressive, even for that age of the fast buck and quick exit. Firsthand memories of the Battle of Shiloh did little to impress his pacifist neighbors. "Turn your other cheek once," he counseled his newly arrived nephew about an imaginary foe, "but if he smites you then punch him." Besides religious unorthodoxy and personal contentiousness, there was something of the buccaneer about John Minthorn, a financial restlessness and tendency to build nonprofitable castles in the air. By the time Bert Hoover left the river steamer that carried him on the final passage through Oregon's Willamette Valley, Minthorn had been a conductor on the Underground Railroad, a U.S. Indian agent, a medical doctor who didn't hesitate to voice disregard for "poor white trash" who wouldn't pay their bills, and superintendent of the Newberg Academy, a small Quaker school where his nephew was soon enrolled.[7]

Hoover described his uncle later as "a severe man on the surface, but like all Quakers kindly at bottom." In November 1885, and for the six years that followed, Bert struggled to maintain uneasy coexistence with one who routed him out of bed to tend horses, expected him to milk cows, split logs, help level a patch of fir forest and be grateful for a monthly allowance of five dollars. One summer, almost as a vacation, the boy weeded onions for fifty cents a day on a farm outside town. At other times, he accompanied his uncle over muddy roads on medical calls to surrounding villages, sampling Civil War stories and impromptu lectures on physiology, a Minthorn specialty that would prove useful when college entrance exams came around. In 1888, age fourteen, Hoover set out on a new career, as office boy in the Oregon Land Company his uncle launched in nearby Salem.

"No Hot Nights in Summer—Grass Grows All Winter" proclaimed John Minthorn's prospectus. It was not a modest document, asserting as well a total absence of cyclones, blizzards, earthquakes, crop failure, grasshoppers and Hessian flies. Dr. Minthorn claimed title to a half-million acres of Oregon countryside. His actual holdings amounted to three thousand acres of prune and pear orchards, to which his nephew conveyed potential buyers in a buggy drawn by one of the horses he detested. Equine transport notwithstanding, Bert made the company his life. Many nights he slept in a room back of his uncle's office. When morning came around, he picked up bookkeeping and typing skills from other employees. He oversaw the promotion of Silver Falls City in a thousand eastern newspapers, hurried to the local depot to head off a rival salesman, and talked a fellow office boy into starting their own enterprise, a resourceful if unprofitable attempt to repair and market old sewing machines.

In the evening he attended business school. "My boyhood ambition," he said while in the White House, "was to be able to earn my own living, without the help of anybody, anywhere." The desire for success hobbled the development of Hoover's personality. There wasn't anyone in Dr. Minthorn's circle to teach him social arts or small talk, and the smothering presence of older people who preached duty and reserve hardened a character already inclined toward moody silences and a short fuse. Hoover chose to put a different interpretation on it: the secret of his success, he once confided to Norman Vincent Peale, was that he soaked up the wisdom of those entrusted with rearing an orphan boy from West Branch.[8]

When an engineer from the East made his acquaintance and guided him around some mining prospects in the Cascades, Hoover's ambitions were quickened. By the end of 1888, his brother Tad and sister May were reunited with him and, in an even greater piece of luck, he was befriended by a Salem banker's daughter and schoolteacher named Jane Gray. "An orphan among uncles," as one friend remembered him, "generating about as much excitement as a china egg," Bert had few friends and a strong sense of class inferiority until Miss Gray invited him to Sunday dinner at her home, where he saw powdered sugar for the first time and had it drummed into his head that money counted for nothing in this world, next to individual determination and persistence.[9]

"Angelic" is the word used by Hoover's best boyhood pal to describe Miss Gray, who opened the boy's eyes to the world of creative literature. First with Scott, then Dickens—David Copperfield would always rank among Hoover's favorites—Jane Gray gave reassurance to the diffident, unspeaking boy who now began to take interest in his appearance and know the mind in which she placed such confidence. For a year, despite his uncle's insistence that he attend a Quaker school in Indiana, Hoover pored over catalogues and textbooks on engineering. In 1891, the Oregon Land Company failed, precursor of the panic engulfing Grover Cleveland's second term. That same fall, Bert gave two dollars to help build a Friends Meetinghouse in Salem, his first benefaction. He also revealed his decision to enroll at Stanford, the embryonic univeristy conceived by California's Senator Leland Stanford as a memorial to his dead son.

The Minthorns were not pleased by his rebellion, and the sting was eased only a little when the mathematics professor who arrived in Portland that summer to conduct entrance examinations turned out to be a Quaker himself. "A young Quaker . . . none too well prepared," Joseph Swain informed his superiors about Bert, "but showing remarkable keenness." Neither faith nor keenness could, by themselves, admit Bert to Stanford. His own education was sadly deficient, Miss Gray notwithstanding, and after failing Swain's examinations, he readily agreed to go to Palo Alto three months before the formal opening of the new school and work with a tutor in preparation for another battery of tests. On the night before his final examinations, still one course shy of the entrance requirements, Hoover thought back to the long hours on his uncle's buckboard and the talk of patients' symptoms and the body's own response. With those memories, and the help of a couple of standard works in the field, he made the grade, aided considerably by the new college's hunger for students to fill its classrooms. With a friend from Salem, he moved early into room 8 of Encina Hall, the red-tiled men's dormitory, and became Stanford's first overnight student. [10]

★   ★

Leland Stanford originally intended to practice law in his native Port Washington, New York. But when his legal office burned down in 1853, he abandoned the courtroom for an alluring Pacific Coast. Taking up residence in a settlement with the appropriate name of El Dorado, within eight years he rose to become governor of California. That same year, Stanford and his friends Mark Hopkins, Charles Crocker and Collis Huntington founded the Central Pacific Railroad. Aided considerably by gubernatorial largesse, the line prospered. So did its president, a post that Stanford assumed when he left the State House in 1863 and which he never relinquished.

Now a wealthy, if not entirely self-made man, the railroad magnate displayed a taste for national politics, which the California legislature duly satisfied in 1885 by electing him to the United States Senate. Back home, Senator Stanford relaxed on a magnificent ranch in the Santa Clara Valley, thirty miles south of San Francisco, where he raised prizewinning racehorses with names like Electioneer and Advertiser, and where he laid the cornerstone for a free university in tribute to the son who died in 1884. Unsparing of effort or cost, Stanford called upon the best men to give expression to his wishes. H. H. Richardson designed a California mission-style quadrangle, with adobe roofs of red tile and plenty of Romanesque archways. Charles W. Eliot, the pioneer of Harvard's elective system, offered advice on curricula. David Starr Jordan, who as president of the University of Indiana was noted for the excellence of his faculty and the vigor of his youth, was recruited to give the unfinished school enough cachet to compete with its established rival across the bay at Berkeley.

Aside from Stanford himself, there was little prepossessing about this college in a hayfield in the summer of 1891, when Bert Hoover, at seventeen the youngest member of the freshman class, took up residence at Encina Hall. Board was twenty dollars a month, a fee he paid off with the help of a job in the registrar's office. When the head of the new geology department, John Caspar Branner, arrived after Christmas, Hoover earned money typing for the man whose Geology I course he savored five days a week. He rapidly impressed Branner with an ability to turn a suggested detail of departmental housekeeping into accomplished fact. The professor, who doubled as state geologist of Arkansas, reciprocated with a summer job mapping geologic outcroppings in the Ozark Mountains. As a result, Hoover saved sixty dollars for himself and took careful note of the dulling effects of the mountaineers' diet of sowbelly and cornmeal.

In 1893 he toughened a frame already used to strenuous exercise by following another geologist, Waldemar Lindgren, on an expedition to Pyramid Peak, near Lake Tahoe. Riding miles through Nevada deserts, sleeping under the stars in the High Sierras, trying and failing to get a Washington bureaucrat to believe his story of a mule that broke its own neck by scratching it with his hind foot, Hoover found ways to satisfy his own need to achieve while enjoying a sense of comradeship. Stanford let him belong, for the first time. It showed he could get ahead while still serving the humanistic gods of his boyhood faith. It taught him far more about himself than about carboniferous rocks or English composition.

Hoover cut no intellectual swath at Stanford. He never managed an A, flunked German and survived English I only when a paleontology professor named J. P. Smith added punctuation and grammer to an otherwise impressive piece of scholarship, then waved the finished product before the English department and demanded to know how a man capable of such logic could justly be denied a Stanford degree.

Hoover's mark was made outside the classroom, as a manager, not a magnet. Lacking the agility needed to be a shortstop, he settled for managing the baseball team instead. He performed similar chores for the football squad. When friends who shared his dislike of fraternity elitists pressed him to run for class treasurer, Hoover refused until they promised that no salary would go with the job. Then he entered the fray with gusto, campaigning for the Barbarian slate throughout The Camp, a ramshackle settlement orginally housing the laborers who built Stanford and more recently set aside for poor students unable to pay campus board charges. The contest was so fierce that President Jordan asked whether he was leading a university or Tammany Hall, but when votes were counted, the Three-H ticket was victorious. As treasurer, Bert wiped out the junior class debt of $2,000, instituted a voucher system to guard against fraud, and wrote a student constitution.

Even in office, Hoover seemed an unlikely campus hero. Gangling and sinewy, with mouse-colored hair, perpetually downcast eyes and the blue serge suits that became a sartorial trademark, he was better known as a promoter and profit seeker than candidate for Big Man status. He launched the Red Star laundry, managed a lecture and concert agency that entertained a then-unknown Nebraska congressman named William Jennings Bryan before a half-empty house, and boasted to a friend of having

"3000000000000 schemes" for future success. Then as later, Hoover was not an easy man to know. Will Irwin, who became a lifelong friend, never forgot the proficiency with which his classmate summoned medical care for Irwin's broken ankle—and the almost physical effort Hoover required to stammer out the words "I'm sorry" as he fled through the door.

Even Hoover's one great romance began prosaically, when Branner invited a tongue-tied senior to comment on the age of some laboratory samples in the presence of the tall, tomboyish Miss Lou Henry. The only woman in geology and, like Hoover, a transplanted Iowan, Lou was somewhat defensive about her unconventional ways ("It isn't so important what others think of you," she remarked to another freshman in Roble Hall, "as what you feel inside yourself"). From her father, a Monterey banker who loved to hunt and fish and who had raised her like the son he always wanted, Miss Henry had gained a passion for the outdoor life. An avid sportswoman—she later founded the women's division of the National Amateur Athletic Association—she was also intellectually eager. With her radiant blue eyes, contagious grin and thick hair worn like a coronet, she dazzled Hoover. Within a week, he was calling on her, inaugurating a relationship that lasted half a century. Whether or not there was any truth to campus rumors that he waited on tables at Lou's Kappa Kappa Sigma sorority, there was no doubt that some of Miss Henry's friends regarded her shy suitor as a blot on her escutcheon.[11]

But Lou was a woman of independent thinking. With her penetrating mind, according to one classmate, she could be skeptical, "even cynical but a very sweet woman withal." Neither she nor Bert felt very comfortable at the parties to which he dutifully escorted her. Later she confessed that she hadn't danced since college because "Daddy doesn't dance." Yes, she informed another questioner, she did indeed major in geology at Stanford, "but I have majored in Herbert Hoover since." This was typically modest, considering the scope of her public activities as official hostess, White House historian, president of the Girl Scouts, organizer of a post–Teapot Dome women's conference on law enforcement, and outspoken advocate of women in politics ("Good women elect bad men," she liked to say, "by staying away from the polls"). As time passed, she gradually acclimated herself to the background. Her devotion to Hoover never wavered. That, along with her evident delight in each new experience that came to the wife of a globe-trotting engineer, whether carrying her five-week-old son along on a trip to western Australia, strapping a Mauser pistol to her hip during the Boxer Rebellion or assisting Bert in translating De Re Metallica, the pioneering work of sixteenth-century metals scholar Georg Agricola, made

Lou as indispensable to Hoover as the air he breathed or the ambitions he nurtured. Providing a gentle buffer between him and a less appreciative world, her love was uncritical through all the years when public criticism replaced the acclaim of earlier times.[12]

Second only to Lou in Hoover's affections was Stanford itself. It had given him an identity to match his need, and he returned the favor with interest. For fifty-two years, he served on its board of trustees. He played a leading role in organizing the School of Business and a Food Research Institute, donated $100,000 anonymously to help build a student union, and housed millions of priceless war documents in a soaring tower modeled after Salamanca's Romanesque cathedral. As an old man, he was both paternal and peevish, denouncing the architecture of a proposed medical school and post office, and threatening to withdraw his papers and patronage, like a bullying father, when the school showed hospitality to left-wingers who took issue with his insistence that world communism and its attendant dangers be the focus of Hoover Institution activities.[13]

All this was unimaginable in May 1895, when a boy still three months shy of his twenty-first birthday accepted a diploma from President Jordan and pondered his economic future in the unpromising atmosphere of Grover Cleveland's depression. Endowed with $40 in his pocket and the likelihood of Lou Henry's hand when he enlarged that meager bankroll, Hoover was lucky in at least one respect. "I had never heard of depressions," he recalled. "No one told me that there was one afoot. . . . Nor did I have to worry about what the government was going to do about it."

Unemotional to the end, Hoover left Palo Alto without tears or lachrymose farewells "which so many writers seem to have experienced." He just assumed, he said, that he would see both friends and landmarks again. It was one of the few safe assumptions he could make in the summer of 1895, when he returned to the field for the U.S. Geological Survey. The atmosphere around Lake Tahoe, he told his sister May, "would energize an Egyptian mummy and give him an appetite like a Florida alligator."[14]

Neither Hoover's appetite nor his energy was ever in doubt. Only his future was.

★   ★

Early in a volume aptly titled *Years of Adventure*, Herbert Hoover conveyed his feelings on the brink of self-support: "I needed at once to find someone with a profit motive who needed me to help him earn a profit." At the risk of striking a reactionary note, he continued, "this test for a job has some advantages. It does not require qualifications as to ancestry, religion, good looks, or ability to get votes." With his prospects for a white collar job

—and Stanford's forty-dollar legacy—soon exhausted, Hoover was content to shovel ore and push a handcar through the bowels of the Reward mine in Grass Valley, California. The pay was two dollars for each ten-hour night shift, but "I did not feel like a down-trodden wage slave," Hoover explained. "I was confident that when I got $40 or $50 ahead again I would have the option of looking for some more open-minded economic despot." [15]

His faith in free enterprise survived even the mine's closing, and a bleak stretch of idleness, "ceaseless tramping and ceaseless refusal" at every employment office he visited. Early in 1896, it was justified in a call at the San Francisco office of Louis Janin, a French-born mining engineer of considerable prominence, who gave the youth a job typing. Soon he was dispatched at $150 a month to smelt gold in New Mexico. In Colorado he made the acquaintance of hard-boiled Mexican miners who "practiced a good deal of original sin, especially after paydays." He assisted Janin's superintendent in Arizona wastelands only recently freed from Geronimo's threat. In hours spared from Janin's office, he began to expand his economic horizons, devouring Adam Smith, Walter Bagehot and John Stuart Mill. He followed with disdain the campaign of William Jennings Bryan. "It was," he said later, "my first shock at intellectual dishonesty as a foundation of economics."

In October 1897 the London firm of Bewick, Moreing asked Janin to recommend someone thirty-five years of age with seventy-five years of experience to help bring American technology to the newly capitalized mines of Australia. Instinctively, Janin turned to his young protégé. The job offered $7,500, triple his current pay, he informed Hoover. Among other things, this would enable Hoover's brother Tad to resume his own engineering studies. Age, however, posed a dilemma. Still only twenty-three, Hoover inflated his credentials, grew a mustache to make himself appear older, and hurried off to acquire a Market Street wardrobe fit for his London interview. Two years later, the friend who talked him into buying a natty tweed outfit received it back in the mail.

"Since you like this damn thing, take it," read an accompanying note. "I haven't worn it yet."

Sealskin would have been as appropriate to the hellish heat of Coolgardie, the half-civilized camp of corrugated iron and burlap to which Bewick, Moreing sent Hoover in the spring of 1897. Five hundred miles from the port of Albany, Coolgardie was a town of 12,000 desperate miners and their dependents, "three yards inside civilization." Less than an inch of rain fell each year to nurse the outback of western Australia, a vast lunar landscape where eucalyptus plants struggled and aborigines scraped out a primitive existence amidst "red dust, black flies and white heat." Even worse was Kalgoorlie, another mining settlement where midnight temperatures often hit a hundred degrees, and relentless winds filled his eyes with dust.

"Every man here talks of when to go home," Hoover informed a friend in Oregon. "None come to stay except those who die, and a few go away as well off as they came." Three men a day perished from typhoid, he reported. Hoover was the exception. Going a week without bathing was no more pleasant than his diet of sardines and cocoa. But his resourcefulness became legendary. Code-named "Textbook," Hoover learned to remove his black shirt and blindfold a reluctant camel at a desert crossroads, bathe in beer instead of prohibitively expensive water (it cost him $500 to grow two cabbages), and overcome the rowdiness and suspicion of hell-raising Aussies, who called him Fatty and Hail Columbia Hoover. Best of all, the young American was lucky. While camping at Mount Leonara, an aggrandized molehill over a hundred miles from Kalgoolie, he came across a fabulously rich vein of gold—the Sons of Gwalia mine. On his advice, Bewick, Moreing snapped up the place for a million dollars, and earned back $65 million in ore and interest.[16]

Hoover further helped enrich his London employers with a filter process that salvaged water and lowered the cost of mining operations. In his memoirs, he claimed near-exclusive responsibility for both the filter and the Sons of Gwalia, accomplishments actually shared with other men. Exaggerating his own successes, denying responsibility for failure, Hoover would later assert that his various nutritional efforts had saved 1.4 billion people from starvation, grossly inflating a number that was impressive enough without embellishment. The same trait colored his presidency.

In appearance, he was still anything but charismatic. A Melbourne reporter sent to interview the rising young manager found a boyish character, with floral tie and long hair parted in the middle, who had the curious habit of averting his eyes from whoever was speaking. He was "dreadfully put out," Hoover confessed, when forced to fire a seventy-two-year-old accountant. "If this were my own business, I would be too tenderhearted to let him go, but I have to get things in shape for the company."

Bewick, Moreing was well satisfied with the shape of its Australian operations under Hoover, as it showed by raising his salary to $10,000. Additional proof came in an offer from Algernon Moreing, late in 1898, to oversee a huge new engineering enterprise in Imperial China. That nation, under the influence of its boy emperor, Kwang Hsü, was embarking on one of its periodic modernizations. Still an economic colony of the West, the Chinese turned naturally to the City of London, which called in turn on its youthful Californian discovery. Hoover proved eager to escape a feud with his Australian partner; an offer of $20,000 didn't dull his enthusiasm. That same evening, he wired Lou Henry a proposal of marriage. She accepted with equal haste, and on February 10, 1899, a civil ceremony performed by a Monterey priest (Miss Henry had converted to Quakerism, but there was no preacher of that faith present to pronounce the vows), united the couple in matrimony. Just as quickly, they set off again, this time for the Far East, and an ancient land wracked by internal dissension and the glimmer of incipient revolution.[17]

Lou established the first of many households in Peking that March. She soon learned the language, unlike her husband, and began to collect the priceless porcelains that would one day comprise the world's finest ensemble. She went with Bert on expeditions, riding behind Manchurian ponies bearing guards to ward off bandits. She slept on brick beds and suffered through five courses after asking for a simple omelet. Her husband taught football to the children of Chinese missionaries. He also oversaw construction of a new port at Chinwangtao and tried to modernize coal mining, before his patron on the Celestial Throne was deposed by the Empress Dowager. Aware of the pressures building up against Westerners, Hoover nonetheless went off in search of mineral deposits, fortifying himself against boredom with paperbacks of Balzac, Zola, Hugo and Rousseau. He brushed aside bedbugs, coped with a Chinese manager who smoked opium daily, and patronized a translator whose fractured English made him announce each piece of bad news with the phrase that soon became his own nickname, Really Damn.

Hoover uncovered no gold deposits in the Gobi Desert or Shansi province. He did pay a call on the Dalai Lama, whom he found in the ungodlike activity of riding a bicycle around the court of his monastery. On Christmas Eve 1899, he stood at the Kalgan Gate of the Great Wall. He examined the Yellow River with an eye toward flood control, and with Lou at his side, he discussed Chinese history while riding down the Grand Canal. But the new year brought with it an eruption of anti-Western feeling, spearheaded by the I Ho Tuan—the Boxers. The Hoovers found themselves under siege in Tientsen, where Bert helped lay barricades of rice and grainsacks and Lou rode her bicycle close to the walls of surrounding buildings to avoid bullets. One day, a shell smashed through the window of their residence. Undisturbed, she went on playing solitaire. Another time, she read her own obituary in a California paper. Then, two weeks after the siege commenced, it was over. "I do not remember a more satisfying musical performance," Hoover later observed, "than the bugles of the American Marines entering the settlement playing 'There'll Be A Hot Time In The Old Town Tonight.' "

The Empress fled Peking, and Hoover was prepared to depart himself when the Chinese Engineering and Mining Company sought his help in its own conversion into a British corporation. He cabled Moreing for approval; his own reward included $250,000 of stock in the new firm. Early in 1901, he was back in Peking, only to discover the new enterprise falling into Belgian hands. He quarreled with Emile Franqui, the dynamic, imperious director, who nullified Hoover's contract with a Chinese board. The two men would make more auspicious partners thirteen years later. Following his decision to leave China that same year, Bewick, Moreing made Hoover a junior partner, traditionally a position calling for administrative talents over derring-do. But Hoover broke with tradition. For the next seven years, he traveled endlessly, to Peru and Japan, Siberia and Egypt, New Zealand and the Yukon. He saw the world of Kipling and Maugham, contracted malaria in a Burmese rice paddy, and sailed the Bay of Bengal. Creeping through a blackened Burmese mine in defiance of superstitious native porters, he noticed strange markings in the mud. Bending closer to the prints, which went in only one direction, Hoover backed out fast when he realized he was following fresh tiger tracks.

Lou accompanied her husband during most of his journeys. She also sank roots of her own in a cottage at Monterey and a small home on the Stanford campus. After 1907, they lived in Red House, in Campden Hill, London, where she could garden and entertain visiting Americans over dinner. Guests often found Hoover and his young sons panning for gold in the courtyard fountain. Other times, he and his friend, fellow engineer and veteran of Australian and Burmese mines Edgar Rickard, all but crawled on their hands and knees through London's legendary fogs. The Hoovers and Rickards saved up money for overseas trips—what they called the "Seeing Cairo Fund"—and toured the English countryside. On weekends, Bert and Lou went to Stratford-upon-Avon, where they kept a cottage and Hoover accepted the chair of an international Shakespearean fellowship. All this notwithstanding, Hoover's own feelings about the British bordered on xenophobia. "Yankees are not well received," he wrote while still sweating it out at Coolgardie, after reporting the camp "simply overrun with young Englishmen," including one Oxford graduate working in the mines for $2.50 a day. "They only have us because they have to. They don't know how to make their mines pay dividends; we do. . . ." Now, he added to the catalogue of British sins an undemocratic obsession with titles and a foolish affection for "the Empire."[18]

To another friend, he described the American as an alien abroad, who could never assimilate, and whose heart must forever remain in his native land, even if his niche there was a shrunken one. He had reached a stage in his career, "where I am playing the game for the game's sake. . . . I am disgusted with myself when I think how much better off you people are who stuck by your own country and place. When you walk down the street you meet a hundred men who have a genuine pleasure in greeting you. I am an alien who gets a grin once in nine months." At times he sounded almost ashamed of his success. "What is an able man like you," he asked a fellow Californian visiting Red House, "doing in an old-world country?" Hoover rejected out of hand an offer to join the British Cabinet during the first world war. "I'll be damned if I'll give up my American citizenship," he replied when asked by Lord Kitchener to become Minister of Munitions.

As a boy, he had wandered in search of friends and family. As a young man, his travels on behalf of foreign mining interests brought him international renown and prosperity to match his prestige. By 1908, when he left Bewick, Moreing to open his own consulting offices in London, Paris, New York, San Francisco and Saint Petersburg, Hoover was an authentic *wunderkind*, his bags always packed, and tailors on four continents alerted to his measurements, in case he needed a new suit on the spur of the moment.

Admirers pointed to the way he assumed responsibility for half a million dollars embezzled by a Bewick, Moreing partner, paying $127,000 out of his own pocket. Later, he would be accused of using slave labor. Australian successors said he cut corners and exhausted machines as well as men. In truth, he had threatened to import Italian laborers to frighten the unruly Aussies into line, and Hoover struck a jarring note early on by callously reporting that Chinese families willingly accepted $30 in exchange for a husband or father snuffed out in the mines. But he told a business audience in the Transvaal in 1904 that the use of coolie labor was unprofitable, and he was known for paying the highest wages in any goldfields. He could be harsh, but his innovations delivered profits, and his reputation soared. By 1913 his various concerns employed more than 175,000 men.

For all this, Hoover was not satisfied. As early as 1907 he confessed to David Starr Jordan that he had "run through his profession." Money alone was not enough of an inducement to fix his attentions. "If a man has not made a million dollars by the time he is forty," he observed without self-consciousness, "he's not worth much." The banality of materialism clashed in Hoover's mind with the Quaker Query instructing him to "create a social and economic system which will so function as to sustain and enrich life for all." His own restlessness reflected that of a people caught up in unregulated competition and a crescendo of unthinking optimism.

Americans, H. G. Wells observed during a 1906 visit, were suffering from what he called "a delusion of automatic progress." And why not? The

Wright brothers had invaded the skies above Kitty Hawk, the cinema age was unfolding with early titles like *The Great Train Robbery* and President Wilson marveled at D. W. Griffith's *The Birth of a Nation* after ordering it shown at the White House. The horse so derided by Hoover was disappearing from the nation's thoroughfares. Between 1910 and 1918, the number of automobiles rose 1,100 percent while horse-drawn carriages became rural curiosities. Not all Americans shared equally in the promise of equality: 1905 saw formation of the radical labor organization, the Industrial Workers of the World, and Colorado miners who failed to emulate Bert Hoover's rags-to-riches tale sang a lusty chorus of discontent.

> God give us men; a time like this demands
> Strong minds, great hearts; true faith and ready hands;
> Men whom lust of lucre does not kill;
> Men whom the spoils of office cannot buy.

Coal miners earned twenty-nine cents an hour in 1910, when Hoover was plumbing Burma's lead and complaining of the "squeeze" native to impoverished China. Less than a tenth of American workers belonged to unions, endorsed by Hoover in a series of Columbia lectures. Not until August 1923, under pressure from Hoover and the Interchurch World Movement, did the steel industry consent to an eight-hour day. Meanwhile, the cost of living far outpaced American wages. The typical family's food bill during the mild depression of 1907–8 was a little over five dollars a week, spent mostly on staples like meat, butter, flour, eggs, sugar and beans. Green vegetables were out of reach of most American workers, a nutritional deficiency that would no doubt have horrified the calorie-conscious Hoover.

The Great Engineer, as he was now called with increasing frequency, was hardly more content with his own fame and comforts than the miners or assembly line workers who lacked both. "I'm getting to the point where I'll soon have an independent income," he informed Will Irwin. His foreign enterprises, Hoover continued, were being handed over to colleagues. For his own part, he was interested "in some job of public service—at home, of course."

Conscious of a defective formal eduction, Hoover began to absorb hundreds of weighty volumes on economics, history, sociology and government. He went on archeological expeditions to Egypt and Italy and wrote at least nineteen articles, most for scholarly geological publications. In 1909 he published his Columbia lectures, which, under the title *Principles of Mining*, became a standard textbook for years to come, and for five years he pursued his intricate translation of Agricola with the help of Lou and a

2,500-volume library of rare books they collected to fill the chinks in their own knowledge of medieval mining. (The widening circle of Hoover's curiosity never brushed up against the arts. Unlike Lou, who organized a music society at Stanford, he had a tin ear, unable to tolerate any melody more demanding than a player piano's rendition of "Barcarole.") In 1912, Hoover joined the Stanford board of trustees; colleagues said more was accomplished during his first hour of membership than in the preceding three years.[19]

As his country struggled to digest a heavy meal of modernity, Hoover was busy developing his own theory of social usefulness. He was influenced heavily in this by the seminal thinker Thorstein Veblen, himself a member of the Stanford faculty after 1906. Beginning 1899 with *The Theory of the Leisure Class,* Veblen outlined the crucial distinction between the rapacious individual's predatory instinct and the ideal of service as embodied by his own caste of engineers. He described in succeeding books a system in which engineers would control both production and distribution—what would later be captioned "technocracy." Hoover embellished Veblen's notion of the engineer as society's management consultant, disinterested enough to know what was best, forceful enough to realize the age-old ambition of a standard combining generosity with practicality. No mere disciple of mechanical utopias would do.

The engineer dealt with exact sciences, Hoover noted. "That sort of exactness makes for truth and conscience. . . . But he who would enter these precincts as a lifework must have a test taken of his imaginative faculties, for engineering without imagination sinks to a trade. And those who would enter here must for years abandon their white collars except for Sundays." The engineer, he continued, was intimately acquainted with hard beds, biting cold, loneliness and disappointment. But he also knew the joys of creation, "the fascination of watching a figment of the imagination emerge through the aid of science to a plan on paper. Then it moves to realization in stone or metal or energy. Then it brings jobs and homes to men. Then it elevates the standards of living and adds to the comforts of life." With the industrial revolution in full swing, he predicted, the engineer might well become a public figure, a powerful advocate for social justice as well as scientific advance.[20]

This was optimism of a high order. It was also utterly unsentimental, the cold-blooded observations of a man who functioned best behind the scenes, imposing an order conspicuously absent in his own early years. A lunchmate of Hoover's during his days as Food Administrator noticed that the great man ate far less than any of his table companions. Asking why, he received a short course in dietary efficiency. "I'm an engineer," Hoover told him, "and I'm not using my body. An engineer does not stoke the engine unless there is a considerable amount of power to be exerted. So, I eat as little as I can to get along." [21]

With similar precision, Hoover calculated the negative effect of his own introverted personality ("I don't think a man makes more than a dozen friends in a lifetime"). One visitor to his London study found him reading William James's *The Varieties of Religious Experience* and doggedly trying to reconcile evolution and his own geological knowledge with traditional theology. Later, he confessed to agonizing over the phrase, "And lead us not into temptation" in the Lord's Prayer, until someone explained it as too free a translation of the original Aramaic. [22]

With so easily pained a conscience, Hoover earnestly debated his future in the spring of 1914. Enthusiastic for progress, yet emotive as a slide rule and temperamentally unsuited for politics, he considered buying the *Sacramento Union* and starting a new life in publishing. Then, on July 28, a band of Serbian assassins took the decision out of his hands. A bullet fired in Sarajevo terminated the California negotiations and set Hoover himself upon what he later called "the slippery road of public life." [23]

★   ★

Hoover was in London, on a fruitless swing to persuade jittery European nations to add their names to the roster participating in San Francisco's forthcoming Panama-Pacific Exposition, when the conspirators of Sarajevo gave way to the guns of August. His salesmanship was abruptly halted on August 3, by an urgent appeal from U.S. embassy officials: with all British sailings to America suspended, thousands of panic-stricken U.S. nationals were fleeing the Continent for a safe haven. Walter Hines Page, ambassador to Britain, invited Hoover to apply his formidable talents of organization to the swelling clot of confused, penniless Americans piling up outside official doors. The next morning, as German troops punched through the Belgian frontier, Hoover was assembling five hundred volunteers from other American business interests in the British capital and transforming the main ballroom of the Savoy hotel into a canteen *extraordinaire.*

During the next six weeks, he distributed food, clothing, transatlantic tickets aboard steamers and in steerage, and cash to 120,000 of his countrymen. He helped Chief White Feather of Pawhuska, Oklahoma, and dowagers in jewels to reach their destinations. When one woman angrily insisted on a written pledge that no German submarine would attack her vessel in midocean, Hoover readily complied. While he improvised, Lou organized a women's division, cared for unaccompanied children and escorted idle, nervous tourists through cathedral towns and Lorna Doone country. Before they were through, Hoover and nine business associates had guaranteed $1.5 million, much of it in personal checks without collateral. Less than $400 went unpaid, impressive testimony to the Great Engineer's faith in volunteerism and the American character.

Across the Channel, 7.5 million Belgians languished under the hobnail boot of their German conqueror. Relying on imports for 80 percent of her food, Belgium was soon hungry as well as humiliated. With the invader already seizing crops and cattle, and a British blockade raising the specter of mass starvation, an American engineer in Brussels named Millard Shaler conceived the idea of a large-scale relief effort under neutral management. Hearing of Hoover's work in London, Shaler went to their mutual friend, Edgar Rickard, for an introduction. More than that, he was rewarded with plenty of advice on how to purchase and load foodstuffs for shipping to Belgium. When the British blockade threatened to abort Shaler's plan, Hoover sought help from Ambassador Page. He also alerted Melville Stone, a friend and general manager for the Associated Press, to the impending tragedy. Starving Belgium was on its way to becoming an international *cause célèbre.*

On October 18, with Antwerp now in German hands and his own return to America booked on the *Lusitania,* Hoover received a call from the embassy. When he got there, he found not only Page and Hugh Gibson, a U.S. diplomat stationed in Brussels as deputy to Ambassador Brand Whitlock, but a delegation of impassioned Belgian patriots, led by none other than his old China adversary, Emile Franqui. With bulldog tenacity, Franqui had attempted to organize relief efforts inside Belgium. Now he generously offered to step aside, serving under Hoover in a broadened campaign to save his homeland. For the American, whose tattered business interests stood to gain immeasurably from a prolonged war, the request came as a shock. Asking for twenty-four hours to think it over, he went home and prayed with Lou. He talked with farflung associates. He pondered financial realities, his own and Belgium's. On the morning of the twenty-first he remarked to Will Irwin over breakfast, "Let the fortune go to Hell." That afternoon, he was back at the embassy, wiring the Chicago commodity exchange for ten million bushels of wheat.

Forty years later, embittered and ironic, he had a different reaction. His decision to go to Belgium's aid in her most desperate hour, Hoover remarked to friends, had been "the worst mistake of my life." Without it, he never would have been elected president. The rest was eloquent silence.[24]

Herbert Hoover's position on October 22, 1914, was analogous to that of a board chairman suddenly designated door-to-door-salesman, without inventory and with only the slimmest prospects of persuading the reluctant belligerents of Europe to open their doors and sample his product—even if it meant the difference between life and death for the children upstairs. In scope as well as concept, the Committee for the Relief of Belgium (CRB) was an unprecedented attempt to prevent the civilian slaughter visited on one third of Europe during the Thirty Years' War. At the outset, prospects for success were bleak. The city of Liège had five days' bread and 80 percent unemployment, Hoover was told; Brussels was down to four days' flour. Without immediate help, Brand Whitlock informed President Wilson, Belgium would starve within two weeks.

By the end of October, Hoover and a band of fellow mining engineers had opened offices in London, Rotterdam, Brussels and New York. They obtained cosponsorship of the CRB from the Dutch and Spanish governments, recruited volunteers to study nutritional needs and conduct diplomatic exchanges, and managed to ram 4,500 tons of food through the British blockade. Hoover himself paid a fleeting visit to the Flemish kingdom and was rewarded with his first taste of military paranoia, strip-searches by British intelligence agents on one side of the Channel, and German soldiers on the other. He drove through rubble-littered streets in Louvain and Antwerp, pausing at street corner soup kitchens dispensing a thin, watery gruel. In the evening, he spent hours negotiating for funds with Belgian financiers, while outside a German sentry stood guard.

A host of miracles were required of the CRB, all at once. It must create an organization capable of gathering, transporting and distributing enormous amounts of food—more than five million tons in all to eleven million inhabitants of occupied Belgium and northern France. It must convince both sides in the savage fighting that it was strictly neutral. And it had to locate vast sums of money to sustain its work, at a time when billions of dollars were being shot away or sunk forever in a bloody, muddy line of trenches 400 miles long or the graveyard of the Atlantic. Nothing came easily. The Belgian government, which still occupied a slice of territory around Le Havre, promised Hoover $9.6 million. Together with charitable contributions and a small grant from the British, this would sustain his work for a few months. But Belgium reneged on its pledge, and appetites proved harder to satisfy than expected. Private charity was clearly insufficient to handle the job alone, and, early in November, Hoover informed the governments of England, France and Belgium that they would have to bear the major burden of humanitarian relief.

The British thought this outrageous. It was the Germans who invaded and occupied Belgium, they argued; let the Germans accept responsibility for feeding the overrun territory. Still more provocative were German attempts to collect $7 million a month in Belgian indemnities. Hoover could forget about help from Whitehall, the Asquith government let it be known, so long as this abominable practice continued. In December, Hoover journeyed to the Kaiser's capital, to plead in vain for an end to the forced payments. In desperation, he hit on two fresh ideas. First, he would tap funds held in Belgian banks overseas. Next, he would penetrate the economic blockade by creating a novel exchange system, allowing anyone outside the beleaguered kingdom to deposit funds with the CRB, to buy food for sale to those with cash of their own. The proceeds would sustain four million or more in genuine distress and liquidate the loans simultaneously. In London, Lord Kitchener and Winston Churchill rejected the scheme angrily. Detesting even the appearance of trading with the enemy, they forced Hoover to appeal personally to Lloyd George, then Chancellor of the Exchequer. It was a desperate time for the CRB, able to count barely $6 million in its coffers, with advance contracts for provisions worth five times that amount signed and sealed. Hoover himself pledged personal responsibility for sums far in excess of his net worth.

His own sense of urgency was communicated to Lloyd George and the British cabinet. "Except for the breadstuffs imported by this Commission," his memo to the fiery Welshman began, "there is not one ounce of bread in Belgium today. . . ." Hoover insisted that the Germans would never take food from their own people to feed Belgium. He revealed a pledge from Berlin to stop requisitioning Belgian supplies after January 1, 1915, and pointed to the fickle nature of U.S. public opinion as a final incentive to back his "practical idealism." [25]

"You have made a good fight," the Chancellor told Hoover, "and deserve to win out." Actually, the fight had barely begun. As the CRB's financial needs rose from $5- to $10- and ultimately $25 million per month, its chairman found himself pulled in a hundred directions at once. When the government of Raymond Poincaré evaded responsibility for feeding more than 2 million residents of northern France trapped behind German lines, Hoover denounced as "perfectly ghastly" a mass evacuation plan for the region, endorsed by Marshal Joffre. He didn't ask questions in March 1915, when a London bank official presented him with anonymous checks totaling 1.4 million pounds. [26]

"No day went by," he wrote afterward, "without a fight to keep part of the mechanism from breaking down." Commandeering 40 ships and 500 canal boats for his independent republic of relief, he suffered in silence when the Belgian government said it lacked the legal authority to seize additional vessels capable of carrying 80,000 tons of barley and bacon, wheat and rye. He designed a triangular, red-lettered flag for the CRB vessels to proclaim their neutrality—and agonized over the German sinking of the *Harpalyce*, a British-chartered relief ship flying that flag. He demanded and got safe passage and special passports for the 350 CRB volunteers, organized 5,000 communes in the occupied territories and support committees throughout the United States. American response to his appeal was phenomenal: Kansas millers gave a shipload of flour, the Rocky Mountain Club of New York City presented the CRB with half a million dollars previously earmarked for a new clubhouse, and thousands of local drives produced cash, food supplies and clothing. Hoover was confirmed in his view of Americans as a benevolent, self-reliant race. "If you tell them what is needed," he recalled, "they will give you anything and everything. The winter I ran the National Clothing Collection Drives, I put new tailcoats and tuxedos on every waiter in Europe."[27]

Gallantry, like the sight of hungry children, moved him deeply. When two English ladies sent him a dozen silver buttons snipped from their gowns, he returned all but one, "which . . . I shall keep as a reminder that there are people like you in the world." Less understanding than its citizens, His Majesty's government stiffly protested German purchases of Belgian livestock—leading the CRB to assume control of the kingdom's slaughterhouses. Before he was through, Hoover also requisitioned dozens of mills, bakeries, factories, railways and warehouses. The British insisted he add all manufacture and sale of cloth to his responsibilities. Otherwise, they worried, a German shortage of wool for army uniforms might be solved with shiploads of clothing donated from America. For their part, German authorities permitted Belgian lacemaking to continue, so long as patriotic motifs were strictly forbidden. CRB personnel dutifully nodded their heads, then wrapped patriotic lace around their bodies for smuggling through the port of Rotterdam.[28]

With organization and finances established, Hoover appealed for Rhodes scholars to donate their services, and Red House was filled with brainy young men for the duration of the war. He poured over the findings of eminent dietary experts including Horace Fletcher, who had instructed Americans to chew every bite thirty-two times, before settling on eighteen hundred calories a day as the minimum required to nourish Belgians. When children in the war zone showed signs of rickets and tuberculosis, he added cocoa to their regimen—and more than two million Belgian and French youngsters enjoyed an extra "Hoover lunch" of white bread and thick vegetable soup every day. He even lured Pope Benedict XV into a public endorsement of the CRB, backed by 10,000 lire and marching orders to the American church hierarchy.

Not all Hoover's thoughts were of the battlefield. On one of forty crossings of the Channel, he read the autobiography of Cornell's Andrew D. White, who early in his teaching career had started a substantial personal library on the French Revolution. Fired by White's example, Hoover realized from his own unique vantage point, as a neutral among combatants, that he could undertake an even broader collection of documents pertaining to the Great War. In 1919 he gave Stanford $50,000 to launch the Hoover Institution and dispatch three scholars from Palo Alto to begin a careful combing of Europe's archives. On his own, he cajoled governments into giving him their wartime papers and eventually gathered up a trunk belonging to Mata Hari and millions of classified orders from Allied commands.

Less satisfactory was his relationship with Emile Franqui and the native Comité Nationale, whom he accused of polluting philanthropy with ward politics. Chemistry among the Allies was combustible, as Hoover strenuously opposed Franqui's scheme to provide a dole to the unemployed. Such a plan, he maintained, was "socially wrongly founded, giving money as a right to the unemployed." Appalled by the petty rivalries between the Belgians and various relief committees, Hoover at times was tempted to wash his hands of the whole project. Early in 1916 he publicly offered to resign and complained in martyred tones that the CRB was being "hammered" from all sides. Personally, he wrote Hugh Gibson, "I find staring me in my dreams a large poster entitled, 'Go back to the lead mines' in which occupation one obtains a modicum of human gratitude and a large liberty from hammers of all sizes." [29]

Lack of appreciation was not confined to Europe. In October 1915, Hoover was forced to return home, where he called on President Wilson and friendly newspaper editors for their help in warding off the attacks of Henry Cabot Lodge. Lodge, eager to prosecute Hoover under the century-old Logan Act, which forbade private Americans from dealing with a wartime enemy, was eventually calmed by the press and his old friend Theodore Roosevelt. The Brahmin from Boston, T.R. told Hoover at an Oyster Bay lunch, could see "involvements" in Europe beneath every bush. "I will hold his hand," he promised. [30]

Hardly was he back in London than Hoover received an urgent message from Hugh Gibson in Brussels: five young CRB workers were being held on espionage charges, and the German field commander, a Colonel Blimpish figure named Von Bissing, wanted to use the incident as a pretext for banishing the entire commission from occupied soil. Hoover rushed to assure the Germans that when it came to even the appearance of partiality, he was "more Catholic than the Pope." Three of the suspects returned to London, a Salvation Army major was set free and the fifth American was hastily deported to the States.[31]

Another crisis passed. But the allegations from both sides never subsided. British naval intelligence accused Hoover of profiteering on the black market. The Germans were gathering up tins filled with condensed milk for Belgium's children and turning them into hand grenades, charged the French. Milk cows could not be allowed within the German zone, insisted Von Bissing. "Trouble 7921," Hoover labeled a snag in the French clothing drive.

When pushed, he pushed back, this most undiplomatic of diplomats. Herbert Asquith called him impertinent, an assessment shared by government officials throughout Europe. Winston Churchill, typically, went further; Hoover, he snapped, was "a son of a bitch." In addition to his not-so-subtle warnings to the German command about future U.S. involvement, Hoover didn't hesitate to lecture British Foreign Minister Sir Edward Grey on his country's moral obligations. King George's government had, after all, entered the war solely to protect its gallant little ally on the Continent. "It would be a cynical ending if the civil population of Belgium had become extinct in the process of rescue," he told Grey. He did constant acrimonious battle with Churchill's Admiralty, what Hoover called "the sanctuary of British militarists." He won few friends among the mighty, but his picture appeared in millions of Belgian homes.

Along with his seat-of-the-pants diplomacy and his own blunt language, Hoover turned for results to "the club of public opinion" and a swelling chorus of worldwide propaganda. Instructing aides to play up the CRB, not him (the first appeal for help went out at his insistence under Millard Shaler's signature), Hoover denounced reporters who did otherwise, refused foreign decorations, and dreaded the day when elderly ladies riding London double-deckers might tap him with their umbrellas and say, "Oh, you are the Relief man, aren't you?" They were working in a ship's hold, the Chief told CRB colleagues, but he was on the bridge and could see the progress being made.[32]

Hoover's leadership of the CRB had its roots in earlier triumphs, from Stanford labs to the wastes of Siberia. It was the Yankee ingenuity and wire-pulling talents of a shy gladiator, born to the backstage and blessed with promotional instincts to match his moralistic fervor. Terrified of public speaking, before small groups he was vinegary and persuasive. William Allen

White, for one, came away from meeting Hoover for the first time "mesmerized by the strange low voltage of his magnetism."

Above all else, Belgium demanded improvisation. Being breadeaters, the Belgians regarded cornmeal as something fit for their cattle. Hoover solved the dilemma this posed by chance, on an inspection trip to Mons. "Hello there," he called out to a black man he spotted, "can you make cornbread?" As a matter of fact, the man replied, he could make cornbread that would stand up and talk. "You have a job," Hoover told him. "Hop in." His passenger, it turned out, was a onetime mess steward from Norfolk named Jim, off to see the world. With Hoover at the wheel, he was sure to see plenty. After kneeling in the back seat at a German patrol point, Jim arrived in Brussels, where the director of the CRB secured him a chef's uniform and dispatched him to the city's largest skating rink (transferred by Hoover's group into a child feeding center). He then began a series of baking demonstrations for hundreds of mothers with infant children. Soon, society women were translating Jim's recipes for cornbread and muffins into Flemish and French. Thousands of their countrymen discovered a hitherto secret longing for maize, and when the fighting ended, Belgium became a cornmeal importer for the first time.

By then, Hoover and his men had spent a billion dollars—carefully audited to guard against fraud—and protected millions of Europeans from malnutrition and nakedness. Administrative overhead for the entire operation came to .4 percent. More than $24 million in profits were plowed back into the rebuilding of Belgian universities, a scholarship fund for Belgian-American exchange students, and an ambitious program of scientific research. Hoover's own reputation soared, and when German submarines in the spring of 1917 provoked Wilson into scrapping his earlier vows of neutrality, there was no question that the "simple, modest, energetic little man," as Ambassador Page described him, "who began his career in California and will end it in Heaven," would assume a domestic role equal to his overseas performance.

★   ★

German submarines were exacting a deadly toll of Allied merchant shipping by the time Hoover moved into the ramshackle structures of wire and wallboard that housed the United States Food Administration. From his position in the capital's new "Foggy Bottom" neighborhood—and at Woodrow Wilson's right hand—Hoover surveyed a food crisis turned military-imperative. British officials were warning that without immediate shipments of at least 75 million bushels of wheat, the war might be lost. At the same time, U.S. stocks were down to 30 million bushels, with Belgium and Cuba competing for the dwindling stockpile. Hoover's job was to organize Americans to increase production, diminish consumption and avert wartime profiteering and inflation, all the while hewing to his own preference for voluntary cooperation over federal fiat.

"We have gone for a hundred years of unbridled private initiative in this country," he told senators at his confirmation hearings, "and it has bred its own evils and one of these evils is the lack of responsibility in the American individual to the people as a whole, the unwillingness of personal selfishness to sacrifice to the national interest." Having made the allegation, Hoover set out to disprove it. The difference between democracy and autocracy, he liked to say, lay in "whether people can be organized from the bottom up or the top down."

His own formula was simple: "centralize ideas but decentralize execution." To control prices without suffocating the economy, Hoover invented Price Interpreting Boards, more than 1,200 in all, bringing wholesalers, retailers and consumers together at the county level. Local newspapers printed the prices voluntarily arrived at, along with the names of businesses in noncompliance. A benevolent dictator, Hoover was everywhere at once, persuading the Navy to adopt a convoy system, stabilizing wheat prices by guaranteeing farmers twenty cents more for their wheat than a congressionally dictated tab, worrying about the size of bread loaves, conferring with Cardinal Gibbons and other churchmen, welcoming a cadre of young men—Robert Taft, Christian Herter and Lewis Strauss among them—who wished to serve him at a dollar a year. He created the U.S. Grain Corporation to purchase foodstuffs and protect American farmers from exploitative European agents. He launched the Sugar Equalization Board, and in partnership with other Allied governments, bought up the entire Cuban sugar crop. In July 1918, he successfully urged Wilson to press for an excess profits tax, the first in U.S. history.

Hoover's influence, like his mandate, seemed limitless. An organizational chart of the Food Administration presented for his review was promptly ripped into shreds. "This is an emergency organization," Hoover explained. "Every day we must meet new problems. . . . My notion on organization is to size up the problem, send for the best man or woman in the country who has the know-how, give him a room, table, chair, pencil, paper and wastebasket—and the injunction to get other people to help—and then solve it. When that problem is out of the way, we shall find plenty more." One subordinate in charge of milk production was a former cigar salesman; his successor came to Hoover's office from a career raising citrus fruit. Hoover himself chafed under the conventional devices of Washington, so much so that Wilson's majordomo, Colonel Edward House, took to the social circuit to plead with hostesses to "be nice to Hoover because he's not happy. He doesn't understand how to work with Congress or politicians."[33]

"The Food Administration is called into being to stabilize and not to disturb conditions," Hoover announced, and it canceled licenses with fewer than one percent of American businesses guilty of price gouging. Instead of the forced planting and rationing common to Europe, Hoover wanted Americans to pull together, voluntarily sacrificing restaurant meals and gorgeous clothes to a larger good. In her Washington library Lou Hoover kept one of millions of Hoover Home Cards. "Save fuel," it read. "Use wood when you can." Hotels and restaurants eliminated wheat products from their menus. Tens of thousands of homeowners started backyard gardens. Under the guise of patriotism—and contempt for German brewers—the sale and distribution of intoxicating liquors was forbidden in September 1918. Not every attempt to foster self-denial was successful. Hoover failed miserably in his "Buy a Pig" campaign. "A properly cared for pig," claimed the Food Administration, "is no more unsanitary than a dog." Suburbia disagreed.

Besides its reliance on the grass roots, another hallmark of the Food Administration was a skillful use of publicity, just then maturing as a tool of mass persuasion. "We are good advertisers," Hoover told Will Irwin. "The world lives by phrases. . . . We need some phrase that puts the stamp of shame on wasteful eating, dressing and display of jewelry." It wasn't long before Hoover discovered what he was after. "Food Will Win The War" took its place alongside "54-40 or Fight" and "Remember the Alamo" in the annals of patriotic instigation. But it was hardly alone. Nearly nineteen hundred press releases poured out of Foggy Bottom over the next two years, exhorting Americans to hooverize 16 million barrels of wheat and wage personal war on kitchen waste. "Do Not Help The Hun At Meal Time" banners proclaimed. Eager to comply, 20 million housewives joined the food army. Fish and vegetables substituted for meat and bread. Blood sausage became "victory sausage" and children sang songs about the "patriotic potato." Nineteen million dollars' worth of free advertising was donated, along with display space in libraries, schools and shops.

The hundreds of thousands who signed pledge cards admitting them to membership in the Food Administration were inspired to still greater efforts at food conservation. So were the 21,000 newspaper editors solicited by Hoover for their gifts of public persuasion. The combination of flattery, propaganda and wartime controls paid off handsomely. Within a year, Hoover could boast of having doubled U.S. food shipments to Europe, without ration cards, interruption of traditional economic freedoms or heavy bureaucratic expenses. Administrative costs for his unorthodox approach ran to less than $8 million.

His name was now a household word, even if Hoover personally directed his publicity department to refer always to "the Food Administrator" and not to himself. He could not so easily suppress average Americans from doing what came naturally. "I can hooverize on dinner," went one Valentine's Day message, "and on lights and fuel too, but I'll never learn to hooverize, when it comes to loving you." Hoover, wrote Walter Lippmann, "incarnates all that is at once effective and idealistic in the picture of America." Yet the object of public acclaim remained a shadowy, omniscient figure, unromantically flipping a half dollar as he paced his office, dictating an endless stream of memos and instructions, in the words of one associate, "as impatient of people who were lacking in understanding or perception as any man I've known." Josephus Daniels, Wilson's Secretary of the Navy— and young Franklin Roosevelt's tolerant superior—scratched his head in astonishment after listening to Hoover describe his Belgian relief work "as coldly as if he were giving statistics of production." Even harsher was the opinion of George Creel, who, as head of wartime propaganda for the Wilson administration, helped popularize the sentimental anthem "Keep the Home Fires Burning" and whipped up anti-German feeling with films like "The Beast of Berlin." Hoover, Creel told the president, gave him the feeling of a cockroach sliding around a porcelain bathtub. [34]

"While the inspiration to reform comes from the human heart," Hoover once stated, "it is achieved only by the intellect." Asked about the possibility that one Hoover-ordered study might conflict with his own publicly expressed views, his reply was typical. "That's all right," he said. "Get the facts. What we want are the facts." There were exceptional moments when his self-control crumbled under the onslaught of barbarous memories. A few weeks after the Armistice, informed that two German officials wished to see him, Hoover adamantly refused. "You can describe two and a half years of arrogance toward ourselves and cruelty to the Belgians in any language you may select," he directed the aide who brought him the news. "And tell the pair personally to go to hell, with my compliments." Later, making his way across a French battleground where the soil had yet to swallow soldiers' shoes and boots, Hoover was grimly silent. There, among the relics of death, he saw graphic, gruesome evidence of what he called the stupidity of war. [35]

At Versailles, he met John Maynard Keynes ("the Puck of Economists" to Lloyd George), Jan Smuts and the Big Four who represented the victorious enemies of German militarism. Witnessing firsthand Old World betrayal of New World idealism, Hoover never forgot the ordeal of Woodrow

Wilson (of whom the cynical French Premier Georges Clemenceau said, "I never knew anyone to talk more like Jesus Christ, and act more like Lloyd George"). "It grows upon me daily," Hoover told the president in a memorandum dated April 11, 1919, "that the United States is the one great moral reserve in the world today and that we cannot maintain . . . independence of action . . . if we allow ourselves to be dragged into detailed European entanglements over a period of years. . . . If the Allies cannot be brought to adopt peace at the basis of the Fourteen Points," Hoover went on, "we should retire from Europe, lock, stock, and barrel, and we should lend to the whole world our economic and moral strength, or the world will swim in a sea of misery and disaster worse than the Dark Ages."

Combatting British, French and Italian moves to prolong the blockade, and oversee American resources on the Continent, Hoover magnified dangers and barely concealed a rising tide of personal hostility. Colonel House detected a strong whiff of pessimism in his colleague. "He takes, as usual, a gloomy view of the situation," House confided to his diary after talking with Hoover that June, when his colleague's shock over the draft treaty with Germany was still fresh. Hoover's relationship with Wilson, like his faith in the negotiating process and European statesmanship in general, would never recover. He returned to the United States in September 1919 a man without illusions.

America could win great wars, he had concluded. But she could not make a lasting peace for Europe, a continent boiling over with ancient antagonisms, racial mistrust, the plague of empire, and ideological infection from communism, socialism and the Fascist embryo. "The duty of European statesmen of goodwill," he wrote later, "is to engage incessantly in adroit power politics . . . in hopes that a tenuous peace can be extended a little longer. It is a delicate job in which national honor and loyalties to agreement by any of them are continuously sacrificed to expediencies and self-preservation." Whether the subject was diplomacy, economics, domestic politics or class structure, Hoover discerned a clear superiority in his own continent, which had grown 300 years apart from the Old World's murderous baronies. Others among his countrymen might be influenced by European culture; Hoover remembered "the deep-seated tribal instincts of nationalism, imperialism, age-old hates, memories of deep wrongs, fierce distrusts and impellent fears" motivating the men of Versailles who broke Woodrow Wilson's heart.[36]

Hoover's contempt for politicians did not smother his compassion for suffering subjects. When peace settled over the ravaged Continent, with misery its attendant and starvation its ironic reward, Hoover organized the

American Relief Association to feed twenty-one prostrate nations from the North Sea to the Urals (including Germany, over Lodge's objections and with Wilson's support). He aided 6 million children through his European Children's Fund, precursor to CARE, and threw political considerations aside in April 1919 when the Bolsheviks sought his help in averting mass famine and lethal waves of typhus, cholera and dysentery for 15 million Russians.

"The Bolsheviki has [sic] resorted to terror, bloodshed and murder to a degree long since abandoned even amongst reactionary tyrannies," he informed President Wilson in opposing recognition of Lenin's government. But he disputed those, like Churchill, who wanted the Big Four to unite for a military invasion of Russia. Contemptuous as he was of Communist revolutionaries, Hoover displayed no tenderness for the Czar. He characterized Russia's turbulence as "the not unnatural violence of a mass of ignorant humanity, who themselves have learned in grief of tyranny and violence over generations."

"Our people," he continued, "who enjoy so great liberty and general comfort, cannot fail to sympathize to some degree with these blind gropings for better social conditions." Eventually, Hoover managed the unlikely feat of persuading Warren Harding and a Republican Congress to appropriate $20 million for Russian relief.[37]

Before he left for home, Hoover suffered through a parade of 50,000 Polish schoolchildren in his honor. In Paris, he was given a gloomy forecast of future conflict. "There will be another world war in your time," Clemenceau predicted, "and you will be needed back in Europe." Clemenceau was right. There would be another war, and Hoover would not return until its eve, twenty years after the guns of Belleau Wood and Verdun fell silent, and a false dawn of normality cast its pale light across a Continent bled and bleeding still.

★   ★

I do not believe that I have the mental attitude or the politician's manner. . . . Above all I am too sensitive to political mud.

—Herbert Hoover, October 1919[38]

Herbert Hoover returned to a nation in turmoil. "We seem to be the most frightened lot of victors that the world ever saw" was the way Walter Lippmann put it. Instead of pride, peace brought an endless round of recriminations and pointed fingers, inflation and strikes, race riots, Red scares, and a nebulous contempt for the European continent bathed in the blood of American doughboys: this and more overshadowed the homecoming parades. Wilson, broken and bitter, clung to office without even the authority of his once ringing words. Liberalism seemed to have died with the Armistice as Kansas legislators prohibited strikes, an Indiana jury required just two minutes to acquit a man accused of murdering an alien who wished the United States would go to hell, and Washington sports fans cheered a uniformed sailor for shooting to death a fellow spectator who refused to stand for the national anthem.

Attorney General A. Mitchell Palmer, like Hoover a Quaker and old Progressive, saw his front porch pulverized by an anarchist's bomb. Then he hired a twenty-four-year-old former file clerk named J. Edgar Hoover to compile 250,000 cards on radical Americans. Palmer predicted a general Communist uprising for July 4, 1919, and Lincoln Steffens returned from a visit to Russia with the words "I've been over into the future, and it works."

Hoover had been there too, and nursed a different point of view. But he steadfastly refused to join in Palmer's Red-baiting. "We shall never remedy justifiable discontent," he told one of the dozens of audiences he addressed in the next year and a half, "until we eradicate the misery which the ruthlessness of individualism has imposed upon a minority." Reactionaries, he warned, more subtle in their methods, more seductive in their platitudes, posed a greater danger to the republic than any ragtag band of radicals. Originally, he had hoped to withdraw to California and start anew the engineering and mining careers abandoned in 1914. Instead, Hoover found himself drawn into the public debate. Ruefully, he concluded that his new home seemed, not the seven-room Hopi-style structure he and Lou designed for San Juan Hill in Palo Alto, but a Pullman car. In a torrent of speeches, magazine articles, and public reports, he called for a national program to lay rails and dig canals, irrigate the earth and conserve national resources, all under the constructive guidance of his fellow engineers. He praised labor unions, stressed the health needs of children, pressed society for greater economic efficiency and less waste. Throughout, Hoover groped his way toward a consensus between modern mass production and the personal happiness idealized in his own agrarian past.

"There is somewhere to be found a plan of individualism and associational activities," he wrote, "that will preserve the initiative, the inventiveness, the individuality, the character of men and yet will enable us to synchronize socially and economically this gigantic machine that we have built out of applied science."

The prose was gray, but Hoover cared nothing for emotional crusades. Like other Progressives, he looked forward to perpetual advance, spurred on by technology, inhibited only by irrational politicians, greedy interest groups, and what he called "individualism run riot." His was an incremental idealism, wherein personal success was tempered and purified by service. "Character," Hoover wrote, "is made in the community as well as in the individual by assuming responsibilities, not by escape from them."

Turning from theory to practice, Hoover walked a tightrope of material progress and an almost mystical cult of personal liberty. Somehow, he concluded, a balance would have to be struck among three central actors on the American stage—capitalists, workers and a public represented by its national government. If any single group should gain too much authority, he warned, the results would be fascism, socialism, or tyranny by bureaucracy. And individualism, the mainspring of American greatness, would be crippled permanently.

Hoover's intellectual odyssey came against a backdrop of accelerating change. His Palo Alto home built of reinforced concrete and fireproof reflected the latest in technology. As an equally modern wife, Lou typed much of her personal correspondence and enjoyed every labor-saving device except a refrigerator (she didn't want the neighborhood iceman to lose his job). Her address at 623 Mirada Drive, with its open air patios and indirect lighting, reflected her love of the outdoors, and a taste for experimentation. "Our home must be an elastic thing," she told her younger son, Allan, "never entirely finished. . . ."[39]

The universe itself was expanding in 1919. Not far from San Juan Hill, the new Hooker telescope poked an eye of polished glass into the heavens. In more distant classrooms, Einstein was expounding relativity. Radiation and the quantum theory yielded their secrets to Niels Bohr and Max Planck. The war had spun off dozens of new products, from helium and antifreeze to drugs consigning malaria and typhoid to grim memory. Chemists laid claim to being engineers of social equality. So claimed the peddlers of rayon, a new fabric made from cellulose. When spun into stockings, salesmen insisted, rayon leveled equally artificial barriers between shopgirls and ladies of leisure.

Hoover gloried in the onslaught of industrial and scientific ingenuity. "There are continents of human welfare," he proclaimed, "of which we have penetrated only the coastal plane." His special joy was a kind of dynamic efficiency. Nothing could be wasted, including words. At family dinners, irreverent youngsters made a game out of Uncle Bert's silences, the winner eliciting a "Pass the salt" or "Yes, it's a warm day." A Hoover companion visiting Yellowstone Park talked about the scenery, the shimmering lakes, and the outdoor cathedral of dense woods—without a murmur in response. Only the subject of fly-fishing began a trickle of conversation, soon broadened to a stream of recollections and comparisons between the fish of Australia and their Siamese counterparts. Coming down a California mountain with his journalist friend Mark Sullivan, the Great Engineer spotted a car broken down beside the narrow, twisting road. Stopping his own vehicle, Hoover climbed out and asked the car's driver if he could provide help. Scanning the machine closely, he concluded it would never run again and asked its owner what it was worth. Every bit of $35 the motorist replied, and maybe fifty.[40]

"Well, I'll give you $75 for it," Hoover told him, "now come here and give me a hand." With that, all three men pushed the auto to the edge of the mountain, then rolled it over the side. The road cleared, his conscience salved, Hoover continued on his way.[41]

With similar precision and far greater urgency, he warned his countrymen of the potential for class conflicts if untended social needs were allowed to fester. Hoover wrote *American Individualism* in the shadow of the Russian revolution. He said as much in its opening sentence. Revolution was not to be confused with a summer thunderstorm clearing the atmosphere, but seen as "a tornado leaving in its path the destroyed homes of millions with their dead women and children." Aware, too, of the recent upheavals in his own country, he spoke out with a passion all but muffled in face-to-face encounters. His message, unlike his syntax, was simple. Americans, he argued, required a new philosophy of individualism, generous enough to promote social justice, self-confident enough to ward off government's deadening hand, rigorous enough to prevent any interest group from gaining dominance.

"We might as well talk of abolishing the sun's rays if we would secure our food," he wrote, "as to talk of abolishing individualism as a basis of successful society." A nation's progress reflected the progress of its citizens. Both come "from out of the womb of the individual mind, not of the mind of the crowd." Yet American individualism was tempered by equality of opportunity which diffused leadership automatically. "Its stimulus," Hoover judged, "is competition. Its safeguard is education. Its greatest mentor is free speech and voluntary organization for the public good." The state could not go too far in stimulating such equality, Hoover told friends. More than patrolling the streets of national life, it should discover, develop and exalt individual leaders and protect the verdant richness of diversity that Hoover glimpsed in Vermont and Texas, music halls and movie houses, cotton fields and western mines. "If we examine the impulses that carry us forward," he had written in 1922, "none is so potent for progress as the yearning for self-expression, the desire for creation of something. . . . But it can only thrive in a society where the individual has liberty and stimulation to achievement."

It wasn't difficult to trace the origin of his faith. Out of his own Quaker background came Hoover's insistence on the divine within each individual. His struggle for professional recognition led to an unshakable belief in "the emery board of competition," plus the fatalistic conviction that "human leadership cannot be replenished by selection like queen bees, by divine right or bureaucracies." For Hoover, the ideal of cooperative association, first tested in Belgium, later honed through the Food Administration and humanitarian feeding of Europe, and now applied in his own land at thousands of Red Crosses, Community Chests, YMCAs and settlement houses, held the heartbeat of what he called the American System. Unlike bureaucracy, "co-operation appraises its methods and consequences step by step and pays its bills as it goes." It was a form of "self-government outside of political government," a fragile inheritance that elected officials were sworn to protect by constantly watering the grass roots of opportunity in what Hoover labeled the Individualizing State. Enlightened, naive and essentially conservative, Hoover's message appealed powerfully to a rudderless nation in the first light of global responsibility.

His attitude toward domestic politics similarly reflected the Progressive's contempt for stale partisanship. "I am not a party man," Hoover announced early in 1920. "There are about forty live issues in the country today in which I am interested and before I can answer whether I am a Democrat or a Republican I shall have to know how each party stands on those issues."

This was somewhat disingenuous, since Hoover had belonged to the National Republican Club since 1909 and informed President Wilson of the fact when he first agreed to become Food Administrator. Wilson told his brother-in-law he preferred Hoover as his successor anyway. So did a young Harvard undergraduate named Archibald MacLeish, and a Yalie who unsuccessfully tried to lure Hoover onto his campus, Henry Luce. The *New York Times* ranked Hoover among the ten greatest living Americans. His very defects—hypersensitivity, an appetite for personal domination and a self-evident contempt for the sonorous expressions and meaningless gestures adopted by most office seekers—became assets to millions who shared Hoover's passion for measured progress, along with his contempt for politics as a profession of piranhas, nourishing themselves by taking bites out of one another.[42]

Hoover didn't shy away from discussing his prospects as a Democrat early in 1920 with the party's national chairman, Homer Cummings. Later, he acknowledged he saw 1920 as a Republican year and had no desire to serve as sacrificial lamb for Wilson's party. That February, he told Colonel House he wanted to make the GOP into the kind of Progressive party that Theodore Roosevelt at one time envisioned, only to abandon in Chicago in 1916.

A month later he revealed publicly his allegiance to the GOP, permitting backers to enter his name in California's Republican primary against the state's militantly isolationist senator, Hiram Johnson. When the votes were counted, Hoover polled enough to cripple Johnson's candidacy and ignite a lifelong enmity without impressing either the Old Guard of his own party or the warring Democrats.

His name was placed before GOP delegates at the convention in June, but a cheering gallery and some amateur enthusiasts were no match for the senatorial cabal and a powerful instinct for conservative retrenchment. America, proclaimed Warren Harding, had had enough of heroes; and Hoover, the biggest hero to emerge from the war, received only a handful of votes.

"I don't agree with the President," Harding informed senatorial colleagues when Wilson requested U.S. help in feeding an exhausted Europe, "that we must establish a new internationalism paralyzed by socialism." His victory in Chicago was regarded by many, Hoover included, as a triumph of expediency over statesmanship. Hoover rebuked the nominee for his ambiguous language over the League of Nations; privately, he called Harding's straddle "a surrender to the worst forces in American public life." Yet he supported the Harding-Coolidge ticket and delivered two speeches on its behalf (assailed by GOP chairman Will Hays as "too objective"). Behind closed doors, the affable, compromise-prone Harding told Hoover he was pro-League. Yet publicly he continued to wobble, embellishing his Edwardian rhetoric even more than usual and promising a return to the frock-coated utopia of McKinley. Woodrow Wilson etched his opinion of the Republican candidate in acid. Harding, said the President, had a "bungalow mind."

Whatever the power of his intellectual light, in November Harding had little difficulty in crushing James Cox and Franklin Roosevelt. Immediately, he set out to recruit the best minds his party could offer. Old Guard senators supporting Andrew Mellon for Treasury balked at the selection of Hoover as Secretary of Commerce. Harding struck a defiant pose. "Mellon and Hoover," he informed his former colleagues, "or no Mellon." Late in February 1921, after securing the president-elect's promise that he would have a hand in all economic policy-making, and that other departments must yield to this remarkable power grab, Hoover accepted the job. The strongest figure in the new administration, he was assigned the most obscure department in government. Hoover saw it otherwise. Commerce, he reasoned, would provide the perfect training ground in which to perfect his vision of a society always advancing through individual genius and warmhearted co-operation.

★   ★

Who kept the Belgians' black bread buttered?
Who fed the world when millions muttered?
Who knows the needs of every nation?
Who keeps the keys of conservation?
Who fills the bins when mines aren't earning?
Who keeps the homefires banked and burning?
Who'll never win presidential position,
For he isn't a practical politician?
Hoover—that's all!

—"A Friend in Need," *Chicago Daily News*, 1923

Much later, when critics turned Hoover's presidency into a fable of failure, portraying the man himself as mired in the concrete of outworn convictions, it was easy to forget *American Individualism* and his seven and a half years at the Commerce Department. No such bout of amnesia affected his countrymen in the 1920s. Frederick Jackson Turner read Hoover's book and pronounced it "the platform on which all genuine Americans can stand, a noble statement of the fruits of our past and the promise of our future." The new secretary shared his optimism, as well as the historian's preoccupation with new frontiers for a restless, inventive people. Believing in the perfectibility of society, Hoover turned Commerce from a themeless hodgepodge of bureaucratic leftovers (wags described its pre-Hoover responsibilities as "turning out the lighthouses at night and putting the fish to bed") into a dynamic laboratory for his theory of a federal government eager to encourage private associations as the surest path to progress for all without domination by any—including Washington itself.

After 1929, much about his years at Commerce would assume an ironic tone. "There is no economic failure so terrible in its import," Hoover told the President's Conference on Unemployment in September 1921, a conference called at his urging, "as that of a country possessing a surplus of every necessity of life in which numbers willing and anxious to work, are deprived of dire necessities. It simply cannot be if our moral and economic system is to survive."

The president faulted for doing too little to combat the Depression had been a Cabinet officer criticized for doing too much. Coolidge especially accused "the wonder boy" of meddling in other agencies, from Agriculture to the Shipping Board. "He didn't care much whether he stepped on people's toes," one observer wrote of Hoover, "being anointed by God to save the country. What did the feelings of a few inadequate incompetents mean to him?" His relations with Congress a few years later were foreshadowed in such assessments.[43]

"The last three years have confirmed me in a constitutional objection to price-fixing in any form," Hoover told one associate in 1920 after grappling with the issue as Food Administrator. So why should it come as any surprise when Hoover as president clung stubbornly to the associational and voluntary ideals that had worked so gloriously for him in the past? More than a whirlwind of activity and a series of personal triumphs, the Commerce Department became for Hoover the frosting on a cake of almost miraculous dimensions. Outside his S Street home, made a striking mélange of black and gold by Lou (when not engaged in fund raising for the Girl Scouts or supervising her younger son's pet alligators, Mrs. Hoover found time to teach "Puss in the Corner" to the harem of a Burmese prince), Hoover promised neighborhood children twenty-five cents if they could stump him with a question. After his first few months at Commerce, few Americans would have been willing to make the wager.[44]

More than the product of any mere efficiency expert, Hoover's reorganization of his sleepy little enclave suggested a rare whiff of progressivism in Warren Harding's Washington. Eschewing White House poker games and the president's oratory—"Damn it," Harding demanded of his Commerce Secretary, "why don't you write the same English as I do?"—he insisted on restoring Civil Service protection throughout his department, added three thousand names to the Commerce payroll, expanded the Census Bureau into an informational treasure trove for business planners, and undertook at Harding's request a study of national petroleum reserves. Commerce added new divisions dealing with housing, radio (whose stations grew from two in 1921 to more than three hundred a year later) and aeronautics. Hoover played godfather to the Railway Labor Mediation Board in 1926, and dreamed of 9,000 miles of inland waterways. He regulated mine safety and negotiated a precedent-making compact among seven southwestern states squabbling over use of the Colorado River, dispatched explorers to South America to undermine British and Dutch monopolies of rubber, promoted environmental restrictions on oil slicks, and looked for ways to preserve the scenic splendor of Niagara Falls. Opposing the McNary-Haugen farm bill, Hoover devised his own alternative to price-fixing. It stressed farm exports and greater use of cooperatives to stem falling prices voluntarily.

Hoover was all for the individual, it was said, only in his case it meant the individual's right to sit on a committee. The gibe contained more than a kernel of truth, as the secretary presided over an endless round of public conferences and private think tanks, all designed to educate decision makers, inspire legislation or promote grass-roots cooperation. He became president of Better Homes for America, wrote a manual for prospective homeowners, and prodded 4,500 local chapters into lowering the average cost of a new home by a third. He churned out a new building code for municipalities—to be accepted voluntarily, of course. He convened a meeting of fishermen and oilmen to preserve Chesapeake Bay. He eased regulations on inventors seeking patents, raised on his own more than a million dollars to further scientific research, and in April 1927 saw his features and voice transmitted to New York over three telephone wires, in the first public demonstration of television. He snatched regulation of the "wireless telephone" away from the Bureau of Navigation and chaired four conferences devoted to the subject, where it was decided that radio licenses would be limited initially to three months, that certain bands would be set apart for public-service broadcasting, and that there would be no British style regimentation of the airwaves.

In the course of his activities, Hoover received an angry telegram from radio preacher Aimee Semple McPherson. "Please order your minions of Satan to leave my station alone," it commanded. "You cannot expect the Almighty to abide by your wavelength nonsense. When I offer my prayers to Him, I must fit in with His wave reception." Another religious sect asked Hoover for permission to build a station from which to disseminate warnings of the world's imminent end. He told them to spend their money for time on existing outlets; if the world was going to end in a month, it would be a far wiser investment.[45]

As befitting the man who added 1,386 miles of airways in a single year and insisted that all runways be equipped with landing lights, radio beams and other safety devices, Washington's first airfield was named for Hoover. Only in Franklin Roosevelt's presidency did it give way to National Airport. His Bureau of Fisheries saved Alaska's salmon from extinction, and after a friend obeying District of Columbia traffic regulations found himself in violation of twenty-four local ordinances en route to New York, the Secretary convened the first national conference on highway safety. In yet another of his highly publicized campaigns, Hoover exhorted American industry to standardize everything from milk bottles to gas meters. The only item not subject to Hoover's obsessive crusade to eliminate waste, he commented at the time, was the padlock key. By reducing manufacturing costs and bolstering productivity, standardization created jobs and made it easier for do-it-yourselfers to build a house or tighten a screw. Critics found fault with homogenized goods, and few Progressives seemed attuned to the deadly boredom of the assembly line, but Hoover was too engrossed in his vision of engineered prosperity to doubt the equation of conformity. "The man who has a standard electric light, a standard radio, and one and a half hours more daily leisure is more of a man," he concluded, "and has . . . more individuality than he has without these tools for varying his life."

All this deepened his faith in American generosity and know-how. Never was it more dramatically in evidence than in April 1927, when the Mississippi River rushed over its bank, obliterating 25,000 square miles under a sheet of yellow water, and leaving 350,000 people without shelter. Instantly, Hoover was on the scene. He was interested in one thing only, he remarked to one reporter who followed him downriver to Vicksburg, and that was human relief. In clipped sentences and round-the-clock interviews with eyewitnesses able to satisfy his hunger for terse reports, Hoover assessed the need. Then he acted, assembling an armada of 600 ships, ordering a trainload of feed from Chicago ("We'll settle this later"), requisitioning vast amounts of corn and tomatoes, organizing tent cities and brusquely telling one group of white businessmen that they would have to get up $5 million by the time his train left at 5 P.M. or he'd start shipping uncared-for blacks North that same night.[46]

"I suppose I could have called in the whole of the Army," he said later. "But what was the use? All I had to do was to call in Main Street itself." He visited ninety-one communities. In each, his message was the same: "A couple of thousand refugees are coming. They've got to have accommodations. Huts. Water-mains. Sewers. Streets. Dining-halls. Meals. Doctors. Everything. And you haven't got months to do it in. You haven't got weeks. You've got hours. That's my train."

Sinclair Lewis might disagree, but Hoover perceived nobility on Main Street. "No other Main Street in the world could have done what the American Main Street did in the Mississippi Flood," he said, "and Europe may jeer as it likes at our mass production and our mass organization and our mass education. The safety of the United States is its multitudinous mass leadership."

The statement might have reflected Hoover's unpleasant if poignant exposure to the dying Warren Harding, a man of relative values torn between loyalty to friends and his own pathetic desire to be at least a well-loved president. "In all the history of this government," Harding confessed to his Commerce Secretary cryptically, "there have only been three Cabinet officers who betrayed their chiefs, and two of them are in my Cabinet." The president's reference to Attorney General Harry Daugherty and Interior

Secretary Albert Fall was unmistakable. So was the anguish he felt on a trip to Alaska and the West Coast in July 1923. If he knew of a great scandal in the administration, Harding asked during a lull in the constant bridge games that provided his only refuge from Teapot Dome, what would he do for the good of the party and country?[47]

"Blow it out at once," Hoover replied. By itself, such an act would demonstrate Harding's basic integrity. The president seemed agreeable, but he was easily swayed, and he said nothing more to suggest a future course. Wrestling with his own conscience, Hoover seriously considered resignation. When Harding fell ill, his Commerce secretary sent for Ray Lyman Wilbur, Stanford's president and an eminent heart specialist. It was Wilbur who signed the death certificate on August 3, and Hoover who phoned Secretary of State Charles Evans Hughes to alert the vice president that he might legally be sworn into office by his father, a Vermont justice of the peace. "People do not die from a broken heart," Hoover concluded, "but people with bad hearts may reach the end much sooner from great worries." In a coincidence of history, the first reporter to learn of Harding's death was Steve Early, who twenty-two years later, as White House press secretary, would announce to the world the passing of Franklin Roosevelt.[48]

Hoover went back to Washington, past a multitude of grief-stricken faces and a hundred trackside renditions of "My Redeemer Liveth," the dead President's favorite hymn. Waiting for Hoover were his blueprints for a grandiose new Commerce building, off-the-record conferences interpreting the new administration for capital reporters and editors, and a steady drumbeat of promotion to convince Americans that their Commerce Secretary was infallible as well as ubiquitous. By 1928, managers for Hoover's preconvention rival Frank Lowden were complaining they couldn't find anything in the weekly press and small dailies but publicity for Hoover and Fletcher's Castoria.[49]

It was hard for thoughtful Americans in 1928 to conjure up anyone more ideally suited to be President. Hoover appeared more realistic than Wilson, more committed to excellence than Harding, more innovative than Coolidge, and more purely American than Al Smith. Dazzled by his achievements, few of his countrymen paused to investigate the price of success or calculate the odds on hero worship without hubris.

CHAPTER THREE

"WHAT RIGHT HAVE WE TO BE OF LITTLE FAITH?"

★

My friends have made the American people think me a sort of superman, able to cope successfully with the most difficult and complicated problems. . . . They expect the impossible of me and should there arise in the land conditions with which the political machinery is unable to cope, I will be the one to suffer.
—Herbert Hoover, December 1928

The very stars seem to have turned in their courses to make your path difficult. . . .   —Henry L. Stimson, December 1930

★

After March 1933 cast him as black bishop to Roosevelt's white knight, Hoover protested the injustice of it all. "Please do not use me as a whipping boy for the New Era," he asked Dorothy Thompson. "I was neither the inventor nor the promoter nor the supporter of the destructive currents of that period. I was the 'receiver' of it when it went into collapse." His 1928 campaign against Al Smith suggested otherwise. "Hoover and Happiness or Smith and Soup Houses," ran one GOP slogan. It was a contest of optimists, "engineer against engineer," to the *New York Times,* in which two self-made men celebrated the glories of individualistic America, and obscured from the electorate their own deeply conservative preferences. Smith's national chairman was a General Motors executive named John J. Raskob, who touched his wealthy friends for more than $5 million in campaign contributions. While Hoover privately warned the Coolidge administration about "this fever of speculation," Raskob was sanguine. "Anyone not only can be rich but ought to be rich," he insisted. Smith himself said nothing to suggest disagreement.

The fall campaign was not devoid of controversy. On the contrary, it was poisoned by whispers about Smith's Catholicism and doctored photos of the Republican candidate dancing with a black woman during his Mississippi flood relief. Hoover denounced his party's national committeewoman from Virginia after she called on American women to hold standfast against the alien forces of Rome and rum. "It does violence to every instinct that I possess," he told the New York World on September 19. "I resent and repudiate it." He could not prevent the Reverend Bob Jones, Senior, from delivering more than a thousand speeches on the theme that no Catholic should ever be elected president, nor restrain supporters who labeled New York's Lincoln Tunnel Smith's direct conduit to the Vatican.

The mudslinging was, in classic fashion, bipartisan. Hoover had to contend with stories dredging up his Chinese labor and financial dealings, and Missouri Senator James Reed's persistent allegation (delivered in appropriately tweedy accent) that he was actually a British citizen. In Jersey City, burglars broke into Hoover's headquarters one night and stole records and voting lists. In retrospect the candidate might have judged his own supporters criminally excessive in their claims.

"He sweeps the horizon of every subject," proclaimed John L. McNab in nominating the Commerce Secretary at the Republicans' Kansas City convention. "Nothing escapes his view. His trained mind marshals every factor and where he proposes a remedy it neglects nothing the omission of which would disturb the final solution." Other advocates found parallels between George Washington's surveying career and Hoover's as an engineer. The Los Angeles Times was reassured by the candidate's mathematical training: the presidency, it concluded, was too important an office for mere emotionalism. Bruce Barton, the New York ad man who created a name for himself by calling Christ "a startling example of executive success," summed up the feelings of many. Imagining himself a prospective employer, Barton was blunt. "I might get more fun out of having Smith around, but I'd make more money with Hoover."

Even liberals, nominally pro-Smith, could find little to disqualify the Secretary of Commerce. According to Walter Lippmann, Hoover was a reformer himself "who is probably more vividly conscious of the defects of American capitalism than any man in public life today" and who would, if given a chance, "purify capitalism of its predatoriness, its commercialism, its waste, and its squalor."

Hoover did nothing to dampen such hopes. Accepting his party's nomination on August 11, before 60,000 cheering supporters in Stanford's football stadium, he pointed the way to future prosperity without ever mentioning his rival. During the previous eight years, he noted, Americans had built 3.5 million new homes, installed electricity in 9 million more, purchased 6 million telephones, 7 million radios and 14 million automobiles. "Upon . . . material progress as a base," claimed Hoover, "we are erecting a structure of idealism," and he called for a shorter workday, additional public works, and "hundreds of millions of dollars" in relief for hardpressed farmers whose median income in 1928 was less than $600. "Given a chance to go forward with the policies of the last eight years," he continued, "we shall soon with the help of God be in sight of the day when poverty will be banished from this nation."

In foreign policy he struck a similarly elevated tone. "We have no hates," Hoover declared. "We wish no further possessions. We harbor no military threats." He committed himself to the enforcement of Prohibition, "an experiment noble in motive and far reaching in purpose"—a statement Smith twisted into permanent misrepresentation and Mrs. Franklin D. Roosevelt judged "a very wise thing." The rest of his campaign polished the theme of a New Day. "The bitter opposition to improved methods on the ancient theory that it more than temporarily deprives men of employment," he told a crowd at Newark, New Jersey, in mid-September, "has no place in the gospel of American progress." He promised to create a Federal Farm Board and endorsed economic regulation to smooth out business cycles, without venturing far enough to the left to satisfy farm state liberals like Nebraska's George Norris.

Unable to hold Norris in his camp, the Republican nominee won the endorsements of Thomas Edison, Henry Ford and Charles Lindbergh. Many workingmen agreed with the titans of industry: Hoover meant good times. At Madison Square Garden on October 22, the candidate glimpsed a promised and prosperous land. "In seven years we have added seventy percent to the electric power at the elbows of our workers and further promoted them from carriers of burden to directors of machines. We have steadily reduced the sweat in human labor. Our hours of labor are lessened; our leisure has increased. We have expanded our parks and playgrounds. . . . According to insurance actuaries since the recent war we have lengthened the average span of life by nearly eight years. We have reduced infant mortality. . . ."

Sandwiching it in among his statistics, Hoover told his New York audience that America's bounties resulted from her conscious decision at the end of the war to reject the temporary regimentation imposed by the fighting. "We were challenged with a peacetime choice," he continued, in words that later dogged his steps, "between the American system of rugged individualism and a European philosophy of diametrically opposed doctrines— doctrines of paternalism and state socialism." Drawing on his own experiences, Hoover denounced the "false liberalism that interprets itself into the government operation of commercial business. Every step of bureaucratizing the business of our country poisons the very roots of liberalism; that is, political equality, free speech, free assembly, free press, and equality of opportunity."

Confronted with a heroic opponent, who took credit for prosperity while vowing to eliminate society's imperfections, Smith's supporters fell back on ethnic and religious appeals of their own. One of the most imaginative, Franklin Roosevelt, portrayed Hoover as the radical and Smith as the true friend of business. "Mr. Hoover has always shown a most disquieting desire to investigate everything and to appoint commissions and send out statistical inquiries on every conceivable subject under Heaven," FDR informed one prospective ally in New York's financial circle. "He has also shown in his own Department a most alarming desire to issue regulations and to tell businessmen generally how to conduct their affairs. . . ." At least one Hoover friend attributed to FDR an unfounded report that both men had attended a dinner at which the supposedly abstemious Hoover became intoxicated.[1]

Whoever tried to sell Hoover as less than he seemed, voters weren't buying. On Election Day, they gave the Republican 58 percent of the popular tally and 444 electoral votes to Smith's 87. In the Deep South, where Republicanism had been equated for sixty years with carpetbaggery, Hoover succeeded in making Smith the carpetbagger. Virginia, Texas, Tennessee and Florida joined GOP ranks. So did New York, and the agrarian Midwest, despite rural discontent that found vocal expression in a dozen rebellious members of the new Senate's nominally Republican majority.

The Hoovers spent election night on San Juan Hill, serenaded by John Philip Sousa and a student throng that sang chorus after chorus of the Stanford alma mater, "From the Foothills to the Bay." Overhead, a plane dropped bombs of red, white and blue stars. Inside, Hoover himself struck the only discordant note of an otherwise joyous evening. "He might have conceded three hours ago," the victorious candidate muttered when Smith's congratulatory telegram arrived, "or even three months ago."[2]

Three days later, Hoover discarded another tradition, announcing his intention to visit eleven Latin American nations prior to his inauguration. On a ship off Rio de Janeiro, the president-elect discovered medicine ball.

He took to the sport with relish. Less successful was his foray into diplomacy. The journey went well, but Hoover betrayed faulty judgment in selecting South American heroes. Exceptionally gifted—so he judged Peru's strongman President Augusto Leguía, sure to remain in power for as far as his American admirer could see. Two years later, Leguía was deposed and placed under arrest.[3]

Back in Washington, conservatives worried about Coolidge's headstrong successor. Chief Justice Taft was one. The president-elect, Taft confided to his diary, was a "dreamer" with "some rather grandiose ideas" about the roles of government and the presidency itself in setting the national agenda. Others thought differently. Bruce Barton told a Hoover friend that when Coolidge took office, few expected anything more than bare-bones administration, "and anything that he did was in consequence hailed with delight." For Hoover, Barton concluded, a different standard prevailed. "People expect more of you than they have of any other President."[4]

In his Inaugural Address, Hoover gave credence to Old Guard fears and hope to the Bartons. "Our first object must be to provide security from poverty and want," he declared to a nationwide radio audience. "We want to see a nation built of homeowners and farmowners. We want to see their savings protected. We want to see them in steady jobs. We want to see more and more of them insured against death and accident, unemployment and old age. We want them all secure." Hoover described America on March 4, 1929, as "filled with millions of happy homes; blessed with comfort and opportunity. In no nation are the fruits of accomplishment more secure. In no nation is the government more worthy of respect. . . . I have no fears for the future of our country. It is bright with hope."

As a man of broad but practical interests, Hoover probably had little exposure to Attic tragedy, wherein Hubris was overthrown by Nemesis and Darius's ghost warned against complacency. "Pride that has blossomed bears the fruit of ruin," it cautioned. Aeschylus put it more pointedly still, in words out of place at the new president's inaugural, but lurking offstage, eager to interrupt a carefully scripted triumph. "There is an old saying among men that great prosperity engenders insatiable woe."

★　　★

True to his instincts, Hoover's first months in office were a whirlwind of reform. Not since Woodrow Wilson, declared the *New Republic*, had so decisive a leader set the nation's priorities. Within thirty days of his inaugural, the new executive announced an expansion of Civil Service protection throughout the federal establishment, declared open warfare on his own party's rotten boroughs in the South, canceled private oil leases on government lands, and issued an executive order opening records of substantial tax refunds. He directed federal law-enforcement officials to focus their efforts on gangster-ridden Chicago, where Al Capone held sway, pledged support to a new immigration policy, and launched his Commission on Conservation and Administration of the Public Domain under James Garfield, once Theodore Roosevelt's militantly conservationist Interior Secretary. In its report, the Garfield Commission called for increased commitment to national parks and wildlife refuges and simultaneously proposed returning grazing lands to state control. The latter idea caused an uproar among some conservationists, and Congress ignored most of Garfield's findings.

Late in May, the President announced another commission, this time to examine under the chairmanship of George Wickersham law enforcement in general and Prohibition in particular. In June he signed the Agricultural Marketing Act, fulfilling a campaign promise to farmers. He used his famed powers of persuasion to populate the eight-member Federal Farm Board charged with carrying out the act designed to build a floor under farm prices by making loans to cooperatives and purchasing surplus crops outright if necessary. At least two of the board's new members abandoned annual incomes of more than a hundred thousand dollars to serve the people. Washington cynics might sneer at "Hoover patriots," but the public and much of the press responded enthusiastically to the new administration and its outreach to the nation's best minds. "The White House has become a positive force," commented Roy Roberts of the *Kansas City Star*.

Planning for the future was a Hoover fetish. The president directed one of his assistants to gather information on how to reorganize all ten of the government's major departments. Another he put in charge of a committee analyzing social trends in America. Hoover's Bureau of Reclamation prepared blueprints for a series of dams in the Tennessee Valley and central California. His view was not restricted to the domestic arena. Henry Stimson, Hoover's Secretary of State, expressed astonishment at the new president's grasp of foreign policy. Hoover, he confided to his diary, had forgotten more about the world than most diplomats, himself included, had ever learned. Together, the two men embarked on a new day in hemispheric relations, withdrawing U.S. troops from Haiti and Nicaragua and publicly pledging Washington to noninterference in the internal affairs of Latin America. In place of the Monroe Doctrine, Hoover mediated a border dispute between Chile and Peru and negotiated treaties of arbitration or conciliation with forty-two countries.

Returning his gaze to the home front, Hoover asked a citizens committee to examine the question of a new federal Department of Education. He ordered the army to cut expenditures to the bone, made public for the first time all endorsers of candidates for federal judgeships, stepped in to prevent a Texas rail strike, and called for sharp reductions in income taxes, graduated to favor low-income Americans. Early in June, the president unveiled plans for a White House Conference on Child Health and Protection, met with GOP congressmen opposing his tariff revisions, and congratulated those who shared his "long view" about agriculture.

"I know there is not a thinking farmer," he told the first session of the Federal Farm Board, "who does not realize that all this cannot be accomplished by a magic wand or an overnight action. Real institutions are not built that way. If we are to succeed it will be by strengthening the foundations and the initiative which we already have in farm organizations, and building steadily upon them with the constant thought that we are building not for the present only but for the next year and the next decade."

"The Kind Lord certainly continues to shower his blessings and support upon your administration," Roy Roberts informed the White House on July 27. In just two months, wheat prices had risen to $1.25 a bushel. Similar increases in cattle and hog prices gave Hoover at least a breathing space in which to pursue his program, Roberts continued, ". . . the biggest break in the world out west." [5]

As the summer of 1929 cooled, Hoover's ardor for the reform did not. "The President now has several very definite plans to advance several great social causes," his secretary and literary assistant French Strother informed philanthropist Julius Rosenwald that July. "As of course you know, he has been studying these matters for years, doing meanwhile what he could in them, and crystallizing his thought about them, hoping for his present great opportunity to give them the backing of the Presidency. Now he is ready to proceed." As one familiar with Hoover's "practical methods," surely Rosenwald would appreciate the significance of the forthcoming national conferences on the Home and Children's Health. Could the generous-minded millionaire see his way to funding part or all of another such meeting, in the spirit of the president himself, to review the recreational needs of the American people at a time when industrialists like Owen Young of General Electric were forecasting a six- or even four-hour workday in the not-too-distant future? [6]

On his own, Hoover undertook a $5 billion program to redirect federal prisons. No more would they resemble Dickensian hovels; the new facility at Lewisburg, Pennsylvania, with its own chapel and modern library, reflected the president's taste for humane treatment and rehabilitation. In a similar vein, he sought to heal the gaping breach dividing the white man from the red, dismissing an insensitive Commissioner of Indian Affairs and stressing vocational skills as well as traditional arts and crafts as the basis for a revived Indian economy. Early in September, Hoover's stock rose higher still, after his public derision of shipbuilding companies that he charged were spending vast sums on propaganda to sway the public against armaments reduction. On the sixteenth, the President lunched with insurance executives and sought their cooperation in devising old-age pensions, the first step toward his plan to pay $50 a month to Americans above the age of sixty-five.

His wife was equally uncomfortable with the status quo. Not until Jacqueline Kennedy entered the White House thirty-two years later would a First Lady lavish so much time and energy on the old house. At her own expense Lou hired Signal Corps photographers to snap every piece of furniture in the place. A book on White House furnishings was projected, but never published. She covered floors with rugs picked up on the South America trip and discovered some of Dolly Madison's chairs, only to have her husband crush one with his bulk and shout while lying flat on his back, "Lou, didn't I tell you not to inflict Dolly's chairs on our guests?" Lou also paid for reproductions of James Monroe's elegant fixtures, located in the Fredericksburg law office of the fifth president, turned the second floor West Hall into a gracious room filled with bookcases and palms, and launched a massive campaign to transform the shabby first floor into a suitable showcase for American art and antiques. She seemed pleased when Helen Keller called, identifying a bust of George Washington by running her fingers over it and crawling on her hands and knees to touch the Great Seal woven into a foyer rug. Lou brought great musicians into the East Room, patronized concerts at the nearby Pan-American Union, and achieved personal elegance with combs in her hair and the rhinestones so admired by her younger son, Allan.[7]

Contrary to later reports, Lou was protective of her thirty-two servants. She told the director of an asylum at Fourteenth and Upshur streets that if he couldn't take proper care of a White House butler suffering from tuberculosis then she would see to it that he was replaced with someone who could. Staff members with the flu found food dispatched to them from the White House kitchens. Maggie Rogers was given brown bread for her blood pressure, and Rogers's daughter Lillian received cookies from the White House Christmas tree and a ride in the presidential elevator as Lou's husband waited for the young seamstress, a polio victim, to reach her destination. The Hoovers personally paid the tab for staff meals; the president instructed the domestic staff not to rise from their table when he entered the kitchen.

Another butler, unable on his monthly wage of $80 to afford cream and milk for his ulcers, was astounded to find them delivered to his house nonetheless, courtesy of Mrs. Hoover, who also offered to pay the college bills of a White House maid.[8]

Privately, the First Lady still preferred the outdoor life of Camp Rapidan to dinners for visiting royalty. The White House exacted much from her, not least of all time alone with her increasingly embattled husband. In the evening, a formally clad president dined with guests and drank White Rock water from a bottle wrapped in a towel, champagne style. Only three times during their first three years in the White House was the pattern of public entertaining broken—on their February 10 anniversary date. A resourceful woman, Lou was more accustomed than her cook to small affairs that turned into last-minute mob scenes. "White House Supreme" was one such culinary improvisation, croquettes of ham, beef, lamb and whatever else the housekeeper could find in the refrigerator when her planned menu of chops for four had to be converted into a repast for forty.[9]

Through it all, Lou maintained her composure. On Sunday mornings, before attending services in the Friends meetinghouse supplied with a preacher recruited by the president (and providing her husband with the $5 for the collection he often forgot), she worked on a book for the Girl Scouts. "Worthy" friends, many of them active in the scout movement, were always enlisting her support in finding a job, and Lou paid special attention to the urgent appeals for help that were sprinkled throughout her mail—"fire alarms," she called them.[10]

Staff members were instructed to make awed visitors to the White House feel at home. "Well, don't ever worry," Lou told a youthful assistant concerned with protocol. "You just always do what will make the other fellow feel comfortable, at ease, and then you will be all right." On June 12, 1929, the Green Room was a very uncomfortable place. Among the First Lady's guests for tea that afternoon was Mrs. Oscar De Priest, wife of a black congressman from Chicago and unwilling storm-center of a national dispute. Southern editors denounced Mrs. Hoover for "defiling" the presidential residence. The Texas legislature publicly rebuked her. Some of Mrs. De Priest's fellow guests refused to shake her hand. But Lou carried the occasion off with dignity, sitting next to the woman in a blue georgette while a black butler barely contained his own astonishment over the turn of events. The incident caused the sensitive Lou much grief, about which her husband consoled her by explaining that one of the great advantages of holding to orthodox religion was "that it included a hot hell." Cruel journalists and politicians would find "special facilities in the world to come," he promised.

He also tried to shift the criticism in his own direction by inviting R. R. Moton, president of Tuskegee Institute in Alabama, to become the first black dinner guest at the White House since Theodore Roosevelt asked Moton's predecessor, Booker T. Washington, thirty years earlier.[11]

Lou's burden grew with the illness of her older son, confined to an Asheville tubercular sanitarium for ten months. The president could spare time for only a single visit to the boy he called Bub, but his wife made the journey more often, and both took pains to guarantee the privacy of Herbert, Junior's, wife Peggy and their grandchildren. Advisers wanted the youngsters brought into the spotlight, if only to humanize the dour chief executive, but he flatly refused. After a promising start the president had seen his relationship with the press go into a tailspin. Larry Richey, who reminded one Hoover associate of a mother hen with a single chick, hid the Chief behind a stone wall of inaccessibility, and kept a "blacklist" of former supporters who had subsequently turned against Hoover. Barely a month into his term, the president himself criticized journalists for violating confidences and lost his temper over trivial exaggerations, such as the time reporters covering his weekend on the Rapidan wrote that he had caught eighteen fish during a thunderstorm. It hadn't rained at all, an angry Hoover informed the press. He didn't want himself or his angling exploits magnified, and if such misreporting persisted he wouldn't hesitate to do something about it.[12]

His distaste for personal publicity was coupled with a shallow understanding of executive-congressional relations. Legislators might win Hoover's attention; they never earned his respect. Accustomed to having his orders followed by a small band of devoted admirers, the president suffered through the special session of Congress he called in April 1929. His farm legislation required seven weeks to pass. Tariff reform came harder still, and then without the authority he demanded to change rates by up to 50 percent.

When the Hawley-Smoot tariff was finally adopted over the objections of more than a thousand leading economists in June 1930, it turned out a perversion of the modest reforms sought by Hoover. The proposed bill mandated to Congress, and not the president, authority to make tariff revisions, a clause eliminated only after Hoover threatened to veto the entire package. As it stood, Hawley-Smoot raised import duties on raw materials by up to 100 percent and hurt American consumers by stifling the flow of cheaper goods. It also raised a permanent wall against trade at a time when desperate worldwide conditions demanded an end to such barriers. Other lands soon retaliated and a locust storm of economic nationalism engulfed the globe.

Hoover's miracle-worker image began to erode. His administrative talents were transformed into a taste for personal dictation. His commissions inspired fear instead of confidence. "Tentacles of the commission octupus will be seen swarming out from the White House to the Capitol," prophesied the usually friendly *New York Herald Tribune* early in 1930, "the liberties of the people will be in danger, the Constitution will be on its deathbed, our republican institutions will be seen falling before an oligarchy of scientists, professors, specialists, and technologists." The presidential honeymoon was suddenly threatened with annulment as Congress rejected Hoover's idea of yet another commission, this time to implement the recommendations of George Wickersham's study group, and the Senate Foreign Relations Committee turned down a presidential investigation of conditions in Haiti.

Hoover went to Capitol Hill in December 1929, where he called for a Federal Power Commission, federal subsidies to county health units, a rural child health program, reform of railroad rates and the banking system, new prisons and the extension of Civil Service protection to tri-level postmasters. Two weeks later, in the face of mounting attacks, he explained his penchant for appointing expert bodies—and his contempt for political swashbuckling.

"The most dangerous animal in the United States," Hoover told the Gridiron Club on December 14, "is the man with an emotion and a desire to pass a new law. He is prolific with drama and the headlines. . . . The greatest antidote for him is to set him upon a committee with a dozen people whose appetite is for facts." Such talk bewildered a Congress already badly split between Old Guard Republicans, instinctively distrustful of Hoover as an intellectual whirling dervish, and insurgent members of the GOP, disappointed by the President's agricultural policies and willing to make common cause with minority Democrats, even if the result was embarrassment for the nonpolitician occupying the White House.

Admittedly lacking in partisan skills (insiders cracked that Attorney General William Mitchell, a Democrat, had at least supported the GOP in 1920 and 1924—which made him more of a Republican then his boss), Hoover permitted himself to be outmaneuvered on the tariff issue, and his own Senate majority leader, Indiana's Jim Watson, openly boasted that he did not talk with Hoover, he talked at him. What he said was not always heard. Hoover refused to heed Watson's warning to withdraw the Supreme Court nomination of North Carolina's John J. Parker in the spring of 1930, after labor and black groups mounted a campaign against Parker for early statements avowing his white supremacist convictions. Hoover turned a deaf ear to the plea and suffered a humiliating defeat on the Senate floor. Like Jimmy Carter, another engineer, he failed to understand the fragile ego of subordinate elected officials. Congressmen who called at the White House were annoyed to find the President staring at the ceiling or out the window instead of at them. "I think he's afraid we Senators will influence him," concluded one member of the upper body, "and he doesn't want to get under our influence." [13]

Policy played as big a role as personality in estranging lawmakers from the White House. Isolationists and militarists alike bridled at Hoover's Rapidan Camp meeting in October 1929 with Ramsay MacDonald, which set the stage for a naval disarmament conference in London early the next year. Most of the key points in the final agreement had their genesis in a conversation between the president and prime minister, held while sitting on a log besides the Rapidan on October 6. (Years later, Harold Ickes would point to a pool at Camp Rapidan and tell his traveling companion, Hiram Johnson, "Now right here is where they sank the fleet.") Six months later, Britain, the U.S. and Japan agreed to reduce their armaments and accept a 5–5–3 ratio of naval strength. The people cheered their president. A Victrola attached to a microphone boomed out "Hail to the Chief" at the World Series in Philadelphia that October, and thousands gave Hoover a standing ovation. The Senate was less enthusiastic about the treaty, but Hoover demanded a special session, and on July 22, 1930, he affixed his signature to the agreement he hoped "will mark a further step toward lifting the burden of militarism from the backs of mankind." [14]

His early burst of activity and the incessant headlines that poured from Hoover's White House inspired comparisons with Theodore Roosevelt. But Hoover was no T.R. He was a strategist of decency, not a pounder of the bully pulpit. In his heart he must have regretted the protectionist tariff he signed into law in the summer of 1930. Yet he stubbornly refused to acknowledge its imperfections. A friendly industrialist cast aside the president's feeble arguments that the bill had been rendered less objectionable than it might have been. What did it matter that Hoover found the bill marginally acceptable when the country found it pernicious? And what of the president's own function as a leader and educator of men? Hoover stopped his doodling. In a voice that barely carried beyond his desk, he justified his actions while apologizing for them. "I'm afraid you'll have to give me up," he remarked to his erstwhile admirer. "I can never be the sort of man you want me to be."

October 1929 began as a month when Hoover's imperfections were as well concealed as the rickety state of the nation's economy. At midmonth, the president boarded a train bound for Henry Ford's recreated museum of Americana at Greenfield Village, just outside Detroit, to pay homage to Thomas Edison on the fiftieth anniversary of his invention of the electric light. On board an exact replica of the car in which a youthful Edison had once sold newspapers and candy, Hoover relaxed, jocularly ordering a peach from the old man. He looked on as Edison recreated the fateful moment in which an old carbon filament lamp blazed to life, and at a banquet in Edison's honor on the twenty-first, the chief executive sounded a note of national pride. By his own genius and industry, the inventor had risen from modest beginnings to "membership among the leaders of men. His life gives renewed confidence that our institutions hold open the door of opportunity to all those who would enter."

Edison himself was less impressed. "I am tired of glory," he told his son, Charles. "I want to get back to work." But the nation would not permit him to escape deification. Nor could Hoover have overlooked the similarities between the scruffy newsboy from Milan, Ohio, and the ore digger from West Branch. For both, Light's Golden Jubilee seemed a confirmation of their social and economic faith. Within a week heroes and commandments alike would tumble from their secure places, and reputations would vanish like rain through a grate.

★   ★

Hoover took office confident of his mandate for change, but concerned about economic speculation he called "crazy and dangerous." He worried out loud to Mark Sullivan about Wall Street gambling, in part the result of the Federal Reserve's policy of deliberately keeping interest rates low in order to aid floundering European banks. During his first frenetic weeks in the White House, he found time to order a reluctant Andrew Mellon before reporters, to urge the purchase of bonds instead of stocks. He sent Henry Robinson, a Los Angeles banker and longtime friend, to convey a cautionary message to the financiers of Wall Street—and received for his pains a long, scoffing memorandum from Thomas W. Lamont of J. P. Morgan and Company. When the Federal Reserve Board that same month took steps to check the flow of speculative credit, Charles E. Mitchell of New York's National City Bank defied Washington, promising to make $100 million of credit freely available. Angered, Hoover let stock exchange president Richard Whitney (in 1938 convicted of embezzling funds from the New York Yacht Club) know he was thinking of regulatory steps to curb stock manipulation and other excesses. Yet he undercut his own threat by placing ultimate responsibility for such drastic measures on New York's new governor, Franklin Roosevelt. Having exerted influence behind the scenes, the president settled for an order to his Justice Department to prosecute market tipsters who used the mails to stir an already bubbling cauldron. Hoover had his own reasons for discouraging the fever gripping Wall Street: his conscience was pained after a friend took his advice to buy an issue that nose-dived. "To clear myself," he later told intimates, "I just bought it back and I have never advised anybody since."[15]

By early September the market was topping out, 82 points above its January first plateau. General Electric hit 396, triple its paper value of eighteen months before. Other blue chips enjoyed similar popularity, fueled by more than $8 billion in brokers' loans. Six weeks later, a series of convulsions set in, exploding the New Era and exposing an economy jerry-built upon predatory instincts. On one day, October 24, radio stock lost 40 percent of its worth. Montgomery Ward surrendered 33 points. Steel stocks declined despite the efforts of Mitchell, Lamont and Whitney to brake their fall. Hoover reassured the doubters. "The fundamental business of the country," he declared the next day, "that is, production and distribution, is on a sound and prosperous basis." Only 4 percent of America's families, claimed Assistant Commerce Secretary Julius Klein at month's end, were affected by the sudden break.

Others agreed. Rockefeller, the House of Morgan and John J. Raskob let it be known that they were buying stocks. The *New York Times* and the American Federation of Labor forecast at worst a temporary slump. The president was less optimistic, his public statements notwithstanding. He said as much to a group of industrialists he summoned to the White House on November 21, part of a round-robin of conferences with business, labor and agricultural leaders. Using the word "depression" to describe current conditions, Hoover predicted a prolonged period of hardship, estimated the number of jobless at two to three million, and asked for cooperation from all sides to prevent the liquidation of labor that had accompanied every previous panic. Most of all, he wanted the line held on wages, an extraordinary demand given the boom and bust theories then prevailing. Instead of allowing deflation to take its toll in jobs, Hoover now moved to stimulate employment, through voluntary pledges from business and a hefty increase in public works and other construction spending.

On November 27 the president of the National Electric Light Association promised Hoover that his organization's membership would spend at least $110 million over and above its healthy investment of 1929. Railroad executives vowed a similar commitment. Organized labor agreed to withdraw its latest wage demands. Henry Ford actually boosted wages and cut prices on his new models. Five thousand approving telegrams deluged the White House. Most echoed the sentiment of Julius Klein, who called Hoover's unprecedented actions "prosperity insurance."

In drawing up a federal response to the crisis of confidence on Wall Street, Hoover combined vigor with restraint. He appealed to all forty-eight governors for a speedup in public works projects in their states. He recommended to Congress a doubling of resources for public buildings and dams, highways and harbors, coupled with a tax cut and a lowering of the federal discount rate. In December his friend Julius Barnes of the U.S. Chamber of Commerce presided over the first meeting of the National Business Survey Conference, a task force of four hundred leading businessmen whom Hoover designated to enforce the voluntary agreements.

As in the past, the president turned to publicity to dispel fear from millions of homes. A conference was organized in January 1930 to convince the public that times were especially ripe for homebuilding. Later that year, with breadlines lengthening, the President's Emergency Committee for Employment was created, with three thousand local chapters coordinating grass-roots relief and resorting to public exhortation to lift Americans by their bootstraps. "Spruce Up Your Home" campaigns were organized, under much the same leadership as Hoover had called upon eight years earlier, during the postwar slump of 1921–22. A Cabinet Committee on Employment was formed under Commerce Secretary Robert Lamont. The Farm Board was directed to cushion wheat and cotton prices, and in April of 1930, Hoover secured $150 million for his crash public works program.

By then, what was later dubbed the Little Bull Market had restored much of the confidence dissipated the previous autumn.

Praise for the president's intervention, so much greater than any measures taken by Van Buren, Cleveland or T.R., was widespread. "No one in his place could have done more," judged the New York Times that spring. "Very few of his predecessors could have done as much." The New York Herald Tribune lauded Hoover's "cool and superlative leadership." By February 18, Hoover was able to announce that the preliminary shock had abated, that over half the outstanding market loans had been liquidated without panic, and that the employment index was showing marked improvement from its 86 percent level of the previous December. Three weeks later, he predicted an end to the economic crisis within sixty days. "We have now passed the worst," he announced at the end of two months, "and with continued unity of effort we shall rapidly recover." The Harvard Business School agreed. When a delegation of bishops and bankers called at the White House early in June to warn Hoover of spreading unemployment, he reminded them of his productive conferences with business and labor, and surveyed the wide range of government activities, from shipbuilding to road grading, all working smoothly to prevent just such suffering. "Gentlemen," he concluded, "you have come six weeks too late." On June 19, William Green of the AFL concurred. Employment, he said, was once again on the rise.

Both men were wrong. Convinced that the recession had its roots in Wall

Street, and buoyed by the wage agreements he had won from industry, Hoover overlooked the fundamental weaknesses of an economic system sliding toward disaster. For one thing, American prosperity was largely bogus, limited to the 5 percent of the population that controlled at least one-third of the nation's wealth. For the average worker in 1929, his income less than $1,500, wages failed to keep pace with the spectacular gains in productivity that marked the decade. Now, with the postwar building boom a thing of the past, with 26 million new cars glutting America's roads, and with other, equally desirable consumer goods flooding the market, production had become embarrassingly overextended. Consumer debt also grew; easily carried in a time of limitless prosperity, it became a mill weight around the neck of an economy staggered by its own excesses.

Hoover's celebration of technology hadn't counted on a day of reckoning. Yet technological advances hadn't been matched by higher wages, shorter hours or restrictions on the employment of women and children, some of whom continued to labor up to 70 hours a week in southern textile mills. When unemployment resulted—and there was plenty of it throughout the twenties—buying power simply disappeared. The Individualizing Society had yet to devise insurance for the jobless or income maintenance for the destitute. The twenties had been bad for organized labor; unions lost a third of their membership during a decade reserved for business. Consolidation accompanied the march of progress. By 1929, a fifth of the country's retail trade belonged to chain stores like Woolworth, Sears and A&P. Thousands of smaller firms vanished, gobbled up by competitors or merged into giant holding companies. There were too many banks (a position Hoover himself argued. It was, he told a friend in February 1932, "a banker's depression," although greatly worsened by Britain's decision to abandon the gold standard), and too many of them played the stock market with depositors' funds, or speculated in their own stocks. Too few, one-third at most, belonged to the Federal Reserve System, on which Hoover placed such reliance. International trade was out of balance. Agriculture was deprived of the cash it needed to take part in the consumer revolution. High tariffs worsened the plight of debtor nations and discouraged exports of U.S. goods.[16]

All this was temporarily drowned out by the throbbing tickers of Wall Street. Yet Hoover persisted throughout the first half of 1930 in seeing the setback as limited in its effects. At that, he was much more energetic in his prescriptions for recovery than Secretary Mellon, who urged complete liquidation. A panic might not be such a bad thing, concluded the man his admirers called the greatest Secretary of the Treasury since Alexander Hamilton. "It will purge the rottenness out of the system," he told Hoover.

"High costs of living and high living will come down. People will work harder, live a moral life. Values will be adjusted, and enterprising people will pick up the wrecks from less competent people."[17]

This was a far cry from the president's critique of "the arbitrary and dog-eat-dog attitude of the business world of some thirty or forty years ago." To the American Bankers Association in October 1930, Hoover denounced "economic fatalists" and insisted that the pestilence of depression was not inevitable or beyond control by what he called "the genius of modern business." Neither would he accept the defeatist notion that Americans were doomed to lower living standards. To do so, Hoover said, would be to condone "perpetual unemployment and . . . a cesspool of poverty for some large part of our people." But Mellon was not alone in falling victim to conventional wisdom—or personal self-righteousness. With economic conditions clearly worsening, Hoover fell back on what came naturally. He appealed to the better natures of industry and labor, called for voluntary cooperation to stem the downward spiral, resorted to publicity and optimistic statements to contain Wall Street's infection before it could poison the rest of America.

Disagreeing with the strategy, financier Bernard Baruch turned down an invitation to join the parade of optimists. You could no more stop the liquidation of prosperity with words, Baruch explained, than Al Smith could halt Niagara Falls with his brown derby. The administration itself acknowledged 4.5 million people out of work in 1930; Cleveland Trust used different criteria and came up with a figure of 6 million. In August, a terrible drought settled in on the Great Plains, sucking the life from farmers' crops and draining off every dollar Hoover's Farm Board could pump into the fields. Hoover canceled a planned western visit—he didn't see his California home once in four years—and remained in Washington to coordinate a program of locally administered relief efforts, coupled with $45 million in federal loans for seed purchases. Immigration was curtailed, and deportation laws applied strictly, but recovery receded and Democrats reaped a bountiful harvest in the 1930 congressional elections by accusing the White House of having caused or prolonged the panic. Things weren't helped by the sudden resignation of Republican National Chairman Claude Hart Houston, the second of four men to hold the post during Hoover's term. Houston acknowledged using lobbyists' funds to carry stock market speculation. His successor, Ohio's Simeon Fess, claimed that there was no such thing as a depression sweeping America. On Election Day, the voters said otherwise.

Apple sellers began to appear on urban street corners that fall. For all the pledges of new construction, actual contracts plummeted by 25 percent.

Instead of stabilizing wages, Hoover's compact with industrial America led
to fewer jobs. Long before U.S. Steel broke ranks with a 10 percent wage
cut in September 1931, building trades officials in Chicago and St. Louis
were reporting three-fourths of their members out of work. Early in 1932 the
president himself joined the rush. He took a 20 percent reduction in salary
—a salary he had already refused. The Cabinet and White House staff
followed suit. Hoover donated $10,000 a year to San Francisco's Board of
Welfare, anonymously, of course. He raised a quarter of a million more to
assist the families of destitute miners—only to rail at the beneficiaries later
for having gone over to Eleanor Roosevelt. He called in a friend and showed
him a bundle of letters from fellow engineers having a rough time of it.
Quietly, he said he would like their appeals looked into. He wanted to help
those he could, Hoover went on, "but I don't want anybody to get help if
he doesn't need it."[18]

A month after the election, his hold on Congress more tenuous than
ever, Hoover lashed out at "gangster tactics" pursued by the opposition
under publicist Charlie Michaelson's generalship. "The table was spread,"
Michaelson explained afterward. "All we had to do was eat." From his
headquarters in the National Press Club, Michaelson, backed by a million-
dollar bankroll, cranked out dozens of vituperative speeches and an
uncopyrighted column called "Dispelling the Fog" for use by anti-adminis-
tration spokesmen. Twelve thousand dollars were paid to a disgruntled Interior Department employee for evidence of a new Teapot Dome scandal;
even the instigating paper, the New York World, was compelled to admit no
such malfeasance, and apologize in fine print. Hoover was falsely implicated
in a sugar-lobbying scandal. An alleged food riot in Arkansas was seized
upon as proof of the president's inhumanity. Herbert, Junior, was accused of
profiteering from a job with airlines delivering the mails; he resigned. The
president's niece was informed by a gardener that the Depression resulted
when "Hoover and Mellon" removed the gold from Fort Knox and buried it
on an island in the Potomac. The Baltimore Sun printed another story, this
time suggesting improper awarding of mail contracts by Postmaster General
Walter Brown, and Hoover lost his temper. Denouncing the report as a
"dastardly attack," he succeeded only in giving it wider circulation.[19]

Will Rogers summed up the mood of a nation. If someone bit an apple
and found a worm in it, he joked, Hoover would get the blame. One
sympathizer sent the president an ironic verse.

Worldwide Depression, Everywhere
Herb Hoover is to blame.

Disaster in the Earth and Air,
Herb Hoover is to blame.

I find my eyes are getting dim,
Herb Hoover is to blame.
My bank account is very slim,
Herb Hoover is to blame;
My oldest boy is running booze,
And little Jennie smokes and chews,
I'm nearly dying of the Blues,
Herb Hoover is to blame.[20]

Later, he maintained that none of the attacks disturbed his equilibrium. As a Quaker, insisted Hoover, he cultivated "peace at the center," allowing him to "drop hostilities in this deep pool of inner quietness." At the time, he seemed anything but peaceful. Hoover told the Supreme Court at a reception in October 1930 that he sometimes envied them "for they cannot do anything to you." At one White House dinner, the president suggested, tongue more or less in cheek, that the man who held his office should be able to execute two people a year "without giving any reason whatsoever for his decision." He dismissed as "bosh" an academic interpretation of the Depression's causes by his son Allan, then enrolled at Harvard Business School, and demanded to know what made a friend "yellow" who had warned him early in December 1930 of the imminent collapse of the Bank of the United States. He complained to Federal Reserve member Eugene Meyer after a contentious session with congressional leaders, "You had no idea how I had to demean myself before those Democratic swine before they consented to agree."[21]

Gradually, as 1930 wound down and the recession turned ugly, it dawned on the president: Wall Street's burst bubble was only the opening round of a much worse conflagration, in which tens of millions might suffer privation and principles that had guided America since her birth might come under attack. Hoover resolved to protect both. His "battle on a thousand fronts" became a life or death struggle, hampered by his own reluctance to rouse emotions. Urged by his press secretary to go on the radio more intimately and appeal to the people over the heads of the press, Hoover blanched; Steve Early passed the idea on to FDR, who made it the basis of his fireside chats. "I only wish I could say what is in my heart," Hoover sighed. His heart went out to those in need. But it never subdued his head.[22]

★   ★

New Year's Day 1931 found Hoover awake before dawn. Informed that two men wishing to see him as part of the annual New Year's reception were already standing outside the White House gates, he ordered them in from the cold—and breakfast for both. Later that morning, he endured the annual handshaking ritual with relative good humor. "Hello, Miss Bluebird," he called out to a young girl in a sapphire-colored hat and dress. Another child was addressed as "Little Red Riding Hood." A boy wearing goggles and scarf was "Mr. Aviator." Midway through the reception, the president turned to Colonel Starling. He wished the Secret Service agent could supply him with some new phrases, Hoover muttered; he was running out of his own. When the festivities were over, he returned to work, to the grueling pattern of conferences, reports, telephone calls and congressional lobbying that filled eighteen hours of each day. Not once in four years did illness keep Hoover from his desk. Only once did he cancel his daybreak game of medicine ball: he rose at 5:30 A.M. that morning in May 1932 to compose a personal message for delivery to the Senate at noon.[23]

His days followed a fixed routine. In his office by 8:30 A.M., not to leave before six-fifteen, he regularly conducted two dozen meetings, tore through piles of documents and met the public for a daily photo session on the South Lawn. "Are you seeing everything you want to while in Washington?" he liked to ask visiting contingents of Rotarians and Girl Scouts. "If not, let me know. I am pretty well known around here. Perhaps I can fix it up for you." Then came lunch. If taken alone, it lasted ten minutes or less. More often, it turned into another group effort at pulse-taking and policy-making. A short nap was followed by dinner and more consultation with political, financial or diplomatic experts until midnight or later. He read late and often awoke from a troubled sleep to pore over the latest reports and prognostications. As the Depression deepened, so did Hoover's resentment of anything depriving him of work time. He testily denied that an Easter Sunday sermon was a grand success: ". . . that preacher had four very good stopping places and went right on by them." His heart sank when he learned that a congressman was to deliver a dedicatory address at the unveiling of a memorial to victims of the *Titanic* sinking. Experience taught Hoover that congressmen never talked for less than half an hour. He suggested half-seriously that the White House should designate a special orator to attend such occasions in the president's stead, and noted wryly after the new ambassador from Santo Domingo presented his credentials that such ceremonies seemed to occupy his time in inverse ratio to the size of the republic being recognized.[24]

With congressional opposition to his program on the rise, Hoover traveled to Puerto Rico in March 1931, and the island's governor, Theodore Roosevelt, Junior, won a rare chuckle with the tale of his father's African safari. "Mr. President," a newsman had told the elder T.R., "you might bring back some of those lions and turn them loose in the Senate." Another reporter interjected that the wild animals might get loose and attack the wrong senators, to which Roosevelt replied they would do no harm, so long as they stayed in the chamber long enough. Then young Roosevelt turned serious. "You must not wear yourself out," he advised Hoover, "and you have done nothing but work day and night for a very long while." [25]

Retainers urged a bone-weary chief executive to have breakfast after one especially worrisome night. He refused. "I want to pump [Federal Reserve Board member Adolph] Miller dry on the Depression before I go any further with the day." At other times, they saw the president walking through the residence arm in arm with Lou, who turned to smooth his hair as a wordless endearment, before surrendering him to the day's business. One night, when the First Lady was away, one of her secretaries was startled by a plaintive request. "Do you mind having dinner with me, Sue?" Hoover asked. What followed was a solemn, mirthless meal, whose only justification was the brief assurance it gave the puffy-faced host that he was not alone. "He had a very hard time when he was by himself," recalled another member of the White House staff. "He could put it off . . . while in the company of others, but I don't think that otherwise he did." [26]

At Lou's direction, rifts within the official family were kept from him. She struggled to fill social dead spots with deliberately cheerful chatter, and camouflaged the long ride to Camp Rapidan with humor and family stories. Yet an air of defeat hung over her home. Allan Hoover said he had to escape the place before it gave him the "willies." Late in 1931, ten thousand Communist-led demonstrators picketed 1600 Pennsylvania Avenue. "The Hoover program," read one of their placards, "a crust of bread on a bayonet." Hoover himself was baffled. "Why is it," he asked one aide, "that when a man is on this job as I am day and night, doing the best he can, that certain men . . . seek to oppose everything he does, just to oppose him?" Railing against Democratic obstinacy, the president managed a metallic whimsy. He mused out loud that the only way to perpetuate democratic government was to put a dictator in power for six months every fifty years and give him unrestricted power to scrape barnacles from the ship of state, while stationing an army close by Washington with sealed orders to march on the capital on the last day of dictatorship and allow the benign despot to slip away. In June of 1931, Hoover was forced to leave the city himself, for the distasteful but obligatory chore of dedicating Warren Harding's mausoleum in Marion, Ohio. The public had no inkling of his developing plan to declare a moratorium on German war debts—a bold alternative to total collapse of the central European economy—and he refused to cancel the trip lest the press suspect something was up.[27]

When he arrived in Marion, Hoover paid graceful tribute to a decent man sold out by venal friends. Harry Daugherty sat barely thirty feet away, but Hoover did not mince words. Those with Harding on his last trip, he told the people of Marion, "came to know that here was a man whose soul was being seared by a great disillusionment. . . . Warren Harding had a dim realization that he had been betrayed by a few of the men whom he had trusted, by men who he had believed were his devoted friends. It was later proved in the courts of the land that these men had betrayed not alone the friendship and trust of their staunch and loyal friend but they had betrayed their country. That was the tragedy of Warren Harding."[28]

Daugherty seethed, but the president's brief display of emotion touched a chord of public sentiment. As usual, he had doubts. "Do you think I did right in hitting that thing head-on?" he asked Charles Dawes, Coolidge's vice president. Dawes assured him that he would always be grateful for the presidential statement at Marion. But the pleasant surprise was short-lived. Hoover himself wrote Dawes that the nation's economic machine, although "in good running order, is running out of gas." The European financial crisis was building to a head, a tentative recovery at home was endangered by overseas turmoil, and Hoover's own position of leadership was being undermined by a chorus of accusation and demand. He told Coolidge, after outlining all the steps being taken to end the depression, that he could understand neither his critics' vehemence nor their rapid numerical growth.[29]

"You can't expect to see calves running in the field the day after you put the bull to the cows," Coolidge told him.

"No," Hoover replied, "but I would expect to see contented cows."

There was little contentment among Americans in the spring of 1931. Amid the mangled wreckage of the New Era, unemployment rose to 8 million, and emotions rose to meet it. There were food riots in New York City and Minneapolis. In Chicago, hundreds of homeless women slept outdoors in Grant Park. Detroit converted a Fisher auto-body plant into an emergency flophouse. It also undertook a sweeping program of relief that put 11,000 men to work, at a cost of $2 million—only to discover relief rolls larger than ever and the mood on the streets turning venomous. In Pennsylvania, a quarter of the state's work force was unemployed. A St. Louis Hooverville featured a church built out of orange crates. In New York, Clifford Odets scripted his first play while living on ten cents a day. People talked of mercy killings for the elderly, and the president of the Wisconsin

Farmers' Union told a congressional hearing that, if his men could afford to buy airplanes, they would undoubtedly fly to Washington that instant "and blow you fellows up."

The editor of *Cosmopolitan* magazine did fly to Moscow to sign up Soviet writers for his publication. Will Rogers praised Russia as a nation where everyone worked. From the pulpit of New York's Riverside Church, Harry Emerson Fosdick preached a eulogy on capitalism. "Individualism in the modern world," he said in January 1931 "is insanity. Optimism is a dangerous lie." Unless capitalism could adapt itself to "the needs of the present age," including social planning and controls, some form of communism would inevitably be thrust upon the next generation.

Henry Ford disagreed. He said that America's poor were recruited from the ranks of the unthinking and shiftless. J. P. Morgan—who paid no income tax at all during 1930, 1931 and 1932—informed a Senate committee that destruction of what he called "the leisure class" would bring down the pillars of civilization. Asked to define the leisure class, Morgan said it consisted of those households able to afford a maid's wages.

Hoover was disgusted. "My own battle," he wrote afterward, "has been constantly with the extremes . . . the disloyal demagogues of the West and the disloyal representatives of special interests mostly emanating from New York City. . . ." Determined to balance a budget bleeding half a billion dollars of red ink by midyear, the president raised the maximum tax on upper-income Americans from 24 percent to 55 percent. He wanted a sales tax, but the Democratic rank and file within Congress rebelled against their own leadership and voted the idea down. It was symptomatic of an increasingly nasty conflict between Hoover and the dim galaxy of Old Guard Republicans, insurgents from the West, and opportunistic Democrats smelling the heady aroma of victory in 1932. Immediately after the 1930 midterm elections, the latter began demanding direct relief payments to the jobless. They were not alone. "For God's sake," cried Idaho's cantankerous Republican William Borah, "get something done to feed the people who are hungry." Later, Ogden Mills, who succeeded Mellon at the Treasury Department early in 1932, concluded that care of the destitute would have required $8 billion in government grants to states and charitable organizations until the economic tide turned, "and we should have done it."[30]

Hoover held differently. "I do not feel," he informed reporters in February 1931, when cries for relief payments were escalating, "that I should be charged with a lack of human sympathy for those who suffer, but I recall that in all of the organizations with which I have been involved over these many years, the foundation has been to summon the maximum of self-help."

The money involved, he continued, was insignificant compared to the national ideals and institutions such a precedent might undermine. Before another audience, he placed his opposition to the dole within the context of the truce on wage reductions. Anything else, insisted Hoover, would "lower wages toward the bare subsistence level and . . . endow the slacker." He refused to agree to a congressional appropriation for Red Cross relief efforts, preferring instead to tap private sources and taking to the airwaves himself to make an appeal for funds. It was Belgium all over again: a man who sent friends live turkeys for Thanksgiving so he wouldn't have their slaughter on his conscience was condemned as heartless. In fact, he was not cruel, merely irrelevant.[31]

In September 1931, his original committee on employment gave way to a new body, under the chairmanship of AT&T's Walter Gifford. "Between October 18 and November 25," Gifford revealed, "America will feel the thrill of a great spiritual experience." Those were the dates of a new fund-raising campaign to tide cities and towns over the approaching winter. This at a time when families in New York received an average of $2.39 a week in public and private assistance, and farm income plunged to less than a third of its 1929 level. Yet for all the evidence of suffering, most Americans held firm against the dole. The National Council of Social Workers condemned it. Congress voted down Senator Robert Wagner's direct relief bill (of which Hoover said, "Never before has so dangerous suggestion been seriously made to our country") early in 1932 by a healthy margin. Yet a few months later, the president himself was compelled to accept $300 million in relief assistance to state and local governments. For Hoover's own position was eroding under the spreading plague of unemployment, and a barrage of skillful, often devastating attacks from congressmen and vaudeville comedians alike.

Alben Barkley of Kentucky took note of Hoover's earlier relief efforts and suggested that the solution to America's unemployed millions was to relocate them all in Russia and China. Sculptor Gutzon Borglum concluded that a rose would wilt in Hoover's hand. On Broadway, a smash musical called "Of Thee I Sing" immortalized a song called "Posterity Is Just Around the Corner," a none-too-subtle reference to the bromide widely and inaccurately attributed to Hoover. Comics announced a rise in the stock market, whereupon their partners asked if Hoover was dead. Or they told the imaginary request of the president to Andrew Mellon for a nickel with which to call a friend. "Here," Mellon was supposed to have replied, "take a dime and call all your friends."

In the White House, Hoover dug in his heels. His critics were concerned with the next election, he concluded. His own thoughts were of the next generation. Painful as current conditions might be, Hoover had little difficulty persuading himself that he was protecting the nation he loved from false values and philosophical hemlock. It would be a mockery of all that America conjured up in his mind should a distressed people sell their birthright for temporary surcease. So Hoover took his stand on principle, only to discover himself perched on a political trapdoor. In February 1931, he vetoed a bill to permit veterans to borrow up to half a bonus scheduled for payment in 1945, with the blunt declaration that "the country should not be called upon . . . to support or make loans to those who can by their own efforts support themselves." Before the month was out, Congress overrode the veto. A week later, Hoover rejected another bill, this one embodying George Norris's pet vision of a vast federal investment in electric power in the Tennessee Valley. "I am firmly opposed to the government entering into any business the major purpose of which is competition with our citizens," he wrote tartly.

It's not hard to see why it took most historians nearly half a century to credit Hoover with the anti-Depression measures he did take, or the foundation they laid for the New Deal. Even ignoring the towering figure of FDR which blocked their retrospective view, Hoover was perceived as a negative force, standing blindly if without malice astride humane efforts and the inevitable growth of government. His presidency, it seemed, was constructed on the shifting sands of wishful thinking, dull nostalgia, and a charmless, almost clinical personality. Hoover clearly did not fit the pattern of strong presidents who swore allegiance to change and thundered their way through tumultuous times. He played a lone hand. But what escaped historical notice was the intellectual and moral power of Hoover's position. Rather than charging forward, he was manning the barricades, defending old values clearly spelled out in a lifelong search for ways to rid individualism of its greed, and government of its deadening acceptance of mediocrity as the price for security. He had more scruples than magic. But a river rises no higher than its source, and Hoover refused to yield to those who cared less about abstract catastrophes down the historical road than about a crippled economy and a doubting electorate.

When in the fall of 1931 Gerard Swope of General Electric called for a relaxation of antitrust laws, an appeal quickly seconded by other businessmen who wanted a period of "stabilization" wherein production could sink to demand, and the old nostrums of liquidation take hold, Hoover was adamant in his refusal. Such ideas, he fumed to the Chamber of Commerce, their warmest advocate, were nothing less than backdoor attempts to smuggle fascism into the American economy. He would not be party to any corporate state and would react with similar fury to Roosevelt's National Recovery Administration in 1933. His contempt for supposed Allies was limitless. "England would like nothing better," he stormed during one crisis over foreign hoarding of gold, "than to tear us down to her level." His own partisanship became shrill, as when he rejected the idea of naming Owen Young to the Reconstruction Finance Corporation in June of 1932. Considering Young a potential rival in that year's election, Hoover told Eugene Meyer, "We can't give the Democrats anything."[32]

For public and politicians alike, it was easy to overlook Hoover's successes. Accustomed to presidents who marshalled fiery words and headline-making actions, they could hardly share in his secret conferences, like those preceding the moratorium declaration in June 1931, or the October 4 meeting at Andrew Mellon's Washington apartment which laid the cornerstone of his National Credit Finance Corporation, and, by inference, its successor, the Reconstruction Finance Corporation. After hearing the president reassure them for two years that the economy was sound and headed for an early recovery, their enthusiasm for his subsequent program was bound to be muted. They resented his apparent eagerness to loan RFC funds by the tens of millions to hobbled financial institutions while dismissing individual relief as an insult to American character. They forgot that he asked Congress to adopt a Public Works Administration in his December 1931 message, only to see the proposal languish on the vine until FDR revived it and made the PWA his own, or that his angry call for a Senate investigation of unethical stock market practices paved the way for Roosevelt's Securities and Exchange Commission. They dismissed as remote from their own misery banking reforms like the Glass-Steagall Act, adopted early in 1932 by a Congress at last energized to the emergency caused by Britain's decision to go off the gold standard the previous September.

Even when Hoover embraced the dramatic, it was capsized in the rush of events. In the fall of 1931, after the American Legion demanded early payment of the veterans' bonus, the president decided to fly to Detroit and deliver a personal appeal against the move. His message lasted just eleven minutes, and he left the hall immediately on its completion, but the effect was galvanizing. The legion recanted, and reporters temporarily hailed a decisive new Hoover—only to have the good news washed out by Britain's desperate plight and the ensuing flight of the U.S. gold reserves. Hoover worsened relations with reporters by admonishing them against misquoting or broken confidences. In October 1931, before a late-night session with congressional leaders called to hammer out fresh legislative initiatives, he halfheartedly asked journalists not to report the meeting at all. Told that any such agreement was out of the question, Hoover backtracked. "I am giving you my feeling and what I think would be in the interests of the American people," he mumbled. "I leave it to you and ask for no promises . . . you are absolutely free to do whatever you please." Not surprisingly, the press did exactly that.

At the heart of the problem lay Hoover's own inability to fill the role of presidential persuader, or play the political games his opponents dominated by default. Added to this was a thin skin and an undeniable streak of self-righteousness. "I know that from the newspaper man's point of view," he told his secretary Ted Joslin in 1933, that "he had to appreciate the fact that his readers want to see the President on a white charger of wrath with a flashing sword of slogans, and that they do not realize that the safety of a nation lies in the infinite drudgery of determination of fact and policy or the patience in co-ordinating the minds of men for a common objective."[33]

Anne O'Hare McCormick was no more patronizing than most of her journalistic colleagues when she described Hoover as "the ideal business manager." But Hoover hurt his own cause by refusing to publicize incidents that might convey to the public the extent of his concern. When three Detroit children showed up outside the White House gates in May 1932 asking to see him about their father, imprisoned on a charge of auto theft, his response was warmhearted. "Three children resourceful enough to manage to get to Washington to see me are going to see me," he informed Joslin. "But first I want the facts." Attorney General Mitchell was ordered to examine the records of the case. Not long after, the children were ushered into the Oval Office, where Hoover asked the oldest, a thirteen-year-old girl named Bernice, to tell him the whole story. By the time she was through, the muscles in Hoover's face were twitching from his effort at self-control. "I know there must be good in a man whose children are so well behaved and who show such loyalty and devotion to him," he told them. "I will use my good offices. You may go home happy." He reached into his desk and presented each with a memento to remember him by. Then he told them to run along home; their father would be waiting for them.

Minutes later, the buzzer in Joslin's office rang. He found the president staring out over the South Lawn, unable momentarily to speak. When he broke the silence, it was in a voice thick with emotion:

"Get that father out of jail immediately."

Joslin asked if he might relate the incident to the press. Absolutely not, said Hoover. Only the barest announcement might be made, and nothing more. "Let's not argue about it. . . . That is all we will say about it. Now we will get back to work."

The flip side of a leader who wouldn't or couldn't personify optimism convincingly was a man who seemed defensive to the point of bewilderment. "No one is actually starving," he reminded reporters at the White House. Personally, Hoover went on, he knew of one hobo who managed to beg ten meals in a single day. His penchant for statistics led him to cite numbers from the Surgeon General purporting to show a drop in infant mortality. His old willingness to hide behind a slogan surfaced anew. Offering Rudy Vallee a gold medal for a joke that would curtail hoarding, to another White House visitor Hoover expressed a longing for "a great poem," in the spirit of "John Brown's Body" or Kipling's "Recessional."

"Let me know if you find any great poems lying around," he concluded. In the most grievous example of insensitivity, some of the president's supporters plastered trackside billboards with the words "Wasn't the Depression Terrible?" In May 1931, Hoover himself left the White House to attempt more direct inspiration of a restless, fearful nation. In an address at Valley Forge, he sought to rouse the nation's conscience through stirring words instead of numbing statistics. "Sirens still sing the song of the easy way for the moment of difficulty . . . but the truth which echoes upward from this soil of blood and tears, the way to the nation's greatness is the path of self-reliance, independence, and steadfastness in times of trial and stress." Valley Forge had posed such a test during war, said Hoover. His generation's challenge was to meet a similar test "in times and terms of peace."

He closed with words from the heart as well as the head, the emotional residue of his own storm-tossed days and an eloquent retort to those he believed guilty of treason in the trenches. "Freedom was won here by fortitude," Hoover told the crowd at Valley Forge. Washington's encampment was "our American synonym for the trial of human character through privation and suffering, and it is the symbol of the triumph of the American soul. If those few thousand men endured that lone winter . . . humiliated by the despair of their countrymen, and deprived of support save their own indomitable will . . . what right have we to be of little faith?"

Words might fortify the spirit; they could not overcome the financial holocaust sweeping a European continent still reeling from the war and its own exhausted diplomacy. One week after Hoover's Valley Forge address, Germany signaled an imminent collapse of its banking system. A bank crisis enveloped Chicago that same week. On the verge of issuing his daring call for a moratorium, Hoover sought private pledges of support from congressional leaders. Joseph Robinson, the Democratic leader in the Senate, told him he was not against the proposal but would not support it on the Senate floor. House Speaker Garner was similarly noncommittal. For hour after hour, Hoover took to the phone, tracking down their colleagues, explaining endlessly what the foreign threat portended and how he proposed to meet it. In the end, fears of a press leak compelled him to go public on July 20, 1931. Immediate reaction was favorable. But France refused to cooperate, the suspension of debt payments proved too little, too late, and the stage was set for a backlash of voter discontent that would bring Adolf Hitler to power in Berlin and send Britain's new government off the gold standard in September.

At the White House, one bleak day fused into another as Hoover's plans were buffeted by events beyond his control. Japan invaded Manchuria. The president's hopes for drastic armaments reduction as a result of global conference in Geneva went glimmering. In New York, Governor Franklin Roosevelt pledged himself to a program of direct relief payments for those in his state without work. Congress delayed for weeks, sometimes months, passing Hoover's latest depression-fighting mechanisms, the RFC and Home Loan Discount Banks. It rejected outright presidential proposals to reform banking and bankruptcy laws, trim government waste, and put teeth in the new Federal Power Commission. At the 1932 convention of Virginia's Girl Scouts, someone cut the radio wires carrying Lou Hoover's message to the delegates. In Washington, a self-proclaimed Bonus Army encamped near the White House, and members of his own party wished Hoover would retire from the scene.[34]

"It is a cruel world," he told Ted Joslin.

CHAPTER FOUR

SWAPPING HORSES

★

All the money in the world could not induce me to live over the last nine months. The conditions we have experienced make this office a compound hell.
                                        —Herbert Hoover, early in 1933

He is so anxious to be a great figure that I fear he will lose everything in the eyes of the historians—even dignity.   —Agnes Meyer [1]

★

Fewer well-wishers than usual came to the White House on New Year's Day 1932. Between greetings Hoover found time to talk about his research into the ancient war between Greeks and Persians, in which Themistocles, relying on Greek lead miners to build and man his ships, defeated the Persians at the battle of Salamis. "But for the miners," proclaimed the president, "the Persians might have won . . . ," with incalculable effects upon Western civilization. The danger to Herbert Hoover's America appeared just as imminent during the first week of 1932, even as her miner-turned-chief-executive was mired in frustration. Britain's decision to abandon the gold standard had been duplicated in forty other lands, destabilizing an already precarious world order and spawning a severe drain on U.S. gold supplies. As the Federal Reserve raised interest rates to keep gold from flowing overseas, it inadvertently tightened credit in an economy already bled to the point of exhaustion. Frightened depositors were hoarding cash and nullifying the mandate of Hoover's National Credit Finance Corporation to keep the banks open. In the single month of October 1931, deposits in U.S. banks plunged by $6 billion. Joblessness was pressing ten million. The farm belt and Congress alike were seething in resentment.[2]

Without a moment to spare, Hoover grasped the last hand outstretched before soaking his own in a special solution ordered by his doctor. Then he summoned seven officials for a round of conferring, holidays or no holidays. It was the start of a grim goal-line stand, accompanied by a torrent of activity suggesting that at last the president was dispelling his cautious demeanor. On January 4, he reminded Congress of his month-old request for depression-fighting measures including the Reconstruction Finance Corporation. Two days later, he met with Father James Cox, the self-proclaimed "Shepherd of the Unemployed," after ordering army barracks in the capital thrown open to the fifteen thousand protestors who answered Cox's call. The priest's army of the hungry was at least better-mannered than another recent band of demonstrators, a milling band of Communists who marched outside the White House singing, "We'll hang Herbie Hoover to a sour apple tree."

On January 7, 1932, a young Texas congressman named Wright Patman, best known for sponsoring a $2.4 billion veterans' bonus, rose to his feet to demand Andrew Mellon's impeachment. The Secretary of the Treasury, it was revealed, had employed government experts to devise a dozen ways to evade income taxes on his personal fortune. That same day, Hoover conducted twenty-two meetings at the White House, including a Cabinet session at which he broke with his own Secretary of State over Stimson's support for economic sanctions against the Japanese invaders of Manchuria. True to his Quaker instincts, the president called instead for the civilized nations of the world to withhold recognition of any territory gained through aggression. "Neither our obligation to them," he wrote of the Chinese, "nor our own interests, nor our dignity requires us to go to war. . . ." Stimson contended that Japan's militancy contained seeds of future conflict with the United States, a theory his chief dismissed as a "phantasmagoria." In March, the League of Nations adopted his tactics of moral pressure in lieu of economic quarantine. The United States stayed out of war, Japan withdrew from the League, and thoughtful people, including Stimson, peered anxiously across a broad Pacific, wondering when and where some future blow might fall.[3]

At home, events fell upon Hoover with trip-hammer force, lending credence to his bitter description of the presidency as "nothing but a twenty-ring circus, with a whole lot of bad actors." Before the end of January, he signed the RFC into law, despite a congressional flank attack stripping it of any role in aiding slum clearance, farm improvements and plant modernization. Manhattan's fiery congressman Fiorello La Guardia denounced the $1.5 billion agency as "a millionaire's dole." At the other end of the ideological spectrum were conservatives who criticized the whole idea as a seamy detour into socialism. Whatever Hoover called it, the new board did represent a radical intervention by Washington in the peacetime economy. By the end of March, it had loaned out hundreds of millions to ailing banks, insurance companies and other financial institutions. It stemmed the tide of bank failures (from 346 in January to 46 three months later) and rescued the nation's railroads in the bargain.

Hoover had neither the time nor the inclination to celebrate. One night after affixing his name to the RFC legislation, he agreed reluctantly to attend the National Press Club's annual show in the capital. He would stay no longer than ten minutes, he told Ted Joslin. When he got there, however, Hoover relaxed, throwing off his cares for a couple of hours. His pleasure was short-lived. Returning to the White House, he received the gloomiest news yet: a confidential report describing a crescendo of hoarding by American citizens. More than a billion dollars in all had been siphoned from the nation's credit pipeline, Hoover learned that night, with the pace of withdrawal accelerating. The gold standard itself, he concluded, might not be able to hold out for another ten days. When Federal Reserve Board Governor Eugene Meyer dropped by the White House to discuss the new RFC, Joslin's son demanded to know what state he governed.

"I am governor of the state of bankruptcy," replied Meyer. The president was close to making the same admission. On February 3, he went public with his concerns, appealing for public confidence with words crafted for their effect on the average consumer, and designating *Chicago Daily News* publisher Frank Knox to head a citizen's committee against hoarding. This time, Hoover's offensive was not restricted to publicity or moral suasion. Before the month was out, he persuaded Virginia's venerable Jeffersonian Democrat Carter Glass to lend his name and prestige to a bill freeing up three-quarters of a billion dollars from federal gold reserves. The hoarding ceased, and Hoover turned his attention elsewhere. To combat growing demands for relief, he directed his Federal Farm Board to make available to the Red Cross 85 million bushels of wheat and half a million bales of cotton. Lou Hoover set a precedent by wearing a gown spun from cotton instead of silk—at Andrew Mellon's farewell reception. The premier liquidationist was at last being bundled off to the Court of St. James's. In his place, Hoover named Ogden Mills, a brilliant, hulking, hard-drinking New Yorker who understood the link between public psychology and any recovery.

Mills said that fear, as much as frozen assets, held the American people

in thrall. To combat both, he prescribed remedies near the president's heart
—a balanced budget, "sound monetary legislation" and unswerving devotion to the gold standard. Such was the price, Hoover maintained, of restoring business confidence and putting a permanent halt to the hoarding
that drained the economy of vital capital and credit. His prescription for
austerity touched off a new and intense battle with Congress. Hoover demanded stringent economies; the legislators responded with a flood of relief
bills. Together, he estimated, they would cost the taxpayers $40 billion. To
close the existing revenue gap, the president and Mills proposed to double
income and estate taxes. No sacred cow could be assured of its place at the
federal trough; the administration's budget cut included a reduction in General Pershing's pension. Congress refused to approve such draconian measures. But it did vote a drastic tax increase, providing economists ever after
with a justification for the Keynesian alternative.

Hoover was hardly alone in his mania for traditional economies. "Cactus
Jack" Garner, the tobacco-chewing, poker-playing Speaker of the House,
won a near-unanimous show of hands in favor of a balanced budget from his
own side of the House aisle. Neither did Garner dispute the president's
attachment to gold, a metal "enshrined in human instincts for over 10,000
years," as Hoover put it. In the canon law of American politics, few things
were more sacred. Yet Garner, more colorful than forceful, fell victim to a
backbench rebellion. Soon the ambitious speaker, with an eye on his party's
1932 presidential nod, was offering fiscally exorbitant measures himself—
including one bill to construct a thousand post offices ("the most gigantic
pork barrel ever proposed" in Hoover's angry words). Senator David Walsh
of Massachusetts next demanded a billion dollars in new currency be
printed. In the ensuing brawl, the president vetoed a bill providing direct
relief payments; the Congress peevishly withheld $120,000 in clerical ex-
penses for his own unemployment commission, and curtailed the White
House telephone allowance. Hoover dipped into his own pocket to pay the
tab.[4]

Demanding absolute authority to reorganize the federal establishment,
Hoover vowed to shrink the deficit and cut his critics off at the knees. Yet
even here he would not engage in gamesmanship. Advisers urged him to
seek half a billion dollars in budget cuts, rather than the $300 million he
thought prudent. Such tactics would be demagogic, replied the president. "I
can see no advantage in setting up a straw man merely to knock him down
again and get into a futile row." In the end, he got into a row anyway—
without mobilizing public opinion or achieving more than a fraction of the
economies sought. He did sign Fiorello La Guardia's anti-injunction bill,

along with a measure directing $125 million to help farmers renegotiate crushing mortgages on their homes and acres.

Early in May, impatient with the pace of congressional action on his economy program, Hoover strode into the Senate chamber himself, to upbraid the world's greatest deliberative body and issue a rebuke that even the Democratic *Baltimore Sun* hailed as fitting reward for those who "missed no opportunity to disembowel . . . orthodox finance." Later in the month, with hoarding again on the rise, and wheat prices falling sharply, Hoover confessed that yet another crash might occur within two weeks. He looked at a chart of stock movements and asked his friend Mark Sullivan what would happen if Bethlehem Steel were to drop another ten points. "It can't," replied Sullivan. "There's the edge of the chart."[5]

He was very nearly correct. By the summer of 1932, General Electric and U.S. Steel were worth just 8 percent of their pre-Crash values. The issuance of corporate securities was down 96 percent, and the nation's total output had fallen from $104 billion to just $41 billion. American Locomotive marketed 600 models a year in the glorious twenties; in 1932, the company sold exactly one. In a cruelly ironic twist, labor-saving devices had resulted in a sharp gain in worker productivity since Black Tuesday. They had not created new jobs. In Buffalo, the president's men conducted a survey of 15,000 able-bodied adults and found fewer than half employed. An Arkansas man earned himself a spot in the news by walking 900 miles for a job. The schools in his native state were closed for ten months of the year; nationwide, a third of a million schoolchildren were turned out of bankrupt educational systems. Worse yet was the estimate that 200,000 young people were drifting around the country. The Southern Pacific Railroad counted 683,000 persons tossed off its cars in a single year, part of a vagabond nation endlessly moving on. California posted guards at its borders to turn away impoverished drifters. Fifteen hundred tramps a day passed through Kansas City.

Secretary of War Patrick J. Hurley thought he had a ten-strike idea when he proposed that the nation's swankier restaurants package their leftovers for the destitute. Dutifully, Princeton eating clubs voted to donate their scraps to the less fortunate. The Commerce Department reported that over half the seats in the nation's commercial aviation fleet were going unfilled. During one five-week period, Swedish industrialist Ivor Kreuger and George Eastman killed themselves, utilities magnate Samuel Insull fled the country after the sudden collapse of his billion-dollar empire, and Hoover himself took to the airwaves to denounce the kidnapping of Charles Lindbergh's baby. And still there were other human tragedies, incessantly if poorly reflected in the numbers measuring economic production and individual suffering. The steel industry clung to life at 19 percent of capacity. All five banks in Iowa City, bordering on Hoover's birthplace, went broke. Lou Hoover played hostess at a concert by the famed Polish pianist Ignace Jan Paderewski, who raised nearly $12,000 as his way of returning thanks for Hoover's wartime efforts to prevent his country's starvation. For his part, the president let it be known early in the year that he would be unable to participate in any formal receptions. He demanded as much from subordinates. When a wife of one exhausted official came to plead her case, Hoover complained that his men were dropping around him.

With the arrival in Washington that spring of nearly 20,000 members of the Bonus Army, there to demand early payment of Wright Patman's fiat currency, the atmosphere turned ominous. Henry Stimson went to pay a visit upon Oliver Wendell Holmes, newly retired at ninety-one, and came away refreshed in mind and spirit. In a year and a half, he confided to his diary, he had sat around the Cabinet table without ever hearing a joke, trapped in the company of men with "apparently no humanity for anything except for business." An admirer asked Hoover if he ever got a thrill speaking over the radio. "The same thrill I get," he told her, "when I rehearse an address to a doorknob." Two friends debating the wisdom of a single, six-year term for presidents asked Hoover for his judgment. Personally, he replied, three and a half years would be sufficient for him. Lou confessed her own unhappiness to friends, even as her husband stepped up his pace and snarled at his detractors. He rejected an overture from Louis B. Mayer to meet the powerful press lord William Randolph Hearst. Hearst's editorials angered Hoover, who was willing to discard a potential ally to satisfy his own standards.[6]

When a secretary casually remarked that a brief honeymoon with Congress seemed at an end, Hoover reproached him sharply. "There has been no honeymoon. You know that perfectly well," he said. "You know the Democrats have taken my program because they had none of their own and because the attitude of the country compelled them to take the one I put forward. They would murder our plans in a moment if they dared. . . ." Upbraided for his lack of small talk when a few pleasantries might smooth the way of congressional relations, Hoover dismissed the whole idea as offensive. "I have other things to do when the nation is on fire." He wished members of his own party would leave him alone to work. "Oh, he's here again," he moaned at the sight of Jim Watson, "telling me what to do." Official Washington shook its head and wondered how it could have so seriously misjudged the man. "He's what the doctors call a worrier," explained Cary Grayson, once Woodrow Wilson's physician. "If you and I started it we'd be dead in no time but he can stand it because he's been doing it all his life." Some were less confident of the President's stamina. H. G. Wells visited the White House, and judged Hoover "sickly, over-worked, and overwhelmed."[7]

Still he went on, improvising, justifying, often sounding an unflattering note of self-pity. He had been "absurdly oversold," he told New Hampshire Senator George Moses that spring. Hoover, concluded even some of his admirers, suffered from an acute persecution complex. Seven weeks before the climactic destruction of the Bonus Army encampment across the river in Anacostia, on July 21, 1932, the president's advisers were speculating on the size of the Communist and criminal element within the demonstration. Then as later, they exaggerated the Red presence. In fact, the Bonus Expeditionary Force was a crazy-quilt array of men and women, nearly 90 percent of whom had actually served in the army. Some were Communists, but most were simply desperate, eager to rally around the sentiment expressed by one typical sign hung outside an Anacostia shack: "War is hell, but loafing is worse." Filthy men cooked beans on Washington sidewalks, laid siege to the political establishment and prompted even an arch-liberal like California's old Progressive Hiram Johnson to warn of a new era dawning, "when fat old men like me stop making speeches to sleepy galleries and [are] lined up against a stone wall." They aroused more resentment than support. On July 15, Congress rejected their demands, voting instead $100,000 to aid the marchers in returning to their homes. Most accepted the offer, but perhaps two thousand remained behind, occupying government buildings and upping the ante in a grim war of nerves.

Hoover stayed in the White House, meeting heavyweight wrestling champions and a delegation from the Eta Epsilon Gamma sorority—but no veterans. He refrained from the customary Capitol Hill appearance on the session's final day. As barricades went up around the White House, much of official Washington assumed the appearance of an armed camp. The First Lady, meanwhile, dispatched coffee and sandwiches to some of the marchers. On July 23, after weekend picketing of the President's home by members of the BEF, Hoover passed word to Police Chief Pelham Glassford that if his forces could not prevent such outbreaks, the Army would be called in. On the morning of July 28, District of Columbia police moved in to clear demonstrators from four buildings not far from the White House. A few bricks were tossed, igniting violence that took the lives of two demonstrators. That afternoon, after receiving certification from local authorities that they could no longer guarantee the peace, Hoover issued a verbal directive to Secretary of War Hurley. In it, he instructed Hurley to avoid bloodshed and "use all humanity consistent with the due execution of the law" in clearing Pennsylvania Avenue with federal troops under General Perry L. Miles. Moreover, Hoover ordered that women and children be singled out for "every kindness and consideration." Hurley turned to Chief of Staff Douglas MacArthur, who quickly assembled a thousand soldiers, including Third Cavalry troopers with sabers drawn under the command of Major George S. Patton, Jr., supported by six midget tanks, tear gas and a machine-gun unit. Dwight Eisenhower, then a colonel serving under MacArthur, pleaded with his histrionic superior to avoid the field of battle. Anything else, he said, would "dignify" the entire incident. MacArthur refused. He saw the ragtag protest as a serious challenge to government strength, he told Eisenhower. By late afternoon, he was on the scene, directing the operation that broke up the protestors' Bonus City in full view of twenty thousand spectators, without casualties.[8]

The real casualty was Hoover himself. A message arrived from the White House (where the president could see flames from the Lincoln study), reiterating Hoover's demand that the army troops not cross over the Eleventh Street bridge into Anacostia, where the veterans had their main outpost. "I don't want to hear them and I don't want to see them," the flamboyant general instructed his aides. "I will not permit my men to bivouac under the guns of traitors." Hoover's orders were purposefully laid aside, and MacArthur's troops poured into the Anacostia encampment, torching makeshift shelters and sending an infant to the hospital (its subsequent death set off a national storm, even though the exact cause has never been determined). MacArthur returned to the capital that evening, a hero in his own generous estimation. Hoover, unaware of the flagrant insubordination, released a statement that he was "pleased." Secretary Hurley poured grease on the fire two days later, telling reporters that not an eye had been blacked by the Army, nor a shot fired once the general took command. "And I want to tell you," enthused Hurley, "Mac was all there . . . like four aces and a king." Hoover himself claimed a victory for the forces of law and order. What he did not do, then or ever in public, was reveal his fury at MacArthur's disregard of his command. Even in his memoirs, Hoover skirted the issue, saying that his orders were not carried out but refusing to point the finger at MacArthur personally. Privately, he told friends, it was years before he discovered exactly how much authority the general had assumed for himself in Anacostia that fetid summer night, intercepting the White House messenger and telling him to get lost. "I upbraided him," he told F. Trubee Davison, Hurley's Under Secretary of War. But he would not level the slightest accusation in public.[9]

Neither was it known until Colonel Starling's memoirs were published many years later, that Hoover and Hurley had prepared another directive to the troops, ordering them stayed until all women and children could be evacuated. Like so much else about the affair, this too fell victim to bad timing, confusion, and signals crossed either accidentally or on purpose. However scrupulous Hoover's conduct, the Bonus Army's violent eviction from Washington all but completed his metamorphosis from hero to scape-goat. The fiasco was heightened when MacArthur told reporters that con-stitutional government would have been in jeopardy had "he [Hoover] not acted with the force and vigor that he did," thus wrapping responsibility still tighter around the hapless president. Finally, the Justice Department attempted in a clumsy report to implicate Communists and criminals as the masterminds behind the demonstration. Far more attuned to the political realities was the President's November opponent, Franklin D. Roosevelt. Himself appalled by the news from Washington, FDR could not suppress a certain fatalistic joy. "Well, Felix," he said to his friend and adviser Felix Frankfurter in Albany, "this elects me."

★   ★

Like Wagner's "Flying Dutchman," Hoover's reelection campaign was unwelcomed in any port. The Chicago convention that renominated the president in mid-June reflected a dispirited party, $200,000 in debt, beset by internal wrangling and bereft of traditional support from farmers and businessmen. Harold Ickes, a disgruntled old Bull Mooser from Chicago, spent $3,500 of his own money to promote a progressive alternative to the president. "I can see no reason why the Republican Party should deliberately run into a smashing defeat merely to satisfy one man's ambition," he wrote to grass-roots workers. Hoover himself said he knew why his chances for victory were rated at no better than one in ten. "We are opposed by six million unemployed," he remarked, "10,000 bonus marchers, and ten cent corn. Is it any wonder that the prospects are dark?"[10]

Yet there was no one to contest Hoover for a nomination few believed worth the effort. Coolidge stoutly refused to prick up his ears when some eastern businessmen tried a lame draft that spring. Hiram Johnson similarly refused to enter the fray from the left; ultimately, he joined with other GOP progressives like George Norris, Wisconsin Senator Robert La Follette and Ickes in supporting Franklin Roosevelt. The convention hall might have been barely two-thirds full, and orators forced to fall back on the bogeys of "stark communism" and "paternal government" to rouse even a feeble cheer, but only 28 delegates bolted Hoover's standard on the final roll call. Still less enthusiasm greeted the renomination of Vice President Charles Curtis, a seventy-three-year-old mediocrity whose penchant for protecting the poultry industry had earned him the nickname of Egg Curtis. As a senator from Kansas, Curtis had accepted money for advertising Lucky Strike cigarettes. His campaign train was enlivened by the frequent appearance of an Indian maid on the rear platform to recite "Hiawatha" in recognition of the vice president's Pottawatamie ancestry. Hoover and Curtis were not close, and the vice president, bone-dry as Carry Nation, reminded voters of the deep split within the party over Prohibition. But the president would not lift a finger to depose his lieutenant, and when Charles Dawes refused to run for the second spot himself, Curtis was reluctantly chosen.[11]

In the end, the only real fight to lift the tedium came over a middle-of-the-road Prohibition plank, a straddle which, as one New Mexico paper put it, made "the Colussus of Rhodes look like a paralytic." Many of the delegates wanted outright repeal of the Eighteenth Amendment, for economic as well as political and personal reasons. Such a step would enhance government revenues and create jobs. It might also take America's mind off the Depression. Personally, Hoover believed the amendment a failure. In New York, he confided to friends late in July that it had compelled bootleggers seeking protection to pay tribute to "rotten police." Yet he believed it his duty to carry out the law, and to that end he filled the jail cells to overflowing with a doubled rate of convictions. Adhering to rigid principle, he denied any role for a president in the amendment process, and told advisers who wanted him to endorse repeal that any such step would make the presidential oath of office itself an exercise in hypocrisy, "the most dangerous precedent I can think of."[12]

At the convention, administration forces led by Ogden Mills (who died five years later after drinking an entire bottle of gin in less than an hour) pushed successfully for a new amendment, reserving to the states ultimate control over the legality of liquor within their borders, while preserving federal authority to stay a return of the old saloon system. All of which led H. L. Mencken to proclaim this convention "the stupidest and most boresome ever," yet one likely to earn a paragraph in the history books if only because it witnessed the death throes of Prohibition.[13]

Hoover was in the Lincoln study when news arrived of his renomination. "Well," he said, "it was not wholly unexpected. Guess I will go back to the office now." He let it be known that he did not expect to stump much for his own cause; the nation's business would keep him in Washington. National party headquarters were soon shifted from the capital to Chicago, while the president busied himself with a dramatic call to the Geneva Conference for a one-third reduction in all armaments. But Prohibition dogged his trail. William Allen White urged presidential advisers to be frank in unstraddling the issue. "I know how agitation irks him," White said of the president, "but he cannot send a boy to do this job." On August 11, Hoover accepted the call of his party with a mild appeal for a program along the lines of the platform. Even this he found a disturbing break with tradition and instinct. Privately, he predicted it would cause his defeat in November, a complete misreading of the public mind. To Secretary Stimson, he went further still. "I feel more depressed and troubled than I ever have been in my whole life," he said. "All my life I have been connected with the God-fearing people of this country. . . . I feel now that I have made a decision that will affront them and make them feel that I have betrayed them." [14]

Meanwhile, in Chicago, the Democrats nominated a man as cavalier in his contempt for what he called "foolish traditions" as Hoover seemed enamored of them. "The country needs, and unless I mistake its temper, the country demands bold, persistent experimentation," Franklin Roosevelt told his inner circle. "It is common sense to take a method and try it. If it fails, admit it frankly and try another. But above all try something. The millions who are in want will not stand by silently forever while things to satisfy their needs are within easy reach." Hoover, judged Robert Moses, "was the country doctor who had been treating a family for years. If you got sick, he would say to you, 'Well you are in bad shape. . . . It's going to be a tough battle but together maybe we can work this out.' Roosevelt . . . was like the Park Avenue gynecologist with a terrific bedside manner. . . . He could tell the American people, 'We're going to get well fast. We're going to fix things up. We're going to make things right again. The only thing we have to fear is fear itself.' " [15]

Flexible where Hoover was adamant, gregarious where the president was withdrawn, Roosevelt was a curious liberal, a man who wanted government to do the decent thing without going into debt. Personally, he boasted, he could get nine shaves from a single razor blade. Hoover himself defined as a weakness his opponent's lifelong wealth and status as "sort of the kept son of his mother." But life had bred security into the handsome governor of New York, whose leonine features broke naturally into a smile, whose voice inspired confidence in millions of radio listeners, and whose own bout with polio had deepened the sympathies and broadened the outlook of a Hudson Valley aristocrat. [16]

Hoover at the time and historians later made much of Roosevelt's inconsistencies during the 1932 campaign—how he called for a 25 percent cut in federal expenditures while simultaneously demanding vast increases in relief programs—and the president scored what he regarded as a telling blow by conclusively demonstrating that his rival's plan to put men to work planting a billion trees would provide barely three days of work. Roosevelt was often vague or contradictory, harassing Hoover alternately from left or right. He had a genius for the haphazard, and when he nodded his big head and cooed "I understand," it was a rare supplicant who failed to go away convinced of the candidate's warmhearted backing. Even Adolph Berle of Roosevelt's famous "Brain Trust" worried about FDR's apparent tendency to be all things to all men, and Hoover effectively attacked the composite speeches written by Albany academics who were "experts in semantics but grievously undernourished on truth."[17]

All of which counted for nothing at a time when desperate people were uplifted by the prospect of a "New Deal," including old-age pensions, unemployment insurance, farm relief, economic nationalism and publicly generated power—and when one industrious hitchhiker got from coast to coast in record time by displaying a sign that read, "Give me a lift or I'll vote for Hoover."

Already, Roosevelt's personality and charm were assuming legendary proportions. Having been a legend himself, Hoover preferred to defend abstract principles. When Roosevelt publicly charged the president with having done nothing to stem the Depression between October of 1929 and the end of 1931, Republican National Chairman Everett Sanders responded that Hoover had banished forever the old economic doctrine of what is to be, will be. To Sanders, the president was like Michelangelo in the Sistine Chapel, working away in silence, oblivious to the critics who saw nothing more than scaffolding. He would be reelected, Sanders continued, because he had maintained the gold standard, exercised economy, promoted a balanced budget and taken the courageous step of raising taxes on the eve of an election. Another party official, still closer to the White House, looked elsewhere for signs of comfort. "Maybe the army intelligence tests of 14 years ago were wrong," David Hinshaw wrote to William Allen White early in August, "and . . . there are more than 20% of our people above 14 years old mentally. If so, the Republicans have a chance; if not, we will be making the fight only because that is the thing to do." White replied with both foreboding and insight. "Roosevelt is going to have the devil's own time electing Hoover."[18]

★   ★

The president had planned to deliver no more than three speeches. But on September 12, Maine voters threw over their historic allegiance to his party, and Hoover changed his mind. "It is a catastrophe for us," he commented. "The thing for us to do is to carry the fight right to Roosevelt whenever the opportunity presents itself. . . . We have got to crack him every time he opens his mouth." Hastily, a speaking schedule was devised, and the Lincoln study was transformed into a literary assembly line, with the president dictating draft after draft of the long, ponderous addresses with which he hoped to convince posterity if not the electorate. His first speech, set for Des Moines on the fourth of October, ran to seventy-one pages. In it, he defended his policies, claimed credit for preserving the gold standard and warned of congressional Democrats who would create a "rubber dollar" and turn the federal government into "the most gigantic pawnbroker in history." For farmers, he outlined a twelve-point program. He spoke of public works and drought relief, international disarmament and a labor policy "which placed humanity before money through the sacrifice of profits and dividends before wages."

To all who listened to him in person or via radio, Hoover tried to convey the frustration of battles fought largely in private, despite "hideous misrepresentation and unjustified complaint." It was, he said, as if the public's knowledge of his fight was limited to the stream of dead and wounded returning from the front. "Let no man tell you it could not be worse. It could be so much worse that these days now, distressing as they are, would look like veritable prosperity." Logic was with the president, but not irony. Here he was, the confident superman of the New Era, who four years before pledged the abolition of poverty from American soil, reduced to asking for a second term with the cry that things might have been worse.

Agnes Meyer caught the sense of impending disaster. "Earlier when I said that I would not care to see him defeated, just because the situation offered great opportunities for misrepresentation," Meyer wrote in her diary, "he looked so deep into my eyes that I could see what a tragedy it would be in his life. . . . He is still consumed with ambition in spite of all that he has suffered. The man's will-to-power is almost a mania. The idea of good will, of high achievement is strong in him, but he is not interested in the good that must be accomplished through others or even with the help of others. Only what is done by Hoover is of any meaning to him. He is a big man but he cannot bear rivalry of any sort."[19]

Later that night, against his own wishes, Hoover was prevailed upon to address a group of Iowa editors, not on Depression measures or the protective tariff, but on his own boyhood in West Branch. It was, agreed those present, perhaps the most effective talk of his campaign. It was also the last display of reminiscence to grace Hoover's stumping. For there was Roosevelt to deal with: Roosevelt with his endless appeals to "the forgotten man"; Roosevelt, who traveled lightly intellectually, swinging wildly between Woodrow Wilson's New Freedom and his fifth cousin's New Nationalism, suggesting in one speech that government regulation would correct economic injustice, only to veer toward more radical reforms and the hint of centralized planning in a later text. FDR vowed to cut a billion dollars from the federal budget, and Hoover responded that it had already been done, and that if the voters would return a cooperative Congress, still more might be cut. Roosevelt called the Hawley-Smoot tariff a "ghastly jest" and sounded a call for reciprocal trade agreements in place of tariff barriers. Hoover counterattacked, winning votes in the Midwest and Northeast with his contention that the tariff had saved jobs—and his opponent was forced to backtrack. Hoover proved that his veto of a public power bill had been sustained with Democratic votes in the Senate, exposed congressional obstruction, and called Roosevelt's promise of work for every jobless American a cynical ploy to win votes from the desperate. To Henry Stimson, the president revealed his strategy: frighten the voters into overcoming their hatred for him.[20]

Early in October, Roosevelt delivered a memorable address at San Francisco's Commonwealth Club, in which he claimed that the American frontier had passed and the nation's industrial plant was largely completed. "Our task now is not discovery or exploitation of natural resources," he continued, "or necessarily producing more goods. It is the somberer, less dramatic business of administering resources and plants already in hand . . . of distributing wealth and products more equitably, of adapting existing economic organizations to the service of the people."

Such assertions struck at the heart of Hoover's philosophy, the idea of immutable progress assured by the foreordained genius of Americans. "What the Governor has overlooked," he said in New York on October 31, "is the fact that we are yet but on the frontiers of development of science, and of invention. I have only to remind you that discoveries in electricity, the internal-combustion engine, the radio—all of which have sprung into being since our land was settled—have in themselves represented the greatest advances in America. [The] . . . philosophy upon which the Governor of New York proposes to conduct the Presidency of the United States is the philosophy of stagnation, of despair. It is the end of hope."

Nor was his campaign limited to a philosophical holding action. For support of his contention that recovery was under way, Hoover could point to the lastest economic indexes, up modestly since midsummer. Prices for farm products rose by 12 percent, according to Federal Reserve measurements. Production of iron and steel went up 20 percent. Textile mills spun 50 percent more of their product. The values of common stock soared by 60 percent between July and October 1932, and the American Federation of

Labor reported an extra 700,000 men at work. Hoarding had been stopped, gold was flowing back into the country, and more banks opened than closed their doors. This set the stage for Hoover's later claim that he had beaten the Depression, only to lose his quarry to a wave of panic attendant on Roosevelt's election and his successor's refusal to pledge fealty to the gold standard. Such a claim ignored other evidence that the economy was spiraling downward toward the collapse of March 1933: the sharp drop in credit, despite purchases of government securities and the best efforts of the Reconstruction Finance Corporation, the steep decline in bank deposits, and the failure of Hoover's encouraging statistics to translate into visible relief for the ten million without jobs.

None of which mattered to the embattled chief executive. He was in the fight of his life, and he wanted every reserve that might be pressed into battle brought up to join him on the frontline. Henry Stimson was appalled early in September when Hoover asked him to make a speech attacking Roosevelt's record as an administrator in New York. Yet Stimson judged the effect of the president's Des Moines defense to be "magical," and others seemed to agree. Coolidge came around with a radio appeal calculated by GOP strategists to have been worth a million votes. Henry Ford, Alice Longworth and Negro activist Mary McLeod Bethune all took to the airwaves on his behalf. Hoover took comfort in a note from a Harrisburg, Pennsylvania, supporter who reported a sign in a local jewelry store that read, "That was a pretty bad depression, wasn't it?" By October 16, with the *Literary Digest* reporting a shift of sentiment in its straw poll, he was telling intimates that the contest yet might be won if only he could raise more funds. Thereafter, in addition to staying up late at night to write his speeches, Hoover took to tapping campaign contributors personally. Two days after his doctor made him leave a reception line because of physical exhaustion, he was stumping through Ohio and Pennsylvania, telling ten audiences a day of his fight to save their industries through the tariff. His back to the wall, he was trading punches like a man revivified, before crowds as large as any seen in local memory. Thirty thousand came out to see the president at Akron at nightfall; 50,000 stood outside an Indianapolis auditorium already filled to overflowing. In Illinois, a predicted Democratic margin of 300,000 was melting fast.[21]

"I don't know how I shall fare," Hoover confided to those on board his campaign special, "but our country will never allow itself to lose." He could not altogether evade suffering or public anger. At Detroit, a handpicked arena crowd cheered him to the rafters, but outside the hall, there were loud boos and chants of "Down with Hoover" and "Hoover—Baloney and Applesauce." Four men were arrested outside the city's train station, including Michigan's Communist candidate for governor, and Ted Joslin feared the worst when he heard a lightbulb crash to the pavement a few feet from the president's car. Hoover himself looked stricken as he drove through hosts of people demanding he be hung. Not far from St. Paul, where the president praised the army for its dispersal of the Bonus Army and caused an audible ripple of dissent to run through his audience, a man was caught pulling up spikes from the rails over which Hoover's train was due to pass.[22]

In New York, he delivered an impassioned plea on behalf of capitalism itself. He claimed for himself the mantle of "true liberalism" and insisted that the proposed new deal of his opponent would endanger ordered liberty. He acknowledged that prosperity had blinded many, and led to economic abuses. But he would not abandon his loyalty to the system that had raised him up. "It is men that do wrong," he cried out at Madison Square Garden, "not our institutions. It is men who violate the laws and public rights. It is men, not institutions, that must be punished." Then, in a specific reference to Democratic calls for tariff reduction—but which subsequent writers interpreted as Hoover's anathema on Roosevelt's election itself—the president predicted that "the grass will grow in a hundred cities, a thousand towns; the weeds will overrun the fields of millions of farms."

He left the East and turned his direction back to the heartland—to Indiana and Illinois, Missouri and Wisconsin. In St. Louis on November 4, he recalled Roosevelt's criticism of him for failing to prevent Wall Street's speculative bubble and said he had little taste for turning the White House into a stock tipster's office. He faulted Roosevelt for proposing securities reform after failing to take action as governor of New York, and quoted Al Smith himself to absolve the Republicans as a party from responsibility for the Crash. Roosevelt, said Hoover, seemed oblivious to the fact that good times had come to an end in at least twenty-two other nations before America awoke to Black Tuesday.

On and on Hoover traveled, flailing out at his rival and defending his record in the face of bitter opposition. At one point, after tomatoes had splashed his train in Kansas, Hoover faltered. "I can't go on with it anymore," he blurted out as Lou put her arm around him. But he quickly recovered. When the president pleaded indulgence of a crowd in Carlin, Nevada, for not speaking (his voice was a husky whisper, and he was due to deliver one final radio appeal to the nation that evening), someone called out, "Oh raspberries." Hoover lost his composure. "If the man who made that remark will step forward I will tend to him." Walter Lippmann pronounced his public comments "the language of panic," while a behind-the-scenes struggle raged over Hoover's defense of the diluted Prohibition plank in the GOP platform. Nevada's governor refused to greet the president, eggs were tossed at his train, and watchmen scared away two would-be assassins carrying sticks of dynamite near the rail crossing reserved for Hoover's Pullman. The president himself said that the mood on board recalled Warren Harding's funeral train.[23]

When the time came for Hoover to make the closing address of his campaign, his manuscript fell on the floor, and then, in the poor lighting, he could barely make out the words that warned Americans to beware of what he called "false gods arrayed in the rainbow colors of promise." On the last day of the campaign, silent crowds stared at the presidential motorcade as it made its way down San Francisco's Market Street. Residents of Oakland hooted openly as Hoover went by. At Palo Alto, he said he was glad to be home, and apologized for bringing back everything from his 11,000-mile journey but his voice. He wanted to say more, had prepared a greeting for his "cherished friends and kindly neighbors. I know that some thoughtless person has said I am not responsive to these demonstrations of human friendship. No more cruel thing was ever said. My heart flows and my soul is nourished by your handclaps and your smiles of welcome."[24]

True as it was, it was too revealing—and too demanding for a man past the point of exhaustion. The Secret Service wanted a reception for Stanford's faculty called off; Hoover might collapse at any moment. Three times, the president shook the hand of an agent he had known ten years, each time addressing him as if he were a voter being met for the first time. "See," Lou Hoover told a crowd let through Secret Service lines, "we are carrying on."[25]

Her husband told the professors that he had renewed sympathy for their efforts. "I, too, have tried to be a teacher during the past four years," he reminded them, "and have sought to teach some of the elements of political economy to my fellow countrymen. What I want to impress on you teachers is this: you don't know how fortunate you are that you do not have to be elected by your students!" In El Dorado, Kansas, Vice President Curtis was telling a friend that he was confident of victory. Never, Curtis went on, had he seen such enthusiastic crowds jamming a campaign progress. On November 8, he was proven wrong. In Albany, Roosevelt predicted a victory margin of ten million, and wondered if an even larger win might force Hoover to resign and hand the presidency over to him four months before Inauguration Day, circumventing the natural order of succession. It was barely nine o'clock in Palo Alto when the Hoovers emerged from their study. Outside, an avalanche of rejection was piling up, eased only by a crowd of students singing college songs and cheering "Sis-boom-bah! President and Mrs. Hoover!"[26]

The president went up on the roof of his house to thank the crowd for their friendship. A girls' choir sang "Taps" and Lou stood at his shoulder as Hoover expressed gratitude for "this demonstration of fine loyalty." He turned away from newsreel cameramen, not wanting them to see the tears glistening in the light of student bonfires. Then he went back inside, put his arm in Lou's, shook the hands of all present, cast a final glance at those assembled around him, and flashed a smile of relief. "Good night, my friends," he called out. "That's that!"

The next morning, bruised by rejection and bewildered by the scope of his defeat, he sent a telegram to Roy Roberts in Kansas. A few days later, Roberts boarded the presidential train en route back to Washington. Inside he found a president much older than the cheerful man he had congratulated for his good fortune with farmers three summers earlier. Now Hoover looked up at his friend, with a singular greeting for the editor of the *Kansas City Star.* "Why?" he asked.

★　　★

Hoover's loss had the resonance of a volcanic eruption, the ordered certainty of the four seasons. Forty-two of the forty-eight states rejected him on November 8, 1932. Fewer than 40 percent of the nation's voters opted for staying the course as chartered by their incumbent president. "Well, it's all over," wrote William Allen White privately. "I still think it wasn't Roosevelt. I think it was the depression, the desire for a change and an instinctive demand for leadership . . . which would take the people into its confidence and not work behind the veil." In public, White sounded a more ambiguous note. No one could guess in the immediate aftermath of Election Day, he told his readers, whether "this battling figure of the President is an emblem of futility crushed by the onrush of new times and strange new ways of men, or whether he is the hero who went down with the blazoned banner that shall rise victorious before the battle ends." Only when a decade or more had passed, concluded White, would American be able to divine for themselves whether Hoover was "the last routed defender of the old order or a leader born before his time."[27]

"It will work out some way," Hoover told associates frightened of the future. Meanwhile, personal as well as public demands crowded in upon the defeated man who made his way cross-country during the second week of November, his wife never leaving his side. Soon, he would be an ex-president, without official platform or position, income or influence. While not dismissing the possibility of running in 1936, Hoover told intimates that he was resolved to remain "entirely out of public life" for at least eighteen months after turning the presidency over to Roosevelt.[28]

Beyond that, he had no plans formulated for life after March 4, only a hope for some rest and some fishing. He didn't want to live in Palo Alto, he confided to Lou; that college town was too provincial in outlook, too isolated from events and their shapers, to satisfy him for more than a few months. It would be "embarrassing" to settle in Washington, as Wilson had before him; he would all too easily find himself drawn into every controversy, however petty, that his successor might kick up. He would maintain an office in the capital, in order to supervise publication of materials vindicating his administration. He might develop a university tie, belated assuagement for having spurned the Stanford presidency. He would devote more time to "Operation Pack Rat," his global search for war documents. He would pull down the blinds, without consigning himself to the shelf.[29]

Worried about his investments, Hoover speculated on entering the transportation field, or investigating the paper industry. "I'm going to look for mercury," he told one friend, who noted the coexistence of the valuable mineral and some challenging brook trout in the same corner of the Northwest. There was no shortage of private offers to enrich a former president. Henry Ford offered $3,500 a week for a five-minute radio broadcast, to air from Palo Alto or any other place of Hoover's desire. The McNaught Syndicate wanted him to write a newspaper column, in the manner of Coolidge. The *Saturday Evening Post* pressed its claim for literary contributions. Other invitations piled up from the National Drug Company, the radio tube industry, South Carolina textile mills and Idaho gold mines.[30]

Edgar Rickard, perhaps Hoover's closest friend and for twenty years his confidant, placed little credence in the president's insistence on a period of rest following Roosevelt's inauguration. "My own view," he wrote in his diary, "is that he can never retire, even for a month, from participation in public affairs. His recreation is hard work, the harder the more he likes it."[31]

No one questioned Hoover's taste for work. But what could he contribute after March 4? Given the public mood, who would listen if he spoke out? "People seem to think the presidential machinery should keep on running," Coolidge had remarked not long before his death, "even after the power has been turned off." Confronted with the sobering example of his predecessor's retirement, Hoover might easily be excused for believing that his power would be turned off permanently once the clock struck noon on Inauguration Day.

★   ★

Once before, there had been an American president confronted with the prospect of national dissolution, a man linked in history's mind with feeble irrelevance. *Vanity Fair* looked at James Buchanan's White House during the crisis months between Abraham Lincoln's election and Buchanan's own departure from office and pronounced the presidential residence a "White Old House" inhabited by a gray old rat. Around Washington, it was said that no one knew better than Buchanan how to keep a secret, and to his niece the president gave advice that had served him well during a thirty-year diplomatic career. "Be quiet and discreet and say nothing," he admonished her. But America was dividing down the center, or, more precisely, rushing headlong for the extremes. Discretion would not reverse the process. Frozen in his passion for constitutional gentility, the fifteenth president denied alike the right of southern states to leave the Union, or the federal government to use force to prevent their secession. Attending conferences, writing letters, resorting to moral suasion at a time when violence threatened his most cherished ideals, in the end he became a figure of pity. "I at least meant well for my country," he told Congress in his farewell message, and to one congressman's wife, he appealed for sympathy. "Nobody knows the heart of a President," he told her.

And once before in the nation's journey there had been a president-elect, faced by an unprecedented challenge and badgered throughout the four-month interregnum between his election and inauguration for at least a tipping of his policy hand. Lincoln responded with the homely story of Fox River, and a band of Illinois lawyers fretting over ways it might be forded after a stream-swelling rain. Eventually, they were put up for the night, at a tavern also frequented by a Methodist presiding elder. Like the lawyers, the preacher traveled in all weather. He knew the lie of the land. So when they asked him if he was acquainted with Fox River, he replied that he had crossed it often. "But I have one fixed rule with regard to Fox River: I never cross it till I reach it."

For twelve weeks, Lincoln refused to divulge how he might cross Fox River, while Buchanan wrung his hands and predicted to a visitor from New York that he was the last president the United States would ever have. Then, on March 4, 1861, the two men climbed into an open carriage, and rode to the Capitol, past sharpshooters set out to guard against public assassination. Lincoln told a city bristling with bayonets that the Union was perpetual and inviolable.

Like a weary phantom, the Lincoln-Buchanan transition has haunted history's view of the far stormier relations between Herbert Hoover and Franklin Roosevelt in the months bridging the end of 1932. At a time when *Barron's*, no hotbed of radical sentiment, was proclaiming its preference for "a genial and lighthearted dictator," and labor leader William Green was declaiming before a Senate committee about "class war" and "the language of force," it wasn't difficult for the outgoing president to wonder if he might not, in fact, turn out to be America's Alexander Kerensky, a moderate precursor of a radical shift in values. To his critics, Hoover was a Buchanan, tragically unwilling to go further than his constitutional scruples in combatting an economic whirlwind that might tear apart the fabric of even that sacred document. In his repeated overtures to Roosevelt for "cooperation," he was really trying to reverse the election results, tarring the president-elect with his own discredited policies. To his defenders, Hoover during the bitter final weeks of his presidency was a man on the verge of victory, who had arrested the downward spiral only to see it slip out of control through the irresponsible behavior of his successor.

It is difficult even now to resist a temptation to personify the events of those bleak months, to measure out blame or award praise. In retrospect, the interregnum is a story of missed opportunities, blatant partisanship, posturing for history. Most of all, it is a simple clash of fundamentally different philosophies. It is an irony of truth that Hoover, celebrated as the apostle of rugged individualism, staked his claim to posterity's favorable judgment on his defense of institutions—and that Roosevelt, the old Wilsonian, was so willing to abandon his mentor's faith in international solutions in favor of economic nationalism. For Hoover and Roosevelt alike, their campaign rhetoric conveyed more of their beliefs than even they recognized. The president held that the Depression was global in scope and origin, and that no domestic recovery could come without international action to restore the gold standard and, with it, the stability of currency worth more than the paper on which it was printed.

For his part, FDR cared less about a world shedding its former idols than he did about domestic reform. As his advisers pointed out, individualism was a cruel hoax in a nation where two-thirds of all industry was concentrated in the hands of six hundred corporations, and where the flow of capital, like the deposits of banks, was dominated by no more than twenty great banks and banking houses. To the Brain Trust, no amount of regulatory tinkering could solve the crisis of American capitalism, which they defined as the inability of purchasing power to match technology's quickening pace of production. Unlike Hoover, they believed that the American frontier was finally closing, economically as well as geographically. Hoover denounced regimentation, but there was regimentation in work, in savings, "even in unemployment and starvation," as Adolph Berle put it for the governor of New York. Roosevelt, who himself liked to distinguish between "Buchanan types and Lincoln types," cared little for the abstruse reasonings that were as mother's milk to his defeated rival. "People aren't cattle, you know," he angrily informed one cold-blooded economist.

Even if endowed with far more good will toward each other, it is unlikely under the circumstances that two other men could have forged a closer working relationship. In fact, both Hoover and Roosevelt came to the transition carrying a heavy baggage of perceived insults and deep-rooted suspicions. Each cast a jaundiced view on the other; neither could see the mote in his own eye. Hoover himself came to have a grand obsession on the subject of Roosevelt that would poison his mind and limit his options for more than a decade: as early as November 17, 1932, he assigned a White House stenographer to secretly record a telephone conversation he had with his rival. Roosevelt, cried the president, had "the bravado of a 15 year old boy," and he told friends that he knew beyond doubt that Roosevelt wrote none of the speeches he delivered during the campaign. For his part, FDR could chuckle till the last day of his life at William Allen White's characterization of Hoover as "a fat, timid capon." Hoover, concluded the president-elect, was "cheeky" in his efforts to ensnare him in defense of old and failed dogmas. Nor could he forget the physical ordeal to which he had been subjected a few months earlier, forced to stand in his steel braces for half an hour while a delayed Hoover kept all those attending the National Governors' Conference waiting in the White House East Room.[32]

Long afterward, mellowed by the years and liberated by Roosevelt's passing, Hoover confessed to personal limitations. "My education was that of an engineer," he revealed. "I do not know all the nuances of economics." Yet no such humility governed his actions in the dramatic confrontations that followed the election. When Roosevelt came to the White House on November 22 for what he termed a "wholly informal and personal visit," he was dismayed to find Hoover's Treasury Secretary, Ogden Mills, in the Red Room. The atmosphere of chill was not eased by the schoolmasterish manner Hoover adopted toward Roosevelt and his economic adviser, Raymond Moley.[33]

For over an hour, the president laid out the dimensions of the war debt crisis, renewed with Britain and France's request for a continuation of the moratorium due to expire before year's end. He floated the idea of reviving the old War Debt Commission, and Roosevelt nodded his head—a signal Hoover was not alone in taking for assent. ("When I talk to him," Huey Long once noted, "he says 'Fine! Fine! Fine!' But Joe Robinson goes to see him the next day and again he says 'Fine! Fine! Fine!' Maybe he says 'Fine!' to everybody.") In fact, the president-elect was more concerned about placating Democratic congressional leaders, who were flatly opposed to any softening on the debts, than the debtor nations of Europe. Before he left, he asked Hoover whether he might endorse a farm plan calling for domestic allotments, and the president replied, more forthrightly if less adeptly, that he was unlikely to do so. Less diplomatic still was his curt rebuke to Roosevelt and Moley, when the president-elect signaled it was time for his advisers to leave the room. "Nobody leaves before the president," he reminded them.

Outside the White House, Roosevelt cheerfully admitted that the war debts issue, like the forthcoming World Economic Conference, was "not my baby." Although factually correct, it was a poor choice of words, guaranteed to inflame Hoover's doubts and deepen the impression of Roosevelt as a man of diffuse vision and vague instincts. The *Baltimore Sun* voiced the opinion of many when it warned that the baby so cavalierly disowned "may soon develop into an unruly stepchild lodged permanently under his roof and disposed to play with matches." When Hoover talked with Democratic congressional spokesmen, he was astonished that no word from FDR had reached them on the debt question. Not that the president-elect was wholly silent: late in December, after Hoover presented a final message to Congress urging government economy, fresh public works, construction of a St. Lawrence Seaway, and reform of the nation's weakened banking system, Roosevelt passed word to his party's lawmakers that he was opposed to the president's call for excise taxes. Balanced budgets themselves had less luster for the New Yorker—and Congress stalled obligingly until March.

A few days later, John Nance Garner, two months away from being inaugurated as FDR's vice president, enraged Hoover with his bill to require public disclosure of all RFC loans to ailing financial institutions. As Hoover saw it, this was an invitation to disaster, at a time when confidence in the banking structure was already undermined by Senate hearings into notorious practices by Charles E. Mitchell's National City Bank of New York. Yet Congress would not adopt his own reform legislation, or his plan to expand RFC lending authority to nonbanking institutions. Hoover's own Attorney General told him that the president's idea of a one-day moratorium on banking operations nationwide would require congressional approval—and that was impossible without Roosevelt's agreeing to the plan.

A second conference between the two men on December 20, again called to discuss foreign debts and how the U.S. might respond to European appeals for cancellation, resulted in a public misunderstanding. Hoover and Roosevelt released conflicting memoranda on the meeting, Roosevelt allowing he was "rather surprised" that the president had taken such a step at all. It was, he concluded, "a pity" for the country and for the prospective solution of foreign dilemmas that any impression might be fostered of his own unwillingness to be cooperative. Hewing to a course of independence, Roosevelt was cheerfully contemptuous of those clamoring for him to spell out a program. "Let's concentrate on one thing," he remarked to one old friend during the interregnum. "Save the people and the nation and, if we have to change our minds twice every day to accomplish that end, we should do it."

A month later, the two protagonists met for a third time. Afterward, Moley described Hoover that afternoon as being close to the breaking point. "He had the look of being done, but still of going on and on, driven by some damned duty." Again Hoover pressed for a commitment to the gold standard at the World Economic Conference. Speaking for Roosevelt, Moley insisted that the issue of concessions to the British could hardly be linked to their tariffs or currency. Besides, Moley felt, none of it was relevant to the real issue at hand—the restoration of domestic confidence. By now, Hoover seriously doubted his successor's commitment to gold. As usual, Roosevelt was sending out contradictory signals, reserving to himself maximum freedom of action. Despite mostly conservative talk during the campaign, and his own appointments of orthodox advisers like Arizona congressmen Lewis Douglas to be head of the Budget Bureau, and William Woodin to succeed Mills at Treasury, Roosevelt as early as mid-October of 1932 had told advisers he was unwilling to guarantee the gold standard. He hadn't "the faintest idea," he snapped, whether or not the nation would be on gold come March 4, 1933. Two months later, meetings in Albany led to rumors of an impending shift away from gold and in favor of a devalued currency, akin in Hoover's mind to seismic warnings prior to a devastating earthquake.

Before the end of January, Roosevelt ignored demands from the *New York Times* and the Federal Reserve Board to give some signal to calm investors' fears. Henry Wallace, slated to be FDR's Agriculture Secretary, publicly called for gold's abandonment. The president's attitude hardened. Stimson, for one, was worried. Hoover, it seemed to his Secretary of State, "is not thinking so much of the welfare of the world," he noted on January 21, "as he is about his own record and party advantage." A few days later, the atmosphere between the outgoing and incoming executives grew chillier still, according to Stimson, because of a report carried in the Hearst press claiming Hoover was trying to trap his successor into a negotiating stance with other nations.[34]

Early in February, the nation's banking system began to totter, with daily withdrawals of currency reported at ten to fifteen million dollars and likely to rise. Hoover found himself drawn into a desperate struggle between two old antagonists, Henry Ford and Michigan's crusty Senator James Couzens. At stake was the survival of Detroit's Guardian Trust Company, in which

Ford maintained large deposits and which was appealing to the RFC for an immediate infusion of cash to stave off bankruptcy. Ford had already invested more than $16 million in Guardian. He would not take the extra step of freezing his deposits, he informed emissaries from the White House. Couzens was less willing still to commit himself or his personal fortune. Out of bitter enmity for the automobile magnate, once his friend and more recently a detested foe, the senator was willing to see Guardian fail—and take with it the rest of Michigan's banking system. What's more, he made it plain that he would block any RFC loan to the bank already secured by Hoover's success in persuading both General Motors and Chrysler to deposit funds in Guardian. Hoover lost his temper.

"If 800,000 small depositors in my home town could be saved by lending three per cent of my fortune even if I lost," he remarked to Couzens, "I certainly would do it."

In the end, neither Ford nor Couzens would yield, and Michigan's governor declared a ten-day bank holiday in that state. On February 13, Hoover spoke in New York, at a Republican dinner in honor of Abraham Lincoln's memory. He used the occasion to make a final appeal on behalf of the institutions he wished to rescue from themselves. "Ever since the storm began in Europe, the United States has stood staunchly to the gold standard. . . . We have thereby maintained our Gibraltar of stability in the world and contributed to check the movement of chaos." But other nations had declared an economic siege of reduced currencies and raised barriers to trade. "If the world is to secure economic peace . . . it must start somewhere to break these vicious fiscal and financial cycles. . . ."

Gold, said Hoover, was a commodity that the world had not yet outgrown. Like a loose cannon on the deck of a storm-tossed ship, he continued, gold went wherever it was wanted, wherever it was safe. Those who feared its discontinuance might easily spread panic among the users of banks. For proof, Hoover drew upon words that might have been composed a decade earlier by Woodrow Wilson. The American people, he said, would soon find themselves "at the fork of three roads. The first is the highway of co-operation among nations, thereby to remove the obstacles to world consumption and the rise of prices. This road leads to real stability, to the expanded standards of living, to a resumption of the march of progress by all peoples. The second road is to rely upon our high degree of national self-containment, to increase our tariffs, to create quotas and discriminations. . . . The third road is that we inflate our currency, abandon the gold standard, and with our depreciated currency attempt to enter a world economic war, with the certainty that it leads to complete destruction, both at home and abroad."

He appealed for unity and closed with a final reference to his hero, in whose study he conducted business and to whom he would be compared derisively in the years to come. "Civilization," said Hoover, "is the history of surmounted difficulties. We of this world are of the same strain as our fathers who built this civilization. They passed through terrible conflicts. They met many great depressions." The next forward step in history, he told his audience, would be greater still. In the spirit of Lincoln, "it is that we perpetuate the welfare of mankind through the immense objectives of world recovery and world peace." Wilson would have approved. But Wilson had lain eight years in his grave. His memory might be fresh, but his ideas seemed dated. Like so much else that Hoover touched, the concept of a world pulling in harness crumbled in his hands.

★   ★

The banking crisis that began in mid-February, 1933, and culminated in national paralysis on Inauguration Day gave Hoover's administration its final aura of failure. It provided Roosevelt with a dramatic launching pad for the New Deal. It completed the poisoning of relations between both men, and set the tone for a generation of Democratic attacks upon Hoover and his party. Throughout, Hoover would claim that the panic was manufactured, akin to Hitler's burning of the Reichstag to create a false emergency. Citing statistics to prove that over 80 percent of the nation's banks had sufficient deposits on hand to comply with public demand, he seized upon an impolitic comment by Roosevelt adviser Rexford Tugwell to the effect that the entire system would collapse on or about March 4, and that the president-elect should do nothing to deny his predecessor both responsibility and blame. For Hoover, this was proof positive that FDR wished a Roman holiday for his inauguration. Allowing for lapses in FDR's personal behavior during the crisis—something Hoover, of all men, was unlikely to do—the reality of the situation was both more sweeping and less conspiratorial than imagined by the embittered man in the White House. "Some people can never understand," Roosevelt once admitted in a moment of candor, "that you have to wait, even for the best things, until the right time comes." For FDR, that time would be 12:01 on the afternoon of March 4, and not a moment before.

With his own notions of virtue in place of the mystical ones of political leadership, Hoover did not seem to grasp this. On February 17, he wrote Roosevelt a lengthy letter, in longhand. It contained some remarkable requests. "A most critical situation has arisen," he began, in reference to "a steadily degenerating confidence in the future which had reached the height of general alarm." There followed a pained litany of instances in which Hoover, fighting the instincts of Congress, had restored confidence and maintained the government's credit. With the election, he continued, had come new uncertainty, deepened by publication of the RFC loans, Congress's failure to cut spending and enact banking legislation, and, as Hoover phrased it, "all the chatter about dictatorship." As a result, hoarding was again on the rise, with capital fleeing and Detroit's bank crisis only a preview of likely developments elsewhere. Credit was available, Hoover insisted, but a lack of public confidence paralyzed borrowers and lenders alike.

"It would steady the country greatly if there could be prompt assurance that there will be no tampering of inflation of the currency," he informed his successor, "that the budget will be unquestionably balanced, even if further taxation is necessary; that the Government credit will be maintained by refusal to exhaust it in the issue of securities. . . . It would be of further help," Hoover went on, "if the leaders could be advised to cease publication of RFC business." For good measure, he concluded that he would welcome announcement of the identity of Roosevelt's new Secretary of the Treasury, "as that would enable us to direct activities to one point of action and communication with your good self." For several weeks in private, Hoover had been hoping for a strong Cabinet to "guard" FDR as he put it; a less euphemistic word would have been "hamstring." [35]

At Hyde Park, Roosevelt let ten days go by, then apologized lamely for a secretary who misplaced his original reply to the president's extraordinary message. "I am equally concerned with you," he wrote, "in regard to the gravity of the present banking situation, but my thoughts is that it is so very deep-seated that the fire is bound to spread in spite of anything that is done by mere statements." Roosevelt's expression was more polite than the delay in making it. Amenities aside, there was little else he could do. It was almost comic to suppose that a citizen on his way to withdrawing his life savings would be stayed by the assurance that government's own borrowing would be halted. As for balanced budgets, Hoover had managed only one in four years. The president himself admitted that his letter amounted to a demand that FDR abandon 90 percent of "the so-called new deal" and ratify Hoover's own agenda for recovery. Nor was the chief executive free of political motivations. On February 21, he wrote to Senator Simeon Fess a letter outlining his efforts and warning that "the day will come when the Democratic Party will endeavor to place the responsibility for the events of this period on the Republican Party." His letter to Fess was insurance; Roosevelt wasn't the only one playing to the historical gallery. Yet to Henry Stimson, Hoover railed against Roosevelt as "a madman" for refusing to agree with his requests. [36]

On February 20, it became known that Carter Glass had firmly rejected Roosevelt's invitation to take the Treasury Department. The job went instead to William Woodin, a birdlike little man who wrote songs , preferred the company of fellow composers like George Gershwin and Irving Berlin, and made no secret of his Republican sympathies. Ogden Mills and others began a covert courtship of the secretary-designate, who soon had in his hands a report of gold payments by the New York Federal Reserve Bank, showing the total for February 15 and 16 alone greater than the entire month of January. Agnes Meyer caught the national mood in her diary during the last tumultuous week of February: "World literally rocking beneath our feet. Michigan banks closed last week, Maryland today, Washington in danger, Cleveland tottering. . . . Hard on H[oover] to go out of office on the sound of crashing banks. Like the tragic end to a tragic story." The president, she continued, had been "a bitter disappointment," even to those with few illusions. "God knows I wished him well," concluded Meyer. "Looking back it seems like nothing but blunder after blunder." [37]

At the White House, the president searched almost frantically for an alternative to disaster. Banks in Cleveland were on the brink of disaster, he was informed on the afternoon of the twenty-third—the same day Mills reported back from his meetings with Woodin that Roosevelt would make no statement before the inauguration. "Perhaps they want a breakdown," he blurted out. "That is always the technique of revolution." As for corrupt bankers themselves, Hoover said they were worse than Al Capone. ("He apparently was kind to the poor.") Mark Sullivan suggested a program to insure all bank deposits of under a thousand dollars. Dissatisfied, Hoover sought guidance from the Federal Reserve Board. He asked Bernard Baruch to get a statement out of Roosevelt; neither overture produced its desired effect. Unearthing the old Trading with the Enemy Act, Ogden Mills prepared an order halting bank payments to depositors except for necessities, and controlling the flight of capital. He urged the scheme on Woodin, only to be told that Roosevelt would say nothing. On Tuesday, the twenty-eighth, Hoover again addressed the Federal Reserve Board, suggesting formally a temporary federal guarantee of each depositor's account. He also wrote a fresh appeal to his successor, asking that Congress be called into session as soon as possible after March 4, and pleading for a declaration along the lines described in his earlier letter, to "save losses and hardships to millions of people." [38]

On March 1, Mills and Woodin met again in New York, fruitlessly. "The boss has a great scheme," Woodin announced at one point. "He has the idea that all we need is a bold gesture of confidence and a demonstration that we don't fear anything. . . . He is going to propose the United States instantly redeem all of its outstanding bonds in paper money, no matter what the maturity of the Bond may be. If it has 50 years to run, just buy it in with nice new printed money immediately." Mills was aghast. If such a scheme were to be approved, he exclaimed, "I'm a fit candidate for Bedlam."[39]

The next day, with banking operations suspended or restricted in twenty-three states, and with daily hoarding up to $200 million, Meyer replied for the Federal Reserve Board, throwing cold water on the idea of deposit insurance as well as Hoover's proposal for using scrip in communities where banks were closed. That night, another Reserve official urged a general banking holiday on the president. Hoover would take no action without the Board's concurrence, and Roosevelt's, and the president-elect held fast to his position of noninvolvement. To Senators Carter Glass and Joe Robinson, Hoover said "that when a man's leg is broken it was immaterial so far as the leg was concerned whether he broke it while drunk or while rescuing a child from under a railroad train." In response, they too criticized FDR, but could offer no hope of congressional action without him. On the third, New York banks alone reported losses of over $300 million.

That morning, Hoover conducted his final Cabinet meeting, after which his colleagues presented him with a desk set including a calendar, clock, and barometer. Wryly, he noted that the forecast was for fair weather—he could not be sure whether that meant fair and dry. Later, he met with the press, gathered in a semicircle around his desk. Hands clasped behind his back, the president spoke in a barely audible voice. "I only want to express my appreciation for your conduct and co-operation," he told them. "I have no news today. I think you will find plenty of news in other quarters." He invited them to visit him on the West Coast, when they might discuss matters more objectively. "And so I will say goodbye." He shook hands all around, thanked a reporter who wished him long life, and returned to work.

On his desk was a letter from Will Irwin. "You have fought the good fight," it said, "but you have not finished your course." A New York admirer wrote from a still broader perspective. "As the Executive of the nation you have had the most difficult task of any President. No one before you has been faced with the situation of a worldwide change. Whether it is to be evolution or revolution—a transfer of power and responsibility or an upheaval—is not yet entirely certain. However, you saw the issue and have steadily fought to preserve civilization as we know it and the standards and forms of our American life."[40]

Congress was adjourning without any action on a banking bill. On Wall Street, the stock exchange was rising, in anticipation of the new administration and the restoration of public confidence. No such optimism lurked within Hoover's White House.

At noon, Stimson called with news from Cordell Hull, his designated replacement at State. Hull reported a long, unsuccessful attempt the previous night to get Roosevelt to join in a common declaration of a bank holiday. At three-thirty, Mills advised the president to demand a three-day holiday—a subject both men would take up when the president-elect arrived half an hour later for the customary inaugural-eve social call.

Prefabricated ramps to help Roosevelt maneuver White House corridors in his wheelchair were hidden in the bushes, ready to be assembled the moment the Hoovers left. Tables groaning under the weight of glassware, china, pictures and other gifts from the American people were laid out by the First Lady for the staff. Lou presented Maggie Rogers with a Victrola. On her own, she sounded a defiant note. "My husband will come back someday to do great things," she told Maggie. The president himself confessed his frustration to a reporter. His reddened eyes fixed on the Washington Monument, Hoover told Turner Catledge that the country was in "a hell of a fix," due in part to the failure of "that man" to join him in a statement of reassurance. "Well," he continued, "from now on it will have to be his responsibility."[41]

Although noncommittal otherwise, Roosevelt did agree to discuss a suspension of banking within New York State at a prearranged conversation with Governor Herbert Lehman at six o'clock. Near the end of his visit, FDR informed his host that he needn't return the call, as custom dictated; he obviously had enough to do as it was. Hoover stalked to the door. "Mr. Roosevelt," he replied, "when you have been in Washington as long as I have, you will learn that the president of the United States calls on nobody." Only the timely intervention of Eleanor Roosevelt prevented a scene. "It's been very pleasant," she said, "but we must go now." The visitors took their leave, Hoover returned to the Lincoln study, and the lights burned late throughout official Washington.

When Mills urged a national moratorium on him, Hoover's temper flared. The object of his life, he told Mills, had been to keep the banks open, and he proposed to fight on that line to the end. Twice that night he phoned Roosevelt, who claimed with Lehman as his authority that no proclamation should be issued, that the governors could take care of the situation on a state-by-state basis. Officials in Chicago echoed the advice. At the Treasury Department, Mills, Woodin and others worked through the night to convince the governors of New York and Illinois to close their states' banks. Hoover was at last in bed when both men did so. At one-thirty in the morning, he was awakened by a letter from Meyer, demanding an executive order to shut down every bank in the land. Gold reserves were virtually depleted, claimed Meyer. Hoover rejected the appeal out of hand. Roosevelt did not wish it, he told Meyer that morning, and without the president-elect, Hoover was standing by his assertion that he had insufficient authority to take such a drastic step by himself. To the end, he remained the compassionate legalist, outwitted by a man who, like Lincoln eighty years earlier, was now willing to become what the crisis and the nation demanded: an American version of Plato's Ideal Tyrant. A few weeks later, Henry Stimson noted a conversation with the new president in which Roosevelt noted his good fortune at entering office during a time when the Congress and electorate alike were desperate, throwing up their hands, as Roosevelt put it, and saying, "Please lead us—tell us what to do!"

Exhausted but not surprised at the news from New York and Chicago, Hoover roused himself from bed at six o'clock on the morning of March 4. If he survived the day's ceremonies, he remarked to his staff, he would go to bed for forty-eight hours. To Ted Joslin, he managed a final word. "We are at the end of our string," he muttered. "There is nothing more we can do."

★   ★

Hoover did not play medicine ball on the morning of March 4. Instead, he presented sixteen 5-pound balls, signed by all the players, to members of his daily workout group. Outside, the day was chilly and gray, but dry as predicted by the president's barometer. "Roosevelt weather," his successor called it. Washington hotels refused to accept checks drawn on out-of-town banks. In New York harbor, dock workers were loading $9 million of gold on a ship bound for Europe. In the *Cleveland News* there was an editorial entitled "Two Men and Fate," lauding Hoover's "brave and almost lone-handed fight" and asserting that in normal times, his activism would have earned a high place for "the most sorely beset, yet most conscientiously energetic President since Lincoln." A Hanover, New Hampshire, paper embellished the theme, saying that Hoover would be remembered "as the man who assembled the facts upon which his successor could act." The *Columbus Dispatch* put it more simply still. "He was not a politician," it concluded.

In his office by nine o'clock, Hoover met with Harvey Couch, director of the RFC. Patrick McKenna, head doorkeeper, admitted three black men in white jackets, to sweep the room and bid farewell to a president they hardly knew. Autos waiting to take their place in the inaugural procession filled the long, curving drive, while Hoover chatted with a Secret Service man who had come to remove his presidential flag. It was, the agent thought afterward, the first time in four years that he had exchanged words with one judged by others on the staff to be a whipped man. A few minutes before eleven, the president and Mrs. Hoover appeared in the Blue Room, where the Cabinet and congressional representatives were drawn up. Then Eleanor Roosevelt came into sight, signaling her husband's arrival and the start of the day's official ceremonies.[42]

The two men rode together down Pennsylvania Avenue, Hoover silent for most of the journey, raising his hat but once to acknowledge applause almost certainly not meant for him. Roosevelt tried to make conversation, pointing out the steel scaffolding on government buildings under construction, but it was no use. Only once did the outgoing president rouse himself to speak, asking his successor to find room on the federal bench for his secretary Walter Newton, a former GOP congressman from Minnesota. FDR promised to do his best. The uncomfortable silence resumed. On the pavement could be heard the clip-clop of Douglas MacArthur's Third Cavalry, part of a massive military presence that included army machine guns and hundreds of security men stationed along the route and atop high buildings.

One hundred thousand persons swarmed around Capitol Hill, including a delegation of 1,500 Tammany braves from New York City, thirty of the nation's governors (excluding those from New York and Illinois), and tens of thousands of expectant ordinary citizens. Inside the Capitol, Hoover removed his hat, lit a cigar and winnowed a last-minute pile of bills in the ornate President's Room. Flanked by aides in gilt braid and morning coats, he laid aside measures to provide nearly a billion dollars in veterans' benefits, aid cotton farmers who promised to reduce plantings by 30 percent, and fund independent offices within the federal establishment. Next door, members of Harvard's Fly Club presented their alumnus with a reproduction of Abraham Lincoln's silver inkwell. Franklin Roosevelt wondered out loud what he might do with the gift. "You certainly never could shake a cocktail in a thing like this," he concluded, to general laughter.[43]

President Hoover left the Senate side of the building, striding glassy-eyed past the diplomatic corps arrayed in the great Rotunda. Outside, he stood surveying the throng as the strains of "Hail to the Chief" greeted him for the last time. A few minutes later FDR appeared on the arm of his son, James, and Chief Justice Hughes (whom Hoover had urged to resign rather than serve under the new administration) stepped forward to administer the oath. Hoover leaned forward to catch the cadence of Roosevelt's inaugural address.

It was, said the new president, a time to speak the truth, "frankly and boldly." Conditions could be faced honestly, and overcome. Revival and prosperity would return. "The only thing we have to fear is fear itself— nameless, unreasoning, unjustified terror which paralyzes needed efforts to convert retreat into advance." When it was over, Hoover jumped up, shook his successor's hand, and climbed into the lead car in a procession that carried him through the Capitol grounds to Union Station, five minutes away.

There were five thousand people gathered at trackside as the former president and Lou appeared just after one-thirty. Clutching his tall hat in his left hand, Hoover advanced slowly through the crowd, surrounded by Secret Service men and Cabinet officers in frock coats. "We won't forget you," someone called out. "You are coming back again—don't worry." "You've done your duty." "We'll see you in 1936!" Hoover's face twisted into a faint smile. He dug his hands deeper into the pockets of his dark topcoat as he followed his family in boarding the four-car special destined for New York. Standing motionless on the rear platform, a quizzical expression on his face, he could see members of the National Capital Republican Club before him, along with the Hoover-Curtis Campaign Club and League of Republican Women. Some Girl Scouts made their way forward with candy and roses for Lou. Henry Stimson stood nearby, along with Mills, Hurley and other intimates.

Larry Richey was worried. The crowd, even though friendly, renewed all his fears about security, doubts that two days earlier led him to arrange police protection for his chief in New York. At the station, he turned suddenly to Colonel Starling and asked him to let Secret Service agents come along on the trip. Starling refused. "I am sorry, Larry," he said, "but you are now a private citizen with no authority to order anyone to do anything." There would be four agents of the railroad to accompany the Hoovers, he went on. In New York, there would be plainclothesmen and a motorcycle escort. For the rest of his life Hoover told friends how the White House refused him adequate protection at a time of inflamed sentiments. "I had all the security in the world going to the inauguration," he remarked to one. "The moment Roosevelt was sworn in, I was nothing." Before the day was out, his suite at the Waldorf-Astoria received a telephoned death threat, and Brooklyn police arrested a deranged veteran carrying a gun.[44]

As Hoover's train began chugging out of the station, and the cheers were lost in the sounds of whistles and engines, Lou waved her handkerchief. Her husband turned away from the station crowd to cover the tears in his eyes. Four hours away was another crowd at Pennsylvania Station, watched over by 125 uniformed men and 50 detectives assigned to guard the former president by the city's police commissioner. At the Waldorf, where Hoover would occupy a ten-room suite guarded full-time by three plainclothesmen, a special switchboard was set up to connect him with Washington. But there were no messages from the White House. Hoover made his way through the lobby of the ornate hotel, with its bronze portals, marble hall-ways and 2,200 rooms, only to encounter a festive tea dance in progress—a celebration of Roosevelt's inaugural.

Quickly, he took an elevator to the thirty-third floor, to disappear from the headlines and begin to assemble a future. A local columnist claimed he would stay in New York because of a brewing scandal "dwarfing Teapot Dome." In Pittsburgh, there were rumors that detectives were guarding Hoover in order to prevent him from escaping with a hoard of gold. He had actually been arrested, it was whispered in Memphis, while the story in Detroit had Hoover on board Andrew Mellon's yacht, which was loaded with gold and destined to leave New York harbor at any moment. For Herbert Hoover, the wilderness years had begun.

AN UNHAPPY
WARRIOR

★

1 9 3 3 – 1 9 4 5

CHAPTER FIVE

"THE GOSPEL ACCORDING
TO PALO ALTO"

★

I knew from the bitter experience of all public men from George Washington down that democracies are fickle and heartless. When the ultimate bump came, I was well fortified to accept it philosophically . . . for democracy is a harsh employer. —Herbert Hoover

I don't know what additional authority Roosevelt may ask, but give it to him, even if it's to drown all the boy babies. —Will Rogers, March 1933

★

Hoover did not sleep the forty-eight hours he promised upon arriving in New York; his prediction was put down as the first of a hyperbolic series that littered the years of Franklin Roosevelt's presidency. Instead, the former president rose after twelve hours in his bed, to exchange calls with Ogden Mills in Washington, dictate a plan of action for dealing with the bank crisis, and dabble in the organizational affairs of pet charities like the American Child Health Association and the Belgian-American Educational Fund. He deeded his Rapidan camp officially to the government, for use as a permanent presidential retreat. (FDR visited the place once, only to discover the steep terrain impassable for a man on crutches; in its place, he created Shangri-la in Maryland's Catoctan Mountains, later renamed Camp David by Dwight Eisenhower.) Hoover's mind was still in Washington. At lunch that Sunday, he confided to a friend his expectation that Roosevelt would rush through Congress a set of conservative legislative proposals to

169

allay eastern fears of inflation, then turn to "radical farm measures and labor schemes" as a truer demonstration of his personal and political sympathies. It was one Hoover prophecy destined to be realized.[1]

When the president that night announced a three-day bank holiday, to be followed by a reopening largely crafted by leftover advisers in Hoover's Treasury Department, his predecessor muffled his private criticisms. FDR's action, he announced, "should receive the wholehearted support and co-operation of every citizen." Not everyone agreed. That same day, Washington police used nightsticks to disperse two hundred communist demonstrators demanding five-dollar-a-week relief allowances, and equal treatment for black and white citizens. More typical of national reaction was Walter Lippmann's column in the *New York Herald Tribune* proclaiming, "There are good crises and there are bad crises . . . the present crisis is a good crisis." The new president, whose inaugural address and subsequent actions would draw half a million letters within his first week in office, was a man "fresh in mind and bold in spirit," wrote Lippmann. ("Some day he will be buried with those who spent their lives in dialectics over the Nicene Creed," snapped Hoover in assessing America's leading pundit. "In the meantime his contribution to civilization is one of boosting nuts and then dissecting their doctrines until they perish under his attentions.") The same paper's editorial page chose to look elsewhere for inspiration. "During the last three years," it concluded, "Herbert Hoover has bled himself to the last drop to compensate our anemia as individuals. He has tried to make up from himself what we lacked in courage, what we denied each other in mutual trust. . . ." The *Springfield* (Massachusetts) *Leader* eulogized "a grim-visaged, weary man, forgotten by the nation that acclaimed him . . . only yesterday."[2]

Few New Yorkers took notice of the gray-haired tourist in dark business suit, a felt hat low on his head, as he strolled each morning before breakfast up Fifth Avenue or past the new Radio City, whose marquee promised newsreels of Roosevelt's inauguration. Hoover confined his shopping to the window variety; caught short of cash as a result of the bank holiday, he relied on friends to take his checks or advance him funds. His bitterness, so well concealed from the public, was stoked by fresh reports of rumors sweeping the capital. His old Assistant Secretary of State, William Castle, phoned the Waldorf with word that "supposedly responsible people" were spreading a story that Hoover was being detained in New York per order of the Justice Department. Others whispered that he was under surveillance—a tale inadvertently given credence when the Roosevelt White House reversed itself and offered to dispatch Secret Service agents to accompany the ex-president on his way back to Palo Alto. Even Steve Early, the new chief executive's press secretary, found himself angrily denying a story that Hoover had been apprehended with a passport and $5 million in gold, bound for England.[3]

On the ninth, Hoover again urged the American people to rally behind Roosevelt, this time in support of his program to reopen the banks, even though he personally thought it unfair to smaller financial institutions and was highly indignant at a delay in implementing his own proposals for deposit insurance and hoarding restrictions that seemed patently political. Despite his misgivings, he urged "support to the utmost of one's conscience" in a letter to Henry Stimson. That week's edition of *Time* carried the headline "Roosevelt Gets Power of Dictator . . . All Protests are Stilled." On the nation's radios, Father Coughlin was jubilantly proclaiming the end of fiscal peonage. Discarding its obstreperous ways, Congress adopted FDR's bank bill—like his first "fireside chat," drafted primarily by old Hoover men —the same day it was introduced, then overrode the strident objections of the veterans' lobby one day later to slash federal spending by half a billion dollars. "Too often in recent history," said Roosevelt, "liberal governments have been wrecked on rocks of loose fiscal policy." The implication was clear: Herbert Hoover had been a financial wastrel.[4]

"Things are taking place," Hoover counseled a friend on March 11— twenty-four hours before the president, on a whim, decided to legalize the sale of beer—"which when analyzed in the cold light of five or six months hence . . . will make a curious picture." For the moment there was nothing to do but "stand behind until public confidence has been restored from a terrible and unnecessary shock." A reporter calling upon him at the Waldorf was startled when Hoover defined his single mistake in dealing with the Depression as the failure to repudiate all debts, both domestic and foreign. On another day, he received a delegation from the American Friends Service Committee, who shared his interest in aiding the stricken coal miners of Pennsylvania.[5]

On March 12, Hoover went to visit Theodore Roosevelt's widow at Sagamore Hill, only to cancel a planned stop at T.R.'s grave when a crowd gathered. His secretary, French Strother, died that afternoon, the victim of penumonia contracted on Inauguration Day. Forty-nine years old, Strother took to his own grave a proposed series of historical and documentary works explaining and justifying Hoover's presidency. For his boss, Strother's death closed off one more source of activity, at least for the foreseeable future.

On March 16, Roosevelt sent Congress his first farm bill, radically extending the old Farm Board's mission by luring farmers into restricting acreage. It was only the prelude to a far more sweeping program that by year's end would see the slaughter of millions of pigs and the deliberate destruction of vast amounts of produce and grain. For Hoover, already a shadowy figure against the swirl of excitement and renewed promise characterizing FDR's Washington, it was a day to fold his tent and slip out of New York. Microphones were set up for him to address a crowd at the Thirty-first Street entrance of Pennsylvania Station, but the former president had nothing to say. Negro porters cheered as his train pulled out. The *New Yorker* tartly wondered if the distinguished visitor had discovered any grass growing in the city's streets.

On March 21, he was back in Palo Alto, nineteen years to the day since he had left on a mission to enlist foreign participation in San Francisco's World's Fair. For all that time, he told a crowd gathered in Oakland to meet his train, "I have been going away from California. . . . Now I hope to reverse that." He had no plans whatever, he informed reporters. Personally, he went on, "I believe I'm entitled to a long, long rest." How long did he intend to stay, they asked? "I hope to remain for the next 20 years."

"On economic and political questions I am silent," he concluded. "Even on fishing I am silent." Then he left, a figure shrouded in defeat, to be driven up the hilly road that led to a white stucco house, on a college campus where twenty thousand letters awaited him and seclusion promised a time for healing.

★   ★

The house on San Juan Hill—no one had ever been able to devise a proper name that would stick—was as eclectic as its owners. Set high above the Stanford campus, on a lot Lou Henry first grew to love during a California summer fifteen years earlier, the residence featured flat roofs converted into terraces for outdoor living, exterior stairways connecting most areas with additional porches, and spacious rooms deliberately designed for flexible use. One interior passageway became "the Belgium Room," a fitting repository for the hundreds of tributes, ornaments and books commemorating Hoover's humanitarian efforts. A dining room was built a step above the neighboring drawing room. With folding doors opened, it could easily become a stage for one of Lou's musicales, or her husband's formal greetings to visiting dignitaries or delegations. In a dark-gold ceiling, three hundred tiny light bulbs were sequestered in a primitive version of indirect lighting. There were also concealed cabinets housing Lou's pewter collection, and a fireplace copied from Red House, the Hoover's beloved London address. The former president spent much of his time in a second-floor study, before a plate glass window looking out on San Francisco Bay, Mount Tamalpais across the Golden Gate, and the blossoming prune orchards of the Santa Clara Valley.[6]

Lou loved no spot more. "It's a beautiful evening," she would inform the proctor of Roble Hall, Stanford's dormitory for freshman women. "Will you bring some of the girls up to enjoy the view? I have 65 coffee cups." The school's Cap and Gown society held meetings on the Hoover terraces, where magnolias bloomed and buffet suppers included grilled oysters and miniature enchiladas. The former First Lady herself liked to carry a shopping bag along University Avenue, swapping stories with old friends and planning picnics in the hilly, moorlike region nearby that she called Scotland. She took an active interest in the Stanford curriculum, preached the virtues of physical education, and anonymously stocked a YWCA room on campus with clothes for needy students. Lou enjoyed vacations at Hobe Sound, bicycling along Ocean Road, dismissing bloody wounds caused by a tumble, cooking and eating the sailfish she caught, and hiking through the towering red-woods around Monterey. When guests stepped aside to let her enter a dining room first, she motioned them on ahead; "this is no longer the White House" was the way she put it. With her gardening, her proselytizing for the Girl Scout movement, her passion for the outdoors and the warm embrace of Stanford itself, Lou was content.[7]

Her husband was not. A friend who called upon the former president early in April 1933 found him "lonely beyond measure," and feeling isolated as a diver in his bell from the great or frightening events unfolding a conti-nent away. Complaining that Washington news was relegated to page three of the local newspapers, Hoover was soon receiving thirty papers a day by air mail. His schedule followed a set pattern, beginning at six o'clock each morning as a solitary figure made its way along Fraternity Row, accompanied only by a German police dog named Pat, and Wejie, his Norwegian elk-hound. Looking neither right nor left, doffing his hat in response to the few who shared his pleasure at such hours ("slept out" was Hoover's self-ap-praisal six weeks after leaving office), the former president then returned to his journals, his books, and a sustaining interest in the university and his library. To a reporter who visited him that summer, he awarded Stanford precedence over writing or foreign travel or commercial endeavors. "Some day, I shall go back to the business of earning a living," he said. "Right now that is not necessary." But he was incapable of idleness, and his alma mater was soon enriched by a stream of gifts, all inveigled by its most prominent alumnus.[8]

According to Ray Lyman Wilbur, Hoover was swooping like a hawk over the War Library. Others predicted that a vast research project on child health might soon engage his interest. In fact, the object of speculation had more prosaic things on his mind. A few days after his return, Hoover left

Palo Alto on the first of many automobile journeys, most impromptu and all designed to avoid ceremony and the press. To Reno or one of his sons' homes near Los Angeles, into the coastal range hills behind Palo Alto or over to Grass Valley, where he had first learned the life of a miner, he traveled eight thousand miles in ten weeks. His first trip was to Nevada, where he and Lou visited the old Comstock mines. Donning a miner's hat and coat, shouldering a shovel and chatting amicably with hardrock men and muckers, his distant colleagues from another time, Hoover could briefly shed his celebrity and overlook his concerns for the new course being followed in Washington. Happier still were the hours he devoted to fishing, for him a pursuit of almost spiritual intensity and one that restored a sense of proportion in a period of excess.

It was on the open road, wading through a trout stream, or bunking down for the night in a country cottage, where Hoover called upon the sense of whimsy his countrymen found indetectable and his friends found irresistible. His approach to catching fish was both methodical and exhausting—days of determined relaxation that went from six in the morning until a noon picnic, followed by a drive of perhaps two hundred miles and still more angling until sundown. On one such journey, not long after Roosevelt took the nation off the gold standard and gave encouragement to those who would inflate currency to counteract the Depression, Hoover arrived at a remote crossroads near Yellowstone Park. There he encountered a stern-faced woman of middle age, carting nothing more than a small weekend case. Halting the vehicle in response to her signal, the former president asked where she was going and what she was doing on the road. Yellowstone Park, she replied, before listing her avocation as a saver of souls in tourist camps. Hers was a simple gospel: "First, soup; second, soap; and third, salvation." Hoover asked how she financed her work, and the woman assured him that the Lord always provided.

When the party reached its destination, the driver stopped his auto at a tourist camp inside the park and asked the woman if she was short of funds. "The Lord always provides," she repeated, and shook her head. He slipped a bill to her anyway, saying it would at least help her buy some soup and soap. "Don't you have any hard money?" she demanded, and Hoover reached into his pocket to give her all he had, perhaps three dollars. Then he turned to his traveling companion. "Glen," he said, "she must be one of the few in the country who still believes in sound money."

On another jaunt, the ex-president stopped to pick up a hitchhiker with ninety-two cents in his pocket, who told of his search for employment as an auto mechanic. When they reached San Francisco, Hoover took the young man into a ferry lunchroom and bought him a meal. Then he pressed a hundred-dollar bill into his hand. "I'm going to take a chance on you," he said. "You have an honest face." Not long after, he got the hitchhiker a job at a local filling station; years later, as head of the Rocky Mountain division of New York Life Insurance, John Wafe Gordon exchanged Easter and Christmas greetings every year with his unlikely benefactor.[9]

A sense of humor helped in those first few months of virtual exile. When an Australian delegation of youthful debaters visited Stanford, they paid their respects at San Juan Hill. Being a child of parliamentary democracy and eager to sound sympathetic, one young man inquired of Mr. Hoover if he had managed to retain his seat. Unable to suppress his laughter, the former president replied that he had retained almost nothing else.

But there were other days, stretching sometimes into weeks, when friends found Hoover playing solitaire in his comfortable retreat, lashing out at his successor and bitterly complaining of smears in the national press. Petty criticisms cropped up in his conversation: of how the Marine band played "Hail to the Chief" for Roosevelt on Inauguration Day before he was actually sworn in, of derogatory comments on the new administration censored out of certain newspapers, and of "malicious lies" interpreting his stop at a Virginia City soft-drink place as a saloon visit. "Would it not be decent public policy," he wrote the United Press, "not to circulate lies, intended to humiliate decent citizens—let alone an Ex-President of the United States?" On a trip through Omaha later that year, Hoover refused to see any reporters. "They probably won't print what I say," he insisted, until his host persuaded him to grant a reluctant interview. That same fall, on a fishing excursion to the Klamath River in Oregon, a grumpy Hoover protested against giving out autographs. "I won't do it," he answered testily when invited to visit a class of schoolchildren. Relenting, he wound up donating fifty dollars so the students might have a lunch their parents couldn't afford to provide.[10]

At the outset, the former president declared a moratorium on public controversy. He held his tongue when gold was abandoned in April, and recognition was granted to the Soviet Union seven months later. He was sufficiently angry late in 1933, following the lynching of a California man suspected of kidnapping—a mob scene openly endorsed by the state's governor—to sign a letter of protest. Governor James Rolph replied with a defense of his refusal to call out troops to quell the lynchers. "Look at the mess we got into when troops were called out in Washington," Rolph continued, jabbing a soft spot. "Men with guns and bombs were sent to attack . . . our world war veterans who fought for us." Hoover shot back that the governor was guilty of "gross ignorance" of the Bonus March, and of advocating lynch law in place of civil liberties. Then he resumed his retreat.

His self-imposed silence on national events boomeranged in at least two ways. For one thing, it deprived conservative critics of the new administration of an authoritative voice, leaving the field to leftwing prophets of disenchantment and Huey Long, Father Coughlin, and the apostle of 200-dollar-a-month pensions for the elderly, California's own Dr. Francis Townsend. On the personal level, it fostered a resentment that chafed within its own restraints, turning venomous as Roosevelt's democratic revolution cast Hoover in the unwelcome role of spokesman and apologist for the *ancien régime*. He had noted, Hoover wrote acidly, that the Brain Trust and its supporters "are now announcing to the world that . . . laissez-faire died on March 4." He wished the Trust would hire a history professor, for laissez-faire had been dead in the United States for half a century. For proof, Hoover pointed to the Sherman Act, not to mention regulation of transportation and public utilities, the Federal Reserve System, the Eighteenth Amendment, and his own creation of Home and Farm Loan Banks, along with the Reconstruction Finance Corporation. Intellectually, it was a powerful argument, but so long as Hoover refused to make it publicly, his own recriminations against New Deal policies remained so much verbal buckshot —and it became difficult to expect other Republicans to raise their voices in protest of his martyrdom.[11]

Hoover's anger was easily roused by correspondents who supplied him with an unending stream of indignities large and small committed against cherished subordinates or programs. Joel Boone, the White House physician, wrote of FDR's duplicity in assuring him he would stay on, only to have him sacked out of the blue, with heavy loss of rank and pay. Personally, Roosevelt assured Boone, he wanted him to remain at his post, but "they" felt he should go for the good of his career. Ted Joslin reported from the capital that Roosevelt had the press corps (to whom he promised to serve the nation's first batch of legal beer) "eating out of his own hand," calling reporters by their first names and providing "oceans of copy": as many as twenty-one separate subjects were discussed at a single press conference. In another letter, Joslin gossiped that FDR had been on the preferred list of Kuhn, Loeb and Company when governor of New York and profited handsomely, that Roosevelt's political assistant Louis Howe was marketing lucrative government contracts, that presidential secretaries were stooping to performing on radio's "Cascaret Hour," and that Ike Hoover was complaining of such a general lack of decorum in the Roosevelt White House, where newspaperwomen had the full run of the place and the First Lady served hot dogs at social functions, that he didn't know whether he was in the presidential mansion or a nickelodeon.[12]

More heartrending still were the thousands of letters that came to Palo Alto from people who were dispossessed, jobless or merely deranged. An eighteen-year-old student in Manhattan, Kansas, wondered if Mr. Hoover could help him defray his $150 a year in expenses while studying agricultural economics. Others sought help in paying their taxes. Eastern Europe sent appeals from the generation once fed by Hoover and now turning to him again to help in feeding their own children. To a friend who agreed to investigate writers' claims and distribute Hoover donations, the former president said he would be glad to put up small sums of cash. "They must be in amounts of less than $100, as I no longer have the means to temporize with people in the present situation." In November 1933, he apologetically noted that he would have to get himself a job where he could earn some money "before I can take care of all the burdens that come up to this desk."[13]

Hoover spent a thousand dollars a month just to open and answer his mail. He searched in vain for any word from the Roosevelt White House. His fifty-ninth birthday came and went in August, unmarked by the customary greeting. Neither was he invited to the Army-Navy game, a courtesy extended to previous chief executives. Then, on September 14, 1933, a wire came from Washington, announcing the sudden death of Ike Hoover. From Palo Alto, Hoover replied with "deep regrets" over the news. No further word would pass between the two men for eight years—until Roosevelt's mother died and Hoover wrote out a note of condolence. His reward was a formal White House card, edged in black and devoid of any personal comment. A third time, death intervened to bridge the gulf between the two antagonists, in January 1944, when Lou suffered a fatal heart attack and her successor as First Lady penned a gracious note of sympathy. Except for these three occasions, the Hoover-Roosevelt relationship itself was marked by a silence of deathlike finality.[14]

★   ★

Seven weeks after Inauguration Day, Hoover's former military aide looked on in amazement as the new First Lady presided with ebullience over an East Room entertainment featuring her friend Mayris Cheney. Miss Cheney introduced "the Eleanor Waltz" that night, a high-kicking, leg-displaying acrobatic exercise which according to Campbell Hodges included "simulated love-kisses. Shades of Lou Henry!" he exclaimed.[15]

The rest of the Roosevelt administration seemed equally indifferent to traditions once hallowed. In his first hundred days in office, FDR won from a pliant Congress fifteen separate measures, the combined effect of which were to alter forever the balance between the American citizen and his government. Acting as an agent of the Agricultural Adjustment Administration, Henry Wallace deputized 22,000 volunteers to fan out into farm country, cajoling the suspicious to plow under one-quarter of their crops for up to 20 dollars an acre. Under Jesse Jones, Hoover's old RFC was radically transformed into the nation's largest bank and biggest investor—a bureaucratic galaxy that included the Commodity Credit Corporation, the Electric Home and Farm Administration, the Export-Import Bank and several governmental mortgage agencies. In the 40,000-square-mile Tennessee Valley, the federal government went into competition with private generators of electric power, building or acquiring two dozen dams, surpassing even George Norris's ambitious visions, and more than tripling the number of rural farms supplied with electricity.

The Securities Act regulated Wall Street by forcing all new securities offered for sale to be registered with a federal agency. The Federal Deposit Insurance Corporation guaranteed the solvency of all accounts of less than $5,000 and sliced bank failures by over 90 percent. A new Home Owners Loan Corporation pumped out nearly a billion dollars in the first year of Roosevelt's term alone, and three million men aged seventeen to twenty-five signed up with the Civilian Conservation Corps to plant trees and fight forest fires, stock fish hatcheries and forsake urban street corners where hopelessness was the rule. Guided by Harry Hopkins, a former social worker devoid of his profession's sentimentality, the Federal Emergency Relief Administration, augmented for the winter of 1933–34 by the Civil Works Administration, paid four million men to construct or renovate roads and schools, teach adult education classes and excavate prehistoric Indian mounds, put on plays, and build privies. "Boondoggle" found its way into the language, and there were plenty of jokes about leaf raking, but a billion dollars entered the economic mainstream, and William Allen White's prescription for a disheartened nation was being realized.

"What this country needs, if we are to shake off the torpor of fear and hopelessness," wrote the homespun editor from Emporia, "is a series of blinding headlines proclaiming action, resolute leadership, a firm hand at the controls. . . ." FDR met that need with gusto, and history has been grateful. Yet few men have ever received more posthumous credit for the ideas of others. Roosevelt came to the White House sincerely wishing to balance the budget (when he tried to at the first possible opportunity, in 1937, he precipitated a severe recession that for a while tarnished even his enormous personal popularity). Doubting the value of massive spending on public works, he argued that Hoover had been able to spend barely $900 million to advantage. He terminated the CWA as soon as possible, asserting that no one would starve in the warm months.

When the World Economic Conference was poised to take up the issues of debt renegotiation and tariff reduction, FDR made supportive sounds, even while pursuing domestic policies (especially in agricultural price-raising) that could only have the effect of walling America off from the rest of a stricken world. Eventually, he torpedoed the conference altogether, convincing his predecessor for one that the New Deal was profoundly isolationist—until 1939. It was, wrote Hoover, "deliberate work preparing the way for a period of emotional economic nationalism and economic war as a smoke screen for failures. Unfortunately, the public will welcome it because of the way the debtor countries are acting."[16]

The president's personal command of the dismal science was such as to leave Lord Keynes shaken after a White House visit in 1934. Roosevelt reciprocated the feeling. "He must be a mathematician rather than a political economist," he remarked of the man whose revolutionary theories of pump priming and deficit spending were at least the unwitting heart of New Deal economics.

Strangely quaint appear Hoover's criticisms today of managed currency and planned economy, since so little was managed and so much was improvised. At one early press conference, Roosevelt likened himself to a quarterback, who knows what the next play will be, but not the course of the game, since "future plays will depend on how the next one works." His administration, not surprisingly, was unabashedly experimental. This was a far cry from his attack on Hoover during the 1932 campaign for pursuing "novel, radical, and unorthodox economic theories." Consistency aside, what made things worse was FDR's inclination to be all things to all people. In one typical snafu, Raymond Moley discovered that the president had asked five separate people to do the same job, and was astonished to find himself swamped with five separate, equally elaborate reports. When a securities regulation bill was needed, the president put at least two groups to work independent of each other. One of the resulting drafts was so bad it required Sam Rayburn's personal intervention to save the White House the embarrassment of its passage. Roosevelt conducted important debt and tariff negotiations with Britain without telling his nominal Secretary of State, treated as mere "details" to be left to warring subordinates decisions such as whether the CCC should include a quarter or a half million men, and never did resolve the fundamental rift between recovery and reform that split his advisers and made so much of early New Deal legislation a thick gumbo of contradictory impulses.

Perceptive capital hands soon took advantage of the situation. When

Labor Secretary Frances Perkins, planning advocate Rexford Tugwell, and liberal legislators like Robert Wagner and Robert La Follette wanted a dramatic expansion of public works, they piggybacked the program on top of the president's own brainchild, the CCC. Within twenty-four hours, Cabinet officers had returned FDR's draft bill with amendments. They warmly approved the concept, they informed him—before slipping in both public works and a half-billion-dollar program of direct grants-in-aid to the states. Roosevelt himself willingly compromised on an amendment introduced by Oklahoma's Senator Elmer Thomas permitting drastic inflation of the currency, without informing either his budget director, Lew Douglas, or other economic advisers (Douglas's comment afterward: "Well, this is the end of Western civilization)."

Perhaps the ultimate witches' brew was the National Recovery Administration, delivered after an exasperated FDR ordered a disparate group of experts locked in a room until they could devise something acceptable to him. What they came up with had something for everyone: a perfect broker state partnership between government, industry and labor cobbled together to forestall enactment of Hugo Black's thirty-hour-week bill. The NRA, like the New Deal itself, was part Theodore Roosevelt's New Nationalism, part Woodrow Wilson's New Freedom, part government regulation of the economy and part government dictation. Adopted on June 13 and placed under the fractious command of General Hugh "Ironpants" Johnson, the NRA "invited" businessmen to draw up codes of fair competition—in obvious violation of the Sherman Antitrust Act. As a result, production might be cut, and prices fixed, hardly a spur to employment or consumer purchasing power. To prevent the latter, the same bill contained minimum wage provisions, along with a forty-hour workweek, a ban on child labor, and guarantees of the right to organize unions. To sell the whole unwieldy contraption, Johnson fell back on the biggest propaganda campaign in the nation's history (ironic in light of the criticism aimed at Hoover for attempting to spark recovery by encouraging words), sending hundreds of thousands of people parading down Fifth Avenue and other thoroughfares, and stamping the NRA's famed Blue Eagle on millions of households and workplaces.

When patriotic blandishments failed, stronger methods were used. In March 1934, Roosevelt issued an Executive Order—one of 1,486 that marked his first term—requiring all government suppliers and contractors to sign up under the NRA codes. In the end, more than two million employers went along. Even so, most Americans grew restive under a bureaucratic arm so long that it manifested itself in arrangements fixing prices in the dog food, horsehair, shoulder pad and burlesque industries. On one of his motor journeys, Hoover was told by a rural merchant ("I have made it a business to buy more articles for which I had no need than at any time in my life," the ex-president informed a friend) that the Blue Eagle "had its fingers tangled in a barbed wire fence on one hand and the other caught in a sprocket."[17]

There was much more to the Hundred Days, including currency tinkering that endowed Roosevelt with virtual one-man rule in determining the price of gold and the value of the dollar. Following a break in the stock market that July, FDR hit on a fresh expedient. Admitting that the idea might prove unsound but embracing it anyway in response to the cries of desperate farmers, he would have the government itself buy up gold. In characteristic fashion, the president, his Treasury secretary and other fiscal planners met in FDR's bedroom to establish each day's gold price. From his three-quarter mahogany bed, Roosevelt sounded a jocular note, suggesting a rise one morning of twenty-one cents. Henry Morgenthau asked why twenty-one. "It's a lucky number," Roosevelt replied, "because it's three times seven." When devaluation occurred, it also had the ironic effect of raising the tariff wall so bitterly criticized by Roosevelt and others just a few months earlier. Promises of balanced budgets turned out equally forgettable, the president managing to claim a balance by the simple expedient of submitting two budgets, one regular and one "emergency." From Palo Alto, Hoover cast a fishy eye on all this whirlwind of activity (what he called "the Washington combination of Coué–P. T. Barnum–W. J. Bryan–Karl Marx–Moody and Sankey") so repugnant to old Progressives like himself, who believed that government's role was to encourage the associational, voluntary ideals that set America apart from other lands, to foster economic freedom for even the smallest competitor, and to preserve the character of individuals and communities alike.[18]

Moralistic and easily convinced of their own rectitude, the old Progressives had joined together to combat undemocratic restrictions on an economy they believed to be essentially healthy, and to graft Jeffersonian values onto a modern, urbanized society. They fought political bosses and unfair business practices with equal fervor. They made government an umpire of fairness, not an arbiter of individual conduct. Social engineers rather than revolutionaries, they planned for rational progress and the orderly elimination of injustices and excesses. Before departing Washington, Hoover left a 1,660-page report by his Research Committee on Recent Social Trends, a historic document that laid the groundwork for unemployment insurance, Social Security, and other reforms credited to the New Deal.

Then came broker-state government under FDR, and organized scarcity in the form of NRA and AAA, and it was no wonder that many of Hoover's contemporaries among the self-proclaimed best men were aghast. As Richard Hofstadter has written, "If the state was believed neutral in the days of TR because its leaders claimed to sanction favors for no one, the state under FDR could be called neutral only in the sense that it offered favors to everyone."

Such generosity was inevitably accompanied by administrative chaos, a vast expansion of the bureaucracy, a shift of authority from legislative to executive hands, the creation of the first truly personal presidency, and something very close to a cult of personality in place of the traditional supremacy of law. Given the national emergency, all this might be forgiven. But when the emergency was over, the changes proved permanent. For the rest of his life they would draw Hoover's fire as a sort of political sorcery, defying logic if not the law. But in the first months of the New Deal, he was reduced to sputtering indignation in purple letters to friends. One day, he forecast, February, March and April would be known as "the winter of the Roosevelt hysteria," marked by "the unnecessary closing of banks for dramatic purposes," an attack on rural banks, an economy program that was pure deception, and assorted "white rabbits" adopted by Congress "in a spirit of total abandonment of responsibility." Before the month was out, Hoover complained of "Bryanism under new words and methods." Thanks to the "terrible conduct of the 72nd Congress," people were in the mood for a whiff of dictatorship. But fundamental liberties were at stake, and even a foolish or obstructive Congress was better than "a march down the course of so many European peoples." [19]

Asked later to assess his own greatest achievement in the White House, Hoover doubtlessly reflected on the New Deal before replying, "Defending constitutional government." In fact for all his shrill comparisons of Roosevelt's program to fascism or communism, he foresaw a contemporary concern about the enlargement and personification of the presidency, as well as the danger posed by an omnipotent federal government to the spirit of community and individual responsibility assumed by Americans since their earliest days on the continent. "The idea that because powers are conferred by Congress . . . they are within the Constitution is a new doctrine to me. If that notion is to prevail," he wrote early in May, "there is nothing left in the Bill of Rights." [20]

The inflationary bill introduced by Senator Elmer Thomas, Hoover commented privately, might temporarily restore prices to normal levels. But either more inflation or a later slump would necessarily result down the road. Worst yet, speculation would be encouraged to the benefit of large corporations; life insurance policies and bank savings would be "more than 50% destroyed"; wages and salaries alike would be effectively reduced; and with real income diminished, taxes would have to be raised to cover government's rising costs. Other criticisms proliferated. Hoover thought it wiser to expand naval construction than plant trees. He fretted that the Triple A awarded too much authority to the Secretary of Agriculture, and would rob urban dwellers of purchasing power by artificially raising prices. By mid-June, he was worrying that an apparent recovery might be misinterpreted as the result of New Deal nostrums, thus permanently fixing the new social philosophy upon America. "I feel so strongly sometimes that it is wrong to keep still when I see the country being misled that I cannot stand it much longer," he confided to a friend that summer. "But we must reserve our fire until we can make it effective."[21]

Most noxious of all was the NRA, which Hoover whimsically joined "as I am the sole occupant of this industry of being an Ex-President," and which he found in his travels to be quickly losing its initial appeal. True to the old Progressive spirit, he was convinced that abandoning antitrust laws would permit big business unfair advantage in the marketplace. "Heaven help the consumers," he noted, before admitting that even public discussion of the NRA seemed useless; "such measures," he said "glow with promise, even though they contain the poison of social destruction."[22]

More to the point, wrote Hoover, all the ballyhoo and code-writing sanctioned by a coercive federal government would do nothing to alleviate unemployment. He had already undertaken a survey of job creation under various plans to reduce the average workweek, and concluded that a forty-hour week would mean less than a 2 percent gain in payrolls. Most people would sign NRA pledges, he continued, only to forget them immediately afterward, or try to beat them if it cost any money to carry them out. "One phase of it distresses me enormously and that is the introduction of the boycott into American life upon the recommendation of the President of the United States. . . . It is immoral and cannot but result in the degeneration of fundamental social relations." For all his anger at what he called "the blue buzzard," however, Hoover was a realist. "It would be a fatal thing," he wrote on August 22, "to interpose my true thoughts at this juncture." So he kept silent, for the record, carrying on a highly personal investigation of the NRA at roadside stands and dusty crossroads. What he found dismayed him.[23]

Any so-called "partnership" with big business, Hoover warned as early as mid-May, would only result in exploitation of the public by big business. "When business fixes prices," he wrote patronizingly, "it will take tender care to cover the cost of the small producers, and the low cost producer, which is big business, will proceed with joy." Moving from the realm of theory to what he could see with his own eyes, the former president judged the NRA guilty of tearing apart the communities he visited, "with feuds, re-awakening of old grudges, and constant spying around. . . . If the motto of this new Administration is to abolish fear, they are doing it by substituting terror." For proof, he cited the northern California woman who ran a hot-dog stand, pouring out the story of a hardscrabble existence garnered by working eighteen hours a day for ten years. An elderly relative, destitute, had come to stay with the woman and her husband. The woman had given her two dollars a week in pin money, along with food and lodging.[24]

Now NRA agents—including one of their competitors who sat upon a local compliance board—were ordering them to stay open no more than twelve hours a day and to pay the old lady a minimum wage of eleven dollars per week. The woman's husband demanded to know if he had any rights, and Hoover directed him to go to the high school library, obtain a copy of the Constitution and read the first ten amendments to the document. He then wrote out a list of at least six violated by the compliance board, which the man should read to the assembled board before defying their orders. A few days later, the woman wrote to tell Hoover that they had followed his advice to the letter, bolstered by her own personal denunciation. "They haven't dared do anything to us since," she revealed.

Still another Californian was ordered to reduce the price of the gasoline she sold by two cents a gallon. With three children to support on four dollars a day, she told Hoover she could ill afford to comply. In response, he gave her the name of a leading San Francisco attorney, promised he wouldn't charge her a dime, and instructed her to refer the NRA to the noted lawyer if agents should ever come calling again. She heard nothing further from the bureaucrats. For his part, Hoover was the recipient of a little cactus in a pot—and the promise that its donor would vote the Republican ticket for as long as she lived.[25]

By November, with much of the New Deal in place, and the economy still refusing to soar, the ex-president was waxing indignant about a new and still more sinister threat. "Suppression of free speech," he wrote to Will Irwin, "is not confined to Germany. You should look into the pressures and intimidations now going on in the radio world. In fact, the spirit of the Bill of Rights is being violated in a dozen ways in every town and village every hour of the day. Some day the American people will awaken to the fact that the agonies and blood of a race over 160 years to establish certain primary bases of human liberty is being traded for a fictitious price of wheat and oil."[26]

By this time, his gloomy, even apocalyptic views mingled personal animus with philosophical distaste. For Hoover, even in his exile, had become an obsession for the men around Roosevelt. And he was fast on his way toward becoming the first casualty of the imperial presidency.

★   ★

Americans were feeling better in the spring of 1933. If recovery had not yet blossomed, the bulb was in the ground, cared for by a man with an exceptional green thumb. Unencumbered by his predecessor's tortured constitutionalism, Roosevelt raised the nation's spirits before the index of its economic performance. Gaiety returned to the White House; five times during his first press conference was the new president, jaunty and casual, interrupted by reporters' laughter. Millions of listeners were entranced by the homely language and conversational tone of a chief executive who began each of his famed fireside chats with the greeting, "My Friends." Hoover's own military aide marveled at the informality of Roosevelt's manner and the way the president made certain to introduce him to guests, something his predecessor never contemplated.[27]

Across the country, people sang "Who's Afraid of the Big, Bad Wolf," and psychologists attributed the song's popularity to relief at Hoover's departure. In an East St. Louis movie house, a man watching newsreels struck his neighbor, a total stranger. He justified his act by professing dislike for anyone resembling the former president. In Washington, FDR's cranky, scene-stealing Interior Secretary, Harold Ickes, complained that next to Hoover's $17 million Commerce Department, his own headquarters resembled "a humble mud hut." In his diary, Ickes recorded a warning delivered to the entire Cabinet on May 2 by Attorney General Homer Cummings. They were being watched, claimed Cummings, and women were being hired to "worm themselves into the confidence of your wives," as part of "a strict espionage" conducted out of the nearby Shoreham Building by Hoover's alter ego, Larry Richey.

Two months later, Roosevelt himself jokingly referred to a plot by Hoover, Eugene Meyer and Bernard Baruch to create a kind of shadow government. Having planted the story with reporters, the president went on to dissociate himself from it. "Really," he said, "the heat has got people down in this town." Ickes was less easily reassured. His personal notion of conspiracies aimed at the new administration was a virtual mirror image of Hoover's own suspicions. Saints need sinners to confirm their identity, and both men found themselves richly blessed with enemies to justify crusading. Six days after the attorney general's warning, Ickes on his own authority directed that the huge reclamation dam under construction on the California-Nevada border—already referred to in five separate appropriations bills as Hoover Dam, in recognition of Hoover's efforts as Secretary of Commerce to launch the project—be known henceforth as Boulder Dam. To honor individuals, especially living ones, according to the secretary was inappropriate. Letters of protest began arriving at Ickes's office. The *Los Angeles Times* wrote that if the same policy were followed across the board, the Washington Monument might soon be renamed Granite Shaft and Jackson Park be known as Mud Hole. His dander up, Ickes retorted that Hoover's contribution to the dam had been "very casual" and his attitude of support "lukewarm."

Will Rogers jumped into the fray, amusing radio listeners—and infuriating "Honest Harold"—by suggesting the whole thing ought to be dubbed Ickes Dam or, better yet, have the names transposed. When the $40 million project was dedicated in 1935, Hoover was not invited. An artist employed to sculpt bas-reliefs listing those instrumental in its planning and construction was told to leave Hoover's name off. At a banquet in Los Angeles, FDR remarked casually that he had considered returning his predecessor's name to the dam. "It would have been good politics, wouldn't it?" he asked a dinner partner. Not only good, the man answered, but fair. Why hadn't he done it? "Because that man over there," Roosevelt said, pointing at Ickes, "wouldn't let me!" [28]

In perhaps the ultimate irony, Ickes's stubborn assertions were challenged, first by the United States Board on Geographic Names, then by Rand McNally and finally by Homer Cummings himself, who wrote a private legal opinion dismissing his colleague's action. But Hoover Dam remained Boulder Dam for fourteen years. It was only the first of a series of noisy squabbles between the former president and his bête noire at Interior whose impressive achievements in office were married to an unattractive personality and a fondness for gloating over fallen rivals. Early in February 1934, Ickes reveled in "a bloodless revolution . . . turning out from the seats of power the representatives of wealth and privilege" and derided Hoover personally as "the champion of that ruthless individualism that was, in the main, responsible for the terrible economic situation in which we found ourselves."

On still another front could the Old Curmudgeon claim victory: the hated Commerce Department, symbol not only of Hoover's faded omnipotence but also of the scientists and statisticians, experts and explorers whom he had summoned into government service, was at last brought to heel. Nowhere throughout the federal establishment did Roosevelt's initial economy drive cut deeper. Even the new secretary's brother-in-law was fired, and Hoover himself mourned the loss of "fundamental benefits" of scientific and economic research that stood in stark contrast with "the fabulous waste carried on through the [CCC]." Adding injury to insult, the administration welshed on its verbal pledge to make Walter Newton a federal judge.[29]

Other events intruded upon the hermit of Palo Alto. In August 1933, Father Coughlin set off an uproar in Detroit, accusing that city's bankers of immoral exploitation of depositors. Senator Couzens echoed the priest's demand that Hoover, as their protector and friend, be called to testify in court. Before he was through, Coughlin resurrected John Hamill's old story about Hoover's English citizenship and his alleged career as a promoter of worthless mines. Pat Hurley warned his former boss that legends were being built up around him. He could strike back at his accusers without openly opposing Roosevelt's economic policies, advised the former Secretary of War. But in public at least, Hoover would do nothing. Instead, he complained about AP coverage of the Detroit proceedings "vomited" over the wires, and wondered abut his chance to get what he called "a square deal out of the American press at the present time."[30]

Ickes and Coughlin were one thing, nuisances that thrived in the spotlight and might best be opposed with silence. But then, early in 1934, Hoover began finding his mail opened before he read it. A letter from Walter Brown, once Postmaster General in the Hoover Cabinet, was returned for expert inspection, which confirmed its having been tampered with. A similar complaint was voiced by William Castle, to which Hoover responded with acidic humor. "If the gentleman who opens this letter could please transmit a copy of it to the President I should be greatly obliged," he wrote in a sardonic postscript. As for tampering with the mails, Hoover predicted that before long "there will be a national demand for an investigation as to who is conducting the United States Cheka."[31]

From Carter Glass came a furtive warning that either Hoover's phone was being tapped, or that he was under personal surveillance. For proof, the Virginian cited the experience of his Senate colleague from North Carolina, Joseph Bailey, who had recently held a secret conference with Hoover at a friend's New York apartment. No one knew of the meeting except for the two principals, their New York host and Hoover's secretary. Two days later, Bailey called at the White House.

"Did you have a pleasant visit with Hoover in New York Saturday afternoon?" Roosevelt inquired.

More tangible evidence arrived in a letter from William Allen White, no friend to paranoia or anti-Roosevelt hysteria. Edna Ferber told White the story of a middle-aged actress playing in Dinner at Eight on the New York stage and staying at the Drake Hotel. Noticing an extra phone, apparently disconnected, in her room, the woman paid it no attention until she heard a faint, persistent ring. One day, curiosity led her to pick it up. What she heard was a conversation between Hoover and Pat Hurley in Chicago, abruptly ended ten minutes later when her dog began barking and the two men realized their predicament. The actress promptly reported the incident to the hotel management, who removed the phone. "But somebody blundered somewhere," wrote White. "Doubtless the phone in the room had been put in for some other purpose and the wiretappers had forgotten that it was tied into some wiretapper's trunkline and there it was."[32]

The evidence of illegal conduct on the part of Roosevelt operatives is circumstantial. What is beyond doubt is the continuing interest Hoover's activities held for those around the president. Hoover himself sighed that if he opened a door, "someone in Washington is bound to get some significance connected with it." A day before an important Hoover political declaration was published in March 1935, Jim Farley was confidentially displaying it for FDR. Earlier still, Farley had informed the president of a private meeting between Hoover and *Des Moines Register* cartoonist Jay Darling, in which the two men supposedly discussed the ex-president's prospects for renomination in 1936. As for the credibility of his informant, judged Farley, "I really think he knows what he is talking about." Nor was Roosevelt himself above gossip. One of his friends claimed presidential authority for a tale of Hoover as a boy, setting fire to his father's barn and refusing to admit culpability—a veiled Freudianism for the adult's supposed unwillingness to acknowledge error.[33]

"I am getting a good deal irritated at the continual misrepresentation which goes on about my Administration," Hoover griped at the end of the year. There didn't seem to be a single member of his own party in Congress or elsewhere willing to stand up and say anything kindly about it, nor even to refute the most flagrant allegations. By then, a special section of the Justice Department was combing through records in an effort to secure evidence of malfeasance by Hoover's appointees. Walter F. Brown, Hoover's postmaster general, was pursued by a Senate committee investigating air mail contracts, and Hoover coached his friend on the presentation of his case. "For all I know," the former president wrote of charges of "fraud and collusion" between Brown and private air carriers, "there may have been some weaknesses on the part of some contractors. They at least deserve a chance to explain themselves." Such efforts were "of course . . . all directed at me and to cover up all these hastily organized Government agencies."[34]

Brown was cleared (after Jim Farley exonerated him under oath), but not before FDR canceled the private contracts and entrusted air mail delivery to Army pilots, at the cost of a dozen lives lost in crashes. Next, the Senate launched a probe of Herbert, Junior, on the old charge that he had tried to use his position to promote air mail contracts for his employer, Western Air Express. Young Hoover revealed that as soon as the story first surfaced, in the summer of 1930, he had submitted his resignation to the company, only to have it refused. The air mail investigation fizzled, but its failure did not end attempts to implicate Hoover or his family in wrongdoing. The ex-president's other son, Allan, was accused by Henry Wallace in an off-the-record session with reporters of profiting from AAA payments at a time when his father was denouncing the agency as an unwarranted intrusion by government into the farming community. As it turned out, the boy did own shares in a land company receiving AAA payments—a handful purchased to secure rights to review the company's annual statements. Instead of the $20,000 in subsidies mentioned by Wallace, Allan was entitled to around two dollars, which he refused to accept. His father told him to inform the public in no uncertain terms that Wallace was not only robbing him of earnings by depriving him of the right to buy feeder cattle and calves, but was also violating the law that forbade any disclosure of government officials of individual subsidy payments.[35]

Andrew Mellon was less fortunate than the Hoover sons. The elderly tycoon, even then preparing to present the federal government with a fabulous art collection and a building to house it—a present worth a hundred million dollars or more—was being investigated for possible income tax evasion. The FBI tried and failed to indict Mellon. Then Robert Jackson, as chief counsel of the Internal Revenue Department, instructed Tax Commissioner Elmer Irey to take up the case. Irey protested, and Secretary of the Treasury Henry Morgenthau himself pressed the order. Again, a grand jury refused to indict Mellon, who died in 1935, after going ahead with a bequest that framed the nucleus of the National Gallery of Art.

By the start of 1934, a cloak and dagger atmosphere pervaded Hoover's inner circle. In April of that year, his secretary's room was broken into while the man was out to dinner. Whoever was responsible came up empty-handed: the secretary's briefcase was purposefully kept locked in a hotel vault. Two days later, IRS inspectors came calling, seeking information on the former president's personal tax returns (angry and vengeful, Hoover told Ogden Mills that Homer Cummings had filed false entries on his own 1930 form). Later that year, Hoover was dragged into Senator Gerald Nye's investigation of the munitions industry. Nye interpreted a meeting of sporting arms' manufacturers at the Commerce Department in 1925 as something other than Hoover's attempt to exempt their industry from the Geneva treaty's proposed global ban on the sale of all offensive weapons. The whole proceeding was ironic, given the fact that Hoover had called loudly and often for ratification of the treaty, while Nye helped block its adoption for nearly a decade.[36]

By then, too, Hoover had engaged in a private but raucous dispute with *American Mercury* magazine, which in its November 1934 issue denounced the American Red Cross as "a first class war machine . . . chiefly interested in preparing for the next war and only incidentally in relief work." The same article charged Hoover with having used his own Russian Relief Administration to compel Lenin to reinstate concessions for a vast conglomerate in which he held a large stake, and with cutting off all aid in October 1922, "although 5,000,000 shadows of human beings were still walking around, slowing dying of starvation." Such lies, Hoover told his attorney, had rattled around in left-wing circles for years, "usually as proof of my personal wickedness and of the wickedness of the 'capitalist' class generally."[37]

In truth, he had held no financial interest in the company described by *American Mercury,* and his Russian relief efforts continued for more than a year beyond the date of their alleged termination. Hoover had a warm letter of gratitude signed by Soviet officials in July 1923 to back up his assertions. The article was, as the ex-president phrased it, "a fouling of the whole American people before the world," and he seriously considered suing for libel. But the Red Cross took exception to the plan. In the end, he agreed not to press a suit, the Red Cross restated the facts to their 3,700 local branches, and Hoover's anger subsided to a dull rumble. There would be more attacks to come, fresh outbreaks of indignation and much consulting with lawyers. Hoover forced *Harper's* magazine to retract its claim that his speeches were ghost-written, by demanding that editors compare his handwritten drafts. He wrote but never mailed a furious letter to Henry Luce, accusing *Life* magazine of spreading the legend of Hoovervilles, "when you know that outside of every American city there has been for the last 75 years a tin can dump inhabited by hoboes and tramps." Only four or five such camps in the nation proclaimed themselves Hoovervilles, insisted their unwilling sponsor—and only then because politicians put up such signs during the 1932 campaign. Such distortions were "dirty and immoral . . . infamous smearing." With depressing frequency did such assertions crop up in Hoover's correspondence during his time of testing.[38]

For much of the 1930s, the nation's journals contributed to personalizing the depression. Liberal publications cartooned Hoover as a coldhearted nuncio from the old order, a self-proclaimed Restoration waiting to happen. That such efforts largely succeeded was due in no small part to Hoover's own choleric response.

In March 1934, he expressed interest in the source of funds for "the corps of sleuths" who were searching files and making charges. After condemning the whole venture as unable even "to make up a plausible lie," Hoover revealed just how far bitterness had propelled him. "One has to bear in mind," he wrote, "that one of the tactics of revolution is to destroy one's predecessors in authority at any cost or hazard." So that was it: FDR was a revolutionary, America's institutions were in imminent danger of subversion, and he, Hoover, would be a lone voice crying out of the wilderness, sometimes persuasive, often ineffective. The New Deal did not succeed in unearthing any evidence of wrongdoing against the former president. But it crafted an image that haunted Hoover and his party, estranging one from the other, and both still further from popular influence or political appeal.[39]

★　　★

Christmas 1933 found Hoover morose and snappish, his pessimism about the future offset only partially by the elfin presence of three grandchildren. One hundred telegrams came to the house on Mirada Drive that day. A month later, when FDR celebrated his fifty-second birthday, the White House was deluged with more than 300,000 messages and gifts. One man hiked a wintry 280 miles from Raleigh, North Carolina, to extend personally his best wishes. Forty thousand Alabamians signed a telegram to the president which took two days to transmit over four separate wires. "In that dark hour when the ruins of reaction heaped high about us," it proclaimed, "you gave us light and leadership." The same day, Roosevelt signed the Gold Reserve Act, giving the government title to the entire stock of monetary gold in the country and permitting further devaluation of the dollar. Six thousand balls and parties were held throughout the nation that evening, raising funds for the president's cherished Warm Springs Foundation and incidentally raising to new heights the reputation of a man dismissed as a lightweight less than a year earlier.

It was an unfortunate human failing, the president liked to say, that a full pocketbook often groaned more loudly than an empty stomach. For much of his first two years in office, he tried to satisfy both. His course of action, Roosevelt claimed, was neatly plotted between the 15 percent of Americans who belonged to the extreme left, and another 15 percent on the far right whose opposition was political or simply a matter of "pure cussedness." Conservative advisers like George Peek of the AAA, Budget Director Lew Douglas and Under-Secretary of the Treasury Dean Acheson disagreed. All submitted their resignations before the end of 1934, a year in which the hectic pace of the Hundred Days yielded to fresh innovations, like a new Federal Housing Administration, pensions for railway workers, a Federal Communications Commission to oversee radio, telegraph and cable traffic, and a Securities and Exchange Commission, which sharpened the teeth of earlier legislation regulating Wall Street.

Even some of the New Deal's most fervent supporters were beginning to harbor doubts about the pace of reform, and the revolutionary advances now sanctioned by law. Walter Lippmann, newly fallen under the spell of John Maynard Keynes, voiced no objection to a federal deficit of $7 billion. As Lippmann told a Harvard audience in the spring of 1934, the modern state must provide a standard of living for its people. Less important than the amount of dollars involved were the devices put to work at the service of a desperate democracy. "Free collectivism" was Lippmann's phrase for a supremely rational government acting to balance the economic scales through spending, taxation and interest rates. "It becomes an employer when there is no private employment," he said, "and it shuts down when there is work for all."

Unlike the *Herald Tribune*'s resident sage, Franklin Roosevelt cared less for theoretical perfection than immediate results. And he had no idea of relinquishing soon his extraordinary hold over Congress and the body politic. "During June and the summer," he confidantly wrote the old Wilsonian, Colonel House, "there will be many new manifestations of the New Deal, even though the orthodox protest and the heathen roar!" Among the orthodox was Herbert Hoover. The economy might be reawakening, with auto assembly lines twice as busy as a year earlier and farmers blessed with 45,000 Triple A checks a day flocking to rural Montgomery Wards, but there was no joy in Palo Alto. Hoover was more depressed over the future than at any time since 1929, he told Michigan's Arthur Vandenburg early in January. Everywhere he looked, there was only artificially inflated purchasing power and a populace rushing to barter their freedoms for the fool's gold of instant security. New Yorkers having just elected Fiorello La Guardia their Fusion mayor, Hoover predicted the city would become "a further clinic for socialism." A friend back from a visit to Mussolini related Il Duce's praise of Roosevelt as "his latest recruit." The NRA was a demonstrable flop, destined for burial in six months time (in fact, the Supreme Court invalidated the program a year later), and the administration was crawling with social revolutionaries taking out the heart and nerve centers of the economic body.[40]

Nowhere was Hoover's self-pity displayed more unflatteringly than in a letter to Simeon Fess, written in the last week of 1933. With his "over developed scruples of conscience," he admittedly was a poor contender for reelection in 1932, the former president wrote. Nor could he repress a gloomy satisfaction "that when the American people realize some ten years hence that it was on November 8, 1932, that they surrendered the freedom of mind and spirit for which their ancestors had fought and agonized for over 300 years, they will, I hope, recollect that I at least tried to save them."[41]

Intense activity could rescue Hoover from his splenetic isolation. In mid-January 1934, Ted Joslin urged such a course on his former chief. Hoover must "cut loose," according to his former secretary. "Only one voice is carrying to the country. That voice calls for further experimentation; it propounds unsound principles of government. Only one voice can reach the length and breadth of this nation. . . . You have kept your counsel almost without precedent," Joslin continued; "I think the people are just about ready to hear from you." The litany of complaints was, by now, familiar: an abject Congress, a pitifully weak Republican leadership, plus Joslin's second-hand quotation of FDR to a Chinese missionary. "If you are going to get money from wealthy people get it now. There will be no wealthy people at the end of this Administration."[42]

From John Callan O'Laughlin, once editor of the *Army-Navy Journal* and more recently Hoover's liaison to the Republican National Committee, came more solid evidence that the administration's optimistic forecasts of five million back at work were bogus. *Harper's* magazine found NRA codes ignored, minimum wage laws disobeyed, and compliance boards packed with industry's friends. Henry Ford obstinately held out from any display of the Blue Eagle, while newspaper mogul William Randolph Hearst flailed away at the becalmed agency as "No Recovery Allowed."[43]

William Allen White, a far more impartial newsman, visited the president that spring. Afterward, he described Roosevelt to Hoover as "the greatest hitchhiker since Andrew Johnson, going a little piece down the road with anyone, backward and forward, zigzagging, covering and recovering . . . mooching his intelligence from his younger associates." For an hour and a quarter FDR had talked without interruption ("Facility under duress may become recklessness," warned White), frankly confessing that currency tinkering had failed, complaining about the inordinate greed of western silver forces, generalizing and simplifying as he went.

"He still smiles too easily for one who shakes his head so positively," wrote White. "I fear his smile is from the teeth out . . . away down in my heart I am scared. He is a fair-weather pilot." Personalities aside, White worried about the centralization of authority taking place in Roosevelt's Washington. On the whole, he told Hoover, he believed politicians to be as honest and effective as businessmen, "but I never saw a businessman or politician whom I would trust with all the power they are generating around the White House. . . . I would like to see the Wall Street dehorned and unclawed, but I don't see much sense in gluing the horns and claws of Wall Street on the politicians. They still remain predatory weapons."[44]

Unlike other advisers, White urged Hoover to maintain his silence. "Your job is to emulate Brer Fox and the Tar Baby—lay low and say nothing." For now, Hoover took it to heart, even at the cost of a pained conscience. When his former Agriculture secretary Arthur Hyde delivered a rousing Lincoln Day address in New York that February, it was only after Hoover turned down an invitation to speak, and Hyde's remarks were virtually ghosted by the former president. His own correspondence included a tart defense of the Bill of Rights and a withering blast at those who would abandon representative democracy in the name of emergency measures. The Constitution for Hoover was not "a legalistic document but . . . a covenant among people" to maintain the freedoms enshrined in its first ten amendments. Those freedoms had been obtained, "not by laissez-faire but by a system of individualism of our own . . . and those who attempt to blacken our American Individualism," he told Hyde, "by calling it 'laissez-faire' or by stigmatizing it as the license to abuse and privilege are the same type of mind as those who defame the Sermon on the Mount because we still have to maintain criminal courts and jails. They would destroy our religious faiths. Instead of a nation of self-reliant people they would produce a nation of sycophants eating at the public trough."[45]

It was, said Hoover, "time for a ringing statement of our own principles," if only to counter the myths created by Washington and a jaundiced press. His own party, enfeebled by its sluggish acquiescence to most of the Roosevelt revolution, and reduced to scattered pockets of resistance, was a constant source of worry. As early as May 1933, Hoover was fretting in print over the fainthearted willingness of Republicans to compete with "demagoguery and socialism," just as he was upset by those "representing the interests of greed." Instead, the GOP must go before the public "as a defender of constitutional methods: of local responsibility, not centralization; of real liberty not abetted by the glitter of radical dictatorship; regulation and not regimentation of men; the representative of sound economic thought, honest currency, and honest private initiative. . . ." It might sound old-fashioned then, acknowledged Hoover, but within a year it would seem new indeed.[46]

In September, while visiting Chicago's Century of Progress exposition, the former president conferred with Ogden Mills, Arthur Hyde, Cal O'Laughlin and others. Out of the meetings came a proposed manifesto for his party, and a plan of more vigorous public opposition for Hoover himself. The former attacked the New Deal for retarding a recovery begun months earlier in other industrial nations; the latter envisioned a series of university lectures and a syndicated column wherein Hoover might combat Roosevelt's mutton dressed as lamb.[47]

But the trial balloon failed to gain altitude, and by early October, Hoover was back in Palo Alto, preparing a new edition of *American Individualism* and expressing mock sympathy for Roosevelt, whose gold-buying had failed to reverse depreciation and check the evil effects of "Old Man Supply and Demand." By the start of December, the former president was telling friends that the safest investment was a gold mine, "and I would not have believed that after a lifetime of mining experience . . . I would have ever said a gold mine had anything safe connected with it." That same month, he urged Republicans to demand equal time on the nation's radio outlets to present their viewpoint of the coming congressional session. He was also casting his hook for a new national party chairman to replace the somnolent Everett Sanders. The new leader should preferably be someone from the Midwest, "free of New York influence," as he put it, and young enough to infuse the moribund party structure with energetic hope.[48]

Three months later, Hoover climbed into his twelve-cylinder touring car and set off on a three-thousand-mile journey through seven states. He was, he told reporters, just visiting a few friends and relatives, but his roster included party officials in Arizona and Missouri, Iowa and Illinois. In Topeka on March 29, he met Governor Alfred M. Landon, a genial, mildly progressive executive already being boomed in a modest way for his party's 1936 presidential nomination. Passing within a few miles of West Branch, the former president didn't bother to pay a visit to his birthplace. His thoughts were on the future, not the past. Wherever he went, Hoover found a party demoralized and divided by the magical man in the White House. Liberal elements of the GOP were attacking Iowa's stalwart Senator Lester Dickinsen. In Nebraska, Senate candidate Robert Smith refused to be pinned down to specific criticisms of the New Deal. Yet another feud rent Pennsylvania Republicans, who leaned to Gifford Pinchot, a progressive who was openly sympathetic to FDR's policies. Such paper allies were distasteful to Hoover, who complained upon his return that the entire Midwest was being subsidized "from stem to breakfast."[49]

Congressional campaigns were brewing as the first national referendum on the New Deal, but Hoover's attention was focused less on the hustings than on the back rooms. On June 7, he wired congratulations to his party's new chairman, Henry P. Fletcher, a sixty-one-year-old former ambassador who said the country must put the brakes on further experimentation. Hoover's own choice for the post, Fletcher presided over a party gathering that wiped out a $200,000 debt clouding GOP prospects, and issued a policy statement that even old Bull Mooser William Allen White calculated as progressive enough for followers of the first Roosevelt. Largely crafted by Ogden Mills, it endorsed old-age pensions, opposed unlimited inflation, denounced government control over agriculture and business, and demanded an end to presidential emergency powers. Still, it amounted to little more than a waging of a new kind of warfare with old and discredited tactics.

His own feelings on the New Deal, Hoover told Henry Stimson in July, were "benumbed." Sometime he would break loose, even if it would do little good. "I have long since resolved myself that just one final blast from me will register my concluding contribution to American life." Remarkably, he predicted that "true Liberalism" would survive in England if not America, "and with this lamp still a light in the world our children may come back to it." "Whatever the future may hold for Mr. Hitler," he wrote late in 1933, "he needs about four or five years to consolidate the German people." Besides, Hoover went on, the fuehrer was "one of the most extreme individualists that has come into high place in government. He is so extreme that he doesn't want anybody else to mention the subject."[50]

When Hoover celebrated his sixtieth birthday on August 10, he did so without cake or crowds. He told the handful of reporters gathered to mark the occasion that the day would pass pretty much unnoticed in his own household "if it weren't for you people." Someone tried to draw him out on public questions and he chuckled. "The interesting things are the ones we can't talk about," he replied cryptically. But his silence was about to end. "My conscience will not stand it any longer," Hoover told a friend that same month. He had written a book, all by himself, and much to the chagrin of some of his friends, he confided. Already, the *Saturday Evening Post* had paid $10,000 for two articles, a fraction of what *American* Magazine was willing to pay, but as Hoover's friend Edgar Rickard put it, the former president cared only for getting his story to the public "in his own way and language."[51]

Far from being "one final blast" to conclude his public contributions, Hoover's manuscript was the opening round in a war without quarter, a savage assault on Roosevelt and his reforms masked by deliberately temperate, even dull, prose. The president's name was not mentioned once in *The Challenge to Liberty*. Neither was the New Deal per se. But no one who read it could doubt the targets of Hoover's wrath, nor the fury that burned beneath a cool, philosophically deceptive surface.

★   ★

It is one of history's enduring ironies that Franklin D. Roosevelt has come down to us as a magnificent cheerleader, whose personal buoyancy offset the deadweight of a nation with twenty million people on relief, while his predecessor and later rival has been cast as a brooding fatalist, confusing wealth with virtue and government oversight with incipient fascism. For it was Hoover the supreme optimist who composed *The Challenge to Liberty* in the early months of 1934. Such a mood did not come naturally, nor could it have been easy to sustain. Roosevelt's coalition of business and the unemployed was breaking apart that spring. A year after capitalism's greatest crisis, a delayed reaction was setting in from the left. Forty million Americans a week tuned in to hear Father Coughlin pronounce the New Deal Christ's Deal. Five million more became followers of Dr. Townsend and his "Old Age Revolving Pensions, Limited." Seven million signed up as adherents of a onetime shortening salesman from Winn Parish, Louisiana, named Huey P. Long in his demagogic "Share Our Wealth" campaign, a vague panacea promising each family its own home, free schooling from kindergarten through college, plus the "reasonable comforts of life" up to $6,000 a year. In New York that April, a Methodist convention insisted that the NRA didn't go far enough; delegates narrowly rejected a motion demanding socialization of banks, transportation and basic industry. A Minnesota congressman introduced an unemployment insurance bill authored by Earl Browder, who usually greeted his followers beneath a banner proclaiming "Communism in Twentieth-Century Americanism."

The world itself seemed eager to leave its axis. In Paris, street riots appeared to presage civil war between right and left. Adolf Hitler carried out a blood purge of his own Nazi followers, while the death of Austria's chancellor opened up new paths to the German adventurer. At home, Americans severed their roots, geographically as well as politically. Highway 66 leading West into Hoover's California was clogged with a million Okies and Arkies, refugees from barren plains and farms destroyed by drought. (Hall County, Texas, lost all but a thousand of its 40,000 inhabitants.) After the relative peace of the Hoover years, industrial violence pockmarked the mines of Kentucky and the auto plants of Michigan. In Des Moines, electrical workers pulled a switch, sending 160,000 of the city's residents into darkness. Not far from Palo Alto, Communist-led strikers in the Salinas Valley refused to pick lettuce. Outside the Waldorf-Astoria in New York, where the former president liked to stay during his eastern visits, picketing busboys sang the Internationale. Repeating a pattern established in Toledo and Milwaukee, Minneapolis and Philadelphia, San Francisco stevedores launched a general strike in July. Two men died on the fifteenth, "Bloody Thursday," and desperate local authorities appealed to President Roosevelt, who was cruising offshore, to intervene on the side of public order. FDR refused. Some of the labor leaders might be "hotheaded," he declared, but even worse were conservative businessmen who sought a strike in order to crush labor once and for all.

Meanwhile, Californians were confronted with the most radical gubernatorial candidate in the history of a rambunctious state, as muckraking author Upton Sinclair won the Democratic nomination and pursued a platform promising communal production and public ownership of idled factories and farmlands. The state was in a "terrible mess," Hoover told a friend in mid-September. To the same correspondent two weeks later the ex-president complained that Republicans were entering the 1934 elections on "a 50% Roosevelt platform," hoping to withstand the Democratic tide. As for his own role in the forthcoming contest, Hoover struck a petulant note. His party's congressional committee in Washington wished to run its candidates "on any local platform that comes handy, . . . I do not wish them to be embarrassed by fundamental opposition to the Administration." But non-politicians were still educable, he believed, and so to his study Hoover now repaired, forsaking the uncongenial world of partisan politics to define the moral imperatives so callously ignored by other critics on the right.[52]

Chief among these was the American Liberty League, chartered in August 1934 by conservative Democrats like John J. Raskob, Irénée du Pont and Jouett Shouse. Hoover was openly contemptuous of the organization and its founders, who in his view owed the American people an apology "for bringing Liberty to such a pass. Had they used their enormous expenditures on propaganda during the past five years to tell the truth about our Administration, and had they also told the public what they thought of their candidate in the terms they spoke of him privately, the country would not be writhing to this condition." "Anyway," he concluded, "I am no more fond of the Wall Street model of Liberty than I am of the Pennsylvania Avenue model." Liberty Leaguers stressed property rights only, the former president complained. The Bill of Rights seemed almost irrelevant in their universe. Neither did they understand the very heart of liberty in the American system, a concept designed "to free the mind, the spirit and the energies of men." For Hoover, the right of property could not be unlimited, nor could it be vested in the state, where it might easily be employed to extinguish other liberties.[53]

It was a theme both abstract and immediate that ran throughout *The Challenge to Liberty*. In many ways the new book was a sequel to Hoover's earlier work on American individualism. Now, as then, he wrote in the shadow of revolution, economic dislocation, nationalistic frenzy and domestic inflation. But the greatest danger to liberty and genuine liberalism, he predicted, would not come in the streets of America. Modern revolution was more subtle than that. "In many democratic states," concluded Hoover, "it has meant the imposition of a new philosophy, changed ideas and changed ideals without their open submission to the people, and often without the people recognizing its approach until it has become a reality. And not a few of these recent revolutions have been stimulated by ambitious men preying upon the suffering of humanity for personal power." What Hoover called "the tragedy of Liberty" followed an inexorable pattern of "idealism without realism, slogans, phrases and statements destructive to confidence in existing institutions, demands for violent action against slowly curable ills; unfair representation that sporadic wickedness is the system itself." Then came the man on horseback, demanding delegation of author-ity from elected representatives, denouncing all opposition and exploiting propagandists in the pay of the state. In the end, "Liberty dies of the water from her own well—free speech—poisoned by untruth."

There followed a familiar tribute to Hoover's American System, with its enthronement of the individual and its insistence on social conscience as the price for personal achievement. He defined as "a hard commonplace truth" a set of economic laws that could not be repealed by official fiat, nor defined away by "amateur sociologists." These included biological inequality —balanced by equality before the law—and individual self-interest, enno-bled in Hoover's lexicon as initiative, leadership and enterprise. Competi-tion must coexist with cooperation. Stratification as well as monopoly must be rejected. So long as these extremes had been avoided, Americans read more books, fathered more innovations, created more leisure time, provided more education, shared more power, and advanced greater justice than any people on earth.

Hoover labeled the current depression itself a "transitory paralysis." He chose to sidestep less-flattering instances of Americanism, including racism, and employers who relied on professional strikebreakers and undercover agents. He paid scant attention to a concentration of wealth confirmed that same year by a landmark Brookings Institution study. Instead, he struck out at those who spoke of capitalism in "ruins" in March 1933, reminding critics that even then the economic structure did not "produce more goods than bureaucracy could tolerate," that children still attended school and their parents continued to find spiritual inspiration in churches, and, in a classic Hooverian aside, "that 23,000,000 automobiles were running about in our 'ruins' at ever increasing speeds."

Hoover criticized opponents of laissez-faire for setting up that dead expres-sion as a straw man. He then did the same thing himself, defining socialism, communism, fascism and nazism as alternatives to his own brand of liberalism. More realistically, the former president attacked the idea of national regimentation, of which he provided a host of examples. Currency had been debased and gold made the province of one man. Sales taxes had been levied on food and clothing; vast sums had been spent on public works and relief without any prior knowledge by Congress of where the money would go; government corporations had been created to compete with private enterprise; production itself had been limited in defiance of basic freedom (not to mention antitrust laws). Civil Service had been emasculated in favor of political appointees, and interest groups instructed in the fine if ignoble art of exerting pressure to make permanent their emergency gains.

Nowhere did regimentation have more pernicious effects, judged Hoover, than in industry and agriculture, where costs were artificially raised and small business ("the very fiber of our community life") deeply discouraged. Setting quotas or levying taxes to limit cotton and sugar production, in Hoover's words, "creates a privilege and destroys a right. . . . The nature of agriculture makes it impossible to have regimentation up to a point and freedom of action beyond that point. Either the farmer must use his own judgment, must be free to plant and sell as he wills, or he must take orders from the corporal put above him."

The same a priori reasoning made Hoover rule out any middle ground between government intervention in the economy and outright socialism. The problem with even the slightest penetration of Socialist methods, wrote Hoover, lay in the demoralizing effect they must have upon the economic system, legislatures and liberty itself. Still worse was the unavoidable next step, a frustrated middle class embracing fascism in disillusionment at social-ism's failure. Similarly abstract was Hoover's treatment of relief. The ex-president laid out an elaborate pyramid of responsibility, beginning with that of the individual to his neighbors, extending upward through local institutions and communities, and then to state governments. Only if all these together failed to relieve the distress of hunger and joblessness should the federal government step in, and risk bureaucratic problem-solving. Hoover the legalist discerned in all bureaucracies "three implacable spirits—self-perpetuation, expansion, and an incessant demand for more power." Just as bad was bureaucracy's betrayal of liberty's innovative spirit. "Does anyone believe that the automobile would have been invented, constantly per-fected, and the enormous industry built up by a bureaucracy?" asked Hoo-ver. "Or the railroads, or the mines?"

Throughout the pages of his book ran a determinist thinking hardly dif-ferent from that displayed in *American Individualism*. In the White House, Hoover had shown himself to be a president with a theory. Having raised him to the office, it shackled his imagination and paved the way for ultimate defeat. Hoover became the victim of his own certainties. But the moralist within him, a side first displayed in the West Branch meetinghouse, could not reject self-evident truths because of a temporary setback. His unshakable belief in his American System, like his distrust of bureaucracy and concentrated power as disincentives to enterprise, had survived even 1933 intact. If anything, as The Challenge to Liberty proved, they were held all the more tenaciously.

For Hoover, the reformer turned critic, America remained a classless society. Her economy retained the potential for fresh scientific and technological expansion. Yet dangers lurked everywhere, above all in Washington, D.C. "Free men pioneer and achieve in these regions; regimented men under bureaucracy dictation march listlessly, without confidence and hope." Hoover diagnosed other ailments as well. For him, "a factory of prayer-wheels directed at Congress" bespoke a people weakened in the virtues of their forefathers, not a nation awakened to participatory democracy. And those addicted to pump priming forgot they were draining the well of public credit.

Liberty was subject to abuse, Hoover wrote near the end of his volume. But a free economy carried its own remedies. Competition was one. "Intelligent self-interest" was another. "Free co-operation" was still a third. Warning his countrymen of "economic hypochondriacs," Hoover offered up his by-now-familiar reiteration of the causes of the Depression—the war and its attendant inflation—plus a defense of his own policies, which he insisted had turned that corner by mid-1932. Subsequent progress was halted by uncertainty among those worried about the gold standard and government-fostered inflation and borrowing. Shifting gears, he acknowledged a need for still wider dispersal of wealth in America. "But this . . . comes slowly, for violent action distributes more poverty than wealth." He was anxious for the future of liberty, Hoover asserted. In their blind groping for solutions to the Depression, some Americans had stumbled into philosophies that would lead to the surrender of freedom. For the appetite for power grew with every opportunity to exercise it, and representative government could not long survive the diseases of regimentation and dictation.

Hoover concluded his summons to national renewal on an appropriately lofty note. The structure of human betterment, he wrote, "cannot be built upon foundations of materialism or business, but upon the bedrock of individual character in free men and women. It must be [built] by those who, holding to ideals of high purpose, using the molds of justice, lay brick upon brick from the materials of scientific research, the painstaking sifting of truth from collections of facts and experience, the advancing ideas, morals and spiritual inspirations. Any other foundations are sand, any other mold is distorted; and any other bricks are without straw."

Reaction to the book was predictably mixed. William Allen White congratulated Hoover on what the former president mischievously labeled "the gospel according to Palo Alto." His attack was "dignified, serene, impersonal," said White, who made sure *The Challenge to Liberty* was chosen as a Book-of-the-Month Club selection. Old Elihu Root pronounced himself in "deep sympathy" with the author and recalled the tale of his grandson who, armed with half a dollar and accompanied by his nurse, strode into a shop where he purchased a toy, only to begin wailing in distress and jabbing his finger at the shopgirl. "That woman took my half dollar away," sobbed the boy. Root discerned a similar attitude growing among the American public.[54]

But others found the book turgid and almost offensive in its irrelevance to the present crisis. To Hoover's amazement, Roy Roberts read an early draft and judged it an eighteenth-century relic. So did Bruce Barton. Even as loyal a retainer as Edgar Rickard advised against publication. Hoover's work outlined a "grand philosophy," Rickard write in his diary that spring, but parts of the book also displayed "unrelenting animus" toward his successor. Rickard was no less dubious about the ex-president's intention to distribute 25,000 free copies, a gesture easily subject to political interpretation. Meanwhile, Hoover's ideological foes made the most of their stationary target. To John Chamberlain of the *New York Times*, *The Challenge to Liberty* was a series of "brooding, bitter essays," with Hoover guilty of hypocrisy in assailing the New Deal for devaluing the dollar and obscuring facts after himself signing the Hawley-Smoot tariff act and issuing a stream of optimistic forecasts during the depths of the economic slump. Hoover's fulminations against inflation seemed almost surreal to this reviewer. If inflation was the devil, concluded Chamberlain, then deflation was the deep blue sea. Others reminded Hoover that Prohibition was a form of regimentation, and saw unfairness in his habit of treating emergency assumption of power as a sustained assault on liberty.[55]

The *San Francisco News* was harsher still, likening the former president to a badly defeated general removed from command when the army is in retreat, only to lecture another commander who is in the process of regaining lost ground. Worse yet, the paper continued, was Hoover's fossilized confusion of liberalism and liberty. In his own administration, liberty had meant "freedom for the few and bondage for the many." From Washington, the venerable and cantankerous William Borah dismissed the whole volume as nothing more than Hoover's declaration of candidacy for a third presidential nomination. Al Smith, by now a mainstay of the Liberty League, announced with curious logic that his 1928 opponent erred in publishing at all. "When a man is out of politics," said the Happy Warrior, "let him stay out."

Hoover lashed back. Of course he hadn't provided a detailed alternative to the New Deal. He had warned a man about to leap from a window to reconsider. As for Chamberlain, he was "an unknown man" employed by a newspaper with "a complex of humiliation from having betrayed American institutions" by supporting Roosevelt in 1932. He wished that "New Deal reviewers" would attack his book front-on, rather than dismissing it as trite and stodgy. Such an all-out assault would sell more copies. But never mind, Hoover went on. "The press away from the pink and sophisticated areas are giving it a good run."[56]

This was not entirely true. By the first week of December, Hoover was forced to admit to his chagrin that only 85,000 copies of the book had been circulated, far below the publisher's hoped for 150,000. That same month, Ted Joslin published his behind-the-scenes account of the Hoover presidency, a fawning tale that even so rankled his former chief and sold still further below expectations. Worst of all, however, were the November elections, in which Roosevelt's party confounded precedent and padded its already top-heavy congressional majorities. The new House would contain fewer than 120 Republicans, the new Senate just 27. Appearing at an Armistice Day ceremony in San Jose a week later, the former president appeared nonchalant, shooing away police who tried to prevent children from getting his autograph. "I was a boy once myself," he told them. No such mood extended to his political commentary. In mid-October, he had hoped to add 30 seats in the House of Representatives; now, he emphasized the fact that over 45 percent of the electorate had resisted the appeal of a federal Santa Claus. Yet he also informed one defeated senator, "I despair that this Tammanyizing of the country can end until all the money is spent."[57]

Hoover took comfort in and claimed some credit for the defeat of Upton Sinclair in his own state. It only whetted his appetite for combat. He asked friends if he ought not begin a regular newspaper column, even if it entailed moving to Chicago for the winter. More plaintively, he inquired how it could be that movie houses reported applause for his image on screen, and yet opinion makers accepted "the combined damnation of the Old Guard and the New Deal as to myself." He suggested that William Allen White and others might orchestrate a public demand for his services, at the head of one hundred "representative men over the country. . . . Many people write me demanding something of this kind." But neither the column nor the demand developed. [58]

Columnist David Lawrence visited Palo Alto in the middle of December and wrote of "a new Hoover," an elder statesman more reconciled to his lot, less inclined to rage against his enemies. Lawrence was not privy to the ex-president's private thoughts. These included the melodramatic revelation that an Albany conference held on December 18, 1932, first signaled Roosevelt's determination to devalue the dollar. To one friend early in 1935, Hoover confessed that his hope for the future now rested with the Supreme Court, then reviewing crucial elements of the legislative New Deal. Until the justices handed down their decisions, he said, he could contribute no advice to the young. Even if he could, he added puckishly, "It will require a cool place to hold it." One week later, however, Hoover did meet with a group of Stanford debaters. He proved a man of his word, attacking the New Deal for destroying long-term credit, claiming for his "Old Deal" a start toward real recovery, and variously labeling Roosevelt's program "just a series of experiments" and "nothing in the world but fascist doctrine." The NRA, no product of "the Forgotten Man" according to Hoover, had merely succeeded in decreasing the standard of living and pleasing the U.S. Chamber of Commerce. Relief programs were shot through with corruption and the spoils system. With all this so firmly entrenched, asked one young man in the audience, how could Republicans possibly hope to compete with Roosevelt's magic? [59]

"We don't," Hoover replied, "not for two or three elections anyway. I believe they've got the people bought off for that long." With this sour assessment, the ex-president sat back and waited for judicial salvation. When it came, it would prove a Pyrrhic victory. For once again, just as he misgauged Roosevelt's true colors and rapport with the public, Hoover underestimated his antagonist's ability to tack with adverse winds. On land as on water, FDR proved a formidable helmsman. [60]

CHAPTER SIX

A SWING AROUND THE CIRCLE

★

The time is coming when you will have to deal with Mr. Roosevelt personally, in the language of the street, a sock in the nose . . . more power to your elbow.
—Ted Joslin to Herbert Hoover,[1] March 1935

There are some principles that cannot be compromised. Either we shall have a society based upon ordered liberty and the initiative of the individual, or we shall have a planned society that means dictation no matter what you call it or who does it. There is no half-way ground. They cannot be mixed.
—Herbert Hoover, June 10, 1936

★

The new year opened on a contradictory note. In his annual message to Congress, Roosevelt acknowledged continuing inequities "little changed by past sporadic remedies." He also asked for $4.8 billion to undertake a vast new program of public employment in place of the "narcotic" dole and promised to quit the business of relief altogether as soon as possible. Within weeks, the Works Progress Administration was paying construction workers and artists, teachers and vaudevillians, three million Americans in all who built New York's Lincoln Tunnel and Washington, D.C.'s, Zoo, Dealey Plaza in Dallas and a storehouse for gold at Fort Knox. Later that same January, the president unveiled his concept of Social Security, a $39-a-month retirement program too modest in its dimensions for diehard Townsendites but the thin end of a repellent wedge to conservatives like New

Jersey Senator A. Harry Moore. "It would take all the romance out of life," cried Old Guarder Moore.

Having ruffled the feathers of his critics, Roosevelt himself seemed genuinely anxious for what he called "a period of good feeling" in the country. Give him the jobs program, Social Security, reforms of holding companies and a two-year extension of the NRA, FDR suggested to Ray Moley, and he would be content to weather the storms of dissatisfaction brewing to his right and left. Roosevelt had not discarded his Hoover fixation. He bet Moley a dollar at one to twelve odds that the former president would be his 1936 opponent.

A Chicago man wrote the White House, urging that Hoover be named to manage the new relief effort. "This is too good a suggestion," Louis Howe noted sarcastically, "not to let the President see it."[2]

The object of all this interest was in New York City, taking a seat beside his old rival Al Smith on the board of the New York Life Insurance Company. (Both men endorsed their $50 checks for board service to the New York Milk Fund.) Hoover also conferred with political associates about the timing of a book vindicating his administration, and his own resumption of partisan activity. On February 12, the former president attended a Lincoln Day dinner at the Waldorf-Astoria. Seven hundred and fifty Republicans gathered in the Starlight Roof greeted him warmly; hotel regulars found more excitement in Janet Gaynor's visit earlier that week. A few days later, in a confusing yet heartening verdict, the Supreme Court ruled unconstitutional Washington's repudiation of the gold clause in government bonds. Yet simultaneously, the justices forebade bondholders from suing federal officials for reimbursement.[3]

Hoover's response to the split decision came in a statement issued en route home from New York. Calling for a return to the gold standard, the former president also proposed retention of the dollar at its current value. Since those without jobs were concentrated in industries reliant upon long-range capital, this would sweep away uncertainty, the greatest single impediment to genuine recovery. It would also repeal the false prosperity engendered through inflation. More important than Hoover's words was the public forum he chose for them, and his unmistakable wish to rally conservatives in what was fast becoming a three-cornered debate. "I have concluded that I will not keep still any longer," he told a friend a few days later. "Everybody says it is not good politics, but I have not noticed any Republican in Washington or New York raising his voice in protest at the moral issue."[4]

Among the letters congratulating Hoover for breaking his long silence was one postmarked Topeka, Kansas. "I hope the country, as well as the party, may have the benefit of a more active interest in politics on your part," it said, above the signature of Alfred M. Landon. "Pay as you go" Landon to his admirers, the Kansan was one of a handful of Republicans to occupy a state house after the massacre of the previous November. Forty-eight years old, as a boy Landon had marched for the Bull Moose in 1912. At college, his political skills earned him the name Fox; others remembered him as a pioneer of dinner jackets on the campus social scene. Later, Landon developed successful oil investments, entered politics full-time as an ally of William Allen White, and was elected governor of Kansas in 1932 after a split in the Democratic ranks. At the moment, his chief asset lay in his very lack of a national reputation or record.[5]

It was a measure of the GOP's internal disharmony that Landon's admirers (including the Hearst press) called him the Kansas Coolidge while presenting him to a skeptical public as a disciple of Theodore Roosevelt. In his youth, Landon had supported the League of Nations. In his 1933 inaugural address, he found fault with "the great industrial plutocracy" allowed to gather strength since the savage depression of the 1890s. He disliked power companies and early in 1935 managed kind words for the New Deal itself as "a modified form of individual rights and ownership of property out of which will come a wider spread of prosperity and opportunity." At the same time, Landon faulted FDR's "slapdash, jazzy method" of governing and ordered his own state to pare expenses to the bone.

A Hoover friend writing to the former president glimpsed something of Grover Cleveland in such steady, unspectacular leadership. "He has Cleveland's rugged qualities of character, his bull dog tenacity, his slow honest mind and his fine courage." Best of all, Landon was the exact opposite of the New Deal and its whirling-dervish progenitor. Should the party select him to carry its standard in 1936, the resulting campaign would be "the country boy, possessor of sound, homely American qualities . . . pitted against the trickster who resorts to magic, European isms and political sharp practices. The former works his way out of his difficulties, practices frugality and neighborliness," the informer concluded; "the latter borrows his way out, revels in wastefulness and paternalism."[6]

Hoover resolved to know Landon for himself. He invited the Kansan to be his guest at a July encampment of California's Bohemian Grove, an annual ritual Hoover called "the greatest men's party in the world." Landon's response came a month later. "More and more," he noted in a carefully worded acceptance, "I am impressed with the fact that the national campaign of 1936 is going to be an exact duplication of our campaign of

1932 here in Kansas." Equally cautious, Hoover replied that he was looking forward to a fuller discussion of such matters at the encampment. In the meantime, "We shall all of us need continue to make ourselves a nuisance to the opposition from now on until the country is relieved from this jeopardy." [7]

In point of fact, the biggest nuisance to Roosevelt in the spring of 1935 came, not from other politicians, but from nine old men in black robes. Following his close call on the gold issue, FDR sat helplessly as the Supreme Court handed down a series of rulings eviscerating the heart of the New Deal. A railroad pension act was invalidated early in May. Then, on the twenty-seventh, four brothers from Brooklyn convicted of violating a NRA code governing their poultry business provided the opportunity conservatives had been praying for. Writing for a unanimous court, Chief Justice Hughes decried the delegation of "virtually unfettered" powers by Congress to the executive. More ominous still was the court's narrow interpretation of interstate commerce, something it judged beyond the power of any federal law or regulation to control.

The president waited four days before responding. When he did, his description of the justices and their "horse and buggy definition" of modern commerce filled the nation's headlines. But it could not prevent the court from dismissing still more of his programs, including the AAA in January of 1936. Before the end of 1935, Attorney General Homer Cummings was warning Roosevelt, "we will have to find a way to get rid of the present membership of the Supreme Court."

Jubilant conservatives, by contrast, fell down on their knees in gratitude at what Arthur Schlesinger, Jr., has labeled "this slot machine theory of constitutional interpretation." Al Smith rejoiced before a Liberty League dinner that the court was throwing out the whole alphabet, "three letters at a time." As for Hoover, he took heart from new and unusual sounds—including spontaneous applause in a New York railyard and an April 1935 column suggesting that he might make a perfect GOP nominee the next year. "Herbert's great mistake," wrote columnist H. I. Phillips, "was that he called a panic a panic and not a sound experiment." The former president boasted of buttons breaking out across the landscape reading, "I voted for Hoover. I am proud of it." Emboldened by such approval, before an audience of twelve hundred California Republicans in March 1935, Hoover was blunt in his call to battle. Their party, he claimed, had its greatest responsibility since the days of Lincoln. "The American people have directly before them the issue of maintaining and perfecting our system of orderly individual liberty under constitutionally conducted government, or of rejecting it in favor of the newly created system of regimentation and bureaucratic domination in which men and women are not masters of government but . . . the pawns or dependents of a centralized and self-perpetuating government.[8]

Unspiking his guns, Hoover attacked the economy of scarcity, the establishment of monopolies and the stifling of opportunity. "I am probably . . . unwise for sticking my head up to be shot at," he wrote unconvincingly, "but it seems to me something is more important here than politics, and that is while the New Deal is sinking we should rally the intelligent people of the country to the belief that there is some hope for stability. . . . If I was a candidate I would certainly keep still instead of exposing myself at the present time." Yet he testily denied any participation in "high conspiracies" to make Ogden Mills a candidate, spread the word that a series of articles was on the way revealing Roosevelt's unreliable behavior during the 1933 bank crisis, and early in April left Palo Alto for a trip loaded with political hobnobbing in the East and Midwest. On his return journey, Hoover stopped off in Emporia to visit editor White, who revealed that his guest had no plans to further his own political destiny. Then, in a shrewd reading of Republican psychology, White assessed Hoover's 1936 chances: "He will become impossible or inevitable."[9]

In mid-May, after denouncing the NRA as "un-American in principle and a proved failure in practice," Hoover reported a flood of approving letters—and took impish delight in the discomfiture his reemergence was causing Old Guard Republicans. Hungry for the latest political gossip, quick to broadcast details of a successful trip to Ohio and Indiana, by the second week in June the noncandidate was off on yet another excursion, this time motoring through the West and farm belt to Chicago. To GOP leaders he met along the way, he urged concentration on the weak links of Roosevelt's regime, especially relief expenditures (more than tripled since 1932, administered by a work force swollen from 200 then to 140,000 now) and financial irregularities. In his own mind, he was defending a set of principles. To others, he was merely pawing the ground.[10]

Close friends understood what Hoover's numerous enemies within the party only dimly perceived, that the former president was serious in pursuing electoral vindication in 1936. As ever, his methods were unorthodox. He told Edgar Rickard on June 9 that he would not actively campaign for anything. If his admirers felt sufficiently keen, they ought to "get out and 'spread the gospel,' " stirring a popular groundswell for his renomination. Any one succeeding Roosevelt in the White House who was intent on doing his duty, Hoover continued, would have to fire thousands of government workers and raise taxes to balance the budget. Soon, he "would be the most hated man in the country," a position no one should subject himself to without the strong and vocal support of his friends.[11]

For other Republicans, the prospect of running on such a ticket was nightmarish. When the party held a midwestern conference in Springfield, Illinois, that June, Walter Newton reported to the former president that he had many well-wishers among the assembled delegates. Personally, Newton confided, he felt "shelved" at Springfield for obvious reasons. He admitted failure in securing two amendments, one castigating Roosevelt for his conduct during the bank crisis and the other placing blame for the Depression itself on World War I and its aftershocks. Newton summed up the attitude of GOP leaders as a desire to keep quiet about Hoover, the Depression and his efforts to combat it, in the forlorn hope that the whole issue might go away without calling for a defense of the last Republican administration. Other friends echoed a defeatist bent attributed to Ogden Mills, whom Hoover came to regard as an ingrate, mindless of the risk taken in naming him Secretary of the Treasury despite his heavy drinking.[12]

Personalities aside, thoughtful observers raised serious doubts about the political appeal of constitutionalism itself. All the alphabet agencies might be struck down by an avenging court, they reasoned, but how many farmers would rejoice in the triumph of constitutionalism if it resulted in fifteen-cent corn? How many union members would celebrate the demolition of their newfound rights? How many consumers would take solace in constitutional purity at the expense of their own purchasing power? While victory-minded members of his own party sought in vain to muzzle Hoover, the man in the White House pronounced "perfectly grand" the prospect of running against his 1932 opponent. Asked at a press conference in the wake of the GOP Springfield conference whether Hoover and Chicago publisher Frank Knox, another 1936 hopeful, were on the Democratic payroll, FDR couldn't resist a humorous jab. "Strictly off the record," he deadpanned, "it is a question of how much longer we can afford to pay them. They have been so successful that they are raising their price." By then, Roosevelt himself was upping the ante in a legislative and political game played with more finesse than conviction.

The more he learned about Andy Jackson, FDR had informed his vice president the previous November, the more he liked him. Now he began to act like the old populist. With his administration becalmed, his partnership with business in ruins, and eleven million people unemployed by the AFL's own reckoning, the president displayed the instincts of both lion and fox reserved for him by his biographers. One week after the NRA's judicial slaughter, Roosevelt informed congressional leaders that his January priorities were being fattened with new bills embodying the late agency's objectives. He reversed his earlier opposition to Senator Robert Wagner's Labor Relations Act, a measure radically redefining the rights of labor to organize and placing the federal government squarely behind collective bargaining. Nor was that the only red flag he wished to wave before the conservative bull, as Ray Moley discovered when summoned to the White House early in June. Fearful of Huey Long's appeal on the left, angered by the resentful bleatings of the Chamber of Commerce and others on the right, the president nimbly proposed his famous "soak the rich" tax plan, draining off "unwieldy and unnecessary corporate surpluses" and sharply hiking tax rates on all incomes over $50,000. Moley tried to dissuade him. Such a program would only accentuate booms and busts, undermine business confidence and destroy any hope for economic stability, Moley argued.

Pleased with himself and the initiative so boldly seized, FDR was immovable. "Pat Harrison's going to be so surprised," he said of his party's Senate Finance Committee chairman, "he'll have kittens on the spot." Surprise did not exhaust the catalogue of reactions to the president's latest proposal. William Randolph Hearst was furious at the man he now labeled Stalin Delano Roosevelt. Will Rogers said he'd like to see the look on the King-fish's face when Roosevelt woke him in the middle of the night and told him, "Lay over, Huey, I want to get in bed with you." In Palo Alto, Hoover's reaction was only slightly less apoplectic. "I don't know how much 'reform' this country can stand before 'recovery,' " he wrote two days after Roosevelt sent his new tax package up to Capitol Hill. "So far there is none of the latter in sight, despite the propaganda to the contrary." To William Allen White, Hoover sounded less angry than bemused. In raising the top tax brackets from 24 percent to 55 percent during his own administration, he believed he had gone as far as possible to collect revenue without destroying wealth. "That was however a popular move!" he added.[13]

By the start of September, having secured congressional passage of his Second New Deal, confounded his enemies and inspired his friends, Roosevelt could well afford to assent publicly to Roy Howard's demand for a legislative breathing spell. Immediately, the stock market rose. So did the president's Gallup Poll rating. Two weeks later, when the son-in-law of a gerrymandered judge fired a single bullet into Huey Long inside the Louisiana state capitol at Baton Rouge, the chief threat to FDR's 1936 prospects disappeared. For Hoover, disabused of his earlier pleasure at the Supreme Court's action, it was a bitter reprieve. Old journalistic supporters like Mark Sullivan, David Lawrence and Frank Kent urged him not to be a candidate.

Early in October, Ogden Mills dropped a bombshell of his own: the former Treasury secretary let it be known that he was for Alf Landon. Other officials in his administration refused to arrange dinners where Hoover might advance his cause. A friend of Edgar Rickard's did agree to invite some women to lunch with the former president, but only after making it clear that her personal admiration should not be misconstrued as political support. California's Republican National Committeeman said he was being excluded from political strategy sessions. His crime—long years of identification as a Hoover partisan.[14]

Notwithstanding Hoover's own lack of availability, a parade of would-be candidates and shapers of party policy made their way to Palo Alto: Frank Knox, the red-haired newspaper publisher who fancied himself a new edition of the first Roosevelt, even to the bared teeth and jerky gestures of his old hero; Governor Harry Nice of Maryland; Pat Hurley and others. Reporters found amusement in the hopeful procession, gingerly sidling up to their titular leader, even while avoiding his outright embrace. George Creel dubbed their host "the head that will not bow."

Growing restless, Hoover resolved to take a swing around the circle himself. On October 5, 1935, he roused an audience of young Republicans in Oakland with a vigorous assault on New Deal fiscal policies. Phrases could be made to scintillate like the aurora borealis, he told his listeners, but in the practical business of governing they counted for no more than the aurora itself. The battle for America was not between phrases, but between "straight and crooked thinking." Hoover's call for common sense included ridicule of Roosevelt's habit of submitting "regular" and "extraordinary" budgets—a juggling act that barely concealed deficits grown by $14 billion in less than three years. At least his own administration, argued Hoover, told the fiscal truth—and made a good-faith effort to balance receipts and outlays. Had FDR been candid with the voters in 1932 about prospective deficits and a swollen bureaucracy, five thousand paid committees and commissions, a devalued dollar and all the rest, he would not have been reelected. "But the wreckage of representative government," noted Hoover, "is strewn with broken promises."

Waste was no mere abstraction. Like the bureaucracy itself, "the most gigantic spoils raid in our history," it would be supported only by higher taxes, further devaluation of the dollar, or inflation. For all the talk of soaking the rich, Hoover insisted, Roosevelt's deficits, like his hidden taxes, meant hardship for the poor, already going without bacon and meat, and fated to see savings, pensions and purchasing power in general diminished by the New Deal's habit of "clipping the coin." Yet when anyone raised his voice in protest, he was met with the peremptory demand: "Would you let the people starve?"

Six weeks later, Hoover was in New York to address the Ohio Society. His topic was "National Planning," and he led off with the assertion that "there are nests of Constitutional termites at work" in Washington. More whimsically, the former president suggested that only four letters of the alphabet remained to be utilized by the New Deal planners, and even those would doubtlessly be exhausted upon formation of the Quick Loans Corporation for Xylophones, Yachts, and Zithers. Hoover faulted the administration for encouraging monopolies and competing with private business. Instead of economic plenty, there was planned scarcity—"the more abundant life—without bacon." Meanwhile the average citizen, unable to compete with government bookkeeping and a bottomless treasury, lost just as surely as a Congress rubber-stamping public works project without even the niceties of debate.

Destroying both self-respect and self-government, the New Deal had converted the treasury into a national grab bag, and replaced old ideals with a new imperative: "If we don't get ours, someone else will." Relief enriched a political bureaucracy and fostered permanent dependency. Strikes were up, the value of the dollar down. Silver mines in other lands were being subsidized by unnecessary government purchases. Managed currency, instead of benefiting mortgages, was impoverishing 65 million life insurance policyholders. It was equivalent, said Hoover, to reducing a yard to 21.2 inches, in the hope there might be more cloth in the bolt. "Instability of currencies and inflation," he charged, "are the green pastures upon which the speculator grows fat." Of what value were savings or unemployment insurance or any other government assistance if devaluation and inflation were pursued at the same time? As a boy in Iowa, said Hoover, he had learned some simple truths about finance. Most of all, "I learned that the keeping of financial promises is the first obligation of an honorable man." What was demanded of individuals held true for governments, or else misery, like dishonor, was inevitable.

In offering up what he called "a constructive fiscal program," Hoover demanded an end to waste of taxpayers' money on "unnecessary public works" and "visionary and un-American experiments." He called for sharp cuts in political bureaucracy, a balanced budget, repeal of presidential authority to inflate currency, and a restoration of confidence in government promises. Forty-one times in forty-three minutes, Hoover's audience interrupted the speaker to register its applause. Harlan Stone, borrowing a phrase from Justice Holmes, pronounced the speech "sockdological" and urged his friend to continue hammering away at bureaucratic abuses and an economy of scarcity. Hoover assured him that he would. "I have no other interest than to see that the issues are put before the country," he added.[15]

This was, at best, an exercise in self-delusion, rendered transparent when Hoover paid to have forty thousand copies of his speech distributed. As early as October 11, Edgar Rickard reported in his diary that his friend seemed interested in little besides his own political prospects. A few days before Christmas, the former president was concerned about gains being made in New York by the Landon forces and preparing to travel to Ohio for a speech if a national radio hookup could be arranged. Meanwhile, the fourth estate listened to Hoover's Ohio Society address, lauded his new, droll style of delivery, and excoriated much of what he had to say. The *Los Angeles Daily News* chose to publish a list of farm prices for 1932 and their most recent counterparts. Wheat, 45 cents then, was 89 cents now. Corn had climbed from 22 cents to 52 cents, hogs from $3.50 to $9.00. Equally eloquent were the statistics of industrial production. According to the *News*, auto output had quadrupled since the advent of Roosevelt, stock prices had doubled, and employment had risen by a third. In November 1932, Cincinnati worried over how to feed a quarter of its 450,000 residents. Ohio schools were closing, their teachers having already surrendered 40 percent in wage reductions. Yet, "the Old Deal's bugleman—in extraordinary" preferred to deal in abstractions.[16]

"It would have been pertinent," judged the editors, "to have asked the speaker, as an engineering problem, if he could tell them how to feed and clothe the starving families of eleven million idle men and women, deprived of their God-given right to earn a living by the sweat of their brow. By handing them the 'provisions of the Constitution'?"

But Hoover kept up his attack. In St. Louis on December 16, he assailed those who claimed that civilization had come to a halt on March 3, 1933, denounced political exploitation of Americans on relief, and hailed the volunteers whose services to the needy under his own administration demonstrated the clear superiority of nonpolitical relief over "those whose major passion was sociological experiment upon a mass of distress." In fact, ten thousand fewer government workers were employed at the end of the Hoover Administration than at the beginning—irrefutable evidence to Hoover that he had succeeded in providing relief instead of red tape. Vowing that only "honest productive jobs" created by a stable currency and balanced budgets would provide permanent relief to the millions out of work, Hoover once more displayed a gift for the snappish phrase. He noted that county supervisors in Los Angeles had named a street New Deal Avenue. Unfortunately, the road was a deadend. He professed his sympathies for "the humble decimal point, lost among an army of regimented ciphers" in New Deal accounts, and predicted that the ultimate alphabet agency would be christened IOU.

In a farm speech at Lincoln, Nebraska, a month later, the former president warned of the opposition's own patented technique of stifling dissent. "They set up a glorious ideal to which we all agree unanimously. Then they drive somewhere else or into a ditch. When we protest they blackguard us for opposing the glorious ideal. And they announce that all protestors are the tools of Satan or Wall Street. When we summon common sense and facts they weep aloud over their martyrdom for the ideal." To stop the production of fifty million fertile acres was not progress, said Hoover, "but goosestepping the people under this pinkish banker of Planned Economy." Progress came about solely by producing more of a variety of things. How logical or progressive was it to reduce agricultural production, only to wind up importing a hundred million bushels of grain, and seven times as much in animal products? "Is that not the principle of the Economic Dog chasing its own tail?"

The only sure principle of New Deal agricultural policies was politics—embodied in 120,000 full- or part-time officials approved by the Democratic National Committee. Bad as it was to impose political agents as a new middleman between the farmer and consumer, Hoover found it still worse to coerce farmers into curtailing crops under a gentle rain of checks. By legislating scarcity, the New Deal had spread "hideous poverty" among southern sharecroppers and fostered unemployment among tens of thousands dependent for their livelihood upon the soil and its economic by-products. Processing taxes mandated by the Triple A redounded against the poor who went without pork and flour, and fed the flames of class conflict and housewife rebellion. As for the contention that farm prices were up, that was easily accounted for by drought, inflation, and recovery in other markets outside the U.S. Give the farmer back his home markets, Hoover demanded. Increased demand for his product would follow a rising curve of employment, made possible by the now-familiar remedies of a stable currency and a balanced budget. Instead of curtailing production, expand crops that might be marketed or improve soil fertility. Vegetable oils, sugar and other commodities now imported might be home-grown. If it required government subsidies to launch such experiments, Hoover was willing to go along. Subsidies at least had the saving grace of stimulating freedom and production, rather than curtailing both. "Stop, look and listen," Hoover concluded his farm address. In the last weeks of 1935, more and more Americans seemed attentive to the message.

Friends might doubt his electoral prospects, but no one questioned Hoover's achievement in refocusing the spotlight. At the Gridiron Dinner in December, there was a sketch featuring a mock Hoover keeping his counsel over 1936—followed by six more Republicans, identical in appearance and bearing, but announced to the audience as Landon, Knox and the other active contenders. The humor lost its gentle edge, however, when Roosevelt got up to speak. Needling a half-dozen Supreme Court justices who sat a few feet away by demonstrating how earlier presidents, Hoover included, had made a practice of stealing at least one plank from the Socialist platform, Roosevelt concluded each example with the stinging rebuke "and it's still constitutional." At this, Hoover's informant detected a chill in the audience. But the country approved, and FDR knew it. What he might do with his knowledge was a subject of no mean interest to his leading rival.[17]

★   ★

Roosevelt and Hoover shared a talent for making enemies. There the similarities ended. For Roosevelt exploited his foes to monopolize debate and transcend political conventions, whereas Hoover, less strategically minded than moralistically quick to anger, consistently boxed himself into situations confirming his public image as a Rollin Kirby cartoon come to life. In the first week of January 1936, FDR rejected the idea of a constitutional amendment to proscribe Supreme Court review of his popular revolution. Instead, he used his annual State of the Union Address to attack forces of "entrenched greed," "our resplendent economic autocracy," and others who would "gang up against the people's liberties."

Those who took at face value his assurance of a breathing spell in New Deal reforms were aghast. Al Smith accused his former protégé of aping Lenin. A fresh cascade of mail swamped the White House, some addressed simply "To the Greatest Man in the World," some directed to "Benedict Arnold 2nd." Roosevelt haters whispered that the president was a syphilitic, at the head of an alcoholic family, dogged for fascism or communism in place of traditional American values. *Chicago Tribune* publisher Robert McCormick likened FDR to Louis of Bourbon. Taking heart from the controversy, Nicholas Roosevelt, once Hoover's ambassador to Hungary, told three hundred GOP activists in New York that their party might evict "that man" from the White House in 1936, but only if it shed Hoover and "the old conservative leaders" associated with standpattism and past failures.

With such friends, Hoover might be forgiven for wondering the identity of his enemies—until Harold Ickes rose up in a speech at Rochester, New York, to declare the former president something of an authority himself on unconstitutional legislation, having signed three such acts during his own presidency. In fact, the three bills in question predated Hoover's term of office, but when Ickes's target demanded an apology, the Interior Secretary sounded as if he were the aggrieved party. It was, he said in a statement heavily edited by Steve Early (who cut out the best parts, according to Ickes), an "honest mistake" of which he was guilty. He fully understood, Ickes went on, "that a politician who is trying to improve a desperate situation will overlook no opportunity to exaggerate an incident with a view to arousing popular sympathy, but I did not expect this of a man who has occupied the very great position with which you were once honored." In truth, Ickes noted in a stinging passage, it was entirely constitutional to do nothing, a stance familiar to Hoover.[18]

Hoover's own position in a simultaneous feud with Walter Lippmann was hardly more defensible. The columnist had accused the former president of opposition to every New Deal measure, a charge Hoover angrily branded untrue. "It don't think I have ever made an important public statement," he told Lippmann, "that I have not specifically referred to things that were right in their objectives." Lippmann fired back, phrasing with infinite delicacy a request for proof, coupled with an offer to make amends should he discover in any of Hoover's speeches a measure of support for Roosevelt's initiatives. He was referred to a three-page passage in The Challenge to Liberty, along with a weak rejoinder that Hoover wished no publicity on the whole matter. "He merely wished you to be informed."[19]

But it was with Alf Landon, or, more precisely, with Landon's most prominent supporters, that Hoover waged his most intense struggle in the early months of 1936. Feverishly calculating his chances for a convention upset, Hoover during the first week of January was awarding Idaho's crusty irregular William Borah two hundred delegates, waxing indignant over a presumed conspiracy among the Republican National Committee and the radio networks to keep him off the air, and cocking a receptive ear to reports of dissatisfaction with Roosevelt among relief workers. A month later, responding to an inflammatory FDR message to Congress, Hoover gloried in his vocation as the new order's chief scourge. Friends should produce "a good thumping article" to demonstrate beyond doubt that the bank crisis "really was not any great crisis after all," he wrote. He delivered his own pronouncements on the state of the union in a speech on February 12 at Portland, Oregon. Having toyed with the idea of renouncing any active candidacy, instead he stuck to his prepared text, describing the New Deal as "a veritable fountain of fear," from its birth in an artificial bank panic to its celebration of a stock market rising from fear of inflation. Roosevelt's denunciation of his enemies was nothing more nor less than a summons to class warfare, "a red herring across the trail of failure," and an attempt to patent for Washington, D.C., all righteousness and compassion.[20]

The greed for money was evil, said Hoover, but at least it could be controlled by law. The greed for power, on the other hand, seized the law for its own ends. When Roosevelt urged Congress to advance instead of retreat, he was reminded of similar words used by Napoleon on the long march to Moscow. To be sure, stock values had been restored to 1926 levels, but with a difference. In 1926, Hoover claimed, unemployment was unknown. Now, there were ten million to attest to its horrors firsthand. In 1926, foreign trade was flourishing; now it was demoralized. In 1926, the budget was balanced, and currency stable; now both were bobbing helplessly on a sea of whim—one man's whim. For all its fine phrases of concern for the forgotten man, the New Deal reserved its keenest power of recollection for political allies. Quoting the *New York Times,* Hoover found twelve thousand employees on the rolls of the Federal Resettlement Administration —giving relief to barely five thousand recipients, at a ratio of six to one in administrative overhead to aid extended.

The *Portland Oregonian* dismissed the speech as "inhuman insinuation" and said there wasn't a thing in it that would put bread in a hungry mouth, shoes on bare feet, or a job into empty hands. "America moves on," concluded the editors. "The world is changing, but not Mr. Hoover." Nor was Roosevelt blind to the target so invitingly presented. A few weeks after the Portland address, the president suggested that aides reprint a critical book entitled *Lest We Forget.* [21]

He had two more speeches approaching, Hoover told Ted Joslin late in February. After that, he would lapse into silence, "unless the President offers me some grounds for sheer debate." As if to cheer his old employer, Joslin quoted Joe Tumulty, once Woodrow Wilson's secretary and confidant. According to Tumulty, Hoover was the New Deal's most effective critic, and the president himself a pagan, whose reelection would bring a halt to future elections and a final chapter in American democracy. Yet Hoover's gloom did not abate. Having rejected advice from numerous friends to pull out of the 1936 race, he halfheartedly sought to buy time. Money for more speeches and their distribution was scarce. An Ohio poll in February showed just 4 percent of the state's GOP voters favoring the former president. Only three thousand listeners asked NBC for copies of a Hoover speech delivered at Fort Wayne, Indiana, early in April, and although three-quarters of the party's national committee and state chairmen agreed that Hoover was easily the best qualified candidate, they also dismissed out of hand his chances of reelection. [22]

Yet others among his entourage encouraged his feeble hopes. Walter Newton reported growing Hoover sentiment in the South. In New York, Hoover's 1928 campaign manager, Alan Fox, promised open support from

Ogden and Helen Reid and their *Herald Tribune* if any move in his direction could be detected. Meanwhile, Fox offered to poll 16,000 Public Works Administration (PWA) workers for their preferences—a curious step at best, illustrative of the naivete with which Hoover's backers confronted the Landon juggernaut. Hoping to fill a vacuum that didn't exist, with a compromise candidate whose nomination might tear the party to pieces, they seized upon an old enemy to revive their flagging hopes.[23]

On September 30, 1935, William Randolph Hearst bestowed his blessing upon Alfred M. Landon. Hearst had been persona non grata in Hoover's White House, the president flatly rejecting a visit by the publisher at a time when his powerful influence might have softened the prospects of defeat in 1932. The feeling was strictly mutual. Hoover was "selfish and stupid," stormed Hearst to Louis B. Mayer. His very presence harmed the conservative cause and emboldened radicals. "If you don't suppress this hoodoo," the publisher warned Mayer, "your party will lose its chance, too, of electing a Congress as well as a President. His name is anathema to the American public."

On the last subject, at least, Hearst might be considered an authority: moviegoers hissed at the sight of Hearst Metrotone newsreels, organized labor detested the man whose annual salary was reputed to be the greatest in America, larger even than Mae West's, and FDR privately designated his soak-the-rich tax scheme as Hearst's comeuppance. So when the hawk-nosed laird of San Simeon threw his arms around Landon, it was an embrace to frighten away more moderate Republicans who recalled the publisher's earlier manipulation of delegates to the convention that nominated Roosevelt in 1932. Worse yet was Hearst's appropriation of the Landon cause in California, where he and Governor Frank Merriam overrode objections from party leaders like Bill Knowland and Earl Warren and entered a slate of delegates committed to the Kansan in violation of Landon's pledge to stay out of Hoover's home turf.

Despite his own suspicions about Standard Oil subsidiaries "suddenly broken out in great enthusiasm" for Hearst's contender, and the feeling that a divisive primary contest would rule victory in November out of the question, Hoover could write as late as February 10 that he was taking no part in the California brawl—"so far."[24]

Within a few weeks, however, he was running up huge telephone bills, contacting California allies several times a day as the date for candidate filings drew near. By the end of March, the former president was resolved: He would go home to fight for an ostensibly uncommitted delegation. He had no choice. To surrender now would end his political life, he informed friends, enshrine Hearst as the party kingmaker, and almost surely taint Landon himself as he prepared to contest Roosevelt.[25]

Into the crusade Hoover threw every available resource. He urged Hearst's rival publisher Harry Chandler to undertake a series of articles exposing the mogul's earlier efforts at political dictation. He dispatched friends to raise $20,000 in New York City and another $35,000 in San Francisco with which to wage battle. In a moment of unrelieved bitterness, he complained of Landon's appearance as little more than Hearst's stooge. "I hope he has the qualities which you mention," he stiffly informed William Allen White. "Of course there is nothing in his public utterances which has yet established that." Railing at the small-mindedness of Landon's Kansas City advisers, Hoover denied knowing as many as ten members of the uninstructed delegation (over half of whom, as it turned out, leaned to Landon anyway). Going a step further, the former president proclaimed that he would sit out the fall campaign should Hearst emerge a winner on May 5. He was even then composing "my last address" for delivery in Philadelphia on May 14. "If Governor Landon is nominated, I do not intend to either embarrass him or take any responsibility for his probable defeat. I do not believe any man can stand up against the Democratic bombardment of linking the Republican candidate with Hearst."[26]

A few days later, Hoover wrote White again, explaining his earlier entreaty as "simply an explosion of my own feelings" and promising to concentrate opposition on Hearst and Merriam rather than the Kansas governor. "How long that will last, I do not know, for while my friends will ignore Hearst's attacks on me, they won't stand it long from the Landon managers. . . ." A moral question was at stake in the balloting, he went on. "If Governor Landon gets 44 delegates from California from Hearst, he has got something that will dirty his entire life—and the Presidency, if he gets that." His own mood wavered from hopeful defiance to a kind of weary compliance with the inevitable. He detected "a certain indignation rising in the state" that might teach his enemies a lesson. But he also criticized the party's national committee for refusing to distribute some "of these painfully produced speeches of mine," even though the RNC had "several hundred thousand dollars in hand." To Alan Fox, Hoover urged that any further polling in New York be put on hold, pending the results of the California voting. "It is always difficult to beat somebody with nobody." His own career in politics was "absolutely dependent" upon the primary's outcome, he conceded on April 18, and a few days before the voting, in a move testifying to his anxiety, he asked Colonel McCormick and his rabidly anti-New Deal *Tribune* to denounce Hearst and praise his own "magnificent job of revitalizing the Republican Party and exposing the New Deal."[27]

But McCormick would not accommodate the former president, who by now professed to see omens of defeat in large sums being spent to support the Hearst slate. Snappishly, Hoover disputed Ted Joslin's warning that his own activities appeared both obstructionist and motivated by personal ambition. "Certain camps have for months tried to capitalize on my presumed unpopularity," he told Joslin. "They have not been content to allow me to go along building the bridge upon which they were to cross into the Presidency." Such declarations failed to carry much weight with reporters, given Hoover's continuing interest in state caucus results, and the ongoing efforts of friends like Walter Newton and Alan Fox to promote him as the only authentic alternative to Roosevelt.[28]

On May 5, California voters repudiated Hearst by a large margin. But they inflicted no mortal wound on Landon. In fact, barely a week after the voting, Hoover was back in New York, jubilant over the "deserved thrashing" administered the newspaperman, yet conceding the nomination to his opponent from Kansas, and promising Landon only perfunctory support, like that extended by Coolidge in 1928. Personally, he told friends, he regarded former Illinois Governor Frank J. Lowden as the better man. But Lowden was seventy-three, too old to be a candidate. Ten days after California, Hoover kept his speaking date in Philadelphia. By then eager to convert this self-proclaimed valedictory address into a warm-up for Cleveland, he pressed his newly pithy oratorical style to the limit. Denouncing the five horsemen of a new Apocalypse, "Profligacy, Propaganda, Patronage, Politics and Power," also known as "Pork-Barrel, Poppy-cock, Privilege, Panaceas, and Poverty," calling for "a nation of proprietors, not a state of collectivists," the former president went further than before in laying out what he called "a platform for America." He compared New Dealers to umpires wanting to pitch the game, claimed for Republican governments at the state level the honor of creating old-age pensions, insisted that child labor had not, as FDR claimed, gone out in a flash under the NRA—"It was mostly a flash in the pan"—and demanded a government that would foster honor and self-reliance in place of "parasitic leaners" and presidential gag rules.[29]

"Is it not time to jerk ourselves out of this," asked Hoover, the embers of ambition still glowing, "and clean out the high priests of these heresies?" Yet even in the wake of this fresh triumph, he had cause to fear what "that bunch in Washington," as he labeled the National Committee, might do to lower his profile at the convention.[30]

★   ★

Long before Hoover, Roosevelt realized the implausibility of his wish for a rematch of 1932. Another Roosevelt-Hoover contest might have been a philosophical brawl, ending in massive justification and a renewed mandate. Now, however, with the prospect of running against the genial but unimpressive Landon sinking in, the president seemed almost disappointed. Spoiling for a fight, FDR in May of 1936 was railing against foes, real or imagined. Most businessmen were very stupid, he informed Ray Moley; they lacked "moral indignation." So did newspapers, which at least did him the favor of ensuring popular resentment. Moley interrupted. It was one thing to welcome the hatred of such rivals, he said; quite another to provoke it needlessly. What's more, such critics played an essential part in the democratic system. No one would contest the point, Roosevelt replied. The problem lay in criticism that was unjust or destructive, and in what he called an "excess of debate." Gradually, it dawned on the original architect of Roosevelt's Brain Trust: FDR intended 1936 to be his blank check from the electorate, an impression solidified three weeks later. "There's one issue in this campaign," an agitated chief executive asserted. "It's myself, and people must be either for or against me." Unlike Roosevelt, who was bored with his own success, Hoover didn't have the luxury of inventing enemies. Barely ten days before the opening gavel of his party's nominating convention, he still didn't have a hotel reservation for Cleveland. Neither did he have what he wanted most: an invitation to address the delegates and dramatically reclaim a measure of lost authority. Frank Knox, believing he could count on the former president's support should a deadlock take place, asked national chairman Fletcher to issue such an invitation. Landon's managers, guided by a skillful Kansas politico named John Hamilton, agreed.

But a snag developed when convention officials asked Hoover to deliver his remarks, not in the evening before a national radio audience, but in the morning, when few would be listening. This was rejected out of hand, as was a second invitation to speak at three o'clock in the afternoon. Hoover threatened to denounce his own party's governing board unless an evening time slot was made available: the arrangements committee caved in. Such behavior did nothing to alleviate Hoover's distrust, nor salve his feelings of persecution. Others agreed with his assessment of shabby dealings. The man who twice led his party and still remained its titular leader deserved better, Henry Ford told a friend. Anything less was like saying, "Well, our last captain wrecked you and the ship, but come aboard again and we'll see what the new pilot can do. . . ." According to Ford, the GOP could win in 1936 only by a willingness to lose for principle.[31]

On May 18, Hoover denied being a candidate for anything. "My concern is with principles," he insisted in Chicago. Privately, he listened to the siren's song of ambition. The convention would be "foundering" without a clearcut preference, John Callan O'Laughlin assured him from Washington.

"It is not at all impossible that a single spark may set it off, and that spark may be a speech." Through O'Laughlin, Hoover let it be known that he was adamant in opposing any platform admission of evils in past Republican administrations as well as his own. Such a repudiation, he insisted, would cost the nominee at least five million votes in November. He passed word to Ruth Simms, a powerbroker from New Mexico, that she might organize female delegates, with whom such other Hoover stalwarts as Walter Brown and Arthur Hyde would gladly cooperate.[32]

On May 23, O'Laughlin informed Douglas MacArthur, then in Manila, that Hoover would accept the nomination if offered it, that personally the former president regarded Knox as having done most for the party, and that Landon was disqualified both on the ground of general competence and because of his oil interests—according to Hoover, Harold Ickes boasted a thick dossier sure to "paralyze" the Kansan should he win the nomination. With assorted friends in California and elsewhere, plus Illinois, where Frank Lowden backed his shadow candidacy, Hoover might yet produce a miracle. Thin as they were, his chances seemed to rest on a single dramatic speech, capable of igniting a firestorm of militant enthusiasm like the one greeting William Jennings Bryan's anathema on gold forty years earlier.[33]

Hoover was working on just such a speech. As he scribbled away, his supporters fanned a dying flame. Nearly a hundred delegates were prepared to vote for him, claimed the *New York Times* on June 3, should the leading contenders deadlock. Yet Hoover persisted in playing Hamlet. He "greatly appreciated" the thoughtfulness of Delaware's delegates, but he would not schedule a meeting with them; he expected to be in Cleveland for only a day. Informants within the huge New York delegation reported only tepid support for Landon. Fourteen of Brooklyn's fifteen delegates were personally opposed to his nomination, but were willing to yield to popular preference in the vacuum created by Hoover's disqualification.[34]

Pragmatism mingled with passionate contempt for Roosevelt, as 25,000 Republicans descended on Cleveland. Their apparent willingness to swallow the Kansas Coolidge reminded some of Roscoe Conkling's long-ago pronouncement on the highly available Ulysses Grant: "When asked what state he comes from, our sole reply should be, 'He comes from some good section of the right geography.'" Such flexibility of judgment did not extend to assessments of the opposition.

> "Three long years," they sang to the tune of "Three Blind Mice,"
> "Three long years.
> Full of grief and tears,
> Full of grief and tears.
> Roosevelt gave us to understand

If we would lend him a helping hand
He'd lead us all to the promised land,
   For three long years."

In his keynote address, convention chairman Bertrand Snell of New York assailed "the bob-tailed eagle" of the NRA and lambasted the president's high-handed attitude toward the Supreme Court. "He runs the true course of the dictator," thundered Snell. Having throttled liberty and seduced Congress, FDR now hoped to usurp "the last bulwark of the citizen against unbridled autocracy." The crowd cheered, grateful to express its emotions over something besides the price of a beefsteak dinner, raised from 60 cents the previous weekend to $1.75 now that the delegates were in town. Off the floor, hopeful contenders tried to strike sparks of their own. Michigan's Arthur Vandenburg criticized evasive tactics, an obvious blow aimed at Landon's managers and insisted, all evidence to the contrary, that "this is not a circus. It is a crusade." Borah of Idaho denounced as unnecessary a proposed plank submitting to the states a constitutional amendment permitting regulation of wages and hours. Landon's own followers were upset with language assailing New Deal farm policies. Everyone was unhappy about something, and few could summon more than ritual optimism about November.

Reporters surveying the scene outside convention hall, in hotel lobbies and rooms filled with wishful schemers as well as smoke, pronounced the gathering a tedious affair. It was, wrote one correspondent, as if everything were suspended, pending Hoover's arrival. Proving his point, thousands of Republicans jammed the city's rail depot to see the former president on Wednesday morning, June 10. Old friends like Pat Hurley and Walter Brown were at the platform, alongside Chairman Fletcher. Outside, another crowd surged around the station entrance. "Hooray for Hoover" someone shouted, in a chant soon picked up by others. Many of his admirers followed their hero to his hotel, where he held open house throughout the day, and turned a deaf ear to those pleading with him to announce his own candidacy. "Chief, how are you?" Vandenburg boomed out. Less auspiciously, Knox managers sought in vain a private audience. Reporters clamoring for advance copies of Hoover's speech were equally frustrated.

All afternoon, rumors fed on speculation. California's delegation was ready to lead a stampede for Hoover, it was whispered. The former president might describe his own ideal candidate in terms clearly fashioned to exclude Landon. Yet as fast as the specter of a Hoover comeback emerged, the huge delegations from New York and Pennsylvania put it to rest. At an afternoon caucus of the Empire State's eighty-five members, Ogden Mills administered the unkindest cut of all. Insisting against any delay in polling the delegates until after Hoover addressed the convention, Mills joined seventy-eight other New Yorkers in publicly endorsing Landon. Only his longtime supporter Ruth Pratt remained loyal to Hoover. For all practical purposes New York snuffed out his ambitions.

But vindication remained a tantalizing possibility. The man who approached the podium a few minutes before nine o'clock that night, in a hall filled to overflowing and hungry to erupt in honest emotion, was eager to remind America that he, at least, had never dipped his colors. Seventeen thousand Republicans shouted and sang at the first sight of him. Texans clanged cowbells. Virginians paraded through the clogged aisles. Everywhere, people were tearing up programs and tossing bits of paper into the air. The object of their ardor stood bathed in floodlights, a wistful smile on his face, his hands held up for quiet. But silence was evasive. This was the moment and the man produced by two years of brooding silence, followed by eighteen months of a cross-country crusade against Roosevelt and his experiments. This was Moses standing atop Mount Pisgah. For fifteen minutes, the tumult went on, and then Herbert Hoover could be heard above the delirium.

"In this room rests the greatest responsibility that has come to a body of Americans in three generations," he began. There was a moral purpose to the universe, he continued, "elemental currents which make or break the fate of nations." Transcending partisanship and issues alike, they controlled a people's destiny; they restricted or unleashed its soul. For four years, he had been a student of the New Deal, trying to determine its ultimate objectives, its guiding light. "To some people it appears to be a strange interlude in American history in that it has no philosophy, that it is sheer opportunism, that it is a muddle of a spoils system, of emotional economics, or reckless adventure, of unctuous claims to a monopoly of human sympathy, of greed for power, of a desire for popular acclaim and an aspiration to make the front pages of the newspapers. This is the most charitable view."

From the floor came cries of "louder" and Hoover stood, left hand on his hip, as technicians adjusted the sound system. Then he resumed his philippic, defining the New Deal through the eyes of others as "a cold-blooded attempt by starry-eyed boys to infect the American people by a mixture of European ideas, flavored with our native predilection to get something for nothing." Which interpretation was accurate was disputed, according to Hoover, even by New Deal alumni "who have graduated for conscience's sake or have graduated by request."

Holding up the specter of central Europe, where dictators of right and left gained power using the very weapons of democratic persuasion, Hoover recalled 1932, "the promises of the abundant life, the propaganda of hate." Must legislation and Planned Economy, regimentation, corrupted currency, a holiday of spoils and a funeral for honest credit; if there were any items in the march of European collectivism left out by the New Deal, it must have been an oversight. But all was not lost, he insisted. "The American people should thank Almighty God for the Constitution and the Supreme Court." The hall erupted in sounds of approval that lasted two full minutes; an applause meter soared to 100. And Hoover was only warming up. "America is no monarchy where the Chief of State is not responsible for his ministers," he asserted, and the very mention of names like Ickes, Tugwell, Wallace and Hopkins stung the audience. He moved on, and the crowd moved with him, rapt and a little amazed at the trumpet call it was hearing.

Hoover the debunker shared the spotlight with Hoover the moralist. "We have seen the frantic attempts to find new taxes on the rich. Yet three quarters of the bill will be sent to the average man and the poor. . . . Freedom to work for himself is changed into a slavery of work for the follies of government." Inflation, relief politicized, an economy of scarcity—all were celebrated by "the little prophets of the New Deal." Yet could democracy withstand the strain of "Mother Hubbard economics" much longer? A wave of laughter swept the hall. Over and over now, Hoover was interrupted by applause as he assailed "the soul of monopoly" embodied in price-fixing and ceilings on production. Even worse, he claimed, the very gospel of brotherhood had been violated by those preaching class hatred from the White House steps.

"There is the suggestion in the Gospels," said Hoover, "that it is the meek who will inherit the earth. That disinherits the New Dealers." No, he went on, Roosevelt's concoction was nothing more nor less than what the three witches brewed for Macbeth, "the poisoning of Americanism." It was time for straight talk and honest answers. Surely propaganda agencies that emitted half a million words a day could inform the people in fifty what would happen after an election to unstable currencies, unbalanced budgets, and measures deemed unconstitutional by the Supreme Court. "I noticed recently that they spent three hundred words on how to choose a hat," Hoover said. "It is slightly more important to know the fate of a nation."

He warned against what he called "a swing from the foolishness of radicalism . . . to the selfishness of reaction." His party must oppose greed for privilege as well as greed for power. It must welcome change within a system protecting the safeguards of free men and women. But first things must come first. "Throughout the centuries of history, man's vigil and his quest have been to be free. For this the best and the bravest of earth have fought and died. To embody human liberty in workable government, America was born. Shall we keep that faith? Must we condemn the unborn generations to fight again and to die for the right to be free?"

Less than twenty years earlier, a great war had been fought, and thousands of American sons had been buried in foreign soil, to defeat collectivism and advance the cause of liberty, Hoover told the nation. Earlier still, the Whig party temporized on the issue of slavery for the black man, and died a contemptible death. Today's Republicans must be no less vigilant than their predecessors who risked war rather than submit to domestic tyranny. It would not be easy. Many Americans doubted the values of their rights when measured against the agony of their distress. They did not see the Constitution as "a fortress for their deliverance. They have been led to believe that it is in an iron cage against which the wings of idealism beat in vain."

In truth, it was their one hope. "Let this convention declare without shrinking, the source of economic prosperity is freedom. Man must be free to use his own powers in his own way. Free to think, to speak, to worship. Free to plan his own life. Free to use his own initiative. Free to dare in his own adventure. . . ." Fundamental liberties were at stake. "Is the Republican Party ready for the issue?" Hoover demanded. The crowd roared back its approval. "Are you willing to cast your all upon the issue, or would you falter and look back? Will you, for expediency's sake, also offer will o' the wisps which beguile the people? Or have you determined to enter in a holy crusade for liberty which shall determine the future and the perpetuity of a nation of free men?" And then he reached for a final salvo.

"Republicans and Americans! This is your call. Stop the retreat. In the chaos of doubt, confusion and fear, yours is the task to command. Stop the retreat, and turning the eyes of your fellow Americans to the sunlight of freedom, lead the attack to retake, recapture, and reman the citadel of liberty. Thus can America be preserved. Thus can peace, plenty, and security be re-established and expanded. Thus can the opportunity, the inheritance, and the spiritual future of your children be guaranteed. And thus you will win the gratitude of posterity, and the blessing of Almighty God."

For a moment, there was a hush. Then a new explosion roiled the floor. People stood on chairs and howled their approval. Visitors in the gallery waved their hats. Californians unfurled a bright blue banner, the first of two dozen states to join a dance of jubiliation. Women wept, as a band played "The Battle Hymn of the Republic." When it finished the party's anthem, and still the noise grew, it struck up "Onward, Christian Soldiers," and

Cleveland's convention hall was transformed into one vast camp meeting. Alabama and Maine, Virginia and New Jersey, bobbed their standards in the air. Below the podium, a woman from New York waved the American flag for half an hour. "We want Hoover" she shouted, in a cry picked up by a few dozen, then a few hundred throats.

Chairman Snell tried to end the demonstration by bringing forward Mrs. Benjamin Harrison, but no one cared about Mrs. Harrison at that moment, least of all Snell. Thirty minutes after he finished, the former president was still receiving his noisy tribute. Finally, at ten minutes past ten, the chairman announced that the proceedings were adjourned for the night. The band played "Hail, Hail, The Gang's All Here" and Alfred Landon's shaken managers met to regroup and reassert their authority. Others, desperate to halt the Kansan short of nomination, turned to Hoover. Three times, the sergeant at arms asked him to return to the hall to acknowledge and subdue the pandemonium created by his speech. Hoover refused. To return now, he said, would be "a cheap thing to do." He had finished his speech; he would not return to milk applause or tilt at windmills. Later, Drew Pearson and Robert Allen ("that scum of Washington") would write that he agreed to a joint statement with Vandenburg and Knox, to be issued the following morning. Its alleged purpose was to block Landon at the eleventh hour. In reality, there was such a proposal from the anti-Landon camp, rejected by Hoover, who rightly assessed it as futile and incendiary. Such an action, he concluded, "would have torn the party to shreds."[35]

Early on Thursday morning, on schedule and as prearranged, Hoover departed Cleveland for New York having lost his gray felt hat and gained readmission to the inner circles of influence. In less than twenty-four hours, he had established himself firmly as the moral guardian of Republican purity, and the party's most magnetic spokesman. Only time would decide whether his speech was a classic on the level of Bryan's Cross of Gold, or a bitter elegy for a dying order. Hoover himself sounded content. He would not be taking the stump for Landon, he informed reporters during a brief stopover at Albany. But when another crowd was on hand to welcome him in New York, the former president couldn't resist asking if the shouts of "We Want Hoover" had gone out on the radio. Assured they had, he smiled and nodded approvingly.

He made peace with former adversaries like Walter Lippmann, who praised his speech and raised a muted cheer for Landon. "I withdraw previous explosive remarks of my own about you," he told Lippmann, as they both were pursuing the same objective, "that is, to make the bridge between economic liberalism and the enlarged public responsibility without falling

into the European water." Hoover's own sense of humor, previously suppressed in the cause of political self-righteousness, resurfaced. "My funeral
eulogies have now been preached by all the press," he informed a friend two
weeks after his triumph. "As a last flower on the grave, they have elected
me Elder Statesman. How would it do to organize that office a bit and make
it a live, militant job?" he asked mischievously, surrounded by a stack of
approving letters and telegrams. "It would surely chagrin the funeral directors and it might be made of some service to the American people." [36]

★　★

Hoover's refreshed spirit did not outlast the sound of Cleveland's cheering
voices. The reason was simple: Alf Landon did not want his help. Despite
assurances from William Allen White that the governor was "a decent,
square, kindly, courageous young man," devoid of vanity and intellectually
promising, Hoover was unconvinced. Landon, he complained midway
through the campaign, was "completely ignorant" of American political
history. He didn't pretend to know anything of foreign affairs, and he
seemed better suited to managing a small business than leading a great
nation. His opinion of the nominee had been poisoned by Landon's own
desire to keep him at arm's length, supported by the Republican National
Committee's cancellation of speaking dates and radio time for the former
president. [37]

Not everyone around Landon wished to ostracize the sage of Palo Alto.
John Hamilton, newly elected national chairman, invited Hoover to confer
with himself and the candidate. More important, Hamilton revealed in a
Chicago speech his intention to defend Hoover's administration. Delighted
with such comments, Hoover warmly praised the young chairman, while
excoriating the New Deal's claim to be a lifesaving crew. "I do not know
how much credit really ought to be given to people who blow up the ship
and then save a few of the passengers," he wrote Hamilton on July 14, "but
I am not disposed to give them any." [38]

But if Hoover was satisfied with such tactics, Landon was not. Distressed
by Hamilton's preference for party conservatives, and keenly aware of his
own need to make inroads among more liberal voters, when the nominee
learned of his chairman's intention to visit the West Coast, he asked Hamilton to refrain from calling on Hoover. Going further, Landon called the
Chicago speech a mistake, destined to hurt the campaign by diverting attention from the progressive victory and fresh faces of Cleveland. Hamilton
persisted, and Landon finally agreed to let him see the man he almost
certainly resented for having tried to derail his own nomination. On August
13, Hamilton paid a call on Hoover in Palo Alto. He told his host that

several more of his "powerful" speeches would be helpful. Hoover asked if Landon shared this view, and Hamilton reassured him he did. Pressing his advantage, Hoover demanded a telegram or letter to this effect, since "there were groups around Landon who were demanding that I take no part in the campaign." If the Kansas governor did not wish his participation, Hoover continued, he would understand. He would not cause any difficulties, since "I want this gang out of the White House for the salvation of the country." Anticipating such a result, the former president had already announced a return to his former profession. Hamilton replied that he would need time to discuss the matter with Landon, and Hoover said this proved his contention of "cross currents" in Topeka, "otherwise he could settle it by a telephone call."[39]

Two weeks passed before Hoover's phone rang. In a gracious yet restrained conversation with Landon on September 2, the nominee assured his prickly ally of the need for his help, "especially in October when the fighting gets hard on the homestretch." Hoover asked for a public declaration; such a statement, he told Landon, would quiet gossip going about "that I am not wanted in the campaign." Landon dismissed such reports but promised "when the time comes I will be very glad to do anything along those lines." He invited Hoover to visit him in Topeka after conferring with Hamilton and scouting out the political landscape back East. Both men sounded an optimistic note about prospects in the fall, and the conversation came to an end.[40]

Barely had he put the receiver down than Hoover took up his pen. "I beg to confirm my answer to your telephone message of today that you urgently want my help and activity in this campaign," he wrote. "Somewhere along the line I shall take occasion to indicate that you have made such a request as certain members of the Republican Publicity organization are giving a contrary color and are damaging the party and your interests."[41]

Having selectively interpreted their conversation, Hoover privately expressed dismay over his own small part in the campaign drama. Landon rejected eleven drafts of a letter before deciding to call, he told friends. His own plans to establish a campaign headquarters in Chicago were in disarray, since local GOP organizations had been instructed to reject his appearances. Meanwhile, the candidate was surrounded by a clique of Topeka liberals, suspicious of if not openly hostile to his own participation. Wishing to remain in public life, Hoover told friends that he had only one alternative —to bring in his own arguments against FDR. Not until the end of September could he look forward to a firm speaking engagement, in Philadelphia, and even then it was uncertain whether the national committee would pay for radio time. After the election, he went on, he might travel to Europe, revisiting the scene of earlier triumphs and returning home to live out his days as a Republican elder statesman. He wanted to leave Palo Alto, Hoover said. The atmosphere was too narrow; even Lou was coming around on that point.[42]

Here as elsewhere, wish might have been father to the thought. Lou enjoyed a near-idyllic life on the Stanford campus. She liked inviting students to gather behind the balustrade at 623 Mirada. She savored drives through the countryside of her girlhood, visiting her sons and grandchildren who lived nearby, watching quail on her lawn or an oriole in a pepper tree. "You know," she mused in a rare moment of revelation, "young people don't understand loyalty." Lou was loyal. In the fall of 1935, she was the driving force behind Allan Hoover's purchase of Bert's birthplace at West Branch. For $4,500 the family retrieved the white frame cottage, more recently turned into a summer kitchen for the R. P. Scellers family. Three years later, it was detached and returned to its original site, close by the Wapsinonac. It was the beginning of a park whose growth over the years mirrored the slow restoration of esteem that came to the man it honored.[43]

Other activities kept Hoover's mind from political morbidness. He made good on his word to resume his mining interests, although on a scale vastly reduced from their prewar levels. Thanks to engineering friends who supplied him with tips, he invested in Utah and Nevada mines, and celebrated deposits of lead and zinc in Guatemala that at first appeared to be the greatest finds of his career. Allan Hoover presided over the Compañía Minería de Guatemala, which began promisingly only to run afoul of political instability (including two revolutions). Whether profitable or not, the subject of mining was a positive diversion. The same relaxed feeling came over him when reminiscing about Belgium, or attending the reunions of his European colleagues, raucous affairs that included catsup-squirting and bread-throwing until more civilized heads prevailed and costumed maidens danced to a Rumanian orchestra. No gathering was complete without a Hoover speech, usually informal and always in the ironic style increasingly shared with public audiences.[44]

After October 1936, the former president's platform included meetings of the Boys Clubs of America. Joining the movement at the behest of his financier friend Jeremiah Milbank and colleagues from the old CRB, Hoover was elected chairman the same night. From then on, he devoted thousands of hours to the organization, building it up from 140 clubs to more than 600 at the time of his death, dictating terse letters to raise funds ("I am not a professional beggar," one stated, "but this is one cause where I break my rule"), and conducting meetings with a highly personal style of parliamentary procedure.[45]

Twice a year, a hundred or more board members convened in New York's University Club, where a black tie dinner was followed by a business meeting of sorts. "I'm sure you're not interested in reading all these minutes," Hoover typically announced, "so I vote that they're approved." When business old and new was transacted, everyone settled in for a Hoover talk, as far-ranging as the speaker's field of interests. At precisely ten o'clock, the gavel fell, even if it interrupted a board member in midsentence.[46]

Hoover relished the entertainment presented by his "pavement boys" at these gatherings. He found ways to put at ease even the most uncomfortable ghetto child visiting him at the Waldorf Towers. He moved to strike the phrase "for white boys only" from the organization's charter, and lamented as the great tragedy of his time the reality of urban lives, in which boys were born and brought up, died and were buried without tapping a quarter of their potential. The former president tried to be present at the dedication of every new Boys Club. But even his devotion knew bounds. "Dear Boyd," he informed a fellow board member bringing him a problem via long-distance mail. "I am fishing for bonefish and desperately trying to catch one. I have no time to worry about board members. Write me later."[47]

For the boys themselves, however, Hoover found time. In one of his most touching addresses, he defined the essence of boyhood, a bundle of paradoxes blunted in his own case by tragedy. Along with his sister, he said in May 1937, "the boy is our most precious possession. But he presents not only joys and hopes. . . . He strains our nerves, yet he is a complex of cells teeming with affection. He is a periodic nuisance, yet he is a joy forever. He is a part-time incarnation of destruction, yet he radiates sunlight to all the world. He gives evidence of being the child of iniquity, yet he makes a great nation. . . . He is an illuminated interrogation point, yet he is the most entertaining animal that is."

Sadly, boys must grow up to live in worlds of reality, where their natural inclination to hunt in packs ran smack into civilization's appetite for cement and slums. "We have increased the number of boys per acre," said Hoover. The modern urban boy had a life "of stairs, light switches, alleys, fire escapes, bells and cobblestones, and a chance to get run over by a truck." The outlets of curiosity opened to rural boys were closed to him, and if he could not contend with nature, he was likely to battle a policeman on the beat. Packs need not turn into gangs, he asserted, not so long as pavement boys had a place to play checkers and learn a trade, swim in a pool and steal nothing more harmful than second base. He was determined to start a hundred new clubs in three years, Hoover revealed. He met his goal, and not long before his death, was embarking on a still more ambitious plan, "A thousand clubs for a million boys."

For his niece, who expressed alarm over dinner speakers overstepping the bounds of their time, Hoover had some advice. "You just pass them up a little note and you just write on it 'your fly is open' and he'll sit down right away." His own public remarks rarely exceeded twenty minutes—a far cry from the days when he insisted on forty-five minutes of radio time as the minimum required to state his case. In his mellower moods, even the New Deal could arouse a chuckle. A visitor once inquired about Hoover's sources of inside information, an invaluable resource for any public speaker. "Well, there's one advantage about these New Dealers," he boasted. "If one of them knows, at the next cocktail party twenty-five will know. I know before the party even starts." [48]

Husbands and wives ought to take occasional vacations away from each other, Hoover advised friends. His own favorite getaway was the Bohemian Grove, a 2,500-acre reserve of redwood trees and conservative politics, easily reached by car from Palo Alto. San Francisco's Bohemian Club was already half a century old in 1924, when Hoover and other members of Stanford's Class of '95 established a temporary camp on Kitchen Hill, not far from the dining circle where all Grove members gathered for their evening meal. Later, they put up an old logger's cabin in a small canyon called Pioneer's Gulch. From a concrete caveman left behind by the producers of the 1910 play put on at the Grove, Hoover's camp took its name. Eventually, the Caveman Camp grew into nine separate cabins, accommodating up to thirty people.

To the outsider, the Bohemians remained as mysterious and vaguely sinister as in the days when the club convened its decidedly informal gatherings at digs rented from another fraternal organization, the Jolly Corks. Exclusively male, heavily populated by men whose success could be measured in financial terms, the club seemed to mix elements of a college hazing, a naturalist's holiday, and a disputatious boardroom, flailing away in comfortable irrelevance at the latest excesses of that man in the White House. Obscure as most masculine fraternities, the Bohemians adopted for their emblems a one-eyed owl, a fourteenth-century Czechoslovakian saint and the cryptic motto "Weaving Spiders Come Not Here." Each year's calendar included an all-male revue entitled High Jinks, primarily an excuse to tell bad jokes and imbibe good liquor. More vulgar still was the Low Jinks, a logical innovation for such early performers as Henry George, Ambrose Bierce, and the *San Francisco Bulletin*'s own poet in residence, Dan O'Connell. Mark Twain and Bret Harte became honorary Bohemians, and Oscar Wilde was impressed during an 1882 visit with the clothes worn and the food eaten by these very worldly ne'er-do-wells.

Over the years, and with the acquisition of a campground north of San Francisco, the club's rituals became ever more elaborate. In addition to High and Low Jinks, each summer's festivities included a ceremonial Cremation of Care, a Grove play worthy of David Belasco at his most bombastic, plus a climactic Lakeside Talk, for years a ready-made platform for Hoover to discourse on domestic politics and global dangers, secure in the knowledge that nothing he said would be carried beyond the gates of Bohemia. (A favorite topic over the years: deficit spending and "fuzzy-minded intellectuals.") Initially, even the forest seemed to carry little recuperative powers. Attending his first camp-out since leaving the White House, Hoover hardly recognized old friends as he passed them on the paths connecting the twenty or so individual camps. He ate his meals in seclusion, or with intimates like mystery writer Clarence Kelland or oilman Bert Mattei. But on Saturday night, when Low Jinks were at hand and more than a thousand men awarded their famous colleague a standing ovation, Hoover was welcomed home. He never felt estranged again.[49]

For all its reverence toward success, the Grove was a place disdainful of mere celebrity. "We're two mining engineers who have gone astray," Hoover informed cartoonist Rube Goldberg. After he talked too long for the crowd's taste, Will Rogers was never invited back. Hoover himself could not escape a heavy-handed humor inspired by masculine camaraderie and his own vulnerability. He roared with laughter when Chauncey McCormick persuaded a valet to supply him with a double-breasted blue jacket, panama hat, white trousers and pipe. Stuffing a pillow under his shirt to heighten the resemblance, McCormick presented himself as a contestant in a Hoover look-alike contest. Bud Kelland wrote a poem for the occasion on toilet paper; Ray Lyman Wilbur read a facetious citation. The former president was not above some mildly bawdy humor of his own, running to the likes of Mae West, Gideon Bibles and Traveling Salesmen. In the evening, when alcohol and memories flowed around the bonfires, Hoover asked a camper to play "Wake Up, America" on his accordion. Another highball, and it was off to bed. If the night was chilly, other campers saw the former president venturing out in his nightshirt to pick up sticks for a fire.[50]

In the morning, Hoover was again surrounded by admirers. Holding court as he munched honey from a comb or demonstrated the scientific way to eat a peach, "the Chief" found himself smoking ashes more often than tobacco, so engrossed did he become in the talk around him. Even here, a certain formality prevailed. When someone presumed to address him as Herbert, the former president gave him an icy stare. For all its determined anarchy, the Grove still enforced some rules. Between meals, Hoover played cards, composed his Lakeside Talk, reminisced or visited back and forth with neighboring camps. There were fish to be caught, redwoods to admire, and dangerous public trends to be spotted and denounced. Hoover's pleasures were not undiluted. "I need some protection," he once revealed, "because so many of my friends, especially in the evening after a generous portion of alcohol, are apt to sit down beside me and tell me about the death of their mother or wife and also of the Republican Party."[51]

It was a recurrent theme, in the dog days of summer 1936, when Alf Landon saw his early advantages melting away and conservatives within his own party succeeded in wrenching away control of the campaign. From the first day, Landon was handicapped, not only by his opponent (a resourceful Roosevelt had already instructed Henry Wallace "up to the fifth of November" to keep cotton prices above twelve cents a pound, and WPA officials to prevent the laying off of a single worker before Election Day), but by the avenging ghost of the Old Guard, who saw 1936 as a referendum on 1932, a chance to repeal the mistaken judgment that contributed so much to the bank panic and subsequent discrediting of Hoover and his party.

Landon disputed such tactics. "None of my campaign speeches will be merely an attack upon the opposition," he informed Senator Borah early in August. ". . . I cannot criticize everything that has been done in the past three years and do it sincerely." To his running mate Frank Knox, the Kansan dismissed the Constitution as a winning issue, and he made no secret of his contempt for those he labeled "the stuffed-shirt leadership" of the GOP. So on October 1, when Landon found himself confronting Hoover in the high-ceilinged living room of Kansas's executive mansion, the atmosphere was bound to be strained. According to one who was there, Landon was "terribly upset" that the former president had come to Topeka at all, and hoped to send his visitor packing as soon as possible. Nor was Hoover any more impressed. He told Landon, as he put it later, "that no one should campaign for the presidency without mastering the subjects on which he spoke and making the opinions which he expressed his own." Having criticized the nominee for delivering canned speeches, Hoover did nothing to warm the atmosphere at a nearby restaurant, where he attended a family-style chicken dinner staged by correspondents covering the Landon campaign, and actually booed the voice of Franklin Roosevelt as it came over a radio. As FDR accused his predecessor of increasing the national debt, a pall of embarrassed silence fell over the room. Landon stared down at the table; Hoover himself attempted a faint smile. Shortly afterward, the guest of honor left early to catch a train—and everyone breathed a sigh of relief.[52]

Earlier that same afternoon, the two men listened to Al Smith assail the New Deal in a New York speech. Businessmen, complained Smith, were "getting kicked all over the lot." As for party loyalty, how could he, a former nominee, be expected to defend a failure in office? The Carnegie Hall audience cheered, and Landon's strategists dreamed of a great coalition of Republicans and "constitutional" Democrats. The *Literary Digest* published a poll (promptly dismissed by Hoover) showing the Kansan ahead of Roosevelt, and even liberals praised the governor for his defense at Chautauqua, New York, of a system of public education that required no teacher to take an oath not required of other citizens.

But academic freedom was not likely to rouse bedrock Republicans. More to their liking were the hard-shell dogmas of John Hamilton, Frank Knox and Hoover himself. On October 16, the former president entered the campaign for the first time publicly. In a speech entitled "Intellectual Dishonesty in Government," he savaged FDR's 1932 promise of a 25 percent cut in government expenses, accompanied by words like "desperate," "shocking," "spendthrift" and "extravagance" in describing Hoover's own depression-fighting efforts. Now, four years later, Roosevelt returned to the scene of this oratorical crime to claim credit for restoring prosperity. Implying that revolution was in the air at the time of his inauguration in 1933, FDR doctored his numbers, said Hoover, ignoring the decline between Election Day and the bank panic and the devaluation brought about by his own monetary policies.

"The President illustrated his views of this period by recounting a story of a nice old gentleman who fell off the dock in 1933 and was rescued. The gentleman was effusive in thanks but three years later he complained that he had lost his hat. I have some inside information about that incident," Hoover told his audience. "The old gentleman was surreptitiously pushed off the dock in order that the hero could gain the plaudits of the crowd as a life saver." Roosevelt liked to use baseball analogies to prove his claims of recovery. But all the time he was really "juggling with the scoreboard," inventing new and immoral means of disguising the record deficits being run up. Quoting from Treasury Department documents, Hoover conducted a seminar in creative bookkeeping, à la Roosevelt. By omitting such budget items as the District of Columbia and veterans' bonuses, and by shifting a host of regular governmental functions from the regular budget to one labeled "recovery and relief," the New Deal held up economies that on closer look turned into profligacies.

To illustrate his point, Hoover resorted to the lowly gypsy moth. "The Republicans pursued these moths over many years at a cost of about $600,000 per annum. And in the old-fashioned way we charged it off and called it a day." Then came the New Deal, and "a grand economy" in moth pursuit. The regular budget item was listed as barely one-quarter of the old amount. But under the heading "Relief and Recovery" was the figure of $1,490,000. "Thus the cost of the chase had really increased by 150%." Such intellectual dishonesty, insisted Hoover, was symptomatic of an administration that claimed a balanced budget by the simple expedient of lumping recoverable loans as revenue. And it could be repealed only by the election of "those honest gentlemen, Alfred Landon and Frank Knox."

Tepid as it was, even this praise outshone Hoover's final speech of the campaign, delivered at Denver on October 30. He didn't mention Landon by name, but kept Roosevelt firmly within target range. Which was just as well, given the incumbent's habit the previous six weeks of campaigning against Hoover and not Landon. In accepting his party's nomination, FDR delighted partisan Democrats with a sizzling attack on "economic royalists" who could be overcome only by a government organized to defeat them. Talk of plans to overthrow American institutions was a smoke screen, said the president. "What they really complain of is that we seek to take away their power." The speech set the tone for a divisive, high-pitch appeal to the discontented. While Landon pursued the specter of one-man government and an end to the profit motive, Roosevelt pirouetted around the Republican candidate, content to allow his self-destruction while he stalked bigger game.

As Al Smith and other Liberty League Democrats painted the bogeyman of communism—Tugwell, said Smith, ought to depart for Russia, where he could sit on a block of ice and plan to his heart's content—their nemesis shrewdly reserved his fire for Hoover. Over and over as the campaign headed into the homestretch, the president ignored Landon and contrasted conditions in March 1933 with those of 1936. October marked the first month in four and a half years without a single national bank failure. The stock and bond markets reached levels not known for five years. Profits, unknown then, were some $5 billion now.

Such a recovery had been the work of "a people's government" in Washington, one willing to use every power at its disposal "to protect the commerce of America from the selfish forces which ruined it." Wall Street might jeer—so did the president's alma mater in Cambridge—and the press might be unremittingly hostile, but a landslide was building. Landon's managers only added to its dimensions by having employers stuff pay envelopes with warnings about Social Security taxes and dogtags for the average citizen. Even this boomeranged against Hoover. "Why didn't the boss put any political propaganda in your pay envelopes four years ago?" inquired James Cox, FDR's 1920 running mate. "Because there wasn't any pay envelopes." In his own final appeal to the voters, made twenty-four hours after Hoover's solemn warning about the threat to American liberty, FDR delivered a virtual declaration of war against the malefactors of wealth.

Never in U.S. history, he claimed, had the forces of business monopoly and class antagonism been so united in condemning a candidate. "They are unanimous in their hatred for me—and I welcome their hatred. I should like to have it said of my first administration that in it the forces of selfishness and of lust for power met their match. I should like to have it said of my second administration that in it these forces met their master."

The delirium his taunt provoked was echoed with only slightly less conviction three days later. Roosevelt swept all but two states, crushing Landon with the greatest electoral triumph since a single elector held out against James Monroe in 1820. Beneath the rubble, the Kansan nursed no bitterness, except against the Old Guard he held responsible for the increasingly shrill tone of his own campaign. A knowing friend said there was only one thing about the result that disappointed him. "I missed seeing the astonishment on the faces of all those stuffed shirts who really thought you would be a Kansas Coolidge."

In New York, Edgar Rickard quoted a fellow club-car passenger: "If Landon had made one more speech, Roosevelt would have carried Canada." Hoover was less amused. The outcome, he told Ogden Mills, was "a mess . . . we haven't either principle or party spirit—at the moment." It was a "bum campaign," he complained to another friend, made worse by Landon's acceptance of Liberty League support and the subsequent appearance of business domination. Worse still was the party's attempt to apologize for its own record since 1912. Every abuse of himself and Coolidge was allowed to go unanswered, "apparently with the idea that all this would make Landon look Progressive." Seven weeks later, the former president was pondering his own role. Should he be like Cincinnatus, or play the part of "an evangelist who is mostly resented." Of one thing he was certain. "Leadership cannot be created synthetically. Men must be what they were made by the Almighty or the American people will find them out in time."[53]

With that none-too-subtle swipe at Landon, Hoover settled back to survey what he called "the broken chinaware" and assay his own chances to resume control of the party. Early in December, he denied published reports that he might take up permanent residence in England. He had no comment later that same month when Madrid newspapers urged him to take on the task of evacuating the war-torn Spanish capital. The European continent was on other minds as well. FDR's ambassador to Paris, William C. Bullitt, was informed by the president of a "delightful game" in New York's subways, wherein financial district employees wore Roosevelt buttons all the way to the Wall Street station, only to replace them with Landon buttons out of deference to the boss. Bullitt's reply ignored domestic politics for the tense field of European diplomacy. With modern bombing aircraft barely twenty-four hours from the gates of Paris, wrote Bullitt, it was more than ever vital that a Franco-German reconciliation be achieved. Yet such a plan was opposed by Italy, Russia and Great Britain, all of which placed a growing burden on his own country to do what had to be done if peace were to prevail.[54]

Peace was beginning to occupy many Americans, none more than Roosevelt and Hoover.

CHAPTER SEVEN

STORM CLOUDS

★

The whole national situation is very discouraging. The economic situation is bad; the total failure of the Roosevelt Administration to grasp the fundamentals of what is needed is worse; and the disintegration of the Republican Party due to the efforts of a dozen pin-heads does not offer much hope for real leadership.
—Herbert Hoover, December 1937 [1]

"It's a terrible thing to look over your shoulder when you are trying to lead—and to find no one there.
—Franklin D. Roosevelt

★

It rained on Franklin Roosevelt's second inauguration, a dismal portent of a stormy second term. Hoover rejected an invitation from the inaugural committee to attend the ceremonies on January 20, 1937. Had he gone to Washington, he might have found a curious satisfaction in the president's eloquent acknowledgment that a third of his countrymen remained ill-housed, ill-clad, ill-nourished. For four years, Hoover had painted his successor in the unflattering pose of aspiring tyrant. As often as not, his attacks on the New Deal had rebounded against their maker. But here was FDR himself, conceding mass poverty and demanding fresh authority from Congress to define wages and expand the generation of public power far beyond the desperate hollows of Appalachia. [2]

Nor had the president forgotten his feud with the Supreme Court. Having taken the oath of office for a second time, Roosevelt bridled at pledging obedience to the Court's Constitution. He felt, he said afterward, like telling Chief Justice Hughes that it was the Constitution as he understood it, "flexible enough to meet any new problem of democracy—not the kind of Constitution that your Court has raised as a barrier to progress and democracy!" To Felix Frankfurter, FDR was even more portentous. "Very confidentially, I may give you an awful shock in about two weeks," he informed Frankfurter. "Even if you do not agree, suspend final judgment.. . . ." The president was a man of his word. When he dropped his bombshell on February 5, 1937, the shock was not limited to legal scholars. It would split his own party asunder, open the door for a Republican resurgence and hand Herbert Hoover the most convincing evidence yet that all his talk about dictatorship and presidential subversion of liberty was more than a personal vendetta.

As early as December 1935, his Attorney General had warned FDR that Chief Justice Hughes and his brethren meant to destroy his administration. "We will have to find a way to get rid of the present membership of the Supreme Court," Homer Cummings added dramatically. Roosevelt bided his time, almost fatalistically. Personally, he told his Cabinet, he expected to see archconservative James McReynolds occupying a seat on the bench at the age of one hundred and five. The 1936 campaign came and went, with Hoover and others demanding that the president tip his hand.

In the first week of February, FDR did exactly that. With studied casualness, he announced a new reorganization package, this one dealing with the federal judiciary. Since the courts were unable to keep up with their present work load, at least in part because some judges remained on the bench "far beyond their years or physical capacity," Roosevelt proposed to assist the magistrates by adding one additional judge for every colleague who failed to retire within six months of his seventieth birthday. "A constant and systematic addition of younger blood" is how he phrased it.

"Packing the Court" is what others, Hoover included, called the maneuver. In a carefully worded statement released the same day, the former president cautioned Americans to be wary of any such change. Their liberties depended on judicial independence, he continued. Surely, it was not asking too much to take a few months to examine the proposal more closely. Others were less temperate. Walter Lippmann wrote that Roosevelt was "drunk with power" and eager to demolish safeguards against dictatorship. Roosevelt's own vice president, John Garner, held his nose and pronounced his chief "the most destructive man in all American history." Democratic congressional leaders berated the White House for providing no advance notice of the proposal. On the other side of the aisle, GOP spokesmen concluded that their best strategy was to lie low and defuse partisanship. With such liberal stalwarts as Burton Wheeler, George Norris and Hiram Johnson hacking away at the plan, they did not wish to risk defeat by raising their own voices.

When Hoover let it be known that he planned to take on the president in a Chicago speech on February 20, Arthur Vandenburg sent word to John Hamilton that he and other Republican senators would appreciate a lower profile from the former president. Just in case, Hoover prepared two speeches, one dealing with the Court, the other addressing American neutrality in a world increasingly polarized by Nazi advances in Europe. Even before he spoke out in public, however, he was on the phone, inciting opposition to the plan among key figures in thirty states, Democrats as well as Republicans. One of the former was a New York utilities executive named Wendell Willkie, who had already shown himself a forceful critic of New Deal business regulation, and who impressed Hoover with some "ghastly stories" of Roosevelt's personal duplicity.[3]

Fired up by such talk, Hoover had little taste for the game being played by congressional Republicans. For four years he had manned the barricades of constitutional government. It had been a lonely outpost. Now, events invited him down from his abstract summit. Dismissing the cautionary warnings, Hoover in his Chicago speech accused Roosevelt of scheming to appoint "an intellectual nurse" to divide the vote of every justice over seventy. He wondered how John Marshall or Oliver Wendell Holmes might have responded to such treatment.

If Roosevelt could alter the Constitution to suit his own purposes, said Hoover, then so could any of his successors. If a troop of "President's judges" could be dispatched to seize political power, then what would prevent future executives from naming equally subservient judges to claim still more power. "That is not judicial process," thundered Hoover. "That is force."

"Hands off the Supreme Court!" he concluded. One of those impressed by the appeal, despite his earlier misgivings, was Wendell Willkie. Not only had the former president presented his case convincingly, adding to the strength of Roosevelt's opposition and improving his own position, claimed Willkie, but "he gave to the Republican party something it had lost. . . . He gave it character."[4]

The battle escalated in March. FDR denied any intention of appointing "spineless puppets." With equal fervor, and less judgment, he directed a heavy-handed lobbying campaign to win back recalcitrant Democrats. Wheeler revealed that his income tax returns were being audited. Others whispered of investigations into senatorial sex lives. Then, on March 21, a

packed congressional hearing listened closely as Senator Wheeler read a
seven-page letter, composed by the Chief Justice and demolishing the contention that the justices were behind in their work load. More effective still
was the Court's own turnabout later that spring on wage and hour laws and
the Wagner Act.

In mid-May, Justice Willis Van Devanter, one of the most incorrigible of
the Nine Old Men, announced his resignation. Roosevelt had a vacancy to
fill. But he still lacked a mandate for his packing plan. On July 14, a hotel
maid discovered the lifeless body of Joseph Robinson, the Senate Majority
Leader who had gamely carried the president's ball, and who hoped to
succeed Van Devanter. Robinson's heart had given out, exhausted by overexertion in a losing cause. Buried with him was any hope for compromise.
When the entire Senate voted eight days later to return the legislation to
committee, Roosevelt suffered the most humiliating defeat of his presidency.

In a rancorous postscript, the president nominated Alabama Senator
Hugo Black to take Van Devanter's place. Black's previous membership in
the Ku Klux Klan came to light, raising hackles in a city grown snappish,
and providing bittersweet memories of John J. Parker's failed nomination
seven years before. Harold Ickes was typically resourceful in turning the
controversy to partisan advantage. When a reporter sought his opinion
about Black, Honest Harold was prepared. "You mean about the Ku Klux
Klan?" he shot back. "Why don't you interview former President Hoover?
He knows more about it than I do," Ickes went on, before labeling Hoover
"the greatest expert on the subject" of the KKK, owing to its support of his
1928 campaign against Al Smith. Even for the Old Curmudgeon, this was
extreme. "We fail to see where Mr. Hoover figures at all in the Black
controversy," said the *Buffalo Courier*, "except insofar as his own Supreme
Court appointments provide a refreshing and inspiring contrast to Mr. Roosevelt's record in the same field."

For his part, the former president barely took notice of the latest verbal
assault from the Interior Department. He was too busy waging a quiet yet
intense campaign against those within his own party whom he regarded as
ideological Trojan horses. Emboldened by the Court fight and subsequent
challenges to FDR's dominance, contemptuous of the pragmatism displayed
to disastrous results in 1936, he wished to make the GOP reflect his own
militancy. Alf Landon had other ideas.

★   ★

The spring and summer of 1937 opened many doors for Republican op-
portunists. Besides bearing with the Court fight, the nation was nervous
about a wave of sit-down strikes in the auto and steel industries. General

Motors was losing a million dollars a day, and Roosevelt pleaded with John L. Lewis and his Congress of Industrial Organizations to call a halt to such tactics. Lewis refused, and FDR himself would say nothing critical in public. GM caved in, and Lewis moved on to the hellish furnaces of Big Steel, where the average worker supported six people a year on an average of $369. There were more than seven hundred strikes in 1937. Perhaps half a million men in all sat down on the job; ten died on a picket line in South Chicago when police charged their ranks. At Ford's River Rouge plant outside Detroit, organizers like Walter Reuther were beaten by company hirelings.

Among those offended by the president's silence was Walter Lippmann. "For the first time in their experience," the columnist complained on March 25, "the American people are not sure whether the party in control of the government respects the law and means to enforce it." No longer could FDR dismiss the crisis, asserted Lippmann, "with any childish prattle about economic loyalists and the dead and damned Liberty League." Hoover's judgment upon the administration was no less harsh. "These people are failing in the primary functions of government," he wrote in June 1937, "and that is to preserve order and enforce the laws in protection of life." [5]

More ominous still for Roosevelt and his followers was a recession that began late that summer, demonstrating just how precarious was the New Deal's claim to having restored prosperity. Early in April, the president hinted to reporters that prices were rising too fast for consumer purchasing power to keep pace. Fifty times, he testily reminded his vice president that spring, he had promised a balanced budget for 1938. Did Garner want him to repeat the pledge once—or fifty times more? As if to show good faith, Roosevelt moved to reduce WPA rolls substantially. Credit controls were instituted by the Federal Reserve, the White House called for additional economies, and the government stepped back from the frontline, only to see hard times regain most of the ground so painstakingly claimed since 1933. The stock market broke in mid-October, surrendering billions of dollars in paper value and signaling the start of a business contraction that sliced the index of industrial production from its August 1937 level of 117 to just 76 the following May. By then, steel production was off 75 percent from its level of a year earlier; auto production and other industries contracted similarly. Unemployment reversed its fall, and soon there were ten million Americans—again—without jobs.

Chagrined by the recession that bore his name, Roosevelt ordered his Commerce Secretary, Dan Roper, to stop giving out so many "Hooverish" statements of good cheer. (Harold Ickes was less concerned; after all, he noted in his diary, "nobody pays any attention to a statement from the

Secretary of Commerce anymore.") The president may have been per-plexed, but he most certainly was not paralyzed. "You'll have to learn that public life takes a lot of sweat," he once confided to a friend. "But it doesn't need to worry you. You won't always be right, but you musn't suffer from being wrong." And with the cheerful acquiescence in experimentation that so distinguished him from his predecessor, Roosevelt took a fresh tack in appearing before Congress in November 1937. The new economic ortho-doxy spun by Professor Keynes called for government intervention on a grand scale. A persuasive if reluctant advocate, FDR now sought measures to stimulate housing construction, revive crop restrictions—especially on cotton—protect the workingman against long hours and low wages, clear urban slums, and reorganize the executive branch of government. The fol-lowing spring, he abandoned permanently the chimera of a balanced budget. On the contrary, he appealed for $3 billion in public works, relief and related programs.

It would be hard for any man of Hoover's inclinations to avoid saying I told you so. Even before the Court fight was over, the former president was grumbling in private that Chief Justice Hughes ought to resign and wage public warfare instead of private stratagems. But his chief alarm lay else-where. It was his own party that Hoover wished to rescue from the pragma-tists who had captured it in 1936. He worried about such forces making for "disintegration" of the GOP, he told John Hamilton, in an April 1937 letter setting forth his idea of a national midterm convention of Republican officeholders and party officials. Free of the pressures of candidates and schedules, such disciples of the true faith could deliberate over a basic credo. They could, in turn, choose committees to draft a blueprint for public policy and party renewal. A two-day conclave, with few speeches, and no proxies, would build upon the Grass Roots Convention of 1934, and prepare the nation for a spirited counterstroke in 1938. So Hoover argued. Privately, he fretted over the prospect that John L. Lewis or some other radical might capture a party not first purged of "socialistic tendencies." This was not welcome music to the ears of other Republicans, including some Hoover loyalists. Ogden Mills opposed the idea. So, more importantly, did Alf Landon.[6]

The Kansan was intrigued by a different kind of political awakening. In delicate maneuverings of his own, the GOP's 1936 nominee was feeling out the prospects of a permanent linkage with conservative, anti–New Deal Democrats. He discussed the idea with Al Smith, Lew Douglas—and Mills. He did what he could to strip away vestiges of Old Guard control within his own party. Bertrand Snell retired as House Minority Leader that summer, to be replaced by Joseph Martin of Massachusetts. In New York, Landon supported the ambitions of a dynamic liberal named Kenneth Simpson, who didn't hesitate to breach tradition and arrange a partnership of convenience with the left-wing American Labor party. He also cast admiring glances at another youthful liberal from the canyons of Manhattan, a headline-grabbing special prosecutor named Thomas E. Dewey.

Landon flatly refused to sign any call for a convention of the kind Hoover wanted. Such a gathering, he noted, would be little more than "ghosts from the boneyard." Hoover agreed to let the issue rest for a while, but he did not disguise his impatience with those men of supple principles who were looking for common points around which to rally disaffected Democrats. "The coalition stuff," as he put it, was obviously evidence of party weakness.[7]

Others were just as certain that a midterm conference would lead to disaster. Far better, they counseled, to concentrate on local issues and candidates. John Hamilton pointed out that the party, with barely enough money in its coffers to pay rent on a Washington headquarters, could not afford the $200,000–$300,000 cost of Hoover's convention. Instead, suggested Hamilton, why not create a policy committee, a select yet representative body empowered with the task of devising the statement of principles which to Hoover and his followers would serve as a warrant for the party's very existence? Dissatisfied, Hoover dismissed the youthful national chairman as no more reliable than Landon himself. Doggedly, he reached out to grass-roots Republicans in thirty states; back came approving statements from men as disparate in outlook as Ohio's John Bricker and young Earl Warren in Hoover's own California. He proposed a summit meeting with Landon, Vanderburg and others, perhaps under the friendly auspices of Frank Lowden.[8]

Other leaders floated trial balloons of their own: Theodore Roosevelt, Junior, urged a new party with a new name. This was impractical, Hoover insisted in a September 1937 article for the *Atlantic Monthly*. No such party could surmount the obstacle of state ballot laws in time for the 1940 election, nor could it overnight swallow the existing Republican organizations or supplant the old faith in 17 million hearts. That faith must be reclaimed, galvanized by youth and dramatized as the only logical alternative to coercion and the death of liberty.

True to his credo, Hoover embarked on a militant courtship of precinct workers. Visiting in Nevada, Wyoming, Montana, Washington and Oregon, he found a heartening response. "They are sick and tired of trying to organize and fight, simply on the basis of being 'against' an idea," he wrote of the GOP foot soldiers. "They want to have some affirmative principles of our own." He would not acknowledge a more painful truth, that what he wished to affirm was long since out of favor with the American people. The Progressive reformer had become a fixed obstacle to the new realities. This, at heart, was the reason Landon and others wished to shorten Hoover's time upon the stage.[9]

Alarmed when Arthur Hyde wrote to hundreds of Republicans urging them to turn to Hoover as the party's conscience, Landon made common cause with congressional Republicans (in Hoover's view "the . . . demagogues in Washington"). Neither was eager to treat the electorate to the spectacle of an avenging Old Guard. As Landon put it, "If you had a Republican convention, who would you have on the front row of the platform? Pat Hurley, Jim Watson, George Moses, Herbert Hoover. Read 'em and weep."[10]

Still optimistic as the summer wore on, the former president took heart from favorable reports in major papers like the *New York Times* and the *Cleveland Press*. He praised Bert Snell's endorsement of the conference, and used the occasion to lob a shell at others in the party, "who believe that we can win this election . . . if we pussyfoot." His hopes persisted even after the *New York Herald Tribune* prematurely revealed the whole project, personalizing it as Hoover's own bid for political reacceptance. He wanted "an intellectual meeting rather than a political one," he insisted. Only the opposition of "certain politically-minded men" who preferred to win as a result of "misfeasance of the other side" rather than a positive appeal to the voters could thwart his crusade, Hoover maintained.[11]

On October 3, Hoover and Landon met secretly, at Frank Lowden's Illinois estate, Sinissippi Farm. Neither man could agree afterward on precisely what took place, ambition and mistrust distorting recollection, but Hoover pushed ahead full speed with the convention, claiming full concurrence from his erstwhile rival. Landon's memory served him differently. Without dismissing such a gathering, he recalled several demands involving delegate representation, agenda and congressional support. "A convention on fundamentals," he wrote, "a re-statement of the Bill of Rights, as I heard discussed, would be worse than no convention." Even this tenuous support evaporated the next morning when Landon heard Hoover's interpretation of their meeting. At midmonth, the Kansan took to the airwaves for the first time since his defeat and with virtually no advance warning to Washington—let alone Palo Alto.[12]

A veritable dance of the elephants ensued as Landon forces on the national committee muttered darkly about replacing John Hamilton with their own hero, as the national chairman sought a middle ground between his party's feuding champions, and as Hoover resentfully tuned in to hear the voice of a man he by now regarded as at best a political accident. "All we can do is to let him hang himself" was the reaction one Hoover partisan passed on to the former president. When Landon's "nationwide mass meeting" concluded at nine o'clock on the evening of October 19, it seemed a fair prophecy. "The dull product of a stupid man," groused Harold Ickes, "a lot of slobbering over the dear Old Constitution." Less-biased witnesses were nearly as disappointed with a rambling speech that made no mention of the current recession. Far more forceful in his correspondence, Landon was toying with a public renunciation of any second chance in 1940, if only to stall Hoover's (to him) obvious desire for vindication.[13]

The former president, Landon wrote that same month, was on his way to being the dominant figure within the GOP, partly because of his time and money, partly out of anger over Landon's failure to defend his administration the previous year. Hoover made a speech of his own one week later, a spirited appeal for his convention, and a none-too-convincing disclaimer of interest in public office. "I shall keep on fighting for those things vital to the American people," he told a Boston audience, before adding, "There is no form of words that will convince a suspicious politician that any man under 85 can have any other purpose for interesting himself in public affairs."

"You will observe that I am trying to get unity despite obstacles," Hoover wrote Helen Reid. He even managed kind words for Landon—in public. But it was not a happy time. The former president broke irreparably with Ted Joslin, after Joslin's paper editorialized against the convention as Hoover's bid for leadership ("It is hardly necessary to point out how disastrous to the Republican Party this would be"). Ogden Mills died the same week. An Iowa judge spoke for many within the party when he bluntly asked Hoover to keep quiet. He had read the man's "carefully framed insult," Hoover replied stiffly. "You will get further animus from the address which I enclose." Joe Martin, griped Hoover, was "blowing himself off as usual," claiming that 90 percent of the party's congressional membership was against his proposal. Even Lowden, loyal for so long, turned negative as time neared for the national committee in Washington to reach its decision.[14]

At the end of the month, Hoover spent a weekend at Henry Stimson's estate on Long Island. The former Secretary of State and his wife, neither of whom had much looked forward to this visit, were astonished at what Mabel Stimson called "a transformed man." Hoover told story after story, tinged with humor and laced with salty character development. He proved thoroughly delightful company, until the subject turned to politics. Then all the old pessimism returned in force. Roosevelt, said Hoover, was pursuing a course that would inevitably lead to the destruction of democracy. Landon opposed the conference out of personal spite. Mills, in his grave only two weeks, was tried in absentia for having once met with FDR when the subject of currency debasement was floated, and for failing to clear Hoover's name of the stigma attached to it during the bank panic. The *New York Herald Tribune* was no longer of any use as a Republican organ; its editorial page was far inferior to that of the *Times*. On only one other front did Hoover display such gloom: France was unlikely to escape revolution, he told Stimson. As for the rest of Europe, its center of gravity seemed to lurch back and forth between London and Berlin.

Then, back to domestic politics. He and Lowden had Landon "thoroughly beaten" on party reorganization, said Hoover. Almost pathetically, he took from his pocket a letter written by a California lumberman, congratulating him on his latest radio speech and thanking him for showing young people the road back to old-fashioned principles. Hoover's own wish was for a shadow government, capable of speaking with authority for a party in opposition. He even used the term "opposition president" to Stimson, and there was little doubt over the prospective identity of such a figure. But when the national committee met in Chicago on November 5, Hoover's confident assertions were disproved. A broad spectrum of party leaders denounced the convention plan. The party's Executive Committee adopted a compromise supported by Landon's forces, as well as by John Hamilton. A policy committee would be established, to number not less than a hundred members. It was to canvass opinion among Republicans of all age groups and geographical locales, then make a report to the national chairman, who in turn would call a meeting to decide the proper forum in which to present the committee's findings.[15]

Hoover's long fight had yielded something less than half a loaf. The committee itself, he warned friends, was endangered by a "general conspiracy" among Landon, Knox and Martin. He accepted membership on the group (among the names he submitted for other places was that of black diplomat Ralph Bunche) and gathered intelligence on efforts by Landon and GOP congressional leaders to block any report until 1940, to elevate Ken Simpson to the party's governing board, and generally to curb his own growing influence. In the capital for the Gridiron Dinner as well as a little strategizing with the anti-Hoover forces, Landon ruled himself out of contention for 1940. His words were aimed with unmistakable accuracy at the last Republican president. "A man who is . . . suspected of being either an active or a receptive candidate," he said, "cannot render the service to his party or to his country that I conceive to be a patriotic duty in the critical situation that now confronts us."[16]

Promptly, Frank Knox seconded his running mate's assessment. "It puts Hoover on the spot," he told his wife with obvious delight. The former president had been there before. Yet he refused to concede defeat at the hands of men conducting a dalliance with false liberalism. An anguished world would provide him with a new theater of operations, and new villains to oppose. "This is just to wish you another year of influence in truth and sanity," he wrote Dorothy Thompson at the start of 1938. Both, he guessed, would be much needed in the months ahead.[17]

★   ★

"The world seems to be reverting to the frontier practice of getting the drop on your man." With these words, Hoover signaled his distaste for those who would amend the Constitution to forestall any American president from leading his nation into war without first obtaining popular approval in a national referendum. Yet his personal opposition to American participation in a new European war was adamant. "The world is living dangerously," he told a Republican women's group in New York City on January 15, 1938. "It is living recklessly." War was tearing at the vitals of China, where Japanese forces were overrunning Shanghai and Nanking, and half a globe away, where the right-wing forces of Francisco Franco were slowly strangling Spain's socialist republic with the aid of Hitler's Germany and Mussolini's Italy. Three months earlier, President Roosevelt had delivered his celebrated quarantine speech, beseeching other peace-loving nations to join the United States in checking the spread of such aggression. "If those things come to pass in other parts of the world," he told a Chicago audience, "let no one imagine that America will escape, that America may expect mercy, that this Western Hemisphere will not be attacked and that it will continue tranquilly and peacefully to carry on the ethics and the arts of civilization."

For once, Roosevelt was out of step with his countrymen, 63 percent of whom protested to George Gallup against any boycott of Japan. This sentiment did not weaken noticeably even after Japanese pilots sank a navy gunboat and killed two U.S. sailors in December 1937. Secretary of State Hull protested the assault, which he called deliberate. With tensions mounting in both Asia and Europe, Hoover's fears were mingled with puzzlement. He couldn't decide, he wrote early in 1938, whether a domestic war drive was on "merely as Machiavelli's number one rule for diversion of a troubled public mind, or whether it leads through to a determination to get us involved. Either one is dangerous."[18]

The former president conducted a clandestine diplomacy of his own. He told Henry Stimson in November 1937 of his desire to see Germany's one-time Chancellor Heinrich Bruning at the Waldorf Towers; he had made arrangements, he remarked, so that he was no longer subjected to "espionage" as to the identity of his guests. A month later, when Belgium's ambassador brought an official invitation from his government to return to the scene of his earlier humanitarian triumphs, Hoover was delighted to accept. Soon, friends who shared his skepticism of Roosevelt's neutrality (as well as his interest in the 1940 presidential campaign) were urging him to expand his itinerary. It would, as one put it, "be more effective from the standpoint of American publicity." By the first week of February 1938, Hoover was back in New York, preparing to visit as many as fifteen European nations, combining calls on statesmen with sentimental visits to aged colleagues and warmly remembered locales where his name still evoked hero worship. One problem remained, as the former president's aide Perrin Galpin explained. Hoover would undoubtedly find himself in situations calling for a toast to the current American executive.[19]

"Well, I can certainly do that," Hoover replied.

But what, Galpin went on, if he were asked to say something in public that might be construed as a defense of Roosevelt's foreign policy course? Hoover's expression never changed. "Oh," he told Galpin, "I think I can keep silent in seven languages."[20]

★   ★

Arriving at Ostend, Belgium, on February 16, Hoover was swept up in the cheers of a grateful continent. To the Europeans, he was no political outcast, nor a prophet without honor, but a reassuring memory of American generosity in a time of desperate want. He was hailed by the Belgian Chamber of Deputies and given the unprecedented title "Friend of the Belgian People" by King Leopold. A stamp was issued in his honor, and crowds gathered to shout Vive l'Amerique whenever the hero of World War I was glimpsed. The former president visited universities aided by his Belgian-American Educational Foundation, laid a wreath on the tomb of King Albert, chatted with Emile Franqui's widow at Ghent, and, at a misty-eyed twentieth-anniversary dinner in Brussels on February 19, greeted forty survivors from the 120 Belgians who had worked with the CRB.

After a week in the little kingdom, he motored to Lille, France, where representatives of fifteen northern French communities were gathered to express belated thanks to the man they called their savior. Deeply touched, the visitor replied with a prayerful wish that no war would ever again lay waste to their native soil. The University of Lille gave Hoover an honorary degree, the first of twelve he picked up along the way, and an enthusiastic student crowd presented him with a *béret d'Honneur*. A street was given his name, and Hoover the chairman of the American Anti-Cancer Committee squeezed in a visit to the city's famed cancer clinic. Correspondents who pressed for his subsequent itinerary and purposes were told, "I intend to look and listen." He did exactly that the next day in Paris, passing up art galleries (yet managing a stop at Notre Dame Cathedral, for which he had a special affection) to question journalists in the French capital on European politics and confer briefly with President Albert Lebrun at the Elysée Palace. He discovered among other evidence of France's decline the government's inability to force northern coal miners to work their own mines. The Socialists overseeing the game of musical chairs that passed for parliamentary democracy in Paris were being compelled to import 65,000 Polish miners to do what Frenchmen refused to do. Hoover came away convinced that the republic might turn Fascist at any moment.[21]

From this disturbing outpost, Hoover moved on to Geneva, where he piqued League of Nations officials by ignoring their new $10 million palace in favor of a private call on his old friend Ignace Jan Paderewski. The two men sat in a room dominated by a pair of concert grand pianos, and Paderewski, old and shaken by the death of his wife, let his American visitor do most of the talking. Later, Hoover confided to friends that the League was practically dead and the Polish patriot deeply discouraged over the current administration of his homeland, a nation reconstituted at Versailles as a testament to democracy by Woodrow Wilson, yet more recently governed by military factions tolerant of mass privation for the country's Jews.[22]

On March 3, Hoover was in Vienna, to receive yet another degree and remind engineering students at the university that their profession might outdo conventional statesmanship in providing what he called "the things that make peace." It seemed a point beyond dispute, that stormy March of 1938. All around him, statesmanship in Europe was breaking down. Nine days after Hoover's visit to Vienna, Richard Schmitz, the mayor, was jailed by occupying Nazi forces, and Austria herself forcibly annexed to the German Reich less than forty-eight hours before a scheduled plebiscite called to determine the question of national independence. Hoover apparently expressed no outrage over Hitler's disturbing of the peace. On the contrary, he told Edgar Rickard after his return, a spirit of fatalism had sapped Austrian nationalism, the people were cowed into accepting Nazi rule and Hitler's decision to send troops to enforce the Anschluss was an unnecessary gesture. He was pleased by Anthony Eden's resignation as British Foreign Minister (in the midst of what Churchill would call "a good week for dictators"), over Mussolini's invasion of Abyssinia and his own government's refusal to respond with more than perfunctory protests. Eden's personal hatred for Il Duce had prevented Prime Minister Neville Chamberlain and Mussolini from reaching an agreement. Now, said Hoover, the impediment to friendly relations was gone.[23]

Hoover was equally certain after three days in Czechoslovakia and a conference with President Eduard Beneš that the Czechs would peacefully surrender territory largely populated by Germans, but fight fiercely, aided by the Russian air force, to hold off any Nazi move against the rest of the country. He had no way of foreseeing the subsequent pact between Chamberlain and Hitler that effectively eliminated Beneš's republic from the map of Europe.[24]

On March 7, the former president motored from Carlsbad to Berlin on one of the magnificent new autobahns built by the National Socialist regime. Hoover, who always liked to push an automobile to its limit, was particularly pleased to find himself speeding along at ninety miles per hour. Far less satisfying was the pervasive security in the German capital. Before Hoover and his party left Berlin's Hotel Adlon, a contingent of Hitler's secret police ripped open a package bearing the former president's name, only to find it contained a framed picture of the late Czarina Alexandra, sent by an admiring partisan of White Russia.[25]

The night of his arrival, American ambassador Hugh Wilson paid a call on Hoover and Hugh Gibson, another traveling companion with whom Hoover hoped to inspect German achievements in low-cost housing. Wilson brought news of a startling nature: Hitler himself wished to receive the distinguished visitor from America the next day at his Chancellery. Hoover was not interested. He was traveling as a private citizen, he told Wilson, and had no business to conduct with the fuehrer. But the diplomat persisted, describing his own frustration at having penetrated no further in the German hierarchy than Foreign Minister Joachim von Ribbentrop and insisting that it would be a real service to the cause of U.S. diplomacy if Hoover would accept Hitler's invitation. Until now, the former president had regarded the German leader as little more than a front man for influential forces, a kind of charismatic shield for the real powers ruling Germany. Now, he began to have second thoughts. Reluctantly, he agreed to Wilson's request. Next morning, when it came time to leave for the Chancellery, Hoover seemed restless and hesitant. Gibson was forced to remind him that an elevator was waiting to take them down to the lobby and the start of their historic call.[26]

It was a few minutes before noon when the two men were ushered into a large room in the Reich Chancellery, without *San Francisco Chronicle* general manager Paul Smith, a Hoover traveling companion, whose presence had been rejected by the Foreign Ministry "because he is a newspaper man." The fuehrer was on hand to greet them in black breeches, varnished boots and a khaki-colored jacket emblazoned with a swastika. Hoover informed his host that he had but twenty minutes until his next scheduled appointment. An hour and a quarter later, the two men were still together, alternating talk of economic and social gains with the American's own assertion that the Nazi regime, however successful it might be within the German context, could hardly be adapted to a democratic nation.[27]

Hoover told Edgar Rickard that Hitler accepted his statement without offense. At the time, divergent accounts of the meeting surfaced, including one by Paul Smith presumably written with Hoover's acquiescence and stressing the fundamental dispute between the dictator and the democrat. According to still another version, the fuehrer replied fatalistically that liberty was a luxury, open only to those lands with abundant natural resources. "You may be able to indulge in co-operation," he remarked. "I just order." And he hinted broadly that Germany's need for additional food would inevitably lead her into armed confrontation with the Soviet army for possession of the Ukraine's breadbasket.[28]

The session was not without its dramatics. Hoover himself recounted a seemingly rational man, able to marshal a considerable intellect to make his case—at least until the word Jew was mentioned. Similarly, references to democracy or communism prompted furious outbursts, complete with gutter language and purple-faced shouting. Hitler leapt to his feet and ranted for several minutes without interruption, until Hoover at one point told him to sit down. "That's enough," he told the Nazi leader. "I'm not interested in your views." An American jury, he concluded, would judge the leader of the Third Reich insane. There were, he confided to a friend, "certain trigger spots in Hitler's mind," and an emotional streak subject to sudden and violent losses of control.[29]

If his call to the Chancellery had been unexpected, Hoover was still more surprised by a fresh piece of hospitality. Hermann Goering, the fuehrer's air force commandant and number one deputy, extended an invitation to visit him at Karinhall, his sumptuous hunting lodge sixty kilometers east of the capital. At the same time, Perrin Galpin learned of a U.S. aviation manufacturer who the previous day was taken to see a factory employing three thousand workers in the construction of airplanes, a facility until then unknown to the air attaché who revealed its existence to Galpin. Hoover's friend made careful notes. "It would prove to be almost impossible for an outsider to learn anything of value about military preparations in Germany unless he were a trained spy," he wrote. "No one knows who is watching you, following you, listening to you and ready to denounce you." Practicing the caution called for under such circumstances, Hoover made no phone calls from his Berlin hotel room. The rest of his party noted that their own conversations were carefully recorded on discs for preservation.[30]

Oppressive as the atmosphere was, even Berlin contained warm memories and light moments. Hoover was introduced to seven-year-old Axel Hoover Gelhard, born on the May 1931 day Hoover had proposed his famous, ill-fated debt moratorium. He gave the boy a piece of silver ore studded with garnets. That night, the former president was honored by the Carl Schurz Foundation—his friends had first to correct his impression that he was to be guest of honor at a dinner thrown by admirers of Karl Marx—and the president of Germany's Reichsbank used rich words of tribute as foreign in Hoover's homeland as the language from which they were translated. "We may expect great things yet from the man who is our guest," announced Hjalmar Schacht, who went on to laud the visitor for his humanitarian motives. "It is in a certain sense tragic," he continued, "that Mr. Hoover has not been able to carry out personally the work he conceived from so humane and so idealistic standpoint."[31]

From the gilded splendor and suave language of the Schurz Society, Hoover made his way on March 9 to Karinhall. He found an establishment as bombastic as its owner, a vast complex of state and private rooms surrounding the Great Hall, a 200-foot-long chamber dominated by hunting trophies and a plate-glass window overlooking Goering's artificial lake, itself half a mile in dimension. At the entrance, the visiting party was greeted by sixteen trumpeteers, dressed in elaborate costumes and performing the Hunting Song from *Siegfried* on horns built to scale with everything else in this oversized retreat. On the walls were hung Gobelin tapestries as well as more modern examples from an apparently inexhaustible collection, and in the place of honor, a painting by the fuehrer himself. Servants dressed in uniforms used by Frederick the Great's foot soldiers served sherry and port. Then it was time for lunch, a stroll through another immense gallery stocked with museum pieces, and more functionaries in powdered wigs and silk stockings. On the table before Goering sat a jewel-encrusted bust of solid gold. It was a memorial to his first wife, the air marshal revealed, before pushing a button that turned the profile to different angles.[32]

In their talks, Goering pressed for ways to emulate Hoover's successful elimination of waste as Secretary of Commerce. Hoover parried the thrust, knowing that the inquiry had already been directed to a cooperative U.S.

embassy in Berlin. He emphasized the voluntary nature of his actions, and assumed they could be carried out still more rapidly and efficiently given present-day German methods. The father of Germany's Luftwaffe was no less interested in Hoover's assessment of Soviet military potential, something the visitor cagily answered with a deliberately rosy portrayal of German prospects to the East. Goering made no effort to contain his pride in the Reich's programs to foster artificial substitutes for such industrial or military necessities as oil, textiles and food.[33]

When luncheon was concluded, the men walked past another example of the Teutonic glitter that according to Hoover would turn a Hollywood mogul green with envy: a wall of glass perhaps two hundred feet long and two feet thick, converted into an enormous aquarium, fronting on a garden ablaze with daffodils and other flowers. Paul Smith never forgot how his lunch companion turned to him and explained of the National Socialists, "We are the party of the people."[34]

Perhaps unnerved by what he had seen, or fearful of the implications of his meetings in the U.S. press, Hoover issued a statement to the press on his return to Berlin, taking aim at those who would portray him as a cat's-paw for the Nazi regime. "I am even more reinforced in my belief," he said, "that the progress of America rests in the principles of intellectual liberty and spiritual freedom, a system of free economy, regulated to prevent abuse, and popular government." He would have more to say regarding U.S. relations with Europe, he concluded, upon his return.

To Edgar Rickard, Hoover portrayed a Germany uninterested in military action against either France or England but eager to move east to acquire territory with a predominantly German population. What's more, he proclaimed, the Germans could undoubtedly provide better government to Rumania, Bulgaria, Hungary and parts of Czechoslovakia than currently prevailed. The notion that the Nazi regime might crack could be dismissed out of hand; it had attained a high degree of self-sufficiency, bolstered by the raw materials of Austria. As for the military situation, Hoover judged Berlin incapable of offensive warfare, preoccupied as it was with a campaign to purify Nazi ranks. A repressive government was also a stable one. At other moments, he was less dispassionate. Whenever a new ideology arose, he told one associate, it was apt to be followed by a bloody war. "I'm quite sure that one is rising in Germany." Mussolini provided far less danger to the peace of Europe. Italian fascism, said Hoover, was only a poor imitation of its more violent neighbor to the north.[35]

The rest of his trip was bound to be somewhat anticlimactic. Hoover had warm words for the Finns and Swedes, drew back in dismay as a Polish count describing the Jewish quarter of Krakow insisted that its inhabitants sacrificed Christian children in their ceremonies, and in a happier excursion acknowledged the cheers of four thousand schoolchildren gathered to greet him in the courtyard of Wawel Castle, Poland's national shrine. He enjoyed an amusing encounter with the dictator of tiny Latvia, educated in Nebraska and eager to return to the United States and provide similarly firm-handed leadership to Americans as soon as he completed a seven-year plan for invigorating his own land. He dined on wild boar and reindeer meat, worried that his old nemesis, French Customs, would deprive him of his beloved cigars, and in England revisited cherished scenes from his days as the world's foremost mining engineer. He spent an hour in the company of U.S. Ambassador Joseph P. Kennedy, with whom he would enjoy a close if controversial friendship. He paid a call on King George VI, in office barely three months since his brother Edward abdicated to marry the American Wallis Warfield Simpson. Hoover noted a painful stutter on the part of the earnest young monarch. His attitude toward Neville Chamberlain was less equivocal. Chamberlain, he decided, was "a dyed in the wool, old time Tory," repelled by America and Americans, anxious to isolate Great Britain and her colonies in order to preserve the Empire should war come. The P.M., Hoover continued, was all for peace, and would never sacrifice British soldiers to protect Czechs, Spaniards or anyone else. England's alliance with France was a flimsy thing, operative only in the event of a sudden attack from the east.[36]

Even though he did not set foot on Russian soil, Hoover nurtured an abiding distrust for Moscow's "gangster regime," backed by a huge yet ineffective army. Informed that the Soviets were building large hangars in and around Vladivostok, he theorized that the Russian bear had renewed his historic designs on Japan, and that following Japanese exhaustion in its own campaign against China, the Soviets were likely to pounce from the air.[37]

Before departing London for home, the former president granted a final interview to U.S. correspondents. European distemper notwithstanding, a general war on the Continent was unlikely anytime soon, he told them. "Statesmen are more generally alive to the danger than in 1914 and all men of good will are doing their best to promote peace. The principal nations are not ready with their war preparations and won't be for two or three years. There are considerable groups in every country that still recollect the terrible parts of the last war. . . . This is not a guaranty of peace, but at the same time the will to peace is much stronger than the will to war." Taken with Europe's economic rebound—something he could attest to after long hours of discussion with leading economists—Hoover could wax optimistic about the immediate future.

He would have more to say, he made clear, as soon as he arrived home.

And indeed, it was soon revealed that the world traveler would deliver a major address on U.S. foreign policy a few days after his transatlantic vessel tied up in New York harbor at the end of March. Whatever he said, it was sure to attract a curious audience, nowhere more than at 1600 Pennsylvania Avenue.

★   ★

Like Charles Sumner, who summed up his philosophy with the avowal "I am in morals, not politics," Hoover looked at the world as an unrepentant sinner, too corrupt to save itself, too important to abandon to its own sins. The continent from which he returned late in March 1938 he described as "a rumbling war machine, without the men yet in the trenches," a natural breeding ground for dictatorships, debt, the cynical and shifting balance of power, and a brutality toward its own people epitomized by what he called "the heartbreaking persecution of helpless Jews." Once before, America had gone to the aid of this self-destructive grab bag of nations, only to see its own illusions shattered and the growth of democratic rule reversed—first in Soviet Russia, then in other lands until, by Hoover's calculation, the fruits of liberty were tasted by only one fourth of those who had known them at the end of World War I. Now, in the face of a new threat from Hitler's "gigantic spartanism," Americans were speaking of quarantines and collective actions. Hoover did not conceal his apprehension.

To join with Britain or France, he told a national audience on March 31, would be to ally ourselves with imperialism, or worse yet, with France's friend Joseph Stalin. "But more than that," he went on, "we would be fostering the worst thing that can happen to a civilization . . . the building up of a war between government faiths or ideologies. Such a combination of democracies would at once result in combining the autocracies against the democracies. It could have all the hideous elements of old religious wars." Americans should have none of it, Hoover insisted. To maintain the peace, they must accept the presence of dictatorships, however hateful. "The forms of government which other people pass through in working out their destinies is not our business. You will recollect we were once animated by a desire to save the world for Democracy. The only result that time was to sow dragons' teeth which sprang up into dictatorships. We can never herd the world into the paths of righteousness with the dogs of war."

Only someone as bitterly familiar with Versailles, the broken promises and crushed hopes of the postwar era, the German republic snuffed out before it could set down roots, and the subsequent rush to rearm and seek vengeance on the authors of Germany's humiliation could wash his hands so thoroughly of a tainted, foolhardy continent. Only one with firsthand knowledge of America's own battles, first with inflation, then depression and now—in Hoover's view—with the forces of one-man rule that promised Utopia and delivered gall and wormwood, could share his alarm at war and the subsequent death of American liberty.

Finally, only someone with Hoover's continuing belief in moral force could make the suggestion that followed. "The greatest force for peace is still the public opinion of the world," he said. "Decency is still news." Specifically, he proposed that America adjust the debts of war-relief countries, which in turn would make payments into a fund to sponsor scientific and educational exchanges with the United States, as well as scholarships for their own student population. The best antidote for fear and hatred was prosperity, said Hoover. Yet the advent of Planned Economy put more and more of foreign trade in the hands of central regimes, which favored barriers more potent than the old tariffs to keep out competitive goods. More than any other factor in Hoover's view, unstable currencies contributed to the blood clots in world commerce. Correct them, and a freer flow of trade would follow.

He did not wish to be misunderstood, he told his countrymen. "I have no doubt that Fascism will fail some time, just as Marxian Socialism has already failed. The stifling of intellectual progress, the repression of the spirit of men, the destruction of initiative and enterprise, will offset all the efficacies of planned economy." Yet America's role in a dangerous world was to continue to set an example. "The protection of Democracy is that we live it, that we revitalize it within our own borders, that we keep it clean of infections, that we wipe out its corruptions, that we incessantly fight its abuses, . . . that we build its morals, that we keep out of war." Such a contribution, Hoover concluded, was the greatest service his country could provide humanity.

A week later, returning to greet a large crowd in San Francisco, Hoover was more explicit about the terrors he had witnessed. Those who lived in authoritarian states found that their souls generally belonged to the state. "If you carry over the old idea that perhaps it belongs to you, then you go to a concentration camp to rest your nerves. . . . Your trade union having been dissolved you can belong to a government recreation project. You will also be taught to sing cheerful songs in the recreation hours and to march all about. You have social security if you conform. If you do not conform you get security in concentration camp. . . . Altogether I am glad Europe is still 7,200 miles from California."

From his wry portrait of a repressed Continent, Hoover easily made the leap to domestic fears, tangible in a continuing recession, with twelve million unemployed and a capital freeze attributable in his mind to the poison of Planned Economy. Nineteen thirty-eight was an election year. Hoover characteristically saw it as an opportunity for both personal and political vindication. There were those who said in 1932 that things could not have gotten worse, he recalled. "But someone said that . . . about forty billion dollars ago. And we must live in the present." There lay the rub, especially to one still fresh in the recollection of old-world tyranny. Regulation of American business had been stretched into government dictation, claimed Hoover. A federal policeman not only expedited traffic but chose the motorist's destination and laid down what he might do once he arrived. Farmers were facing jail for flouting orders from Washington. He did not announce the arrival of fascism at America's shores, said Hoover. He did foresee a course which would lead to the demoralization from which fascism invariably sprang.

More and more now, Hoover's private preoccupation with government morality was coming to the surface. He would be sixty-four in August 1938, and the conservative certainties of old age were beginning to show through. But there was far more to Hoover's fondness for Holy Writ than advancing years.

For one thing, it was soon apparent that Europe's cheers had not drowned out the voices of his own critics at home. At a Yale Club dinner a few days after his return, Hoover sat next to a tipsy associate from CRB days who was less than diplomatic in his welcome. "Chief," the man said somewhat groggily, "there are many who consider you to be a so and so, but I don't." The guest of honor silently rose and moved to another place, farther down the table. There he found Ken Simpson, Manhattan's rising spokesman for liberal Republicans who found inspiration in youthful heroes like District Attorney Thomas E. Dewey. Someone remarked on the sad state of the U.S. economy, still in the throes of the Roosevelt Recession. Hoover agreed, only to hear Simpson chime in with an observation that things were worse yet back in 1932.[38]

The smearing had not stopped, Hoover complained to friends. Columnists like Jay Franklin took to the air and accused the former president of spending people rather than dollars, and of ignoring a national suicide rate increased by 35 percent during his four years in office. "You lie, you lie," he muttered back at his radio set. His indignation did not end there. "It is rather unendurable having to stand this stuff being periodically spread over the country," Hoover informed the president of NBC in March 1939. Four months later, he was embroiled in another controversy involving the network, this time winning a retraction of a broadcast claim that he was buying up southern delegates for the 1940 Republican presidential nomination. Alben Barkley accused Hoover's administration of having added $6 billion to the national debt with no public buildings to show for it. This, replied Hoover, showed that Roosevelt's Senate Majority Leader had been "grievously misinformed by the Liars' Research Bureau," and he went on to demonstrate that the real figure was less than one twentieth the debt run up under the New Deal.[39]

A reader of *Life* magazine scanned pictorial coverage of the former president's European travels and noted a startling resemblance between the top-hatted expatriate and Mr. Heinz Tomato on the facing page. Lou Hoover refused to send her portrait to hang in the White House until Congress appropriated funds for one of her husband; not until August of 1939, on its fourth attempt to resolve the issue, did the legislators find money for such a tribute. Hoover's personal feelings spilled over in an impromptu breakfast with Ray Moley, the disgruntled ex-Brain Truster whom he encountered on a train outside Los Angeles in May 1938. A porter had just finished telling Moley an off-color story about the current occupants of the White House, when Hoover appeared at his table.

"Mr. Moley," the porter asked, "do you think that Mr. Hoover would like to hear this story about Mr. Roosevelt?"

"I don't like to hear stories about presidents," Hoover snapped.[40]

To one friend in the summer of 1938, Hoover wrote that he found consolation in reading the history of the post-Napoleonic and post–Civil War eras, "where we had all the moral degeneration and demagoguery which has again appeared in this post world war period. The apparent reason why we have come out from the previous holes was not so much a re-gathering of spiritual strength as the discoveries in pure science and the consequent advance in invention. It may be that the scientists and the engineers will save us again."[41]

He hadn't changed at all.

Year after year, he had held to his course, defying, accusing, taunting an administration that used the words of democracy while encouraging the methods of undemocratic Europe. Now, in the spring of 1938, with the economy turned sour, the judiciary breathless from its narrow escape, and Roosevelt casting anxious glances at troublespots around the world, Hoover seized on fresh evidence of domestic transgressions.

With the index of economic activity down to 79, only 10 points above its 1932 trough, and the winds of political adversity roaring around his head, Roosevelt that April cast aside his preference for orthodox finance and demanded a return to the free-spending ways he had so recently shunned.

The PWA was resurrected from its shallow grave, and given nearly a billion dollars. Harry Hopkins's WPA got $1.4 billion more, and there were generous subsidies granted to agriculture, housing and the National Youth Administration. The president narrowly secured his wages and hours legislation, over the combined opposition of Republicans and southern Democrats. He was less fortunate when it came to a government reorganization plan, swept away in an overwhelmingly Democratic House amidst cries of incipient dictatorship. If such a bill were to pass, claimed New York's Hamilton Fish, then Congress would retain no more authority to legislate than India's Mahatma Gandhi had clothes.

For the increasingly strained coalition of northern liberals and southern conservatives, urban bosses and western insurgents who comprised Roosevelt's base, the breaking point was at hand. "Democrats," cried Carter Glass in contemptuous reference to the planners and spenders surrounding the president. "Why, Thomas Jefferson would not speak to these people." FDR himself was out of patience with those who claimed membership in his party yet voted like Republicans. Late in June 1938, he publicly denounced those Democrats he called "Copperheads," and launched a determined effort to purge recalcitrant legislators like Georgia's Walter George, South Carolina's Cotton Ed Smith and Millard Tydings of Maryland. The resulting controversy was fed by well-documented charges that WPA workers were being coerced into voting for administration favorites at risk of their paychecks.

For Hoover, all of this amounted to proof positive that his worst premonitions were on the verge of fearful realization. Will Irwin found the former president sitting behind a desk at the Waldorf Towers that July, twirling a lock of his hair as he bore down with a lead pencil, deep in literary composition. Plucking a pipe from the mantelpiece, dropping into a padded chair, he opened himself up for questions. "Fire away, Bill," was the way he put it. "Let's see your stuff!" He told Irwin that Americans were suffering, not a recession but a repression, a throttling of their normal energies and faith in the future. He quoted Rudyard Kipling's tale about rewards and fairies, attributing the paralysis of business to those who had locked up the rewards and poisoned the fairies. Restore confidence by ending the attacks on judicial independence, he urged, along with the corruption of the electoral process, the hostility toward investors and the expansion of bureaucracy.

"Have I sounded too much like an Old Testament prophet?" Hoover wondered of his friend. Perhaps he had talked too much about fear, he acknowledged, but there was a reason for that. "When you see a car coming at you, it's fear that makes you jump and save your life." The forthcoming congressional elections, he concluded, were the most important since 1860.

In the same spirit, Hoover decried fellow Republicans who made speeches "the basis of which seems to be that all of the humanitarian actions lie in the New Deal, that the Republican Party ought to be sorry for its misconduct, that it ought to forget its past, that it ought to weep in sackcloth and ashes for its misdeeds, that now it will change and adopt the New Deal with a few improvements." [42]

His own utterances betrayed no such accommodation with the new order. Everywhere he went that summer and fall, Hoover found phrases to singe the New Deal and occasionally dishearten less adamant Republicans. Alf Landon, for one, thought his rival's addresses "terrible" and took solace in the fact that neither he nor Hoover could have any hope of snaring the party's 1940 nomination. Such a contest, were it to occur, wrote Landon, would be "like two undertakers fighting over the corpse." Yet the Kansan was hardly without bias as an observer. Thousands of rank-and-file members of the GOP thrilled to Hoover's vocabulary of resentment tinged with wit. In Philadelphia, he paid honor to Benjamin Franklin by quoting the homespun philosopher's observation that "he that kills a breeding sow destroys all her offspring to the thousandth generation." In modern day America, it would not be a happy theme to pursue, said Hoover, who also believed that Franklin's observation about God helping those who helped themselves had been "distinctly limited" ever since, "especially as to the public utilities."

He chose harsher words to kick off his own campaign for Republican candidates in the fall elections. "When citizens are crooked among themselves the damage falls mostly upon themselves," he said in Kansas City on September 28, "and it may affect their chances in the Life Eternal. But when government is immoral, it damages the morals of a whole people." And the New Deal, with its enshrinement of the spoils system, its "Praetorian Guard" of political appointees 400,000 strong, its resortment to class hate and relief politics, its purges and its pork, its president who sold his autograph to corporations to enrich the Democratic National Committee to the tune of $250 per book, its dishonest budgets and partisan use of the mails, its dictation and its debts; these were hardly the stuff of true liberalism. If they were, continued Hoover, "then George III, Hitler, Stalin, and Boss Tweed are liberals."

Americans should worry less over what was liberal than what was honest. "Integrity lives not alone in the pocket," said Hoover. "It lives also in the mind." As alternatives, he proposed the return of relief administration to local officials, even if Washington continued to pay 95 percent of the tab. He insisted that every official except for a few at the very top of the public pyramid be placed under Civil Service—and that all those appointed during the previous six years be required to take merit examinations. He wanted the Corrupt Practices Act amended "to provide instant dismissal and jail for any of these job holders who speaks out loud on politics," and a sweeping repudiation of the whole idea that ends justified means, a grim doctrine that violated Christian ethics and common decency alike.

Three weeks later, Hoover resorted to a low blow of his own, telling a Hartford audience that he would not refresh their minds on the "liberal" attack on the Supreme Court—nor raise the question of liberalism within the Ku Klux Klan. He focused instead on the dangers of a rubber-stamp Congress and quoted the New York Times on Roosevelt's efforts, largely blunted, to purge opponents within his own party: ". . . How great an intellectual servitude the President now requires from his followers."

He recruited a thirty-four-year-old farmer named John I. Anderson and helped raise $35,000 to elect Anderson in place of a faithful New Deal congressman from the California district that included Palo Alto. He solicited more money to aid Thomas Dewey's campaign for the governorship of New York—even though Hoover's friends noted how Dewey personally kept his distance from the former president. He conferred with organization Republicans, especially on the West Coast, and two days before the balloting, Hoover returned to Spokane, Washington, to complete his verbal assault on the New Deal with his own measurement of its economic consequences. The price of grain was down 40 percent, he noted; cotton 36 percent. Eleven million were jobless. All of which moved him to suggest a new slogan for the advocate of Planned Economy—"two families in every garage." Other lands had snapped out of depression long ago; Britain, for example, enjoyed a level of business activity higher than before 1929, while the United States was struggling 30 percent below that benchmark. Again, Hoover's prescription for recovery was limited to general principles, designed to restore confidence to the man he called John Q. Public.[43]

On November 7, a restless electorate rewarded the GOP handsomely. The party gained seven seats in the Senate and sixty-seven in the House. It swelled its own gubernatorial ranks in key industrial states and nearly toppled the previously unbeatable Herbert Lehman in New York. Lehman's opponent would have won his race, Hoover believed, were it not for Dewey's reluctance to introduce national issues into the statewide campaign. Dewey's organizational ally, Ken Simpson, was still less acceptable to the former president, especially after Simpson pronounced the GOP ready to govern, subject only to the realization that it was no longer under the sway of "Mr. Hoover, the Liberty League and some of the reactionary influences of the past."[44]

Others within the party were more complimentary. West Virginia's national committeeman, Walter Hallinan, spoke for many in awarding Hoover substantial credit for standing up against "demagogues and pseudo-liberals." Hoover agreed on the headway being made as the country began to realize for itself what he called "the foolishness of all this stuff." But he could not resist a shot at those Republicans who, two years before, had failed to hammer home a fundamentalist message. He was receiving "an enormous amount of mail," he told Will Irwin a week after the voting, most of it claiming that it was he who had carried the election, "but I haven't seen any account of that in the newspapers."[45]

In a brief time-out from partisanship, Hoover joined Landon, his old nemesis Harold Ickes, and clergymen from Protestant and Catholic Churches in a radio appeal on behalf of Germany's persecuted Jews. It was not the German people, he said on November 13, who were taking their nation back 450 years to the time of Torquemada's expulsion of Spanish Jews. It was, rather, "the political agencies in power." So long as those agencies refused to emulate the civilized traditions of Germany herself, "it is the duty of men everywhere to express our indignation not alone at the suffering these men are imposing upon an innocent people but at the blow they are striking at civilization itself." When Ickes's turn came, he delivered remarks carefully sanitized by Roosevelt to remove any mention of Hitler or Mussolini personally. The situation was too delicate to play with diplomatic matches. But as 1938 came to a close, with Hitler savoring his latest peaceful conquest in Czechoslovakia, and the stockpiles of war continuing to escalate, Hoover did not doubt where the president's sympathies lay, nor his inclination to ultimately do battle with Europe's dictators. Such certainty, accompanied by fear, promised to bump domestic alarms from his own calendar for 1939.[46]

★　　★

A world hell-bent for destruction would not allow America the indulgence of isolation. Having already recalled the U.S. ambassador to Berlin in protest over the latest pogrom against German Jews, Roosevelt in his annual address to Congress on January 4, 1939, asked for repeal of a compulsory embargo on arms shipments to foreign adversaries, along with $2 billion to bolster his own country's defenses. "Some boob," said the president, was responsible for misquoting him in a private session with senators to the effect that America's frontier now lay on the Rhine. No such refuge could shield administration claims of neutrality when a French pilot was pulled from the wreckage of a late model American bomber crashed to earth in California. Cold steel and hot words kept Americans uneasy company as they paced the diplomatic waiting room in the spring of 1939.

A scarred veteran of earlier operations, Hoover prepared a new salvo against both the president's defense budget and his appeal to come to the aid of Europe's democracies. "Effective protest at acts of aggression against sister nations," he told Chicago's Council on Foreign Relations, was fine in the abstract. But what actions existed short of war and more effective than words? Either the United States would supply one side with food, munitions, raw materials and finance, or it would deny these tools of battle to the other side through boycotts and embargoes. In any event, such policies would award America the right "to determine who are the aggressors in the world." And inevitably they would hasten the day when his countrymen burned their fingers in the European flame.

Any hint of U.S. coercion, Hoover insisted, spelled a death knell for genuine neutrality and would invite retaliation. Nor could he find any easy line dividing what he called legitimate expansion and wicked aggression. Moreover, said Hoover, even in Europe itself, ground fortifications had reached a point nearly impregnable to assault. "It is my belief that the Western democracies of Europe can amply defend themselves against military attack." He found incredible the notion that any civilized leader would countenance barbarities like air raids upon helpless cities; world opinion would not tolerate it. The totalitarian states themselves suffered from "grave internal weaknesses." Finally, "the common people in no country of Europe want war. They are terrified of it." His own hemisphere was protected by a moat of ocean, 3,000 miles to the east, 6,000 to the west. No airplane yet built could cross such a sea, drop bombs and return to its home field. It was "sheer hysteria" to think otherwise.

Most urgent, however, were Hoover's warnings of the dangers to liberty from the kind of war now envisioned. Neither personal liberty nor economic freedom were likely to survive the mass mobilization and temporary resort to dictatorship that such a conflict would demand. "It means that our country must be mobilized into practically a Fascist state," he forecast. "It went some distance in the last war. . . . It would have gone much farther if the war had extended longer." In the aftermath of his address, *Los Angeles Times* publisher Harry Chandler invited Hoover to undertake a weekly column of a thousand words. "I can think of nothing that America needs more at this critical time . . . ," Chandler wrote. Agreeing to consider the idea, Hoover also said it would be "awfully hard for me to work against a deadline." Perhaps his distaste for the daily press was also influenced by a controversy between himself and Eleanor Roosevelt. The First Lady in her own column, "My Day," had taken Hoover to task for criticizing her husband the same night FDR sent a message to Munich, inviting a peaceful settlement between Chamberlain and Hitler. "I cannot help but wonder," Mrs. Roosevelt told Larry Richey in response to his own note of protest, "what encouragement Mr. Hoover's remarks . . . gave to the forces responsible at that time for conditions which threatened the peace of the world."[47]

Bleak as the prospects were, Hoover hedged his bets. He engaged a scholar from his Stanford library to gather up documents from Russia, Spain and France, lest a new war obliterate evidence of the last one. He deplored the cheers which greeted his name at a February 1939 meeting in New York of the German-American Bund. And whatever he might say publicly about no more Guernicas, Hoover was far more concerned than he let on. To one friend at the time, he descended from the summit of philosophical abstraction long enough to ask if a new war would bring with it indiscriminate bombing of Europe's cities. The friend said it would, and Hoover, deeply shaken, muttered his agreement.[48]

It was with the conscience of a West Branch Quaker that he wrote for *Liberty* magazine's July 1939 issue a moving description of combat stripped of its glory. Others might forget the horror of the first world war, he noted, or choose to dwell solely on the courage, heroism and spiritual greatness of those called on to do the fighting. His own view was less selective. He recalled the filth and stench, the death and the trenches, the dumb grief of mothers and children. He penned a haunting memoir of the Battle of the Somme, and a muddy battlefield occupied by a million and a half men.

"Here and there, like ants, they advanced under the thunder and belching volcanoes of 10,000 guns. Their lives were thrown away until half a million had died. Passing close by were unending lines of men plodding along the right side of the road to the front, not with drums and bands, but with saddened resignation. Down the left side came the unending lines of wounded men, staggering among unending stretchers and ambulances. Do you think one can forget that?" he asked plaintively. "And it was but one battle of a hundred."

He remembered roads clogged with refugees, old men and small children dropping from fatigue; civilians executed by firing squads and winds that carried away every shred of justice or human decency; air raids that sent the innocent fleeing to shelters, terror written on their faces; politics and diplomacy conspiring to foster starvation by blockade and submarine warfare. "It is an idiot who thinks soldiers ever starve," Hoover snorted. "It was women and children who died of starvation. . . . And after the Armistice came famine and pestilence, in which millions perished and other millions grew up stunted in mind and body. That is war. Let us not forget."

Powerful images, unmatched by the logic that followed. Europe itself had invited a general war every century since the Roman-kept peace, claimed

Hoover. A new conflict would be a savage joke on democracy so long as democratic powers were aligned with totalitarian ones. The democracies themselves had the resources to wage their own defense. Whether they prevailed was simply a question of willpower. "We are told that if they fall we shall be the next victim," Hoover noted. "I do not agree that they will fall. But if they do fall the exhaustion of the dictators will be such that these countries will leave us alone for a quarter of a century at least."

Convinced as he was of Roosevelt's folly (as well as a Jewish influence over his own nation's policies which he told Edgar Rickard was excessive), Hoover did not retreat from the moral challenge of the age. A wave of grateful letters followed in the wake of his radio denunciation of Jewish persecution in Hitler's Reich. Actor Edward G. Robinson spoke for others: "Your broadcast will not be in vain . . . moral forces are not impotent," he wired the former president. In January 1939, Hoover began a correspondence with Harvard president James B. Conant over Conant's plan to rescue Jewish academics from Nazi Germany before it was too late. The educator sought Hoover's cooperation in raising funds. The former president promised to do his best. He affixed his name to a statement of the group's principles and served on a committee promoting their advance. He acquiesced when Conant asked his help in approaching Nelson Rockefeller as a possible chairman. In mid-March, he looked on favorably as Bernard Baruch tried to negotiate with the administration a new homeland for dispossessed Jews in the plains of Kenya. Lewis Strauss as go-between was soon able to report FDR's statement to Baruch that "there was no man but [you] who had the experience and ability to do what is proposed." The president also vowed to bring the matter personally before Neville Chamberlain, thereby avoiding his suspect London ambassador, Joe Kennedy.[49]

"I add my entire collection of fingers and toes to those that are to be crossed," Hoover replied on March 25, ten days after Hitler seized the rump of Czechoslovakia, and Roosevelt applied new economic sanctions against the Reich. "But we will wait for news." That summer, Strauss left for Europe, anxious to secure Continental backing for what Baruch would call the United States of Africa, a haven for refugees created under British sovereignty in Kenya, Tanganyika or nothern Rhodesia. Hoover assured both men of his willingness to visit the new nation and to aid in developing its transportation, communications and mineral resources. Strauss proposed to finance the project through a self-imposed tax of 10 percent on all the world's Jews. But the plan collapsed in the face of opposition from the British Colonial Office. The Chamberlain government had its own favored site for this new Jewish homeland—the unlikely Canaan of British Guiana, with its fetid swamps and lifeless soil. Even this was postponed when war broke out, and it was "in the light of the present chaotic situation in Europe," wrote Under Secretary of State Sumner Wells in July 1940, that Roosevelt felt compelled to put the whole issue on a back burner.[50]

The aborted rescue was one more bit of evidence to confirm a man with Hoover's suspicions that peace itself might soon be sacrificed. By April the Gallup Poll showed two thirds of those questioned in favor of selling Britain and France planes and other war materials. Roosevelt himself caused a stir that Easter, telling a crowd gathered to see him off from the Little White House at Warm Springs tht he would be back in the fall "if we don't have a war." On April 15, the president addressed a public appeal to Berlin, seeking Hitler's guarantee that he would refrain from any attack on twenty-one nations of Europe. Unimpressed, Hoover hoped that the British, "the only outstanding skillful group of world diplomats," could yet avert war. He told Cal O'Laughlin at the start of April that he wished Roosevelt would maintain at least Chamberlain's tone of voice. Had this been done, the president might have brought Europe's adversaries to sit around a council table, "and . . . make the greatest contribution to peace in this generation. As it stands, there is no one to make this contribution." More cynically, he suggested to another colleague that politics were being played, the worst yet.[51]

Politics of another variety were not far from his own thinking.

A year before, Hoover denounced as "a rotten kind of thing to put about" the forecast distributed in Roger Babson's "Washington Report" that the former president would use his European travels as a springboard for electoral vindication in 1940. In his anger, Hoover threatened, only half in jest, to inform the public of Babson's "general unreliability." Yet his closest friends could see for themselves the interest with which he followed political developments. Edgar Rickard noted lunches with District Attorney Dewey, as well as Hoover's evident fear that Dewey's undeclared candidacy was gaining entirely too much momentum for any hope of a convention stalemate to have credence. In April 1939, Hoover's Iowa supporter Harrison Spangler told the ex-president flatly that the fearless young Gangbuster had caught the public fancy. Beyond the appeal of a spectacularly successful prosecutor, avenging society against the likes of Lucky Luciano and Tammany boss Jimmy Hines, Spangler noted a desire for new faces, the ancient appetite for New York's huge electoral vote, the feeling that Washington could use some of the same scouring applied to corrupt Manhattan, and a reaction against the Old Guard, whose lukewarm enthusiasm for the DA only brightened his prospects with rank-and-file voters.[52]

Hoover admitted that Dewey's campaign was "growing to serious proportions." He read a letter from John Hamilton, just back from attending the Gridiron Dinner at which Ohio's Senator Robert Taft, a Hoover protégé now interested in 1940 for himself, delivered a dismal speech that Hamilton predicted would put a serious dent in Taft's presidential ambitions. On his own, Hoover had already reprimanded Taft for accepting without question "one of the favored New Deal lies," namely, that his administration had added $5 billion to the nation's debt.[53]

Rickard noted his old friend's reluctance to discuss politics whenever Lou was present. Otherwise, there seemed to pour from his lips a torrent of plans, calculations, accusations and schemes to keep his name before the public. That summer, Hoover returned to Palo Alto to help organize the Republican Circles, ostensibly the latest in his party-building efforts but in fact a network of friends and supporters eager to reward their hero for his long years of faithfulness by placing him at the head of the Republican ticket in 1940. Half a continent away, Alf Landon was no less emphatic in his demand for change, or his distaste for any Hoover comeback. In his eagerness to see anyone but Roosevelt occupy the White House, the Kansan was willing to drop his first choice, Dewey, and align himself with such constitutional Democrats as Virginia's Harry Byrd, Burton Wheeler, even Secretary of State Cordell Hull.[54]

Early in August 1939, Hoover recounted a series of off-the-record meetings between himself and western Republicans. With more than a touch of wishful thinking, he said he was unable to discern strong enthusiasm for any particular candidate. "But there is a determination to enter the battle such as we have not seen in 70 years." The same week, Cal O'Laughlin informed his patron of a conversation with old Hiram Johnson, once Hoover's bitter enemy, now willing to be reconciled over foreign policy. O'Laughlin urged that Hoover be given control of the big California delegation to the next year's convention, and Johnson voiced no objection. More good news arrived from New York, where a savage fight was brewing between Dewey and Ken Simpson, Simpson who was conversant with the art of Matisse and Modigliani, Simpson who numbered Gertrude Stein and Alexander Kerensky among his personal friends. Papered over in the name of temporary unity and long-range ambition, the Dewey-Simpson feud had national ramifications. Desperate to retain a hammerlock on his own state's delegation, the DA was willing to placate the New York County leader by withholding any support for dissident elements angered over Simpson's courtship of the Left. Hoover's friends were much less willing to concede control. Late that summer, Alan Fox was able to report $18,000 already raised with which to wage combat among GOP primary voters.[55]

If all else failed, Fox noted, a different kind of war might finish off the dapper prosecutor whose achievements had taken a weary nation by storm. "In the fact of a world situation like the present little Dewey looks so insignificant." A jaundiced view, it was nonetheless accurate. And as the heat of August tested men's tempers on both sides of the Atlantic, Hoover again turned his attention to Europe, where a diplomatic bombshell went off, encased in a nonaggression pact cynically negotiated between Berlin and Moscow. Hoover was not alone in wishing that the two dictatorships, Nazi and Communist, might destroy each other like modern-day Kilkenny Cats. For now, the prospect appeared remote. Once again, German troops were massing, this time along the Polish border, and once again, Hitler was protesting his peaceful intentions.[56]

Five years later, their alliance forged in adversity and confirmed in popular rejection, Joe Kennedy and Hoover had breakfast in New York. Kennedy told of a book he was writing, using nine hundred diplomatic dispatches to illustrate his experiences as Roosevelt's ambassador to London. He could not publish such a volume without the approval of the American government, said Kennedy, but he was not at all bashful about sharing his information with an old friend like Hoover. According to Kennedy, following the German occupation of Prague and Hitler's subsequent demand for Polish territorial concessions, Neville Chamberlain had wished to enter into a new round of talks with the fuehrer. (The same Chamberlain who a month earlier described Winston Churchill, in Kennedy's words, as "a fine two handed drinker" of irresponsible judgment and warlike tendencies. Had Churchill been a member of his Cabinet before, intimated a weary P.M., England would already be at war.) But his plans were frustrated when Roosevelt, through Kennedy and his Paris envoy William Bullitt, told the Poles not to agree to any terms that might emerge from such negotiations. The American president implied to the British prime minister that U.S. support would be sure to follow a principled stand. In Kennedy's words, FDR cabled him to "put a poker up Chamberlain's back and . . . make him stand up."[57]

In the end, Chamberlain caved in. He gave the Poles the guarantees of British assistance counseled by Washington but not without gloomy forebodings. He hoped that the Americans and Jews would now be satisfied, he told Kennedy; personally, he felt as if he had signed the doom of civilization.[58]

At least one such communication sustaining Kennedy's view can be found in the Roosevelt Library at Hyde Park, a diplomatic message dated August 25, 1939, sent to Cordell Hull and conveying Chamberlain's hope, even at that late hour, to avoid conflict over Poland, a nation, in the British view "with no future anyway." England would agree to Hitler's demand for

Danzig and a slice of the Polish Corridor separating the Fatherland from that much-coveted port city. Germany, it was confidently forecast, would in return respect and even fight to preserve Britain's empire abroad. Hitler would limit his armaments, return to peaceful pursuits and perhaps even take up his neglected palette and brush. Otherwise, reported Kennedy, the worst conflagration in five hundred years would engulf the continent.

"Writing this out," the American emissary concluded, "it looks like a ridiculous proposition to make Great Britain quit or cut away from the Poles but to hear the text as read it seems much more reasonable." A day later, Kennedy was reporting Hitler's remark to British ambassador Nicholas Henderson that the only beneficiary of a conflict between their two nations would be Japan. On the twenty-eighth, the Poles signified their own willingness to negotiate, and within twenty-four hours Kennedy was cabling news that a skeptical Hitler would accept one final attempt to mediate his differences with Poland. Three days later, the world learned how elaborate a hoax had been played.[59]

Even Hoover admitted at the time that Hitler's seizure of Prague had damaged the atmosphere for peaceful diplomacy. The move had left the world "without any confidence" in the Nazi leader's stated intentions. But the longing for peace was too strong to be suppressed. "As I read between the lines of Hitler's note to [French Premier Edouard] Daladier," he wrote on August 28, "he would hold to a compromise on the City of Danzig, to which I think the world would concede, and some connection across the Polish Corridor. As I have said," he went on, "divested of the Prague background, this is no issue for Europe to go to war about."[60]

Like Chamberlain, a decent man undone by his own equanimity, Hoover had believed in Hitler's openness to reason. For a man who so easily diagnosed evil all around him, his moral antennae seemed strangely insensitive to evil abroad. Or perhaps he cared so much about a return to the pre-1914 Eden he never stopped mourning that he was willing to deny the serpent's presence. On September 3, Chamberlain yielded to reality at last, proclaiming a state of war between his own ravaged government and the Nazi regime that two days earlier had crossed the Polish frontier. In America, a noisy new debate was launched. "We shall be preoccupied chiefly with trying to keep the United States out of such a conflict," Hoover prophesied. In this, as on so many fields of battle, his chief antagonist was to be Franklin Roosevelt. The latest chapter of their historic rivalry began, however, with an unusual twist. FDR, so it seemed, had plans to recall his predecessor to national service.[61]

CHAPTER EIGHT

THE PEACEMONGER

★

This nation will remain a neutral nation, but I cannot ask that every American remain neutral in thought as well. . . . Even a neutral cannot be asked to close his mind or his conscience.
—Franklin D. Roosevelt, September 3, 1939

As far as I'm concerned, I'm willing to feed women and children. I don't care what nationality or race they are.
—Herbert Hoover, February 29, 1940

★

With Nazi storm-troopers thundering across Poland, with Britain and France belatedly mobilizing to halt their advance, with American emotions aroused and American fears deepening, a surface rally of public opinion sustained both president and Congress. A special session of both houses was called for September 21, at which time Roosevelt would respond to the new danger by demanding repeal of old restrictions; more precisely, the embargo on military sales to combatants that effectively favored the land power, Germany, over the sea power, Britain. In New York, Hoover debated briefly over whether he might lead Republican opposition to the move, then dropped his plans when it became clear that the party's congressional leaders wished him to stay out of the controversy.[1]

An invitation to become involved in another war-related effort reached him from the most unlikely of quarters. On September 11, Hoover was visited by Myron Taylor, ambassador without portfolio from the Roosevelt White House. The president, said Taylor, wished to have his predecessor's views on how best to organize relief on the war-racked Continent. In fact, he would like Mr. Hoover to come to Washington within forty-eight hours for consultations at the White House. Hoover's reply was prompt if wary. His advice was to entrust any relief campaign to the American Red Cross, vastly expanded in the 1920s from its old, parochial status as a military adjunct. Hoover himself knew firsthand of the invaluable work performed by Red Cross chapters during the Mississippi River floods of 1927, as well as their European counterparts that he thought might initiate relief activities within hours. A dubious Taylor listened as he warned of precious time that would be wasted in creating any new body to aid the war's victims. Then the former president authorized his visitor to transmit all he had said to Roosevelt.

He would be delighted to advise the president further, should Roosevelt have questions. For himself to come to Washington just then, concluded Hoover, "would only create speculation and unnecessary discussion in the country." He mentioned to Taylor responsibilities to his party and then, with what must have been sublime pleasure, pledged unequivocal support for any administration policy that would keep the United States out of the war. GOP opposition, Hoover guaranteed, would be entirely constructive, limited to methods of achieving that noble aim.[2]

Six days later, Hoover entertained another emissary from FDR's Oval Office: Norman Davis, veteran diplomat more recently turned chairman of the American Red Cross. Davis began with an attempt to sooth relations strained by eight years of public recrimination and private suspicion. Roosevelt himself could not understand Hoover's seeming hostility. According to Davis, for example, he had never heard of Secret Service protection withdrawn on Inauguration Day 1933. Hoover parried the thrust, recommending that Davis's own Red Cross undertake the relief assignment, and volunteering to serve on both its Executive and Central committees. He provided his guest with a detailed relief blueprint that might be implemented speedily. Four hours after it began, the meeting ended, Davis to return to Washington, Hoover to remain at the Waldorf, from which he tried fruitlessly to persuade Belgium's King Albert to agree to his plan to avoid civilian bombings, and sought cooperation of the neutral powers in policing belligerents for actions against civilians.[3]

On the eighteenth, the Red Cross Executive Committee met as scheduled and agreed that no such campaign as Hoover proposed could be successfully concluded by the present organization. Could the former president come to the capital and discuss possible alternatives? Hoover could not. To Edgar Rickard, he theorized that Roosevelt was anxious to sidetrack him into relief work. His own priorities included the coming struggle to keep America out of the war—and a possible presidential nomination in 1940. He was disappointed, he now told Davis, that Red Cross chapters were unwilling to assume responsibility for "one of the greatest obligations that has ever come to them." Considering the situation in Poland, where German forces were overwhelming local resistance, no one else could possibly reach the hungry or homeless as soon. Again he asked Davis to create a European Relief Division "under some experienced man as I have already suggested to you."[4]

Davis responded in a frosty tone. He had "hoped and understood" that Hoover would attend the Washington meeting, and found unfortunate the former president's reluctance to do so unless his own letter stipulating the conditions of his involvement was first made public. As for the counsel contained in the letter, "the situation in Europe had not yet developed to the point where it was possible to lay out a general program of relief" for civilian victims. Aware of Poland's agony, Davis was equally cognizant of a combined Russian-German blockade. Even then, he told Hoover, the International Red Cross was dispatching two representatives to Poland, with Berlin's approval, to report on the situation. But Davis would not accept any obligation beyond what he called "emergency relief." It was simply not possible for the Red Cross to undertake mass feeding over an extended period, "which requires such substantial outlays of money as to necessitate Governmental financing."[5]

Hoover was no more flexible. He had given Davis a plan. "I see no reason to depart from it. The more I see of the situation the more I am convinced that the Red Cross is the only American agency that can give leadership and take these responsibilities." His suggestion regarding publication of letters was made "to clear the public mind as to the purpose of my coming to Washington and to avoid useless speculation." Deep as his distrust of Roosevelt ran, in this instance, he might have looked beyond the president. For the voice might have been that of Franklin, but the hand was that of Eleanor, who had devised a plan of her own to share responsibility for European relief with the former president. "Mr. Hoover turned us down," she reported to a friend on September 27; "said he probably would be busy organizing a political campaign next year and did not feel he could support the setting up of anything else. . . . He refused to call on the President."[6]

Perhaps, as Mrs. Roosevelt saw it, Hoover was too enthralled with his own political prospects to yield gracefully to her husband's invitation. Edgar Rickard noted during the first week of October that his friend was eager to enter the Republican fray, and a few weeks later recorded Hoover's prediction that if he failed to win his party's endorsement this time, he would leave Palo Alto for good and retire from active politics.[7]

But there was more to the story than that. As early as the ninth of September, Roosevelt remarked to Harold Ickes that all the talk of inviting Hoover, Vandenburg, Taft, "even Dewey," into his official family was nothing more than preconvention puffery by hopeful Republicans. Nor was Davis without political motivations of his own. On the fifteenth, he passed word to the president that Hoover would indeed be coming to Washington for the Red Cross meeting three days later and conveyed his wish to report personally the content of their New York conversations before the former president reached town. What he said was evidently unfavorable, for yet another go-between, this one what the White House staff would label "an Eleanor person," told FDR that Davis was wrong, that Hoover was interested less in his own campaign than in keeping America out of the war. The truth, according to this informer, was that Hoover could claim a large measure of responsibility for transforming the old Red Cross into "a great civilian relief agency in order that we should be prepared for just such emergencies as this." The president should ask for a copy of the written recommendations given to Davis. "You will find in it a real plan of action."[8]

Nothing happened, and the entire affair only deepened the mistrust endemic to both camps. FDR came away believing his rival a small-minded partisan, plotting electoral revenge at the cost of suffering Poles. Hoover was confirmed in his assessment of a chief executive too clever by half, harboring no conviction nobler than political advantage. When the president finally convened an ostensibly nonpartisan gathering to discuss the Neutrality Act on September 20, Landon and Knox represented their party. Hoover was conspicuous by his absence. Afterward, even Landon felt used, while Harold Ickes preserved Frank Knox's description of a dinner party at which the former president lauded Neville Chamberlain as the greatest statesman of his generation—a performance followed by Knox's spirited disagreement, and yet another assessment of the European cauldron by Chauncey McCormick, who for good measure added his belief that Hoover shouldn't run in 1940.

The next morning, according to Ickes, McCormick approached the publisher in a quizzical mood. "Frank," he blurted, "did I say anything last night that was not all right?"

"No Chauncey," Knox responded. "You did fine."[9]

The damage done, both contenders retreated to their corners, Roosevelt to persuade Congress to grant him repeal of the embargo, Hoover to enlist

Charles Lindbergh and Eddie Rickenbacker in a new scheme to limit U.S. shipments to strictly defensive materials. When the plan was rejected by the Senate, 56–36, Hoover was encouraged. The margin, he told Rickard, was "not bad" given the mood of the country and the persuasive skills of the president. By then, other developments were crowding a mind already teeming with ideas and resentments. Poland was falling apart. Despite his earlier protests, Hoover was about to be sidetracked after all.[10]

★   ★

Late in September, Poland's anguish, part military humiliation, part civilian destitution, drew Hoover into the maelstrom of relief politics. With the Red Cross unwilling or unable to come to his country's aid, Poland's ambassador to Washington, Count Jerzy Potocki, appealed to the former president, whose earlier crusades to feed war-torn Europe had made him something of a folk hero. Hoover agreed to do what he could, then turned to familiar faces from the old CRB. His own participation, he told them, should be as low-key as possible. Anything else risked attacks from the New Deal. On September 25, 1939, the Commission for Polish Relief came into being. It sent emissaries to Berlin and Warsaw, determined priority needs and identified ghettoes crowded with underfed children, set up canteens to distribute 200,000 meals a day, and supplied both clothing and food to the Polish government-in-exile. Until Hitler's invasion of Norway in April 1940, Hoover's men shipped supplies to Sweden and then on to Hamburg or Danzig. The new escalation in fighting forced a change of route, involving ships bound for Genoa or Lisbon, and a long rail passage into the beleaguered war zone.[11]

Hoover assured a packed Madison Square Garden on October 11 that Poland would rise yet again from the ashes of war. "There is more to nations than their soil, their cities, their wealth, and even their governments," he said. "There is a soul in a great people. . . . It is steeled in their sufferings. They may be occupied by armies; they may be oppressed; they may be enslaved; they may be impoverished. But the soul of a great people cannot be crushed." At such gatherings in New York, Chicago and other centers with substantial Polish-American populations, the former president and his colleagues raised more than a million dollars.

It wasn't the only challenge confronting the hastily improvised CPR. Once more, friction between Hoover's men and the Red Cross threatened to become public knowledge. Early in December 1939, the Soviet Union invaded tiny Finland. On the fifth of that month, Hoover received word that Finnish leaders hoped he would raise a fund to help their war casualties. The next day, he gave a favorable response, influenced no doubt by his contempt for Moscow as well as his admiration for the hardy Finns, virtually unique in faithfully meeting payments on their World War I debt. He called Norman Davis, asked if the Red Cross had any plans to undertake Finnish relief, and promised support if they did. Davis denied his own organization's capacity to feed the Finns, and Hoover suggested splitting responsibility fifty-fifty. Davis said it was against Red Cross policy to join in any drive not exclusively its own. Hoover then read a proposed statement soliciting public support for both funds, existing and proposed.[12]

On December 7, he went public with a request for Finnish aid. Within two hours of his arrival in New York, he was rejecting a quiet office at a makeshift headquarters for a cubbyhole in a noisy room shared with two dozen typists. "This is where things are going on," he explained, "and this is where I can be most easily reached, so this is where I shall be." In Washington, the administration was nearly as quick to respond. To his Cabinet, the president expressed displeasure with Davis for having abandoned the relief field to Hoover. What Davis needed, said FDR, was a good publicity man, a vacuum he was personally trying to fill. Meanwhile, friendly columnists, including Drew Pearson, Jay Franklin and Raymond Clapper, were suggesting in print that Hoover's interest in relief was less than met the eye. Roosevelt's press secretary Steve Early fanned the flames with a statement on the thirteenth, recounting the president's invitation to Hoover to become "general manager" of the U.S. relief activities at the start of the fighting. New stories began to circulate: Hoover might replace Davis at the Red Cross; Davis's ouster was Hoover's price for participating in any relief campaign. To quiet the wagging tongues and busy typewriters, the former president deputized Larry Richey to show the Washington critics his complete correspondence with Davis.[13]

Nor was that all. In New York, an angry Hoover pounded his desk as he denounced those "out to poison the wells of charity." Their insinuations didn't hurt him, he went on, but they might cause serious harm to Finnish Relief and the Red Cross. He hoped that the press itself might ferret out the source of such malicious tales and investigate their validity. For once, a wave of journalistic sympathy came to his rescue. The New York Journal American assailed what it called "shoddy politics," including a group of Democratic governors who were withholding support from Hoover's organization after obtaining "private advice" from Washington. For the Baltimore Sun, Frank Kent composed an article entitled "A Smear That Failed." One did not have to like Hoover or agree with his politics, wrote Kent, to feel anger at those who would belittle his current relief activities. Given Hoover's key role in forming the Finnish republic twenty years earlier, and the

warm reception awarded the old war hero on his 1938 visit there, the facts
as Kent interpreted them refuted those out to malign a man who for ten
years had tasted opprobrium.

Newsweek went further still, dismissing the earlier overtures from Roosevelt as of at least questionable authenticity. "Few administrations in American history," the magazine judged, "ever went to greater lengths to smear a
predecessor than this one." Little wonder that Hoover might regard as
fraudulent a sudden peace offering, "particularly at a time when President
Roosevelt was making considerable capital of the so-called national nonpartisan front."

The tempest quieted, and Hoover pressed forward. He startled his old
friend Hugh Gibson with word of a peace feeler from Hitler, delivered
through the German consul in San Francisco. Gibson urged extreme caution. In any event, now that the Finnish relief campaign was under way,
there was an avalanche of work to keep the former president busy in New
York. From the fourth floor of the Graybar Building, at 420 Lexington
Avenue, Hoover and his staff issued a stream of requests and exhortations.
Correspondence alone kept a contingent of volunteers working until three
o'clock most mornings. Their chief typically was in his office by nine-thirty
(having already convened a working breakfast), ready to begin a series of
conferences that might last until the dinner hour. At noon, box lunches
were sent in, and questions from the labor or women's economic divisions
settled over sandwiches and pie. The simple meal gobbled, Hoover leaned
back. "What's on your mind today?" he would ask.[14]

There was no shortage of replies. Something had to be done to find
gainful employment for a flood of volunteers. There were fourteen hundred
newspapers to solicit, not only for their editorial support but also for their
willingness to serve as collection agencies for relief contributions. There
were benefits to arrange and attend—Washington's flamboyant hostess Ev-
alyn Walsh McLean bought out the entire theater when *Gone With the Wind*
first opened in the capital, and Tallulah Bankhead that same evening raced
around demanding money with which to purchase guns for Finland. Ordinarily reticent in the face of photographers who demanded publicity shots,
Hoover dutifully posed with a man dressed in a Popeye costume, part of the
Hearst syndicate's campaign to promote itself as well as the Finns. The
world's foremost spinach eater had a decidedly informal greeting. "Hiya
Herb," he said as the flashbulbs went off. More welcome was actress Gertrude Lawrence, who showed up at the Graybar Building wearing huge fur
mittens. "Well, Mr. Hoover," she explained, "I wore my boxing gloves. I
don't know whether I needed them or not." Charmed by the British musical

star, Hoover was sufficiently appealing himself that Lou ordered extra copies of the final print. It was, she said, the best picture ever taken of her husband, with a rare look of spontaneous mirth on his face.[15]

The whole experience seemed to revive him. Grim as the work of relief might be, it was a puritan's tonic, something outside the treacherous ground of domestic politics. But even a moralist could keep a sense of humor. Before a rally at Madison Square Garden, the former president was met by a group of New York sportswriters, one of whom promptly introduced himself by recalling a 1932 rally "when the whole crowd booed you and set up a chant, 'We want beer.' What do you think about that?"

"It was a good ballgame, wasn't it?" Hoover replied. When the meeting ended, he told Hearst columnist Bob Considine that he might have done better in life had he known sportswriters earlier in his career.[16]

By then, the same Norman Davis who had earlier turned thumbs down on a joint fund-raising effort was asking Hoover for a status report. Told that money was coming in pretty well, he expressed pleasure. "I want to get some of it," he informed Hoover, who complained that Red Cross chapters in some states were attempting to block his campaign altogether. He had 600,000 Finns on rations, said the former president, "and it is just keeping me humping." In more elegant language, he pleaded with Congress to appropriate $50 million for European relief. It was, noted reporters, the first time Hoover had set foot on Capitol Hill since March 4, 1933. That same day, he met with Secretary of State Hull, the two men privately disparaging Finland's less-than-reliable ambassador to the United States.[17]

A month later, he confided to Davis that Polish relief could not continue much longer unless he received $5 million immediately from the government-in-exile. With such funds at his disposal, he insisted, ships loaded with relief supplies might set off for Europe within a week. And Hoover admitted that it was useless to rely on public giving. "The whole thing," he told Davis, "should be on donations from governments."[18]

That same month of March 1940, Finland surrendered before the Russian onslaught. Hundreds of thousands of her people were expelled from Finnish territory now ceded to Stalin. Hailing the "heroic defense" doomed from its start, Hoover promised to continue assistance, now more than ever required by fatherless children and hungry families. Finland had set an example that must not be forgotten. Subjected to unspeakable aggression from the east, its people had fought nonetheless, bravely and against impossible odds. "A star has risen which lights the No-Man's Land of civilization," Hoover said in his eulogy of the Finnish republic. "Its glow will light the minds of men and women and give hope to liberty for a thousand years to come."

He continued funneling what aid he could through a distant war zone. At the start of the Polish relief operation, Hoover had negotiated through the German embassy in Washington a non-aggression pact of his own. Mindful of his global reputation, the Germans even guaranteed the safety of neutral vessels from submarine attack. In London, the Chamberlain ministry was similarly cooperative. Then came the Nazi attack on Norway and Denmark, the invasion of France, the collapse of Chamberlain's government, and the belated recognition of Winston Churchill. The latest development held no appeal for Hoover. The new prime minister, he wrote afterward "was a militarist of the extreme school who held that incidental starvation of women and children was justified if it contributed to . . . victory." Memories rankled, of Churchill holding out against Belgian relief in 1914, and of the long, discouraging struggle to commit Herbert Asquith's government to at least tacit support for the CRB.[19]

As if to confirm Hoover's fears, Churchill let it be known that no relief vessels would be permitted to reach a continent in temporary thrall to Nazi tyranny. "Let Hitler bear the responsibilities to the full," he told the House of Commons in August 1940 (the same month Noël Coward tried for two hours to persuade Hoover to abandon his relief efforts) "and let the peoples of Europe who groan beneath his yoke aid in every way the coming of the day when that yoke will be broken. . . ." Hoover's rationale for Finnish relief was keyed to a higher pitch. Unless peace could be achieved soon, he told a reporter in January 1940, a long war was inevitable. "And it will be a war such as the world has never witnessed." Thus far, American emotions had been restrained. But self-control might easily crumble under the weight of horrors bound to ensue. In helping Finland, he maintained, "we are supplying an outlet for feelings which might well otherwise lead us into war."[20]

As aid to Poland diminished to a trickle, and Finland counted its losses, Hoover looked for fresh outlets of his own. The day after his Washington conference with Hull, he reported to a dubious Rickard that the New York Herald Tribune would soon endorse him for the presidency. He pointed to newspaper polls to buttress his claims of popular support, responded angrily when longtime supporters like his friend Jerry Milbank advised against his candidacy, and crafted strategy with the likes of Frank Knox and former national party chairman Will Hays. Hoover's suite at the Waldorf became a frenzy of calculation, trial balloon raising, and stubborn resistance to fact. A friendly journalist reported at the end of February that Dewey's groundswell was astonishing. The GOP was "insane," wired radio commentator Boake Carter, if it failed to heed the message from its own ground forces.[21]

Yet within a week, Hoover claimed no consensus for any one contender. On the contrary, he insisted, most Republicans wanted an open convention in Philadelphia. Concerning his own plans he was coy, telling a group of legislators in Washington, "about the 24th of May I probably would begin to think about the subject." In mid-April, he rejoiced over the continuing Dewey-Simpson feud in New York, and a new poll suggesting Dewey slippage in his own bailiwick. "Just as the fever blew over in Minnesota," he went on, "so it has blown over in Oregon, where I am informed the delegation has not a single Dewey man on it." [22]

Clearly, Hoover was not waiting until May 24 to ponder his own course of action. In his hands, he held a survey of expert opinion, showing Dewey and Bob Taft running neck and neck among Republican delegates, with himself staking out a beachhead of a dozen or so, easily expandable on succeeding ballots. Out of this emerged a strategy: foster a deadlock and wait for delegates of faltering loyalty to their first choice to turn Hoover's way—most likely after the third ballot. A very similar game-plan was laid out by a still more unlikely contender, the utilities president, business champion and former Democrat named Wendell Willkie. Had he seen a letter Willkie wrote on April 8, Hoover might have easily dismissed the charismatic Hoosier. "I agree with you that Hoover is the ablest man in the country," Willkie informed his correspondent, "and should be our next President." Events would endow his words with a bitter irony. [23]

Spring came to America, a land still applauding a peace taking its final bows. Even before the Nazi invasion of the Low Countries on May 10, 1940, some Republicans who shared Hoover's alarm or coveted his experience began shifting their loyalties. A poll of Landon supporters from 1936 put the former president in third place among GOP contenders, behind Dewey and Vandenburg, ahead of Taft and Wendell Willkie. His newfound prominence as director of Finnish relief played a part in Hoover's resurgence. So did a vacuum within the party, glaringly evident as Europe's war intensified and both Dewey and Taft competed for isolationist votes. Only too delighted with his new status, Hoover pulled strings and devised scenarios. He passed word to Vandenburg that he should make a couple of nationwide speeches late in May; the Michigan senator might yet rebound from crushing losses to Dewey in Wisconsin and Nebraska. Ken Simpson offered his hand if not his heart in a stop-Dewey movement, whose existence Hoover urged the New York Herald Tribune to deny editorially. [24]

Professing noncandidacy, Hoover at the start of May mailed a barrage of speeches to delegates from Minnesota, Wisconsin and the Dakotas. The German march into Holland and Belgium, he predicted on May 11, would focus unflattering attention on Dewey's youth and lack of international experience. Regarding Willkie, as unorthodox a candidate as ever sought a major party nomination, the former president was incredulous. Wall Street's hero might enjoy backing from a number of Dewey's erstwhile financial angels, he wrote, but "I cannot conceive that it will get anywhere in a convention." Two weeks later, Harrison Spangler was warning his friend of "extreme internationalists centered in the lower part of New York City" who were moving heaven and earth to secure Willkie's nomination. This time, Hoover accepted Spangler's facts. By the time he lunched with Dewey on June 4, his earlier resentment of the aggressive Gangbuster was diluted by the new threat. A few weeks before, he regarded any appeasement of Dewey's followers as an exercise in crocodile feeding. Now, united in their fear of a common foe, the two men were temporarily reconciled.[25]

For all his private ambitions, Hoover remained diffident to political organization. The convention was less than two weeks away by the time he finally named Perrin Galpin to gather information on the thousand delegates who would anoint the party's new standard-bearer in their Philadelphia conclave. Edgar Rickard noted a swarm of Hoover volunteers beseeching the amateurs around the former president for ways to advance his cause; "terribly at loose ends" was Rickard's charitable description of Hoover's supportive network. Behind the scenes, Rickard's friend went on collecting data, on the war, on Roosevelt's political ambitions, on the new Churchill government in London and the prospects for American intervention on its side. He conspired with Taft to "keep the pot boiling in good shape" by preventing Dewey supporters in Oklahoma from invoking the state's unit rule. (He dismissed as "pre-convention stuff" a report that the Ohioan wished him to serve as his Secretary of State, and noted that other Cabinet slots "are being unusually well-distributed.") He listened as Charles Lindbergh insisted on May 25 that the Allies would surrender to Hitler within two weeks. He accepted an invitation from his party's national committee —seconded by Ken Simpson—to address the forthcoming convention. And all the while, like Mr. Micawber, he waited for something to turn up.[26]

Nineteen forty for Hoover was to be a rerun of 1920 and 1936. The same fatal streak of passivity, rooted in his own disdain for the political trenches, further distorted by misjudgment of the popular mood and its apparent softening toward his administration, led him once more to calculate the movements of a shadow army. John L. Lewis told Hoover he could count on his support. But what influence could a militant labor chieftain like Lewis wield at a Republican convention? The former president moved to patch up his tattered relations with Landon, advising convention managers to reserve a place on the speaker's platform for the 1936 nominee. But Landon was irreconcilable, and leaning toward Dewey anyway. Indeed, on the Friday before Joe Martin slammed down the opening gavel, Hoover discovered from Lewis that the Kansan was furtively seeing Burton Wheeler in Baltimore, investigating the likelihood of Democrat Burton accepting the GOP nod for vice president. There were friendly delegates to reach in Massachusetts and Ohio, Georgia and Tennessee, according to Hoover's friends. Later, it would be estimated that 150 to 200 such potential allies were on the floor of the convention hall, lying or hiding in wait for the moment when they might throw off their previously stated preferences and launch a blitzkrieg for Hoover. New York's Ruth Pratt went so far as to stash banners and placards in the basement of the Bellevue-Stratford Hotel, in readiness for the coming battle.[27]

Yet the general would not command. He offered a terse "no comment" when asked by a Philadelphia newspaper on the convention's second day if he would accept the nomination. "I do not believe in 2 o'clock conferences," he replied, after asserting confidence in open deliberations. To the end, he denied his own candidacy. Candidates gave themselves away, he told reporters, by their constant stumping, their open solicitation of popular support and their tolerance for what he called "whoopee at the convention." Uncommunicative as he was on the subject of politics, Hoover had plenty to say about Europe. The totalitarian countries "have already won the war on the continent," he said, little more than a week after France's humiliating capitulation to Hitler. Yet Hoover opposed compulsory military training for the sons of America. Raising his voice in competition with a passing band on Broad Street, the coy candidate urged construction of a new tariff wall around the Western Hemisphere. He criticized President Roosevelt's characterization of Italy's entry into the war as a "dagger in the back" and revealed his own private contacts with Germany, Britain and Belgium in an effort to avert mass starvation in the Flemish kingdom.

Just as he had four years earlier, the former president hoped to galvanize the delegates with a spectacular display of speechmaking. Two weeks before the convention opened, Hoover was asking for help from friends "as it is an occasion that may be of great importance to the American people." But when he rose to deliver an eloquent appeal for salvation from "totalitarian liberals" who threatened to extinguish liberty's lamp overseas, and warn his own countrymen that America could not forever exist "two-thirds workers and one-third dependents," the effect of his oratorical crashing symbols was muted by a sound system almost certainly tampered with by Connecticut's Sam Pryor. As chairman of the arrangements committee and an open

Willkie supporter, Pryor had well-developed plans for his own dark horse. As if Hoover didn't have enough grudges to nurse, Pryor added another by packing the galleries on Willkie's behalf—a historic achievement inadvertently proven when the printer's bill was sent to Larry Richey by mistake. For the moment, Hoover was too busy railing against friends to devote much attention to his enemies. Helen Reid wrote to defend her newspaper's embrace of Willkie. In doing so, she ransacked her memory to link diplomatically two men so dissimilar in the public's sight.[28]

"You were not the machine politicians' choice in your first campaign," she told Hoover on the day after his failed address. "You had had no legislative officeholding experience. There was distrust of your party conviction, your party allegiance. You could have been nominated by Democrats or Republicans—so they said at the time. You had the support of business."[29]

Inside convention hall, the heat, the noise, and the pulsing rumors added up to bedlam. Little appeared certain; anything seemed possible. On the first ballot of voting for a nominee, Hoover won a sprinkling of votes, but as tally followed tally, hoped-for support in Nebraska, Idaho and other delegations failed to break his way. Instead, Willkie and Taft battled each other for the dwindling ranks of Dewey delegates. On Thursday, the twenty-seventh, with his own hopes dependent on a deadlock, Hoover talked by phone with a frantic Dewey. He could not now enter the fray in good conscience, he told the New Yorker, whose own candidacy was rapidly evaporating. Dewey himself later recalled an admonitory Hoover telling him to stand fast against the Willkie onslaught. The former president's forces were reaching out to the Taft camp as well, hoping to adjourn the convention after the third ballot, which effectively ended Dewey's chances and narrowed the contest to Taft, Willkie and Hoover. Clarence Kellington, the Chief's Bohemian Grove campmate, sought out Dave Ingalls, Taft's cousin who was also his convention manager. Would Ingalls commit himself to adjournment? Ingalls would not. By the time other spokesmen for Taft were ready to agree to such a motion, chairman Joe Martin—himself pledged to Willkie—delighted the obstreperous galleries by overruling it.[30]

Four thousand "Draft Hoover" buttons disappeared within two hours of their display in a Philadelphia hotel lobby. Political operatives still hoped to swing New York City delegates away from Dewey. But the galleries persisted in chanting Willkie's name, backed by a flood of supportive telegrams. Hoover himself received hundreds, part of a potent mix of journalistic pressure and eastern money. And so, early on Friday, June twenty-eighth, the Republican party meeting in convention at Philadelphia endorsed the claims of Wendell Willkie, erstwhile Democrat, Tammany brave, utilities executive and Roosevelt partisan. In the galleries Lewis Strauss stopped distributing Hoover buttons and surrendered to tears. Strauss recognized his hero's last chance to be president. So did Hoover. Whatever his own emotions, he behaved manfully in public. He wired congratulations to Willkie on "the result of a free convention in a free people." And to friends who offered consolation on this latest crushing blow, Hoover sounded a note beyond resignation. Perhaps he felt a burden lifted when he wrote: [31]

"There are things in the world that cannot be brought about. There are mistakes that cannot be repaired. But there is one thing sure—that loyalty and friendship are the most precious possessions a man can have. You have given it to me unreservedly, but it is my wealth and you make it." [32]

Hoover being a stranger to serenity, his forbearance was not likely to last. Nothing would test it more severely than his own party's presidential candidate.

★   ★

For Hoover, frustrated in attempts to feed the Poles and Finns, still more alarmed at the ominous drift of events that included the first peacetime draft, stiff U.S. warnings against Japanese movements in French Indochina, and a growing convoy of arms and aircraft to beleaguered Britain, the 1940 campaign was a legitimate crusade. (At one point, he even made the slightly fantastic suggestion to Chief Justice Hughes that he should resign his seat on the bench and take to the hustings on Willkie's behalf.) Yet Hoover's brand of evangelism was not in demand among the youthful irregulars who gathered under Willkie's banner. The nominee himself seemed cordial, if slightly confused about the myriad details that must be mastered overnight if he was to translate personal charisma into a campaign leading to victory against the opponent Willkie himself called the Champ.

Hoover's suspicions fed on those surrounding the candidate, from Sam Pryor and *Fortune* magazine's Russell Davenport, to Henry Luce and the Reids. They were further stoked by a flood of letters bemoaning the death of what one correspondent called "the Republican Party as we have known it." But more than balancing his own precarious position within the GOP was a barrage of Democratic grapeshot. Alben Barkley sounded the dominant theme in his speech keynoting the convention that renominated FDR for an unprecedented third term. "We inherited chaos eight years ago," said Barkley on July 16. "We inherited fear, which was almost universal. We inherited lack of confidence. . . . The American people had been led to the brink of precipice by the fallacies of a smug and blind regime, which found itself impotent to draw back or to avert the disaster which it had contrived."

Mentioning Hoover repeatedly by name, Barkley likened his administration to "that backward flying bird which never knows where it is going but can only see where it has been."[33]

It was obvious that Roosevelt and his party intended to make him their central target, Hoover remarked soon after, "first to build up the usual false comparisons of revolution marching, etc. by the usual lying campaign; and second, to make Willkie think he better be free of political lepers and the Republican Party, and thus drive away Republicans in this campaign. These are the same tactics as used with Landon." Personally, he had dispatched three messages to the candidate from his Oregon fishing camp, without a reply. "I am willing to do whatever they want to help get Blum out of Washington," he confided, in a derisive comparison of Roosevelt and France's ineffective socialist leader, Léon Blum. "But I need to know direct if they want it and when." He had no intention of "imposing myself on anybody," he told another friend early in August. Yet his appetite for combat was undisguised.[34]

Less apparent were Willkie's own intentions. From Colorado Springs, where the candidate was vacationing, filtered word that he not only wished to have a personal conference, but that he agreed with much of Hoover's critique of administration foreign policy. According to Charles Halleck, who had placed Willkie's name in nomination at Philadelphia and remained on close terms with him, the affable Hoosier was anxious to aid the British "within the law as it exists . . . and within the rules of international law." This was all well and good from Halleck's standpoint, but the public was unlikely to learn of it unless the candidate found the right forum in which to publicize his cautious views. Hoover's friends thought they had the perfect solution—a face-to-face meeting between the two men. Halleck acted as intermediary, and on August 12, Hoover arrived at Willkie's retreat, a salesman for the kind of frontal assault on Roosevelt's policies that Landon avoided and most of Willkie's own close advisers were counseling against.[35]

The meeting did not go well. Impulsive as always, Willkie took the occasion of Elliott Roosevelt's presence nearby to invite the president's son to join him for pictures. An irate Hoover did little to conceal his displeasure. Only slightly more encouraging were the candidate's vague plans to involve the former president in his campaign. Hoover would be making "some major talks," Willkie told reporters, who later discovered that they would number no more than two or three at the most. Hoover himself told Edgar Rickard that he was satisfied with his party's presidential candidate, a man of immense charm and equal candor, but dismayed at the organizational chaos engulfing the infant campaign. He made a number of suggestions, he revealed to another colleague, none of which were accepted. One involved Joe Martin, as green a recruit in national political wars as Willkie himself. Another concerned the contentious presence of hundreds of Willkie Clubs, spontaneous chapters of amateurs who clashed with the senior party structure and promoted disunity in a campaign already notorious for dishevelment. From the speechwriters' car—dubbed the Squirrel Cage—to the candidate's own penchant for nonstop oratory, Willkie's cross-country tour would assume legendary dimensions. Few who traveled with the rumpled candidate ever forgot the excitement, or the frustration generated by his restless, grab-bag mind.[36]

"Only the strong can be productive," he liked to shout, "and only the productive can be free." But Willkie's strategy of accepting most of the New Deal, while faulting Roosevelt for excessive claims to executive power and unceasing hostility to free enterprise, disappointed many of his original backers. Hoover himself advised the candidate to ignore talk of a September slump. It "is always the month of grouches and complaints," he cautioned, before urging similar proportion in assessing the loyalties of "highly emotional saviors of the world"—this at a time when some of Willkie's most prominent journalistic supporters, Walter Lippmann and Dorothy Thompson among them, fell by the wayside over the candidate's shift from his outspoken internationalism. When Roosevelt announced a deal swapping fifty aged destroyers for British bases in the Western Hemisphere, the former president could only fault the methods used to consummate the deal. He wished that Congress had been consulted. But as for the bases themselves, Hoover pronounced himself "very glad" over this acquisition. Privately, he was less sanguine about the president's policies toward the Japanese. Economic reprisals limiting Tokyo's access to scrap iron and octane gas, wrote Hoover, were deliberately "sticking a pin in a rattlesnake."[37]

New friction arose with the party organization in Washington. Hoover wondered if Joe Martin would allocate him funds to make a radio address on behalf of the GOP ticket. On September 12, he listened as Tom Dewey complained of being similarly ignored. Rickard noted his friend's growing anger at being denied permission to speak. Soon, Hoover was seriously contemplating a public break with Willkie. The candidate compounded the split when he failed to phone the former president during a day-long visit to New York City on the twenty-eighth. In frustration, Hoover appealed directly to the campaign train. Willkie replied the next day, confirming "my very urgent request" for three Hoover speeches, and promising to secure financial backing from the national committee. Relations improved somewhat, to the point where Hoover dashed off a fatherly letter to the candidate, warning him against overexertion. He wrote, said Hoover, "not . . . in a spirit of criticism but in one of anxiety for you." His cause was too important to permit local functionaries to sap his strength or silence his already hoarse, croaking voice.[38]

Willkie answered with gratitude for Hoover's concern, reassured the older man that he felt fine and promised to take a fresh look at his schedule. For Hoover himself, fresh indignities arose almost daily. He rebuked *New York Times* publisher Arthur Sulzberger for printing an inordinate number of letters spreading lies about earlier relief to Belgium. Alerted that Mrs. Florence Harriman carried a request for Hoover to help occupied Norway survive the coming winter, he rushed up to her in a restaurant and assumed he could count on her support in fighting the British blockade. But he was wrong; Mrs. Harriman had already been to the White House, where Roosevelt won her over by describing the blockade as Britain's first line of defense. Party officials in Connecticut did not want him to speak for the ticket in the Nutmeg State. Alexander Woollcott found humor in the ex-president's membership alongside Booth Tarkington, Rex Beach, Ida Tarbell and others on a writers' committee supporting Willkie. After reading the chairman's rebuke to Woollcott, reciting Hoover's literary activities from Agricola on, the former president and sometime author pronounced himself delighted with this education "of the ill-read and ill-bred." He was informed by Russ Davenport that, in common with other Republican speakers, he should lavish praise on Willkie rather than "slam the New Deal." And in his own state of California, Hoover was forced to read the candidate's handsome tribute to Hiram Johnson—and endure his embarrassing silence when it came time to mention the state's only president. Even Johnson was outraged.[39]

When he finally did deliver three speeches for Willkie, late in October, Hoover received a warm response. The candidate himself wired congratulations on a pungent Columbus, Ohio, address, attacking the third term and questioning the long-range implications of Roosevelt's acquired powers. Just as encouraging was the praise lavished by his old friend Mark Sullivan ("It was," wrote Sullivan, "an unanticipated and highly agreeable experience to hear an audience laugh at practically every second or third sentence of a speech by Herbert Hoover"). A few days later, Hoover scored again, denouncing the president's foreign policy before a Lincoln, Nebraska, audience. America's moral influence was being undermined, said Hoover, by FDR's practice of scolding foreign powers. Far from deserving another term on the basis of his global competence, Roosevelt should be retired as the mastermind behind the wrecking of the London Economic Conference, the fiasco of Geneva's disarmament talks, the extension of recognition to Moscow, and the incendiary policies pursued since Munich. A third and final address at Salt Lake City on November 1 reiterated old themes of domestic coercion and economic malaise.[40]

Willkie himself pronounced the speeches "masterpieces." He was "deeply grateful" for the former president's timely assistance, he assured him. They may, in fact, have helped the GOP nominee solidify his support in the isolationist Midwest. But they also presented Roosevelt with an irresistible bull's-eye. Stung by Willkie's counterattack, the self-professed "old campaigner" struck back in Philadelphia late in the campaign—not at Willkie, but at the shadowy figure already a receding memory for many younger voters. FDR wished to jog their recollections. "The tears, the crocodile tears, for the laboring man and laboring woman now being shed in this campaign come from those same Republican leaders who had their chance to prove their love for labor in 1932—and missed it. Back in 1932," the president continued, "these leaders were willing to let the workers starve if they could not get a job. Back in 1932, they were not willing to guarantee collective bargaining. Back in 1932, they met the demands of unemployed veterans with troops and tanks."[41]

And on it went, a magnificent piece of political irrelevance, perfectly timed to electrify laggard partisans and tar Willkie with the Hoover brush. The Roosevelt tide crested on Election Day, November 5, carrying the incumbent to a five-million-vote margin over his challenger and renewing Hoover's lease in purgatory. In the aftermath, Hoover asked his reporter friend Paul Smith, who had traveled aboard the Willkie train, for some insights into the defeated candidate. Smith echoed the general line that Willkie was personally attractive, although without intellectual depth or philosophical background. What's more, according to Smith, the vanquished nominee was "obsessed" with the notion of his own liberalism. "Altogether," Hoover noted of the conversation, "it was not a pleasant picture."[42]

A week later, the former president lunched with Willkie himself. The two men spent most of their time discussing war fever, Hoover asserting the inevitable collapse of democracy should the United States enter the fighting, Willkie agreeing that aid to the British ought to be limited to financial support. Emphatically, Hoover said that the Churchill government must be told how far Washington would go, since the battlefronts themselves suggested at best a stalemate and the British held out only through hope that Roosevelt would rescue them. (Hoover had no patience with those like William Allen White, whose pro-British activities, in his view, prolonged the fighting, and drained off financial support for his own stalled campaign to feed occupied Europe. White asked the former president what he might do to be helpful. "All I want of you folks is to keep your damned mouth shut!" was Hoover's blunt response.) Predicting a Nazi invasion of Russia, he said only its date was in question and repeated his assertion that the British "if they could get that through their thick heads" might yet be able to salvage their Empire.[43]

Willkie mentioned Roosevelt's efforts to lure him to Washington, ostensibly to discuss the situation with Hull and other members of the Cabinet. Hoover warned against any negotiating with "No. 2 men." Simultaneously, he cited his own experience after the 1932 election to justify extreme caution in any dealings with FDR personally. Willkie should have "two or three honest men" present in the room as protection against "a mass of smearing liars." The conversation ended on a typically forthright note, Hoover pointing out that his guest ran far behind his party in most states. "If you follow the pea around among the four shells," was the way he put it to Mark Sullivan, "I think you will at least come to the conclusion that Mr. Willkie failed to secure a large section of the Regular Republican vote." As in the past, the implication of insufficient loyalty to Republican—i.e., Hooverian—principles, was less than subtle.[44]

In Washington, Roosevelt expressed concern over Hoover's campaign to inflame public sympathy for the conquered democracies of Europe and against the British blockade that prevented them from obtaining outside food. "Ever so many thanks," he wrote Thomas Lamont on November 29 after Lamont assured him in private conference that he would, in Ickes's phrasing, "do whatever he could to keep Hoover in control." As for himself, the president told Lamont, he was confident Hoover's crusade would "fall of its own weight, especially if you are able to carry out your wise plan of letting condensed milk into France. . . ." Ickes himself couldn't resist tacking on an explanation of his own. "There must be something," he jotted in his diary, "to the report that Hoover has always hated England."[45]

★   ★

Willkie's defeat marked a turning point in Hoover's life. Had the result been different, he would have returned to Washington, and the S Street residence he and Lou had occupied during happier times. Now, he decided to sell the house and take a permanent suite of rooms at the Waldorf beginning in December 1940. Henceforth, Hoover's address was Suite 31-A in the Waldorf Towers, fourteen floors of elegant accommodations set aside for full-time residents of the hotel, including the Windsors, the future Queen Juliana of the Netherlands, the Shah of Iran, as well as the royalty of New York's sophisticated entertainment world. Cole Porter spent the last thirty years of his life in the Towers. Elsa Maxwell staged a burlesque ball in the Empire Room, complete with stripteasers and vaudeville acts from Broadway's knockabout hit *Hellzapoppin*.[46]

The Waldorf was a self-contained community, whose citizens could eat plovers' eggs or drink champagne at $66 a bottle, dance in the Astor Gallery or be paged by one of 155 operators, be protected by a small army of security men or greeted at an East Side dock by a member of the hotel's protocol-conscious foreign department.

The Waldorf supplied interpreters conversant in dozens of languages. Its 200 cooks prepared chicken in 71 ways. On the nineteenth floor, a white-tiled "home kitchen" served up all-American dishes, much preferred by Hoover. When he tired of hotel cooking, he told guests, he liked to send out to the nearest Horn and Hardart for some baked beans. Nothing flattered his palate like corn bread and beans.[47]

His own suite consisted of four rooms, one of which was occupied by his secretaries, up to five in all. He was careful to introduce the women to visiting dignitaries. "I was his first experiment," New Jersey Governor Charles Edison informed one of the women who was unaware of his famous parent. In an adjoining room Hoover sat at a desk, furnished with a telephone and ashtray, and flanked by tall windows overlooking Manhattan's towering profile. During a blackout, one guest climbed thirty-one flights of stairs only to find the former president still at his desk, toiling with the help of two searchlights. In one drawer was a box of cigars. Another box was filled with Hoover's "hairshirts," disagreeable subjects hidden away until such time as he felt like dealing with them, and still another was crammed with the change he staked in ferocious games of canasta. Here he convened informal meetings of Stanford trustees or the Boys Clubs directorate. Here he scribbled away most of each day, fortified by a simple lunch of lamb stew or goulash. The hotel supplied him with a waiter, and Hoover told Daniel Rodriguez that he was now a member of the family and thus entitled to call him Chief. He asked Rodriguez about his family, his work history and his wages. Discovering that the man was supporting a family of four on sixty dollars a month, Hoover raised his own payment, and encouraged guests to be similarly generous.[48]

During the Christmas season, one room of the suite was dubbed "the Commissary" for the food and liquor which poured in from friends and admirers. A small maid's room was "the Black Hole of Calcutta," reserved for ornaments and sets of Hoover's memoirs, gifts of which he was apt to make whenever a boy or girl wrote asking him to interpret some historical development for them. As a cherished part of a vast correspondence, such letters were awarded priority treatment. The former president enjoyed writing out longhand replies to children in the middle of the night, a welcomed substitute for sleeping pills. Each December, Hoover's desk gave way to a tree, always immense, which he liked to dress with an engineer's precision. Occupying an armchair, he reminded one regular in 31-A of Molière directing the Comédie-Française, directing the handing of tinsel in spirals rather than loops. "You go against nature if you loop it," he explained. Lou had a party for hotel employees. It was her pleasure, she told Daniel Rodriguez, to wait on him for a change. Christmas Eve was marked by a special dinner party, followed the next morning by a well-organized ritual of unwrapping, note-taking, ribbon-saving and exclamations of delight or dismay, depending on the presence of macadamia nuts or bad cigars in the mountain of packages. For his secretaries, the day brought presents of stocks or jewelry, complementing Hoover's practice of splitting checks he received for articles with the women whose research he held to be indispensable. Likewise, each August 10 Hoover donated a raft of birthday cakes to the Waldorf's telephone operators and elevator men.[49]

His new home was a comfortable base of operations for the man whose thinning gray hair and bushy eyebrows provided the only apparent testimony to advanced age. He liked to attend the Oldtimers Game at Yankee Stadium or root for Branch Rickey's Dodgers. When in need of fresh air, Hoover simply donned a hat—he was rarely glimpsed bareheaded—and strolled two miles up Park Avenue, then down Fifth. He admired new styles in fashion and architecture, just as he startled a journalist one day by rhapsodizing over such technological discoveries as the atom smasher, the electron microscope and the cathode ray tube. Even Lou managed to adapt to big city life, where her practical knack was put to advantage. Friends calling for dinner one night were surprised not to see her at the door. "She's there," her husband explained, "under the table . . . a light went out, and she knows all about these things so I let her fix them." Without missing a beat, the former First Lady climbed to her feet and said, "How do you do?"[50]

Hoover enjoyed his newfound proximity to newsmakers. In addition to reading a host of papers, the former president listened each evening to Ray Henle's "Three Star Final" on NBC, followed by commentator Fulton J. Lewis at seven. Then came cocktails, dinner, canasta, and suddenly Hoover was walking his guests to the door. Once a week he strode a block to the Dutch Treat Club, where he could relax in exclusively masculine company and speak whatever was on his mind without fear of its being quoted outside. He was less partial to the University Club, even if it did provide him with unlimited library privileges and his own special blend of tobacco. Hoover quoted Lowell Thomas's observation that the University Club was so stuffy a man couldn't bring his mistress into its sacred precincts unless she was the wife of a member. Joining the board of the Waldorf himself in 1949, the former president mused over the irony of himself, a Quaker and the president who had enforced the Volstead Act, winding up overseeing "the biggest bar in the world."[51]

He started work on his memoirs, aided by Bunny Miller, a Stanford girl originally hired as a companion for Lou. Bunny was a tiny woman, handicapped since childhood by a riding accident, fiercely devoted to the Chief and almost maternal in her protective embrace. Once a week, she stuffed a suitcase full of his jottings and scrap paper, and accompanied a bellman to the Waldorf's incinerator. She refused to permit other secretaries serving her boss to take his picture or keep diaries. She ordered a colleague who purchased a black cloth to cover a bridge table to banish it at once; Hoover couldn't abide black. Ultimately, Miss Miller became a problem for the doctors who attended the former president in his final years. After twenty years of service, she was demoted to supervising Hoover's research activities. But if Bunny could be "a little czar," as recalled by some, she was also selfless in making Hoover's comfort and welfare synonymous with her own.[52]

Others, equally given to hero worship, began to hover around the Waldorf. Neil MacNeil, night editor for the New York Times, was one. H. V. Kaltenborn was another. Other journalists began appearing frequently, along with Jerry Milbank and his wife, Bill Nichols of This Week magazine, Richard Berlin of the Hearst organization, and the former president's son Allan. At the start of 1941, at least one familiar face departed the inner circle. He was through with active politics, Hoover informed Larry Richey. He would no longer require his professional services. A handsome financial settlement was arranged, the two men severed their twenty-year partnership, and remained intimate friends. Edgar Rickard became more than ever Hoover's sounding board, available at all hours, so it seemed, to hear the Chief's gloomy forecast of Britain's imminent defeat (in mid-March, he predicted her capitulation within sixty days) and eavesdrop on a motley collection of isolationist paragons, from Charles Lindbergh, whose intemperate remarks about Jewish influence disturbed the former president, to Joe Kennedy, who reported his own warning to FDR that "whatever aid you extend to Britain you must regard . . . as a bet on a losing horse."[53]

When Roosevelt proposed Lend-Lease early in 1941, permitting the British to augment their own dwindling stockpiles with U.S. military equipment, Hoover was enraged. As Robert Taft put it, "Lending war equipment

is a good deal like lending chewing gum. You don't want it back." Burton
Wheeler went further still, calling Lend-Lease the New Deal's "Triple A"
in foreign policy. It was, said Wheeler, the president's plan to plow under
every fourth American boy. Hoover confined his own anger to private conversations. Turning down the request of Robert Wood, founder of the isolationist group America First, to make a critical speech over the nation's
airwaves, Hoover said he was exerting himself "day and night" to try to kill
or water down the proposal. "At this moment," he concluded, "I think I
can do better to let the situation develop a little." He asked Tom Dewey,
unsuccessfully, to speak out against the idea in a cross-country tour. In
nearly constant communication with GOP leaders in Congress, he helped
line up other radio speakers who shared his aim of at least deleting the bill's
near-dictatorial powers.[54]

"The American people have been so fooled as to the purpose and character of this bill," he complained at the start of March 1941, "that there
remains no hope of adequately amending it. It is a war bill, yet 95% of the
people think it is only aid to Britain." But even "Boatman Roosevelt" might
soon find himself too far out in midstream to control the direction of his
vessel. And, Hoover guessed shrewdly, once the bill was passed, "we shall
hear the cry, 'Why provide all this material and have it sunk in the Atlantic?
We should convoy it with our navy!' Then we will have American boys
torpedoed," he continued, "and war is on."[55]

At the same time he fought the administration over Lend-Lease, Hoover
was seeking in vain any kind of favorable signal permitting his Committee
to Feed the Small Democracies to proceed with its relief plans for conquered
Belgium, Holland, Norway, Poland and Finland. In February 1941, he proposed a trial run—a network of soup kitchens in Belgium, with supplies
passing through the British blockade one ship at a time, and the Germans
supplying breadstuffs to go with the soup. He pleaded with Lord Halifax,
the new British ambassador, to allow the feeding of three million adults and
children. Halifax refused. There was already enough food in Europe, he told
Hoover; the problem lay in equal distribution. Furthermore, any food taken
into the area of invasion, no matter its purpose or amount, provided indirect
assistance to the enemy. Hoover tried every argument at his disposal—the
intellectual resistance of the small democracies to Nazi tyranny, the need to
lay a groundwork for post–Hitler Europe, American public opinion, the
disinclination of the Germans to reduce their own rations in order to feed
occupied nations. Nothing worked.[56]

Hoover was no more successful when he called later that month on
Secretary Hull at the State Department. Hull informed him that the Wehr-

macht was massing more than a million troops along the Russian border. An invasion of Greece appeared likely as soon as spring arrived. In the Far East, the Japanese were eager to annex a region stretching from Singapore to India. Only his own policies, Hull implied, were holding the warlords of Tokyo in check. When his turn to speak came around, Hoover explained his recent contacts with German authorities, who had permitted him to dispatch three observers into Belgium for a firsthand review of the food situation. Working through Hugh Gibson and the Belgium government, he had tried to apply moral pressure against the British Foreign Office. Ten to twenty million civilians might be saved, he insisted, if only 20,000 tons a month were allowed through the blockade immediately. The Germans had agreed to his plan; indeed, they already had provided an initial 80,000 tons of breadstuffs to Belgium. Hull seemed surprised at the attitude of the Belgian government. Concerning Hoover's project, he had little to say.[57]

A month later, following adoption of Lend-Lease, and Congress's mandate for a $7 billion armaments program, Hoover tried a fresh approach. The United States now had a duty, he told Hull, "to see that the policies pursued by the British are in the interest of both winning the war and winning a peace. . . . I have considered the humanitarian question of saving millions of lives as the transcendent purpose, and so long as our Government had no responsibilities I felt it should be solved by private action. But it now has other important and different aspects." The hostile powers could not be starved through blockade, he said—but the democracies might be. Eighty million people, friendly to the U.S. and allied with democratic principles, faced death or crippling illness. Belgians already were subsisting on 960 calories a day. Poles were hungry because their agricultural breadbasket was occupied by Soviet forces. America must come to their aid, not only for reasons of humanity, but to assure their later friendship and membership in the family of democratic peoples once Hitler was defeated.[58]

Walter Lippmann criticized his efforts, and Hoover was quick to respond. Relief committees had appealed to him, the former president wrote, poignantly and persuasively. Officials in exile had joined the chorus seeking emergency assistance. "Would you have refused to respond?" he asked Lippmann. Having secured protection of British interests, only to have the British suppress such facts, in the face of their arbitrary refusal to permit any relief to reach the Continent, he, Hoover, had been compelled to wage his case in the court of American opinion, "the only remaining place for help." If he failed, catastrophe would engulf "a generation of people who have done their best to hold the fort of freedom in Europe. Don't they deserve at least one advocate somewhere? Perhaps they were wrong in their choice, but they had already been refused consideration by governments in power."[59]

By the start of April, his relief plans riddled by the combined opposition of the White House, State Department and Downing Street, Hoover decided that only "a great reaction from the middle west" could prevent American entry into the war. Privately, he forecast that within the coming six months, Hitler's forces would overrun Yugoslavia and Greece, the U.S. would begin convoying ships to Britain, even at the risk of combat with German submarines, Japan would edge closer to military confrontation despite Hull's efforts, and a domestic war psychosis would mount, until "every word of caution uttered by honest Americans will be denounced as . . . 'a call from Hitler.' "[60]

"Western civilization has consecrated itself to making the world safe for Stalin," was Hoover's melancholy postscript. He thought Roosevelt mistaken in offering words of encouragement to the Yugoslavs, "a simple minded people [who] will be looking for American planes and American soldiers within a week." Denied access to the BBC, Hoover appealed to the British public in a letter to *The Times* of London. His relief plan was actually pro-British, argued the former president, since its adoption would further please an already sympathetic American population, and because the Germans would bear the brunt of ensuring a cessation of requisitioning and the provision of foodstuffs.[61]

At home, he made a final attempt at enlisting Hull's support. But by now, the Secretary of State was as immovable in his opposition as Churchill himself. Hoover's doubts about his own government's peaceful intentions were magnified late in April when Japan's ambassador to the United States sent word that Tokyo wished to make peace in China, only to run afoul of Mrs. Roosevelt, to whom Hoover ascribed blame for preventing the diplomat from seeing Hull personally. That same month, the U.S. seized Axis shipping in its ports and revealed its own navy's plans to patrol sea-lanes in defense zones. This was but a prelude to still sterner measures, including the freezing of Axis assets in America, the transfer of fifty oil tankers to the British, the closing of all Axis consulates and Roosevelt's proclamation in June of an "unlimited national emergency."[62]

Blocked by men he dismissed as militarists and adventurers, Hoover redoubled his efforts to keep America out of the war. In his race with time and emotion, he asked General Pershing and former Vice President Dawes to raise their voices. His own, he wrote Dawes, was "pretty well worn out." Urging stepped-up aid to Britain (in a speech that drew ten thousand letters to his Waldorf office), he nonetheless denounced convoys as an inevitable prelude to the sending of expeditionary forces. He told one friend that, while many members of America First were extremists, "there are even wilder extremists on the other side—so they make a good antidote for each other." Early in June, thirty-seven members of the Senate introduced a resolution backing Hoover's relief plans and calling on Secretary Hull to persuade the British to cooperate. The California Methodist Council announced its support. So did *Commonweal*, the Episcopal Church, and hundreds of newspaper editors. But Hull would not budge. Only Hitler's overthrow would prevent all Europe from starvation, he informed Hoover. The former president was equally blunt in his reply. "History will never justify the Government of the United States aiding with the starvation of these millions," he wrote Hull. [63]

For now, the fight was over. But new battles were being waged almost daily. In Washington, Roosevelt asked his under secretary of State for advice on how to handle reports privately circulated by Hoover and vehemently denied by Lord Halifax and the British government, to the effect that Rudolph Hess's stunning solo flight to Britain was made for the purpose of carrying German peace proposals. What's more, according to Halifax, Hoover was telling people that Churchill's own Conservative supporters in the House of Commons had threatened to withdraw their allegiance unless the Prime Minister agreed to discuss Hess's proposals, and that Churchill had sought Roosevelt's permission to do so, after having previously rejected similar peace feelers sent via Dublin. [64]

That same week, Hoover was in Palo Alto, for the dedication of his new library tower. The world's greatest collection of diplomatic documents, including the secret minutes of Germany's Supreme War Council, czarist archives from Moscow, Haile Selassie's unpublished memoirs, hundreds of thousands of feet of film, and carloads of maps, books, pamphlets, coins, medals and photographs, Hoover's cache was topped off by a carillon, where the bells that had once rung out from the Belgian pavilion of the New York World's Fair now found permanent refuge. For the former president himself, the occasion was a grim platform from which to deliver an impassioned warning to those who might yet heed the lessons contained in his library's stacks.

If America joined the war, he said, and was rewarded with victory, "then we will have won for Stalin the grip of communism in Russia and a greater opportunity for it to extend in the world. We should at least cease to tell our sons that they will be giving their lives to restore democracy and freedom." That same weekend, Hoover entertained visitors on the terrace of his Stanford home. Surveying the Santa Clara Valley amidst lengthening shadows, the group chatted away, oblivious to the former president's silence.

Finally, he announced his intention to return to New York that night. For the first time, Hoover continued, he was flying in darkness to reach his destination. And for good reason.

"You know that I'm still a custodian of the remaining funds of several nations of Europe after World War I," he remarked, "I have to be in New York Saturday morning, and there must be certain final changes in the disposition of those funds. About six o'clock Pacific Time, Sunday morning, Hitler will invade the Ukraine." [65]

Whatever the source of his information, Hoover was uncannily correct. In Washington, Lord Halifax was composing his note of protest to Sumner Welles. In Berlin, Adolf Hitler was counting the hours until 120 divisions and three thousand guns could pound Stalin's Russia into submission. "You have only to kick in the door," the fuehrer told his generals, "and the whole rotten structure will come crashing down."

★   ★

Hitler's invasion of Russia evoked bewilderment among many Americans. Hoover hoped to muddy the waters further. In the week since Operation Barbarossa's launching, he declared on June 29 "that call to sacrifice American boys for an ideal has been made as a sounding brass and a tinkling cymbal. For now we find ourselves promising aid to Stalin and his militant Communist conspiracy against the whole democratic ideals of the world." Hoover wished his countrymen to ponder carefully the moral implications of such an alliance. He reminded them that Stalin's government had been refused recognition until November 1933, only to break treaty commitments to refrain from domestic instigation among Americans, direct the U.S. Communist party in violation of global etiquette and political decencies, and inspire American workers to strike in key defense industries. It was Stalin, said Hoover, who cynically carved up Poland with the very dictator from whom he now sought relief, who devoured democratic nations like Lithuania, Latvia and Estonia, who made war on tiny Finland, and nurtured fifth columns in France and elsewhere.

Even a tacit alliance with the Russian dictator would debauch American values and ratify Soviet aggression against freedom. All Roosevelt's eloquent talk of four freedoms was so much cant if American boys were now to die defending so hateful a status quo. "War alongside Stalin to impose freedom," Hoover proclaimed, "is more than a travesty. It is a tragedy." In what the former president regarded as the most important speech of his life, he begged Americans to let the two tyrants destroy each other, after which the United States, "the most powerful and potent nation in the world, can talk to mankind with a voice that will be heard." [66]

His words provoked thunderous reaction, both friendly and critical. But

Hoover did not stop there. He sounded out Alf Landon, Joe Kennedy, Bernard Baruch and others about a public declaration reiterating the hypocrisy of aiding Stalin, while renewing America's pledge to serve as Britain and China's arsenal. "We believe that American lives," the proposed statement went on, "should be sacrificed only for American independence, or to prevent military invasion of the western hemisphere. . . . We are fully behind the President in his recently expressed hope that we will be able to stay out of war."[67]

The conclusion was a shrewd bit of deception. For Roosevelt remained suspended between belligerency and inaction. His Secretary of War urged him to immediately approve U.S. convoys, joined by British vessels. "The door is opened wide," Henry Stimson wrote in the aftermath of Hitler's eastward lurch, "for you to lead directly toward the winning of the Battle of the Atlantic." But FDR held back. He did dispatch Harry Hopkins to confer with Stalin, and committed U.S. matériel to the hard-pressed Russian front. He directed Stimson and Frank Knox to prepare a blueprint for ultimate victory. A forty-four-year-old infantry major named Albert C. Wedemeyer asked if he should plan for a two-front war. "You decide," his superior answered. "What are our aims and objectives?" Wedemeyer persisted. "You write them out," he was told. On August 14, it was discovered that the president and Winston Churchill had met off the Newfoundland coast, amidst strict precautions, to draft a common strategy and unveil an idealistic Atlantic Charter. The latter pledged that both countries would renounce territorial gains and renewed Roosevelt's mandate to pursue his Four Freedoms internationally. A few weeks later, the president revealed an unsuccessful German submarine assault against the destroyer Greer off the coast of Iceland. He said nothing to indicate that the ship had taunted the U-boat for three hours. Instead, he denounced the affair as Nazi piracy, likening German raiders to oceangoing rattlesnakes. "When you see a rattlesnake poised to strike," said Roosevelt, "you do not wait until he has struck before you crush him." Henceforth, U.S. vessels would pursue a policy of "shoot on sight."

Such language only confirmed Hoover's opinion that the president was determined to find a backdoor into the shooting war. He now urged Robert Taft and other Senate Republicans to consider limiting all military appropriations to the Western Hemisphere. He divined an overwhelming majority "who do not want to go to bed with Stalin, who fundamentally dislike any British dictation, and who hate Hitler, and yet they are being dragged into war." He promised to continue making "nasty remarks until Congress finally declares war—even though it may only be a confirmation of a declaration of war." To another friend, Hoover held out the hope that if America could keep her powder dry until year's end, she might yet avoid the conflagration altogether.[68]

On August 12, with FDR still off the Canadian shore, the House extended Selective Service by a single vote; Republicans came down decisively against the measure. At the Bohemian Grove, Hoover outlined to General Robert Wood, head of America First, a plan to enlist the GOP minority in Congress in a blunt statement of opposition to any direct intervention in Europe's battle. "As I see it," wrote an encouraged Wood, "the Republican Party has absolutely no chance unless it comes out as the Isolationist Party." Accordingly, interventionists like Willkie ought to be drummed out of GOP ranks.[69]

A new irritant disturbed Hoover's vacation. He was enraged, he told John Callan O'Laughlin, at Roosevelt's handling of Japan. A few weeks earlier, the president had issued a stern warning to Tokyo, promising stiff opposition to any Japanese move against East Indies oil. Two days after that diplomatic shot across the bow, Roosevelt froze Japan's assets in America and throttled trade between the two countries, endangering up to 80 percent of Tokyo's oil supplies. While the administration bluffed, Hoover asserted, "the Japs occupy Indochina and stay there. . . . The Japs will hold their takings, we will threaten and fulminate. When Hitler wins in Russia—as he will eventually—and when the British make their peace with him . . . the Japs will still be there." Far better, in Hoover's view, for America to have remained inactive on the Far Eastern front. Then the Japanese warlords would have collapsed from within. "There is nothing so good for the dictators of Japan," he concluded, "as outside pressure." In his hatred for the Soviets, the former president sympathized with Japanese demands for eastern Siberia. He even suspected the Japanese would abandon claims to Chinese territory south of the Great Wall in exchange for this vast new region into which to expand.[70]

Hoover stirred still more controversy in mid-September when he told a Chicago rally that Hitler was well on his way to defeat. "Actual dangers" posed to Americans, the former president insisted, were less than at any time since the war began. "If Hitler had all the shipyards in Europe," declared Hoover, "he could not in five years build an armada big enough even to start across the Atlantic." His own priorities were simply stated. The four freedoms must be protected at home. Aid must be provided to the democracies alone—pointedly excluding Stalin's regime. No warlike steps could be permitted without congressional approval.

Dorothy Thompson reacted for many of her colleagues in the press. The man who once proclaimed that prosperity was just around the corner, she wrote bitterly, was now predicting victory to be similarly near. Walter Lippmann went a step further. In his obsession with Hitler and Stalin, Hoover appeared oblivious to both Japan and France's presence in the war zone. Hoover, "who has consistently misjudged the realities of this war," continued Lippmann, "is still misjudging them. In the first autumn of the war he advised us not to sell bomber planes to Great Britain and France because he thought they were not needed for defense. When France fell, he told us in a carefully prepared address that we must now adjust ourselves to a total victory of Germany, Italy, and Japan in Europe and Asia. Now he tells us that Hitler's aggression is stopped and that there is a stalemate. He is as wrong now in his optimism as he was a year ago in his pessimism."

About one thing at least, Lippmann was right: Hoover's crystal ball revealed a country turning his way. Nothing else could account for what he called "the rabidness" of Roosevelt's public comments. Three things might yet prevent U.S. entry into the war, Hoover predicted. "God is sometimes good to drunk people and children. We are both." The realization that Roosevelt's administration would not successfully prosecute a war might also slow the momentum toward U.S. participation. So would the prospect that Hitler would make a separate peace with either Stalin or Churchill. If only his party would stay true to its isolationist stand, Hoover forecast a gain of fifty House seats in 1942—by which time the apostate Willkie would no longer be a factor within the GOP. At his most apocalyptic, the former president thanked Joe Martin for the fight being waged by House Republicans, then looked down the road to an inevitable day of reckoning. "When it comes," wrote Hoover, "the future of America will depend on whether the people are willing to go to the ballot box for the revolution or to the man on horseback." If they chose the latter, it would be a sign of confidence "in some group of men, 122 or 150 or 300, who have stood steadfast in opposition to all this stuff."[71]

As events gained a momentum of their own, Hoover threw himself into the battle for peace with near-reckless abandon. He was forced to curtail press access to his speeches after one was leaked to the opposition, and promptly transmitted overseas, where portions were approvingly broadcast by Radio Berlin. Hoover found himself in a row with Stanford's faculty, which disputed the accuracy of a poll he conducted on campus purporting to show a majority against the use of U.S. ships to convoy munitions to Britain. Gertrude Lawrence rejected a medal from the Finnish government, to be presented by Hoover's relief committee. Much as she sympathized with the Finns, said the British actress, she could not accept honors from a vassal of Nazi Germany. His Committee to Feed the Small Democracies was stymied by the president's own organization, a Committee on War Relief Agencies, which Hoover himself dismissed as a smoke screen. Whatever its mission, the White House committee administered a *coup de grace* to Hoover's dwindling hopes to penetrate the British blockade. After Pearl Harbor, he abandoned the effort altogether.[72]

Early in October, Roosevelt asked Congress to permit the arming of U.S. merchant ships passing through combat zones. A week later, the destroyer *Kearney* was torpedoed by German submarines off the western coast of Iceland. Eleven American sailors died in the incident, which fanned the flames of resentment against Nazi Germany and sent Hoover into a new tailspin. The *Kearney* was actually convoying British vessels from Iceland to Newfoundland, he wrote Arthur Vandenburg, in urging a Senate investigation of the ship's mission and mandate. That same week, the moderate government of Prince Fumimaro Konoye fell in Tokyo, after Roosevelt rebuffed his request for a Hawaiian summit conference, and militant officers led by General Hideki Tojo scorned any Japanese pullback in China. "If we go to war with Japan," Hoover declared, "it would be God's gift to Hitler." He fretted over a report that Roosevelt was commissioning plans for a five-million-man expeditionary force to invade Europe. Meanwhile, the American people had no idea "that we have a large fleet between Canada and Iceland daily yearning for incidents which will draw us into war."[73]

Amidst the storm of accusation and rebuttal, some voices were raised in Hoover's defense. The *Christian Century* took note of a fresh appeal on behalf of Europe's women and children and judged him back where he belonged—outside politics, inside humanitarian efforts, "where divine providence has always intended him to be." Norman Thomas overlooked a lifetime of political differences to congratulate the former president for his leadership in the fight for "common humanity and common sense."[74]

By the first of November, Hoover was again predicting peace talks between Germany and England within three months. The idea of Americans going to war "with no determined objectives except certain platitudes of crushing Hitler is one of the most appalling phases of the times," he wrote. He planned a new Chicago address, designed to shift the focus of opposition away from the Neutrality Bill, and onto the idea of expeditionary forces. "To land a force of a few hundred thousand Americans in Persia or Africa or other places," he announced, "would simply invite another Dunkirk." He felt certain that Roosevelt would deny any such intention in public. "But he cannot go on fanning war in the United States without ultimately landing in exactly that position."[75]

Hoover embarked on another mission as well, as risky and potentially explosive as anything in his career. Distraught, yet still nourishing a hope that reason might overcome emotion, he decided to intervene personally, to avert a war between Japan and his own land. In Tokyo, Tojo prepared a final offer to be sent Cordell Hull and his White House superior. At the same time, however, military contingencies were not neglected. Hull had four weeks in which to respond favorably to his latest ultimatum, Tojo had decided. Otherwise, Pearl Harbor would be attacked on December 7.

★   ★

Beneath her placid exterior, Lou Hoover harbored fierce resentments. Never forgiving Japan for overrunning her beloved China, the former First Lady crossed a Palo Alto street to avoid contact with a Japanese merchant. But she shared her husband's abhorrence of war, and she broke her usual silence governing political matters long enough to shock her niece, late in November 1941. She was terribly upset, she told Hulda Hoover. "We're going to have war with Japan." The younger woman asked for an explanation. "Cordell Hull has written a note to the Emperor that means war," Lou replied. In the main, she was right. By then, her husband had already been engaged in nearly a month of tantalizing, highly dangerous negotiations of his own. [76]

More than a year earlier, Hoover had encouraged two Maryknoll clerics in their own unorthodox campaign to establish an avenue of understanding between the State Department and Japan's Foreign Ministry. Now, he was heavily involved in a peace effort that began on October 31, with a dinner invitation from New York attorney Raoul Desvernine. Once counsel to the American Liberty League, Desvernine had more recently represented the interests of Japanese bankers. He had also agreed to advise the Japanese embassy in Washington as Ambassador Kichisaburo Nomura, aided by special envoy Saburo Kurusu, sought to preserve the frail peace still enjoyed by both nations. Now Desvernine wanted Hoover's counsel. Foolhardy as war would be, the former president told the lawyer turned diplomatic trouble-shooter, it was all but guaranteed so long as Secretary Hull and others in the administration employed economic sanctions to corner the Japanese and turn their attention to Malaya and Borneo, rich in raw materials missing from the home islands. The problem, said Hoover, was how to convince Roosevelt and his aides "that they could not bluff, pinch, or stick pins in this tiger without getting bit." [77]

The impasse continued, with Nomura increasingly fearful that it might break down at any time, with a shooting war the result. On November 23, Desvernine phoned Hoover again, this time to impress upon him the desperation of both envoys' plight, and to testify to the sincerity with which

Japan's diplomats wished to avoid war while saving face. Hull, in their opinion, was determined to bring on hostilities. Personally, they found the Secretary of State's conduct bordering on insolence. Nomura, in particular, had reason to distrust the aging Tennessean, widely fingered as the man who shot down a Roosevelt-Konoye summit. Desvernine then recounted interviews between the president, Hull and his clients before asking Hoover's help. Did he have a diplomatic miracle in his pocket? The former president suggested a six-month standstill agreement, freezing military action, relaxing U.S. sanctions and laying the groundwork for a big power conference at Honolulu which could hammer out a durable peace in the Pacific. If Nomura and Kurusu would accept the package, he went on, then the next challenge was to persuade Roosevelt that he make it his own or, as Hoover phrased it, "take the glory."[78]

On his own, Hoover appealed to Nomura through third parties for support of his proposal. Meanwhile, Desvernine was in Washington, conferring regularly with both Roosevelt and Hull, trying to repair the damage done on November 26 when the Secretary summoned both Japanese representatives and presented them with an unsigned memorandum reiterating his hawkish views. The diplomats interpreted Hull's note as an ultimatum, sure to be seized upon by militarists back in Tokyo anxious for a pretext to justify attack. Hoover shared their apprehensions. He now suggested that Roosevelt be called back from a Warm Springs holiday. Bernard Baruch might provide the best avenue of approach, said Hoover, and Desvernine agreed to contact the financier. For his part, the former president relayed a message to Basil O'Connor, once FDR's law partner and still a close friend, who was in Warm Springs at Roosevelt's side.[79]

The call to Baruch was placed through Ray Moley, and a meeting arranged in Washington. It took place on the morning of Monday, December 1, with Desvernine unspooling his tale and Baruch stoutly resisting his entreaties to intervene with FDR. He did consent to have lunch with Kurusu that afternoon, where it was agreed that a memorandum outlining the proposed settlement be composed for the president's review. Then a face-to-face meeting with Roosevelt might be scheduled. Desvernine, Nomura and Kurusu worked feverishly that night, drafting a plan that would gradually withdraw Japanese soldiers from China, weaken the Tripartite treaty with Berlin and Rome, negotiate new treaties of commerce in place of existing embargoes, and authorize both an international conference and a standstill agreement to function pending its convocation.[80]

On Tuesday, the second, Baruch received the memorandum. The Japanese received an appointment with the president, who, at Baruch's urging, had cut short his Warm Springs sojourn and hastened back to the capital. In a private session with Desvernine, Roosevelt told the lawyer that the memorandum contained a "basis of solution" to the war fever endangering both nations. Twenty-four hours later, following his conference with the Japanese diplomats themselves, Desvernine felt relief for the first time. Snags remained: would Tokyo, for instance, talk to Chiang Kai-shek? Roosevelt said that he might introduce them to Chiang, and Kurusu suavely answered that no one introduced by the president of the United States could fail to start a conversation. The November 26 ultimatum, it now appeared, was inoperative. Peace might yet be salvaged. [81]

But the hourglass was nearly empty. By the time the potential breakthrough was sifted by Tokyo's leaders, and a reply drafted for transmission to the embassy in Washington, it was December sixth, and a lethal armada of Japanese warships swarmed like angry bees a few hundred miles from Hawaii. It was nine-thirty at night when a naval courier presented the decoded reply from Tojo's government to Roosevelt. The president scanned the documents for ten minutes. At his side was Harry Hopkins, who finally broke the tense silence. "This means war," he said. Only the exact location of the coming assault was in doubt. Hopkins guessed Indochina. Neither man mentioned Pearl Harbor. Nomura and Kurusu were swept along in the irrational tide. Hoover was equally powerless.

He spent the weekend visiting friends in Bucks County, Pennsylvania, a tranquil outpost in a world infatuated with hate. Late in the day, preparing to depart for the ride home to New York, he asked Lou to turn the car radio off. "We've had such a peaceful and happy weekend," was the way he put it, "do we have to listen to that thing?" Near Washington Crossing, New Jersey, state police apprehended his car, or tried to—but Hoover kept his foot on the gas pedal, one step ahead of a small army of would-be informers. As it was, he walked into the Waldorf Towers to find two dozen reporters camped out. [82]

"Mr. President," one asked, "what do you think of the war?"

"What war?" Hoover replied, six hours after Japan's devastation of the U.S. naval base at Pearl Harbor. That same night, Walter Winchell denounced him on the radio. The next day, Roosevelt asked Congress for a declaration of hostilities, and Hoover backed him with a strong public statement calling for unity. The former president informed Bob Taft that he would be glad to come down to Washington himself if he could provide helpful information regarding prices in the last war. He praised FDR for limiting his war call to Japan, and expressed a hope "that we can even yet limit the area of the war." [83]

But his gloom did not abate. "The day will come," he wrote to one supporter, "when this war will be put into the scales of judgment, and when this time comes you and I will be found to have been right." He had done his best to keep America from sinking into the European bog. "I only wish I could have been more successful in it, but at least our consciences are clear. . . . I am not ashamed of anything we have done and have no apologies to make." On a still more melancholy note, he answered the son of a friend who wrote looking for war work. "There is not the remotest possibility that I will have anything to do with the conduct of this war," Hoover told the young man. However employed in the prewar period, his powers of analysis did not now desert him.[84]

"FOUR YEARS OF FRUSTRATION"

★

I am afraid that we are the lepers in a country which has gone over to the unspeakable intolerance of war psychosis. . . . Truth has never been timed to suit the tastes of the people who do not want to hear it. In view of the way the Preacher was treated, it would seem that the Sermon on the Mount was badly timed.
                                                    —Herbert Hoover, January 1942[1]

★

"I am convinced," Hoover wrote to a political colleague ten days after Pearl Harbor, "that you and I and our kind are not going to be allowed to take any part in this war whatever, so we will have to make up our minds to employ ourselves with our own thoughts as best we can." A painful prophecy, it relegated World War I's heroic centerpiece to the outskirts of influence, pinning badges on Boys Clubs brigades, attending stage door canteens and supporting dictatorial powers for the commander in chief. It meant long days of writing, disciplining the syntax of his Stanford experience (Hoover confessed to one research assistant, "They were not going to let me graduate, because I had flunked freshman English"), to frame the issues of a lasting peace. It led him to pump dry dinner companions and a honeycomb of official sources for facts to prove his theories or justify his biases. It took him to rallies and congressional hearings, where the former president condemned root and branch the Allied policy of denying food to occupied democracies, and pleaded for a more unified structure of command on the domestic front.[2]

    The effect of his compassion was nearly spoiled by the hardening of his emotional arteries. He began work on three volumes of memoirs, the last to be entitled "The Years of Acknowledgment." (Eventually, it was called, with even greater precision, *The Great Depression, 1929–41.*) The books were meant to be withheld from publication during Hoover's life, but their author outlived his own expectations, and they reached the market in 1951. He launched a still more massive literary endeavor, an exhaustive history of U.S.–Soviet relations first called "The Crucifixion of Liberty," later dubbed *Freedom Betrayed.* "The War Book," as *Freedom Betrayed* originally was known, was designed as an indictment of U.S. entry into the second world war. In it he drew an unflattering portrait of both Roosevelt and Stimson, the latter of whom he was convinced sought war with Japan as early as 1931. Hoover, who professed indifference to stories about presidents, listened closely as right-wing journalists like George Sokolsky and Fulton Lewis claimed membership in the Communist party for Eleanor Roosevelt, speculated about FDR's health and alleged ambitions for global leadership, or gossiped about the private morals of the Roosevelt clan and the president's jack-of-all-trades, Harry Hopkins.[3]

Roosevelt was hardly more charitable in his attitude toward the nation's only living ex-president. Shortly after war was declared, the chief executive invited Bernard Baruch to the White House for a discussion of manpower shortages and ways to streamline a chaotic home front. If he ever wanted to put together a smoothly functioning organization, said Baruch, then the first man he would send for would be Herbert Hoover. What's more, Baruch continued, he had already spoken to the former president, who desired just such an opportunity to contribute his services.

Roosevelt was not impressed. "Well, I'm not Jesus Christ," he told Baruch. "I'm not going to raise him from the dead." A year later, FDR was inquiring if the War Department planned to make use of a Hoover memorandum dated October 27, 1917, to Colonel House, in which the food czar advised against sending U.S. troops to France. A few weeks after that, the president displayed a letter asserting that Hoover had promoted at least fifteen failed companies during his heyday as a mining engineer, at a loss to investors of $15 million. The same letter exhumed the old allegations conceiving Hoover's alleged role in the death of Edith Cavell. "No one need ever fear a libel suit from Hoover," its writer concluded; "the crook is too afraid of the truth leaking out." Under a "very confidential" heading, Roosevelt sent the letter to Herbert Lehman, his newly appointed director of postwar relief. He also directed the FBI to look into reports that his predecessor might be consorting with Vichy France and its collaborationist elements. On a lighter note, the president chuckled in August 1943 over the story of a New Orleans doctor visited by a ten-year-old boy named Herbert. The physician asked if he knew of Hoover, and the boy said no. He was president before Franklin Roosevelt, the doctor explained. "And is he still living?" the young patient demanded. Delighted, FDR acknowledged in response that "he had rather a fellow feeling."[4]

The president was not wholly intransigent; he allowed Assistant Secretary of War John J. McCloy at the urging of Henry Stimson to brief Hoover on war developments, some of them top secret in nature. After April 1942, he was persuaded by Harry Hopkins to send Albert Wedemeyer, now a general, to New York for regular explanations of Allied war plans. Wedemeyer was authorized to provide the Waldorf Astoria's resident sage with information he requested, even during a period when his own stubborn insistence on continuing the campaign to feed Greece and other conquered democracies was blocked by Churchill and derided by the administration in Washington.[5]

But there was a limit to the courtesies Roosevelt would extend. Joe Martin publicly demanded a position for Hoover at the head of a price commission. Nicholas Murray Butler advised centralization of food aid under the former president. Walter Lippmann was less specific but more persuasive in calling for reorganization of the present government. "Success not amiability," proclaimed Lippmann, "efficiency not Auld Lang Syne" were needed in this darkest hour of the war, when Japanese forces chased Americans out of the western Pacific, and blackout curtains darkened White House windows. When Bunny Miller went to pick up a sugar rationing card for the Hoover household, she was bluntly told that the former president must stake his claim in person. Ironically, Hoover himself provided much of the emotional rationale for his own exile from responsibility. The war was hardly a few weeks old when he published a small volume entitled *America's First Crusade*. Based on four articles that appeared a few weeks earlier in the *Saturday Evening Post*, this recounting of his experiences at the Versailles Peace Conference of 1919 could not have come at a worse time. For Hoover did more than describe his own frustration at Woodrow Wilson's crushed hopes, and Europe's reliance upon her newest savior as a "golden-egged goose."[6]

More than an exercise in historical reminiscence, *America's First Crusade* promoted the idea that Wilson's League had failed because it was too formal in structure, too imbued with Old World jealousies to survive in any event, too obsessed with the sound of its own voice to promote genuine cooperation. It became the public platform for big power domination, and an incentive to German nationalism, wrote Hoover. But beyond the tangle of personalities who met to debate Europe's peace, he discerned fundamental reasons why America had failed. Her civilization had grown three hundred years apart from the Old World's, Hoover concluded. Her naivete regarding European superiority was as misplaced as her ignorance of the racial tensions that simmered within ever-shifting borders. To preserve its fragile peace, he went on, Europe could not contain its urge to construct alliances and build stockpiles of weaponry. Unlike the United States, it had no oceans to protect it from hostile neighbors, and no democratic foundation on which to build the Wilsonian house.

To Hoover, American isolation was not responsible for Europe's present terror. The Europeans themselves were.

However logical the argument, it fell on ears deafened by buzz bombs and the tramp of soldiers' boots. The *New York Herald Tribune*'s Walter Mills found it extraordinary "that a man to whom there attaches the responsibility, no less than the honor of being an ex-president should permit the publication at this moment of a pamphlet like this . . . with the United States locked in the death struggle declared upon us by the most savage military power in history, it becomes a piece of irresponsibility not easy to describe."

Again, the cry of smear issued from Suite 31-A. This time, Helen Reid had a sharp rebuke of her own. "That word simply does not belong among our standards of work," she admonished her friend. "I hope you are feeling some regret for your letter of January 29th. I could not feel it was characteristic of you." Hoover accepted Mrs. Reid's reprimand. "I am so inconsistent as to discontinue argument with one to whom I am so devoted," he wrote, before mentioning that more than a thousand letters from readers agreed with his position. On one point he would not yield: the anger he detected among average citizens over the sloppiness, confusion, and wishful thinking imbuing Washington. Somewhat ironically, he warned that a continuation of such "puerilities" would frighten the people into demanding a pullback from any foreign involvement. And he renewed his ardent plea for a realistic assessment of the postwar world, a subject that would come to obsess him in the months ahead.[7]

Buffeted by events, moored to his own prejudices, he presented a tempting target to those in search of scapegoats. A Minnesota farmers' group wired the White House that it would never accept Hoover in charge of agricultural production or price-setting. The former president, charged one union local, was "a potential fifth columnist."[8]

Cal O'Laughlin reported Roosevelt's personal pique with his predecessor, to which Hoover replied that he was "somewhat taken aback" by this latest lapse in White House etiquette. No other man had been subjected to so many personal attacks by a successor, he told O'Laughlin. Personally, he explained in the accent of a scorned suitor, FDR's attitude was not unwelcome, "as it relieved me from being involved in any possible responsibility from events." The nation was at war. He would continue to provide any support possible, including defense of the president himself from partisan or unfair attack. "If I find it necessary to engage in comment on the conduct of the war," wrote Hoover, "it will be entirely constructive, upon no petty issue and never below the belt. The White House is of course at liberty to depart from courtesy in my case. . . . I can hardly be expected to lower the traditions of the great office with which I was entrusted by making overtures which might give the mis-impression that I was trying to force my way into office or into publicity."[9]

That same week, he confided to Edgar Rickard his wish to be consulted, if only as an elder statesman. He would not desire a minor post in the war effort; yet neither could he refuse any honest invitation to sign up for the duration. He didn't expect to be asked. Instead, he would content himself with his writing. It didn't come naturally. Hoover's style tended to freeze-dry historical events. "An historical fact," he liked to tell assistants, "is not confirmed unless somebody else confirms it." Larded with documentation, his serious works suffered as well from their author's literary insecurity. Instead of permitting an early draft's casual flow to remain, Hoover worked over the prose—tortured it, some said—until it was drained of vitality. Even this was costly; the former president never relinquished his White House habit of having proofs made overnight, even at eleven dollars a page, and even if little of what was so elegantly printed was likely to survive another twenty-four hours. He was, not surprisingly, a difficult man to edit.[10]

"I may split my infinitives," he reprimanded one aide, "and I may murder the King's English, but when you and Hugh [Gibson] get through with it, it 'taint me." His addiction to words like "gadget" and "secure" drove collaborators to distraction. "Don't you ever obtain anything?" one asked. "Yes," Hoover answered, "I secured . . ."[11]

His grand obsession became the Magnum Opus, an all-purpose indictment of his enemies at home and abroad which would involve him in more than two decades of research and writing. One of its several incarnations was to be a volume on fifteen crucial blunders of statesmanship. "And I am going to tell you what should be the first chapter," Hoover related to a visitor. "When Roosevelt put America in to help Russia as Hitler invaded . . . we should have let these two bastards annihilate themselves." Years after FDR's death, an overnight guest discovered the ex-president scribbling furiously at his desk long before dawn. What could he possibly be doing at such an hour, the intruder asked?

"I'm making my Roosevelt book more pungent," Hoover replied. Nothing more had to be said.[12]

★   ★

The world held its breath in the decisive spring of 1942. Hitler's mechanized armies were bogged down on the Russian front, while Rommel's Afrika Corps was checked by the British Eighth Army at El Alamein. In Washington, George Marshall and Henry Stimson conferred with the president about a possible invasion of Europe as early as April 1943. Off the American coastline, however, German U-boats claimed a supremacy of their own, ranging from the Gulf of Mexico to Nova Scotia and destroying more than a million tons of Allied shipping in a single month. War production lagged until midsummer, and morale suffered under a bruising array of reports from the battlefields of Asia and North Africa. At the White House, Executive Order 9066 consigned thousands of California's Nisei to imprisonment, their crime being their ancestry during a period of national hysteria. "Our standard of living will have to come down," Roosevelt proclaimed that spring in asking Congress to adopt a new and burdensome tax program; no one should have an after-tax income of more than $25,000, the chief executive asserted. Acknowledging the demise of the New Deal, FDR did not abandon his reforming instincts. The GI Bill of Rights was a monument to his political gifts, as well as a headstone for the historic decade whose hard times were forgotten now in the rush of war-induced prosperity.

Bureaucratic snafus mounted as 1.7 million retailers sought relief or release from the heavy hand of the Office of Price Administration. In Philadelphia, one OPA office shut down after it forgot to ration fuel for future operations. By mid-1944, auto suppliers claimed no more than a three-day inventory on hand, and the Republican National Committee made hay with stories of domestic diapers sent overseas to Arab recipients who liked to wear them as turbans. Congress forced Roosevelt's hand on the rationing issue and demanded a rubber czar to promote synthetic production of a vital war material in short supply. Before the end of 1942, inflation came to life, as farmers insisted on 100 percent of parity for their produce and politicians sensitive to the rural vote imposed their greed on national policy-makers. Point rationing was instituted for meats, butter, fats and oils, cheese and other processed foods. Meanwhile, the president was forced to seize eastern coal mines after John L. Lewis led his men out on strike. Later that year, the Army took possession of the railroads for three weeks, a desperate measure resorted to by desperate men.

This wasn't like 1933, Roosevelt complained to reporters, "when the country was economically on its back" and he was able to rule virtually at will. Eventually, he sought fresh powers to control both prices and wages.

The Office of Economic Stabilization was created, with South Carolina's Jimmy Byrnes at the throttle; agriculture was supplemented by urban victory gardens; and Henry Kaiser and his revolutionary methods of mass production eased the crisis of supply. By the spring of 1943, FDR was at least a little freer to turn his attention to the military and diplomatic fronts. Hoover was already there. Having failed to keep his country out of war, the former president was now intent on persuading her to avert the peacekeeping tragedies of Versailles. Along with Hugh Gibson, his old friend and recent coauthor, he was writing another book.

They made an unlikely team. Hoover, homespun, with the twang of Iowa still in his voice, a moralist adrift on a choppy sea of political realities, given to Biblical injunctions and profoundly suspicious of what he called "an unreal world of perfect words," initially found it difficult to mesh his own style with that of Gibson, the worldly, striped-pants diplomat who had cut his stylish teeth as private secretary to Charles Evans Hughes and later carved out a thirty-year career in a variety of foreign assignments. But by the start of May 1942, this odd couple had completed a draft which they called "The Problems of Lasting Peace." Both men took pleasure in the knowledge that soon, more than five million subscribers to the *Reader's Digest* would have instant access to their analytical collaboration.[13]

With the engineer's skills of precision, Hoover and Gibson divided the "dynamic forces" of civilization into seven parts: ideologies, economic pressures, nationalism, imperialism, militarism, fear that sowed the seeds of national hate and revenge, and the will to peace. Encapsulating centuries into pages, the authors traced these forces back to the Thirty Years' War and an even longer period of unease that included the American Revolution and the storming of the Bastille. The League of Nations failed to control them because it sought to impose a big-power peace upon the shattered Continent. Instead of serving as an instrument of cooperation and collective security, the organization reflected all the old antagonisms and ambitions of prewar Europe. Disinterested in what they called "the drama of peace negotiations, the gilded halls, the pomp and circumstance surrounding these scores of nations with their celebrated representatives and their protocols of politeness," Hoover and Gibson portrayed Woodrow Wilson as an earnest but doomed reformer, crushed by fate and centuries of European power politics. The shades of Machiavelli and Talleyrand had sat at the table of Versailles, they wrote, caring less for crusades than for crisis management.

The peace settlement that emerged from their deliberations made enthusiastic noises in the direction of representative government. But it first extracted its ritualistic pound of flesh. Assessing guilt for the war to Germany, maintaining a postarmistice food blockade against the defeated nation, bleeding a feeble economy dry with $40 billion of reparations, changing boundary lines to isolate and fragment the German-speaking peoples; in these and other ways, the victorious Allies had made a mockery of Wilson's Fourteen Points, like the American leader's commitment to open covenants arrived at openly.

History taught lessons, or else its study was wasted. Now, even as Stalin and Hitler were locked in mortal combat on the frozen steppes of Russia, Hoover and Gibson were preparing for the next peace. They felt certain that the seven dynamic forces would again attend the conference table. If they were not to poison this peace as they had the last, they must be anticipated and defused in advance. Without proposing the specific contents of a final treaty, the authors did set forth a number of steps that ought to shape the postwar world. First, there should be no Armistice, no repeat of the nine-month interregnum of 1918–19, during which a hornet's nest of rivalries and resentments was allowed to gather and demand admission to the innermost diplomatic precincts. There should be no Versailles type of conference, either. Rather, Hoover and Gibson proposed that the United Nations make agreements in advance as to the principles for which they fought, and the kind of peace that would be worthy of their sacrifice.

Representative government and economic liberty: these must become the foundation for a lasting peace. Disarmament of the vanquished should be quickly followed by disarmament of the victors. All blockades should be lifted with cessation of hostilities. Interim boundaries should be set down on paper, for later copying on the maps of Europe. The methods of future peacemaking should also be agreed upon as soon as possible. Those who made war ought to be punished, but those who were conscripted into the armies of aggression, like the civilian populations that supported them, should be let alone. Relief should not be withheld from enemy lands; indeed, the victors must cheerfully accept their moral responsibility to lay the basis for a newly democratic Europe. Loans between governments, like reparations between winners and losers, should be dismissed as impractical and uncollectible.

A cooling-off period should follow the silencing of the guns. During this time, regional councils might be established—an idea given tacit support by Winston Churchill in May of 1943. Commissions composed of representatives of the victorious Allies would be assigned different parts of the new global equation and asked to solve them in ways both more practical and less provincial than the Versailles Conference had. Then, and only then, would a world organization per se come into being, and a lasting peace become more than the visionary's impossible wish. "In the making of that peace," wrote Hoover and Gibson, "will come a fleeting chance for the leaders of mankind to bind the wounds, to restore faith, and to bring new hope to the world."

His book was no exercise in treaty making, Hoover informed columnist Westbrook Pegler, but an attempt "to say some things that may stimulate sanity . . . a contribution to less emotional and more real thinking." In campaigning for acceptance of his ideas, Hoover compared the Atlantic Charter, with its sweeping promises of self-determination and individual freedom, to the Declaration of Independence. His own plan for peace, he felt, more nearly resembled the hardheaded doctrines contained within the United States Constitution. It took eleven years to reach from one to the other; it might take just as long for the world to reorder its priorities and fashion the tools of enduring peace. A threat to his vision came from others, men like Wendell Willkie and Franklin Roosevelt, so taken with their own dream of "one world" as to miss the forces dividing one into many. The president warmly welcomed the suggestion of a New York publisher that June that Vice President Wallace write his own volume ("to set Hoover's book back on its heels"). "I do not underestimate the usefulness of inspiring words," Hoover said in Minneapolis in September 1943, a few days after his own party's Mackinac Island conference rejected Willkie's vaguely messianic internationalism for a coalition of major powers as police officers of the peace. "But most of this is exactly the same verbal road which led to Versailles. When we got there we had high ideals, high aims and great eloquence." For the coming peace, "we must have something far more specific and definite. . . . And that path must leave the century-old bright lights of eloquence and nebular words and explore the hard road of experience." [14]

Increasingly, Hoover was critical of what he called "the Freedom House group," a veiled reference to Willkie's followers, many of whom were determined to read out of the party all its officeholders who opposed war prior to Pearl Harbor. Flagship of the liberal Republican fleet was the *New York Herald Tribune*, which editorialized against "isolationists and appeasers" within GOP ranks, earning Hoover's dissent and echoing Roosevelt's own attacks upon "turtles" and "ostriches" within the American family. He had canvassed Republican opinion widely, Hoover wrote Helen Reid in March 1942. Whatever their feelings before Pearl Harbor, party spokesmen now in Congress were determined to push on to complete victory. The real issue before the country, he asserted, was the efficiency of the war effort and what, if anything, was being done to prepare a future peace. It was a disservice to the party and the country to imply a lack of patriotism to those who had disputed administration policies before December 7. "I would like to see a healing process . . .," wrote Hoover, and his antipathy to Willkie and his followers was scarcely concealed.[15]

Willkie himself was indiscreet in denouncing prewar isolationists. "Our friend is breathing fight," Hoover revealed to Landon that same month, "and holding private meetings, but nothing much comes of them." In the 1942 congressional campaigns, he rendered no assistance to GOP candidates but instead embarked on a long and romantic journey around the globe, the nucleus of his stirring volume *One World*. Warning that Willkie's supporters would rush to do battle the moment the former president's own book appeared, Hoover appealed to Landon for an endorsement of its precepts. He did the same with Chief Justice Harlan Stone, and a now-retired Charles Evans Hughes. He sought in vain a few lines of public approval from Hughes, a man of towering probity and legendary frostiness. Robert Taft, although worried lest Roosevelt and Hull commit the nation to free trade "and a kind of international W.P.A.," found cause to hope that Hoover's "few cold hard facts" might rally the GOP against "Utopian thinkers, whose interest appears to be more in foreign peoples than in the welfare of our own." From across the years, Woodrow Wilson's widow wrote to thank him for her copy of the book "with the earnest hope that light may soon dawn on this dark world." Norman Thomas took exception to the author's dedication to free enterprise but strongly approved of global cooperation and an immediate lowering of food blockades.[16]

"Your fight is so honest and steadfast for the essentials of national life," Hoover informed the old Socialist leader, "that I can forget your [mistaken] economic views!"[17]

He could afford to be gracious to Thomas, a man still more removed from power than he. The book was selling "astonishingly well," he chortled, aided by a battery of "most heartening reviews" to a fifth printing by July 11. His gloom lifted. He contemplated the purchase of land near Hugh Gibson's new retreat on Quaker Hill, the verdant country development planned by radio broadcaster Lowell Thomas. He wished Thomas might find Gibson a radio showcase. "You might get thrown off later, but it would help as long as it lasts." Hoover spent August in the trout streams or mineshafts of the Rockies and his adopted California. "The neighbors insisted on sitting on the bank everywhere I was fishing, and talking about the war," he reported to a friend, "so that was not much!" He got an earful of complaints about price controls and the shortage of skilled labor, excessive taxes and a chaotic food production system. "Universally, the people say, 'You cannot believe a word Washington says,' " he concluded. They perceived politics at a time when partisanship should be reserved for the war effort. They saw mismanagement spoiling America's rubber search, and labor demands robbing the consumer blind. His own faultfinding was more expansive. Americans shouldn't deceive themselves into thinking of the Soviet Union as anything more than a temporary ally. Hearing of an Allied landing at Dieppe in August 1942, Hoover dismissed the idea of a second European front. It was, he stormed, nothing more than "a bloody sacrifice to Stalin," and he prophesied a political conflict to follow the shooting one. "Five years after this war," he insisted, "we'll be arming Germany and Japan to help protect us from Russia." [18]

"If I wanted to escape the world," the former president noted in mid-September, "and one has tendencies that way these days—I would build a cabin where I could look at the Tetons and in a dead spot from radio reception." His spirits were buoyed by the November elections, which confirmed his hunch that domestic tensions would find a voice in substantial Republican gains. The party had two great opportunities handed to it, he told Joe Martin: first, to reorganize blundering war agencies, and next "to stop the use of war measures to permanently collectivize this country." Still more explicit were his complaints about the nation's food program. It was being grossly mishandled, he told a visitor to Suite 31-A. Too much grain was piling up in America's granaries, while too little meat and fats reached domestic tables. The OPA refused to cooperate with the Agriculture Department. There should be a single overseer of the entire campaign, replacing the fragmentation of jealous baronies that now passed for a food organization. On another note, Hoover staked out unfamiliar territory for him, defense of the British Empire, when he assailed Willkie's typically undiplomatic criticism of the British. Should London withdraw from its outposts east of the Suez, as the 1940 nominee on his recent journey implied it should, then at least twenty million people would have to emigrate. From top to bottom, said Hoover, British society was imperialist. Why bother picking quarrels with a wartime ally? [19]

That same month, word filtered back from Bernard Baruch that Roosevelt might yet issue an invitation for his predecessor to supervise the food operation, just as Wilson had reached across party lines a quarter century before. Hoover pricked even this trial balloon. They wouldn't ask him to do anything once they read his latest article for *Farm* magazine, he declared, in which he advocated consolidation of all food activities under the Secretary of Agriculture. Nor was this the limit of his assertiveness. In a new *Collier's* appeal, the former president warned his countrymen of hundreds of millions of mouths to feed once the war ended. One third of Europe perished after the Thirty Years' War. Only one nation, his own, had prevented a similar pestilence in 1918. Now was the time to begin planning for a similar postwar rescue, as well as ensuring domestic supplies equivalent to meeting the needs of America and her allies.[20]

★   ★

In Britain, such a voice would have been brought into the governmental family, heeded as an authority and set to work at its unique expertise, past politics notwithstanding. But Washington was not London, and Roosevelt was not Churchill. Late in November, the White House let it be known that it was appointing Herbert Lehman, then in his final weeks as governor of New York, to administer a United Nations Relief and Rehabilitation Administration (UNRRA). Well concealing his own disappointment, Hoover set out to woo Lehman to his point of view. He considered sending an angry "open letter" to Lehman, calling attention to the plight of the small democracies. At the last minute, reason prevailed, and he composed a private appeal, the work of a humanitarian rather than a partisan.[21]

The people of Belgium were down to two pounds of meat and fats per month, a tenth the American diet and a harbinger of mass starvation throughout Europe's overrun democracies. Millions of the Continent's aged, diseased and children were already being victimized. Yet even now, in the third winter of war, Hoover saw a way out. Since the previous August, he wrote, Greeks had been receiving relief under a plan almost identical to his own. The Allied blockade had been opened to permit Swedish vessels to carry supplies to the mountain kingdom for distribution by neutrals. The State Department itself had expressed satisfaction with the process, and with German allegiance to promises that the food would reach the Greeks and no one else. Similarly, supplies had also been shipped to British prisoners inside Germany, under the auspices of the International Red Cross. In Hoover's eyes, it was hard to tell which group confronted the more dire threat. He concluded with a quote from a recent Belgian publication: ". . . were the United Nations fighting to liberate oppressed peoples," he asked, "or a vast cemetery?"[22]

On December 3, 1942, Hoover had lunch with Lehman. (Later, the former president complained that his host tipped off the press to what was supposed to be a private affair.) Again, he tried to speak for the millions without a voice in the councils of war. When the British and American governments the previous winter rejected his proposal to permit neutrals to organize and supervise a relief effort, he had stepped back into the shadows. Now, with Greece receiving aid through just such channels, yet Washington and London remaining intransigent on the issue of a broader program, Hoover appealed to Lehman. He was not successful and left their meeting in a sour mood. The New Yorker, Hoover groused, was a mere publicity-seeker, incapable of doing a job that should be reserved for a former food administrator. Nor did he have much help from others around Roosevelt. The Secretary of Agriculture, for instance, lacked authority over the Office of Price Administration, merrily spinning its spider's web of red tape (including one 46,000-word directive to meat packers). Neither was able to tackle a labor shortage in the situation in the San Joaquin Valley, where a third of the crops went unharvested. During the first world war, Hoover noted, prices had been controlled at the source: witness his own single-handed purchase of the domestic sugar crop. No such coordination existed now, with distressing consequences. Americans would barely be able to feed themselves once hostilities ceased, the former president speculated, let alone a famine-plagued Europe.[23]

With or without Lehman's help, Hoover refused to yield. On January 8, alerted that the British Ambassador to Washington, Lord Halifax, might be susceptible to reason, the former president lunched with the diplomat at the University Club. It proved a false alarm, Churchill's minister avoiding relief as a subject of conversation, focusing instead on America's likely postwar stance. Hoover astonished Halifax by predicting that a British-American air force might easily police the peace, supported by a noncoercive Council of Nations. The former president did have a complaint to lodge: British censorship of *The Problems of Lasting Peace*. Lord Halifax promised to investigate. He was silent, however, when Hoover concluded with a final warning about his own plans to resume agitation on behalf of European relief. The Belgians, said Hoover, were "going through a very dreadful time."[24]

He followed his schedule to the letter. "I confess a desire to expose the realities of the great humanitarianism of this Administration," he wrote Arthur Vandenburg on February 1. A few days later, before a Senate subcommittee, he predicted anarchy unless a food surplus was rushed to Europe the moment peace was declared. He urged the immediate diversion of a million men to ease bottlenecks in the oil, shipping and agricultural industries. He foresaw at least three more years of warfare ahead, Hoover told the senators, possibly five. That same month, he wrote an eloquent appeal for the *Christian Advocate*, insisting "there can be no atom of reason why the Belgians, Dutch, Norwegians, Poles and Yugoslavs should not . . . have relief." People did not lie down to die from starvation, he explained. Before that point, malnutrition paved the way for disease. "The children weaken first, the women and old men next." In a single Belgian industrial city, a third of the childhood population suffered from tuberculosis or rickets, with an even larger share held to be susceptible. Hoover was in no mood to accept military excuses for such neglect. "There are things in this world that are not silenced by ideological argument or declamation as to who is responsible. They are not to be settled in these ways because of the teachings of Christ which have resounded down these two thousand years. The greatest Teacher of mankind did not argue and debate over the ideology and the sins of the two thieves. . . . Can you believe that American public opinion or the spiritual leadership of America has so lost its bearings as to be opposed even to an effort to aid those who lie in the ditch of war?"[25]

During the third week of February, the improbable event of Hoover's sudden return to office seemed a real possibility. Rumors reached the Waldorf that Hiram Johnson, old and ailing, was about to resign his Senate seat. He had been approached by "two or three responsible groups" wanting to know if he would accept an interim appointment, Hoover informed Cal O'Laughlin. "I am not sure but what I could do a job if I got a chance." A still more tantalizing job flickered in front of Hoover a few weeks later, when Bernard Baruch passed on the news that Frank Knox, his Navy Department surrogate Adlai Stevenson, and Jimmy Byrnes had all proposed designating the former chief executive as overall food administrator, only to have FDR display anger whenever the suggestion was renewed. In the end, nothing came of either report, and Hoover rounded out his month of intense activity beseeching 2,500 supporters of overseas relief that America owed an obligation of service to the suffering democracies of Europe. Together, they must open what the former president called "a decency front."[26]

Some of those he wished to assist had ideas of their own. Hoover replied testily when a group of Zionists rejected his plan for a Jewish nation on the eastern African highlands. Their long-range geographical aspirations interested him less than immediate relief for their persecuted brethren closer to the war zone, he told George Sokolsky. No Arabs could be moved out of Palestine until after the war, he maintained. Meanwhile, the important thing was to get food to hungry people concerned with their own survival. That July, Hoover addressed an emergency conference called to rally support for Europe's persecuted Jewry. No language existed adequate to describe either their agonies or their oppressors, he said. But heated rhetoric was not his purpose. He would speak in practical, not emotional terms. In the immediate sense, Jews escaped to neutral lands ought to be rescued and sheltered by the United Nations. They should be fed, as part of a larger relief campaign. In the longer run, Palestine could accommodate some of the uprooted. Still more might find a permanent home in his cherished

African resettlement scheme, a corner of the globe he called "sentimentally an annex to Palestine." [27]

Nor was military strategy beyond the perimeter of Hoover's private criticism. Roosevelt was doing all in his power, he told intimates that spring, to keep Douglas MacArthur as invisible as possible in his undernourished island-hopping of the Pacific. The president was superseding his own Supreme Commander, Dwight Eisenhower, leaving the general with plenty of visibility but less actual authority than his presumed subordinates in British uniforms. The British didn't want a military command anyway, he told the faithful O'Laughlin, but a "High Commissioner." Late in February, Hoover told MacArthur's intimate Bonner Fellers that while the Russian front remained something of an enigma to him, the Soviet stand around Stalingrad seemed to mark the highpoint of Hitler's invasion. Still, he diagnosed exhaustion within the Russian forces and expected the Red Army to content itself with pushing the Germans back a few hundred miles west to the Dnieper River. [28]

Equally pessimistic, Fellers disputed the plans of George Marshall and others to launch a cross-Channel invasion of the Continent. Eighty percent of the troops involved in such an attack, he predicted, would be American, with the balance Canadian. British participation, he felt certain, would be limited to air and naval attacks. In any event, such an assault would be for political rather than military purposes. The same day, Pat Hurley dropped by to inform his former chief of his own recent conversations with Stalin, replete with bitterness over British intentions, and Roosevelt's failure to keep his promise of a 1942 invasion of the Continent. Hurley confirmed Hoover's picture of Eisenhower as a figurehead, and MacArthur as a neglected genius, under whom even the temperamental British would have gladly served. He also played a tune recently popular in suite 31-A, lambasting the naive Willkie for his recent pronouncements supportive of Moscow and its constant demand for a second front. Willkie, said Hurley, was the laughing stock of Europe for his recent travels, during which he was supplied with American Communists for interpreters, and given a wildly optimistic depiction both of Russian military prospects and of home conditions generally. [29]

By now, Willkie was replacing even Roosevelt as the evil villain in the ex-president's political morality play. One World was published to glowing reviews that spring, while Hoover's own crusades to relieve Europe's civilian population and reorganize domestic food production were bogged down. The country would likely be on bread rations by war's end, he forecast late in March. He was only slightly mollified when Lord Halifax reassured him that his book had not been banned in Britain, and had, in fact, been warmly reviewed by the *Spectator*. "Probably the German submarines are our most earnest censor," Hoover replied. But if he kept to his resolve to avoid any public criticism of Roosevelt's war policies, Hoover could not contain his frustration among old friends. His natural combativeness stifled along with his need to be useful, the former president sounded a despairing note. What was the use of even trying to untangle the domestic snarls, he asked that June. "It's the most god-awful mess in history." His words were exaggerated, unlike his sense of waste.[30]

★   ★

Unable to breach the walls of wartime Washington, Hoover gathered his bolts and sought new targets. He continued to call for a National War Council, to bring order to administrative chaos and thereby shorten the fighting. America's enemies had formed the picture of "a disordered country, a declining country," and this complicated the already formidable task assigned the nation's fighting men. Throughout the summer of 1943, the former president drew a sharp distinction between the optimistic food reports issuing from the capital and banner headlines warning of shortages in American cities and an excess of black marketeers clogging American courtrooms. So long as Roosevelt's administration failed to bring all 47 million fallow acres into production, Hoover insisted in a speech that June, the 1944 harvest might fall disastrously short of what a hungry world demanded. Yet control over food was divided nine ways, "too many cooks for too little food," as he put it. Administration ought to be centralized under the Secretary of Agriculture, while the work of his minions ought to be decentralized—the same formula pursued to dazzling success by Hoover himself during the first world war.[31]

Besides the drumbeat of criticism and alternatives offered on the food front, Hoover busied himself with Republican politics and postwar organization. As early as December 1942, he was active in electing Iowa's Harrison Spangler GOP national chairman, a rebuff by party traditionalists to Willkie and his increasingly errant views. As Landon wrote the former president, "Spangler will make a good careful, detailed organizer, and he won't be talking all the time." But the Old Guard could not possibly hope to silence the 1940 nominee, fresh from his global excursion and eager to get on with the work of purifying his party from its own isolationist elements. "Willkie continues to stir up damaging nonsense," Hoover wrote early in January 1943, "by demanding a Council of 26 or 29 Nations to run the war. As only three (or perhaps four) are contributing any war effort, I don't expect he will realize his aspirations as to Costa Rica, Venezuela, and 20 odd others."[32]

A few days later he urged Joe Martin and fellow Republicans in Congress to emulate his attacks on the food snafus. Unreported yet worrisome, meat and milk famines were cropping up, and Hoover proposed to deliver a major address on the farmers' slight—"with the indignation I feel left out." He told Martin that the American people might be appalled if those who were really running the war were daily exhibited in a War Council. He used still harsher language with Arthur Vandenburg. "These people are making an unholy mess of the food situation," wrote Hoover. "They can mess up planes, howitzers and tanks, and the public does not feel it. But mismanagement of food hits them three times a day." The latest example of bureaucratic incompetence was a government statement that no butter was being rationed, since there wasn't enough on hand to warrant it. Hoover was more than puzzled. "We have ten times as many milk cows as Britain," he told Vandenburg, "and they . . . are able to give every family some butter every week." [33]

Early in February, the former president conferred privately with nine newly elected Republican senators, a meeting expanded a few weeks later to include freshmen congressmen as well. Once again, he toyed with the idea of retaining the S Street house in Washington. He met with Landon, their old rivalry buried beneath a common antipathy to Willkie, and with Spangler at the Waldorf. With Willkie's visionary *One World* nearing the million mark in sales, Hoover and other Republican leaders conspired to limit the author's influence within his adopted party. According to the former president, barely a dozen GOP members of Congress supported the Hoosier's 1944 ambitions. That same summer, in a short respite from politics, Hoover went prospecting out West, scouring the desolate countryside of Idaho, Nevada and Utah for gold and copper. He authorized his agents in Guatemala to withhold bribes for a contract; he would rather lose a million dollars, he explained, than pay one cent in graft. He ground out new appeals for his peace plan, decrying those who would settle for "general aims and ideas," and turning for supportive evidence to Versailles. Only five of Woodrow Wilson's Fourteen Points survived that nest of diplomatic intrigue, Hoover told the readers of *Woman's Day*, "mostly because we did not realize that we were part of a very realistic world." [34]

Why repeat the tragic farce of 1919, where a thousand diplomats from forty nations had been forced to hammer out a new world order in the space of a few weeks? Such a schedule invited "dark-corner trades and deals" and planted the seeds of future conflict. Again and again, Hoover spoke up for his two-stage peace, with its conditional solution of pressing issues, and its transitional period during which the fate of the defeated Axis could be determined, along with new boundaries, the protection of ethnic and religious minorities, creation of an international court that would merit the world's respect and obedience, and a companion structure designed to preserve the new peace from future dangers.

His own party was scheduled to discuss postwar issues at a special conference of its most prominent leaders on Mackinac Island in September 1943. In anticipation of the gathering, Hoover labored on a speech embodying his own approach for strategically timed delivery in Minneapolis. He wrote to Dewey, Ohio's John Bricker and others to be wary of "buying a cat blind," his expression for any declaration embracing the still-undetermined policies of the administration. Roosevelt had no peace plan, declared Hoover. He couldn't so long as Allied jealousies continued. Worse yet, "he is likely to flash something to which we cannot agree the minute firing ceases." Not surprisingly, the former president had a better idea. He advised Bricker to avoid "loose words" that might be interpreted as blanket support for any White House plan, particularly since the thorny issue of American sovereignty was at stake. Still, he expressed anxiety for "some bold, constructive, specific proposals that will get outside of words and their traps and will give the Party some distinction." He wanted the conference to adopt a call for his Provisional Peace, in which leading nations would assume responsibilities as trustees of the new order, resume political order and normal economic life, and only then take up the vexing array of problems, including an international peacekeeping body.[35]

Among other reasons for adopting such a proposal, said Hoover, was its demonstration that Mackinac was not the exclusive domain of "certain destructive persons." In case anyone doubted the target of his euphemism, Hoover appealed to California friends (and Tom Dewey) to elect an uncommitted delegation to the 1944 convention. Governor Earl Warren seemed unwilling to accept the challenge hurled down by Willkie's partisans in the state, who had already set up a paid organization to blitz the June primary. On a still more personal level, the former president complained that Willkie had "cribbed almost verbatim" a speech purporting to speak for the loyal opposition. He had new cause for complaint when Thomas Dewey, an undeclared candidate whose draft was widely predicted by party professionals, endorsed at Mackinac a permanent military alliance between the United States and Britain, with Russia and China subject to inclusion later. He was sorry that Dewey took such a line, Hoover informed Landon after the conference ended. And in his sorrow he was scribbling away at an article demolishing the alliance idea "in nine different ways" for Collier's magazine.[36]

He told Bob Taft that his transitional period represented far more than a chance for world powers to cool off. "The major thing is to get a situation where these gigantic long-view problems can be solved, one by one, without a general peace conference and all its intrigue and compromise—and above all, where the American people can have an opportunity to understand, deliberate and protect our own interests." He was angered that Roosevelt had been able to take advantage of Mackinac, snapping up his own proposal the moment it was rejected by the conferees. Meanwhile, his distaste for Dewey's alliance was heightened by a lifelong suspicion of the British. He chastised Walter Lippmann for writing of Great Britain as America's historic partner. Lippmann, wrote Hoover, "belongs to a great clan developing in the United States who would like to see our re-entry into the British Empire." FDR himself might proceed cautiously to a permanent union after 1944, but personally, "I have never believed that the growth of the United States owed one atom to the helpfulness of the British Empire." For proof, Hoover cited British opposition to Texas's entry into the Union, her thinly veiled hostility during the Civil War, and her encouragement of France's invasion of Mexico during the same period.[37]

By the start of November, Hoover was upset anew, this time because no one credited him for the peacekeeping formula contained in the recent Moscow Declaration, even though the document reflected his own preference for provisional accords, trusteeships, a transition period and no general peace conference. On the same day he met with the Duke of Windsor (who seemed to Hoover out of sympathy with the present British government), the former president issued a fresh blast against Churchill's ministry for refusing to lift its blockade of the Continent.[38]

He turned his attention to domestic politics, advising Chairman Spangler to hold the party's convention later than usual, urging Republicans to campaign for the votes of Jeffersonian Democrats, and encouraging every possible contender who could whittle down Willkie's delegate tally. Personally, he told friends late in November, he expected Dewey to be nominated. But he hoped that Ohio's Bricker would wage an effective campaign, if only to cut Willkie down to size. He cultivated Alf Landon, telling the Kansan that Willkie was treacherous and unseemly in associating Landon's name publicly with that of Gerald L. K. Smith, Huey Long's former lieutenant who now commanded his own fringe group, the America First party. Hoover wanted a public denunciation of such tactics, to which Landon calmly took exception. "We must have reasonable amity in the Republican Party," wrote its 1936 standard bearer. But Landon too distrusted the Hoosier, especially in the wake of Willkie's explosive overseas travels. "When he said in China that he talked as he damned pleased it was either more campaign oratory or showed his lack of fitness for public leadership in a Republic. Men can't talk as they damn please and be effective either in politics, business or religion. Furthermore," wrote Landon, echoing a widespread complaint, "ingratitude is one of the unforgivable sins in politics," and Willkie was guilty of nothing more offensive to the party that had entrusted him with its supreme prize, only to reap a bitter harvest of finger wagging and ridicule.[39]

A few weeks later, Landon dismissed the Willkie threat. "For the life of me I can't see where he is going to get any delegates to speak up," he told Hoover. By years's end, the former president agreed. Neither Arthur Krock nor the *New York Times,* for which he wrote, seemed to realize that Willkie "has talked himself completely out of" any possibility for 1944. With the combined support of the *Times, Tribune* and *PM* as well as Henry Luce and the Cowles family, "most men would have blitzed the country," Hoover continued. "The man who has been stopping Willkie is Willkie." Aside from past speeches and impolitic statements, including threats to bolt the party if it failed to adopt his positions and a closed-door denunciation of former business supporters as "a bunch of political liabilities," Hoover himself found plenty to criticize. "His attacks upon Dewey, Bricker and Landon together with his designation of all-aspiring Republican Governors as phony candidates," he concluded, "and the smearing tactics of his allies on Republicans generally, have cumulated to make his political funeral." An objective canvass of delegates would award Willkie no more than a hundred supporters, scattered through the Far West and New England. Yet even there, Willkie's partisans were losing heart. "The *Times* had better find another candidate quickly," said Hoover, "for this one is lost."[40]

★ ★

The Hoovers leased their Palo Alto home that summer of 1943 to the president of Stanford. For Lou, strange surroundings were nothing new. For forty-five years, she had coped with sudden disruptions and unseen houses. "You know," she liked to say, "I've never yet seen a room I didn't want to do something *to.*" And the fresh flowers or favorite pictures testified to her knack for creating a home from a hotel room. Now, she was grateful just to return to keep appointments with the setting sun, to picnic on Mount Tamalpais, to follow the winding roads she loved and whose transformation into sleek, straight highways she mourned. Hoover homes were always littered with maps, in a silver rice bowl, in desk drawers, in coatpockets and handbags. But for all the advance planning, Lou was a roving spirit, unable to resist the latent adventure of an uncharted road. For her, the outdoors was meant to be explored rather than looked at. She complimented a friend on her new shoes, but not without regrets. After all, you could hardly walk a mile in them. Personally, she preferred her "whee shoes," a pair of white elkskins that signaled to everyone around her that the workday was over, and some exploration about to begin. She was asked why she wore so little jewelry, a logical question for an ardent geologist, and she answered that when she was young, she couldn't afford such adornments, and now, she preferred to use the money for better ends—like helping someone through college.[41]

Her appetite for living was matched only by her circumspection as a public figure. She liked informal parties better than receiving lines; best of all, she liked to spontaneously collect a couple hundred Girl Scout leaders and bring them to lunch at the White House. Intimates said she was the woman they'd like to meet in the middle of an earthquake—and being married to Herbert Hoover brought plenty of convulsions. For nearly half a century she remained at his side, uprooting her family whenever a new mine or continent beckoned. She eased his torment, salved his wounds, and introduced him to an entirely new generation of journalists, beginning with Frank Mason of the International News Service, whose wife served with Lou in the Girl Scout movement. Hoover himself took pride in the one he called "my good lady who already knows all about a thing or else finds it out." And if there was much that he guarded from the public, much withheld even from friends, there were no places secret from Lou. When he fell out of favor with the public, she drew still more protectively to him. After every speech he made, he could expect an approving telegram from Lou. When the former president visited the open range and the scruffy little mining towns that dotted the Rocky Mountain states, she was there too, knitting endlessly, laughing easily with leather-skinned westerners. She much preferred Palo Alto to New York, and the casual pursuits of a college town to the feverish engines of the big city. She even taught one pair of Stanford women how to pan for gold in her back lawn, complete with a hose for a river and a baked bean lunch for nourishment. But she accompanied Bert East, where he could be closer to political events and keep his hand on the national pulse.[42]

"I wouldn't know what to do with a daughter," she confessed, she who mothered nearly a million girls in green uniforms. "I am a lucky woman to have had my life's trail alongside the paths of three such men and boys," she wrote, early in the last autumn of her life. At Christmastime, she mailed money to a former White House maid, with instructions to buy "some little things for the children for me." In her Waldorf desk she kept a thick stack of uncashed checks, repayments of assistance lent to strangers as well as friends, students seeking college tuition, mothers worried about infants, old people shunted aside to find for themselves.[43]

The holidays passed, and Lou early in January went to a concert by Mildred Dilling, a harpist who had once graced the East Room of the White House. Leaving the performance, she told Bunny Miller that the air felt good; why not walk home? A short while later, she guessed she had better get a taxi, and when the women arrived back at the Waldorf, Bunny was surprised that her friend did not invite her in for dinner. Inside Suite 31-A, Bert was present, along with Edgar Rickard. Both men were about to leave for a dinner honoring Perrin Galpin. Lou went to her room, and Bert followed to kiss her good night.[44]

He found her sprawled on the floor, her heart beating feebly. A house doctor was sent for, and Lou was tenderly lifted to the bed, but within a few minutes her husband reappeared in the living room. "She's gone," he said. The news was flashed far beyond Park Avenue, just as Calvin Coolidge's passing eleven years ago this week had rapidly become public property. In Washington, another president dictated another condolence note, the first formal communication with his longtime antagonist in over a decade. "The radio has brought me word of the sorrow which has come to you with such overwhelming force," Franklin Roosevelt wrote. "To you and all who mourn with you the passing of a devoted wife and Mother, I offer the assurance of heartfelt sympathy in which Mrs. Roosevelt joins me." Three weeks elapsed before Hoover penned a reply, a single sentence expressing appreciation for "your most kind message."[45]

Lou died on a Friday evening. The following Monday morning, fifteen hundred mourners jammed into St. Bartholomew's Episcopal Church, just across the street from the Waldorf. Downstairs the former First Lady rested in a small chapel. Now, her casket was carried into the nave of the Byzantine church, where a choir sang her favorite humns and the chairman of the American Friends Service Committee read passages from First Corinthians, Revelation and the Gospel of Saint John. There was no eulogy. The coffin lay bathed in a thin wintry light, blanketed by smilax, sweet peas, lilacs and red roses. Along with the celebrated, the pews of St. Bartholomew's were occupied by two hundred Girl Scouts and Alex Sampson and Leo Thompson, black ushers fondly remembered by the Hoovers from their White House days. Joe Kennedy was there, along with Roy Howard, Mrs. Wendell Willkie, Eddie Rickenbacker and of course, Rickard, Gibson and Strauss. Hoover's two sons sat on either side of their father, spared the ordeal of greeting people by a thoughtful rector, who led them to a side door when the services were over.[46]

At four-twenty that afternoon, the three men, joined by Bunny Miller, left Grand Central Station for the West Coast. Lou was going home, to Palo Alto, not so far from the haunts of her girlhood and the mountain trails she loved to hike. Twenty years later, her rest was disturbed when Bert himself was buried on an Iowa hillside and another train carried her back to lie at his side. On his deathbed, the former president reached out in a final protective embrace. He asked that none of her personal papers be divulged for at least twenty years. Lou, he explained, was capable of sharp words when defending loved ones. He wouldn't wish her memory to be marred by any unintentional hurt done the living.[47]

★   ★

Hoover returned to New York two weeks later, alone and bereft of Lou's stabilizing presence. Within two weeks, he and Edgar Rickard dissolved the Seeing Cairo Fund, thirty-five years after the two couples established it in hopes of becoming world travelers; most of the fund was donated in Lou's memory to the war library at Stanford. Then the former president was off again, this time to spend time with the Duke and Duchess of Windsor in the Bahamas, where the exiled ex-monarch, like Hoover condemned to stalk the fringes of authority, was serving an unhappy term as governor. Unlike that essentially frivolous man, Hoover was neither drugged by memory nor blinded by slights, real and imagined. "I have now returned from the tropics," he informed Alf Landon, "and am moved to take up the battle again." He stayed young by working, as well as by nurturing the animosities of a lifetime.[48]

Nineteen forty-four was another presidential election year, with Hoover unleashing strong gusts of anger at Willkie, whom he compared to Roosevelt. Willkie, he wrote, was "the same sort of exhibitionist, has the same lack of administrative ability and is no more reliable intellectually." The 1940 nominee, whose candidacy faced a crucial test in the April 5 Wisconsin primary, had to be exposed, or else the GOP would be mired as the Democrats were for years under the hypnotic spell of William Jennings Bryan. His own strategy was to urge on a host of favorite sons, who together might amass enough delegates to block the ambitious Hoosier. He had words of encouragement for Ohio's John Bricker, the conservative favorite. For Thomas E. Dewey, who behind a façade of disinterest was hopefully calculating his own chances, Hoover had a distant admiration.[49]

Late that March, the two men dined privately, and Dewey all but predicted his nomination on the first ballot at the coming convention. He pressed for California's Earl Warren to be his running mate (Hoover preferred Douglas MacArthur), and when the former president suggested that following his election Dewey appoint a special bureau of six hundred lawyers and two thousand detectives to expose "at least one case per day of the corruption of the present regime," Dewey went him one better: six thousand lawyers and twenty thousand detectives would be needed, he said, "and some new jails." The governor sought Hoover's advice on a key foreign policy speech he was to deliver a month later, and was rewarded with a blast at John Foster Dulles, Dewey's shadow Secretary of State. Dulles, said Hoover, was filled with a lot of fuzzy ideas, inhabiting "a dream-land which had been completely knocked into a cocked hat by Joe Stalin." Any notion of a world government after the war, he went on, would surely founder on the opposition of both Great Britain and Russia. When the session ended, Hoover noted Dewey's intellect, his energy and political gifts, "but in some way I have a reservation as to his character. . . . He has fewer of the human qualities than Bricker has. Whatever humanitarianism he has is coldly calculated in the terms of votes." Yet Dewey was a brilliant manager, widely admired for his combination of tax cutting and social progressivism in New York, and still regarded with something like awe for his remarkable performance a decade earlier as New York City's fearless Gangbuster.[50]

Whatever hesitation he might have harbored over Dewey, Hoover could not conceal his delight when Wisconsin Republicans decisively rejected Willkie. It was, he told a friend, "a public revulsion from Hollywood demagoguery" and a triumph for intellectual honesty. In between editing Bricker's speeches and waiting in vain for similar courtesies from the Dewey camp, Hoover took time out to urge Cordell Hull to adopt his own plan to redeem the freedom of Finland. Hull, understandably, replied that Finnish freedom was more imperiled by Helsinki's cooperation with Hitler than by the Russian forces who since 1939 had occupied much of the country. Hull also revealed that the administration had sought to broker a peace settlement between the two governments a year earlier, only to run aground on the rocks of Finnish intransigence.[51]

The former president could claim a victory of sorts, when both houses of Congress approved a resolution urging the administration to negotiate relief efforts for occupied Europe. By then, according to George Gallup's pollsters, two-thirds of the American public endorsed Hoover's position. But the White House shrugged off the hint from Capitol Hill, and Hoover was left sputtering at earlier, weighted wordings of Gallup's questions. A flap arose involving Douglas MacArthur's possible candidacy for the GOP nomination, and the hero of Corregidor was assured by his former commander in chief that Drew Pearson, a persistent critic, was "the most complete skunk in American journalism." A more ominous face from the past surfaced early in May when word reached the Waldorf that Charlie Michaelson had been lured back into the political wars by organized labor. Far more militant than the AFL, Philip Murray's CIO was organizing the first political action committee to bolster Roosevelt's reelection prospects. Michaelson told the labor bosses, led by Sidney Hillman, that the best way to stop Dewey was to tar him with the Hoover brush. (As Tommy Corcoran remarked to a group of Democratic planners that spring, "We ought to be eternally grateful to Herbert Hoover, who has been our meal ticket for twelve years.") In the White House itself, FDR puckishly informed reporters off the record of "a wonderful story" involving "a former President [who] had lost his hair—shirt," then would say no more.[52]

The governor of New York, a man of icy genius and sensitive antennae, picked up the danger signals early and kept his distance. By the end of May, Hoover was telling in aggrieved tones of new rebuffs from the Dewey camp and its chief strategist, Herbert Brownell. "I do not pretend that you are adopting my ideas," he wrote the likely nominee after Dewey's foreign policy address of April 29, "but the central theme of it has been my steady agitation for the past two years and therefore I could not help but approve."[53]

Hoover was rewarded with an invitation to refrain from any public efforts on Dewey's behalf. Late in May, he was forced to issue a statement disclaiming support for any candidate. Two weeks later, when third parties approached him about persuading Warren to accept the vice presidency, Hoover was dubious. When Dewey himself repeated the request—after first asking that he conceal his own participation in the matter—the former president concluded that Dewey was not, as he put it, "a big man." Still, he promised to do what he could with Warren. Early in June, with the convention only days away, John Bricker visited Suite 31-A, to fan his own dying hopes of nomination and reassure Hoover that many delegates shared his doubts about Dewey. Urged on by friends, Hoover dropped from his convention text a renunciation of further political activity, apparently inserted at the behest of Dewey's allies. His speech became instead an eloquent plea on behalf of a realistic peace, and a new generation of leadership personified by forty-two-year-old Tom Dewey.[54]

Twelve million young men who had fought and suffered on the beaches and in the mud would soon come home, Hoover told the delegates. They would insist upon a reckoning, and a justification for their sacrifice. "They will reject the easy language of politics, the straddlings and compromises, and the senseless phrases of skilled ghost-writers. And they will be watchful of political leaders lest they again be led into the giving of blood and risking the future of their families from failures in international statesmanship. . . .

I rejoice that this is to be." For his own generation, Hoover chose a coun-seling role. His message was to young America, whom he wished to carry the torch "bravely and aloft. Carry it with the dauntless assurance of your forebears who faced the chill of the ocean, the dangers of the forest and the desert, the loneliness of the pioneer to build upon this continent a nation dedicated to justice and liberty and the dignity of the individual man. Watch over it. Vigilantly guard it. Protect it from foes, within and without. . . . Youth of the Republican Party!" he nearly shouted, "I, representing the generation of your fathers, greet you and send you forth crusaders for freedom which alone can come under a Constitutional Republic—a Consti-tutional America."

Following Dewey's nomination, and the pairing of the New Yorker with Bricker of Ohio, Hoover sat on the platform with his sons to hear the latest torchbearer proclaim his gospel of efficiency and fresh blood. Both boys were ushered out of a reception line lest photographers snap their picture with Dewey. Brownell renewed his request for noninvolvement in the coming campaign; Hoover was forced to deny that he had met privately with the new nominee at the home of a friend. "You know what his motive it," he explained almost matter-of-factly to a companion. "He's afraid that associa-tion with me will be brought up against him by the Democrats." He did not expect to be asked to participate in the campaign, Hoover told others—but that didn't prevent him from advising Bricker to push for a coalition govern-ment, including prominent conservative Democrats who might be ap-pointed to half the major Cabinet and agency positions. It was an idea he had explored for several months, wrote Hoover. Depending on the outcome of the Democratic convention, it might be unveiled as a contribution, not to partisan victory, but to the war effort. Dewey rejected the scheme on his own, as soon as the opposition dumped Vice President Henry Wallace in favor of the less radical Harry Truman.[55]

The campaign stirred to life, and true to its prediction, labor made Hoo-ver its chief target. Sidney Hillman called Dewey "mouthpiece of Herbert Hoover and the GOP Old Guard," and attacked the former president for his "unregenerate nationalism . . . and stubborn nostalgia for the discredited past." Other labor spokesmen dubbed the GOP contender "Little Sir Echo" and disseminated pictures of Hoover as ventriloquist to Dewey's dummy. The CIO rushed out millions of copies of that old chestnut Lest We Forget, complete with references to apple sellers ("the only independent business-men ever put out of work by the New Deal"), and prosperity around the corner. Hillman upped the ante, labeling the New Yorker "the crown prince of Hooverism," surrounded by "tools of reaction and selfish greed." The

hand of Charlie Michaelson was visible behind the daily barrage of invec-
tive. Yet Dewey himself rose to the bait, telling reporters in Spokane that
he had not seen Hoover since the convention and had no plans to see him
again. A veteran wrote the former president of a recent American Legion
convention, where his proselytizing on Dewey's behalf had been met with
bitter denunciations of the last Republican president, who had greeted the
heroes of World War I with army bayonets in the streets of Washington. It
was difficult to catch up with such smears, Hoover replied; he was "greatly
obliged" for the man's efforts to clear his name.[56]

His seventieth birthday came and went virtually unnoticed. Ed Sullivan
found room for the great event in his column, right after the Duchess of
Windsor's recent appendectomy. The former president himself seemed
mindless of the milestone. In Utah to inspect mining properties, he dined
on silver-dollar hotcakes and dispatched slices of cake to kitchen workers.
He told reporters that he was too busy to celebrate. "Besides," as he put it,
"there is no interest in this sort of thing." He reserved his attention for
public affairs. The CIO, he concluded, "is the hatchet organization for the
New Deal and improves every shining hour." Much about the campaign
would depend on the war itself. "If it should be over by September or early
October," Hoover forecast, "Uncle Joe's activities are going to be plain to
the American people and they will be pretty distasteful." Meanwhile, he
couldn't refuse FDR a compliment on his political skills. It was a stroke of
genius, Hoover concluded, for the wily executive "to go around over the
Pacific and to lift the idea of Commander-in-Chief . . . to greater public
attention." It also called attention to Dewey's civilian status.[57]

The Republican effort was certain to be the best organized in years, he
told another friend in mid-August. But what Hugh Gibson contemptuously
labeled "the Youth Movement" within Dewey's circle came in for more than
its share of criticism. First, Dulles snapped up Cordell Hull's invitation to
meet with him in Washington and reserve a nonpartisan stance for the
forthcoming United Nations organization. Dewey's speeches, sensitive to
the polyglot realities of New York, but grating to a purist like Hoover,
seemed tired rehashes of Willkie's 1940 platitudes and apologies. Worse yet,
when Willkie died suddenly in October, and both men found themselves
occupying the same pew at his funeral, Hoover was furious at Dewey's
studied ignorance of his presence. Even Eleanor Roosevelt had displayed
sufficient manners to come over and greet him—but not his own party's
candidate for president.[58]

Still, his contempt for FDR easily outweighed his suspicion of the aggressive Dewey, who seemed conciliatory to everyone but his own party's right

wing. "Having relieved all anxious minds by bowing myself out in favor of the youngsters . . . ," Hoover wrote on October 13, "now I am back into it, praying hard for Dewey's election." If Hillman and Roosevelt kept making mistakes, he hoped, "Dewey will win. And this country will be saved." An old friend visiting the Waldorf tried to deflect Hoover's attention from politics and what Rickard called his "peeved attitude of neglect." Brownell came by, and Hoover complained that no one in the campaign was defending his administration or seeking his advice. Then, as if to confound his critics and defy mortality, Roosevelt impressed observers doubtful of his health by riding six hours in a driving rainstorm through all five of New York's boroughs. The sensitive issue of American sovereignty in a global peacekeeping body was submerged to FDR's benefit. Dewey's chances plummeted. "The situation requires constant prayer," Hoover noted in the closing days of the campaign.[59]

The night before the election, he dined with Arthur Krock, who echoed his own criticism of Dewey's attempt to be all things to all people. Harry Byrd, Bernard Baruch, Joe Kennedy and other leading anti-New Deal Democrats had been prepared to endorse the Republican's candidacy, said Krock, until they heard him lavish praise on the Wagner Act and other Rooseveltian reforms. "Too much bird shot, too little concentrated fire" was Krock's description of Dewey's campaign attacks against sluggishness and administrative chaos in Washington. The next day, 47 million voters agreed, awarding Roosevelt his fourth term and fattening Democratic majorities in both houses of Congress. Hoover penned a gracious note to the loser and claimed to find consolation in the fact that the New Deal "will have to take the bumps for four years. We do need for our younger Republicans to stop fighting their elders," he interjected. Steeled to defeat, Hoover did something characteristic. He decided irrevocably to sell 2300 S Street. He was seventy years old, locked in a losing contest with time and Roosevelt's magic hold over the people. He would never live in Washington again.[60]

★   ★

In December, Hoover alternated between cryptic references to the "fabulous power" contained in uranium, even now the object of a race for its development, and a vague plan to consult with GOP congressional figures, a belated elder statesman valued for more than his memories. Dewey made efforts at reconciliation, calling Hugh Gibson personally and sending Herb Brownell to talk with Hoover at the Waldorf. The former president reported early in January 1945 the defeated candidate's failure to write a party charter backed by congressional Republicans; the resulting clash of ideologies and egos prevented the GOP from casting off its by now ingrained reputation for negativism. Harboring suspicions in his own house, Hoover fell out with the director of his Stanford Library over his personal preference for pure scholarship. Caught up in his own crusades, Hoover wanted the War Library to engage in what Edgar Rickard called "current propaganda." It began a dispute consuming more than a decade, at times nearly estranging Stanford's most prominent alumnus from the school of his youth.[61]

An example of what Rickard might have had in mind was Hoover's unwavering opposition to those who demanded unconditional surrender from a shattered Germany. "That can result in nothing except the complete destruction of any Germany which is able to resist a future Russian expansion," he insisted. Yet he managed words of praise for the Yalta agreements, as first announced to the world in February 1945. He admonished Alf Landon not to abandon hope, nor yield to "blind and futile opposition to the central thing we all want—a workable, effective machinery that will at least help preserve peace." The Atlantic Charter, Moscow Pact, Dumbarton Oaks, and Yalta all contained principles which, if carried out in good faith, laid a foundation for a global peacekeeping organization. The odds were against it, he conceded, and in time, their potential was likely to come to nothing. "But at least we can hold up the ideals and promises as a basis of real peace . . ."[62]

Perhaps nations in bondage might yet appeal to the structure fashioned at Dumbarton Oaks in the summer of 1944. Build on what was started there, Hoover urged his ally in Topeka. "Put another way," he concluded, "I am for helping design an experiment. If it has the elements of success, to support it; if it is hopeless, then to damn it. And I want to see it succeed." Within weeks, however, his hopes were beginning to fade, corroded by Cal O'Laughlin's interpretation of what FDR had really agreed to at Yalta. A Triple Alliance loomed large in postwar affairs, only one of many departures from Hoover's own prescription for peace. Secrecy still shrouded much of the Yalta pact from the American public, but O'Laughlin heaped scorn on Roosevelt's concessions, including a large slice of Poland to the Soviets, and voting privileges within the proposed Security Council. "The world is bumping badly," Hoover concluded a month later as he put finishing touches on a series of articles interpreting Dumbarton Oaks and pressing the case for his own kind of international body.[63]

The world would gather in San Francisco that April to translate the broad principles of that earlier conference into a workable plan for keeping the peace. Hoover perceived a number of ways to shorten the odds on their success. First of all, he wished the charter of the new organization to embody a lengthy list of individual rights, including freedom of the press and religion, democratic elections, and protection of minorities. Alongside the proposed World Committees to promote economic and social welfare, Hoover suggested a third, devoted to ensuring political rights. He wanted the new charter to provide for flexibility and periodic revision of treaties. "Peace can be preserved," he wrote in the *New York Times*, "not by preventing change and putting the future in a straightjacket, but by seeking to control change and direct it. . . . Each and every plan for preserving peace, whether it be the Pax Romana, the balance of power, the legitimist theory at the Congress of Vienna, or collective security of the League . . . [has] this one thing in common. They set up a new order, and knowing it to be good, they provide that the new boundaries and other conditions shall be kept and anyone who violates it is evil. Never yet, however, have settlements been made after firing ceases that held against growing and changing forces after the war."

That did not exhaust his agenda. Hoover advocated organization of the world body on a regional basis, governing affairs in the Western Hemisphere, Europe and Asia, and building on the example of the "concert of Europe" that once prevented world wars for nearly a century. Only if such regional associations failed should the Security Council intervene. This way, smaller nations might preserve their influence and find their voice, and the United Nations would shed the appearance of a military alliance conceived by and for a few great powers. It would also relieve American anxieties over being involved "in secondary problems all over the earth." He proposed the disarmament of the defeated and their policing by hundred-thousand-man forces placed in German and Japan for a generation. He dusted off his own 1932 suggestion that all aggressive weapons be suppressed, applying it to the victors as well as the vanquished.

On the most difficult issue of all, whether or not the U.S. delegate to the Security Council would have personal authority to commit American troops to battle, "I cannot bring myself to the delegation of such power to any one human being," wrote Hoover. It negated the democratic process itself. Yet neither was he blind to the need for haste in confronting aggression before it occurred. His own solution, offered tentatively, was to permit the president, backed by majority vote of the foreign relations committees of both houses of Congress, to determine whether or not the full Congress should be consulted. In conclusion, Hoover again appealed for caution in designing a postwar world. "We should take time to cool off from the hot emotion of war," he advised readers. "Our indignation may lead us away from stern justice into vengeance. Victory with vengeance means ultimate disaster to the victor. We cannot have both peace and revenge." No sooner had the articles appeared than their author was denounced as a threat to peace by *Pravda*. It was, for Hoover, a badge of honor he wore proudly, even militantly.

Early in April, the Japanese government was replaced by a new regime, which Hoover and others believed sincerely interested in peace. Ideas for a possible early end to the fighting, short of a massive American invasion of the Japanese islands (and conceding nothing to the Russians, who were still formally at peace with Tokyo), began to germinate in Hoover's head. Their chance of becoming more than a historical curiosity was elevated dramatically on April 12, 1945, when Franklin Roosevelt died at Warm Springs, Georgia, the victim of a cerebral hemorrhage. "The nation sorrows at the passing of its president," Hoover said in a carefully worded statement. "Whatever differences there may have been, they end in the regrets of death." In a personal note to the widow, he was more unguarded. His heart went out to her in sympathy, he wrote. Her own courage needed little support; yet the entire country was extending it to her. "With Mrs. Hoover's passing I know the great vacancy that has come into your life and I cannot forget your fine courtesy in writing to me at that time." Eleanor Roosevelt replied promptly. "I know that you understand only too well the overwhelming sense of loss which is mine. . . . My appreciation and thanks go to you for your kind message." [64]

The night of Roosevelt's death, Hoover attended a previously scheduled party at the home of a New York friend. While others did little to conceal their relief at the day's news, the former president said nothing, a dour observer of a tasteless tableau. He composed a warmly supportive note to the new chief executive, adding his own willingness to serve in any capacity should it be useful, and he told friends that Harry Truman represented a change for the better. "He is pledged to carry out the Roosevelt policies," O'Laughlin noted in a letter dated April 13. "You will recall that this was the pledge also of Mr. Taft when he succeeded T.R., and Mr. Taft carried them out—on a shutter." [65]

Roosevelt was gone, replaced in the Oval Office by a graduate of Missouri's notorious Pendergast machine, a man lacking his predecessor's eloquence and Machiavellian flair. Only time would reveal whether Harry Truman had more in common with Hoover than a rural childhood, and whether the passing of Hoover's bête noire marked the end of his ostracism as well as an era dominated as no other by the elegant, puzzling, incomparable FDR, the democrat-aristocrat whose legacy now devolved upon a most unlikely successor.

EVENING STAR

1945 – 1964

CHAPTER TEN

THE ODDEST COUPLE

★

All Americans will wish you strength for your gigantic task. You have the right to call for any service in aid of the country.
  —Herbert Hoover, to Harry Truman, April 12, 1945[1]

If you should be in Washington, I would be most happy to talk over the European food situation with you. Also it would be a pleasure for me to become acquainted with you. —Harry Truman, to Herbert Hoover, May 24, 1945[2]

★

Memory endowed the Hoover-Truman relationship with unique poignancy, but it never entirely eliminated Hoover's doubts. Oblivious to his own contradictions, he easily diagnosed Truman's. Over and over, he told friends, Franklin Roosevelt's successor was a split personality, "a funny little fellow," as he put it to one. "One day I find in him a devoted public servant who really comes from the people and who is not putting on a show when he stops in a store and talks with the employees and the customers, because he likes the average man and likes to mingle with him; the next time I find him to be a Pendergast-machine politician who will do anything for a vote." Capable of hailing one Hoover speech in 1948 as the greatest since the Gettysburg Address, a few weeks before launching personal attacks on the Great Engineer under whose leadership America backed into her worst depression, Truman could also disarm the chronically thin-skinned former president by dismissing the latter as a "damned canned speech" released to the press before he'd had a chance to revise it. Hoover was not alone in his puzzlement over the essential Truman, so obvious and yet in some ways as unfathomable as his Olympian predecessor. To be sure, Hoover noted, HST lacked Roosevelt's sure touch with Congress—or as he put it, his "adroit coercion and bribing with political spoils." [3]

One quality that stood out to contemporaries as to historians was Truman's decisiveness. When Speaker of the House Sam Rayburn raised doubts over inviting the perennial Democratic whipping boy back into public life, Truman put his foot down. Hoover, said the chief executive, was "the best man that I know of, and he'll do the job for me. . . . You politicians leave him alone and we'll get an organization in this government. Now Sam, that's all—you help!" Blunt as Hoover himself, Truman reacted with typical saltiness when his new friend gently twitted him about spending so much time at his Key West vacation getaway. None of the other presidents Hoover had known could have spent so much time at play. [4]

"I guess I'm a damn sight better manager than my predecessors whom you have known," Truman blurted. [5]

The implied rebuke to Roosevelt's memory was another underlying, if subtle, bond between the two men. Truman had chafed in ignorance of FDR's policies during his brief vice presidency (he had also cast a vote in favor of Hoover's European relief scheme in February 1944). Because he succeeded Roosevelt, his innate modesty was misinterpreted as self-doubt by some of the late president's most devoted followers ("professional liberals" in Truman's derisive phrase). Holdover Cabinet members like Henry Wallace and Harold Ickes proved too heavy a cross to bear for the party regular from Missouri, more comfortable with meat and potato Democrats than the starry-eyed idealists gathered around Roosevelt and now sworn to carry his standard. Hoover's own attitude toward the dead leader was barely concealed beneath the polite solemnities of formal condolence. In later years, he liked to tell of an unlikely appeal from Elliott Roosevelt to John D. Rockefeller, Junior. The younger man hoped for financial assistance with which to transform his father's Hyde Park estate into a national park. Rather than approach Rockefeller himself, Elliott went to Hoover, who drily remarked to friends that he felt no particular obligation to make FDR's burial place a shrine. Nevertheless, he drove up the Hudson Valley one afternoon to see for himself. The estate seemed frayed and unkempt, its shabbiness made more objectionable still when his lawyers checked up on its ownership, and discovered title to the property resting with Elliott and his mother. [6]

His obsession with Roosevelt did not end there. He was much interested in Westbrook Pegler's research into the business dealings of another Roose-

velt son, James, Hoover informed the columnist in August 1945, including
FDR's personal solicitation of advertising for the boy's radio chain. His rival
had been in the soil of Hyde Park barely a month when Hoover was advised
by Joe Kennedy of his own plans to publish an explosive book detailing
Roosevelt's alleged duplicity in guiding a reluctant nation in World War II.
Throughout his 1940 campaign against Wendell Willkie, Roosevelt pledged
peace; yet Kennedy revealed that joint military preparations were going
forward between London and Washington all the while. Indeed, before
Neville Chamberlain's death in the fall of 1940, the desperately sick man
had written the ambassador a nine-page letter in his own hand, insisting
that if their common policies had not been sabotaged by the warmongers,
the world might have been spared its present agony.[7]

Years later, friends could find Hoover checking and double-checking lists
of Rooseveltian falsehoods, the core of his proposed Magnum Opus. "Libel
mixed with propriety," said one editor privy to its intents. For one thing,
Hoover never forgave his successor for aiding Stalin in the war. He followed
closely the congressional investigation of events leading up to Pearl Harbor,
felt vindicated in his belief that the Atlantic Charter had merely camouflaged a U.S.–British military alliance, and looked forward to a spate of
volumes reassessing the father of the New Deal. His own enmities colored
the memoirs to which he devoted sporadic attention. As long as the prospect
of influencing the present shimmered in his eyes, the past could engage him
only fitfully.[8]

Just ten days after FDR's death, he told a friend, "Now that there has
been a change in Washington, I may be on the air more often." He was
contemplating a regular radio series of his own. He was also toying with
feelers, at first maddeningly faint, from the Truman White House. He
wished out loud that he might be named Secretary of War in Henry Stimson's place. Only the War Department, Hoover argued, could avert mass
and imminent famine in the rubble of Europe. "It is a kind of non-ideologi-
cal Republican job," was the way he put it.[9]

Ironically, this came only two days after Stimson himself invited his old
chief out to his Long Island estate. By the beginning of May 1945 the
Secretary of War was raising Hoover's name in private meetings with the
new president, urging Truman to avail himself of Hoover's expertise regarding the chaotic situation in Europe, and the looming threat that Herbert
Lehman and UNRRA were unable to avert. Truman was instantly agreeable. He had been thinking of just such a step on his own, he told Stimson;
in fact, Hoover would soon be paying him a visit. Yet two days later, when
Stimson again contacted the former president, no formal invitation had

been issued. Hoover had no desire to, as he put it, "ride on the horse of my pride." On the other hand, he rumbled, he had been told of a Steve Early remark to the effect that "if Hoover wanted anything he would have to come down on his knees to get it." [10]

Stimson had long regarded him as stubborn, acknowledged his onetime superior. This time, he was right. There needn't be three minutes between him and Truman, but he was adamant about refusing to come to Washington until the courtesy of a personal invitation was extended. To others, he explained his intransigence in a different light: having been made a Democratic scapegoat in four national campaigns, he would insist that Truman make at least this gesture of respect. His position was buttressed by intense opposition to any Hoover role in postwar relief by men close to the president, including Stimson's own deputies Robert Lovett and Brehon Somervell. (Meanwhile, at least one senator, New Jersey's H. Alexander Smith, was urging Truman to appoint Hoover to the U.S. delegation attending the organizing conference of the UN in San Francisco, a job Hoover himself rejected as too constrictive.) [11]

On May 12, Hoover on his own called Stimson to arrange a luncheon for the next afternoon. From at least three different sources, he had been told that "a big job in Europe" awaited him. If so, Stimson's visit shed no light on what it might be. For three hours the two men talked, the host making clear his opposition to Henry Morgenthau's plan to defang Germany by turning her into a pastoral, agricultural cipher in the European family. He pressed his own vision of the Army undertaking immediate relief. Most important of all was the impetus that within forty-eight hours led to an extraordinary document—Hoover's personal formula for an early end to war with Japan. [12]

"Very interesting, rather dramatic and radical" was Stimson's characterization of a four-page memorandum outlining Stalin's wartime gains and the economic adversity they posed to the United States and Britain. As a result of the fighting and his own negotiating skills, the Russian dictator had added 200 million subjects to his Communist empire. What's more, guessed Hoover, the Soviets were likely to annex Manchuria, North China and Korea in the Far East, a base camp from which to extend their ideological domination over all of China and a prostrate Japan. Ultimately, Britain's own Asian possessions would be endangered. The threat grew with each day the Japanese war continued. Yet the Russians themselves were unlikely to enter the fight anytime soon because, as Hoover told Stimson, "She can take what she wants after we have defeated Japan." [13]

Should the U.S. be forced to battle the Japanese military to ultimate extinction, it would require a million men on the home islands alone. "And we are likely to have won the war for Russia's benefit just as we have done in Europe." He had a better idea. Suppose Chiang Kai-shek, "in order to assure the preservation of Manchuria to China and the ascendency of his own government . . . should make peace on these terms:

"1. That Japan withdraw from all of China, including Manchuria, and hand the government of China to Chiang Kai-shek.

"2. That the Chinese government receive all of the Japanese Government railways, ports, mines and factories in Manchuria as reparations.

"3. That Japan be confined to Korea and Formosa. Neither of these people are Chinese and China has no particular moral rights in these countries."

As for the U.S. and Britain, they too should be lenient, forgoing reparations or territorial concessions in exchange for complete disarmament. As a result, Hoover predicted, hundreds of thousands of lives would be saved, America's own economy would be preserved to aid in the relief of other nations, Russian expansion would be halted, and Japan might return to a cooperative stance with Western civilization. No one could know how his proposals would be received in Tokyo, he concluded. But a new and relatively moderate ministry was in place, the emperor was a reasonable man, and if the suggestions came from Chiang himself, they just might stave off disaster.[14]

Nor was his attention riveted on the Pacific. In a major address before the "Save the Children" organization in New York on May 9, Hoover warned of the urgency confronting Europe's starving civilians. Children of the Old World were stunted in their growth, prey to tuberculosis, rickets, and other nutritional diseases. Their parents were little better off. For four years, he had tried to penetrate the British blockade and help these innocent victims of war. More recently, the United Nations themselves had promised abundant food on liberation, a pledge yet to be redeemed. But criticism would achieve nothing. "The dead are beyond our reach." The greatest danger posed now, said Hoover, was to the working class populations of Belgium, France, Italy, Holland, Norway and Poland, none of which had produced sufficient food in the previous harvest to last through the summer months. Farmers would keep enough of what they had to avert starvation; the well-off in the cities would always manage to survive. "The real sufferers from this shortage will be the poor of the large cities." With 450 million bushels of North American wheat available for export, the U.S. might yet provide Europeans with the cereals that made up 60 percent of their diet. Bread, too, could be shipped across the Atlantic. Together, these products could save the adult population.

The biggest problem lay in a shortage of animal fats, meat and dairy products, precisely what undernourished children most required. If UNRRA could not inaugurate the immediate flow of millions of tons of food—and Hoover was not sanguine about the prospect—then only the U.S. Army, with its command of transportation and swollen ranks of personnel, could do the job. Relief would have to start flowing within two weeks, warned Hoover. "It is now 11:59 on the clock of starvation." Whatever men might debate or propose in the form of peace treaties, he was convinced that the preservation of Europe's children was of greater importance, both now and in the long run. "After all," he declared, "peace, prosperity and freedom will not arise from stunted minds or stunted bodies."

As if in response, Stimson on May 23 dispatched Under Secretary of War John J. McCloy and a bevy of military men to see Hoover at the Waldorf and refute his notion that the armed forces could assume relief responsibilities during the next ninety days. Confirming the existence of an emergency, as well as the Communist danger that accompanied hunger, the men in uniform pointed a finger at UNRRA, a lack of cooperation between the liberated nations, and a bottleneck within domestic transportation that prevented any large shipments of U.S. food supplies during the critical period. Hoover refused to accept defeat. Set up a dictator to rule the area from Norway to Sicily, he told the men in uniform, with strong men beneath him overseeing shipping, transportation, food and coal supplies. Appoint a domestic counterpart to direct American agencies, along with a railroad executive capable of cutting through red tape and getting supplies to East Coast ports. Persuade Congress to appropriate funds, or run the risk of seeing Europe's liberation plant the seeds of Communist triumph.[15]

Frustrating as the meeting turned out, Hoover within twenty-four hours had a new straw to clutch: the long-awaited personal invitation from Truman to call upon him at the White House. By now, he was telling friends that Truman was a pleasant surprise, likely to make a better president than Dewey. He had done exactly the right thing in appointing Clinton Anderson Secretary of Agriculture, with added authority over domestic production and prices. Even Truman's decision to send Harry Hopkins to Moscow to see Stalin earned his approval. Hoover was, Rickard noted in his diary, "elated" by the latest gesture in his direction and prepared to remain in Washington for several days if necessary.[16]

Much has been written about his visit to Truman on May 28, the first time in more than twelve years that he set foot in the White House. Truman himself described, late in his life, a teary-eyed old man requiring several minutes to compose himself and quiet his emotions. Hoover recalled a less lachrymose encounter. In response to Truman's questions, he set forth his view of the famine threat as well as the armed forces's own obligation to combat it. With a million tons of wheat per month until the next harvest, bread rations might be lifted and the Communist appeal blunted. He outlined his own role following World War I when the Big Four, sitting in Paris, were able and willing to permit him nearly single-handedly to remove obstructions and slice through bureaucratic delays. He stressed anew the critical importance of the next ninety days, and urged Truman to call for an economic council, with an army man like Lucius Clay representing the victors in rushing needed supplies to the war's human fallout.[17]

America ought not be saddled with total responsibility; coal and transportation, for example, must be left in large part to the Europeans themselves. But food was justifiably a U.S. priority. General Marshall should appoint an officer to procure and ship supplies during the emergency period, aided by a railroad executive like the Pennsylvania line's Walter Franklin. Truman interrupted to say that Stimson was against all this, but that having heard Hoover's explanation, he would like the former president to make his case with renewed urgency to the Secretary personally.

Talk turned to the domestic food situation, which Hoover described as "terrible." Hog production was down 30 percent, and price-fixing was a mess. If anything, the new Secretary of Agriculture required still more power, including complete control over all buying, distribution and production. On foreign affairs, Hoover described the Russians as Asiatics, without the West's reverence for keeping agreements. (Privately, he denounced Molotov and other Soviet diplomats as "hoodlums" disdainful of conventional ethics and the bonds of honor.) Yet we could not think of going to war with Moscow. "A war with Russia," he insisted, "means the extinction of Western civilization or what there is left of it." For the moment, the U.S. must be content to uphold the banner of freedom, to persuade and to cajole where necessary. He had no patience, said Hoover, with people who formulated policies regarding other nations "short of war." Experience showed they always led to war in the end.

Finally, he raised the subject of Japan, setting forth the plan already outlined in his memorandum to Stimson and going one step further: "I am convinced that if you, as President, will make a shortwave broadcast to the people of Japan—tell them they can have their Emperor if they surrender, that it will not mean unconditional surrender except for the militarists— you'll get a peace in Japan—you'll have both wars over." Truman tossed him a pad, instructing him to write down what he might say. Hoover outlined terms consistent with later peace feelers, and the president remarked that any such broadcast would be sure to incur opposition from his own advisers. Would Hoover provide him with a detailed memorandum? [18]

The former president rushed to complete a draft. But he was not optimistic about the results of his fifty-five minutes in the Oval Office. Truman's invitation, he told Rickard, was "wholly political," a shrewd gesture designed to show the new president's own broadmindedness. For his part, he judged it the end of any role he might play in Harry Truman's presidency. Yet even if disappointed in the hope of official responsibilities, Hoover had gained something from the session. From now on, he suggested, those who had smeared him would be at least somewhat cowed; Truman was no Roosevelt. [19]

Hoover did not tarry in Washington. The next day found him back in New York, transferring his theories onto paper for presidential review. Though it satisfied his compulsion to be active, it did not mask his doubts or erode his suspicions. He had been courteously received at the White House, the Army was directed to provide stopgap relief and Truman himself was anxious to pass along word of his gratitude. Autograph seekers and smiling well-wishers flocked to congratulate the former president on the train carrying him north from Washington. Yet he hungered for more tangible signs of popular acceptance. The passing landscape told of spring at its most glorious. Hoover yearned only for Indian summer. [20]

★   ★

Though out of Coventry, he was not yet in vogue. The Communist *Daily Worker* chastised the new president for the affability displayed toward such a notorious "Fascist beast." Nor were Hoover's troubles restricted to the far Left. Only a few days before his meeting with Truman, he vigorously congratulated John Hamilton on his censure of recent Republican candidates whose barometric instincts led them to make peace with the new order. When the GOP abandoned defense of its own conservative administrations, he told Hamilton, permitting them to be "defiled, smeared and lied about unceasingly," the party was guilty of cowardice and betrayal "to the very basic philosophic principles upon which (it) was and must again be founded." That same week, word reached him from J. Edgar Hoover of a scurrilous biography of the former president entitled "The Great American Failure," financed by a California Communist, and designed, as Hoover put it, "to prove that I am 'a born Fascist.' " The FBI director felt confident that publication could be enjoined. In the meantime, he promised his old friend photostats of the manuscript as it evolved. No such protection could shield him from Walter Winchell's gaucheries, including the printed forecast of Hoover's imminent remarriage.[21]

The international scene was little more encouraging. Hoover signed his name to a memorial deploring Soviet domination of Poland and pleading with the White House for release of a dozen Polish underground leaders. "He's always been an adventurer," Hoover rasped of Winston Churchill, whose stunning electoral defeat in July 1945 seemed to him both morally justifiable and the portent of a further swing to the Left in his own land. Still smarting from Churchill's opposition to humanitarian relief in two world wars, Hoover cried foul when the first volume of the former prime minister's war memoirs was published in 1948. Both Stanley Baldwin and Neville Chamberlain had been historically libeled, he insisted, savaged for their adherence to the traditional British policy of Continental balance of power. In his view, Munich was designed to give Hitler easier access to Stalin, until Churchill, Roosevelt and others raised such a hue that Chamberlain was compelled to backtrack, guaranteeing Polish frontiers and making a new war all but certain. For proof, Hoover cited Joe Kennedy's prewar dispatches, and the revelation that Poland's former ambassador had wished to provide copies of the explosive messages to the Hoover Library, only to buckle under pressure from a hostile State Department.[22]

July was the month of Potsdam, where the Big Three essentially ratified the Soviet empire in Eastern Europe and questioned the economic future of the shattered Reich. Hoover made no effort to conceal his doubts. At the Bohemian Grove, he drew a whimsical picture of what he called "woodsy instrumentalities now working toward peace among mankind. . . . Dumbarton Oaks and its adjoining forest, the San Francisco Charter, from little IKONS grew. Bretton Woods grew from the irrepressible American desire to loan all their money to foreigners." The former could barely be seen for all its reservations, "independence with reservations, liberty with reservations. And Bretton Woods undergrowth has poison oak." Only the Bohemian Grove, said Hoover, "is a place of open spaces openly arrived at." Moreover, he told his fellow campers, in describing the annual ritual through which their cares were eliminated, he was replacing the word "cremate" with "liquidate" "in order that we embrace at the same time the spirit of the Bohemian Club and appeasement of Uncle Joe Stalin."[23]

Still more disturbing was the news that American planes had dropped two atomic bombs on two Japanese cities, killing 95,000 people instantly and incinerating four square miles of Hiroshima. "This is the Second Coming with Wrath" muttered Churchill. For once, Hoover was in agreement. Such action, he confided, "revolts my soul." Use of the bomb had besmirched

America's reputation, he told friends. It ought to have been described in graphic terms before being flung out into the sky over Japan. It was, he remarked to a gathering of newspaper publishers in New York six weeks later, "the most terrible and barbaric weapon that has ever come to the hand of man. Despite any sophistries its major use is not to kill fighting men, but to kill women, children and civilian men of whole cities as a pressure on governments. If it comes into general use, we may see all civilization destroyed." Pending solution of mankind's predilection to make war, he suggested that the U.S. keep its atomic secret, while proposing new treaties patterned on those outlawing use of poison gas and possible control of uranium ore at its source by the United Nations Security Council.[24]

In other ways, Hoover hoped to speed the process of normalization. He urged Truman to exempt college age boys from the draft. The future defense of the nation, he wrote Robert Taft, depended on trained engineers, doctors, scientists and others who might undertake public service. "We have already lost four crops of these men and it looks as if we would lose another crop because of the general confusion at the present moment." His own chance to join Taft in the Senate, briefly renewed when Hiram Johnson died early in August, was snuffed out a few days later. Governor Earl Warren appointed Bill Knowland, a young newspaper scion, to fill Johnson's seat. Though disappointed, Hoover grew bolder in his efforts to influence the postwar world.[25]

He passed word to MacArthur, just beginning his tenure as Japan's military shogun, that he should consider a timely retirement from a post that if retained too long "will bring only routine and embarrassment." He tried to untangle the Mideast knot, arguing in print for his plan to recover nearly three million acres of land in Iraq, the basis for resettling Palestinian Arabs there. Afterward, Palestine itself could be turned over to Jewish immigrants in search of a homeland. It might, he concluded, prove "the model migration of history," transferring Arabs to an Arab nation, restoring agricultural prosperity to the ancient valleys of the Tigris and Euphrates, and providing persecuted Jews with a refuge and a beacon. "It would be a solution by engineering," said Hoover, "instead of by conflict." Within a few days, he received a warm note of appreciation from Albert Einstein, thanking him for sponsoring a fund-raising campaign for the Palestine Medical School.[26]

Hoover was deeply troubled by the swift currents of global politics. "Did you ever notice that at every meeting with the Russians," he told a friend late in 1945, "Hull in Moscow, Roosevelt at Teheran and Yalta, [Texas Senator Tom] Connolly at San Francisco, Truman at Potsdam and Byrnes at Moscow—we have appeased every time at the expense of the liberty and freedom of more and more human beings?"[27]

It was the leitmotif of his later years, stated with the prophetic intensity of an Isaiah or John the Baptist. Yet Hoover's Old Testament fierceness was balanced by a New Testament compassion. Early in 1946, Truman again invited him to visit the White House. This, more than anything else, launched the elder statesman on a new career as America's most esteemed healer and humanitarian. As he acknowledged himself, Roosevelt's home-spun successor, who shared his taste for blunt talk and sharp judgments, had added ten years to his life span.

★   ★

Truman's honeymoon with the American people was long since over, terminated abruptly in a noisy babble of domestic restlessness and foreign treachery. His Cabinet was roiled with controversy, as Henry Wallace and other unreconstructed New Dealers were shown the door. Hundreds of thousands of labor union members defied the president and risked legal action matching the ferocity of Truman's private anger. (Hoover himself likened the situation to revolution, and wanted strikes halted as had been done in Britain in the bleak thirties.) Price controls chafed more than ever now that the fighting had ended. Inflation was smoldering away, waiting to burst into flame once the artificial restraints were lifted. Overseas, Stalin was consolidating a vast empire, discarding promises as he annexed nation after nation in Eastern Europe. On top of everything else, much of the world was faced with impending disaster, the product of economies torn apart by war, its hideous aftermath and a wave of natural disasters that followed perversely in its wake.[28]

In Berlin, people chopped down the leafy sentinels that once stood guard along the Unter den Linden; firewood came before esthetics. Columnist Marquis Childs was asked to describe postwar Belgrade. "Like North Dakota bombed," he replied. Ninety percent of Warsaw's housing was obliterated. Italy counted barely a month's supply of grainstuffs in its depleted granaries. Much of Belgium was under water, the destructive legacy of dams blown up a year earlier. Drought was accentuating the usual misery of China and India. Shanghai's warehouses bulged with food; yet there was not transportation to move it into a desperate countryside. In Yokohama, dazed survivors clung to life in shacks of tin and sticks. Even they were fortunate compared to their fellow countrymen in the cities forever marked by atomic destruction.[29]

Early in February 1946, Truman made a public appeal to Americans to conserve food in order that mass starvation might yet be averted in Europe and Asia. Hoover, alerted to the crisis by Agriculture Secretary Clinton Anderson, rallied to his side. UNRRA was devoting much of its efforts to feeding Eastern Europe, he explained, while undernourished mothers and children on the rest of the Continent, Germany included, were staring into the jaws of death. He was convinced, said Hoover, that voluntary action could eliminate wasteful consumption at home and pave the way for a great Christian mission abroad. On the twenty-fifth, in Florida for some fishing, he was summoned to the phone. Anderson was calling again, this time with urgency in his voice. Would the former president be willing to come to Washington and lend his name to a national committee formed to grapple with the emergency? Hoover replied that committees might inspire domestic conservation, but that only governments could overcome the impending famine. "Single-headed leadership" was called for. Truman's praise notwithstanding, he was loath to provide advice from a subordinate position. Anderson agreed, and within four days Hoover was back at the White House, accepting the honorary chairmanship of the Famine Emergency Committee, arguing successfully against a reimposition of the card rationing abolished by Truman only the previous summer.[30]

"I have a job for you that nobody else in the country can do," the president informed his visitor. He feared that a million people might starve to death during the coming winter in Europe unless something was done immediately, "and you know more about feeding nations and people than anybody in the world." He wanted Hoover to go to Europe and judge the situation for himself. He, Truman, would put his private plane at his disposal. Hoover would be given a staff of his choosing and as much time as he needed. In response, Hoover said that he couldn't possibly refuse such a request. Yet he told Edgar Rickard a few days later that the president was "really dumb" in his failure to grasp vital points of any issue. Clinton Anderson understood. So did other members of the Emergency Committee. Together with Dennis FitzGerald of USDA, Hoover estimated a cereal shortfall of eleven million tons and a disparity of three million tons in necessary fats. But until price controls were turned over to a single food administrator, Hoover insisted, nothing much could be accomplished. He was still fuming a week later, wondering how America ever got to be governed by such a mediocre type of man. Yet, uncharitable as he sounded in private, in public he shed his dourness for the more appealing stance of humanitarian.[31]

Half a billion people were in danger, he told a national radio audience on March 14. Countries producing surpluses of grain could supply perhaps half the amount needed. Only a drop in Western consumption would cover the deadly gap remaining. "Today we must transform the world from this era of killing to an era of saving . . . lives," said Hoover. "Saving of human life is a moral and spiritual duty. If your neighbors and their children were hungry, you would instantly invite them to a seat at the table. These starving women and children are in foreign countries, yet they are hungry human beings— and they are also your neighbors. . . . Will you not take to your table an invisible guest?"

Three days later, the former president, accompanied by veterans of his earlier food campaigns, boarded a C-54 aircraft at New York's La Guardia Airport. Just before taking off, Secretary of State James Byrnes asked Hoover and his party to extend their travels to India. Hoover himself announced his willingness to sit down with the Russians to coordinate food supplies in suffering Germany and elsewhere. He spent the rest of the day cruising at 185 miles per hour, playing gin rummy and conferring with Agriculture Department officials on what he was likely to find once he arrived in Paris.[32]

"Here's how I see my job," he told reporters in the French capital. "After the last war I directed food supplies for a large part of Europe. Now I've been called back like an old family doctor."

If anyone doubted the peril facing the European family, Hoover's presence confirmed it. In Paris he watched as three hundred Frenchmen filed into a distribution center: their reward, a cup of potato gruel and a quarter pound of beans. His arrival in Rome, the next stop on a thirty-eight-nation, eighty-two-day journey, coincided with a food riot at Messina. In Hamburg, dozens of people collapsed in the streets as the former president compiled less dramatic evidence of their plight for transmission home. Meanwhile, Soviet occupation forces in the eastern zone of Germany refused to reduce the daily ration there, even though American and British authorities were forced to cut back to a thousand calories a day in the territory under their control. Neither would Moscow share with her recent allies the relative abundance of East Germany.

Back home, Herbert Lehman quit UNRRA with a blast at Hoover, Anderson and others for opposing rationing. An indignant Truman called the New Yorker "very much mistaken." Privately, he scorched Lehman as a dilettante who had "sat on his fanny for years," failed at UNRRA, and now hoped to win a Senate seat in the fall elections. Five thousand miles away, Hoover persevered, a seventy-three-year-old man embarked on a fifty-thousand-mile voyage of relief. His unpressurized plane was ordered to fly as low as possible. The Flying Cow, he dubbed the craft, in honor of the mooing sound made by its wings each time they were lowered. In Quito, Ecuador, it climbed over the Andes to land in a cow pasture. One stretch alone, a nonstop hop from Tokyo to Midway Island, was a grueling 19.5 hours. In Caracas, Venezuela, the distinguished visitor slipped in a bathtub and cracked his ribs, yet insisted on keeping his scheduled appointments, including a meeting with President Rómulo Betancourt. Throughout his trip, Hoover sat without complaint in unheated rooms, sometimes all but buried in blankets and shawls, conferring with food experts, military men and heads of state, wearing out dozens of his stubby pencils along the way. In Prague, he took a look at the lavish banquet prepared for his arrival and groused that it would have provided meals for a thousand hungry children. On a lighter note, he informed the British Cabinet that it had no food problems that ten thousand French chefs couldn't cure.[33]

He canceled a planned motor tour of Berlin, saying he preferred to get to work immediately. "My God," exlaimed a colonel used to visiting dignitaries, "this is the first guy coming out of America who doesn't want to go sightseeing and shopping." He did squeeze in a visit to the bombed-out Chancellery of Adolf Hitler. The vast imperial structure he had last glimpsed in 1938 was gone now. "Exposed by bombs," Hoover noted, "it was as ersatz as Hitler himself." A Russian officer took him down into the bunker where Hitler and Eva Braun had ended their lives. Hoover came up with a stone for a souvenir. It wasn't for himself, he explained. It was for Lowell Thomas's community fireplace back at Quaker Hill, the same masonry that already included pieces of the Parthenon, China's Great Wall and Cheops's pyramid. (Hoover's aide Maurice Pate did nearly as well in the souvenir stakes. Boys in Berlin streets traded him three military medals for a cigarette apiece.) What he saw in Germany confirmed the former president in his opposition to Morgenthau's "pastoral and partitioned state," a plan he also noted ran counter to the wishes of Dwight Eisenhower and Lucius Clay. Before leaving, he took pains to review the hitherto secret "protocol" attached to the 1939 Hitler-Stalin pact. Not surprisingly, the Russians had banned its publication; the paper cynically awarded control of the Baltic states, eastern Finland, Bessarabia, Bulgaria and Yugoslavia to Moscow, along with the Dardanelles. Hoover was not permitted to take notes, but he dictated a memorandum of what he had seen before departing Berlin for Vienna on April 14. There he asked Justice Robert Jackson, soon to join the Nuremberg Tribunal, if he had uncovered any evidence of Hitler's plans to attack the West. Jackson confirmed that he had not. He secured from General Mark Clark a cache of diplomatic and military papers discovered in Berchtesgaden and Salzburg. Clark also revealed that UNRRA supplies earmarked for Austria were instead being shipped to Russia.[34]

Hoover found the French lethargic and dispirited, subsisting on 1,600 calories or fewer per day. In London, he discerned an atmosphere of "total mediocrity" within official circles, including a mendacious minister of food and a grasping attitude that refused to part with agricultural stocks despite a diet nearly twice as nourishing as their brothers' across the Channel. In the end, however, Hoover was able to pressure the British into sharing some of their supplies with Poland. In Prague, he talked with Foreign Minister Jan Masaryk ("He is frankly very anti-Russian but manages to cover it with a good deal of buffoonery—deliberate I think"). The Russians held up permission for his party to cross their German zone of occupation for seven hours; when Hoover finally reached Polish soil, he was forced to curtail elaborate plans including a state dinner and decorations. This was a working visit, he informed his hosts, and so it remained.[35]

His itinerary included visits with seven kings, thirty-six prime ministers, dozens of cabinet officers and military men, forty-two press conferences, and twenty-four public addresses. On March 23, Pope Pius XII, a man who shared his unflinching hatred of communism, and whose prewar equivocations had given rise to the same kind of resentment directed in his own land toward Hoover, offered to lend the Vatican Radio in an effort to persuade heavily Catholic Latin America to join the food crusade. His Holiness asked the former president, whom he had known in his earlier travels as papal Secretary of State, to provide him with a comprehensive review of the world's suffering. Hoover began by stating his own fear for the future of Catholicism, threatened by "the tide of Red agnosticism sweeping over western Europe" as well as the Soviet authorities to the East. It was a welcome statement, Pius responded, but unusual coming from a Quaker. Hoover replied that although the Quakers were but a small minority of the world's faithful, they too depended for their existence upon "the moral foundations of the world."[36]

Pius agreed to direct his nuncios and Cardinals in South America to cast the famine relief effort as an official expression of church concern, and to stress the need for sharing in his coming Easter pastoral letter. Before leaving, the former president presented a group of forty Americans in uniform, some of them members of his own party, others enlisted to drive or guard the Hoover group. All went well until a Protestant from Illinois blurted out his religious affiliation and refused a papal blessing. Pius smiled indulgently. "Young man," he said, putting his hand on the boy's shoulder, "any young man is better for the blessing of an old man."[37]

And off the party dashed, to the capital of Poland, where future Communist party boss Wladislaw Gomulka was introduced as one of thousands of Polish children saved from starvation by Hoover's earlier relief campaigns. Walking through the rubble of Warsaw's Jewish ghetto, now the tomb of more than 200,000 Jews, Hoover saw horrors that haunted his dreams for years. But he could not pause or linger. For fifteen hours a day, he worked, scrambling back to the *Flying Cow* to calculate precisely the number of calories in a pound of corn, or the population of Yugoslavia, and transmit his reports before each day was out. He found a surplus of fish in Scandinavia, and salt in Germany, subtly criticized reporters for failing to convey the dire situation to the folks back home, took exactly three minutes out of his schedule in Athens to accept a university degree and honorary Greek citizenship, suffered in silence as Egypt's Falstaffian King Farouk laid out a sumptuous meal on a hundred-foot horseshoe-shaped table draped with Herbert Hoover roses. He ordered his pilot to dip low over the Tigris Valley and to circle Tel Aviv while he picked out Gethsemane and other Biblical holy places. On April 22, he accepted *Look* magazine's offer to cable back a five-thousand-word article on his travels—on condition that the $5,000 check attached be sent to the Boy's School in Bagdad.[38]

In Cairo, he telephoned Truman to protest reports that his mission was being recalled so that he, its leader, might be enlisted in the campaign for domestic conservation. The president said he had heard Hoover was tired, but that if his envoy wished to continue around the world, he was welcome to do so. The next day, Hoover warned Truman of "a very active propaganda campaign" being waged to suggest that nations other than the United States were responsible for food supplies already shipped to the Old World. He had been careful to set local journalists straight. Then, enriched by an Egyptian offer of 300,000 tons of grain, he returned to the skies. On April 23, he was in New Delhi, visiting the Viceroy ("not a surpassing intelligence," he concluded) and comparing dollar watches with Mahatma Gandhi, whom he had known as a foppish young lawyer in long-ago South Africa. "Gandhi is no more a 'religious esthete' than I am," wrote Hoover. "He is a soap box politician. . . . But he has the most effectual soap box in India." Far out in the desolate countryside around Bangalore, Hoover was ushered in to meet a maharajah. A swarthy little man with an Oxford accent, he bluntly informed his guest that "my people expect your people to do their duty . . . and . . . that if your people do not do their duty by my people, my people will hate your people for all time." A long pause followed as Hoover silently removed the ever-present pipe from his mouth. A ring of smoke drifted upward. Finally Hoover broke the silence. "I think I should inform you, sir," he said crisply, "that my people don't give a good goddamn whether your people hate them for all times." The pipe returned to its former place of honor. "And I think that I should furthermore inform you, sir, I doubt whether my people would ever even know it." He left the subcontinent firmly convinced that its independence would lead to bloodshed, first between Hindu and Moslem, then between Indian castes.[39]

Less contentious was his visit to the youthful king of Siam, or the eleven-course banquet which capped the call, designed to find ways to get Siamese rice to hungry mouths elsewhere. Manila was next, then a stopover in Nanking to see Chiang Kai-shek and his Madame. In Tokyo, Douglas MacArthur laid out a royal welcome for his old chief, taking Hoover by the hand and introducing him around a dinner table that allowed neither place cards nor protocol. The two men spoke of Australia and the Philippines, and Hoover urged the five-star general to return home to assume the role of a domestic John the Baptist. He admired MacArthur's policies for disarming Japan and for constructing a democracy in place of the old feudal warlordism. "It is useless to build a democracy," he judged, "over a cesspool of poverty, starvation and its consequent breeding of hate and antagonisms." What Hoover labeled "a debacle of starvation" in the coming winter might give pleasure to "the Japanese-haters in the United States," but it would spell disaster for long-range stability and his country's own strategic interests in the vital Far East. Perhaps MacArthur might borrow a million tons of shipping to transport a motley collection of Indochinese rice, Manchurian beans, North American wheat and U.S. cotton. Such measures would be justified, not only on humanitarian grounds, but as the necessary down payment on economic revival and future productivity. [40]

From Tokyo, Hoover flew on to Honolulu, where he presented watches to all the men of his party and bracelets for their wives. He thanked the plane crew and told stories for much of the evening, before returning to work on his report to Truman. On May 10, he was back home in San Francisco, and three days later, he strode into the Oval Office, noticeably more robust than when he departed two months before. He had discovered ways to reduce the shortfall of cereals by two-thirds, he told Truman, if surplus-producing countries would pool their excess grains, and self-sufficient nations would share even a little of their sufficiency. He also presented the chief executive with a draft telegram to Stalin, seeking Russian grain for Finland, Poland, Czechoslovakia, Yugoslavia and the Far East. Truman confessed his difficulties with Moscow, and Hoover said the only way to deal with Stalin's regime was to be truculent. "Even if he were to present a gold watch, it should be presented in a truculent mood." That way, said Hoover, "it would be more highly appreciated." [41]

On May 17, he addressed the American people via radio. "Of the Four Horsemen of the Apocalypse, the one named War has gone—at least for a while," he began. "But Famine, Pestilence and Death are still charging over the world." More than 800 million homes were without adequate food. "Hunger," said Hoover, "is a silent visitor who comes like a shadow. He sits beside every anxious mother three times each day. He brings not alone suffering and sorrow, but fear and terror. He carries disorder and the paralysis of government. . . . He is more destructive than armies, not only in human life but in morals. All of the values of right living melt before his invasions, and every gain of civilization crumbles. But we can save these people from the worst, if we will."

"We do not want the American flag flying over nationwide Buchenwalds," he proclaimed. Compared with the specter of hungry children and suffering families, revenge was unthinkable. UNRRA could supply but a fifth of the world's needs. Yet if the American people reduced their consumption of wheat products to two pounds per week, and cut their intake of fats by 20 percent, it might work miracles overseas. And he repeated the message first broadcast from Cairo three weeks earlier: "If every source of supplies will do its utmost, we can pull the world through this most dangerous crisis. . . . Such action marks the return of the lamp of compassion to the earth. And that is a part of the moral and spiritual reconstruction of the world."

On May 25, Hoover was once more aloft, this time headed south for a diplomatically perilous mission to Juan Perón's Argentina and ten other Latin American nations. Before leaving he secured an introduction to the Argentine dictator from Pope Pius, assuring Perón that Hoover represented suffering humanity rather than the United States, with whom Buenos Aires enjoyed a frosty relationship. Almost everywhere he went—in Mexico ("controlled by a plunderbund whose political machinery and policies are directed to remaining in power"), Venezuela ("The American ambassador is a job"), and above all, in Perón's own backyard—the former president found alarming evidence of State Department bungling, matched only by native ineptitude. He judged Ecuador's inhabitants "the most God-forsaken, Church impoverished, downtrodden people on earth," half serf and a quarter elite. Panama and Colombia were ruled by honest men, he concluded, a rare thing south of the border. In Cuba a taxing schedule featured eleven separate events in a single day, complete "with a mighty painful back," the legacy of his bathtub fall in Caracas.[42]

Hoover spent five days in Buenos Aires. The State Department hadn't wanted him to go at all, but Truman deliberately announced the visit before a striped-pants protest could be mounted. The controversy did not end there. Discourtesy was in evidence, even if the American ambassador to Argentina was not, when Hoover's plane touched down on June 5. After that official representative voiced hesitation about an early meeting with Perón, Hoover went through the Mexican envoy, who arranged it within twenty minutes. The session lasted thirty-five minutes, during which he tried to set the dictator straight about the nature of his mission. He hoped for an extra 1.6 million tons of Argentine foodstuffs to close the gap in worldwide supplies. He would be grateful for an appointment of someone to expedite the request; otherwise, nine separate departments stood poised to generate reams of delaying red tape. He also expressed sympathy for the enormous tasks confronting Perón, officially in office for barely forty-eight hours.[43]

Impressed and disarmed by the old man, Perón made certain Hoover was invited to his inaugural dinner—seated 196th out of 216 honored guests in attendance. Going at all was bound to offend American liberals, but as Hoover put it later, "I was resolved . . . to eat even Argentine dirt if I could get the 1,600,000 tons." Hugh Gibson fared worse yet. Invited at the last moment but provided no place to sit, Hoover's traveling companion finally took his leave after being insulted by an Argentine army officer. Two days later, Hoover and Perón met yet again. Hoover flattered the dictator, promising to tell reporters of his fine cooperation and solicitude for a hungry world. The two men spoke frankly of their countries' tattered relations, Hoover listening sympathetically as Perón complained of a quarter billion in Argentine gold frozen in the U.S. He needed oil-drilling equipment to prevent the burning of large quantities of linseed, corn and wheat. He protested against U.S. restrictions on rubber shipments to his nation. But he also promised to divert meat supplies to Europe, on top of 400,000 tons of grain given outright to the Vatican and other governments. And he promised to issue the necessary decrees immediately that would free up still more of the Argentine stockpiles. At the lunch which followed, Hoover met Eva ("an intelligent woman and very cordial"), who displayed a worldly grasp of realpolitik by assuring him that in the event of war between the U.S. and Russia, Argentina would side with her neighbor to the north. After all, as she explained, America had the atom bomb.[44]

When Hoover again reported to Truman on June 20, he included State Department obstructionism in his report, as well as food shortages. Truman quickly released Argentine deposits and canceled the blacklisting of Perón's economy. The former president was now relatively certain that mass starvation could be averted everywhere except China. American conservation alone had produced nearly three million tons for export. But the chief reason the U.S. was able to ship one-sixth of its food supply overseas was both ironic and costly: a sharp hike in federal price supports for corn and wheat. Hoover said nothing of this on June 28, when Canada invited him to address its Parliament, the same week Radio Moscow assailed him as an implacable reactionary. Instead, he criticized the Yugoslav regime of Marshal Tito and proposed a halt in U.S. relief shipments until promised elections were held. Truman himself saluted Hoover's "service to humanity . . . I know that I can count upon your co-operation if developments at any time in the future make it necessary for me to call upon you again," the president wrote him late that fall. It turned out to be a prophetic letter.[45]

★   ★

First, however, Hoover had more partisan concerns clamoring for his attention. As early as July 1946, he learned that Truman was seriously considering changing the name of Boulder Dam back to its original designation. A bill to accomplish this had been introduced in the House; passage seemed likely. But 1946 was also an election year, a testing time for the New Deal coalition which had lost its founding father, and a striking opportunity for long-denied Republicans. Putting his friendship with the president to one side, Hoover committed himself hammer and tongs to electing a GOP Congress, the first in fourteen years. He invited Douglas MacArthur to return home and make a series of speeches outlining the moral and political perils overtaking the republic. The country would listen to MacArthur, he wrote, as to no one else. For his own part, Hoover diagnosed philosophical rot affecting the body politic. "The leftwing regimentation of recent years has created a million bottlenecks in production and distribution and is at last breaking down in shortages of food and other supplies in the midst of plenty." Yet Truman's administration continued to cling to the Rooseveltian idea "that it is possible to have totalitarian economics and at the same time preserve other freedoms." Meanwhile, labor leaders had grown arrogant in their newfound power. A false impression of prosperity, fed by inflation and the wartime boom, sustained higher taxes and the mirage of wealth. More encouraging, Hoover perceived his countrymen "beginning to shake off the various domestic red tinges" painted at a time of naivete regarding Soviet intentions. They were seeing for themselves the disaster brought on by what he called "appeasement policies that have made Russia the sole victor in this war" outside the Far East.[46]

MacArthur rumbled back a wordy refusal ("I believe the merit of anything I might attempt would be vitiated by the charge that it represented not so much a patriotic but a political effect"). Hoover turned to other avenues. In Pasadena, California, he asked, along with his elder son, if there was anyone in Jerry Voorhees's congressional district who might defeat the left-wing congressman. Someone mentioned "a young attorney named Nixon," and both Hoovers asked to meet him. The young attorney was less than eager to make the run. Just returning to a legal practice interrupted by the war, Nixon said he was without funds for politicking. Herbert, Junior, replied that it needn't cost him a cent. What's more, he promised that he could, through contacts with local businesses, ensure enough legal work for Nixon so that it would be worth his while, even if Voorhees won in November. Nixon agreed, and a pivotal career was launched. "I have grown stronger and stronger in my belief in your immense value to the American people," Hoover wrote Dwight Eisenhower's vice president, ten years after their first encounter. But Nixon was never his protégé; he was too shrewd, and Hoover too prickly, for that kind of relationship.[47]

The young lawyer's surprise win over Voorhees contributed to a GOP sweep in November 1946 that ousted Democratic majorities in both houses of Congress. America, rejoiced her thirty-first president, was the first country to repudiate planned economy. Most voters held less exalted views of the result. As usual, they voted their frustrations more than their philosophies of government. At the time, howver, 1946 seemed a death knell for the New Deal. The Eightieth Congress would be guided by the likes of Robert Taft and Joe Martin. It would apply strict standards of economy to domestic programs and foreign aid initiatives alike. It would restrict the right to strike, slice welfare rolls, cut taxes. It would also dig its own political grave, helped along by the scrappy Missourian who understood the electorate so much better than Hoover and his ideological allies.

The former president missed the first few weeks of the new order. He was traveling again, at Truman's behest, seeing what the ravages of war had done to Germany and Austria, the linchpin of Europe where recent enmities were easily obscured in the face of Soviet aggressiveness. Splintered by its occupiers and divested of the tools to develop a modern economy, the former Reich suffered through a terrible winter. The daily ration of 1,550 calores was 60 percent bread and potatoes. A flourishing black market charged 400 marks for a pound of butter officially priced at one mark. Austrian food supplies were expected to run out by mid-April. Yet when Truman sought his help late in January 1947, Hoover persuaded him to broaden the scope of the mission. This latest journey, what he called his "positively last job," would become an economic as well as a food survey, one designed to relieve American taxpayers as well as German children. Hoover wanted Germany to become self-sustaining. He also wanted to dissolve the State Department clique of New Dealers and appeasers, from Dean Acheson and Ben Cohen to outside advisers like Felix Frankfurter and Tommy Corcoran. Their influence adversely affected U.S. interests far beyond the Argentine, Hoover believed. Before departing on February 2, the former president paid his respects on George Marshall, the new Secretary of

State and a man in whom he had the utmost confidence. Among other offers of help was Hoover's promise to place his own contacts with Republicans in Congress at Marshall's disposal.[48]

His travels took him to Frankfurt, Berlin, Hamburg, Stuttgart and Vienna. He preached the utility of cornmeal, a dish previously shunned by Germans, secured a shipment of 250,000 tons of seed potatoes, and appealed to British authorities to release skilled workers imperative to German recovery, yet now held as a part of a general de-Nazification program. He uncovered $19 million worth of warehoused food that could form the basis of his Children's Feeding Program, a series of soup kitchens aiding 3.5 million school-aged youngsters with one hot meal a day (it was immediately dubbed the Hoover *Speisung*). General Clay complied ("If it were not for your report, I know that we would face disaster in the months ahead"), and soon, the next generation of Germans were writing thank-you notes and drawing pictures for the man they called Onkel Hoover. The former president also played a key role in the establishment of UNICEF, whose first director was his old CRB colleague Maurice Pate, and whose $15 million endowment by Congress came only after Hoover testified before Capitol Hill committees. CARE, created in November 1945 with Army surplus food and contributions from U.S. charities, was another by-product of Hoover's relief efforts. It fell under the guidance of General William Haskell, who had previously aided the Great Engineer in meeting the needs of post–World War I Russia.[49]

In Rome, the former president renewed his acquaintance with Pope Pius. He paused in London long enough to brief an inattentive Clement Attlee. His return flight was marred by a sudden drop in altitude over the Newfoundland coast. Hoover's eardrum burst and he wore the inevitable hearing aid that followed as a badge of honor. He hadn't known a warm moment during his three weeks abroad, he confided on his return, but his stamina astonished others unable to match his pace or keep his hours. "It's the old horse for the long race," Theodore Roosevelt's daughter-in-law told him. Those who traveled with Hoover, who heard him turning pages and taking notes at four in the morning, were not about to dispute her.[50]

Hoover sent the White House three thick reports, outlining the desperate condition of German industry, stripped of manpower and raw materials, and decrying the pastoral state originally proposed by Henry Morgenthau and still supported by elements within the State Department. No such realm could be created, he wrote, unless its occupiers were willing to exterminate or remove 25 million of its inhabitants. Neither should fears of industrial war potential repress the restoration of plants and mines. If Western Civilization was to survive in Europe, it must survive in Germany. "After all," Hoover concluded, "our flag flies over these people. That flag means something besides military power." [51]

Halfway around the world, he urged similarly lenient treatment for Japan. "When I think of the white crosses over tens of thousands of American boys in the Pacific and the millions of butchered Chinese," he wrote to Secretary of War Robert Patterson, "I sympathize emotionally with the Draconic measures of punishment. But when we look to the real interest of the United States and the future peace of the world, we must confine punishment to the war leaders and realize that we must live with this [sic] 80,000,000 people." Only by restoring the building blocks of economic productivity, he advised Washington, could peace be assured and communism warded off. [52]

He was willing to provide $725 million in continued relief to defeated nations. He testified to that end before a House committee in May 1947, persuading its isolationist chairman, John Taber of New York, that it was the logical purchase price for a reconstructed, democratic Europe. His own reservations, expressed in the shadow of European politicians "more desperately selfish than ever before," included American control over the distribution process, limitation of relief supplies to food, medicine, fertilizers and seed (a separate clothing drive was launched in the spring of 1947, with Hoover appealing to American children to assist their European counterparts), and a commitment to repay U.S. aid either now or later. Hoover's soft heart did not crowd out his hard head. When Secretary Marshall unveiled his sweeping blueprint for the rebuilding of Europe at Harvard's 1947 commencement, Hoover's first reaction was negative. "Why issue an invitation to Europe to gang up on the United States?" he demanded. "Why ask Russia to join them in view of the Truman Doctrine which was a flat declaration of a Western Civilization block?" [53]

Bob Taft echoed his doubts. Personally, he wrote Hoover that summer, he was prepared to support some additional loans, but only to prevent starvation and provide materials to restart European industry. "In short," as Taft put it, "to help them work harder." A U.S. loan to Britain seemed wasteful to Mr. Republican, used largely to maintain a higher standard of living than necessary. Hoover was glad to hear from his old friend, then in the throes of shepherding the Taft-Hartley Bill with its restrictions on striking workers through Congress. "It is unnecessary for me to tell you how much I have rejoiced over the steadfast character, the magnificent leadership and generalship you have shown," Hoover told him. "You have restored representative government to mastery in its own house." [54]

His own influence in Congress was substantial, extending from Speaker

Joe Martin's acceptance of a committee to investigate every aspect of the Marshall Plan to adoption of "my favorite gadget" of a secret worker-ballot prior to any strike endangering the public welfare. He was in the capital often now, refusing to stay at Blair House because he thought it bugged. That was vintage Hoover. Yet if his suspicions did not mellow, Hoover's personal bearing did. At last his prodigious energies were being channeled into constructive purposes. He was saving lives instead of defending his record. His waspish sense of humor resurfaced, in public as well as behind closed doors. He spoke to Princeton's bicentennial celebration, reminding his audience that the school was founded by Presbyterians, who clung to "a fifty-fifty chance of a hot fire. Being in the neighborhood of the Quakers of Philadelphia, Princeton was naturally weaned away from the predestination part. Sometimes I regret the doubts which are arising about the hot fire end of the ideology," he went on. "I have at times had great consolation in holding to that part of orthodoxy, because I despaired of an adequate heating place on this earth for some people. However," he concluded puckishly "I will not dwell upon their names at this time."[55]

One of those for whom he undoubtedly wished such a Hell was Charlie Michaelson, his old nemesis from the Democratic National Committee. But Michaelson had fallen on hard times. Though Hoover was not one to kick a man when he was down, he might distill humor from an ancient rivalry. Someone told him of an incident in which a fishing rod had been used to steal Michaelson's pants from the hotel room in which he draped them. "Well, the fishing rod is a noble instrument," Hoover replied, "and I hate to think of it prostituted to other ends." At the 1947 Bohemian Grove encampment, he sat next to right-wing oilman Joseph Pew. Afterward, without a trace of irony, he said he had never known a man who opposed more things. He got into an argument between a young American army officer and the head of the British Information Office in New York. "Well," he exclaimed after tempers cooled, "that was the first time I had to go to the defense of the British Empire!" He could joke at his own expense. "I'm the only person of distinction," he informed visitors, "who's ever had a depression named after him." He repeated the anecdote of a young autograph seeker who demanded three of his signatures. Asked why he needed three, the boy informed Hoover that that was how many it took to trade for one Babe Ruth.[56]

In a rare moment, he allowed as to how his 1932 defeat had not been altogether bad. If nothing else, its scope was designed to instill humility. And when the Bohemians commemorated forty years of his company by inducting him into their Old Guard, he welcomed this "tender push into oblivion" with a pointed whimsy. "There is something to be said for all the Old Guards in the world. They are men past the time when they want anything on this earth but the welfare of those whom they guard. Their tempers have been softened in the solution of experience. They have learned that virtue is a more stable currency than the commodity dollar. They are a menace to the fuzzy-minded, the foolish, and all New Deals." He wished it known, concluded Hoover, that "the Old Guarders of the world are generally able to pay their own expenses, including their funerals."[57]

Other satisfactions greeted him. "The President always speaks to me as the President," he said of Harry Truman. The First Lady won his heart by unveiling a White House portrait of Lou. He was moved by Congress's unanimous resolution of gratitude for his humanitarian services, as well as its decision, in the spring of 1947, to restore his name to the huge dam in Nevada in whose construction he had played such a major role. Harold Ickes fulminated in print, but Truman signed the bill into law on April 30, and Hoover contacted the Gridiron Club to do an uncharacteristic thing: he invited himself to the club's annual dinner, to be held ten days later. It was the first time he faced the Gridiron since his farewell address of February 1933, and his tone was deliberately light.[58]

He spoke of his recent travels, and of statesmen along the Iron Curtain who "shook my hand smilingly and looked me straight in the pocketbook." He brought down the house with a joke about Soviet Foreign Minister Molotov and his Western counterparts. He expressed sympathy for the beleaguered Truman, even while taking pains to avoid "an indelicate implication that I am seeking a recruit to my exclusive union of ex-Presidents." The incumbent had already come to realize Congress's preference for advice over consent, said this authority on both. "However, he has not yet probed the depths of their capacities in these directions." Then he turned to the president and expressed gratitude for the chance to say publicly a word of thanks for the high services Truman was performing. "Amid the thousand crises which sweep upon us from abroad, he has stood firm with his feet rooted in the American soil. He has brought to the White House new impulses of good will toward men." Noting that he had sat through more windy speeches in the last twelve months "than anyone not in the United Nations," he quickly reclaimed his seat. The journalists in attendance rose to their feet to applaud him. Truman himself, in an impulsive moment, reached out for Hoover's program. He scribbled an inscription: "With high esteem and keen appreciation to a great man."[59]

More and more Americans were beginning to share Truman's judgment.

★   ★

It fell to Winston Churchill, the war's greatest hero and most ironic victim, to assess the bleak aftermath of victory. "We shall not make the same mistakes after this war that we made after the last," he said with roguish conviction. "We shall make a lot of new ones." It was one of the rare certainties with which Churchill's contemporary from West Branch was prepared to agree. "Peace is Hell," Truman informed a Gridiron Dinner late in 1945. There were shortages at home, famine abroad, and a growing unease about America's wartime ally, the Soviet Union. By the fall of 1947, one national poll indicated that 64 percent of the American public wished to bar any Communist from high office in the public or labor's pay. Churchill himself coined the phrase Iron Curtain in bitter tribute to Stalin's successive triumphs. Truman noted in his diary that he was tired of "babying the Soviets." Only one kind of language, he wrote, was understood in the Kremlin: "How many divisions have you?"

A destitute Germany afforded old comrades new opportunities for misunderstanding and ideological dispute. The Russians, committed to emasculation of the German economy, flooded the western sector with paper money, forcing the United States, Britain and France to combat the resulting inflation. It was a strange note of gratitude for the $11 billion poured into Russia by UNRRA. Churchill's own Britain hovered on the brink of catastrophe as one of the harshest winters on record gripped the nation early in 1947. Electricity lit London homes and the Houses of Parliament for only a few hours each morning. Englishwomen were rationed to a single dress per year, while unemployment reached six million and the scanty rations of wartime began to look positively generous by comparison with the bittersweet fruits of peace.

Alerted to the dangers confronting her closest ally, the United States approved a $3.75 billion loan for Clement Attlee's government. Billions more helped to capitalize the World Bank and International Monetary Fund. Gradually, as a shocked Britain retrenched, Washington came to assume much of her old responsibilities in Europe, Palestine, the Far East and, as of March 1947, in Greece, where Russian-backed insurgents threatened to topple a pro-Western regime.

Resorting to blunt language, Truman set forth his famous doctrine of containment. He demanded $400 million with which to aid both Greece and Turkey against Communist insurgency. His new Secretary of State returned from a devastated Europe in a dour mood. "The patient is sinking while the doctors deliberate," he warned. Within five weeks, he had a miracle cure in mind. Enunciated in a fifteen-minute commencement address in Harvard Yard, George Marshall's vision of the New World coming to the economic and political rescue of the Old struck instant sparks of gratitude on the Continent, smoldering resentment in Moscow, and a mixture of statesmanship and nativist suspicion in the United States Congress. Robert Taft led the fight against Marshall's generous scheme; he proved a formidable adversary. A man of maddening brilliance and withering scorn, who liked to skewer less intelligent colleagues as much as he enjoyed off-key verses from Gilbert and Sullivan, Taft raised clouds of suspicion over Greece, the role of the United Nations in dealing with such self-evident aggression, American overcommitment and the dangers posed to the domestic economy should U.S. largesse be extended beyond the immediate crisis. Ultimately, he backed down on Greece, but Taft's obsession with inflation on the home front did not abate.

Like his old mentor Hoover, Taft did not approve of the new bipartisanship in foreign policy. Indeed, he told one friend, overseas developments should play a decisive role in the 1948 election, "and the sooner we get free from the idea that we are bound to cooperate in everything, the better off we will be." Cooperation had paved the way for Teheran, Yalta and Potsdam, "which set Russia up as the power it is today." Hoover's position was only slightly more fluid. He urged Marshall to downplay chances for any breakthrough at a Moscow conference in the spring of 1947, and advised Arthur Vandenburg, then fighting Truman's battle among congressional Republicans, to be frank in defining aid to Greece as the only way to forestall a Soviet-backed dictatorship in Athens. Simultaneously, he appealed to his countrymen to curtail their diets and combat the gnawing hunger he had witnessed firsthand during his travels abroad.[60]

"The fundamental law of our civilization is based upon compassion and charity," he proclaimed at a public rally in New York. "And compassion and charity do not ask whether the sufferer has always been good or bad, whether he had brought his misery upon himself, or is the innocent victim of forces beyond his control. . . . We are, thank God, sentimentalists. We know that the great bounty that has been placed in our keeping must not be hoarded while others starve and are in pain. We dare not, even in this age of gross and abject materialism, forget that our consciences were forged by tender women and strong men who have built for themselves a world to their liking, always setting aside a mite for the charity that they knew God enjoined upon good people."

A curious parallel with his own White House record now emerged. Charity was one thing, beggaring oneself quite another. Churchill called the Marshall Plan "the most unsordid act in history." Hoover thought it a badly flawed blank check, endorsed to an ungrateful, undisciplined continent. The General's friends put the best light on the subject. It was perfectly reasonable to argue, John Callan O'Laughlin told the former president in the summer of 1947, that the loss of Western Europe would radically alter the balance of power, eliminate free trade, and open vast new resources to the Soviet war machine within the sixteen countries Marshall hoped to stabilize short of revolution.[61]

Hoover saw folly in such reasonableness. Greedy Europeans might "work the two now competitive Santa Clauses," he told O'Laughlin at a time when the nation's debt exceeded a quarter trillion dollars and the average citizen could claim a share of that unpaid bill multiplied a hundredfold since the Spanish-American War. Taft and others in Congress he rewarded with similar candor. "The time has come to stop dodging the truth," he wrote that summer. The United States should provide help "to the full extent which does not disrupt our own economy or weaken our ability for national defense." Yet the nation ought not sentimentalize the recipients of its aid, nor deny the poisons of "socialist nationalization and fascist regimentation" being introduced to Europe's postwar economies. Any assistance to such governments would be futile without substantial efforts to boost the productivity of their people. So-called loans should be called by their proper name, "gifts," and recognized for the privation they indicated. Commodities produced inside the United States should form the nation's list of exports. "There should be no illusion," wrote Hoover, "that we are underwriting the food supply of any nation." What's more, Americans should remember that Marshall's sixteen countries represented only a fragment of their global obligations: Germany, Japan, China and Latin America required and deserved shipments of U.S. food and fuel.[62]

Hoover advised that all aid be divided into two categories, food, fertilizers, coal and the like to be known as "relief goods," while precious metals and other substances taken from the country's limited storehouse of natural resources would be called "depletion goods." The former should be paid for, if at all possible, with domestic currency set aside for future credits. The latter should produce cash on the barrelhead, or funds at least secured by collateral such as U.S. property registered in the name of foreign nationals. No aid should be extended to any government failing to cooperate in the pacification and renewal of Germany and Japan—a euphemism for Moscow and further testimony to Hoover's insistence on the recovery of both defeated nations as essential to future security and reduced burden on American taxpayers. Industry must again supplant the ashes of wartime destructions. "It is simply crazy for us to build up productivity in foreign countries out of American resources, and at the same time, to tear down productivity" in the leading Axis powers.[63]

To these conditions, Hoover added still another when he replied to Vandenburg's request for a public statement early in 1948, one that would have ominous implications for State Department traditionalists and internationalist-minded Republicans alike. "The front against Communism lies not alone in Europe," said Hoover, in the twilight of Chiang Kai-shek's sway over the Chinese mainland. "It stretches through Latin America and Asia."[64]

The former president wanted the Plan restricted to a fifteen-month trial, rather than the four years envisioned by its authors. He thought Marshall's appropriation of $17 billion impossibly high; even the $9 billion called for in a first installment would amount to more than a third of all the personal income taxes paid by American citizens. "Yet the country surely needs tax relief if its productivity and employment are to be sustained." When Congress adopted instead a more liberal bill supported by Vandenburg, the Michigan senator insisted that all facets of Marshall's program would be subject to public scrutiny at the end of a year. "A thin look," groused Hoover, who objected as well to "a window-dressing, bi-partisan board" lacking both investigative and determinative powers, and the inclusion of such unscathed nations as Ireland, Denmark, Portugal and Iceland in the federation of open hands created by the European Recovery Program.[65]

Neither did he succeed in enlisting other countries with strong economies —including Canada, Argentina and Brazil—to relieve Americans in ministering to Europe's grievous wants. Unduly alarmed at the potential for domestic ruptures, Hoover was shrewd in grasping the dangers of a Europe dependent for its military defense and economic survival upon an overextended U.S. He wanted Germany to start its own program of exports, subject to foreign taxation, by the summer of 1949. And he stood his ground against any long-range commitment to hold a defensive umbrella over the heads of Europe's contentious, unreliable powers.

The Marshall Plan ultimately bore at least a few of his fingerprints. Many of his technical and administrative suggestions were adopted by a wary Congress. By March 1948, he was even willing to endorse the final draft of Marshall's "gigantic experiment" as "a major dam against Russian aggression," something that stood a good chance of success if entrusted to a capable administrator. That same spring, he launched a fresh public appeal to prevent famine in Germany, then suffering a hellish combination of bad harvests, a swollen population, and virtual cessation of Russian cooperation in refiring the engines of industry and commerce. On the surface, it seemed a contradiction, this ruling passion for hungry people mingled with a steely-eyed contempt for their governments. But Hoover had devoted half a lifetime to sharpening the dichotomy. His distrust for the feudal warlords of Europe was too great to dissolve amidst the sentiment attending victory. The United States, he had long since concluded, could not unilaterally prevent Europe from rushing headlong into war. It could not impose the kind of peace, rational and humane, that first Woodrow Wilson and later Franklin Roosevelt, wished for the Continent.

He had been disillusioned, after all, by earlier triumphs. Yet he wanted the suffering to stop. He wanted those in positions of authority to assume their obligation to a starving populace. A practical idealist, Hoover would save men, women and above all children from the dogs of war. Yet he rejected as both impractical and naive the idea that America might save the Old World's prime ministers and parliamentarians from themselves.

By mid-1947, his global travels behind him and the organization of U.S. charity occupying most of his attention, the former president was once more an object of public admiration instead of scorn. But a still greater service lay ahead, and with it new accolades from a people both blessed and cursed with short memories.

CHAPTER ELEVEN

"COUNSELOR TO THE REPUBLIC"

★

You have had the acclaim of the American people; you have had the criticism of the American people; and now, in the twilight of your life, the American people have come to realize that Herbert Hoover is one of our few . . . outstanding men in the public life of this generation.
— Joseph P. Kennedy, to Herbert Hoover,[1] July 1949

There is no joy to be had from retirement except in some kind of productive work. Otherwise you degenerate into talking to everybody about your pains and pills. . . . The point is not to retire from work or you will shrivel up into a nuisance to all mankind. — Herbert Hoover

★

In spare moments, when he wasn't speed-reading thick volumes of theory and statistics, inventing his own rules for gin rummy or pursuing bonefish and rainbow trout, Hoover liked to take apart radios and telephones. His mind found pleasure in the intricacies of machinery, even government's. He liked to compare Congress to a father who reproved his son for dismantling a clock, only to have the boy reply, "If you do not like it, you can fix it. I want to play with my soldiers."

Congress liked to play with its soldiers almost as well as it liked to leave clocks unassembled. Six presidents, Hoover included, had tried and failed to persuade the legislators to reorganize the executive branch of government. Red tape and costly confusion were easily denounced on the cam-

371

paign platform—and all but impossible to eliminate in the bureaucratic hen's nest of Washington, fouled by special interest groups and tainted with corruption. Hoover's entire career had revolved in one way or another around organizing people for the public good: as food administrator and secretary of commerce, he created bureaucracies from the ground up or cobbled together new ones from the scattered fragments of competing departments. He was the first president to seek reorganization powers subject only to congressional veto. Even his antipathy to FDR did not blind him to the basic value of Louis Brownlow's groundbreaking 1939 report, lost amidst the furor over Supreme Court packing. "The President needs help," Brownlow proclaimed. In the fall of 1945, Hoover agreed.

That October, he expressed interest in another attempt at executive housecleaning. Truman responded with hearty approval. The overlapping, waste and conflict of policies among executive agencies had been a scandal, wrote the president, for at least thirty-five years. Truman's own interest in the subject was nothing new. During World War II, he had chaired a Senate committee investigating flaws in mobilization and defense contracts. Five weeks into his presidency, he sought from Capitol Hill an extension of his own powers to promote government efficiency. But it took the Republican Eightieth Congress, anxious for retrenchment as well as reorganization, to create the Commission on Organization of the Executive Branch of Government—the Hoover Commission. Its motives were not difficult to fathom. Clarence Brown, the Ohio congressman who introduced the bill in the House, insisted that any commission report be delayed until after November 1948. By then, it was widely assumed, there would be a new man in the Oval Office, a Republican. And Hoover's own conservative preferences were reflected in his recruitment of staff, his designation of nineteen outside task forces assigned specific areas of the government to review, and his regular liaison with Governor Thomas E. Dewey, who appeared a sure winner over Truman even before he was nominated by Republican delegates in Philadelphia in June 1948.[2]

Dewey was not his first choice; Hoover much preferred Robert Taft to the diminutive, self-assured New Yorker, who four years earlier had asked him to stay out of the national campaign and who seemed no more likely to post a defense of the Hoover presidency now. Still, Dewey displayed signs of growth. Before his nomination, he visited the Waldorf, asked questions and sought advice. Hoover professed pleasure but entertained few illusions. "Dewey has no inner reservoir of knowledge on which to draw for his thinking," he remarked to one friend. "A man couldn't wear a mustache like that without having it affect his mind." As the campaign progressed, he became increasingly alarmed at the somnolent tone adopted by his party and its candidate. He unsuccessfully sought a commitment from Dewey to denounce the economic policies that were costing American taxpayers $600 million a year "to keep Germans alive in idleness and constant degeneration." Such a hot potato, replied Dewey, needed "further study." Yet there seemed no doubt at all what should be done "as soon as we have the power to stop the costly and dangerous practices launched by this Administration." It was a clever straddle, unlikely to placate Hoover. It suggested the dangers of overconfidence, of being all things to all people, and the vulnerability such an approach displayed to the fiercely partisan, scattershot tactics of an embattled Truman.[3]

As early as July 27, a mutual friend told Hoover that the Dewey game plan called for only a handful of major speeches. Perhaps three-quarters of the candidate's time between then and Election Day would be spent at his country retreat in Pawling, the same neighborhood where the former president had, a few years before, briefly considered buying a home. Hoover was able to contain his enthusiasm. From all that he could see, he concluded in mid-August, the campaign was unlikely to differ much from that of 1944. "But even so, I don't see how it is possible to lose the election." Dewey's belated support of the Taft-Hartley Act encouraged him. Yet it didn't resolve his doubts or cancel his fears that the governor of New York, a liberal Republican of internationalist bent and more than average flexibility on domestic issues, would do little to eliminate New Deal graftings on the body politic. Added to this was a personal disdain sharpened by years of slights, real or imagined. Why did women dislike Dewey, someone asked Hoover late in the campaign. The response was direct. "Because he is arrogant, ruthless and supersensitive."[4]

The former president played no public role in the campaign. Instead, he labored away with his eleven fellow commissioners, a distinguished panel which included the likes of Dean Acheson, James Forrestal, Joseph P. Kennedy, Vermont's Senator George Aiken, and University of Michigan political scientist James K. Pollack. Communism was much in the news in 1948; the case of Alger Hiss was bannered on the nation's front pages. Conservative Republicans pressed Dewey to seize the initiative, while Truman moved to defuse the issue by demanding a stringent program of security checks throughout the federal establishment. A group of Hoover's admirers wished him to visit Moscow and talk with Stalin face-to-face. Personally, he was receptive to the idea of soliciting such an invitation from the Truman White House—but only if Dewey agreed. In the end, the president dispatched Chief Justice Fred Vinson instead. But the issue persisted. Hoover came to

Washington for the first meeting of the commission that would bear his name. A loyalty oath was put before him, fingerprints were demanded. An outraged secretary protested. No former president should have to submit to such indignities, she said.[5]

Hoover came close to losing his own temper. "At no time do I have any objection to taking an oath of loyalty to my country," he told her. "At no time do I object to having my fingerprints taken."

He reserved his indignation for other things, above all a government besotted with waste. From around 600,000 employees distributed among 350 agencies and bureaus during his own presidency, the federal establishment had swollen to more than 2 million persons, staffing five times as many offices. Washington claimed title to one-fourth the continental United States. It would take 1,250 Empire State buildings to match federal floor space. The Army alone had five million items in its warehouses—and no inventory. Duplication was rampant: one task force assigned to investigate the nation's water resources found open warfare between the Bureau of Reclamation and the Army Corps of Engineers, while moneylending activities were divided among a dozen instruments of fiscal power, competing with private enterprise and costing taxpayers as much as $200 million annually. Public health policies were determined by a hodgepodge of competing bureaus, including the Army, Navy, United States Public Health Service and Veterans Administration. The result was 255,000 hospital beds for 155,000 patients. In New York City alone, four hospitals might be closed and 80 percent of existing medical officers reassigned—and yet there were plans on the drawingboards for a hundred million dollars in new hospital construction, and a doubling of capacity.

The government not only collected taxes and maintained the nation's defenses—it also provided ten million meals a day and seven million uniforms to the Armed Forces. It ran paint factories and sawmills, meat-cutting plants and auto repair shops. It manufactured ice cream, helium and retreaded tires. It repaired watches and operated a railroad in Panama. It counted 366 laundries, a distillery in the Virgin Islands, and a $20-million-a-year fertilizer operation in the Tennessee Valley. The Army supervised and subsidized 450 post exchanges; Hoover wanted them restricted in number and scope, their prices raised to cover the cost of doing business, and consideration given to contracting to private industry their operation and maintenance. The military controlled 170 million square feet of excess storage space. The Army was guilty of shipping 807,000 pounds of tomatoes from California to New York at the same time the Navy sent 775,000 tons of the same product via the same route—in reverse.

For two years, Hoover's task forces poured over the ramparts of bureaucratic resistance. What they found did not surprise the former president. Uncle Sam owned $27 billion in personal property, including a million motorized vehicles, but no one could account for more than a fraction of the whole. Since there was no central office overseeing government purchases, the paperwork often cost more than items bought. More than seventy different government divisions operated storage facilities in metropolitan Washington alone. A central records facility could reduce by half Uncle Sam's mountain of useless paper. In all, the General Services Administration called for by the Hoover Commission might save a quarter billion dollars a year, while shrinking inventories by ten times as much.

The confusion didn't end there. What purported to be a federal budget was more likely to be a confusing series of dodges and dead ends. The Forest Service, for example, was down in the budget for $27 million. Hoover's sleuths did some digging and discovered it was actually spending $43 million. The Post Office was, as he put it, "wrapped in red tape and politics," so Hoover wanted Civil Service strengthened and extended, not only to postal workers but to tax collectors as well. The utmost probity was called for in the revenue business. "It is always unpleasant to 'render to Caesar the things that are Caesar's,' " he noted. "It is even worse when Caesar can't impose this high standard of morality on his own agents."

Impressive as all this was, it turned out to be only part of the commission's legacy. Hoover himself originally expected his review to be an aggrandized pruning job, consolidating functions and pursuing the holy grail of economy. He pitched it to the public and Congress as such. When told that the Armed Forces Medical Library needed more federal funding, his reply was concise. "This Commission was established to save money, not spend more." His administrative concepts were equally stark. "Definite authority at the top, a clear line of authority from top to bottom, and adequate staff aids to the exercise of authority do not exist," he announced in the first of sixteen separate reports he authored—each of which ran approximately 9,000 words, a perfect length, as he put it, to be carried on a single page of the New York Times. "Authority is diffused, lines of authority are confused, staff services are insufficient." By adopting all 273 of his recommendations, estimated Hoover, the Congress might save $4 billion a year. To most Americans, that was the essence of the Hoover Commission, an exercise in reshuffling boxes on Washington's chart, an attempt to reduce the flow of red ink associated with big government.[6]

It wasn't that simple. Hoover himself recognized another priority in claiming for his own province the commission's study of the presidential office. His action was typical. He made it clear at the outset that he would join the commission only as its chairman. Unlike his professional colleagues, the former president could devote all his time and formidable intellect to the work at hand. Combined with a forceful assertion of authority, and a crafty willingness to keep other commissioners too busy to interfere with his own oversight, Hoover was soon in complete control, his mastery subject only to the occasional dissents of vice-chairman Acheson and other liberals who detected a deliberate confusion between government's form and its proper functions. Hoover complained in private that Acheson was giving him problems. Other subjects were at least as worthy of complaint. The schedule of commuting back and forth between Washington and New York each week, followed by hours of grueling meetings and days of tedious report-writing, would have been brutal enough for a man half Hoover's age. On top of it all, the former president contracted a case of shingles in the fall of 1947, attending conferences with his right arm in a sling. His physical impairment did nothing to weaken his resolve to have his own way. Even so minor a matter as the suggestion that the Bureau of Indian Affairs integrate the native and white populations attracted his attention. The word should be "assimilate," he insisted.[7]

Hoover gave far more than his name to the commission. He also built a bridge, as political scientist Peri Arnold has noted, over which congressional conservatives could migrate into the camp of a strong presidency. Throughout the Roosevelt era, many of Hoover's own supporters on Capitol Hill equated such a prospect with a visit to Hell. They had history on their side. Traditionally, presidents yielded to congresses when managerial responsibilities were in question. Yet now the pendulum had swung in reverse. Hoover himself, before the Depression crushed his hopes, had sought to launch reforms along a broad front. Their success would have required firsthand supervision, not delegation to an obstreperous and easily influenced legislature.

Then came FDR, and for some conservatives, the office became as much an object of suspicion as the man who held it for so long. No other reason could account for the quick death of Louis Brownlow's most sweeping recommendations. Yet, as power necessarily flowed to the White House, its occupant needed more staff and more authority. Without them, accountability could be blurred beyond recognition. This was even more crucial, Hoover wrote in his final report, given the dangers abroad and the importance of executive response to them. He quoted Hamilton's Federalist Paper 70: "An energetic and unified executive is not a threat to a free and responsible people." Far more worrisome, he continued, were disunity or administrative chaos—and yet both plagued the president's house like the physical weakening that forced the Trumans to abandon 1600 Pennsylvania Avenue for nearby Blair House in 1949. Between sixty-five and eighty different bureaus, agencies, commissions and departments reported directly to the president. Giving each an hour of his weekly schedule would leave no time for policy development. Then too, Congress over the years had attached strings to many executive agencies.

"The idea that Congress is the board of directors and the President the executive seems to have been lost somewhere." His own prescription was for the establishment of authority "from the office boy up."

Might a Cabinet secretariat, patterned after Great Britain's, do the trick? Hoover dispatched his aide Don Price to study the Canadian Cabinet and Standard Oil of New Jersey. The Joint Chiefs of Staff were pointed out as one example of such administrative theory in effect. Hoover was skeptical. He had seen such systems for himself throughout Europe, "always associated with the most backward looking elements of bureaucracy." His own preference was for an administrative vice president, entrusted among other tasks with oversight of the budgetary process. Former Vice President Charles Dawes joined Price in a strong dissent. Hoover gave way; his thinking evolved around fresh lines. Perhaps the problem of the modern presidency wasn't merely irrational organization, or departments insufficiently under its sway, but a lack of human resources to allow chief executives to carry out their enlarged mandate? Hoover proposed a presidential agency for policy clearance and departmental coordination. Whatever one called it, it looked suspiciously like a secretariat.[8]

Meanwhile, outside the former president's suite of rooms at Washington's Wardman-Park Hotel, the 1948 campaign escalated in temper and tone. Earl Warren, Dewey's running mate, predicted that Truman would soon join Hoover as an ex-President. Warren's running mate was less willing to mention the sole member of that exclusive club. In the final days of the campaign, a shrill Truman resorted to the same device that earlier Democratic candidates had made their calling card: he opened fire on Hoover. In one speech alone, the incumbent mentioned his predecessor's name sixteen times. At Boston, he did leave out of his formal remarks a sniping reference to Communist party strength in 1932. But he claimed credit for his own party in having "licked the Hoover depression." And he recalled the grim specter of Hoovervilles before a packed audience in Madison Square Garden. Dewey, too, was an efficiency expert, said Truman, and his presidency was likely to lead to the same disastrous results. Then he taunted his GOP opponent for not mentioning previous Republican presidents by name.

"He's afraid to discuss them," he told a Connecticut whistle-stop. "He can't point to them with pride, because whenever they have had a chance, they have tried to give the country to special interests."

Reporters traveling with the president ascribed his verbal ferocity to last-minute jitters. Yet Truman was right about one thing at least. Dewey had no intention of defending Hoover. Before his own climactic rally in New York on October 30, its chairman slipped the governor a paragraph for insertion in his remarks. "I do not personally mind Mr. Truman's campaign of abuse, misrepresentations and smears against me," it read. "I can defend myself. But when Mr. Truman directs such statements at former President Hoover, who is not in this campaign . . . that is something unparalleled in American politics. And the reason Mr. Hoover is not in this campaign makes Mr. Truman's conduct even more reprehensible. That reason is that Mr. Hoover undertook a great nonpartisan service for the American people at the request of both Republican and Democratic leaders in the Congress and, in the conduct of this work, he has scrupulously remained out of all partisan conflict."[9]

Dewey wouldn't use a word of it. Far ahead in the polls, his sleek electoral machine confident of victory, the cautious New Yorker also realized the fluidity of the contest. For days his sensitive antennae had detected slippage. A man with little predilection for taking chances, he wasn't about to endanger his third and final lunge for the presidency with a gracious but impolitic tribute to Hoover. The former president himself seemed more hurt than angry. "I really believe that by 1948 the people of this country had reestablished me in their affections," he later told a friend, "but apparently the governor held to the opinion that I was still political poison."[10]

On November 2, 1948, thirty-five close friends gathered in Suite 31-A to listen to the returns and celebrate the long-delayed exodus from power of those who had seized it sixteen years before. But the polls were wrong. By midnight, it was apparent that Dewey's landslide was evaporating. Against all odds, and with an undoubted boost from his own fear mongering, Truman was scoring a historic upset. Angered by his own party's tactics, Hoover faulted Dewey for running away from the Eightieth Congress, Taft-Hartley, price supports and tax cuts—all cleverly portrayed by Truman as the work of "big business and private interest." Dewey failed to excoriate Roosevelt's domestic policies, Roosevelt's foreign policies, and Truman's surrender at Potsdam "which wrecked peace in the world and [caused] enslavement of hundreds of millions of people." Worst of all, the New Yorker had failed to educate the electorate or touch the mystical chords of emotion that hold a party together.[11]

The immediate consequence of Truman's vindication held still more personal dangers as Hoover forecast rough sledding for his own commission's report. Only a few weeks earlier, he told Rickard that opponents within the group were ganging up to prevent its publication. If they were unwilling to make such a move prior to Election Day, there was now nothing to forestall such an administrative coup d'etat. Originally tailored to the administrative specifications of President Dewey, Hoover's finding might now have to be altered to fit Truman and his ambitious view of government. In the capital, Don Price called another member of the commission on this historic morning after.[12]

"What are we going to do?" he asked.

His friend hung up, dialed the president in Missouri, and called Price back within an hour. Hoover's aide-de-camp was authorized to tell his general that the commission's recommendations "are not going to be lost." With that, Price phoned the former president in New York, who could barely contain his pleasure. What's more, the newly confirmed Truman would soon make a public statement in support of the commission's work. Historians would be equally generous. Twenty years after Congress was presented with the first of Hoover's nineteen reports in February 1949, Don Price, by then a distinguished professor of public policy at Harvard, credited the chairman with having contributed "something approaching a workable theory on the fundamental nature of the Presidency." Thanks to reorganized line agencies and enlarged staff, the expansive office was institutionalized and accepted by even its most vociferous critics among congressional Republicans. Later, GOP executives Eisenhower, Nixon and Ford would themselves draw upon the resources of the managerial presidency, an office haphazardly designed by FDR, continued by Truman, but refined and made permanent by Hoover himself.[13]

Of his own voluminous reports, part of a package of 2.5 million words, Hoover said they reminded him of the little girl given a book on pelicans. "This is indeed a very interesting thing," she wrote its author. "It contains more about pelicans than I really need to know." Congress responded more favorably, adopting nearly three-fourths of the commission's recommendations. (Not until Eisenhower's presidency, however, would Hoover's vision of a Department of Health, Education and Welfare be realized.) When the Korean War broke out in June 1950, the federal budget ballooned again, from $40 billion to $70 billion. Suddenly, the few billions salvaged through Hoover's crusade for efficiency seemed a paltry sum. In fact, they were a fiscal footnote to the real, if unintended, achievement of the first Hoover Commission. And they helped make 1949 the highest point yet in the former president's slow ascendancy from scapegoat to what one newspaper called "counselor to the republic."

★   ★

Hoover began the year with a warning to the Truman White House. The state of Israel was in its militant infancy, having survived attack from its Arab neighbors the previous year. Yet half a million Palestinians, the forgotten people of the Middle East, were living in "deplorable conditions," inadequately supported by foreign relief and subject to the opportunistic appeals of unfriendly powers. For perhaps $50 million they could be resettled on several hundred thousand acres of Iraqi soil that would be newly irrigated. "Even with no return of the money," concluded Hoover, "it would seem to be a small item to be fitted into the billions of European Co-operation appropriations." Truman responded favorably to this reprise of Hoover's old Tigris Valley initiative. In fact, he told the former president, he was working on just such a plan himself, and in conversations with engineers had reached the conclusion that Hoover's irrigation scheme was feasible.[14]

No such harmony prevailed within Hoover's own party. Truman's friend was highly critical of the Lincoln Day remarks delivered by a finger-wagging Dewey, whose blunt declaration of a split within the GOP reminded Hoover of Theodore Roosevelt and his Bull Moose in the political china shop. It suggested as well the long migration to the Right of the young engineer who backed up his verbal support of T.R. in 1912 with a thousand-dollar contribution. Not long after that, the son of the man who bested the first Roosevelt gave him a shock by introducing a federal housing bill. Most astonishing of all, Dewey that July offered Hoover the vacant Senate seat of Robert Wagner.[15]

He had given the matter "prayerful consideration," the former president replied, only to conclude that a younger man should be appointed. His personal contribution in the few weeks that remained of the current session would necessarily be limited to promoting his own commission's recommendations—and that was something he could pursue just as effectively outside the world's greatest deliberative body. "For some years I have thought my best service to the American people was occasional special investigation or advice in fields where I have some experience, and with an entire independence of view," he wrote Dewey. "I also have many activities as a trustee for public institutions. I hope to finish in that harness."[16]

He wasn't exaggerating. Lunch was served in Suite 31-A in five minutes' time, "and I want to make use of those five minutes" said Hoover. He was kept busy accepting awards and citations—from the Dutch Treat Club and a group of French scientists, the New York Trade Board and the Salvation

Army. He became a great-grandfather in August 1949, the same month he turned seventy-five amidst a chorus of praise from editorial writers and officeholders alike. He reproached a friendly author for bringing out a biography entitled *Our Unknown Ex-President*. His friends disliked the word "unknown," he explained to Eugene Lyons. His own memoirs were now scheduled for publication in 1951. "I'm not as rich as everybody thinks I am," he protested to visitors, yet he invested $70,000 in printing costs as part of preparing three volumes of autobiography. The much revised Magnum Opus now had a working title—*Freedom Betrayed*—and that suggested much about his continuing animus toward Roosevelt and his policies. Eleanor Roosevelt acknowledged publicly that Hoover had not been personally responsible for the Great Depression, moving the former president to accept her statement with the wry declaration "the pardon came too late." When the former First Lady, writing in the July 1949 issue of *McCall's*, raised the old tale of the Bonus Army and Hoover's alleged orders to the troops under MacArthur, the target of her casual criticism bristled. His friend Pat Hurley prepared a detailed rebuttal, a copy of which went to Hearst columnist George Sokolsky, in case "you took a notion to take a crack at the lady." In the end, Mrs. Roosevelt issued a pale apology: "I am glad to have an authentic account published and I only wonder why it was not done much sooner." [17]

That fall, the former president again urged MacArthur to come home from Tokyo. "We need reinforcements if our own way of life is not to be lost in this wilderness of a 'Welfare State.' " He delivered a commencement address at Ohio Wesleyan University, entitled "Give Us Self-Reliance—or Give Us Security," in which he recalled the night before his own graduation, when he and fellow Stanford students amused themselves with multiple choruses of "Into the Cold, Cold World." He remembered as well the distractions of self-support and Miss Lou Henry that kept him from focusing on the speaker's ritualistic tributes to the Founding Fathers, Herbert Spencer, John Stuart Mill and the race of life. Since then, Hoover continued, many more New Eras had been proclaimed. The old liberalism was somehow equated with reactionary thought. Even the race had changed, now that "each step must be dictated by some official or unofficial bureaucrat with Stop and Go signals. They hold the attraction that with this security you will finish with an old-age pension and your funeral expenses from the Government." [18]

Indeed, he wished to remind his young listeners, all those Americans who lived in new houses and operated complex machinery would one day die. Then the jobs, the plant and equipment would be theirs. Opportunities would abound. "But the best of these jobs are never filled by security seekers."

"Even during these troubled years," said Hoover, science and technology had spun off a thousand new products and opened as many frontiers for intellectual and personal adventure. "I know you are champing at the bit to take your chance in an opening world," he concluded. "Do not fear it will be cold to you."

Death invaded his own circle that summer. Will Irwin was gone. Hoover himself borrowed one of his older son's hearing aids; soon, he had one of his own. In June 1949, "my devoted and constant friend from our boyhood," Ray Lyman Wilbur, died at Palo Alto. Edgar Rickard's precarious health led the former president to suggest a financial arrangement with a San Francisco-based firm, permitting his old friend to shuttle between both coasts. Still another companion of long standing, Mark Sullivan, became a Hoover houseguest in the spring of 1947, after slipping in a Waldorf tub and returning to recuperate after a hospital stay. Sullivan's convalescence was complicated by the zealous pursuit of two staunch Catholics, Clare Boothe Luce and Archbishop Fulton J. Sheen, both of whom were anxious to reunite Sullivan with his church. [19]

"Mark," Hoover told his friend, "don't you worry; I'll handle that damned woman." He proved a man of his word. Ultimately, Hoover's Irish parlor maid brought her parish priest to call, and the elderly columnist died within the Catholic fold. "Arsenic and Old Luce" was foiled. Before then, however, the ambulance and oxygen tents spotted going in and out of the Waldorf led Walter Winchell to broadcast a report that the former president was himself at death's door. Only later did Winchell phone Suite 31-A to seek confirmation. He asked the man who picked up the receiver if Herbert Hoover was still present.

"He's here," snapped the object of Winchell's curiosity, "and he's very much alive." [20]

For additional evidence, there was Hoover's heavy schedule of public appearances. As he neared his seventy-fifth birthday—a milestone he proposed to mark alone, on a California train—the former president addressed one of his favorite themes, the sad perversion of the common man so beloved in American mythology. Most Americans, he argued, especially women, would simply get mad if called "common." This was a hopeful sign, for equal opportunity to Hoover included the opportunity to rise to leadership, "in other words, to be uncommon. . . . I have never met a father or mother who did not want their children to grow up to be uncommon men and women. May it always be so. For the future of America rests not in mediocrity, but in the constant renewal of leadership in every phase of our national life."

He reveled in a vast correspondence with young people, informing a girl who asked for his favorite quote that it was the Sermon on the Mount. He agreed with another young woman that the chances of a female president were improving; after all, "the men have not done too good a job of govern-ment . . . in the last forty-seven years," and wishing her well "if you are a candidate for President about thirty years hence. A ten-year-old sought the former president's advice on fishing. "Nowadays I mostly fish for bonefish with a live shrimp for bait," Hoover replied. "Bonefish are not good to eat. I put them back in the water so they can grow bigger. Bonefishing around the Florida Keys is especially adapted to older gentlemen who can no longer clamber among the rocks and brush. Keep this in mind when you are eighty-seven."

Then there was Kathleen, who informed him that she was not yet born when he occupied the White House, and confided her ambition to become, not a president, but a doctor. "My dear Kathleen," wrote Hoover in re-sponse. "You were saved a lot of trouble by not being born earlier. I am glad you want to be a doctor and not President. We do not have enough doctors, and there seems to be a sufficient number of candidates for President." The public did not know when he sent $500 to help pay for an operation on his sister May—or fifty dollars to an elderly California woman making ends meet on her $25.18 a month in Social Security. The latter was signed only "from a fellow Republican who wishes you good times and a Merry Christmas." [21]

His mood was much fiercer in August 1949 when he arrived at Stanford for his birthday party, and found Encina Hall drapped with a red-and-white banner proclaiming, "Hoover Slept Here." Newspapers across the political spectrum contested with one another in paying him tribute. William Allen White's old *Emporia Gazette* called his comeback "a fine example of poetic justice." A paper in Appleton, Wisconsin, marveled at his Quaker serenity in the face of persistent attack. "Perhaps he realized that in the fullness of time he would tower like a gigantic mountain peak over the scrawny hills when comparisons were made. . . ." The *Washington Post* hailed him as "the most characteristic American of his generation, deeply devoted to all the native pieties." The *New York Times* likewise focused on Hoover's character. "In one era glorified," it wrote, "in another bitterly criticized, he has found the inward strength to follow a true course as he saw it." Even John Nance Garner weighed in with a compliment, calling Hoover the wisest statesman in the country when it came to foreign affairs. "He may be on domestic affairs too," said Garner, who rued the fact that Hoover's presidency began in 1929 and not 1921 or 1937.[22]

At Stanford, a national television hookup had been arranged to carry his speech to millions of viewers. Arkansas and Maryland proclaimed "Hoover Day," and there were more than ten thousand people gathered in the Frost Amphitheatre to hear the school's most distinguished alumnus warn of the dangers of expansive, expensive government. A generation earlier, said Hoover, one American in forty drew his pay from Uncle Sam. Now the figure was one in twenty-two. The average citizen worked sixty-one days each year to pay his federal taxes, twenty-four to shoulder the burdens of cold war defense alone. "Think it over," he repeated throughout an address in which he dismissed domestic Communists as "a nuisance." The real danger confronting America in 1949 came from "fuzzy-minded people" who were willing to compromise with economic and political collectivism.

The crowd approved; left-wing columnist I. F. Stone was unmoved. The remarks at Stanford, sneered Stone, were exactly "the kind of chrome-plated Barton, Batten [sic], Durstine and Osborne guff which made Hoover seem a tiresome old bore before." Stone went on to deride "the mumblings of outraged Victorian gentlemen" revived and given new respectability when emerging from the mouth of a former president.

But Hoover's focus was shifting. His friend Albert Wedemeyer said it best. "America," the general said, "fought the war like a football game, after which the winner leaves the field." Dissatisfied as he might be with domestic conditions, it was foreign policy that claimed most of his attention and generated most of his public indignation. The years since V-J Day had shattered the illusions of others; Hoover held none to begin with. As far back as Potsdam, W. Averell Harriman had amiably remarked to Stalin that he must be pleased to have Soviet forces inside Berlin. The Russian dictator shrugged his shoulders. "Csar Alexander got to Paris," he replied, with awesome indifference. Then followed, in rapid succession, the crisis over Poland and the Greek civil war, in which fifteen hundred villages were burned and 85 percent of the kingdom's children were left tubercular. Soviet troops remained stubbornly perched in northern Iran. Soviet diplomats demanded return of the Bosporus Strait. Early in 1946, Stalin launched his latest Five-Year Plan, predicated on the assumption of a superpower clash in the decade to come. Even so staunch a liberal as Justice William O. Douglas denounced the speech as "the Declaration of World War III."

At home, the 1948 election was played out against a portentous backdrop as congressional committees investigated domestic spy rings and Hoover's young Californian discovery, Richard Nixon, touched off a furor with his sensational questioning of Alger Hiss, once a top State Department official, now on trial in the court of public opinion after allegations by *Time* editor Whittaker Chambers that both men had belonged to a Communist cell. Chambers's own credibility was soon demonstrated, and external events convinced many doubters of a global conspiracy to impose Moscow's theology on the rest of the world. A Communist undercover network was revealed in the Canadian capital of Ottawa. In response to assertions about similar activities in Washington, Truman established his Loyalty Review Board, charged with hearing appeals from government employees themselves labeled threats to national security. In September 1949, the president announced that Moscow had successfully tested an atomic bomb of its own. A few months later, he let it be known that American scientists were working on a still more destructive weapon, the hydrogen bomb.

Finally, and most alarming of all, 1949 marked the end of Chiang Kai-shek's tenuous hold over the Chinese mainland. The new government in Peking was Communist, the fruition of Mao Tse-tung's thirty-year struggle for the soul of the world's most populous nation. Suddenly, U.S. diplomats and politicians alike confronted thorny questions: Should Red China be recognized? Should it be admitted to the United Nations? And what could be done to salvage the world body from a series of Russian vetoes, more than sixty by the spring of 1950, which all but paralyzed the Security Council and rapidly eroded public faith in the organization as anything more than a forum for big power obstruction?

Hoover's response came on several fronts. After receiving from the congressman copies of at least four documents taken from the famous "Pumpkin Papers," he congratulated Nixon in January 1950. "The conviction of Alger Hiss was due to your patience and persistence alone. At last the stream of treason that existed in our Government has been exposed in a fashion that all may believe." A few days later, Nixon sent along a list of 108 names of those applying for work at the State Department—a pale forecast of things to come. For on February 9, Wisconsin's junior senator, Joseph McCarthy, down on his political luck and anxious to find a winning issue for his own reelection campaign in 1952, unleashed a volley of charges, vague of detail yet frightening in their implications. He knew at least fifty-seven Communists nestling in the State Department's clubby confines, charged McCarthy. Adding insult to injury, Tail Gunner Joe fired off a telegram to the White House restating his case. In an unsent reply, Truman excoriated McCarthy as "not even fit to have a hand in the operations of the Government of the United States."[23]

"A pathological liar . . . from Wisconsin," he wrote a few weeks later, "and a block headed undertaker in the same 'great body' from Nebraska are going along with the Kremlin to break up our bipartisan foreign policy." They weren't alone in their efforts. Hoover himself was telling senators of his opposition to any recognition of the new Chinese government, and the need to continue aid and support for the beleaguered Chiang, including naval protection of Formosa, where the defeated Generalissimo established his own regime in opposition to the mainland. Not only would this prevent Chinese legations in the United States from "becoming nests of Communist conspiracies" and reduce the disruptions already corroding the UN; but "by maintaining at least a symbol of resistance," Hoover wrote William F. Knowland, "we would have a better basis for salvation of Southeastern Asia." Three weeks later, he was back in print, warning of the dangers as long as America took it upon herself to fight the cold war in Europe, the Mediterranean and Far East, and as long as Red China was allowed to repeat the example of other Communist states, "their agents boring within our institutions, revolutionary plots over the world, maltreatment of our citizens, conspiracies, threats, national insults, international embarrassments, and refusal to cooperate in bringing peace to the world." Such an attitude had been constant in the Soviet camp, "except for a short respite from Russia while we were furnishing her with $10 billions worth of supplies."[24]

His resort to the written word was deliberate. He no longer wished to speak in public unless a major opportunity arose to contribute to public thought, Hoover informed a friend in February 1950. Such occasions required weeks of advance thought and careful research, not to mention twenty minutes of clear radio time. In the previous six months alone, he had declined more than fifteen hundred speaking invitations. "I am no longer young nor looking for glory," he added. But for the American Newspaper Publishers annual meeting that spring, he would make an exception, offering "four minutes of persiflage versus a major address. You can have your choice!"[25]

The publishers chose, and got, the latter. On April 27, Hoover presented eighteen hundred newspapermen in his audience with a capsule review of Russian history, from Peter the Great to Stalin's "malignant government." He recalled his June 1941 warning against any collaboration with Moscow, even in halting the scourge of Hitlerism. He cited thirty-five "solemnly signed agreements" violated by the Russians since recognition was first extended to their regime in 1933. He spoke in sorrowful tones about the UN. Despite all its verbal pledges of human liberty and national sovereignty, "the Kremlin had reduced the United Nations to a propaganda forum for the smearing of free peoples," he proclaimed. The time had come to recognize that this was not one, but two worlds: "One world is militaristic, atheistic, and without compassion. The other world still holds to belief in God, free nations, human dignity and peace."

Thus far, Hoover had said nothing new. But when he called upon his countrymen to take "a cold and objective look" at both the UN and a global battle in which most of freedom's defense was supplied by a single country, with but 6 percent of the world's population, and when he proposed the reorganization of the worldly body minus its Communist members, then Hoover was setting off a keg of his own, with results as spectacular as anything shouted by McCarthy. He didn't intend such a result; on the contrary, said Hoover, he wished to "redeem the concept of the United Nations to the high purpose for which it was created." He wanted a grand coalition of free nations to pool their moral, spiritual, economic and military weapons against Communist aggressors. "By collective action we could much more effectively keep their conspiring agents and bribers out of our borders and out of our laboratories." What he proposed, Hoover claimed, "is the logical and practical end of total diplomacy."

The speech stirred a national response. Even before he left the dais, Hoover received word that he was wanted on the telephone. Three times he declined, hopeful of deceiving reporters already buzzing over the source of the call. Finally, he was told that the message was urgent. He left the hall, and those behind learned the real purpose of Hoover's abrupt departure —to take a congratulatory call from Harry Truman. The president heartily approved of Hoover's message, which he had heard on the radio. He hoped to see his friend soon. Government reorganization was not likely to be the chief topic of conversation. [26]

Hoover's fears were multiplying. Much of Europe, he contended, had regained its prewar economic strength, and yet Stalin could throw four times as many divisions at Western Europe as America's Allies might muster. Spain could help redress the imbalance, but was shunned by her democratic neighbors. Meanwhile, at home both deficits and long-range debt were mounting. "Before we appropriate more money we should know a lot more about where we are going," Hoover advised Kenneth Wherry, Truman's "block headed undertaker" from Nebraska. "What are our policies? What are the policies of the European countries for whom we are making huge sacrifices and efforts?" [27]

He listened as McCarthy assailed unnamed State Department officials for treasonous behavior, then confided to friends that the Wisconsin senator might indeed be right about Owen Lattimore, mainstay of the left-wing Institute of Pacific Affairs, and a much-published target of the China Lobby.

Lattimore's FBI file failed to sustain McCarthy's allegation that he was "the top Russian spy" in America. Henry Stimson and Drew Pearson, among others, rallied to the defense of Secretary of State Dean Acheson. But McCarthy kept up the attack, calling Acheson "the voice for the mind of Lattimore" and lumping together the State Department's Far Eastern division and the Voice of America as Communist playthings. Taft joined in, lambasting as "the greatest Kremlin asset in our history" the same clique of suspicious State Department operatives. To McCarthy himself, Mr. Republican offered congratulations, along with words of advice to sustain the crusader. "Keep talking," he told McCarthy, "and if one case doesn't work out . . . proceed with another." [28]

The air was filled with such talk, and Washington became a haven of pointed fingers and poisoned pens. "I am so disturbed at the situation," a distraught Hoover wrote Alf Landon in June 1950, "that I hesitate at any public or private appearance—I hate to be perpetually pessimistic!" Yet ten days later, when North Korean forces crossed the 38th Parallel and Truman responded by committing American troops to their defeat, he issued a strong statement of support. "It was great of you" to come to his aid, the president responded. His reaction was premature. Hoover's own formula for ending the war did not include U.S. ground forces. At one point, he called Lewis Strauss with the idea of spreading radioactive dust along the Yalu River dividing Korea from China. At that summer's Bohemian Grove encampment, he struck another note in his Lakeside Talk. His recommendations, he acknowledged, "will have more effect on these trees than officials in Washington." But he would make the effort anyhow. [29]

The Russians had just announced their intention to return to the Security Council, whose meetings they had been boycotting. "If you have an optimistic imagination," said Hoover, "you may believe they are coming with assorted doves of peace. If you are realistic, you may expect them to propose some device which will divide the United Nations. Or alternatively, they will come bearing sheaves of vetoes and slander." This time, Hoover urged the U.S. to cast a veto of its own should Red China's admission to the peacekeeping body become reality. In a broader sense, he was concerned that Stalin hoped to exhaust the United States in fights with his satellites. Europe lacked the will to fight a general war with Russia. "We could no more occupy Moscow than the Communists could occupy Washington." Yet the UN itself might still play a useful role, if only it would impose sanctions against nations aiding the North Korean invaders and was willing to bite the bullet and expel the Communists for vetoing such sanctions. "I suggest that if you have a murderer in your house," Hoover told his fellow Bohemians, "you can at least start legal proceedings for his eviction."

To prevent domestic ruin, he called for fiscal retrenchment. "I just leave the thought in the trees," he added. "It won't happen." As for Fifth Columnists within the country's borders, Hoover said he put little stock in registering schemes. Instead, he favored "amplifying" conspiracy and treason laws, making it possible to move against anyone engaged in subversion. "If our intellectuals want to continue to believe in or to sympathize with abstract Communism as being freedom, they could do so. That could be called academic freedom," he said with discernible irony. "But the moment they make a move to discuss any subversive action they might be in the toils of the F.B.I." His reluctance to go witch-hunting might have been a subconscious reflection of his own unwitting role in having nurtured the danger. Drew Pearson was not alone among thoughtful observers who looked at tarnished idealists now held up as public enemies, and saw over their shoulders "the Hoover depression when young people were groping for something and when the breadlines were blocks long in most of our big cities."[30]

Hoover's own views, never subtle, were hardening into bellicosity. He reassured J. Edgar Hoover that "the country is behind you" and he should pay no attention to "the smear gang." He told Taft that his reelection that November left him "unexpressibly relieved," and Taft responded with appreciation of his own. Taking pride in the heavy blue-collar vote he won, despite union efforts to pillory him for Taft-Hartley, the Ohio senator said it showed "that even the American workman will not listen to a class appeal." Taft shared his old friend's concern about the foreign scene, as well as the inflation and taxes such commitments ensured. He evinced a curious kind of optimism: "I doubt if the American people will stand for a regimented garrison state for any long period of time." Even from Taft, such language was extreme. But it was a hyperbolic era. Early in November, three Puerto Rican terrorists tried to assassinate Truman at Blair House. Hoover expressed relief at their failure, and the president warmly thanked him for his sentiments. It was impossible to convey his gratitude for such words, wrote Truman, "especially because they come from you."[31]

Later that month, he wrote Hoover again, this time with a fresh appeal for help. Considering all the talk about infiltration of Communists in the government, he had decided to appoint a bipartisan commission, including churchmen, lawyers, business executives and labor leaders, which he hoped the former president might be willing to chair. Hoover was "greatly troubled" by the request. For one thing, "I doubt if there are any consequential card-carrying communists in the Government, or if there are, they should be known to the F.B.I." What's more, admirable as Truman's stated intention might be, it was far too narrow in its scope. Lack of public confidence arose, not from the presence of Communists in federal ranks, but from a public belief that non-Communists had pursued disastrous policies regarding the Soviet Union. What was needed was "a widespread inquiry into the past and present of such men," complete with investigative staff and unlimited access to official files. He wished to be helpful, Hoover stressed, and he regretted having to turn down the president's original request. Yet perhaps Truman would be willing to publicly commit himself to cooperation with a more sweeping probe, should the Congress create such a commission or assume the task for itself. Truman responded as graciously as one could expect to such an invitation, and the commission died aborning.

His next encounter with Hoover was far less polite.[32] On December 20, 1950, the former president ignited what later historians dubbed the Great Debate. Ostensibly, he took to the airwaves that night to oppose Truman's plan to send four divisions of American soldiers to aid in the European security efforts of NATO, the collective security outpost overseen by Dwight Eisenhower. But Hoover's perspective reached beyond the headlines—even those announcing the onslaught of Chinese forces in Korea—to embrace history. What he proposed bore striking resemblance to Great Britain's old policy of conserving its manpower and ensuring its independence by relying on ships and shrewd diplomacy to prevent the rise of any single Continental power to dominant status. Hoover's view was more expansive still. Totting up the Communist versus non-Communist populations, he found hardly 300 million of the latter imbued with either sufficient military force or the will to use it. To commit such sparse resources to a land war against either Russia or China would be foolhardy. Nazi Germany had thrown 240 "magnificent" combat divisions into battle, and lost. How could the West hope to prevail against Stalin with an army one-fourth the size of Hitler's legions?

At the same time, his country did command sufficient air and naval power to promote Hoover's real objective: to convert North America, "this Gibraltar of Western Civilization," into an impregnable fortress. Controversial as that concept might be, the former president topped it with two more. The atomic bomb, he declared, "is a far less dominant weapon than it was once thought to be." What's more, it seemed obvious to Hoover that the United Nations had lost in Korea, proof positive that ground wars were intrinsically weighted in favor of Communist numbers. Still more questionable was his blunt assertion that economic disintegration loomed should the United States continue bearing the defense burden of a selfish, unprepared Europe. This at a time of record-breaking prosperity, output, employment and personal income—even after taxes. Real income had doubled its fabulous 1929 levels while workers earning $21.44 in 1940 were taking home over seventy dollars a week in 1951. New York State was forced in August of 1950 to lay off five hundred workers in the state unemployment office, so buoyant was the economy.

Yet Hoover persisted. For three years, he said, the United States had poured funds into Western Europe. Yet money alone could not purchase the willpower necessary to successful defense. Even then, Britain's labor government was flirting with Peking. Ninety percent of the men killed defending South Korea were Americans. "It is clear," said Hoover, "that the United Nations is in a fog of debate and indecision on whether to appease or not to appease."

His own prescription was simple. Through proper use of air and sea power, the U.S. could establish its new frontiers on Britain and the Pacific outposts of Japan, Formosa and the Philippines. Large armies were not needed, "unless we are going to Europe and China." Japan should be encouraged to develop her own defenses. Then Americans might reduce their expenditures on armaments and cut taxes at home. "We are not blind to the need to preserve Western Civilization on the Continent of Europe or to our cultural and religious ties to it," Hoover told his listeners. "But the prime obligations of defense of Western Continental Europe rests upon the nations of Europe."

Europe, said Hoover, must fashion its own military divisions. It must "erect a sure dam against the red flood . . . before we land another man or another dollar on their shores." As for America's role, the former president prescribed "a period of watchful waiting." No such pause followed his own remarks. No one, it seemed, lacked an opinion, or was reluctant to share it. It had been a long time, Alf Landon wrote Hoover, "since a talk by anyone has rung the bell as your last one has done. . . . We can't save people who are unwilling to save themselves." Richard Nixon told the former president that he had received more than one hundred messages approving the speech, which he thought augured well for "a more realistic approach" to the whole foreign policy conundrum. "At least we have the animals stirred up," Hoover responded.[33]

For once, he was guilty of understatement. Across the Atlantic, British observer Harold Nicolson expressed fears that "even the United States is affected with cold feet, taking the form of Hoover isolationism. . . . It is sad to become old amid such darkness," concluded Nicholson. "Where does this leave us poor Europeans?" wondered the *Manchester Guardian*. The *Christian Science Monitor* took exception to Hoover's emphasis on military strength. Had such attitudes prevailed in 1940, then Britain would have been deemed indefensible. At the White House, a reporter asked Truman if Hoover's speech smacked of isolationism, and the president replied that it was nothing but. Secretary of State Acheson denounced the whole thing as an invitation to Moscow to seize Western Europe, with all its resources of men and matériel—not to mention air bases critical to the very supremacy celebrated by Hoover.

Acheson's Republican counterpart, John Foster Dulles, was similarly inflexible. "A defense that accepts encirclement quickly decomposes," said Dulles. Only collective security and the deterrent of powerful retaliation could avert the kind of peril foreseen by Hoover. Dulles's mentor, Tom Dewey, offered up a plan of his own, including immediate creation of a one-hundred-division army, or what Walter Lippmann called "the Truman Doctrine carried to its logical extreme." Such a force could not be raised, trained or equipped for at least several years, wrote Lippmann, nor was there any logical reason to believe that Russia or China would calmly look aside as it took shape on their borders. Yet Hoover's ostrichlike proposal was worse. "The withdrawal of our guarantees," said Lippmann in biting tones, "is a surrender greater than any Stalin or Mao have [sic] ever called for." Why should it come as any surprise that Germany and France, "both disarmed in the war, both bled white in the war," were unable to conjure up sufficient combat divisions to fulfill Hoover's dream of a human wall against further Communist expansion? Western Europe, said Lippmann, would be fortunate to protect itself from internal subversion, civil war and guerilla activity, while America must recognize and grasp its own obligations to hold out a shield of deterrence over the stricken continent.

Early in January, a New York congressman introduced a resolution embodying Hoover's opposition to sending U.S. troops overseas without the consent of Congress. Ken Wherry followed suit in the Senate and the Great Debate reached boiling point. In the Florida Keys for some fishing, Hoover read transcripts of congressional testimony. "The day I read the Pentagon Generals' attempt to fool the country," he said afterward, "I never got a bite. Even the fish were repelled by that fishy four division story." Hoover signaled Taft on his own willingness to appear before the Senate Foreign Relations Committee. In the meantime, he took to the radio again, this time to amplify his charge that no four-hundred-mile line of defense in Europe could be maintained. He demanded to know from the nation's civilian leaders whether the four divisions represented only the first installment of much larger forces to be sent abroad later. If Korea had taught anything, said Hoover, harking back to Douglas MacArthur's brilliant amphibious landing at Inchon the previous September, it demonstrated the potency of air and naval might. Dewey said it proved just the opposite.[34]

Chinese forces had intervened in Korea, and a nervous White House was rethinking U.S. objectives on the Korean peninsula, by the time Hoover spoke to the Foreign Relations Committee on February 27. He acknowledged the weariness of Europe, as well as the suspicions of both Germany and Spain that were harbored within democratic circles. Yet these were luxuries at a time of immense peril. The U.S. had already created NATO. Americans bore the vast majority of expense in promoting a common defense. Their heroic stand against thirty-three well-armed Chinese divisions in Korea hardly needed mention. And now they were being told that a few more divisions would somehow supply Europe with the crucial element of national will thus far lacking. Hoover was no more impressed with deterrence theories. Even fifty divisions would be inadequate for anything more than a Dunkirk-style delaying action, he told the committee.

Not since the depths of his own cold war with Roosevelt had he sounded so bitter a note. Eisenhower hoped that 200,000 fresh American troops would lift European morale, and hasten the day when the Continent might boast its own army, 4 million men strong. Such a force might not be anywhere in sight, Hoover told friends, "but the boys have no doubt lifted the morale in certain very limited circles with cigarettes at 6 cents a pack." He declared bipartisan foreign policy itself anathema: "The whole recent history of bipartisanship in foreign affairs is a record of failures for lack of proper ventilation and criticism." Truman's administration, declared Hoover had gone to war in Korea "under the most specious reasoning," and at extreme risk to Constitutional guarantees of congressional involvement. He was similarly critical of the stalemate developing on the peninsula. In mid-November 1950, Hoover extended some advice of his own to MacArthur, "that he should stop and dig in on the short line across Korea—and then use his air force on any armies north of that area." A few days later, however, Chinese forces poured across the 38th Parallel, and Hoover was left with his pleas for Fortress America and "a poignant recollection" of what might have been in Korea.[35]

Within a few months, MacArthur would no longer be able to act on Hoover's military injunctions. But he would listen closely as the former president sought to transform the five-star hero of Inchon from Truman's scapegoat into his successor.

★   ★

Hoover's brother was eighty years old in April 1951, an occasion the former president forgot to commemorate. He wasn't at all certain, he belatedly informed Theodore Hoover, that such milestones were deserving of much celebration. "Nevertheless," he concluded, "I am glad you continue to live and work." The letter suggested preoccupation as well as emotional reserve, during a month when outside events and figures larger than life crowded mere birthdays off the stage. In the White House, Harry Truman angrily canceled a peace feeler to the enemy in Korea, after Douglas MacArthur issued his own insistence on Communist surrender. Dean Acheson convened an emergency meeting at his Georgetown address to ponder the fate of "the big General." Acheson, as usual, had a classical allusion for what was about to happen. "Whom the gods destroy they first make mad," he told his guests that evening.[36]

MacArthur was no less frustrated. Making no secret of his disagreement with Truman's desire to reinstate prewar boundaries, baffled by theories of limited war at a time when his foes practiced unlimited slaughter, anxious to pursue victory as he defined it, the proconsul of Japan had come to believe himself indispensable. Politically, at least, he fitted Acheson's description of madness, and when Joe Martin took to the floor of the House on April 5 to read aloud a MacArthur endorsement of his own position favoring the use in Korea of Chiang Kai-shek's forces, as well as a flat-out assertion that communism's victory in Asia would ensure the fall of Europe, the general sent shockwaves through the ranks of America's already uneasy Allies. He also enraged Truman, George Marshall, Omar Bradley and others who were now determined to carry out Acheson's wish.

A weekend of reconsideration changed no one's mind, and by April 10, Truman was cutting an order, frostily worded by Marshall, relieving MacArthur of all his commands. As often happened in the Truman White House, execution was botched. Alerted that the *Chicago Tribune* might print the story before the president's decision was made public, Truman abandoned the niceties for an abrupt, even brutal sacking. "The son of a bitch isn't going to resign on me," he exclaimed. "I want him fired!"

Truman had his wish. At one A.M. on the morning of April 11, the news officially broke in Washington. Three minutes later, wire services carried it to Tokyo. Before noon, Taft, Martin and other Republican leaders were caucusing on Capitol Hill, debating the impeachment of both Acheson and the president. Joe McCarthy said the decision must have been the product of a night's worth "of bourbon and benedictine." A flood of negative messages inundated the White House. A Worcester, Massachusetts, crowd burned Truman in effigy. In Houston, flags flew at half-mast. A Gallup Poll reported disapproval of the president's action, 69 percent to 29 percent. In New York, Hoover entered the fray. Telephoning Bonner Fellers, once among MacArthur's closest aides, more recently a mainstay of the Republican National Committee, the former president instructed him to get MacArthur on the phone and insist that he fly back home as soon as possible, before his enemies could engage in a smear campaign. Fellers relayed the message to Jean MacArthur in Tokyo, who replied that she and her general were coming home via boat. That was impossible, Fellers told her. "Mr. Hoover is the one who is determined that you fly back and you have got to take his advice." Jean turned to her husband for a brief conference. "We will fly," she finally told Fellers.[37]

MacArthur got on the line. "You tell the Chief that I'm bewildered about what's going on in the United States. I don't understand much about it and I haven't been there in a long time, but if he will advise me what I should do and say when I get back, tell him I'll take his advice and that of no one else." Fellers of all people ought to have recognized this for the empty flattery it was, but he dutifully conveyed the message to Hoover, who promptly issued his own string of orders: MacArthur should refuse the hundred-thousand-dollar-a-year position with Remington Rand rumored to be his stateside destination. Hoover suggested he write his memoirs instead. *Collier's* magazine, he informed MacArthur aide Courtney Whitney, would pay six figures for serial rights alone. Next, the former president contacted Richard Berlin of the Hearst organization and asked if he and Roy Howard could guarantee a big homecoming in San Francisco, where MacArthur expected to arrive in virtual disgrace. Half a million delirious Californians provided his answer—and a tumultuous kickoff to a month-long explosion of the national emotions.[38]

Three hundred thousand Washingtonians lined Pennsylvania Avenue to see the general on his way to Capitol Hill, where he delivered his famed "Old Soldiers Never Die" speech to a packed joint session of Congress—a session arranged in part by Hoover, who had sent word to the president that such a courtesy was in order. Graciously, Truman agreed, whereupon Hoover again flashed instructions to the general's road show. His Washington speech should be deliberately nonpartisan, focused mainly on the Far East and only implicitly critical of Truman's Korean policies. Hoover even scribbled out two paragraphs that might set the tone of the address. "The objective of every war is peace," he wrote, "a swift war toward a prolonged peace. The object of war is victory, not uncertain, targetless, stalemated action." MacArthur accepted the advice, and ennobled the language.[39]

"Once war is forced upon us, there is no alternative than to apply every available means to bring it to a swift end," he declared to one of thirty-four bursts of applause that greeted his appearance. "War's very object is victory —not prolonged indecision. In war, indeed, there can be no substitute for victory."

Then he left for New York City, where seven million persons poured into the streets to proclaim their admiration for the old warrior, with his simpler code of victory and defeat, his unwavering adherence to the values of an America vanished like a morning dew while he had spent a generation defending them in distant rain forests and snow-topped mountain ranges. Hoover, equally devoted to the departed nation, dubbed his new Waldorf neighbor "a reincarnation of St. Paul . . . who came out of the East." Yet even the general could not ride roughshod over his sensitivities. When the sycophantic Whitney visited Suite 31-A to inform the former president that MacArthur would be glad to receive him, Hoover blew up. "You go back and tell MacArthur that I'm the man who made him Chief of Staff of the United States Army and if he wants to see me he can come down here." [40]

There were more parades, more ticker tape, more fustian proclamations to a land that could not be recaptured. Then came a derisive congressional inquiry, and by year's end, MacArthur at last seemed to be fulfilling his prophecy about old soldiers. Meanwhile, Hoover was writing his columnist friend George Sokolsky about the dangers of electing professional soldiers to the presidency. Andrew Jackson initiated the spoils system, he reminded Sokolsky, destroyed the Bank of America and launched an inflated currency. Grant countenanced corruption while in office. "You might also mention the flop of General Fremont as a candidate and the flop of General McClellan . . . also the remarks of General Sherman when the devil tempted him." Yet Hoover was thinking of a general other than MacArthur when he composed his stinging rebuke to the military man in politics. [41]

Ironically, it was MacArthur himself who reassured the Chief that Dwight Eisenhower would not run in 1952. NATO's commander suffered from serious kidney problems, explained his old superior. Ike's health would keep him out of the ranks of those contending for the GOP nomination. For a while, Hoover believed the story, but only for a while. It soon became apparent that Eisenhower would accept a draft, and that just such a wind was being puffed up by Tom Dewey and his cadre of eastern internationalist supporters. Hoover made no effort to conceal his displeasure. "A conscientious political leper must be careful not to infect his friends," he observed in the spring of 1952. He asked why the Gridiron Club had invited him to return to address its dinner that May: "I do not represent the Republican Party. Some of you are old enough to recollect that I was retired to the sidelines by that Party long ago." The balance of his talk dealt with fishing, with time out for fond recollection of his first such dinner, forty years previous, "in that quarter of a century of the world's last Golden Age." [42]

A similar nostalgia seemed to wrap itself around the partisans of Hoover's own presidential choice, Bob Taft. Taft himself was careful to distinguish between his foreign policies and those of his most prominent supporter. His platform was adorned with previously heretical positions favoring federal aid to education and housing. He was less inclined to lacerate the man in the White House, and even attempted halfhearted overtures to Dewey and others backing Eisenhower. He assured Ike personally of his support for "the European Project." But his enthusiastic backers, who sang "Onward, Christian Soldiers" as they marched into Chicago's convention hall early in July 1952, who booed lustily the sight of Dewey and the sounds of their own impending defeat, who wished with all their fervor to restore a Golden Age that excluded New Deals and Fair Deals, were less willing than their hero to accept changed conditions and heightened expectations about the role Washington might play in the domestic economy.

Hoover's time was not totally given over to the Taft crusade. In April, he issued a whimsical challenge to the inventor of the radio tube to devise a push-button mechanism to squelch commercial advertising on television. Yet his attention remained focused on the growing struggle for the soul of his party. He hosted a meeting of New York Republicans flirting with open rebellion against Dewey's hammerlock, but the meeting itself had to be kept secret for fear an unforgiving Dewey might learn of it and deprive the rebels of state patronage jobs. In the end, the governor found out anyway, and directed minions to meet a train carrying the New Yorkers to Chicago. They needn't have bothered. Dewey's unspoken threat was potent enough to scare away most Taft sympathizers in the Empire State. A new flap arose when Texas sent competing delegations, one for Taft, the other for Eisenhower. On June 19, Hoover met with Henry Cabot Lodge, the general's nominal campaign manager. He reasonably offered to join two other "eminent citizens" selected by the opposing camps for the purpose of examining all contested delegations on a case-by-case basis. The entire process might be kept secret, Hoover added, its ultimate recommendation telegraphed to the regular credentials committee. "Do you still think such an approach is hopeless?" he asked plaintively.[43]

Lodge thought exactly that. Along with the rest of Eisenhower's management team, he recognized the emotional appeal of the Texas issue, in which Taft and his supporters were accused of stealing delegates by excluding the general's supporters from precinct caucuses throughout the state. He could find nothing to compromise, Lodge stiffly informed the former president. "Frankly, I cannot imagine anything more undemocratic than for three men in a private meeting to arrogate unto themselves the power to disenfranchise many thousands of American citizens." Checked, Hoover replied with a patronizing air of his own. Knowing of Lodge's zeal, he wrote, "I refuse to construe your remarks as an insult to my integrity." No such insult was intended, said Lodge. The issue at stake was the integrity of the process, not of any individual. If Taft supporters in Texas were willing to deny Democrats for Eisenhower from voting in GOP caucuses, then what about Democrats who had crossed party lines to support the Ohioan in Wisconsin's primary? Only the convention could rightfully decide the issue; thus the famous "Fair Play" Amendment was born, and Hoover checkmated.[44]

Still he tried to negotiate a compromise. He persuaded Taft partisans to drop challenges of their own in Connecticut, New Jersey and Washington. Yet Eisenhower showed no similar inclination to avert a potentially bloody floor fight over the disputed southern delegates. A few days before the convention opened, a dispirited Hoover concluded that his old friend could not prevail on its floor. Despite a formal endorsement of Taft on July 9, Hoover convened a meeting of like-minded Republicans at 31-A. Someone should approach Taft and tell him forthrightly that victory was beyond his grasp. The group would stick with him to the end if there was any chance of success. Yet events had conspired against his candidacy, and Hoover now wished to throw conservative support to MacArthur. Albert Wedemeyer was assigned the unenviable task of breaking the news to Taft, who offered to reconsider his options after the first ballot. A phone call was placed to MacArthur, who reiterated his support of Taft, as well as his willingness to accept the vice presidency. "Al," he said to Wedemeyer, "Bob Taft is our captain, and you and I must do whatever he wants us to do." Another call from the Waldorf revealed that the number two man was sitting in Suite 37-A, a prospect that delighted Taft. Meanwhile, Hoover sent a bitter memo to both Taft and MacArthur. "One misguided group in this convention," he wrote, wished to "continue bitterness and strife in the party despite every generous, conciliatory proposal and action."[45]

On the second night of the convention, Hoover rose to address the delegates. Confronted for the first time with a teleprompter, he was further unsettled when chairman Joe Martin accidentally crushed his glasses beneath a pounding gavel. But nothing could prevent him from assailing the decline of American moral and spiritual grandeur "corroded by intellectual dishonesty and corruption among public officials. The drip, drip, drip from dishonor in high places," a reference to the minor scandals plaguing Truman's administration, "plays a part in the increasing of crime among the people." Taxes were exceeding the total levies of 170 years of American history. The shades of Mussolini, Lord Keynes and Karl Marx were poisoning the American system. "Man was created somewhat lower than the angels," said Hoover, "but to him the Creator gave the right to plan his own life, to dare his own adventure, to earn his own reward so long as he does no harm to his fellows." The choice was stark and unavoidable: "Either we shall have a society based upon ordered liberty and the creative energy of free men or we shall have a dictated society."[46]

Lavish in his denunciation, he reviewed the policies of Teheran and Yalta, Potsdam and the Atlantic Charter. "The ghosts of the Four Freedoms now wander amid the clanking chains of a thousand slave camps," he said. "I need not remind you that we have lost the peace despite the valor and the sacrifice of our manhood on a hundred battlefields. . . . There is less freedom in the world today than at any time for a whole century." America had already surrendered 120,000 casualties in Korea; yet appeasement argued against any crossing of the 38th Parallel. Western Europe was no closer to self-sufficiency or credible defense than before the $35 billion in military and economic aid poured into the Continent by a naive U.S. NATO had failed to spark anything more than a feeble European response and phantom armies that would crumble in the face of a Stalinist invasion. At home, all this resulted in inflation and hardship, as air and naval power were neglected and taxes reached confiscatory levels. "I do not propose that we retreat into our shell like a turtle," Hoover told the convention. "I do propose the deadly reprisal strategy of a rattlesnake." For good measure he assessed the coming election as perhaps the final chance for freedom's survival in America.

Sentiment as much as philosophical agreement dictated the cries of approval that greeted him that night. Even liberals joined in the frenzy. Wayne Morse, the maverick Republican from Oregon, seized his state's standard and launched an impromptu demonstration of his own. But conventions award ovations to those who lack votes, and when the chips fell, Dewey and his colleagues had sufficient strength to prevail in Texas, Georgia and other credentials contests. Taft was wrong: there wouldn't be a second ballot. Eisenhower won on the first after Minnesota switched nineteen votes from Harold Stassen to the World War II hero, ending permanently Mr. Republican's hope to occupy the White House and redeem the Old Guard theology rejected in 1932 and scorned ever since.

Hoover, deeply disappointed, managed a telegram of condolence for his friend and ideological ally. "I am sorry beyond expression," he wrote at one o'clock on the afternoon of July 11. "We did our best." For the Eisenhower-Nixon slate, he issued a terse statement of support. "Being a Republican I shall vote the Republican ticket." But he also told George Sokolsky that a stiff fight lay ahead for the new nominee. Adlai Stevenson's acceptance speech to the Democratic convention had risen to the heights of Wilsonian eloquence, he went on, and Stevenson was likely to attract a whole new constituency of supporters. "Truman, the C.I.O., the P.A.C. and the A.D.A. will provide the supplementary poison squad," he predicted. As for himself, principle dictated his course of action. "I am going fishing," he wrote. He could not support the idea of garrisoning U.S. troops in Europe. "Stalin has only to take them ground hostages and we are in a ground war which will bring not only defeat but a loss of all free civilization." Neither could he forgive the tactics employed by Dewey, Lodge and others in securing Eisenhower's nomination. As he put it, "No man can set up a megaphone opposite my rooms to yell, 'Thou shalt not steal' and expect me to love him." As the campaign got under way in earnest, Hoover's fishing seemed unlikely to be interrupted by any appeal for help.[47]

Yet Eisenhower adroitly courted his preconvention rivals. Allowing passions to cool, he waited three weeks before expressing regret over not seeing Hoover in Chicago, as well as his own interest in discussing the Hoover Commission and other topics. "With my sincere and respectful regards," he signed his letter. Hoover responded with the gift of his memoirs, and Ike confided that he was under siege "by people who argue in favor of particular or special groups. . . . I spend my days trying to convince all of them that the only true yardstick by which to measure any proposal is for the good, both present and future, of the entire United States." He was certain, the candidate went on, he would find similar convictions expressed in the former president's autobiography. Such tactics paid off. Before long, Hoover was wholeheartedly behind the new ticket, his partisanship bolstered by Stevenson's echo of the now-familiar refrain about "the Hoover Depression" and Democratic attacks on Nixon for maintaining an $18,000 fund with which to pay political expenses in California. The night Nixon went on the air to deliver his celebrated "Checkers speech," Hoover delivered a testimonial of his own. "If everyone in the city of Washington possessed the high level of courage, probity and patriotism of Senator Nixon," he said, "this would be a far better nation." In response, the vice presidential candidate wrote that none of the other thousands of messages he received had meant as much.[48]

One issue remained a bone of contention. Should Hoover himself make a televised appeal on behalf of the ticket? The former president himself shied away from offering his services, he told one friend, "because I am afraid they might be considered the kiss of death." Actually, Len Hall, Sherman Adams and others around the candidate were worried that his own support for Eisenhower might be less than total. Finally prodded into calling Hall, Hoover was pleasantly surprised to learn of this. "Oh, I wanted to do it!" he exclaimed when invited to go on television; he had been too modest to offer on his own. All went well until Dewey sought to limit the talk to domestic issues. The necessary money was not available to purchase network time, Hoover was informed, and it was no simple chore to raise $50,000 virtually overnight. Then Everett Dirksen of the Republican Senatorial Campaign Committee learned of Hoover's plight. Still smarting from his own rancorous confrontation with Dewey at the convention, Dirksen was only too willing to pony up the cash. First, however, Hoover sought assurances from Eisenhower. If the general thought it better for him to remain outside the campaign, he wrote, "it will in no way dim my prayers for your success."[49]

Ike wished nothing of the kind. When Hoover finally did speak over CBS on Saturday night, October 18, he made a vigorous defense of past Republican policies, aimed largely at the 40 million eligible voters who had never lived under a GOP administration, yet had been subjected to decades of what he called misrepresentations and false slogans. Within forty-eight hours, 35,000 viewers wrote in, seeking copies of the address. That same week, he urged Nixon to uncork "a rough machine gun attack" on the Democratic theme "You never had it so good." He argued, in vain, that MacArthur should remove his name from the ballot in several states where fervent admirers had placed it. The general flatly refused to dissuade his supporters in Texas and California.[50]

In the end, it didn't matter. Eisenhower continued his courtship of the old man on election night, phoning Hoover as soon as he received a congratulatory telegram from the Waldorf. The former president was delighted with the general's landslide. The election of Eisenhower, he wrote a friend, "represents a turning in American life away from bad taste, corruption, Communism, and to some extent, from socialism." Yet a narrow Republican majority in Congress could hardly stamp out "the leftwing opposition," and Hoover and those who shared his views must necessarily remain vigilant.[51]

Just twelve months earlier, an admiring reader of his memoirs quoted to their author some lines from Tennyson's "Ulysses":

> "We are not now the strength which in the old days
> Moved earth and heaven, that which we are, we are—
> One equal temper of heroic hearts,
> Made weak by time and fate, but strong in will
> To strive, to seek, to find, and not to yield."[52]

Hoover might be forgiven, late in 1952, as he anticipated the inauguration of the first Republican president since his own ill-fated administration collapsed in national bitterness a generation earlier, for taking such words to heart. His views were unlikely to mellow. They were too ingrained, too fiercely held for that. Yet he was an old man, whose growing taste for the historian's art instilled perspective in place of anger. Perhaps he might at last find contentment in what he liked to call his years of acknowledgment.

CHAPTER TWELVE

THE SAGE OF 31-A

★

*The world has gone by you and me. However it is some satisfaction that you and
I have gone through the agonies of these years without deviations.*
　　　　　　　　　　　　　　　—Herbert Hoover,[1] April 1962

★

Invited by the president-elect to oversee the transition of power from Harry
Truman's administration to his own, Herbert Brownell discovered that all
documentation pertaining to the old Colorado River Commission was missing. He wrote Hoover, instrumental in its formation, on the off chance that
the former president might have the papers. He most certainly did, replied
the sage of 31-A. "I'll be damned if I was going to give them to any of those
Democratic administrations but I'll be glad to give them to you." Not long
afterward, Hoover attended the first presidential inauguration since his own
stormy departure from office. Riding at the front of Dwight Eisenhower's
parade, he was cheered by jubilant Republicans celebrating a return to
power if not the past. Hoover himself brooked no concession to either age
or climate. He had never worn a coat or hat at previous inaugurals, he told
friends; he wouldn't wear them now.[2]

　　The next day, he departed for his regular winter stay in Florida, where
there were bonefish to catch and books to write and a cottage at the Key
Largo Anglers Club was set aside for his comfort. "Fishing is the chance to
wash one's soul with pure air," he wrote, "with the rush of the brook, or
with the shimmer of the sun on the blue water. It brings meekness and

inspiration from the decency of nature, charity toward tackle makers, patience toward fish, a mockery of profit and egos, a quieting of hate, a rejoicing that you do not have to decide a darned thing until next week. And it is discipline in the equality of men," he concluded on a whimsical note, "for all men are equal before fish."

At Key Largo, Hoover did the unthinkable: he attended other people's cocktail parties. He reminisced about Lou, who had loved the area, and it was apparent that not even the affection a forgiving nation showered upon an old man would fully compensate for her loss. Dubbing a neighbor's three-year-old Winnie because to Hoover the child resembled Churchill, he also presented a fishing guide with a temperamental gold-plated lighter initially given him by the great British leader. "Take this thing before I throw it overboard," he told Calvin Albury. When Harry Truman came to call, his fellow member in their exclusive club stalled him long enough to put on some shoes; one should never greet a man who had been president—especially one for whom he confessed "a sneaking admiration"—in stocking feet. On board his chartered vessel *Captiva* or in one of the flat-bottomed boats propelled by poles and outfitted with a swivel chair and a floppy hat to ward off the sun, Hoover counted his catch (at age eighty-five he was on the water for twenty-one days in a row, with 196 fish to show for it), read and wrote, posed for pictures with fellow anglers and exuded the patriarchal manner of a crusty Dutch uncle.[3]

Patient with fish, Hoover was impatient with men. One day, a military training jet from nearby Homestead Air Force Base dove down on his party, knocking the former president's hat off and spewing smoke and fumes in his face. Hoover lapsed into silence for a few minutes, apparently oblivious to anything but the languid beauty of azure sea and a distant shore that seemed to melt into it. Abruptly, his temper flared. "I wish he'd stick that flying blowtorch so far in this mud flat that it would take twenty-five years to find it."[4]

His standards of personal conduct reflected the spartan code of an orphaned boyhood and a globe-trotting career. He had never spent a night in a hospital when he contracted pneumonia a few days after Eisenhower's inaugural. Too stubborn to acknowledge the cost of his own defiant gesture, he was equally adamant in refusing medical treatment. He had come to Florida to fish, he told his younger son, and that's what he intended to do. When an ambulance arrived to take him to Saint Francis Hospital, Hoover would not lie down. But when it deposited him into the care of Mother Magdalena, Saint Francis's superintendent, he was ready with a request.

"Sister," he inquired, "can you make a good dry martini?"

"You bet I can," the nun told him. She proved a woman of her word.[5]

Hoover lived his final years like that, often grumbling about his country's course, more often aiming shafts of dry humor at the body politic or his own cantankerous image. He was the only man in recorded history, he liked to say, who had been credited with the fabulous economic knowledge to start a worldwide depression all his own. He informed Truman that he had written something nice about him in a forthcoming book, and wondered mischievously if it would hurt sales. Invited to address yet another function, he turned down the appeal, having no expectation that anything he might say would penetrate "beyond the over-fed folks who haunt public dinners." When the President Lines fixed his name to their latest liner, Hoover was pleased if not overly impressed. He remembered a river tugboat already named for him, "which led an uncertain life with an upright wood-fired boiler."[6]

"Old reformers never die," he told his fellow Bohemians, "they get thrown out." Undaunted, he offered up a list of his own proposed reforms, including four strikes in baseball "so as to get more men on bases . . . the crowd only gets worked up when somebody is on second base"; a shortened burial service "eulogizing the Dead instead of listening for an hour to what was going to happen to us if we don't look out"; and abolishment of political ghostwriters ("Alternatively we should require an advance notice of who the ghost is. If it is a good speech, we could elect him instead of the Charlie McCarthy"). He urged that after-dinner speeches be made before dinner "so that the gnaw of hunger would speed up terminals." He wanted singing commercials eliminated from the airwaves. He wished photographers might at least hang a strip of numbers around their victims' necks, since most newspaper pictures already conveyed criminal appearances.[7]

This was the Florida angler, dapper in white flannel trousers and double-breasted gray jacket, who decided after a ride through the garish tourist districts of Miami Beach that its hotel and motel titles were inspired by residents of an insane asylum, who presented a friend's wife with an amethyst and then, "Now that I've taken care of your health," gave her one of the old five-dollar gold pieces ("pre-Roosevelt currency") that Lou had always slipped inside a child's shoe as a precaution. A little more stooped in the shoulders, his white hair thinning, his brows frosted over deeply set eyes, Hoover retained an outlook of bemusement, at least about himself. "I will file these papers," he solemnly told a visitor to 31-A, then dropped a sheaf of his own writings into a nearby wastebasket. "My filing cabinet," he explained. Surrounded by grandchildren and great-grandchildren, accustomed to room service and a comfortable pattern that included summers in

California and winters in Florida, he lived out an existence marinated in memory.[8]

Old men are often inflexible; that is their privilege. Hoover was more brittle than most. His unyielding opposition to communism abroad and what he called creeping socialism at home lent a harsh tint to some of his public utterances. His Magnum Opus drove him relentlessly to expose the perfidies of others; yet when asked if he would proceed with publication, he held back. It was too soon, Hoover told H. V. Kaltenborn. "I can't hurt people who are still alive." He claimed to have outlived his time, to be at a stage in life where he existed "from pill to pill." Yet a reporter who dropped by the Waldorf in 1960 was astonished that Hoover worked eight to twelve hours each day. How was such a schedule possible, the journalist asked a secretary. After all, Hoover was nearly eight-six years old. "Yes," the woman responded, "but he doesn't know that."[9]

He was not the sort to let old grudges die without a struggle. When James Roosevelt invited him to attend his mother's seventy-fifth birthday party, he received a frosty "Dear Mr. Congressman" letter in reply. A friend saw the lighter side of his Roosevelt obsession. Casually asked to change the stamps he used on his correspondence with 31-A, the man puzzled over the curious request until he discovered his secretary had been pasting an Eleanor Roosevelt issue to his letters. Then he broke into laughter, knowing of the chuckle that Hoover himself must have enjoyed over the predicament he'd caused. The old man's personality mellowed even as his politics hardened. He praised young William F. Buckley, then in the process of launching *National Review,* as "a dedicated American boy" and judged the *New York Daily News* possessed of the best editorials in any major newspaper. He raised a storm of protest in the academic precincts of Stanford, with his insistence that the Hoover Institution be detached from the regular university administration and set to work on its chosen priorities, which over the years came increasingly to focus on the Communist danger.[10]

Even this late in life, Hoover flirted with controversy. In April 1953, he gave a speech urging the leasing of public power to private companies for resale to the consumer. Immediately, editors and congressmen alike attacked the proposal as the first step in the dismantling of TVA and other public power authorities. Hoover protested that his views were being misinterpreted. He simply wished to halt the advance of socialism and relieve some of the 32,000 bureaucrats currently employed in operating dynamos and distributing their product. He opposed government health insurance as a perversion of his "American way." When an interviewer asked if it was really Communistic to apply to government for such favors, Hoover said it suggested a mind receptive to that godless creed.[11]

"The essence of Marxist doctrine," he went on, " is that you surrender your freedom to the state in return for services rendered by the state. The more services you accept, the less freedom you retain. The more nationalization, the less private enterprise." Socialism, he insisted, softened a people's will to resist, part of a process that led to democracy's ultimate extinction. Yet his dogmatic views were leavened with humor. All his life, he explained to visitors, he had been warned by doctors of the evil of smoking, "but I have noted that these physicians with their good advice have long since departed from this earth." Neither was he immune from humility. One day, in a thoughtful mood, the former president even professed to see silver linings in the black cloud of 1932. Perhaps it had been a good thing that FDR won so decisively, had knocked him off the summit and into the valley. Having weathered ostracism and emerged a figure of popular veneration, such proportion came more naturally now. [12]

And so he spent his last years, hailed by a nation that respected his contributions but could hardly bring itself to embrace his prescriptions for the future. As the hourglass emptied, he would have to content himself with a land wistful for the old ways he represented, yet unable to do more than proclaim its wistfulness in public tributes that grew more touching and ironic with each passing year. Nowhere was this frustrating dichotomy more apparent than in Hoover's friendship for the new president, with whom he was to enjoy a mixed brew of personal warmth approaching awe, and political disappointment that drew him still closer to Harry Truman, that most unlikely of soulmates.

★   ★

As the outset of his term, Hoover warned Eisenhower of rough seas ahead. "You're going to have one of the most frustrating jobs that any president ever had," was the way he put it. Governing in the shadow of Roosevelt, the first GOP executive in twenty years was likely to find himself pulled in competing directions, between advocates of a planned economy and others who, in Hoover's phrase, "want you to go right square back to before McKinley." Eisenhower kept his door open. He invited Hoover to a White House stag dinner that May, an intimate gathering of congenial company that included Lewis Strauss, Douglas MacArthur and the conservative Secretary of the Treasury, George Humphrey. A few weeks later, the president offered congratulations on Hoover's seventy-ninth birthday, adding his own gratitude that recent events had brought them together and looking forward to a still closer association in the year to come. In August 1954, Ike attended the Iowa state fair as part of the national salute to Hoover on his eightieth birthday, and jocularly invited the former president to join him for several days of relaxation in his Colorado fishing retreat. "I assure you that you

don't need to be especially terrified at the prospect of living on my cooking
for a couple of days," Eisenhower wrote. "My culinary reputation is pretty
good—but my repertoire is limited. It is only after about four days that
my guests begin to look a little pained when they come to the dinner
table." [13]

Even this courtesy evoked less than wholehearted enthusiasm. In fishing
as in politics a fundamentalist, Hoover didn't think much of Eisenhower the
angler. It wasn't even genuine fishing in which the two men were engaged,
he claimed afterward, since "the brook had been stocked with fish that
hadn't been fed in six weeks. You couldn't keep them off the hook." Eisenhower spent an hour fixing breakfast and twice as long preparing dinner,
near-torture for one accustomed to ten-minute meals. More substantively,
Hoover judged his visit "purely a political arrangement" to placate his own
party's right wing. [14]

Eisenhower persisted. He provided the ex-president with a plane to transport him between New York and Washington during the two-year life of his
second commission on government reorganization; it was a great relief, said
Hoover, from ten to twenty hours each week spent commuting by train. In
the fall of 1954, Ike asked him to travel to Germany to carry his message of
encouragement to Konrad Adenauer's democratic republic. It was hard for
him to imagine "at this decisive moment in the history of American-Ger-
man relations" that any of his countrymen were more ideally suited to
convey the feelings of friendship which America harbored on Germany's
return to the Western family of democracies. When the former president let
it be known he did not plan on attending his party's 1956 convention in
San Francisco, Eisenhower dispatched a personal invitation to reconsider. [15]

"You exemplify in more ways than I am sure you realize the dignity and
the spirit of the Republican Party," wrote its leading figure, "and I know
that every delegate to the Convention would be keenly disappointed, as
would I, if you were not there to lend your counsel and advice." Hoover
relented, won a thunderous ovation from the party faithful, and when the
sounds of their approval had faded to comforting memory, wrote to express
his gratitude "for a President who has, amid stupendous difficulties, kept the
world at peace and lifted American public life again to the levels of integrity." He might also appreciate the president's selection of Herbert, Junior,
to serve as under secretary in John Foster Dulles's State Department—even
if he disapproved of U.S. support for colonial powers in Africa and the Far
East, and believed the foreign aid program the captive of naive "do-good-
ers." His own advice to his diplomat son was droll. "Herbert," he said,
"keep a bottle of whiskey in your bottom drawer and after the day is over,

when you're tired and before you start for home, take a swig . . . and it'll pep you up." [16]

All this reflected the personal side of the former president's relationship with Eisenhower. Yet anyone who knew Hoover realized that personal considerations alone were likely to count for little if public policy failed to match. For Hoover, Eisenhower's presidency represented a disturbing evolution of New Deal and Fair Deal programs, within the gray, button-down style favored by the military men and corporate executives who now replaced Roosevelt's brain trusters and Truman's cronies from Missouri. "He is a very expensive President," was the way he put it. In fact, spending in every department of government was up from the Truman years. The former president continued to lob shells at U.S. foreign policy, arguing in the fall of 1954 that many former allies were now seeking peaceful coexistence with Moscow. "We should cease to jabber about leading the world," he wrote in a private memorandum. "Sometime the world will turn on us with remarks as to where we have led to." But it wasn't just the $70 billion budgets that nettled him, or the continuing American commitment to the defense of a Europe that seemed intent on neutralism. "No one really is hitting at the issues," he remarked in October 1954. To him, the issues were evident— socialism and all its attendant ills. His party should be offering bold colors instead of pale imitations of Democratic largesse. Hoover found fault with Eisenhower's handling of the school desegregation crisis in Little Rock in 1957, recalling his own technique of using federal marshals to quell disorder among Iowa's cattlemen rather than the more drastic step of employing the National Guard. And recalling Taft's habit of remaining behind for private conferences with the president after larger meetings broke up, ("I only wanted to be sure I was the last one to see Ike," explained Taft, "for the last one who talks with him always gets what he wants"). Hoover defined the president as both decent and sincere in his desire to do right, but with little knowledge of economics, politics or the governing process itself. Besides, said Hoover, "The last ones who see him are the liberals in the White House." [17]

The major source of his disappointment, however, stemmed from the second Hoover Commission, which Congress authorized in the spring of 1953, and to which Eisenhower readily gave his assent. There the misunderstanding began. For Hoover's view of his new mandate was far more extensive than political reality dictated. "Last time we were limited to repairs of existing agencies," he explained at the Bohemian Grove that summer. "Now we are called upon to make recommendations for surgery on everything except the Congress and the Judiciary. We are even authorized to make recommendations for amendments to the Constitution." The scope of the commission's inquiry seemed as broad as the federal establishment itself—at first. Eisenhower encouraged such a view, specifically requesting it to examine navigation and flood control, irrigation and electric power.[18]

At his age in life, Hoover remarked to friends, men ought to go fishing instead of reorganizing governments. Yet once more he set out, accompanied by high hopes for something more than the first commission's pruning operation. He desired "an exhaustive investigation of the whole method of aid to the aged," he told one colleague. He wanted to create an Administrative Vice President, to relieve the chief executive of time-wasting duties from disposal of naval vessels to the presentation of certificates to graduating classes of the Capitol Page School. As an example of the federal pork he was out to slaughter, Hoover pointed to the $5 billion Upper Colorado River Storage Project. Eisenhower demurred. Hoover's figures on the cost of the project didn't square with those of western congressmen. Hoover countered that they were supplied him by the president's own Bureau of Reclamation. Moreover, Truman had rejected the scheme three different times because of its expense. To Hoover, the irrigation plan was nothing more than a plum for Colorado's governor Dan Thornton, then interested in a Senate seat. When Eisenhower intimated his sympathies, the former president was heartened. His pleasure was short-lived. Ike flew over the sluggish ribbon of water en route to Denver and afterward told newsmen that the project was essential and should proceed as soon as possible.[19]

Other complaints proliferated. "Ike gave me a couple of left-wingers," he said of his colleagues on the new commission. One of them was Chet Holifield, a congressman from California who strongly favored public power, and just as fervently opposed Hoover's intention to alter federal policy as well as structure. In common with an unlikely ally, conservative Clarence Brown of Ohio, Holifield tempered the commission's plans, reminding Hoover and others that the House would never accept some of its more dramatic proposals for scaling back federal involvement in the economy. Still another member—at least for a while—said the second Hoover Commission reminded him of the Union League Club in Philadelphia, where his host had once apologized for inviting a Democrat to lunch. "A more reactionary group could not . . . have been gathered to destroy liberal gains that had been made . . . during the previous twenty years," wrote John Carmody. "TVA was anathema, as was REA. Nothing liberal escaped their attack; even the American Medical Association sought to curb the limited medical service the Veterans Administration gives to veterans." In fact, Hoover opposed those who wished to sell TVA. But his words and actions inflamed staunch New Dealers, who were convinced that Hoover II was an attempt to administratively repeal Roosevelt's legacy.[20]

As the fourteen new task forces took up their work, the skirmishing began. Holifield demanded representation for public power advocates. Jim Farley, by now one of Hoover's neighbors at the Waldorf, pounded his fist on the table in opposition to the chairman's plan to have all postmasters appointed by committee. The administrative vice president idea got nowhere. Fearing that Joseph McCarthy, still crusading against Communists in government, might weaken the nation's intelligence-gathering activities with a public probe, Eisenhower invited the former president to set up an investigation of his own. Hoover agreed, entrusting the sensitive operation to General Mark Clark. Later, word was flashed from the White House that McCarthy had been contained, and Hoover's task force should call off its digging. This time, Hoover refused. In the end, he submitted one public report, and another, a confidential one.[21]

Near the end of its work, commissioners wrangled during three night sessions over how to word their findings on the sensitive issue of water and power resources. Outside the room where they met, Joe Kennedy discovered his friend slipping digitalis pills into his mouth. Had it reached such a stage as this, Kennedy asked. "Well," Hoover told him, "I'm afraid it has." With that, Kennedy returned to the meeting to argue successfully on behalf of Hoover's draft. It was one point won by the chairman. Kennedy's son, Robert, was among the commission's 130 staffers; Ethel Kennedy wrote an affectionate note to the former president, suggesting that since their first son had been named Joseph during Bob's stint with Joe McCarthy, their next boy might be given the name Herbert. As late as 1960, Hoover told Henry Cabot Lodge, soon to be Richard Nixon's running mate, that Robert's brother John could claim far more credit for implementing his commission's program than anyone else in the field. He thanked the Massachusetts senator personally, and when JFK left a hospital bed after the latest operation on his back, Hoover dispatched a cheering note.[22]

"It doesn't matter much what the politics of good men are," he told Kennedy. "What does matter is that they get out and keep out of hospitals. Therefore I rejoice at your escape."[23]

Inevitably, the commission's final report struck the same themes of economy and administrative overhaul as its predecessor six years earlier. Hoover himself liked to tell of the twelve agencies that gave contrary advice on the weather, the twenty-two years' supply of toilet paper stored in government warehouses, and the army barn containing a Civil War wagon. "Very interesting," he said when told of the last. "Now I want you to go out and find the stores where they keep the bows and arrows." By reorganizing thirty-four agencies dealing with overseas economic operations, Hoover calculated that the taxpayers might save $360 million. A third of a billion more could be shaved from federal power operations. By requiring federal lending agencies to become self-supporting, another $200 million might be carved out of a flabby government. And so it went. End postal savings. Raise administrative salaries to reduce turnover in the federal work force. Streamline purchasing and stockpiling of food and clothing for the armed forces. Move less material by air, and more by cheaper methods like rail, truck or ship. [24]

Tom Dewey, himself retired from office, labeled the reports "one more magnificent monument to the lifetime of public service you have lavished upon the American people." Eisenhower was more guarded. He appointed an eight-member oversight board to watch the CIA. The Post Office mechanized much of its own paper handling. The Bureau of Mines sold off its shale-oil refinery at Rifle, Colorado. But of the 314 recommendations made by Hoover II, fewer than a third achieved the status of law. When Senator J. William Fulbright tried to hold hearings on Hoover's proposal for greater consistency among federal loan programs, he was stymied because Eisenhower's own Budget Bureau refused to comply with his requests for information on its likely impact. [25]

Undaunted, Hoover gave his blessing to a national citizens committee, a pressure group against pressure groups, to rouse public sentiment in favor of the report. His early confidence didn't last. Shortly, even Harry Truman was deriding the White House for its inaction. His successor wasn't raising a finger on behalf of the reorganization proposals, wrote Truman; Ike needed a little "Hail, Columbia" to stiffen his backbone. Hoover himself remarked in later years that he had been able to get action out of Truman—but not Ike. A little defensively, the president early in 1957 reminded Hoover that he had urged Congress on more than one occasion to enact legislation in the spirit of the commission. He was sending a fresh letter to the President of the Senate and Speaker of the House reiterating this support. But no special message followed. A year passed. Hoover lodged another not-so-gentle reminder that Congress must get on with the job of reorganization, implying that the president himself must prod legislators more forcefully. [26]

Tragically, one of the few men who might have bridged the gulf between Eisenhower and Hoover was no longer on the scene to lend his prestige to the commission's findings. Early in June 1953, Bob Taft confessed to his old friend that he was having "a rather hard time with my hip." When Hoover learned the truth, that Mr. Republican was dying of cancer, he refused to believe it. He promised to enlist the finest medical help in the world on behalf of Taft's recovery. The senator was equally defiant—but in a different direction. On June 16, Hoover paid a visit to Taft's hospital bedside in New York. He was amazed to see him again a few days later in his Washington office, where a meeting had been called to ponder the names of congenial helpmates who might serve on Hoover's new commission. [27]

As the session broke up, Hoover protested his presence: Taft should be in the hospital where last they had met. The senator disagreed. "You should know me," he told Hoover, "and that when I die I want to die with my boots on." A few days later, they spent a couple of hours in Suite 31-A, Taft on his way to a hospital bed he would never leave alive, Hoover about to embark for the annual Bohemian Grove encampment. Both men recognized their meeting for what it was, the final encounter in a partnership that had spanned thirty-six years, since the day in 1917 when a young man rejected for combat duty because of flat feet applied for a position under Woodrow Wilson's wartime Food Administrator.

When Taft died on July 31, 1953, Hoover called him the most nearly irreplaceable man in public life. A more formal eulogy was delivered six years later, on a soft April day in Washington, when an old man stood on the brow of Capitol Hill to dedicate a monument to his friend and staunch ally. Hoover had generous words for Taft's integrity, a rare quality "in a day when men compromised their souls for the crumbs of popularity." Taft had been denounced during his lifetime as a reactionary, an isolationist, a defender of the rich and an enemy to the poor. But however inflamed his public image, his conscience had remained clear. "He was one," said Hoover, "who lost no sleep nights worrying that he would be found out. He lost much sleep over the fate of his country. He knew to the end that his was a moral attitude toward life and men and that he had given to his country his last full measure of devotion." Taft's memorial, concluded his onetime associate and lifetime admirer, would stand to remind others, not of his greatness, but of his virtue. It was a fitting farewell. [28]

★   ★

A visitor calling on Hoover in June 1954 found the old man voluble on a favorite subject, foreign affairs. Dismissing any thought of sending U.S. ground forces to Indochina, where the French colonial regime was collapsing, Hoover insisted that militarily, such a course would be even worse than Korea. Politically, he claimed, it would spell the death knell of the Republican party. Neither did he support a southeast Asian military alliance. The real problem in the region, according to Hoover, was economic. Japan alone faced a balance of trade deficit of $1.5 billion. A coalition of trading partners, including India and Burma, seemed the only realistic path to the kind of regional network he had always favored. It was, he maintained, "silly" for American policy-makers to treat Soviet Russia as a global superman, or interpret his own call for North American solidarity as the signal for a fatal retreat. Such an attitude overlooked Asian nationalism. It ignored the strong antipathy of other nationalities condemned to live under the Russian yoke. It promoted U.S. intervention in blithe ignorance of foreign habits and religions. Nowhere in the Good Book, Hoover concluded, had he found any directive from the Almighty to his countrymen to either feed the world permanently, guarantee external boundaries, or prop up tottering governments inside free nations. Later that year, he appealed in vain to Dulles to apply more stringent controls on U.S. aid abroad.[29]

He never yielded his belief that global intrigues could be met head-on by moral suasion and economic expansion. On the home front, he declared "that anti-Christ, Karl Marx" to be less of an immediate threat than those who would centralize governmental functions in Washington, deprive wage earners of income through exorbitant taxes and foolish spending programs, compete with private enterprise and dull the incentives that rewarded society with a higher standard of living. "Only a drop of typhoid in a barrel of drinking water sickens a whole village," he insisted.

His stern warning was delivered in the bucolic setting of West Branch, where twenty thousand people gathered to celebrate his eightieth birthday in August 1954. Two hundred invited guests assembled at a Boy Scout shelter in Hoover Park, a twenty-eight-acre preserve cleared of elderberry bushes by local residents, where the birthplace cottage would soon be joined by Jesse Hoover's blacksmith shop and the Hoover library and museum, which took shape in the early 1960s. A homely affair, with fried chicken and new corn prepared by the ladies of the Methodist church, it was also a chance for West Branch's favorite son to revisit the scenes of a rugged boyhood now softening in the solution of time. Hoover paused at his parents' graves, planted a tree at the first of four schools given his name that day, listened as congratulatory messages were read from the White House, and then mounted the platform to deliver his own appeal for the protection of freedom, "not in the tones of Jeremiah but in the spirit of Saint Paul."[30]

The life of free men, he said, included constant struggle to prevent the abuse of power, whether by individuals or governments. Those who devised the American republic had recognized this, and responded with a series of restraints, divisions of authority that had become thoroughly confused during the previous twenty years. The executive had encroached on the legislature and judiciary. Judges had usurped the powers accorded to states. Congress had spun a web of its own around the presidency, while Washington grabbed some of the most important functions previously reserved to state and local governments. Such erosion of checks and balances pointed a dagger at the heart of republican government. "They must be wiped out," said Hoover, "if you would remain fully free." He was just as uncompromising in spotlighting "the Socialist virus" generated by Marx and Engels. "Their dogma is absolute materialism which defies truth and religious faith. . . . The recruiting grounds for their agents are from our minority of fuzzy-minded intellectuals and labor leaders." Already, more than a thousand such traitors had been plucked from responsible positions. Many subsequently took the Fifth Amendment, for Hoover a clear implication of guilt and reason enough to deny them voting privileges.

Offensive as their message, card-carrying Communists were easily containable. The greater corruption by far traced from the less dramatic acceptance of modern government's responsibility for individual security. The judgment of the Lord to Adam about sweat had not been repealed, he told the crowd at West Branch. "When we flirt with the Delilah of security for our productive group, we had better watch out, lest we pull down the pillars of the temple of free men." He closed on a more optimistic note. Eighty years, he said, was a long time for any man to live. Yet even as the shadows lengthened for him, his hopes and dreams for America were undimmed. He had never forsaken his confidence in material progress allied to spiritual values. Its flame burned undiminished. "This confidence is that with advancing knowledge, toil will grow less exacting; that fear, hatred, pain, and tears may subside; that the regenerating sun of creative ability and religious devotion will refresh each morning the strength and progress of my country."

One Iowa paper compared his eloquence to Churchill's. The *Boston Post* called the speech a "lucid and urgent rallying cry for the American people." The *New York Herald Tribune,* so often at odds with him in the past, expressed delight that Hoover had exposed "the myth of the common man."

The day after his birthday celebration at West Branch, the former president received a fresh tribute from a packed Madison Square Garden in New York. The same week, it was announced that he would travel to Germany in November. In Bonn, Stuttgart and Tübingen, the ancient university town that conferred Hoover's eighty-first honorary degree, he was greeted by thousands of children. "Vergelt's Gott!" exlaimed the burgomaster of Bonn ("God's reward to you!"). At a state dinner, Chancellor Adenauer thanked the American for taking a week from his reorganizing work at home. He hailed the former president as a true friend of Germany who twice had come to the aid of a defeated adversary and more recently argued strenuously on behalf of German reconstruction. Basking in the applause, Hoover did not hesitate to lecture his hosts on their obligation to participate in a military front to deter Communist aggression.

"Neutralism is no answer to the security of free nations. . . . Our American people have joined in the defense of Western Europe. It is an illusion of some European statesmen that we have . . . spent huge efforts for the selfish purpose of defending ourselves." In truth, his nation could defend herself much more cheaply than the Continent. "Nor is there an atom of truth in the assertion that American action is animated by imperialist ambitions."

He expressed disappointment in the United Nations, acknowledging its usefulness as a forum "whereby with electronic equipment we can denounce the ways of the Communists in five languages all at once." He lavished praise on the supposedly outmoded concept of nationalism. "It springs from a thousand rills of inspiring national history, its heroes, its common language, its culture and its national achievements. It rises from the yearning of men to be free of foreign domination. . . ." It fashioned strength and hardened resolution. It contributed, not to isolation, but to common action "for defense more secure and more potent." Resort to such glowing terms with a people whose nationalism had often been distorted and even murderous was a calculated risk. But, like many old men, Hoover had little to fear from plain speaking.

On his return to New York, he found on his desk the kind of recognition denied him in purdah. Arthur Krock spoke for many others who had disagreed with Hoover in the past, only to marvel at his rediscovery. "What a wonderful life!" Krock wrote to Bunny Miller. "And it goes on." [31]

★   ★

With publication of the second Hoover Commission's final report in May 1955, the former president completed forty-three years of public service. He was resolved, Hoover told a friend in the summer of 1956, to make no more speeches longer than three minutes. Whatever time remained, he would hoard jealously for his writing, for Stanford, and for the circle of friends who gradually replaced the shrinking band familiar to a man in his eighties. When Congress voted to give former presidents an annual pension of $25,000, he reluctantly accepted. Any other course might have embarrassed his friend of more modest circumstances, Harry Truman. Besides, he mused, "I think maybe I've got it coming." His own out-of-pocket expenses for research and secretarial staff averaged $14,000 a year, with nearly $2,000 more for stationery and postage, an inevitable burden given the twenty thousand letters that flowed into Suite 31-A annually. [32]

No less persistent were the demands of passing years. In February 1955, Hoover's brother Theodore died. Later that year, Bert's boyhood home in Newberg, Oregon, was opened to the public. Hoover spent his eighty-first birthday in Newberg, where he managed to heal whatever scars might linger from his days with John Minthorn. He stood silent in the upstairs chamber where he had slept in a big wooden bed, eyes moist with emotion. "This was my room," he finally remarked to his guide, and after another glance at the rag carpet and whitewashed walls, he turned to descend the narrow staircase that led to the front door and a friendly crowd outside. He accepted membership on a committee preparing to commemorate Woodrow Wilson's centennial. He represented Eisenhower on Veterans Day 1955 when illness kept the president from laying the traditional wreath at Arlington Cemetery. He appeared on an hour-long broadcast, a sort of televised autobiography, that aired over NBC that same week. A month later, he was Lawrence Spivak's guest on "Meet the Press." [33]

More and more of his hours were allotted to the historian's routines of research and reconstruction. First came The American Epic, a fact-choked chronicle of his own activities in various relief movements from Belgium to Hungary, where he advised Eisenhower on U.S. aid following the brutal response of Russian tanks to an uprising in the streets of its rebellious satellite. It wasn't simply his intention to record the story of Europe and its various flirtations with famine, he explained to a visitor. "I want to be sure that America's part in this is remembered. . . . Americans don't get much credit abroad these days for what they do." Launched in 1956, the four volumes were interrupted when the figure of Woodrow Wilson entered Hoover's story. Within three weeks, he had ground out another manuscript, too short for book form, and as of yet too lacking in personal color or interpretive detail to warrant publication, but a beginning that Hoover quickly expanded upon. The result was The Ordeal of Woodrow Wilson, a sympathetic account of the wartime leader's exposure to diplomatic cynicism at Versailles. It was the first time an American president had composed a book about one of his predecessors, and it surprised no one more than its author by immediately taking up residence on the best-seller lists. [34]

Hoover wrote biography that read at times like autobiography. Wilson, he noted, had often been described as obstinate, a term Hoover found misleading. "His mind ran to 'moral principles,' 'justice' and 'right,' " asserted his admiring subordinate. Wilson had retained the flinty character of the original Presbyterians; "what they concluded was right, was thereafter right as against all comers." He liked to date his own ancestry to the Scotch Covenanters of 1638. Slow to budge, even when confronted with the realities of European power politics, Wilson easily became impatient. He often confused legitimate argument with personal criticism. "He was not a snob," wrote Hoover, "but he had little patience with small minds."

But there was more than Scotch intransigence to Wilson's makeup. He was, Hoover concluded, "a man of staunch morals. He was more than just an idealist; he was the personification of the heritage of idealism of the American people. He brought spiritual concepts to the peace table. He was a born crusader." America, he went on, was the only nation on earth since the Crusades to have fought other peoples' battles at her own loss. Even if mankind had yet to sample a permanent peace, Wilson the crusader had expounded ideals unknown in the thickets of pre-1918 diplomacy. He set an example as well as a standard.

Edith Bolling Wilson was grateful. So many others who tried to explain her husband seemed apologetic about Wilson's stubborn streak, "but you seem to have really understood him." Wilson's daughter Nellie called the book "a fine and very moving appraisal." Thus buoyed by popular as well as critical reaction to his work, Hoover returned with a vengeance to his *American Epic*. Volume One appeared in 1959, with two more volumes following annually, and a fourth published in 1964. If anything, he stepped up his literary output. Although a projected biography of Robert Taft never materialized, a book of letters to and from children appeared in 1962, along with a small, whimsical manuscript entitled simply *On Fishing*. Now when he went to the Bohemian Grove, secretaries brought research material and typed drafts to the entrance gate—women being strictly barred from this exclusive preserve of masculine camaraderie. "I just keep on working," he informed a Grove visitor who discovered him at six o'clock on the morning of his eighty-third birthday, fully dressed and scribbling away on a card table in his two-room cabin. Or he sat in a hotel room at San Francisco's Mark Hopkins, writing all day without pausing long enough to speak to his research assistant, who sat facing him just a few feet away. Instead, questions were put in note form, as were answers. The mail piled up, filled with speaking invitations, and Hoover noted in the margin of most, "Decline gently" or "Decline with thanks." His single-mindedness was attributable to "The War Book," as *Freedom Betrayed* was called before 1953.[35]

Hoover sent aides scurrying to review all thirty-one volumes of testimony in the Pearl Harbor inquiry conducted by Congress after V-J Day. They examined transcripts of the Nuremberg trials, along with German diplomatic messages stashed for safekeeping at the library in Palo Alto. Herbert, Junior, opened up State Department archives, while other, still more confidential information was gleaned from private diaries and correspondence.

Hoover himself pumped friends like General Leslie Groves, who had super-vised the top secret Manhattan Project that resulted in the first atomic bomb, for their views on espionage and Communist influence. From Douglas MacArthur he got broad confirmation of a substantive Japanese peace feeler seven months before the war actually ended—on terms almost precisely in line with the ultimate accord. Slowly, in the course of reviewing 350,000 documents, he assembled a vast mélange of historical accusation and per-sonal recollection, a sprawling tapestry of American foreign policy that began with Roosevelt's recognition of the Soviet Union in 1933 and contin-ued up to Mao Tse-tung's triumph on the Chinese mainland sixteen years later. There were a dozen different versions of the monumental text, in-tended to fill four thick volumes and convincingly indict his Democratic successors in the court of history.[36]

The *Chicago Tribune* sought serial rights. So did the Hearst Corporation. But Hoover refused to allow publication during his lifetime. Instead, he turned the manuscript over to a committee of journalistic allies. A bitter debate erupted over potentially libelous statements. Might not quick publi-cation result in a flood of critical reviews, they wondered, grouped around a common, depressing theme—that a senile old man was seeking revenge against enemies, in the process jeopardizing his own position in the history books so recently and painstakingly regained? Ultimately, the manuscript was sent to Stanford, for further checking and deletion of its harshest judg-ments, including the author's singling out of individuals as Communists. Allan Hoover assumed final authority, and it was decided not to show *Freedom Betrayed* to Doubleday's Ken McCormick. Today, the manuscript remains locked up in the Hoover Institution vaults.[37]

"I am a collecting fiend for the War Library at Stanford," the former president wrote Chester Nimitz in July 1956 by way of prefacing a request for the admiral's papers. A year later, following the death of Joseph Mc-Carthy, Hoover penned a generous tribute to McCarthy's widow, followed after a decent interval by an appeal for McCarthy's own files. Offering to place them within his personal archives, hidden away from public view, Hoover tried to reassure Mrs. McCarthy. Not only was the institution free of "leftwingers," but he had made arrangements to prevent such intrusions "for at least twenty years." Yet less than two years later, he told another friend, "The library is a complete mess. We have disposed of the Director but will not have a new one for sometime."[38]

It was true. C. Easton Rothwell, for seven years director of the prestigious facility, where William Shirer did much of his research for *The Rise and Fall of the Third Reich*, where Barbara Tuchman prepared *The Guns of August*, and where Alexander Kerensky was a familiar figure out of the past, resigned in the spring of 1959. Rothwell had been a friend to Alger Hiss. If that weren't sinful enough in Hoover's eyes, he seemed insufficiently energetic in raising money. He was even prepared to dip into special funds and curtail both staff and publications. Confronted with such apostasy, Hoover resolved to find himself a new director. Contrary to what he told Mrs. McCarthy, he did worry over possible infiltration of the place from the Left. In his anguish, he turned late in 1957 to the FBI for help. Entrusted with one last secret mission, Larry Richey turned over a list of seventy-eight names to the Bureau's Domestic Intelligence Division.[39]

That done, Hoover pressed forward with a major fund-raising campaign. Liberal faculty members at Stanford disputed his emphasis on Communist studies, what one resolution called predetermined scholarship. But Hoover prevailed with university trustees, who in March of 1958 created a separate board to govern the newly renamed library. "The name of our place has been changed to comport more with its purposes," he informed Truman. "It is now the Hoover Institution on War, Revolution and Peace. So you can have the future any way you wish." The trustees' vote was "a good start," judged their long-standing colleague. But it was only that. A new director must be recruited from a list of a hundred names. Late in 1959, Hoover found his man: W. Glenn Campbell, a conservative economist then working with Washington's American Enterprise Association (forerunner of the American Enterprise Institute), a former member of the Harvard faculty who shared his patron's interest in Communist history and who demonstrated his commitment by launching a three-year examination of Third International activities between 1919 and 1943. The *New Republic* attacked Hoover's stated intention to do academic battle with Karl Marx, and the *Stanford Daily* wondered aloud about his legal claims in the matter, but the former president shrugged off the controversy. He could afford to. Having turned down an invitation to join the board of the new Americans for Constitutional Action because he nurtured hopes of raising funds among eastern foundations (he would be more outspoken in support of another conservative group, Young Americans for Freedom), in April 1960 he wrote a brisk note to the ACA's cofounder, Admiral Ben Moreell:

"My dear Ben:

"1. Now that the liberal foundations have turned me down in my raising funds for the Institution at Stanford;

"2. Now that the faculty of my own university have proclaimed me a 'reactionary' for opposing 'the infection of Karl Marx';

"3. Now that I have raised, within the last seven months, about $1,250,000 for my Institution from righteous foundations;

"4. You can add my name to your collection of reactionaries."[40]

A far happier experience came in July 1957 when Hoover joined Harry Truman, Eleanor Roosevelt and others in dedicating the Truman Library at Independence, Missouri. "One of the important jobs of our very exclusive Trade Union is preserving libraries," he responded when Truman first invited him to the ceremony. Rearranging his own travel plans, he promised to attend "except for acts of God or evil persons." He spoke just four paragraphs at the dedication, lauding Truman for opening up a treasure trove of documentation. Then he joined America's only other ex-president for a personal tour of the collection. Their friendship never faltered. After learning of Hoover's operation for removal of his gall bladder in April 1958, Truman urged caution. "I have been through the same procedure and got up too soon and it cost me three more weeks in the hospital. Please take care of yourself."[41]

A year later, when Bess Truman fell ill, there arrived from New York a bouquet of white mums and yellow roses, "just to show my own convictions," in the words of its sender. He invited Truman to the Bohemian Grove, and called the former president's Waldorf visit "my intellectual stimulant of the month" after Truman came to call in March 1960. When Lewis Strauss's nomination to be Secretary of Commerce foundered on a wave of Democratic charges, he appealed for help from Independence—but even Truman's defense could not prevent Strauss from becoming the first Cabinet appointee since 1925 to fail Senate confirmation. "I treasure your letter as proof of the character of one Harry Truman," Hoover wrote in reply. He thanked Truman for a copy of his own recent book: ". . . it goes into the file of most treasured documents." The Missourian responded with open affection. "I didn't receive a single birthday telegram that I appreciated more than I did yours . . . ," he wrote in July 1963. "We understand each other." A month later, he told an ailing Hoover, "You must reach 100 as I intend to do" and the sage of 31-A replied through his son Allan that he would race his friend to their common goal. Two elderly presidents, writing to each other in a correspondence reminiscent of the autumnal reconciliation of John Adams and Thomas Jefferson, Hoover and Truman did indeed understand each other. It was a happy winter solstice for both men.[42]

★   ★

In April 1958, a few days after his gall bladder operation, Hoover took a call from Eisenhower's White House. It was the president himself, wondering if perhaps the old man would do him the honor of representing the United States at the July 4 commemoration of America's national day at the Brussels World's Fair. The request had a certain poetic justice. It marked the closing of a circle that had begun with Hoover's promotion of another exposition, in San Francisco, even before his wartime exploits had earned him a lasting place in Belgian history. By the end of the month, he was able to report good news: his doctors were agreeable to his going. It was a poignant journey, and a taxing one as well. At a dinner with the Belgian royal family, the former president nearly fainted, and had to be helped to his feet by King Baudouin. Only two of the CRB veterans remained to answer the roll when Hoover called it on July 5, Emile Franqui's widow and the visitor from America.[43]

The day before, he had visited the U.S. pavilion, with its wraparound cinema and filmed tribute to "America the Beautiful." An Air Force band played "Hail to the Chief," and the crowd inside burst into loud applause when the screen showed Hoover Dam. His own speech was a spirited defense of traditional American values, including compassion and a generous sharing of scientific genius with an advancing world. He struck out at "vicious propaganda" being circulated about his countrymen, recalling three wars in the previous forty years in which America's sons had served in the cause of freedom. "Never after victory did we ask for an acre of territory, except a few military bases to protect the free nations. We have never asked for reparations or economic privileges. On the contrary, we made gigantic gifts and loans to aid nations in war and reconstruction, including Communist Russia. . . ."

The Belgians cheered. From Moscow came a wintry blast. Hoover was guilty, huffed *Izvestia* a few days later, of "nasty propaganda." Unearthing the old charge made a quarter of a century before by John Hamill, the Soviet paper of record denounced the former president as a plunderer of Chinese resources and a politician elevated to his nation's highest office "by the kind persuasion of the Morgans, the Duponts, and Lamonts."

Hoover said nothing publicly. His reply came later that month, when he strongly backed Eisenhower's deployment of U.S. Marines in war-torn Lebanon. It was, he said, the only possible response "if the freedom of nations is to be protected from militarist conspiracies."

Closer to home, he worried about the effects of affluence on the moral fiber of his countrymen. He cited alarming statistics suggesting a wave of burglaries and murders. He criticized progressive education as a disincentive to learn mathematics and other skills required of a nation in the wake of Russia's *Sputnik*. Some Americans, he remarked sorrowfully, seemed more mindful of entertainment than religion. Yet Hoover did not retreat into a hermit's disdain. For every fault diagnosed he also urged a solution—a national crime census to be undertaken prior to reforms in the criminal justice system, tougher educational standards and less individual choice for youngsters "who have no ability to choose their own life when they are thirteen years old," and more local efforts like his own beloved Boys Clubs, which according to Hoover reduced juvenile crime in one St. Louis neighborhood by 75 percent.[44]

The nation embarked on another presidential campaign; Hoover predicted John Kennedy's election. Personally, he thought Lyndon Johnson might be a more formidable contender for the Democrats, a southerner able to siphon off conservative Republicans. Richard Nixon, he believed, would make a "splendid" president. Eisenhower's second-in-command had his feet on the ground, Hoover told a visitor in the spring of 1960. He could boast of more foreign policy experience than anyone next to Ike himself. Besides, he went on, he regarded Nelson Rockefeller, Nixon's only prospective rival, as a dangerous man. On July 25, Hoover stood before his eighth Republican convention. Three times before he had bade delegates an affectionate farewell. "Apparently, my goodbyes did not take. And I have been bombarded with requests to do it again for a fourth time. Unless some miracle comes to me from the Good Lord," he added, "this is finally it."[45]

In the ensuing campaign, Nixon passed through the Waldorf several times without pausing to ask for his help. When finally he did call 31-A to invite Hoover up for a visit, the fiercely loyal Bunny Miller protested that her employer didn't call on people—they called on him. "Oh, Bunny," Hoover interrupted, "we won't stand on dignity. I'll go up and see him." He found Nixon pacing the floor, pondering Kennedy's offer to join in a fourth televised debate. "You had three debates," Hoover told the vice president. "Wasn't that enough for you?" Privately, he found the GOP nominee entirely too willing to concede Kennedy's goals, which to Hoover were "evil. . . . By every implication he is determined on a new and greater New Deal." Besides, next to the youthful, vigorous Kennedy, Nixon looked bad on television. "One broadcaster who favors the Republican side," he noted, "said Nixon looked like a made-over stiff." More substantively, Hoover urged a clearer definition of differences between the two parties: Nixon should call for reduced government expenditures, less foreign aid, more attention to the Hoover Commission agenda.[46]

Following Kennedy's paper-thin victory in November, Hoover took a call from the victorious candidate's father. His son was at Palm Beach, according to the ambassador, and Nixon was staying in a Miami hotel. Wouldn't it be a good idea to have both men meet and shake hands in front of photographers? Hoover agreed instantly. Joseph Kennedy would arrange for Jack to go to Nixon if his rival would agree to receive him. Hoover said it should be the other way around, and took it upon himself to persuade the vice president. Nixon wasn't taken with the idea. It was "a cheap publicity stunt," he told Hoover over the phone.[47]

For once, the old man lost his temper. Did Nixon understand what he was saying? The incoming president of the United States didn't need anyone else to win him publicity; he would get all he wanted and more on his own. "This is a generous gesture on his part," he reminded Nixon, "and you ought to meet it with equal generosity."[48]

Nixon agreed, and the meeting took place on November 14. Other courtesies followed. The new president invited his elderly predecessor to attend his inauguration. Hoover flew into Washington, only to find the nation's capital paralyzed by a blizzard. Back in Florida, he praised Kennedy's inaugural speech as "vital, decisive . . . a great address." JFK asked the old man to serve as honorary chairman of his new Peace Corps, and Hoover reluctantly declined, citing his age and other commitments (which had expanded to include a hundred-million-dollar fund-raising campaign for Stanford). Neither was he able to be present when the president of Finland dined at the White House that fall, or when Winston Churchill was made an honorary citizen of the United States, in the spring of 1963. Kennedy's thoughtfulness did not stop there: he dispatched John McCone of the CIA to provide Hoover with a detailed briefing on national security issues and paid his own visit to the Waldorf early in his administration. It was both a reassuring sign of continuity and a personal tribute to one who had served as a convenient foil for Democratic attacks for thirty years.[49]

In 31-A, a gentle decrescendo began. Its occupant continued to work on his books every day. But outside activities were gradually curtailed. In April 1962, he paid a final visit to Key Largo. He presented his favorite guide with his own rod and reel. If he ever got back, he told Calvin Albury, he'd make use of them himself; otherwise, they were a gift. The next morning, Albury walked over to Hoover's cottage to say goodbye. He found his friend close to tears. "Well," said Hoover, "if it's the Good Lord's will, I'll see you again." He instructed his Waldorf visitors to be sure to tell him everything they saw on foreign travels. "I depend on my friends to bring the news to me," he explained. More than ever now, his secretarial staff became a kind of surrogate family. When one woman had a pocketbook containing $150 stolen, she later found a note attached to a check for that amount. "Buy a combination lock," it read. Her coworkers received gold clocks, and, on

Hoover's ninetieth birthday, strands of pearls. In his will, he distributed $140,000 among them, including a $50,000 trust fund for the faithful Bunny Miller. They reciprocated one August with a globe, into which they had stuck red pins to mark every exotic location in which their employer had passed previous birthdays. Hoover was grateful for the company of a podiatrist who came nearly every Friday, long after there was any medical need. "I don't know what to do for you, Dr. Petti," Hoover responded before presenting him with a radio identical to his own, and a tensor light, ideal for old men with failing eyes.[50]

A friend fell ill in the summer of 1962, and Hoover urged a speedy recovery. Hospitals had many useful advantages, he wrote, "but they have no sense of humor." Joe Kennedy suffered a stroke, and the two old warriors managed a final meal of fish and baked apples, punctuated by Rose Kennedy's conversation and the distant memory of his own departed wife. He turned down an appeal to endorse the John Birch Society, accepted membership in the new Calvin Coolidge Memorial Foundation. He sent a message of congratulations to John Glenn, after *Freedom 7* made America's first orbital flight in Feburary 1962. Nine months later, word came of another milestone of sorts. "Mrs. Roosevelt was a lady of fine courage and great devotion to her country," he scrawled in response to news of the death of Franklin Roosevelt's widow. He hadn't forgotten her own courtesy of January 1944.[51]

In other ways, time pressed heavily upon him. That August, Hoover made one more trip to West Branch, to dedicate his own library. Harry Truman returned his courtesy of 1957, and both men were warmly received by 45,000 spectators gathered under the broiling Iowa sun. It was a severe test of an eighty-eight-year-old's stamina. Hoover felt ill during the ceremony, and on his return to New York was immediately placed in a hospital. Doctors diagnosed anemia. They also discovered a malignancy in the right side of his colon. In June of 1963, the former president sustained an attack of internal bleeding only to astonish those around him with his rapid recovery. Worse than illness was disillusionment. Confined to a wheelchair, his daily work schedule cut to five or six hours, Hoover was trying to regain his legs with the help of two nurses. Fortunately, he told Rose Kennedy that fall, "my means of communication are good for expression of indignation when needed, such as, the suppression of prayer in the schools."[52]

He was displeased over more than the Warren Court. In March 1963, a fight erupted in his old American-Belgian Educational Foundation. Over the years, it had provided scholarships for eleven hundred Belgian graduate students and several hundred more American scholars. It had also been generous in funding the Hoover War Library and the Committee to Feed the Small Democracies. In the fall of 1962, trustees appropriated $900,000 to expand the library at West Branch, where CRB records would be stored as part of a larger collection that would eventually top five million documents. A furtive campaign was launched to overturn the vote by packing the board with new trustees. Perrin Galpin emerged as the insurrection leader. His own vulnerability became obvious after a special committee faulted the ABEF for excessive administrative overhead and a bloated staff. Galpin, feeling threatened by the prospect of such retrenchment, joined the dissidents, only to quit his position in June 1963. Lawsuits were filed, including one challenging the library gift. Hoover was shaken. Never before, he confided, had he been more saddened by the "disloyalty and dishonesty" of men he had trusted and provided with a living through the years through the various organizations he'd created and staffed.[53]

Another blow came with John Kennedy's assassination that fall. So upset was his father, Allan decided, that he would spend the night of November 22 at 31-A himself. Shortly after eight o'clock, he took a call from Richard Berlin of the Hearst organization. The new president had tried to reach Allan's father; both Truman and Eisenhower were coming to Washington to provide continuity during the crisis, and Lyndon Johnson wished to touch base with Hoover as well. The next morning, the former president passed on a message: "I am ready to serve our government in any capacity, from office boy up." He conveyed his genuine sorrow to Kennedy's widow, and she replied with equal sincerity. "You were always wonderful to my husband and he admired you so much." She had succumbed to "hero worship" of her own, she wrote, after hearing the ambassador talk about Hoover, likening him to Churchill. Now she paid her own call on 31-A, where the old man indulged his fondness for children by playing with the boy he called John-John.[54]

After listening to Johnson's first address to Congress, he extended his support to the new president. He was certain, Hoover wrote LBJ, "that all Americans who heard your stirring words will evidence appreciation by their co-operation and response." On December 9, in New York for Herbert Lehman's funeral, Johnson surprised Secret Service men by suddenly announcing his intention to visit 31-A. They protested, to no avail. "We'll go to see Mr. Hoover—period." And with Earl Warren and Mayor Robert Wagner in tow, the towering Texan paid his respects. Two weeks later, Johnson telephoned with Christmas greetings. Such courtesies helped at least a little to compensate for the ravages of time. "When you get to this age," Hoover complained a few days after Kennedy's death, "they won't let you have any fun." His intake of "old character builder" was sharply curtailed, he informed fellow Bohemians, on doctor's orders.[55]

Nineteen sixty-four overtook him, still another election year. He received Richard Nixon but told the former vice president that he was unlikely to endorse any candidate. He waved aside Eugene Lyons's offer to let him see the manuscript of his new book, scheduled to reach the public in time for Hoover's ninetieth birthday in August. "Your conclusions will probably contain overstatements which will just trouble me," he informed the author, "and being 90 years old I just don't want any more trouble."[56]

Trouble, of course, was an occupational hazard for men of Hoover's age. In February 1964, he rallied after a five-day contest with pneumonia and a bleeding kidney. He dashed off an encouraging note to Douglas MacArthur, who was waging his own, losing battle at Walter Reed in Washington. "My dear Friend," he wrote. "From experience I can assure you the Waldorf Towers are much more desirable than any hospital, so I send warm good wishes that you'll soon be back in our neighborhood." It was not to be. MacArthur died on April 5, and another human link to the past snapped. Hoover chose to look ahead. He suggested to the Johnson White House that a third reorganization commission was in order. He apologized to the Dutch Treat Club for missing their luncheon meetings, expressing suspicion that his picture in the club's latest yearbook "marks a new era in discretion and decorum." His own theme song for 1964, he informed a friend, was "Off Again, On Again."[57]

Friends sought to involve him in the divisive primary battles between Barry Goldwater and Nelson Rockefeller. Hoover held back. But he was fond of Goldwater, whom he had known since 1933, and he was touched when the Arizona senator phoned during the course of the convention with news of his running mate, New York congressman William Miller. Hoover said he could not take an active part in the ensuing campaign but would gladly issue a public statement of support whenever it might be helpful. It was the first convention he had missed since 1936. His presence was felt anyway, not only in the rock-ribbed conservatism of the new nominee and his platform, but in a six-hundred-word statement dictated by Hoover and read to the delegates by Illinois's Everett Dirksen. When Goldwater came calling on August 9, he found an old man imbued with the righteousness of his cause. He would sell the TVA himself, the former president announced, "if I could only get a dollar for it" and allow state governments to operate the network of dams and power plants bequeathed by the New Deal.[58]

Another visitor that summer was told flatly that he was going to Europe shortly. "Yes, Chief," Walter Trohan replied, "but I don't know how you found it out." Was there anything he could do for his friend while on the other side of the Atlantic? "Well," Hoover told him, "you can tell the British to take their hands out of our pockets." Lucius Clay dropped by, expecting to stay for fifteen minutes; Hoover kept him for an hour and a half. "I just want to talk," he explained to the general. "I sit here most of the day with these nurses and we don't speak the same language. I don't mean to be critical . . . because they're really wonderful to me and do everything they can, but that isn't my type of talk." The president of Stanford and his wife nearly broke down when the old man delayed their departure long enough to retrieve a small gift for Ann Sterling. "It's the Chinese equivalent of a Saint Christopher's medal," he said, handing over one of the handful of Lou's collectibles still in his possession.[59]

August 10 was his ninetieth birthday. Sixteen states declared "Herbert Hoover Day." Richard Nixon stopped by for a chat. The *Reader's Digest* published his own birthday greeting to the American people. "The time has come for Americans to take stock and to think something good about themselves," he wrote, and for a few paragraphs, it was possible to believe that a half century never happened, that the optimistic engineer of social progress was unaffected by personal rejection and ideological isolation, war abroad and secularization at home. Being Hoover, he could even find statistics to ameliorate the lot of the black man in America. Deeply as he felt the inequalities pressed down on such minorities, "I cannot refrain from saying that our 19 million Negroes probably own more automobiles than all the 220 million Russians and the 200 million African Negroes put together."[60]

Certainly the political arena held little cause for cheer. Goldwater's campaign stumbled badly, and Hoover entertained no hope of victory in November. Instead, he clung to the rituals of life, modified by the technology he had long celebrated. He watched the 1964 World Series on a new color television. Learning of a domestic accident involving his friend from Independence, Hoover dispatched a message. "Bathtubs are a menace to ex-presidents," it stated, "for as you may recall a bathtub rose up and fractured my vertebrae when I was in Venezuela on your world famine mission in 1946."[61]

It was one of his last communications. On Saturday, October 16, he suffered massive hemorrhaging in the stomach and intestine. Refusing to be hospitalized—it took one doctor forty-eight hours to persuade him to install a hospital bed—Hoover only reluctantly agreed to the first of two hundred blood transfusions. For the next five days, the hotel became a virtual hospital annex. Blood was smuggled into the Waldorf through a back door. Inside 31-A, oxygen was available, and tubes were placed to Hoover's stomach in a desperate attempt to halt the bleeding. Two bulletins each day were released to the press, while five doctors and six nurses tried to ease the pain and sooth the agonies of dying.[62]

From Truman came fighting words for his friend's recovery. If he weren't in a hospital bed himself, he'd be on his way to New York to provide personal encouragement. By then, however, it would have done little good; Hoover had slipped into a coma. A few old friends were admitted to the sickroom, among them Lewis Strauss. The aging admiral came away in tears. He had gone inside, he explained, and found the Chief asleep, but in turning over Hoover heard a nurse announce Strauss's presence. From somewhere in the depths of consciousness the old man stirred. "Lewis Strauss was one of my best friends," he murmured, before lapsing again into a deep slumber.[63]

Lyndon Johnson wired his own concern. "My thoughts are with your father and you during these difficult hours and we are hoping for the best," he informed the Hoover sons. Early on the morning of October 20, Herbert, Junior, expressed gratitude. His father was putting up "a rugged fight," he reported. A few minutes before noon, the fight ended. The cause of death was not cancer—an autopsy showed no recurrence of the earlier malignancy —but excessive bleeding from the lower esophagus. Hoover had simply been too old for corrective surgery.[64]

The tributes began taking shape, from the famous and obscure alike. From Truman: "He was my good friend and I was his." From Nixon: "For sixty years he walked proudly with the giants of the earth." Barry Goldwater expressed satisfaction that Hoover had lived long enough to see his position in history vindicated. Hubert Humphrey and Dean Burch, Adlai Stevenson and Thomas E. Dewey: from across the political spectrum came words of condolence and fond memory.

In Washington, Chief Justice Earl Warren recessed the Supreme Court. In Monte Carlo, the Paris editor of the *New York Herald Tribune* went back to his room overlooking the Riviera and thought of Europe's restoration. The *Knoxville Tennessee Journal* called Hoover "a martyred President, the victim of the greatest political misrepresentation of this century." Others evoked a common theme: the man who came back.

Walter Lippmann was more measured. The dead man might be remembered since 1932 as "the great objector," Lippmann wrote, but that was the result of his being "run over by the great depression. His negativism was not in harmony with his generous, liberal and magnanimous nature." In the field of war and peace, however, Hoover had remained always true to his real self, "that of the bold and brilliant philanthropist who binds up wounds and avoids inflicting them." Destiny had marked him as natural heir to Woodrow Wilson; yet by choosing to declare himself a Republican in 1920, concluded Lippmann, he had opened a breach with progressive forces that steadily widened, until it became a yawning gulf, traversable by no man.

Others reacted in their own way. William Miller restrained his attacks on Johnson and White House aide Walter Jenkins, the object of a storm of censure following his arrest in a Washington, D.C., men's room that week. Instead, the Republican vice presidential candidate invited a San Jose, California, audience to rise for a moment of silence. Miller was joined by his running mate, as well as the Johnson-Humphrey ticket, at a twenty-five-minute service in Saint Bartholomew's Church in New York on October 24. Twenty years earlier Lou had been memorialized there. Now, heavy security prevented many mourners from getting inside, where Jean Mac-Arthur and Eddie Rickenbacker, John Connolly and Jim Farley were among the four hundred, mainly elderly, guests who slipped through the cordon of city police and secret service men.

Seventeen thousand average New Yorkers filed by the bier before the church was closed that night. The next morning, a motorcade carried the casket and members of the Hoover family to Pennsylvania Station, where a train waited to make the short trip south to Washington. The rotunda of the Capitol, so recently filled with mourners for John Kennedy and Douglas MacArthur, was again the scene of the nation's formal obsequies. "America the Beautiful" filled the Capitol plaza as servicemen removed the casket from its horsedrawn caisson and bore it gently up the steps of the Senate. Twenty-one guns were fired, and fifty Air Force planes flew overhead, an incongruous salute to the Quaker who despised militarism.

But the most moving of all farewells came on Sunday, the twenty-fifth, when a C-30 Hercules aircraft set down in Cedar Rapids. Thousands of ordinary people lined the thirty-three mile route from the airport to West Branch. They stood in silence, in farmhouse yards and newly shaved corn-fields, old men who had survived the distress of 1932, and children too young to recall Herbert Hoover except from their history books or the stories told by their parents.

The sun was beginning to slip away as the cortege made its way around the circular driveway of Hoover Park. Between 75,000 and 90,000 people were assembled in the tiny village, their eyes fixed on the gentle knoll called The Overlook, a quarter mile from the two-room cottage where Hoover's life had begun, ninety years and a world away, and where a National Guard band now played "Fight the Good Fight" and "The Battle Hymn of the Republic." Shielded from the prairie wind by a billowing stand of cypress trees, the gravesite witnessed a simple requiem. This time, there were no military displays to mar the pastoral stillness. Instead, Dr. Elton Trueblood, a leading Quaker theologian and longtime friend from Palo Alto, spoke a brief eulogy. "The story is a great one and a good one," he said. "It is essentially . . . triumphant." Herbert Hoover would be remembered for as long as the American dream was cherished. "He has worked hard; he has been very brave; he has endured." A soldier perched on a nearby hillside played Taps.

The dusk was coming on now, and still the air held the soft, beguiling fragrance of Indian summer. From the village one could hear the chimes of the Methodist Church, pealing out a musical tribute of their own. Ninety-three-year-old Ruth Hoover, widow of the late president's cousin, sat on the front porch of her home, near forty cub scouts drawn up in solemn formation. Other children clambered into oak trees, just as Jesse Hoover's boy must have before the nineteenth century gave way to its tormented successor. Like the rest of the crowd, they seemed reluctant to depart, unwilling to do the logical thing and return to their homes. And why not? For they knew they were burying more than a man that afternoon. They were placing in the loamy soil of Cedar County much of their past, and perhaps more of their future.

APPENDIX

AMERICA'S POSITION—III

The text of Hoover's "very interesting, rather dramatic and radical" plan to bring an early end to World War II, transmitted to Secretary of State Henry Stimson before his own meeting with President Truman.

New York, New York
May 15, 1945

We should today take stock of the position of the United States and Britain.

A. Hitler, Mussolini and their allied dictators in Hungary, Bulgaria and Roumania are crushed. The British, French, Belgian and Dutch Empires are safe for a while.

B. Stalin has annexed Latvia, Estonia, Lithuania, Eastern Poland and Bessarabia. He has set up Communist governments responsible to him in Poland, Roumania, Bulgaria, Yugoslavia, Finland, Czechoslovakia and Austria. He will set up governments that are largely Communist and likely to become more so in Italy, Greece and Northwest Germany.

Thus Stalin's sphere of political domination has been extended over 15 non-Russian peoples in Europe as a result of this war. They embrace a population of about 200,000,000 people.

C. This expansion will have economic effects upon the United States and Britain. The economic life of those countries under Russian sphere will be socialized and there will no longer be an opportunity for American or British private enterprise therein. Their foreign trade will be conducted through government agencies and thus American and British exporters and importers will need to deal, in effect, with gigantic monopolies. Those monopolies will compete with us in other markets.

D. There are only three great areas in the world where the Americans and British might have freedom and opportunity in economic life. That is, in (a) the British, French, Belgian and Dutch Empires, (B) the Western Hemisphere, and (c) Asia outside of Russia.

E. We will defeat Japan. But Russia will likely annex Manchuria, North China and Korea. From this base she is likely to expand over the balance of China and over all Japan by ideological penetration. The British will be unable in this case to stop the penetration of Communism into her Asiatic possessions.

F. The likelihood of this increases every day the war with Japan continues, both because Russia will soon clarify her implied demands for Manchuria and North China and as the war goes on she spreads more Communism in those countries.

433

II

Despite any qualified promises that have been made Russia will not come into the Japanese war at least until the major fighting is over because:

    1. She is tired.

    2. It is a difficult operation at the end of a six thousand mile single-track railway.

    3. She can take what she wants after we have defeated Japan.

III

If we fight out the war with Japan to the bitter end, we will need put 1,000,000 men to attack the Japanese home islands and possibly 2,000,000 on the Asiatic mainland, as Japan has armies of 3,500,000 men left. And we are likely to have won the war for Russia's benefit just as we have done in Europe.

IV

In all these lights which now shine out from Europe, Russia and Asia, a revolution in policies is needed for America and Britain. Russia, not being at war with Japan, has no direct rights in the settlement of the Japanese war.

Suppose Chiang-Kai-shek, in order to assure the preservation of Manchuria to China and the ascendency of his own government in the organization of China, should make peace upon the terms:

    1. That Japan withdraw from all of China, including Manchuria, and hand the government of China to Chiang Kai-shek.

    2. That the Chinese Government receive all of the Japanese Government railways, ports, mines and factories in Manchuria as reparations.

    3. That Japan be confined in Korea and Formosa. Neither of these peoples are Chinese and China has no particular moral rights in these countries.

V

Suppose America and Britain made peace with Japan upon the terms:

    1. That she be totally disarmed and a disarmament commission be established in the country to see she is kept so. By naval and air fortifications on certain Pacific islands, we can see that the disarmament commission is able to perform.

    2. That we ask no reparations or other concessions from her.

VI

What are the results to the United States and Britain?

    1. America will save 500,000 to 1,000,000 lives and an enormous loss of resources.

2. Another 18 months of war will prostrate the United States to a point where the Americans can spare no aid to recovery of other nations.

3. We gain everything that we can gain by carrying on the war to a finish.

4. It would stop Russian expansion in the Asian and Pacific areas. Japan, in these circumstances, would not be likely to go Communist.

5. Those areas would be kept open to free enterprise.

6. Japan could make economic recovery which is to the advantage of all free nations.

7. If we fight Japan to the bitter end, there will be (as in Germany) no group left who are capable of establishing government and order. We will be confronted with establishing a military government in which China, Russia and France will demand participation with all the dangers that that involves.

8. Under such terms there would be the hope that Japan would return to cooperation with Western Civilization and not agitate for revenge for another century as is likely to be the case otherwise.

Thus, China, Britain, Japan and America would be better off.

VII

The question at once is, would Japan accept these terms? If she has military and economic sense, she would. Nobody knows how she would react. The person to find this out is Chiang Kai-shek who, no doubt, has channels to do it. And if proposals came from China, there would be no case for a charge that she had been abandoned.

NOTES AND SOURCES

★

In this text as before, I have followed a somewhat hazardous middle course in noting sources that provide the raw materials of biography. Since this is designed as a work for the general reader, I have restricted footnotes to primary sources—personal papers, diaries, interviews, and the like. Although this approach creates a certain distortion at times—suggesting a preponderance of oral history in the early chapters, which cover a period already described in a wealth of published works—this seems clearly preferable to padding an already lengthy manuscript.

In the end, a biographical portrait must be convincing on the cumulative force of its own credibility. No number of citations can justify a shallow portrait; by this point, the reader has made up his own mind on that score. Besides, I have tried to provide an extensive listing of both books and articles used in the course of my research.

The bulk of documentation can be found in the Hoover Library's Post-Presidential Papers, especially the Individual Correspondence and Subject Files. There are also collections devoted to Hoover's postpresidential travels, his campaign activities after 1932, his government reorganization work, the Hoover Institution at Stanford, the Boys Clubs and other charities with which he involved himself. I found helpful the Clipping and Reprint Files, as well as a special collection devoted to Hoover misrepresentations. No review of the wilderness years would be complete without the correspondence between Hoover and John Callan O'Laughlin, which is housed in more extensive form at the Library of Congress. Equally invaluable to Hoover scholars is "the Bible," a massive compendium of the man's public statements, off-the-record remarks (including his Bohemian Grove talks), plus a varied assortment of personal correspondence collected by the archivists at West Branch. With regard to the White House years, both the President's Personal and Secretary's File were useful. Selected papers for the pre-Commerce period (1895–1921) shed light on a phase of Hoover's life brought to attention magnificently in the first volume of George Nash's recently published official biography. A selection of documents bearing on the Hoover-Roosevelt relationship made available by the Roosevelt Library is revealing, and there are valuable nuggets in the papers of Frederick Croxton, Hugh Gibson, James H. MacLafferty, Neil MacNeil, Lawrence Richey, Maud Stratton, Walter Trohan and Robert E. Wood. Henry Stimson's diaries are located at the Yale University Library; William Allen White's papers are at the Library of Congress along with those of Calvin Coolidge, Charles McNary, Theodore Roosevelt, Jr., Everett Sanders and Robert A. Taft.

PROLOGUE: OLD MAN IN A HURRY

1. Interview with Joseph Binns, December 2, 1968, Hoover Oral History Project (hereafter referred to as HOHP).

2. Interview with Robert Considine, December 12, 1968, HOHP; Binns interview.

3. Interview with Walter Trohan, November 18, 1966, HOHP.

4. Interview with Van Ness Leavitt Hoover, September 27, 1967, HOHP.

5. Interview with Helen d'Oyle Sioussat, November 2, 1968, HOHP.

6. HH–Dwight D. Eisenhower (hereafter referred to as DDE), December 25, 1961.

7. Binns interview, interview with Lowell Thomas, October 7, 1965; interview with Mrs. H. V. Kaltenborn, February 16, 1968; interview with Alan J. Gould, October 27, 1970, HOHP: HH–Burt Brown Barker, December 10, 1963.

8. Interview with Frank Mason, November 19, 1966; interview with Rose Kennedy, February 1, 1968, HOHP.

9. Interview with Michael J. Le Pore, December 5, 1966, HOHP; Binns interview.

10. Le Pore interview; interview with Frank Caro, December 2, 1968; interview with Mrs. Frank Surface, December 4, 1969, HOHP; Mason interview.

11. Caro interview.

12. Interview with Mary Elizabeth Dempsey, July 13, 1967; interview with George Gould Lincoln, November 29, 1966; interview with Vincent K. Antle, January 1, 1972, HOHP.

13. HH–J. Edgar Hoover, December 10, 1960; interview with Mr. and Mrs. Boris Kosta, October 2, 1966, HOHP.

14. Interview with Irene Kuhn, November 20, 1969, HOHP; Binns interview.

15. Interview with John W. Hill, December 2, 1970; interview with Mr. and Mrs. William I. Nichols, October 5, 1968; interview with Charles Edison, December 6, 1966, HOHP.

16. HH–HST, December 19, 1962.

17. Trohan interview; interview with Katherine Milbank, November 6, 1967; interview with Madeline K. O'Donnell, July 7, 1969; interview with Mark Hatfield, July 22, 1971, HOHP.

18. HH–Richard M. Nixon, January 22, 1961; JFK–HH, March 2, 1961; HH–JFK, January 8, 1962; interview with Nicholas Tierney, April 12, 1967, HOHP.

19. Interview with Andrew McNamara, March 12, 1971, HOHP; HH–George McGovern, April 25, 1961.

20. Interview with Richard Berlin, December 5, 1966, HOHP: Kaltenborn interview.

21. Interview with Adeline Fuller, September 29, 1967; interview with Neil MacNeil, February 25, 1967, HOHP.

22. Nichols interview.

CHAPTER ONE: A DEATH IN NORTHAMPTON

1. C. D. McKean–J. Edgar Hoover, December 19, 1929; Edgar Rickard memo, August 25, 1930; Will Irwin memo, "Report on Smear Books," May 25, 1944.

2. Campbell Hodges diary, November 10, 1930; interview with John K. Stewart, October 2, 1967; interview with Levi T. Pennington, October 18, 1967, HOHP.

3. Interview with Mildred Hall Campbell, September 24, 1966, HOHP.

4. HH–Brand Whitlock, January 28, 1916.

5. Interview with Mrs. Preston Davie, October 5, 1969; interview with Fred Clark, October 29, 1969, HOHP.

6. Interview with Ray Lyman Wilbur, Jr., November 24, 1971, HOHP.

7. HH–Frank J. Hogan, October 2, 1939; interview with Mr. and Mrs. Edward Anthony, July 17, 1970; interview with George Akerson, Jr., March 11, 1967, HOHP.

8. Edgar Rickard diary, October 25, 1932.

9. Interview with James H. Douglas, October 13, 1969, HOHP.

10. Interview with Russell V. Lee, October 9, 1967; interview with J. Clifford Folger, June 3, 1967; interview with Leon Chandler, January 23, 1970, HOHP.

11. Hodges diary, February 6, 1930, October 2, 1931.

12. Interview with Ruby Price Staton, October 13, 1967, HOHP.

13. Interview with Mrs. Helen White, October 27, 1966; interview with Susan Dyer, September 29, 1966, HOHP.

14. Hodges diary, January 15, 1931.

15. Interview with Peter Grimm, November 7, 1967, HOHP; MacNeil interview.

16. Interview with Mark Sullivan, Jr., November 30, 1968, HOHP.

17. Interview with Byron Price, March 21, 1969, HOHP.

18. Hodges diary, March 21, 1932.

19. Agnes Meyer diary, June 6, 1932, p. A-50, Columbia Oral History Collection (hereafter referred to as COHC). COHP; Hodges diary, January 14, 1932.

20. Interview with Lawrence K. Requa, October 4, 1966; interview with Forydice B. St. John, February 29, 1968, HOHP; Hodges diary, July 1, 1930.

21. Interview with Alonzo Fields, July 24, 1970, HOHP.

22. Interview with Sallie McCracken, September 1, 1970, HOHP.

23. Interview with Bradley Nash, July 31, 1968, HOHP.

24. R. L. Wilber, Jr. interview.

25. Herbert Hoover, *American Individualism*, Doubleday, New York, 1923, pp. 10–11.

26. Ibid., pp. 25–26, 66.

27. Herbert Hoover, *The Cabinet and the Presidency, 1920–1933*, MacMillan, New York, 1952, p. 157 (hereafter referred to as Memoirs II).

28. Calvin Coolidge, *Autobiography*, Cosmopolitan, New York, 1929, p. 190; Meyer diary, November 20, 1932.

29. Interview with Robert F. Creighton, January 28, 1979; interview with George Drescher, June 1, 1967, HOHP.

30. Memoirs II, p. 55.

31. HH–Calvin Coolidge, October 12, 1932.

32. Calvin Coolidge–Everett Sanders, November 25, 28, 1932.

33. HH–FDR, June 12, 1923, FDR Library.

34. "My Personal Relations with Mr. Roosevelt," Hoover memo, undated.

35. FDR–C. E. Hustis, September 20, 1928, FDR Library.

36. HH memo of meeting with FDR, November 22, 1932.

37. Fields interview; Hoover told Campbell Hodges in January 1933 that his successor was "too dumb" to understand the intricacies of international finance; Henry Stimson diary, January 3, 1933.

38. Stimson diary, January 5, 1933.

39. Interview with John P. Mitchell, September 14, 1967, HOHP; White interview; interview with Mrs. Edwin Bowman, November 6, 1966, HOHP.

40. HH–Grace Coolidge, January 5, 1933.

41. Hodges diary, January 31, 1933; Stimson diary, January 7, 1933.

42. Interview with Joseph S. Davis, October 11, 1967, HOHP; Stimson diary, January 7, 1933.

43. Hodges diary, March 11, 1930.

44. Stimson diary, January 7, 1933.

45. Hodges diary, January 31, 1933; Grace Coolidge–HH, January 9, 1933; John C. Coolidge to author, August 31, 1983.

CHAPTER TWO: THE PRICE OF SUCCESS

1. Interview with Elton Trueblood, July 12, 1971, HOHP.

2. HH–Mort Wiessinger, August 15, 1957.

3. Herbert Hoover, The Years of Adventure, MacMillan, New York, 1951, p. 7 (hereafter referred to as Memoirs I).

4. Interview with Preston Wolfe, August 18, 1967, HOHP; Chandler interview.

5. Memoirs I, p. 7.

6. Interview with Mary Minthorn Strench, July 12, 1968, HOHP.

7. Interview with Burt Brown Barker, October 17, 1967, HOHP.

8. Interview with Hulda Hoover McLean, September 25, 1967; interview with Norman Vincent Peale, September 16, 1971, HOHP.

9. Barker interview.

10. St. John interview.

11. Interview with Ira S. Lillick, October 2, 1966, HOHP; Mrs. Charles A. McLean–Raymond Henle, August 1, 1966.

12. Interview with Jackson Reynolds, p. 14, COHC. COHP; interview with Thomas A. Campbell, November 30, 1971; interview with Paul R. Leach, March 14, 1969; interview with Helen B. Pryor, November 2, 1971, HOHP.

13. HH–Lloyd Dinkelspiel, August 30, 1957. Admittedly pessimistic about reforming Stanford's architectural tastes, Hoover told the trustees he was writing his criticism to clear his own name "from the avalanche of opprobrium that will be showered down from all Stanford people during the next hundred years"; interview with Raymond Moley, November 13, 1967; interview with H. Dudley Swain, October 15, 1967, HOHP.

14. Memoirs I, p. 24.

15. Ibid., p. 25.

16. HH–Burt Brown Barker, October 5, 1897; "Hoover and His Camel," George J. Bancroft, April 10, 1957; interview with Arthur Curtice, October 8, 1967, HOHP; Memoirs I, pp. 125–126.

17. As Lou herself put it later in a reminiscent sketch entitled "Pioneering," "I was married one day and sailed for China the next"; M. H. Campbell interview.

18. Interview with Victoria F. Allen, October 5, 1967; interview with Marguerite Rickard Hoyt, May 30, 1967,

HOHP; HH–Burt Brown Barker, October 5, 1897.

19. Hoyt interview; Bunny Miller–Mrs. Clarence M. Fisher, September 28, 1958; interview with Dwight C. Wilbur, October 6, 1967, HOHP.

20. Memoirs I, pp. 132–33.

21. Holman interview, p. 46, COHC.

22. Interview with William H. Meserole, March 12, 1969; interview with Hugh A. Moran, January 15, 1970, HOHP.

23. HH–Ben Allen, April 23, 1914; Allen interview.

24. Folger interview.

25. Herbert Hoover, *The American Epic*, Henry Regnery Company, Chicago, 1959, Vol. I, pp. 74–76 (hereafter referred to as AE I).

26. AE I, p. 86.

27. Charles Lucey–Raymond Henle, February 24, 1967; Mason interview.

28. Interview with Milton M. Brown, March 21, 1969, HOHP.

29. HH–Hugh Gibson, June 26, 1916.

30. Memoirs I, p. 202.

31. AE I, pp. 148–53.

32. Interview with Gilchrist B. Stockton, March 13, 1969, HOHP.

33. Holman interview, p. 59; interview with Florence J. Harriman, p. 27, COHC.

34. Interview with Elmore R. Dutro, July 13, 1971; interview with Morris Doyle, January 22, 1970, HOHP.

35. Davis interview; Fuller interview.

36. Memoirs I, pp. 476–79.

37. Memoirs I, pp. 412–13.

38. HH–Burt Brown Barker, October 6, 1919.

39. Interview with Clark Birge, January 19, 1970, HOHP.

40. Interview with Horace Albright, p. 423–24, COHC.

41. Interview with Jameson Parker, November 21, 1969, HOHP.

42. Interview with Bascom Timmons, March 13, 1970; Stockton interview; interview with Edgar E. Robinson, September 15, 1967, HOHP.

43. Interview with Eugene Meyer, p. 452, COHC.

44. Interview with Mrs. Jameson Parker, June 2, 1969, HOHP; R. L. Wilbur, Jr., interview.

45. Interview with HH, pp. 11–12, COHC.

46. Interview with Turner Catledge, September 15, 1969, HOHP.

47. Interview with Clarence Dill, December 13, 1967, HOHP.

48. Memoirs II, pp. 49–51; Pennington interview; interview with Earl C. Behrens, August 1, 1971, HOHP.

49. Interview with Alfred Kirchofer, April 4, 1969, HOHP; Anthony interview.

CHAPTER THREE: "WHAT RIGHT HAVE WE TO BE OF LITTLE FAITH?"

1. FDR–Ward Melville, September 21, 1928; Robinson interview.

2. Davis interview; Lee interview.

3. Interview with Harold C. Train, p. 159, COHC.

4. George Barr Baker–HH, January 18, 1929.

5. Roy Roberts–HH, July 27, 1929.

6. French Strother–Julius Rosenwald, July 9, 1929.

7. Campbell interview; interview with Frederick Bates Butler, October 6, 1967; White interview; Dyer interview; interview with Katurah and Phillips Brooks, September 1, 1970.

8. Interview with Lillian Rogers Parks, February 12, 1971, HOHP; Fields inter-

view; interview with Carrie B. Massenburg, December 1, 1968, HOHP.

9. Interview with Charles F. Adams, July 24, 1970.

10. Interview with Ruth W. Durno, March 4, 1970, HOHP; Fuller interview; White interview.

11. White interview; interview with Ruth F. Lipman, September 26, 1967, HOHP.

12. Interview with Robert T. Wall, April 11, 1967, HOHP; Nash interview; Lewis Strauss–Larry Richey, October 17 and 25, 1932; French Strother–Larry Richey, September 12, 1932; interview with James P. Selvage, February 22, 1967, HOHP.

13. Dill interview.

14. Albright interview, p. 537, COHC.

15. Meyer interview, p. 556, COHP; Sullivan, Jr., interview; "Measures and Actions Taken in the Recession and Depression During the Hoover Administration—1929–33"; interview with Charles W. Halleck, March 6, 1968, HOHP.

16. MacNeil interview.

17. Herbert Hoover, *The Great Depression, 1929–41*, MacMillan, New York, 1951, p. 30 (hereafter referred to as Memoirs III).

18. Interview with Lydia Murray Huneke, October 11, 1967, HOHP; Staton interview; McLean interview.

19. Interview with Franklyn Waltman, November 27, 1967, HOHP.

20. John A. Rapelye–Larry Richey, December 29, 1930.

21. Peale interview; Hodges diary, October 13, 1930; Sullivan interview; interview with Thomas P. Pike, July 11, 1968, HOHP; Reynolds interview, p. 145; Meyer diary, February 13, 1932, p. A-28–29, COHC.

22. Akerson interview; interview with David Lawrence, February 14, 1967, HOHP.

23. Hodges diary, January 15, 1931.

24. Hodges diary, April 8, May 28, May 31, June 27, 1931.

25. Theodore Roosevelt, Jr.–HH, March 6, 1931.

26. Brooks interview; Dyer interview; interview with Dare Stark McMullin, September 11, 1967, HOHP.

27. Interview with Agnes Thompson, November 16, 1966, HOHP; Meyer diary, June 6, 1932, p. A-48, COHC.

28. Memoirs II, pp. 52–53.

29. Hodges diary, June 22, 1931.

30. HH–Simeon Fess, May 9, 1933; Davie interview.

31. Nash interview.

32. Meyer diary, June 6, June 8, 1932, p. A-51, 55, COHC.

33. HH–Theodore Joslin, December 9, 1933.

34. T. Campbell interview.

CHAPTER FOUR: SWAPPING HORSES

1. Meyer diary, August 22, 1932, p. A-80, COHC.

2. Hodges diary, January 18, 1932.

3. Memoirs II, p. 369; Stimson diary, March 9, April 5, 1932.

4. Edgar Rickard diary, July 23, 1932.

5. Mrs. J. Parker interview.

6. Robinson interview.

7. Meyer diary, February 25, 1933, p. A-92, COHC.

8. Hodges diary, July 23, 1932; Brooks interview; interview with DDE, July 13, 1967, HOHP.

9. DDE interview; Hodges diary, July 30, 1932; interview with F. Trubee Davison, September 14, 1969, HOHP.

10. Harold Ickes–Mrs. Walter H. Newton, March 14, 1932.

11. Interview with Robert S. Allen, November 11, 1966, HOHP.

12. Rickard diary, July 23, 1932; Bunny Miller–Henry Lee, October 30, 1961.

13. Interview with Robert Moses, October 29, 1969, HOHP.

14. William Allen White–David Hinshaw, July 9, 1932; Rickard diary, August 11, 1932; Stimson diary, August 11, 1932.

15. Moses interview.

16. Interview with Edward T. Folliard, August 6, 1968; interview with Leslie R. Groves, August 9, 1968, HOHP.

17. Adolph Berle diary, October 6, 1932, FDR Library.

18. David Hinshaw–William Allen White, July 5, 1932; White reply, July 18, 1932.

19. Meyer diary, June 6, 1932, p. A-52, COHC.

20. Stimson diary, September 25, 1932.

21. Stimson diary, October 18, 1932; John R. Gaverich–HH, August 26, 1932; Rickard diary, October 16, 1932; Stimson diary, October 13, 1932.

22. Interview with Albert L. Warren, November 11, 1966, HOHP.

23. Drescher interview.

24. Behrens interview.

25. Drescher interview.

26. Interview with John D. M. Hamilton, February 11, 1967; interview with Mr. and Mrs. Frederick C. Loomis, January 20, 1970, HOHP.

27. William Allen White–David Hinshaw, November 12, 1932.

28. Brooks interview; Rickard diary, November 16, 1932.

29. Rickard diary, November 16, November 26, 1932.

30. Nash interview; Henry M. Snevely–T. G. Joslin, January 16, 1933; Charles B. Driscoll–Larry Richey, November

10, 1932; George H. Lorimer–HH, November 11, 1932; Charles E. Carr–HH, January 13, 1933; Leonard Minthorn–Larry Richey, January 31, 1933; John T. Woodside–HH, December 27, 1932.

31. Rickard diary, November 16, 1932.

32. The story of Hoover's eavesdropping secretary, first published by Professor Frank Friedel in the Watergate summer of 1973, was retold with fresh detail in the April 2, 1982, edition of the Houston Chronicle; Robinson interview; Hodges diary, February 10, 1933.

33. Interview with Edward A. Keller, November 4, 1969, HOHP.

34. Stimson diary, January 21, January 27, 1933.

35. Rickard diary, January 22, 1933.

36. Moley interview.

37. Douglas interview; Reynolds interview, p. 167; Meyer diary, February 25, 1933, p. A-92, COHC.

38. Much of my account of Hoover's final days in office is taken from a diary the president himself kept for the period from February 9 to March 4, 1933, and published as Supplement I in Hoover's public papers for 1932–33.

39. Reynolds interview, pp. 168–69, COHC.

40. Will Irwin–HH, March 3, 1933; Herbert L. Satterlee–HH, February 27, 1933.

41. Butler interview; Brooks interview; Parks interview; Catledge interview.

42. Hodges diary, March 4, 1933: interview with William J. Hopkins, August 8, 1968, HOHP.

43. Warren interview.

44. Colonel Starling recounted the scene at Union Station in his memoirs, Starling of the White House (New York, 1946); Drescher interview; interview with Mrs. John A. Brown, December 6, 1966; interview with Charles W. Fischer, July 31, 1971, HOHP.

CHAPTER FIVE: "THE GOSPEL ACCORDING TO PALO ALTO"

1. Albright interview, p. 402, COHC; Rickard diary, March 5, 1933.

2. HH–Will Irwin, November 18, 1933.

3. Castle to Richey telephone conversation, March 13, 1933; Richey phone conversation with Kyle Palmer, March 14, 1933; Richey phone conversation with Secret Service, March 14, 1933; H. E. Negley–Steve Early, March 11, 1933; Early reply, March 25, 1933, FDR Library.

4. HH–Henry Stimson, March 14, 1933.

5. HH–Samuel Crowther, March 11, 1933; "Ex-President Hoover in New York," reminiscences by John M. Carmody, August 1, 1958, FDR library.

6. "Lou Henry Hoover Home," Post-Presidential Subject File, Hoover Homes.

7. Pryor interview; Jeremiah interview; Milbank interview, December 12, 1966; interview with Louise Stevenson, January 1970, HOHP; Fuller interview.

8. Rickard diary, April 6, April 14, 1933; HH–Cal O'Laughlin, March 25, 1933; Creighton interview, HH–Louis B. Mayer, April 21, 1933.

9. Interview with Hope Brown Gordon, January 12, 1970; interview with Kari Gordon, January 12, 1970, HOHP.

10. J. Milbank interview; Rickard diary, May 22, 1933; HH–Carl Bicknell, April 4, 1933; interview with Marvin M. Meyers, December 23, 1969; interview with Nicholas Roosevelt, October 14, 1967, HOHP.

11. HH–Arch Shaw, July 26, 1933.

12. Joel Boone–HH, April 24, 1933; T. G. Joslin–HH, April 5, 1933; Joslin–HH, June 1, 1933.

13. Elmer Winner–HH, September 12, 1933; HH–Mrs. Frank B. Odell, September 16, November 14, 1933.

14. Interview with Morton Blumenthal, December 8, 1966, HOHP; FDR–HH, September 14, 1933; HH reply, September 15, 1933; HH–FDR, September 8, 1941; Eleanor Roosevelt–HH, January 8, 1944.

15. Hodges diary, April 23, September 16, 1933.

16. Robinson interview; HH–Simeon Fess, July 5, 1933.

17. HH–Mrs. Ruth Pratt, August 22, 1933.

18. HH–Henry Stimson, May 16, 1933.

19. HH–O'Laughlin, March 25, March 29, April 19, 1933; HH–Arthur Hyde, March 31, 1933.

20. Robinson interview; HH–O'Laughlin, May 9, 1933.

21. HH–Ashmun Brown, April 25, 1933; HH–Samuel Crowther, June 19, 1933; HH–O'Laughlin, August 27, 1933.

22. HH–Lewis Strauss, July 31, 1933; HH–Simeon Fess, July 5, 1933.

23. HH–Arch Shaw, July 26, 1933; HH–T. G. Joslin, August 2, 1933; HH–Will Irwin, August 22, 1933.

24. HH–O'Laughlin, May 16, 1933; HH–Ruth Pratt, August 22, 1933.

25. Memoirs III, p. 423–24.

26. HH–Will Irwin, November 18, 1933.

27. Hodges diary, undated.

28. Albright interview, p. 552, COHC.

29. HH–T. G. Joslin, July 3, 1933; HH–Walter H. Newton, June 12, 1933.

30. Patrick J. Hurley–HH, August 25, 1933; HH–Harry Chandler, August 27, 1933; HH–Hurley, August 27, 1933.

31. MacCracken interview; Rickard diary, April 2, 1934; HH–Walter F.

Brown, March 7, 1934; Brown reply, March 12, 1934; HH–O'Laughlin, March 16, 1934; HH–William Castle, May 8, 1934.

32. William Allen White–HH, May 3, 1934.

33. Interview with Perrin C. Galpin, p. 36, COHC; James Farley–FDR, March 21, 1935; Fred Davis–Farley, September 29, 1933; Farley–FDR, October 12, 1933, FDR Library; Howard McLenna–Larry Richey, September 10, 1935.

34. HH–O'Laughlin, December 27, 1933; HH–Will Irwin, February 16, 1934.

35. Memoirs III, p. 415.

36. Rickard diary, April 3, April 5, May 16, December 12, 1934.

37. Interview with Herman Phlegar, March 16, 1970, HOHP; HH–Phlegar, November 9, 1934; HH–Frank J. Hogan, October 25, 1939.

38. HH–Phlegar, November 9, 1934; Selvage interview; HH–Henry Luce, February 19, 1939.

39. HH–Ashmun Brown, March 13, 1934.

40. HH–Arthur Vandenburg, January 9, 1933; HH–Ruth Pratt, December 1, 1933; HH–Will Irwin, December 1, 1933; HH–Patrick J. Hurley, January 4, 1934; HH–Simeon Fess, December 18, 1933.

41. HH–Simeon Fess, December 27, 1933.

42. T.G. Joslin–HH, January 13, 1934.

43. O'Laughlin–HH, September 16, 1933.

44. William Allen White–HH, May 3, 1934.

45. White–HH, May 3, 1934; HH–Arthur Hyde, January 19, January 27, 1934.

46. HH–Simeon Fess, May 9, 1933.

47. HH–Walter F. Brown, October 22, 1933; O'Laughlin–HH, October 9, 1933; HH reply, October 12, 1933.

48. Rickard diary, October 3, 1933; HH–Ashmun Brown, November 16, 1933; HH–Samuel Crowther, December 1, 1933; HH–Simeon Fess, December 9, 1933; HH–Harrison Spangler, December 28, 1933.

49. HH–Ruth Pratt, May 2, 1934.

50. HH–Henry Stimson, July 9, 1934; HH–Will Irwin, December 1, 1933.

51. HH–Ashmun Brown, August 23, 1934; Rickard diary, April 29, June 5, July 9, July 14, 1934.

52. HH–Arthur Hyde, September 17, October 1, 1934; HH–Walter H. Newton, October 24, 1934.

53. HH–Charles G. Dawes, September 1, 1934; HH–Mark Sullivan, September 1, 1934.

54. HH–William Allen White, August 23, 1934; White–HH, August 15, 1934; Elihu Root–HH, January 14, 1935.

55. HH–William Allen White, August 23, 1934; Rickard diary, June 5, April 29, 1934.

56. HH–Lewis Strauss, October 1, 1934; HH–Ashmun Brown, October 17, 1934.

57. HH–T. G. Joslin, December 7, 1934; HH–Walter H. Newton, October 18, 1934; HH–Simeon Fess, November 9, 1934.

58. HH–Ashmun Brown, November 23, November 9, 1934; HH–Arthur Hyde, November 23, 1934.

59. HH–William Allen White, January 12, 1935; "Remarks of Honorable Herbert Hoover, January 19, 1935," passed on to FDR by Jim Farley, August 1, 1935.

60. Hoover "Remarks," op. cit.

CHAPTER SIX: A SWING AROUND THE CIRCLE

1. T. G. Joslin–HH, March 1935.

2. Louis Howe–Missy LeHand, January 29, 1935, FDR Library.

3. Interview with Henry Hicks, October 4, 1967, HOHP; Rickard diary, February 11, 12, 13, 1935.

4. HH–Arthur Hyde, February 25, 1935.

5. Alfred M. Landon–HH, February 22, 1935.

6. David Hinshaw–Harold B. Johnson, December 19, 1935.

7. HH–Landon, February 26, 1935; Landon reply, March 23, 1935; HH–Landon, April 22, 1935.

8. Rickard diary, April 6, 1935; HH–Arthur Hyde, May 3, 1935; HH–R.B. Creager, May 16, 1935.

9. HH–Arthur Hyde, March 19, 1935; HH–Ashmun Brown, April 27, 1935.

10. HH–O'Laughlin, May 20, 1935; Rickard diary, April 15, 1935.

11. Rickard diary, June 9, 1935.

12. Walter H. Newton–HH, June 13, 15, 1935; Lewis Strauss–HH, September 17, 1935; Rickard diary, August 12, 1935.

13. HH–T. G. Joslin, June 21, 1935; HH–William Allen White, June 24, 1935.

14. Rickard diary, September 25, October 10, November 4, December 4, 1935.

15. Harlan Stone–HH, November 19, 1935; HH reply, November 22, 1935.

16. Rickard diary, October 11, 1935; Charles Hilles–Henry P. Fletcher, November 18, 1935; Rickard diary, December 21, 23, 31, 1935.

17. O'Laughlin–HH, December 16, 1935.

18. HH–Harold Ickes, January 10, 1936; Ickes reply, January 15, 1936.

19. HH–Walter Lippmann, January 11, 1936; Lippmann reply, January 16, 1936; Mrs. Stark MacMullin–Lippmann, January 18, 1936.

20. Rickard diary, January 8, 9, 1936; Alan Fox–HH, January 18, 1936; HH–Will Irwin, February 3, 1936; Rickard diary, February 26, 1936.

21. FDR–Emile Hurja, March 19, 1936, FDR Library.

22. HH–T. G. Joslin, February 24, 1936; Joslin reply, March 1, 1936; Rickard diary, February 18, 26, March 11, April 8, 1936; Alan Fox–HH, April 23, 1936.

23. Walter H. Newton–HH, February 17, March 16, 1936; Alan Fox–HH, April 28, 1936.

24. Interview with William S. Knowland, October 4, 1967, HOHP; HH–Lewis Strauss, September 23, 1935; HH–R. B. Creager, February 10, 1936.

25. Rickard diary, March 18, 27, April 18, 1936.

26. HH–Harry Chandler, February 1, 1936; Rickard diary, April 24, 1936; HH–William Allen White, April 14, 1936; HH–Chauncey McCormick, April 22, 1936

27. HH–William Allen White, April 17, 1936; HH–Ashmun Brown, April 22, 1936; HH–Alan Fox, April 22, 1936; Rickard diary, April 18, 1936; transcript of telephone conversation between HH and Chauncey McCormick, April 30, 1936.

28. Chauncey McCormick–HH, May 4, 1936; Rickard diary, May 5, 1936; T.G. Joslin–HH, April 11, 1936; HH reply, April 16, 1936; Lewis Strauss–HH, February 24, 1936; Walter H. Newton–HH, March 19, April 9, 1936.

29. HH–Ogden Reid, May 7, 1936; Rickard diary, May 21, 1936.

30. HH–Ashmun Brown, May 7, 1936.

31. Rickard diary, June 9, 1936; John Hamilton memo, March 9, 1956; Samuel Crowther–Larry Richey, June 3, 1936.

32. O'Laughlin–HH, May 11, 1936; O'Laughlin–Ruth Simms, May 19, 1936.

33. O'Laughlin–Douglas MacArthur, May 23, 1936.

34. HH–T. G. Joslin, June 2, 1936; Alan Fox–HH, June 23, 1936.

35. Edgar Rickard–Westbrook Pegler, June 13, 1936; Jameson Parker interview; Lewis Strauss–New York Times, October 13, 1936; HH–William Allen White, June 27, 1936.

36. HH–Walter Lippmann, June 19, 1936; HH–Walter Brown, June 23, 1936.

37. William Allen White–HH, July 1, 1936; Rickard diary, August 14, October 5, 1936.

38. HH–John Hamilton, June 24, July 14, 1936.

39. Hamilton interview; Hamilton memo, August 13, 1936; HH–Arch Shaw, August 18, 1936.

40. Transcript of telephone conversation between HH and Alfred M. Landon, September 2, 1936.

41. HH–Landon, September 2, 1936.

42. Rickard diary, September 9–17, September 23, 18, 1936.

43. McLean interview.

44. MacNeil interview; J. Milbank interview.

45. Milbank interview; interview with Boys Club officers, August 8, 1968, HOHP.

46. Boys Club officers interview; interview with Albert C. Cole, September 23, 1971; interview with John C. Burns, August 8, 1968, HOHP.

47. McLean interview with Ralph Lutz, September 15, 26, 1967, HOHP; Boys Club officers interview.

48. Interview with William O. Fuller III, July 16, 1968, HOHP; Chandler interview.

49. Interview with John P. Falter, February 28, 1968, HOHP; St. Forydice interview.

50. Interview with Rube Goldberg, October 3, 1968, HOHP; Birge interview; Falter interview.

51. Trohan interview; interview with Henry Hazlett, November 18, 1967, HOHP; Hatfield interview, St. Forydice interview.

52. James T. Williams interview, p. 846, COHC; Stimson diary, November 1, 1937; additional descriptions of the Hoover-Landon meeting can be found in columns by Drew Pearson and Robert S. Allen (October 10, 1936) and by Arthur Krock, New York Times (October 13, 1936).

53. Rickard diary, November 10, 1936; HH–Ogden Mills, November 4, 1936; HH–Will Irwin, November 16, 1936; "Forces in the Campaign," HH memo to Cal O'Laughlin, undated; HH–Norman Beasley, December 26, 1936.

54. HH–O'Laughlin, November 10, 1936; Rickard diary, December 2, 1936; FDR–William C. Bullitt, November 9, 1936; Bullitt reply, December 20, 1936, FDR Library.

CHAPTER SEVEN: STORM CLOUDS

1. HH–Ashmun Brown, December 29, 1937.

2. Rickard diary, January 5, 1937.

3. Hamilton interview; Rickard diary, February 15, 1937; John Bricker–HH, February 24, 1937; HH reply, March 12, 1937; Rickard diary, February 7, 1937.

4. Norman Beasley–HH, February 27, 1937.

5. HH–Harrison Spangler, June 24, 1937.

6. Rickard diary, April 13, 1937; HH–John Hamilton, April 15, 23, 1937; Rickard diary, April 20, 22, 1937.

7. HH–Ashmun Brown, July 2, 1937.

8. Hamilton interview; Rickard diary, April 28, May 2, 1937; John Bricker–HH, June 1, 1937; HH–Harrison Spangler, August 28, 1937; HH–Bricker, June 21, 1937.

9. HH–Bertrand Snell, August 23, 1937.

10. HH–Harrison Spangler, November 25, 1937.

11. HH–Bertrand Snell, August 23, 1937; HH–John Bricker, August 24, 1937; HH–Ashmun Brown, August 28, 1937; HH–Albert and Ruth Simms, September 8, 1937.

12. Alfred M. Landon–John G. Townsend, October 6, 1937.

13. Harrison Spangler–HH, October 8, 1937.

14. HH–Helen Reid, October 25, 1937; the Joslin editorial that caused a final rift between its author and the former president appeared in the *Wilmington Morning News* for August 10, 1937, Hoover's sixty-third birthday; HH–T.G. Joslin, October 13, 1937; Joslin reply, October 14, 1937; M.H. Kepler–HH, October 22, 1937; HH reply, October 29, 1937; HH–Harrison Spangler, November 3, 1937; Rickard diary, November 3, 1937.

15. Stimson diary, November 1, 1937.

16. HH–Harrison Spangler, December 2, 1937; Hamilton interview; undated memo.

17. HH–Dorothy Thompson, January 1, 1938.

18. HH–O'Laughlin, February 8, 1938.

19. Stimson diary, November 1, 1938; Rickard diary, January 7, 1938; Alan Fox–HH, January 17, 1938; HH reply, January 21, 1938.

20. Galpin interview, p. 21, COHC.

21. "Through Europe with Mr. Hoover, February and March, 1938," confidential notes dictated early in April 1938 by Perrin Galpin (hereafter referred to as Galpin report); "Resume of Mr. Hoover's European Trip," Galpin to Suda Bane, September 23, 1938.

22. Galpin report; Edgar Rickard's impressions garnered from talks with HH, dictated April 5, 1938 (hereafter referred to as Rickard memo).

23. Rickard memo; Galpin report.

24. Rickard memo.

25. Galpin report.

26. Interview with Samuel Arentz, October 5, 1966, HOHP; in truth, Hugh Wilson had met Hitler on only one occasion before the Hoover visit. It moved him to describe a "lack of drama in this exceedingly dramatic figure," Wilson–FDR, March 3, 1938, FDR Library; interview with Louis P. Lochner, March 2, 1968, HOHP.

27. Hugh R. Wilson diary, March 8, 1938.

28. Rickard memo.

29. Arentz interview; John E. Fetzer memo of conversation with HH, August 15, 1939; Lochner interview; Hugh R. Wilson–FDR, March 12, 1938.

30. Rickard memo; Galpin report; HH–Hugh R. Wilson, March 20, 1938.

31. Galpin report.

32. Galpin report; Rickard memo; Wilson diary, March 9, 1938; Arentz interview.

33. Galpin report; Rickard memo; Arentz interview.

34. Galpin report.

35. Rickard memo; Clark interview.

36. Galpin report; Fetzer memo; Rickard memo.

37. Rickard memo; Galpin report.

38. Interview with Clare M. Torrey, December 9, 1966, HOHP.

39. HH–Ashmun Brown, August 16, 1939; HH–O'Laughlin, August 16, 1939; interview with William B. Coberly, September 21, 1969, HOHP; HH–Dr. James R. Angell, March 11, 1939; HH–David Sarnoff, July 30, 1939.

40. Moley interview.

41. HH–Ashmun Brown, July 28, 1938.

42. Will Irwin's article appeared in *Liberty* magazine for July 16, 1938; HH–John Hamilton, July 26, 1938.

43. Interview with John Z. Anderson, January 19, 1970; interview with George N. Keyston, July 18, 1968, HOHP; Rickard diary, October 27, 1938; HH–William R. Castle, July 14, 1938.

44. Rickard diary, November 23, 1938.

45. Walter S. Hallinan–HH, December 1, 1938; HH reply, December 2, 1938; William R. Castle–HH, November 10, 1938; HH–Will Irwin, November 16, 1938.

46. O'Laughlin–HH, December 28, 1938.

47. Lutz interview; Harry Chandler–HH, February 7, 1939; HH reply, February 11, 1939; Edgar Rickard–Larry Richey, February 9, 1939.

48. Interview with Bonner Fellers, June 23, 1967, HOHP.

49. Rickard diary, June 5, 1939; Edward G. Robinson–HH, November 16, 1938; James B. Conant–HH, January 23, 1939; HH reply, January 24, 1939; Conant–HH, February 6, 1939; HH reply, February 8, 1939; Conant–HH, February 18, 1939; HH reply, February 19, 1939; Conant–HH, February 20, 1939; HH reply, February 22, 1939; Lewis Strauss–HH, March 15, 1939; HH–Conant, April 21, 1939.

50. HH–Lewis Strauss, March 25, 1939.

51. HH–O'Laughlin, April 14, 1939; HH–William R. Castle, April 10, 1939; HH–Ashmun Brown, April 3, 1939.

52. HH–Lewis Strauss, April 9, 1938; Rickard diary, January 18, May 3, 4, 1939; Harrison Spangler–HH, April 17, 1939.

53. HH–Harrison Spangler, April 19, 1939; John Hamilton–HH, April 17, 1939; HH–Robert A. Taft, February 13, 1939.

54. Rickard diary, March 10, May 24, July 18, 1939; interview with Sinclair Weeks, July 16, 1970, HOHP.

55. HH–Boake Carter, August 2, 1939; O'Laughlin–HH, August 8, 1939; Alan Fox–HH, September 6, 1939.

56. Fox–HH, September 6, 1939.

57. HH memo of conversation with Joseph P. Kennedy, May 15, 1945; Kennedy to Cordell Hull, July 20, 1939, FDR Library.

58. HH memo, May 15, 1945.

59. Joseph P. Kennedy–Cordell Hull, August 25, 26, 28, 29, 1939, FDR Library.

60. HH–O'Laughlin, August 28, 1939.

61. Ibid.

CHAPTER EIGHT: THE PEACEMONGER

1. Rickard diary, September 11, 1939.

2. Hoover memos, September 11, 18, 1939.

3. Rickard diary, September 14, 1939; HH–Norman Davis, September 15, 1939; Rickard diary, September 16, 18, 1939.

4. HH–Norman Davis, September 20, 1939; Rickard diary, September 19, 1939.

5. Norman Davis–HH, September 22, 1939.

6. HH–Norman Davis, September 24, 1939; Eleanor Roosevelt–Martha

Gellhorn, September 27, 1939, FDR Library.

7. Rickard diary, October 6, December 16, 1939.

8. FDR's comment about bringing prominent Republicans into his administration is contained in Harold Ickes's diary; E. M. Watson–Franklin D. Roosevelt, September 15, 1939; Rickard diary, September 19, 1939; undated memo, Marie Maloney–Franklin D. Roosevelt, FDR Library.

9. Ickes diary, September 23, 1939.

10. Rickard diary, October 7, 26, 1939.

11. HH memo, undated (Norman Davis File); AE IV, pp. 1–7.

12. "Finnish Relief Fund," undated HH memo.

13. Transcript of telephone conversation between HH and Norman Davis, December 19, 1939.

14. Rickard diary, December 22, 1939, January 11, 1940; Selvage interview.

15. Selvage interview; M. M. Brown interview.

16. Considine interview.

17. Transcript of telephone conversation between HH and Norman Davis, January 8, 1940; Rickard diary, February 29, 1940.

18. Transcript of telephone conversation between HH and Norman Davis, March 22, 1940.

19. AE IV, pp. 17–21.

20. Interview with Payson J. Treat, September 19, 1967, HOHP.

21. Rickard diary, March 1, 10, April 17, 27, May 20, 1939; Boake Carter–HH, February 24, 1940.

22. HH–Walter H. Newton, March 1, April 18, 1940.

23. Delegate tally sheet, 1940 campaign folder; Rickard diary, April 15, 1940; Wendell Willkie–Frank Putnam, April 8, 1940.

24. Rickard diary, April 27, 30, May 16, 1940; O'Laughlin memos, April 28, 29, 1940; HH–Helen Reid, May 2, 1940; Reid reply, May 3, 1940.

25. Walter H. Newton–HH, May 1, 1940; HH reply, May 11, 1940; Harrison Spangler–Larry Richey, May 27, 1940; HH–Spangler, May 30, 1940; Rickard diary, June 4, 1940.

26. Rickard diary, June 12, 13, 1940; O'Laughlin–HH, May 11, June 8, 1940; Robert A. Taft–HH, May 31, 1940; HH reply, June 3, 1940; Mark Sullivan–HH, May 2, 1940; HH reply, May 3, 1940; Rickard diary, May 25, 1940.

27. Rickard diary, June 18, 1940; HH–R.B. Creager, June 11, 1940; Hamilton interview; Walter H. Newton–HH, June 14, 1940; Carlyle S. Littleton–HH, June 21, 1940.

28. HH–Arch Shaw, June 5, 1940; interview with Thomas E. Dewey, November 29, 1940, HOHP; Selvage interview; Allan Hoover–Thomas T. Thalken, March 23, 1978; Andrew Galagan–HH, July 24, 1947; affidavit of Dorothy Emerson, July 3, 1947.

29. Helen Reid–HH, June 16, 1940.

30. Rickard diary, June 25, 1940; memo of HH telephone conversation with Thomas E. Dewey, June 27, 1940; Dewey interview; Herbert W. Clark–HH, July 15, 1940.

31. Alan Fox–HH, August 6, 1940; Hamilton interview; Jameson Parker interview; HH–Wendell Willkie, June 27, 1940.

32. HH–Alan Fox, June 28, 1940.

33. Rickard diary, June 29, 1940; Walter H. Newton–HH, July 1, 1940; George Sokolsky–HH, July 26, 1940.

34. HH–George Sokolsky, August 5, 1940; HH–William R. Castle, July 11, 1940; HH–Walter H. Newton, August 5, 1940.

35. George Sokolsky–HH, August 24, 1940; Bernice Miller–HH, July 11, 1940; William R. Castle–HH, August 11, 1940.

36. Rickard diary, August 12, 1940; HH–Walter H. Newton, August 26, 1940.

37. HH–Wendell Willkie, September 11, 1940; HH–O'Laughlin, October 4, 1940.

38. William R. Castle–HH, July 11, 1940; Rickard diary, September 12, 15, 20, 21, 28, 1940; Wendell Willkie–HH, September 29, 1940; HH–Paul Smith, October 19, 1940.

39. Paul Smith–HH, October 11, 1940; HH–Arthur Sulzberger, September 1, 1940; William R. Castle–HH, September 4, 1940; Harriman interview, p. 27, COHC; Rickard diary, October 11, 1940; Alexander Woollcott–Mark O. Prentiss, September 20, 1940; Prentiss reply, September 27, 1940; HH–Prentiss, October 3, 1940; Russell Davenport–Dudley White, September 20, 1940; O'Laughlin–HH, September 27, 1940.

40. Wendell Willkie–HH, October 26, 1940; Mark Sullivan–HH, October 26, 1940.

41. Wendell Willkie–HH, November 3, 14, 1940.

42. HH memo, November 8, 1940.

43. HH memo on conversation with Willkie, November 16, 1940; William Allen White–HH, December 3, 1940.

44. HH memo, November 16, 1940; HH–Mark Sullivan, November 9, 1940.

45. Ickes diary, December 1, 1940; FDR–Thomas W. Lamont, November 29, 1940, FDR Library.

46. Rickard diary, September 25, December 4, 1940.

47. Nichols interview.

48. Interview with Ellen Brumback, June 5, 1967, HOHP; Surface interview; interview with Scott Turner, October 8, 1968; interview with Robert C. Tyson, June 12, 1970; interview with Daniel Rodriguez, February 10, 1971, HOHP.

49. Nichols interview; interview with Naomi Yeager, January 28, 1970, HOHP; K. Milbank interview; Rodriguez interview; Dempsey interview.

50. Thomas interview; Brumback interview; Anthony interview.

51. Dempsey interview; Gould interview; Curtice interview; interview with George K. Funston, November 5, 1969, HOHP.

52. Huneke interview; interview with Solomon C. Hollister, October 26, 1967; interview with John A. Chapman, October 7, 1968, HOHP; Bunny Miller–Lewis Strauss, July 17, 1936; interview with Marie Louise Pratt, January 24, 1970, HOHP; Brumback interview; Dempsey interview; Gould interview.

53. Mason interview; Dempsey interview; Rickard diary, January 27, February 26, March 14, April 17, 1941; HH memo of conversation with Joseph P. Kennedy, November 22, 1940.

54. Robert Wood–HH, January 11, 1941; HH reply, January 14, 1941; Dewey interview; HH–Walter H. Newton, January 25, 1941.

55. HH–William R. Castle, March 1, 1941.

56. HH memo of conversation with Lord Halifax, February 4, 1941.

57. HH memo of conversation with Cordell Hull, February 28, 1941; memo by Elizabeth Gray Vining, April 25, 1957.

58. HH–Cordell Hull, March 27, 1941.

59. HH–Walter Lippmann, April 6, 1941.

60. Cordell Hull–HH, April 11, 1941; HH–O'Laughlin, April 7, 1941.

61. HH–O'Laughlin, April 13, 1941.

62. HH–Cordell Hull, April 24, 1941; Rickard diary, April 30, 1941.

63. HH–Charles G. Dawes, May 1, 1941; HH–Walter H. Newton, May 20,

1941; Cordell Hull–HH, May 10, 1941; HH reply, June 3, 1941; Hull–HH, June 28, 1941.

64. Sumner Welles–Franklin D. Roosevelt, June 24, 1941; Roosevelt reply, June 25, 1941, FDR Library.

65. Chandler interview.

66. Fellers interview.

67. HH–Alfred M. Landon, July 1, 1941; Rickard diary, June 30, 1941; HH–Landon, June 27, 30, 1941; HH–Joseph P. Kennedy, July 1, 1941; Kennedy reply, July 11, 1941.

68. HH–Robert A. Taft, July 14, 1941; HH–Boake Carter, July 14, 1941; HH–William R. Castle, July 23, 1941.

69. Robert E. Wood–HH, August 21, 1941.

70. HH–O'Laughlin, August 3, September 6, 1941.

71. HH–William R. Castle, September 4, 1941; HH–O'Laughlin, August 23, 1941; HH–Harrison Spangler, September 17, 1941; HH–Joseph Martin, November 18, 1941.

72. HH–Norman Chandler, October 18, 1941.

73. HH–Arthur Vandenburg, October 29, 1941; HH–O'Laughlin, October 19, 1941; Rickard diary, November 8, 1941.

74. Norman Thomas–HH, November 8, 1941.

75. HH–Alfred M. Landon, November 1, 1941; HH–Charles G. Dawes, November 3, 1941; HH–Robert E. Wood, November 12, 1941.

76. Coberly interview; MacLean interview.

77. HH diary of events preceding the attack on Pearl Harbor, October 31, 1941.

78. O'Laughlin–HH, November 15, 1941; HH diary, November 23, 1941.

79. HH diary, November 25, 29, 1941; Payson J. Treat memo, August 10, 1942.

80. HH memo, February 10, 1942.

81. Ibid.

82. Hamilton interview.

83. HH–Robert A. Taft, December 8, 1941.

84. HH–Boake Carter, December 11, 1941; HH–William R. Castle, December 8, 1941; HH–R. Douglas Stuart, Jr., December 18, 1941.

CHAPTER NINE: "FOUR YEARS OF FRUSTRATION"

1. HH–Boake Carter, January 23, 1942.

2. HH–Ruth Simms, December 18, 1941; interview with Walter Livingston, November 13, 1969, HOHP.

3. Interview with Eugene Lyons, October 4, 1968; interview with Arthur Kemp, July 13, 1968, HOHP; Adams interview; Rickard diary, February 22, April 26, June 9, 30, 1942; January 16, 1943.

4. Fields interview; Robert Patterson–FDR, February 20, 1943; FDR–E. M. Watson, March 8, 1943; John McCormick–Marvin McIntyre, March 1, 1943; FDR–Herbert Lehman, March 8, 1943; Lehman–McIntyre, March 16,

1943; Dr. Julian Granbaurth–FDR, August 9, 1943, FDR Library.

5. Interview with John J. McCloy, December 2, 1970; interview with Albert Wedemeyer, November 1966, HOHP.

6. Nicholas Murray Butler–FDR, June 19, 1943, FDR Library; Rickard diary, May 4, 1943.

7. HH–Boake Carter, January 17, 1942; HH–Helen Reid, January 29, 1942; Reid reply, February 12, 1942; HH–Reid, February 14, 1942.

8. St. Joseph Farm Bureau–FDR, January 19, 1942; Joseph McNaughton–Roosevelt, January 27, 1942, FDR Library.

9. HH–O'Laughlin, February 24, 1942.

10. Rickard diary, February 22, 1942; MacNeil interview; Lyons interview.

11. Kemp interview.

12. Hill interview; Fellers interview.

13. Interview with Felix Morley, June 20, 1967, HOHP; Rickard diary, January 30, May 2, 1942.

14. HH–Westbrook Pegler, June 15, 1942; George R. Brett, Jr.–FDR, June 15, 1942; Roosevelt reply, June 16, 1942; Brett–FDR, June 18, 1942.

15. HH–Helen Reid, March 10, 1942.

16. HH–Alfred M. Landon, March 19, May 29, June 2, 1942; HH–Harlan F. Stone, June 7, 1942; Robert A. Taft–HH, July 14, 1942; Edith Wilson–HH, June 30, 1942; Norman Thomas–HH, June 30, 1943.

17. HH–Norman Thomas, November 4, 1942.

18. HH–Lewis Strauss, July 11, 1942; Rickard diary, June 3, 21, July 23, 1942; HH–Hugh Gibson, August 20, 1942; HH–George Sokolsky, August 21, 1942; Sioussat interview; Payson Treat memo of conversation with Hoover, August 10, 1942; Stewart interview.

19. HH–M. M. Meyers, September 14, 1942; HH–Sokolsky, August 21, 1942; HH–Joseph Martin, November 6, 1942; Harold M. Fleming, notes of conversation with HH, November 18, 1942.

20. Rickard diary, November 5, 1942.

21. Ibid., November 23, 1942.

22. HH–Herbert Lehman, November 25, 1942.

23. HH memo on conversation with Lehman, December 3, 1942; Harold M. Fleming notes on conversation with HH, December 15, 1942.

24. HH memo on lunch with Lord Halifax, January 8, 1943; Rickard diary, January 9, 1943.

25. HH–Arthur Vandenburg, February 1, 1943.

26. HH–O'Laughlin, February 21, 1943; Rickard diary, June 22, 1943.

27. HH–George Sokolsky, May 12, 1942.

28. Rickard diary, March 29, 1943; HH–O'Laughlin, January 20, 24, 1943; HH memo of conversation with Bonner Fellers, February 28, 1943.

29. HH memo re Fellers, February 28, 1943; HH memo of conversation with Patrick J. Hurley, February 28, 1943.

30. Harold M. Fleming memo of conversation with HH, March 23, 1943; Lord Halifax–HH, March 12, 1943; HH reply, March 20, 1943; Harold Fleming memo of conversation with HH, June 17, 1943.

31. HH memo "Reorganization of the War Administration," September 12, 1942.

32. Rickard diary, December 7, 11, 14, 1942; Alfred M. Landon–HH, December 11, 1942; HH–O'Laughlin, January 3, 1943.

33. HH–Joseph Martin, January 18, 19, 1943; HH–Arthur Vandenburg, February 1, 1943.

34. Rickard diary, February 9, March 29, April 13, 24, May 27, 1943; Requa interview; interview with Alan Probert, September 22, 1966, HOHP.

35. Rickard diary, August 24, 1943; HH–John Bricker, August 30, 1943.

36. HH–Bricker, August 30, 1943; HH–Michael Shannon, August 3, 1943; HH–Thomas E. Dewey, October 26, 1943; HH–James H. Selvage, August 17, 1943; HH–Alfred M. Landon, September 20, 1943.

37. HH–Robert A. Taft, September 25, 1943; Rickard diary, September 8, 1943; HH–J. Reuben Clark, October 6, 1943.

38. Rickard Diary, November 2, 1943; HH–Alfred M. Landon, November 2, 1943; Rickard diary, November 12, 1943.

39. HH–Harrison Spangler, November 16, 1943; HH–John Bricker, October 2, 1943; Rickard diary, November 23, 1943; HH–Alfred M. Landon, June 5, 1943; Landon reply, June 8, 1943.

40. Alfred M. Landon–HH, July 19, 1943; HH–Lewis Strauss, December 13, 1943.

41. Campbell interview; Dare Stark McMullen tribute to Lou Hoover for Girl Scout Wild Life Sanctuary, 1944.

42. McMullen tribute; McMullen article "Lou Henry Hoover," Girl Scout Book of Memories; Catledge interview; McLean interview; Bowman interview.

43. McMullen article; Lou Hoover–Agnes Thompson, December 19, 1943.

44. Bowman interview; Blumenthal interview; Hoyt interview; Rickard diary, January 7, 1944.

45. Hoyt interview; Franklin D. Roosevelt–HH, January 7, 1944; HH reply, January 28, 1944.

46. Mrs. G. L. Bauer–Sue Dyer, January 11, 1944.

47. Confidential source.

48. Rickard diary, February 7, 1944; HH–Duchess of Windsor, March 6, 1944; HH–Alfred M. Landon, March 7, 1944.

49. "The Forthcoming Willkie Blitz," undated Hoover memo; HH–John Bricker, February 12, 1944.

50. HH memo on conversation with Thomas E. Dewey, March 29, 1944.

51. Rickard diary, April 5, 1944; HH–Eugene Lyons, April 8, 1944; HH–Emory Glander, April 12, 1944; Rickard diary, April 18, 1944; HH–Cordell Hull, April 3, 1944; Hull reply, April 8, 1944.

52. HH–George Sokolsky, February 15, 1944; HH–Douglas MacArthur, April 26, 1944; Rickard diary, May 1, 1944.

53. Rickard diary, May 29, 1944; HH–Thomas E. Dewey, May 1, 1944.

54. John Hamilton memo, March 9, 1956; Rickard diary, June 9, 11, 1944; HH memo of conversation with John Bricker, June 4, 1944; Rickard diary, June 27, 1944; Hugh Gibson–HH, undated.

55. Rickard diary, June 28, 1944; Thomas interview; Mason interview; HH–John Hamilton, July 12, 1944; HH–John Bricker, July 7, 1944.

56. Rickard diary, September 13, 1944; Otto Schuler–HH, August 11, 1944; HH reply, August 16, 1944.

57. Interview with Gire Gin Wah, July 17, 1971, HOHP; HH–George Sokolsky, August 14, 1944.

58. HH–Boake Carter, August 15, 1944; Hugh Gibson–HH, August 24, 1944; Rickard diary, October 10, 1944; Hamilton interview.

59. HH–Alfred M. Landon, October 13, 1944; Rickard diary, October 19, 30, 1944; HH–Landon, October 23, 1944.

60. HH memo on Arthur Krock dinner, November 7, 1944; Rickard diary, November 7, 1944; HH–Thomas E. Dewey, November 8, 1944; HH–Alfred M. Landon, November 14, 1944; Rickard diary, November 8, 1944.

61. Rickard diary, December 5, 7, 13, 1944, January 12, 18, 22, 1945.

62. Morley interview; HH–Alfred M. Landon, February 18, 1945.

63. HH–Landon, February 18, 1945; O'Laughlin–HH, March 3, 1945; HH–Arch Shaw, March 19, 1945.

64. O'Laughlin–HH, April 9, 1945; HH–Eleanor Roosevelt, April 12, 1945; Roosevelt reply, April 18, 1945.

65. Interview with Walter Hoving, October 18, 1969, HOHP; HH–Harry S. Truman, April 12, 1945; Rickard diary, April 14, 1945; O'Laughlin–HH, April 13, 1945.

CHAPTER TEN: THE ODDEST COUPLE

1. HH–Harry S. Truman (hereafter referred to as HST), April 12, 1945.

2. HST–HH, May 24, 1945.

3. John Hamilton memo, June 8, 1960; HH–O'Laughlin, December 27, 1945.

4. Fields interview.

5. Curtice interview.

6. MacNeil interview.

7. Westbrook Pegler–HH, August 2, 1945; HH reply, August 6, 1945; Rickard diary, May 15, 1945; HH memo of conversation with Joseph P. Kennedy, May 15, 1945.

8. Nichols interview; HH–Charles Beard, December 28, 1945; Rickard diary, December 26, 1945.

9. HH–May Shockley, April 24, 1945; Rickard diary, April 14, 20, 1945; HH–Lewis Strauss, April 24, 1945.

10. HH memo on conversation with Henry Stimson, undated; Stimson diary, May 2, 1945.

11. HH memo re Stimson; Rickard diary, May 8, 13, 1945; Stimson diary, May 4, 1945; interview with H. Alexander Smith, p. 92–93, COHC.

12. Rickard diary, May 8, 1945; Stimson diary, May 12, 1945; McCloy interview.

13. Stimson diary, May 16, 1945; HH–Douglas MacArthur, December 1, 1960. Hoover had obtained information through Cal O'Laughlin, including a radio discussion with Japanese officials suggesting a willingness on the part of the new ministry in Tokyo to settle on terms similar to those ultimately ratified; HH memo "America's Position III," May 15, 1945.

14. HH memo re "Position III."

15. Stimson diary, May 23, 1945; HH memo on conversation with John J. McCloy, May 23, 1945.

16. HST–HH, May 24, 1945; Rickard diary, May 14, 24, 27, 1945.

17. HH memo on conversation with HST, May 28, 1945.

18. Fellers interview.

19. HH–HST, May 30, 1945; HH memo, May 28, Rickard diary, May 30, 1945.

20. HST–HH, June 1, 1945; O'Laughlin–HH, June 2, 1945; Perrin Galpin–Bunny Miller, June 8, 1945.

21. HH–John Hamilton, May 20, 1945; HH memo, May 21, 1945; Rickard diary, December 26, 1945.

22. Hazlett interview; Kemp interview; Rickard diary, July 27, 1945; Payson Treat memo, August 2, 1948.

23. "Informal Remarks at Bohemian Grove," August 4, 1945.

24. HH memo, "The Outstanding Effects of Potsdam, "August 8, 1945; Payson Treat memo, August 21, 1945.

25. HH–HST, August 22, 1945; HST reply, August 24, 1945; HH–Robert A. Taft, September 1, 1945; Rickard diary, August 10, 14, 1945.

26. HH–Bonner Fellers, October 15, 1945; Albert Einstein–HH, December 7, 1945.

27. HH–O'Laughlin, December 31, 1945.

28. Rickard diary, January 4, 1946.

29. Maurice Pate diary of 1946 journey (hereafter referred to as Pate diary), March 23, April 9, May 1, 6, 1946.

30. AE IV, pp. 113–15.

31. Interview with Harry Vaughn, June 4, 1969, HOHP; Hugh Gibson diary of 1946 journey (hereafter referred to as Gibson diary), March 3, 1946; Rickard diary, March 7, 13, 1946; HH memo on World Food Emergency, March 11, 1946; AE IV, p. 117.

32. Interview with Dennis A. Fitz-Gerald, March 14, 1969, HOHP;

Mason interview; Grimm interview; Pate diary, March 29, 1946.

33. Pate diary, April 11, 1946; Lochner interview; HH diary of 1946 journey (hereafter referred to as HH diary—1946), April 11–13, 1946; Thomas interview; Pate diary, April 13, 1946; Rickard diary, January 29, 1946; HH memo, April 14–15, 1946.

34. Interview with Mark Clark, March 23, 1968, HOHP; HH diary—1946, March 26, April 4–6; Pate diary, April 5, 1946; HH diary—1946, March 28; Pate diary, April 22–25, 1946.

35. HH diary—1946, undated.

36. HH diary, undated entry on Rome portion of journey.

37. Ibid.; Berlin interview.

38. AE IV, p. 144; FitzGerald interview; Pate diary, April 1, 3, 17, 20, 21, 22, 1946.

39. AE IV, p. 173; HH diary—1946, April 18–20; HH–HST, April 21, 1946; HH diary—1946, April 22–26; Mason interview.

40. Pate diary, April 27, May 5, 1946; HH memos on MacArthur and Japanese occupation, undated.

41. FitzGerald interview; Pate diary, May 8, 1946; Vaughn interview; HH memo on conversation with HST, May 16, 1946.

42. HH diary—1946, on Mexico, undated; on Venezuela, June 17, 1946; on Argentina, June 6–10, 1946; HH diary —1946, May 31–June 1; on Cuba, June 18, 1946.

43. HH diary—1946, June 6–10.

44. Ibid.; Pate diary, June 8, 1946; memo by Julius Klein on Hoover-Peron lunch, June 10, 1946; HH diary—1946, June 20; Curtice interview.

45. AE IV, pp. 218–19; HST–HH, November 29, 1946.

46. O'Laughlin–HH, July 13, 1946; HH–Douglas MacArthur, October 17, 1946.

47. Douglas MacArthur–HH, October 31, 1946; Funston interview; John Hamilton memo, June 8, 1960; HH–Richard M. Nixon, November 9, 1956.

48. Rickard diary, January 20, 1947; HST–HH, January 18, 1947; HH reply, January 19, 1947; HH memo, January 22, 1947; HH memo on State Department, undated; O'Laughlin memo, January 22, 1947.

49. Interview with Lucius Clay, October 9, 1968, HOHP; HH memo, February 20, 1947.

50. Rickard diary, February 23, 1947; Eleanor Roosevelt–HH, February 26, 1947.

51. HH–HST, March 18, 1947; AE IV, p. 230–43.

52. HH–Robert Patterson, May 7, 1947.

53. HH–John Taber, May 25, 1947; HH–O'Laughlin, June 16, June 23, 1947; HH–Styles Bridges, June 15, 1947.

54. Robert A. Taft, July 11, 1947; HH reply, June 24, 1947.

55. HH–Taft, June 24, 1947; Rickard diary, May 22, 1947.

56. Strauss interview; Rickard diary, July 19–August 2, 1947; Kaltenborn interview; Pratt interview.

57. Bess Truman–HH, March 22, 1949; Vaughn interview.

58. HH Gridiron Club speech, May 10, 1947; HH program, May 10, 1947.

59. Rickard diary, March 1, 2, 1947.

60. O'Laughlin–HH, July 19, 1947.

61. HH–O'Laughlin, July 23, 1947; HH–Christian Herter, October 30, 1947.

62. HH–Herter, October 30, 1947.

63. Arthur Vandenburg–HH, December 20, 1947; HH reply, December 24,

1947; HH–Vandenburg, January 18, 1947.

64. HH–Vandenburg, January 18, 1947; HH memo on Marshall Plan, February 18, 1948; Rickard diary, February 9, 1948.

65. HH–Joseph Martin, March 24, 1948.

CHAPTER ELEVEN: "COUNSELOR TO THE REPUBLIC"

1. Joseph P. Kennedy–HH, July 26, 1949.

2. HST–HH, October 11, 1949.

3. Fellers interview; HH–Thomas E. Dewey, July 7, 1948; Dewey reply, July 8, 1948.

4. George Sokolsky–HH, July 27, 1948; HH–Hugh Gibson, August 12, 1948; Rickard diary, October 13, November 1, 1948.

5. Rickard diary, September 21, 1948.

6. Interview with Theodore G. Klumpp, December 2, 1969; interview with Don K. Price, July 20, 1970, HOHP.

7. Hollister interview; Rickard diary, September 7, 1948; interview with Carter Manasco, June 12, 1971, HOHP.

8. Price interview.

9. Thomas Curran note to Thomas E. Dewey, October 30, 1948, Dewey File.

10. John Hamilton memo, March 9, 1956.

11. HH memo on 1948 election, November 17, 1948; Hoover's assessment of the upset was conveyed to Ruth Hurley, wife of his old Secretary of War, who had lost a Senate contest in New Mexico. He didn't have the heart to write his friend directly, said Hoover, about an election that was "thrown away. A good overall campaign would have enabled Pat to win," HH–Ruth Hurley, December 9, 1948.

12. Rickard diary, October 8, November 2, 1948.

13. Price interview.

14. HH–HST, June 21, 1949; HST reply, June 25, 1949.

15. Rickard diary, February 10, April 22, 1949.

16. HH–Thomas E. Dewey, July 6, 1949.

17. MacNeil interview; HH–Eugene Lyons, May 1, 1948; Nash interview; Rickard diary, December 9, 1949; HH–George Sokolsky, July 11, 1949.

18. HH–Douglas MacArthur, October 19, 1949.

19. Rickard diary, April 9, 1950; HH–Edwin P. Shattuck, November 28, 1949.

20. Sullivan interview; Kemp interview.

21. Hoover's correspondence with children can be found in his 1962 book On Growing Up, published by William Morrow Company, New York; Stewart interview.

22. Interview with J. E. Wallace Sterling, July 28, 1971, HOHP.

23. Richard M. Nixon–HH, January 19, 1950; HH reply, January 22, 1950; Nixon–HH, January 30, 1950.

24. HH–William Knowland, December 31, 1949, January 20, 1950.

25. HH–Edwin Friendly, February 10, 1950.

26. HH–HST, April 28, 1950.

27. HH, confidential memo to Kenneth Wherry, May 6, 1950.

28. Rickard diary, April 1, 1950.

29. HH–Alfred M. Landon, June 18, 1950; HH–HST, July 1, 1950; HST reply, July 3, 1950; Lee interview.

30. Off-the-record Bohemian Grove speech, July 30, 1950.

31. HH–J. Edgar Hoover, November 27, 1950; HH–Robert A. Taft, Novem-

ber 8, 1950; Taft reply, November 21, 1950; HH–HST, November 2, 1950; HST reply, November 8, 1950.

32. HST–HH, November 25, 1950; HH reply, November 26, 1950; HST–HH, December 7, 1950.

33. Alfred M. Landon–HH, December 26, 1950; Richard M. Nixon–HH, December 22, 1950; HH reply, December 29, 1950.

34. Off-the-record remarks to Republican Dinner, Washington, D.C., March 13, 1951; Fellers interview.

35. HH remarks to Dutch Treat Club, December 18, 1951; HH confidential memo on the Essentials of Bipartisan Foreign Policy, July 7, 1951; HH–Bonner Fellers, December 3, 1950.

36. HH–Theodore Hoover, April 3, 1951.

37. Fellers interview.

38. Fellers interview; HH–Courtney Whitney, April 23, 1951; Berlin interview.

39. Berlin interview; HH–Bonner Fellers, April 13, 1951; HH–Douglas MacArthur, April 15, 1951.

40. Hamilton interview.

41. HH–George Sokolsky, November 29, 1951.

42. Hamilton interview; HH–Arthur Krock, April 4, 1952; Hoover talk before the Gridiron Club, Washington, D.C., May 10, 1952.

43. Blumenthal interview; HH–Henry Cabot Lodge, June 26, 1952.

44. Henry Cabot Lodge–HH, June 26, 1952; HH reply, June 29, 1952; Lodge–HH, July 1, 1952.

45. HH–Guy Gabrielson, July 3, 1952; Wedemeyer interview; Fellers interview; HH–Robert A. Taft, July 5, 1952.

46. Interview with Edward F. Mansure, October 12, 1967, HOHP.

47. HH–Robert A. Taft, July 11, 1952; HH–George Sokolsky, July 30, August 18, 1952.

48. DDE–HH, July 29, August 4, 1952; Richard M. Nixon–HH, September 25, 1952.

49. Sioussant interview; Fellers interview; HH–DDE, October 8, 1952.

50. HH–DDE, October 21, 1952; HH–Richard M. Nixon, October 25, 1952; Weeks interview.

51. DDE–HH, November 12, 1952; HH–Joseph Pew, November 10, 1952.

52. Edgar E. Robinson–HH, November 27, 1951.

CHAPTER TWELVE: THE SAGE OF 31-A

1. HH–Walter Trohan, April 13, 1962.

2. Interview with Herbert Brownell, March 20, 1969, HOHP; Tierney interview.

3. Interview with Virginia Green, April 14, 1967; interview with John Kluytmans, May 11, 1967; interview with Edward O. Bodkin, March 9, 1970; interview with Calvin Albury, April 14, 1967; interview with James Blocker, April 14, 1967, HOHP; Robinson interview; interview with Kathryn Ann Campbell, April 15, 1967, HOHP.

4. Albury interview.

5. Wall interview; Tierney interview.

6. Behrens interview; HH–Charles Edison, October 28, 1955.

7. Off-the-record remarks by HH to Afterglow Party, October 15, 1954.

8. Antle interview; Moley interview.

9. Kaltenborn interview; Fellers interview; interview with George P. Harrington, November 13, 1969, HOHP; Dempsey interview.

10. James Roosevelt–HH, May 1, 1959; HH reply, May 4, 1959; interview

with Michael J. Petti, February 29, 1968, HOHP.

11. HH–George Sokolsky, April 21, 1953; Klumpp interview.

12. Morley interview; Robinson interview.

13. DDE interview; DDE–HH, May 29, December 6, 1953, August 6, 1954.

14. MacNeil interview; O'Donnell interview.

15. HH–DDE, February 26, 1954; DDE–HH, December 2, 1954.

16. HH–Leonard Hall, June 15, 1956; DDE–HH, July 2, 1956; HH–DDE, August 14, 1956; interview with Robert C. Hill, p. 60, COHC.

17. Moley interview; John Hamilton memo, July 21, 1955; "Our Present Foreign Situation," HH memo, September 4, 1954; O'Donnell interview; Moreell interview.

18. HH remarks at Bohemian Grove, August 1, 1953; DDE–HH, June 9, 1953.

19. MacNeil interview; HH–Clare Hoffman, undated; Moreell interview.

20. John Hamilton interview, July 21, 1955; interview with Chet Holifield, June 14, 1971, HOHP; "Hoover Commission—1954," by John M. Carmody, July 31, 1958, FDR Library.

21. Moreell interview; interview with James Farley, December 3, 1966, HOHP; MacNeil interview, May 9, 1967, HOHP.

22. Interview with Paul F. Grady, February 24, 1967, HOHP; Ethel Kennedy–HH, February 2, 1954; HH memo to Henry Cabot Lodge, April 25, 1960; HH–John F. Kennedy (hereafter referred to as JFK), May 12, 1956.

23. HH–JFK, December 21, 1954.

24. MacNeil interview.

25. Thomas E. Dewey–HH, July 6, 1955; HH memo to Lodge, April 25, 1960.

26. MacNeil interview; Hazlett interview; DDE–HH, June 17, 1957; HH–DDE, February 13, 1958.

27. Robert A. Taft–HH, June 5, 1953; Le Pore interview.

28. HH remarks at Bohemian Grove, August 1, 1953.

29. Memo of conversation with HH, Mrs. Kenneth C. Batchelder, June 25, 1954; HH–John Foster Dulles, September 23, 1954.

30. Interview with William B. Anderson, October 6, 1966, HOHP.

31. Arthur Krock–Bunny Miller, November 30, 1954.

32. HH–George Sokolsky, August 7, 1956; Loomis interview; HH–Edward H. Rees, March 10, 1957.

33. Mrs. John A. Sprouse–Raymond Henle, February 11, 1968.

34. Kuhn interview; Livingston interview; MacNeil interview.

35. Edith Bolling Wilson–HH, April 8, 1958; Eleanor Wilson McAdoo–HH, May 7, 1958; interview with Felix B. Stump, June 28, 1971, HOHP; Hazlett interview; Livingston interview; Kemp interview.

36. Kemp interview; MacNeil interview; Groves interview; HH–Douglas MacArthur, September 3, 1953; MacArthur reply, September 9, 1953.

37. MacNeil interview; Robinson interview; interview with Robert Morris, January 9, 1970.

38. HH–Chester Nimitz, July 10, 1956; HH–Mrs. Joseph P. McCarthy, May 5, 21, 1957; HH–Louis P. Lochner, March 4, 1957.

39. Lutz interview; J. Edgar Hoover to SAC, New York, November 17, 1957; Edward J. Powers–J. Edgar Hoover, December 2, 1957; unknown to Clyde Tolson, December 2, 1957.

40. HH–HST, July 17, 1957; Lloyd W. Dinkelspiel–HH, March 20, 1958; HH

reply, March 23, 1958; Moley interview; HH–Ben Moreell, April 2, 1960.

41. HH–HST, May 10, 30, 1957; HST–HH, April 21, 1958.

42. HH–Bess Truman, June 15, 1959; HH–HST, March 6, 1960, April 15, 1959; HST–HH, April 20, 1959; HH–HST, June 15, 1961, December 19, 1962; HST–HH, July 10, August 9, 1963; Allan Hoover–HST, August 14, 1963.

43. HH–DDE, May 1, 1958; Folger interview.

44. John Hamilton memo, June 8, 1960.

45. Pratt interview; Hamilton memo, June 8, 1960.

46. Farley interview; MacNeil interview; Knowland interview; undated HH memo "The Great Debate"; HH–Thruston B. Morton, September 15, 1960.

47. Undated HH memo; JFK interview; HH memo to Joseph P. Kennedy, November 14, 1960; MacNeil interview.

48. MacNeil interview.

49. HH–JFK, January 19, 1961; JFK–HH, March 2, 1961; HH reply, March 4, 1961; HH–JFK, October 12, 1961, April 7, 1963; Bunny Miller–HH, January 12, 1962.

50. Albury interview; Kuhn interview; interview with Loretta Camp, March 19, 1969, HOHP; Berlin interview; Petti interview.

51. HH–Jack Pew, August 1, 1962; JFK interview; Bunny Miller–Robert Welch, May 3, 1961; HH–John Coolidge, July 12, 1962.

52. HH–Rose Kennedy, September 21, 1963.

53. Torrey interview; interview with Baron Robert Silvercruys, November 7, 1968; HH–Hallem Tuck, April 23, 1963.

54. Mason interview; Berlin interview; interview with Lyndon B. Johnson, January 8, 1971, HOHP; Jacqueline Kennedy–HH, February 16, 1964.

55. HH–LBJ, November 27, 1963; Berlin interview; Kemp interview; HH–Bert Mattei, July 16, 1964.

56. HH memo on Nixon visit, undated; HH–Eugene Lyons, January 20, 1964.

57. HH–Douglas MacArthur, March 3, 1964; HH–LBJ, April 27, 1964; Sioussant interview.

58. J. Milbank interview; Funston interview; interview with Barry Goldwater, November 30, 1971, HOHP; HH–Goldwater, July 16, 1964.

59. Trohan interview; Clay interview; Yaeger interview; Sterling interview.

60. Richard M. Nixon–HH, August 6, 1964.

61. HH–HST, October 14, 1964.

62. Le Pore interview.

63. MacNeil interview.

64. LBJ–Herbert Hoover, Jr., October 19, 1964; HH, Jr., reply, October 29, 1964; interview with Rudolph N. Schullinger, October 27, 1964, HOHP.

INTERVIEWS

Material from the Oral History Collection of Columbia University is used with permission of the Trustees of Columbia University in the City of New York. Horace Albright (copyright 1972), Perrin J. Galpin (1972), Florence J. Harriman (1972), Robert C. Hill (1984), Charles Holman (1975), Herbert C. Hoover (1975), Eugene Meyer (1975), Jackson Reynolds (1972), A. Alexander Smith (1972), Harold C. Train (1975), James T. Williams, Jr. (1972).

Hoover Oral History Project: Charles F. Adams, George Akerson, Junior, Calvin Albury, Robert S. Allen, Victoria F. Allen, John Z. Anderson, William B. Anderson, Mr. and Mrs. Edward T. Anthony, Vincent K. Antle, Samuel Arentz, Burt Brown Barker, Earl C. Behrens, Richard Berlin, Joseph Binns, Clark Birge, James Blocker, Morton Blumenthal, Edward O. Bodkin, Mrs. Edwin Bowman, Boys Clubs officers, Mr. and Mrs. Phillips Brooks, Mrs. John A. Brown, Milton M. Brown, Herbert Brownell, Ellen C. Brumback, John C. Burns, Frederick Bates Butler, Loretta Camp, Kathryn Campbell, Mildred Hall Campbell, Thomas Campbell, Frank Caro, Turner Catledge, Leon Chandler, John A. Chapman, Fred Clark, Mark Clark, Lucius Clay, Willam B. Coberly, Albert C. Cole, Robert Considine, Robert F. Creighton, Arthur Curtice,

Mrs. Preston Davie, Joseph S. Davis, F. Trubee Davison, Mary Elizabeth Dempsey, Thomas E. Dewey, Clarence Dill, James H. Douglas, Morris Doyle, George Drescher, Ruth W. Durno, Elmore R. Dutro, Susan Dyer, Charles Edison, Dwight D. Eisenhower, John P. Falter, James A. Farley, Bonner Fellers, Alonzo Fields, Charles W. Fischer, Dennis A. FitzGerald, Harold M. Fleming. J. Clifford Folger, Edward T. Folliard, Adeline Fuller, William O. Fuller III, George K. Funston, Rube Goldberg, Barry Goldwater, Hope Brown Gordon, Kary Gordon, Alan J. Gould, Paul F. Grady, Virginia Green, Peter Grimm, Leslie R. Groves,

Charles W. Hallack, John D. M. Hamilton, George P. Harrington, Mark Hatfield, Henry Hazlett, John W. Hill, Chet Holifield, Solomon C. Hollister, William J. Hopkins, Van Ness Leavitt Hoover, Walter Hoving, Marguerite Rickard Hoyt, Lydia Murray Huneke, Lyndon B. Johnson, Mrs. H. V. Kaltenborn, Edward A. Keller, Arthur Kemp, Rose Kennedy, George N. Keyston, Alfred Kirchofer, Theodore G. Klumpp, John Kluytmans, William S. Knowland,

Mr. and Mrs. Boris Kosta, Irene Kuhn, David Lawrence, Paul R. Leach, Russell V. Lee, Michael J. Le Pore, Ira S. Lillick, George Gould Lincoln, Ruth F. Lipman, Walter Livingston, Louis P. Lochner, Mr. and Mrs. Frederick C. Loomis, Ralph Lutz, Eugene Lyons,

Hulda Hoover MacLean, Neil MacNeil, Carter Manasco, Edward F. Mansure, Frank Mason, Carrie B. Massenburg, John J. McCloy, Sally McCracken, Dare Stark McMullin, Andrew McNamara, Marvin M. Meyers, Jerimiah Milbank, Katherine Milbank, John P. Mitchell, Raymond Moley, Hugh A. Moran, Ben Moreell, Felix Morley, Robert Morris, Robert Moses, Bradley Nash, Mr. and Mrs. William I. Nichols, Madelaine K. O'Donnell, Mr. and Mrs. Jameson Parker, Lillian Rogers Parks, Norman Vincent Peale, Levi T. Pennington, Michael J. Petti, Herman Phlegar, Thomas P. Pike, Marie L. Pratt, Byron Price, Don K. Price, Alan Probert, Helen B. Pryor, Lawrence K. Requa, Edgar E. Robinson, Daniel Rodriguez, Nicholas Roosevelt,

Forydice B. St. John, Rudolph N. Schullinger, James P. Selvage, Robert Silvercruys, Helen d'Oyle Sioussat, Ruby Price Staton, J. E. Wallace Sterling, Louise Stevenson, John K. Stewart, Gilchrist B. Stockton, Mary Minthorn Strench, Mark Sullivan, Junior, Mrs. Frank Surface, H. Dudley Swain, Lowell Thomas, Agnes Thompson, Nicholas Tierney, Bascom Timmons, Clare M. Torrey, Payson J. Treat, Walter Trohan, Elton Trueblood, Scott Turner, Robert C. Tyson, Harry Vaughn, Gire Gin Wah, Robert T. Wall, Franklin Waltman, Albert C. Warren, Albert Wedemeyer, Sinclair Weeks, Mrs. Helen White, Dwight C. Wilbur, Ray Lyman Wilbur, Junior, Preston Wolfe, Naomi Yaeger.

NEWSPAPERS

The West Branch collection includes thousands of clippings that span the range of Hoover's activities and a long life lived in the public eye. Perhaps the most valuable finding aid for researchers is a thick compilation of the former president's place in the *New York Times*, a detailed chronology that reflects the heavy coverage according his public statements and political crusading during the wilderness years and later.

In addition to the *Times*, the *New York Herald Tribune* provides a useful counterpoint, the liberal Republican flagship trying to maintain an often uneasy alliance with the nation's only living Republican president. Much further to the Left, the *New York Post* took a doggedly anti-Hoover line, while Hearst's *Journal-American* and the *Daily News* were enthusiastic in their approval.

Outside New York, the *Chicago Tribune* voiced the feelings of those who shared Hoover's passionate opposition to the New Deal and Roosevelt's foreign policy. The *Kansas City Star*, edited by Hoover's friend Roy Roberts, provided a less strident view; not surprisingly, Hoover's regard for the paper cooled as it took up Alf Landon's cause. The *Washington Post* and *Baltimore Sun* are just two of dozens of other journals well represented in the collection. The *San Francisco Chronicle* is useful for its inside view of the former president's motivations; it was no accident that the only authorized journalist traveling with Hoover's party through Nazi Germany in 1938 was the *Chronicle*'s editor. The *Palo Alto Times and Standard Daily* contain further nuggets from Hoover's own backyard. The *West Branch Times* and *Iowa City Press Citizen* devoted many pages to Hoover's death and funeral. Roy Roberts's memoir of his friend, which appeared in the *Kansas City Star* of October 25, 1964, is revealing. Finally, a somewhat infrequent publication of special interest was the *ARA Association Review*, composed by veterans of the great relief campaigns that marked World War I and its aftermath; the final edition, published in May 1965 and devoted in its entirety to memories of "the Chief," is fascinating.

PERIODICALS AND OTHER ARTICLES

It is virtually impossible to compile a complete listing of such sources, so extensive is the Hoover file. Among the most helpful publications were such regular news weeklies as *Time, Life, Newsweek*, the *Literary Digest*, and opinion journals like the *New Republic*, the *Nation*, *American* magazine, *Liberty*, *Harper's*, the *Atlantic Monthly*, the *Saturday Review of Literature*, *Fortune*, the *Saturday Evening Post*, and *Business Week*. Hoover's own byline appeared frequently after 1933 in *Collier's;* he and Hugh Gibson waged diplomatic and humanitarian wars in its pages while the rest of the world battled according to its own standards. Still later, Hoover contributed a number of whimsical pieces to *This Week*. The *Reader's Digest* was another favored platform. Among scholarly reviews, *Mid-America* and the *Annals of Iowa* have devoted considerable space over the years to the boy from West Branch. The Hoover library holds, in addition to the primary source materials of historical assessment, hundreds of assessments already rendered, in book or dissertation form. Again, space permits only a fragmentary list.

Especially revealing pieces from the White House years include Will Irwin's "Those Whispers About Mr. Hoover," which appeared in *Liberty* for May 21, 1932; "Hoover's Eighteen Hour Day," by Chester T. Crowell, *New York Herald Tribune*, June 19, 1932; a three-part profile of Hoover appearing in the *New Yorker* for December 27, 1930, January 3, and 10, 1931; "The Personality of President Hoover," by Robert P. Lamont, in the September 1932 *Review of Reviews*; the *Literary Digest*'s worried comments about "Mr. Hoover's Commissions," February 15, 1930; "The Strange Attacks on Mr. Hoover," by Arthur Train, in *Collier's* for February 20, 1932; "Herbert Hoover, An Intimate Portrait," also by Will Irwin, in the May 1930 issue of *American* magazine; "Our Whispering Campaigns" by James Truslow Adams, *Harper's*, September, 1932; a profile of Charley Michaelson, by the *Baltimore Sun*'s Frank Kent, in the September 1930 edition of *Scribner's*; and *Newsweek*'s own look at Michaelson, December 7, 1942.

"President Hoover's Bad Press" by Fauneil J. Rinn, is an interesting review of Hoover's stormy relations with the fourth estate; it was published in *San Jose Studies*, February 1, 1975, and is only one of a number of similar studies rooted in academic research among the West Branch collections. Perhaps the most useful single work is *Herbert Hoover Reassessed*, a compilation of nearly thirty such articles, published on the fiftieth anniversary of Hoover's 1929 inaugural. Among the more helpful for my purposes: J. E. Wallace Sterling's personal recollection, "Herbert Hoover"; Darwin Lambert's profile of the president as naturalist, "The Rapidan Facet of Herbert Hoover"; George Nash's "The Social Philosophy of Herbert Hoover"; and Joan Hoff Wilson's title study.

W. Glenn Campbell examines "Herbert Hoover and the Hoover Institution," and various aspects of Depression America and the man in the White House are covered in essays by James S. Olsen, Martin L. Fausold, and Albert U. Romasco. Donald J. Lisio's study of the Bonus Army, "A Blunder Becomes Catastrophe," is of groundbreaking significance. The interregnum between Hoover and Roosevelt is described by Frank Friedel, while Hoover's postpresidential years receive thoughtful treatment from George T. Mazuzan and Gary Dean Best. Donald R. McCoy's article on Hoover and U.S. foreign policy during World War II is helpful, as is Ellis W. Hawley's assessment of Hoover's place in his own country's history books fifty years after he took the oath of office and claimed to see the abolishment of poverty within the reach of a dynamic, individualistic nation.

Other useful sources include Arthur Ballantine's "When All the Banks Closed," in the March 1948 *Harvard Business Review*; "Hoover, the Presidency in Transition," by Victor L. Albjerg, *Current History*, October, 1960; Gerald Nash's "Herbert Hoover and the Origins of the Reconstruction Finance Corporation," in the December 1950 *Mississippi Valley Historical Review*; Clair E. Nelsen's Stanford doctoral dissertation, "The Image of Herbert Hoover as Reflected in the American Press"; and "President Hoover as a Legislative Leader," a paper delivered at an April 1970 meeting of the Organization of American Historians by Jordan A. Schwartz. *Ohio History*, Volume 91, Annual 1982, contains a revealing account of a president close to the breaking point, "A Hoover Vignette," based on the recollections of RFC member Atlee Pomerene and written by Phillip R. Shriver. Joseph S. Davis, a trained economist, contributed "Another Appraisal" of Hoover, whom he knew well, to the summer 1969 issue of the *South Atlantic Quarterly*. Rexford Tugwell did the same in looking at two highly dramatic figures in his "The Protagonists: Roosevelt and Hoover," in the *Antioch Review* for Devember 1953. *Time*'s February 1, 1982, cover story on FDR and the New Deal legacy is helpful as subsequent interpretation on men and events which still retain after half a century their capacity to provoke hero worship or outrage.

The early years of Hoover's trek through the political wilderness are reported in "The New Hoover," by George Creel, in the October 12, 1935, edition of *Collier's;* "Hopefully the Republicans Look About" by Delbert Clark, in the *New York Times Magazine* for September 15, 1935; "Who but Hoover?" a biting portrait of the former president as logical rival to FDR in 1936, written for the December 4, 1935, issue of the *New Republic* by John T. Flynn; articles on the former president's Palo Alto routine which appeared in *Newsweek* for April 27, 1935; and Duncan Aieman's "Portrait of Our Resting Ex-President," the *New York Times Magazine,* May 28, 1933. More philosophical is Anne O'Hare McCormick's "Hoover Looks Back—And Ahead," in the same magazine, for February 5, 1933.

Also: Gary Dean Best's "Herbert Hoover as Titular Leader of the GOP, 1933–35," in *Mid-America,* for April–July, 1979; Donald R. McCoy's "Alfred M. Landon and the Presidential Campaign of 1936," in the same publication, October 1960; Hoover's own article "The Crisis and the Political Parties and an American Program," in the September 1937 edition of the *Atlantic Monthly;* Frederick Rudolph's "The American Liberty League, 1934–40," which appeared in the October 1960 *American Historical Review;* and "The Republican Congressional Comeback of 1938," by Milton Plesur, *Review of Politics,* October 1962. Especially helpful is Henry E. Everman's Ph.D. dissertation on "Herbert Hoover and the New Deal" for Louisiana State University, 1971.

Hoover expressed his views in print often and forcefully during the pre–Pearl Harbor years. His own travels abroad were well covered in such mass publications as *Life* ("Herbert Hoover Looks at Europe," April 11, 1938), *Time* and *Newsweek.* The April 15, 1939, issue of *Liberty* carried "Foreign Policies Today," by Hoover, making arguments refined in

the July 15, 1939, *American* magazine, the *Saturday Evening Post,* October 27, 1939, and *Liberty,* June 5, 1940. *Pathfinder's* April 13, 1940, issue examined the former president's chances of winning his party's nomination in the face of mounting European hostilities. Later, Hoover and Hugh Gibson published a series of articles in the *Saturday Evening Post,* which subsequently appeared in book form, a few weeks after the Japanese attack, as *America's First Crusade.* This, in turn, led to a second, longer volume, *The Problems of Lasting Peace.* A new debate erupted, with Rebecca West contributing a scathing critique, "The Hoover Frame of Mind," in the *Atlantic Monthly's* June, 1943, issue.

Supported by such journals as *Commonweal* and *Christian Century,* Hoover fought back with his pen. *Collier's* published his warning "We'll Have to Feed the World Again" in two installments, November 28, and December 5, 1942. The same magazine provided a forum for his attack on the idea of a permanent coalition involving the U.S., Great Britain, the Soviet Union and China, the proposal floated at the Mackinac Republican conference by Thomas E. Dewey. "The Futility of Military Alliances" appeared in *Collier's* November 6, 1943, edition. "Let's Go Fishin' " was Hoover's thoroughly different contribution to the same publication for April 22, 1944. More extensive information on his writings of the period can be found in Hoover's *Addresses Upon the American Road,* eight volumes published between 1936 and 1961 and containing most of his significant public speeches as well as many articles and some correspondence.

Articles of special interest to Hoover students include Richard Remhardt's history of the Bohemian Club, in the June–July 1980 *American Heritage;* Horace Sutton's anecdotal report on "The Fabulous Waldorf-Astoria," in the January 1952 *Reader's Digest; Time's* report on the Hoover Library, June 30, 1941; Frank J. Taylor's piece in the May 4,

1957, *Saturday Review*, "Herbert Hoover's Operation Pack Rat"; and another article by Taylor on "Stanford's Man With the Midas Touch," in the December 3, 1960, *Saturday Evening Post*. Both the *Palo Alto Times* and the *Stanford Daily* covered the controversy surrounding the Hoover Institution's commitment to studying global communism. The *New Republic* of May 2, 1960, published its own critical essay on the subject, "Mr. Hoover Leaves His Mark."

Benjamin Rogers was the author of "Dear Mr. President: The Hoover–Truman Correspondence" in the September–October 1974 issue of *Palimpsest*. Hazel Lyman Nickel wrote an unpublished piece on Hoover's 1946 travels to prostrate Germany, "The Lamp of Compassion." An interesting interpretation of "The First Hoover Commission and the Managerial Presidency" appeared in the *Journal of Politics*, February 1976, the work of Peri E. Arnold. Hoover's own efforts to rally public opinion behind his commission and its mandate to reorganize the federal establishment were, if anything, stepped up by the mid-fifties, when Hoover II tackled a number of Washington's sacred cows. He gave a lengthy interview to *U.S. News and World Report*, which appeared in the August 5, 1955, issue, nearly a year after "Big Government: The Hoover Team's Attack" outlined the problem in the October 18, 1954, *Newsweek*.

Hoover's later years were filled with journalistic profiles, many as uncritical of the old man as earlier pieces had been negative. One of the best is Jim Bishop's "Herbert Hoover: A Birthday Salute," in the *American Weekly* for August 9, 1959. His old friend Jay Darling wrote "My Years with Herbert Hoover" for *Look*'s August 14, 1954, issue. Ben Hibbs contributed still another birthday tribute in the July 28, 1962, *Saturday Evening Post*, while the winter 1965 edition of *Annals of Iowa* featured a fond reminiscence by Bill Wagner, who helped design the Overlook resting place at West Branch and found out, to his vast amusement, that the former president insisted on striking matches against the samples of stone dispatched to the Waldorf for his personal inspection. Hoover's own ninetieth-birthday message appeared in the August 1964 *Reader's Digest*. A revealing article based on conversations with Hoover intimates was Herbert G. Klein's "The President That Few Americans Really Knew," in the October 21, 1964, *San Diego Union*. Hoover's own writings in his final years ranged from "How to Stay Young" (*This Week*, August 8, 1954), to his humorous "It's Tough to Be a Statue," in the same publication's February 18, 1960, issue.

Since his death, a host of revisionist pieces have appeared. Earlier still, Yale's Carl N. Degler began the trend with "The Ordeal of Herbert Hoover," in the June, 1963, *Yale Review*. Some of the useful articles since include "Hoover and the Historians: The Resurrection of a President" by Patrick G. O'Brien and Philip T. Rosen, in the *Annals of Iowa* for summer 1981; "Herbert Hoover: A Reinterpretation," by Robert H. Ziegler, in the October 1976 *American Historical Review*; "The Restoration of Herbert Hoover," by Lee Roderick and Stephen W. Statkis, the *Wall Street Journal*, August 5, 1974; Steve Neal's portrait of "Herbert Hoover: Unluckiest President," printed in the September 1, 1974, *Philadelphia Inquirer*; the autumn 1964 issue of Stanford's *Alumni Almanac*; Henry Hazlett's *Newsweek* column on "Hoover as Scapegoat," August 17, 1964; and R. Gorden Hoxie's commentary on "Hoover and the Banking Crisis," in the *Presidential Studies Quarterly* for fall, 1974.

BOOKS

Abels, Jules, *In the Time of Silent Cal,* New York, 1969.

Allen, Frederick Lewis, *Since Yesterday,* New York, 1940.

Allen, Robert S., *Washington Merry Go-Round,* New York, 1931.

Alsop, Joseph, and Turner Catledge, *The 168 Days,* Garden City, N.Y., 1933.

Barber, James David, *Presidential Character,* Englewood Cliffs, N.J., 1972.

Baruch, Bernard, *The Public Years,* New York, 1960.

Beard, Charles A., *American Foreign Policy in the Making 1932–40,* New Haven, 1946.

Bendiner, Robert, *Just Around the Corner,* New York, 1967.

Best, Gary Dean, *Herbert Hoover: The Post-Presidential Years,* Stanford, 1983.

———, *The Politics of American Individualism,* Westport, Conn., 1975.

Burdette, Franklin L., *Readings for Republicans,* New York, 1960.

Burner, David, *Herbert Hoover: A Public Life,* New York, 1978.

Burns, James MacGregor, *Roosevelt: The Lion and the Fox,* New York, 1956.

Cantril, Hadley, *Public Opinion, 1935–46,* Princeton, 1951.

Creel, George, *Rebel at Large,* New York, 1947.

Crowther, Samuel, *The Presidency vs. Hoover,* Garden City, N.Y., 1928.

Dexter, Walter P., *Herbert Hoover and American Individualism,* New York, 1932.

Divine, Robert, *The Illusion of Neutrality,* Chicago, 1962.

Eisenhower, Dwight D., *At Ease: Stories I Tell My Friends,* New York, 1967.

Emerson, Edwin, *Hoover and His Times,* Garden City, N.Y., 1932.

Emery, Anne, *American Friend: Herbert Hoover,* Chicago, 1967.

Fausold, Martin L., and George T. Ma-

zuzan, *The Hoover Presidency: A Reappraisal,* Albany, 1974.

Farley, James A., *Behind the Ballots,* New York, 1938.

Feis, Herbert, *1933: Characters in Crisis,* New York, 1966.

Fields, Alonzo, *My 21 Years in the White House,* New York, 1961.

Friedel, Frank, *Franklin D. Roosevelt: The Triumph,* Boston, 1956.

———, *Franklin D. Roosevelt: Launching the New Deal,* Boston, 1973.

Galbraith, John K., *The Great Crash, 1929,* New York, 1955.

Goldman, Eric F., *Rendezvous with Destiny,* New York, 1956.

Guerrant, Edward H., *Roosevelt-Hoover, Comparisons and Contrasts,* Cleveland, 1961.

Hamby, Alonzo L., *The New Deal, Analysis and Interpretation,* New York, 1969.

Hamill, John, *The Strange Career of Mr. Hoover, or Under Two Flags,* New York, 1931.

Handlin, Oscar, *Al Smith and His America,* Boston, 1958.

Hard, William, *Who's Hoover?,* New York, 1928.

Hargrove, Erwin C., *Presidential Leadership: Personality and Political Style,* New York, 1966.

Hicks, John D., *The Republican Ascendency, 1921–33,* New York, 1960.

Hinshaw, David, *Herbert Hoover: American Quaker,* New York, 1950.

Hofstadter, Richard, *The American Political Tradition and the Men Who Made It,* New York, 1948.

Hoover, Herbert, *Fishing for Fun and to Wash Your Soul,* New York, 1963.

———, *On Growing Up,* New York, 1963.

———, *The Ordeal of Woodrow Wilson,* New York, 1958.

———, *Memoirs,* New York, 1951–52.

———, *The Challenge to Liberty,* New York, 1948.

———, *Hoover After Dinner: Addresses Delivered by Herbert Hoover Before the Gridiron Club of Washington, D.C.,* New York, 1933.

———, *The New Day: Campaign Speeches of 1928,* Stanford, 1928.

———, *American Individualism,* New York, 1922.

———, *Principles of Mining,* New York, 1909.

Hoover, Herbert H., and Hugh Gibson, *The Problems of Lasting Peace,* New York, 1945.

———, *The Basis of Lasting Peace,* New York, 1945.

Irwin H. Hoover, *Forty-two Years in the White House,* Boston, 1934.

Hull, Cordell, *The Memoirs of Cordell Hull,* New York, 1948.

Hutchinson, William T., *Lowden of Illinois,* Chicago, 1957.

Huthmacher, J. Joseph, and Warren I. Susman, *Herbert Hoover and the Crisis of American Capitalism,* Cambridge, Mass., 1973.

Ickes, Harold L., *The Secret Diary of Harold Ickes,* New York, 1954.

———, *The First Thousand Days, 1933–36,* New York, 1935.

Irwin, Will, *Propaganda and the News,* New York, 1936.

———, *Herbert Hoover: A Reminiscent Biography,* New York, 1928.

Johnson, Donald B., *The Republican Party and Wendell Willkie,* Urbana, Ill., 1960.

Johnson, Hugh, *The Blue Eagle from Egg to Earth,* Garden City, N.Y., 1935.

Johnson, Walter, *William Allen White's America,* New York, 1947.

Jordan, David Starr, *The Days of a Man 1900–21,* Yonkers on Hudson, N.Y., 1922.

Joslin, Theodore G., *Hoover off the Record,* Garden City, N.Y., 1934.

Kaltenborn, H. V., *Fifty Fabulous Years,* New York, 1958.

Keller, Morton, *In Defense of Yesterday,* New York, 1958.

Kellogg, Vernon, *Herbert Hoover, The Man and His Work,* New York, 1920.

———, *Fighting Starvation in Belgium,* New York, 1917.

Kennedy, Susan Estabrook, *The Banking Crisis of 1933,* Lexington, Ky., 1973.

Kent, Frank, *Without Gloves,* New York, 1934.

Krock, Arthur, *Memoirs,* New York, 1958.

Lane, Rose Wilder, *Making of Herbert Hoover,* New York, 1920.

Lash, Joseph, *Eleanor and Franklin,* New York, 1971.

Latham, Edward Connery, *Meet Calvin Coolidge,* Brattleboro, Vt., 1960.

Leuchtenburg, William, *Franklin D. Roosevelt and the New Deal,* New York, 1963.

Lindbergh, Charles A., *The Wartime Journals of Charles A. Lindbergh,* New York, 1970.

Lippmann, Walter, *Interpretations, 1931–32,* New York, 1932.

Lisio, Donald J., *The President and Protest: Hoover, Conspiracy, and the Bonus Riot,* Columbia, Mo., 1974.

Lloyd, Craig, *Aggressive Introvert: A Study of Herbert Hoover and Public Relations Management,* Columbus, Ohio, 1972.

Lochner, Louis P., *Herbert Hoover and Germany,* New York, 1960.

Lubell, Samuel, *The Future of American Politics,* New York, 1951.

Lyons, Eugene, *Herbert Hoover: A Biography,* Garden City, N.Y., 1964.

———, *Our Unknown Ex-President,* Garden City, N.Y., 1948.

Martin, Joseph, *My First Fifty Years in Politics,* New York, 1960.

McCoy, Donald, *Landon of Kansas,* Topeka, 1967.

———, *Angry Voices,* Lawrence, Kan., 1951.

McGee, Dorothy Horton, *Herbert Hoover: Engineer, Humanitarian, Statesman,* New York, 1959.

McLean, Hulda Hoover, *Uncle Bert: A Biographical Portrait of Herbert Hoover,* 1974.

Meltzer, Milton, *Brother, Can You Spare a Dime?,* New York, 1969.

Michaelson, Charles, *The Ghost Talks*, New York, 1944.

Miller, Dwight M., *Public Papers of Herbert Hoover, 1932–33*, Washington, D.C., 1977.

Miller, Nathan, *FDR: An Intimate History*, Garden City, N.Y., 1983.

Mills, Ogden, *The Seventeen Million*, New York, 1937.

Mitchell, Broadus, *Depression Decade, 1929–41*, New York, 1942.

Moley, Raymond, *The First New Deal*, New York, 1966.

———, *27 Masters of Politics*, New York, 1949.

———, *After Seven Years*, New York, 1939.

Myers, William Starr, *The Foreign Policies of Herbert Hoover, 1929–33*, New York, 1940.

———, and Walter H. Newton, *The Hoover Administration: A Documented Narrative*, New York, 1936.

Nash, George H., *The Life of Herbert Hoover, The Engineer, 1874–1914*, New York, 1983.

Nevins, Allen, *The New Deal and World Affairs*, New Haven, Conn., 1950.

Nixon, Richard, *Memoirs*, New York, 1977.

Parks, Lillian Rogers, *My Thirty Years Backstairs at the White House*, New York, 1961.

Peel, R. V., and T. C. Donnelly, *The 1932 Campaign*, New York, 1935.

Perkins, Frances, *The Roosevelt I Knew*, New York, 1946.

Phillips, Cabell, *From the Crash to the Blitz, 1929–1939*, New York, 1969.

Prange, Gordon W., *At Dawn We Slept: The Untold Story of Pearl Harbor*, New York, 1981.

Pringle, Henry F., *Big Frogs*, New York, 1928.

Pryor, Helen B., *Lou Henry Hoover: Gallant First Lady*, New York, 1969.

Pusey, Merlo J., *Charles Evans Hughes*, New York, 1963.

———, *Eugene Meyer*, New York, 1974.

Robinson, Edgar E., *The Roosevelt Leadership, 1933–45*, Philadelphia, 1955.

———, and Vaughn Davis Bornet, *Herbert Hoover, President of the United States*, Stanford, 1975.

Romasco, Albert U., *The Poverty of Abundance*, New York,, 1965.

Roosevelt, Nicholas, *A Front Row Seat*, Norman, Okla., 1953.

Rosen, Elliot, *Hoover, Roosevelt and the Brains Trust*, New York, 1977.

Rothbard, Murray N., *America's Great Depression*, Los Angeles, 1963.

Sayles, Ross, *The West Branch Story*, Volume II, West Branch, Iowa, 1980.

Schlesinger, Arthur N., *The Politics of Upheaval*, Boston, 1960.

———, *The Coming of the New Deal*, Boston, 1959.

———, *The Crisis of the Old Order, 1919–33*, Boston, 1957.

Schwarz, Jordan, *The Interregnum of Despair: Hoover, Congress and the Depression*, Urbana, Ill., 1970.

Seldes, Gilbert, *The Years of the Locust, America, 1929–33*, Boston, 1965.

Sherwin, Mark, and Charles L. Mackham, *One Week in March*, New York, 1961.

Smith, Gene, *The Shattered Dream*, New York, 1970.

Smith, Richard Norton, *Thomas E. Dewey and His Times*, New York, 1982.

Spargo, John, *The Legend of Herbert Hoover Who Did Nothing*, 1939.

Starling, Edmund, *Starling of the White House*, New York, 1946.

Stimson, Henry J., *On Active Service in Peace and War*, New York, 1948.

Stoddard, Henry, *It Costs to Be President*, New York, 1938.

Stokes, Thomas L., *Chip off My Shoulder*, Princeton, 1940.

Sobel, Robert, *Panic on Wall Street*, New York, 1968.

Strauss, Lewis L., *Men and Decisions*, Garden City, N.Y., 1962.

Sullivan, Lawrence, *Prelude to Panic: The Story of the Bank Holiday*, Washington, D.C., 1936.

Sullivan, Mark, *The Education of an American*, New York, 1962.

Tonsill, Charles, *Back Door to War*, Chicago, 1952.

Train, Arthur, *The Strange Attacks on Herbert Hoover*, New York, 1932.

Truman, Harry S., *Years of Trial and Hope*, New York, 1956.

Tugwell, Rexford G., *Roosevelt's Revolution, The First Year, A Personal Perspective*, New York, 1977.

———, *The Democratic Roosevelt*, New York, 1957.

———, *The Art of Politics*, New York, 1956.

Warren, Harris, *Herbert Hoover and the Great Depression*, New York, 1959.

Waters, Walter W., *BEF: The Whole Story of the Bonus Army*, New York, 1933.

Wecter, Dixon, *The Age of the Great Depression, 1929–41*, New York, 1948.

Watson, James, *As I Knew Them*, Indianapolis, 1936.

White, William Allen, *The Autobiography of William Allen White*, New York, 1946.

———, *A Puritan in Babylon: The Story of Calvin Coolidge*, New York, 1938.

Wilbur, Ray Lyman, *Memoirs*, Stanford, 1960.

———, and Arthur M. Hyde, *The Hoover Policies*, New York, 1937.

Williams, T. Harry, *Huey Long*, New York, 1970.

Williams, William Appleman, *The Contours of American History*, New York, 1966.

———, *Some Presidents: Wilson to Nixon*, New York, 1972.

Wilson, Carol Green, *Herbert Hoover: A Challenge for Today*, New York, 1968.

Wilson, Joan Hoff, *Herbert Hoover, Forgotten Progressive*, Boston, 1975.

Wolfe, Harold, *Herbert Hoover: Public Servant and Leader of the Loyal Opposition*, New York, 1956.

Wolfskill, George, *The Revolt of the Conservatives: A History of the American Liberty League, 1934–40*, New York, 1962.

———, and John A. Auden, *All but the People, FDR and His Critics, 1933–39*, New York, 1969.

Wood, Clement, *Herbert Clark Hoover, An American Tragedy*, New York, 1932.

Zucker, Norman L., *George Norris: Gentle Knight of American Democracy*, Urbana, Ill., 1966.

INDEX